THE CAMBRIDGE COMPANION TO
THE COUNCIL OF NICAEA

Every Sunday, Christians all over the world recite the Nicene Creed as a confession of faith. While most do not know the details of the controversy that led to its composition, they are aware that the Council of Nicaea was a critical moment in the history of Christianity. For scholars, the Council has long been a subject of multi-disciplinary interest and continues to fascinate and inspire research. As we approach the 1,700th anniversary of the Council, *The Cambridge Companion to the Council of Nicaea* provides an opportunity to revisit and reflect on old discussions, propose new approaches and interpretative frameworks, and ultimately revitalize a conversation that remains as important now as it was in the fourth century. The volume offers fifteen original studies by scholars who each examine an aspect of the Council. Informed by interdisciplinary approaches, the essays demonstrate its profound legacy with fresh, sometimes provocative, but always intellectually rich ideas.

Young Richard Kim is Associate Professor in the Department of Classics and Mediterranean Studies and the Department of History at the University of Illinois at Chicago. He is the author of *Epiphanius of Cyprus: Imagining an Orthodox World* (2015), which won the North American Patristics Society Best First Book Prize (2016).

Other Titles in the Series

THE CAMBRIDGE COMPANION TO

THE COUNCIL OF NICAEA

Edited by

Young Richard Kim
University of Illinois at Chicago

CAMBRIDGE
UNIVERSITY PRESS

CAMBRIDGE
UNIVERSITY PRESS

University Printing House, Cambridge CB2 8BS, United Kingdom

One Liberty Plaza, 20th Floor, New York, NY 10006, USA

477 Williamstown Road, Port Melbourne, VIC 3207, Australia

314–321, 3rd Floor, Plot 3, Splendor Forum, Jasola District Centre,
New Delhi – 110025, India

79 Anson Road, #06–04/06, Singapore 079906

Cambridge University Press is part of the University of Cambridge.

It furthers the University's mission by disseminating knowledge in the pursuit of
education, learning, and research at the highest international levels of excellence.

www.cambridge.org
Information on this title: www.cambridge.org/9781108427746
DOI: 10.1017/9781108613200

© Cambridge University Press 2021

First published 2021

A catalogue record for this publication is available from the British Library.

Library of Congress Cataloging-in-Publication Data
NAMES: Kim, Young Richard, 1976– editor.
TITLE: The Cambridge companion to the Council of Nicaea / edited by Young Richard
Kim, "The University of Illinois at Chicago".
DESCRIPTION: Cambridge, United Kingdom ; New York, NY : Cambridge University
Press, 2021. | Series: Cambridge companions to religion | Includes bibliographical
references and index.
IDENTIFIERS: LCCN 2020035128 (print) | LCCN 2020035129 (ebook) |
ISBN 9781108427746 (hardback) | ISBN 9781108448116 (paperback) |
ISBN 9781108613200 (ebook)
SUBJECTS: LCSH: Council of Nicaea (1st : 325 : Nicaea, Turkey)
CLASSIFICATION: LCC BR210 .C35 2021 (print) | LCC BR210 (ebook) | DDC 262/.5–dc23
LC record available at https://lccn.loc.gov/2020035128
LC ebook record available at https://lccn.loc.gov/2020035129

ISBN 978-1-108-42774-6 Hardback
ISBN 978-1-108-44811-6 Paperback

For Ewan and Rhys
여호와를 경외하는 것이 지혜의 근본이요
거룩하신 자를 아는 것이 명철이니라
Prov. 9:10

Contents

Figures

Contributors

Mark DelCogliano is Associate Professor, Theology Department, University of St. Thomas (Minnesota, USA).

H. A. Drake is Research Professor, Department of History, University of California Santa Barbara (California, USA).

Geoffrey D. Dunn is a Fellow of the Australian Humanities Academy, Associate Professor, John Paul II Catholic University of Lublin (Poland), and Research Associate, University of Pretoria (South Africa).

Mark J. Edwards is Professor of Early Christian Studies, Faculty of Theology and Religion, Oxford University (UK).

Paul L. Gavrilyuk is Aquinas Chair in Theology and Philosophy, Theology Department, University of St. Thomas (Minnesota, USA).

David M. Gwynn is Reader in Ancient and Late Antique History, Department of History, Royal Holloway University of London (UK).

Ine Jacobs is Stavros Niarchos Foundation Associate Professor of Byzantine Archaeology and Visual Culture, The Ioannou Center for Classical and Byzantine Studies, Oxford University (UK).

Aaron P. Johnson is Associate Professor of Classics and Humanities, Lee University (Tennessee, USA).

Young Richard Kim is Associate Professor in the Department of Classics and Mediterranean Studies and the Department of History at the University of Illinois at Chicago.

Rebecca Lyman is Samuel Garrett Professor Emerita of Church History, The Church Divinity School of the Pacific (California, USA).

Daniel P. Mc Carthy is Fellow Emeritus and former Senior Lecturer, Department of Computer Science, Trinity College Dublin (Ireland).

Sara Parvis is Senior Lecturer, School of Divinity, University of Edinburgh (UK).

Kelley McCarthy Spoerl is Professor, Theology Department, Saint Anselm College (New Hampshire, USA).

Raymond Van Dam is Professor Emeritus, Department of History, University of Michigan (Michigan, USA).

Andreas Weckwerth is Professor of Ancient Church History and Patristics at the Catholic University of Eichstätt (Germany).

D. H. Williams is Professor of Religion in Patristics and Historical Theology, Department of Religion, Baylor University (Texas, USA).

Acknowledgements

Oddly enough, the first step in the production of this volume, an invitation from Beatrice Rehl at Cambridge University Press to become the editor, came in the autumn of 2016, on a day when I was waylaid by a sudden case of vertigo and recovering in an emergency room bed. The journey since then, of course, has been dizzying to say the least. All bad puns aside, I will say that how I had envisioned the volume, and how it ended up, of course, are very different. For one, I deeply regret that I was ultimately unsuccessful in recruiting more diverse scholars – especially persons of color – to contribute to this collection of essays. As we approach the 1,700th year since the Council of Nicaea, I can only hope that in the next centennial anniversary we will see another *Cambridge Companion* with as diverse a team of writers as I hope that the humanistic disciplines will actually be with its teaching and research practitioners. This of course in no way reflects negatively at all on the authors contained herein; they are, in a word, stellar. I am deeply grateful to each of them, without whose willingness to work with me, patience, good humor, insights, expertise, and superb writing, this volume would not exist. Ultimately, as the editor, any infelicities with respect to format, typographical errata, and more seriously, gaps in the actual content, are entirely my responsibility. If I had free rein, this volume would have had double the number of essays, covering many other interesting subjects and exploring several different trajectories, but there are wordcount limits, unforeseeable circumstances, and in the end editorial decisions that shall in the end remain unknown to you, the reader. Still, I am proud of this volume, and I am hopeful that it will generate further inquiry and continue an ongoing conversation about the Council of Nicaea and its lasting legacy.

This project began when I was on faculty at Calvin College (now University), and I am grateful for the support of colleagues and friends I received there, and it continued through my time at the Onassis Foundation, to which I am equally thankful. I want to offer particular thanks to Anthony Papadimitriou for the life-changing opportunity. I am fortunate to have a position as a Research Affiliate at the Institute for the Study of the Ancient World with NYU's superb research resources, which contributed greatly to the groundwork for this volume. Finally, I have found my professional home at the University of Illinois at Chicago, and I wish to thank in particular Dean Astrida Orle Tantillo for trusting me to lead the department of Classics and Mediterranean Studies. I also want to express my appreciation for my colleagues in the School of Literatures, Cultural Studies and Linguistics, my home department and my other department, History, and my students, who already in a short time have inspired and challenged me as a teacher and mentor.

In addition to Beatrice Rehl, I would also like to recognize and thank the team, past and present, at Cambridge University Press, whose members helped and guided me at various points along the publication process: Shalini Bisa, Eilidh Burrett, Becca Grainger, Edgar Mendez, Caroline Morley, and Victoria Parrin. I am also grateful to Akash Datchinamurthy at Integra Software Services. Finally, I must thank Nigel Hope, who copyedited the entire volume with precision, proficiency, and professionalism.

Our academic endeavors in many ways seem of lesser significance in light of the challenges we face today – inequality, violence, racism, authoritarianism, climate change, amid other forms of injustice. Still, I believe they contribute to the record of our shared human experience, and I maintain the conviction that the sum total of our efforts can meaningfully cultivate mutual understanding and humility. The quality of what we do while immersed in our books, articles, and critical editions, pounding away at our keyboards, is of course profoundly shaped by what we do away from them, and more importantly, with whom. Friends and family remind us that we are so much more than what we produce. My wife Betty is a boundless source of inspiration, and there simply are not enough words to communicate my gratitude to her. I dedicate this scholarly effort to our beloved sons, Ewan and Rhys, and I will do all that I can to pass on to them a world that I pray is at least a little more than today on its way to healing and restoration. *S.D.G.*

Abbreviations

Ancient Sources
In the footnotes, whenever possible I have edited all contributions to follow generally the orthographic and abbreviation conventions (with modifications) of Lampe 1961 for Greek authors and titles of primary sources and Blaise and Chirat 1954 for Latin authors and sources. For ancient authors not in Lampe, I have adopted those of Liddell and Scott 1996 and Glare 1968.

Ambrose of Milan	Ambr.
Epistulae	*Ep.*
Apollinarius of Laodicea	Apoll.
De fide et incarnatione	*De fid. inc.*
De unione corporis et divinitatis Christi	*De unione*
Kata Meros Pistis	*KMP*
Canones Apostolorum	*Can. App.*
Athanasius	Ath.
Apologia ad Constantium	*Apol. Const.*
Apologia (secunda) contra Arianos	*Apol. sec.*
De decretis Nicaenae synodi	*De decr.*
De sententia Dionysii	*De sent. Dion.*
De synodis Arimini et Seleuciae	*De syn.*
Epistula ad Afros episcopos	*Ep. Afr.*
Epistula ad Epictetum	*Ep. Epict.*
Epistula festivalis	*Ep. fest.*
Orationes tres adversus Arianos	*Ar.*
Tomus ad Antiochenos	*Tom.*

(cont.)

Augustine	Aug.
De Trinitate	*De Trin.*
Basil of Caesarea	Bas.
Contra Eunomium	*Eun.*
Epistulae	*Ep.*
Collectio Avellana	*Coll. Avell.*
Cyril of Alexandria	Cyr.
Epistulae	*Ep.*
Epiphanius	Epiph.
Panarion	*Pan.*
Eusebius of Caesarea	Eus.
Contra Marcellum	*Marcell.*
De ecclesiastica theologia	*De ecc. th.*
De vita Constantini	*VC*
Epistula ad Caesarienses	*Ep. Caes.*
Epistula ad Euphrationem	*Ep. Euphrat.*
Historia ecclesiastica	*HE*
Praeparatio Evangelica	*PE*
Eustathius of Antioch	Eust.
Fragmenta	*Fr.*
Gregory of Nazianzus	Gr. Naz.
Epistulae	*Ep.*
Orationes	*Orat.*
Hilary of Poitiers	Hilar.
Collectanea antiariana Parisina	*CAP*
De synodis	*De syn.*
Fragmenta Historica	*FH*
Liber contra Auxentium Mediolanensem	*Aux.*
Lactantius	Lact.
De mortibus persecutorum	*DMP*
Leontius of Byzantium	Leont.
Adversus fraudes Apolloniaristarum	*Apoll.*
Origen	Or.
Commentarii in Johannem	*Jo.*
Contra Celsum	*Cels.*
De principiis	*De princ.*
Pamphilus	Pamph.

(cont.)

Apologia Origenis	*Ap. Orig.*
Panegyrici latini	*Paneg. lat.*
Philostorgius	Phil.
Historia ecclesiastica	*HE*
Phoebadius of Agen	Phoeb.
Liber contra Arrianos	*Ar.*
Socrates	Socr.
Historia ecclesiastica	*HE*
Sozomen	Soz.
Historia ecclesiastica	*HE*
Sulpicius Severus	Sulp. Sev.
Chronicorum libri duo	*Chron.*
Tertullian	Tert.
Aduersus Praxean	*Prax.*
Theodoret	Thdt.
Historia ecclesiastica	*HE*

Modern Sources

ACO	*Acta Conciliorum Oecumenicorum*
CCSG	Corpus Christianorum Series Graeca
CCSL	Corpus Christianorum Series Latina
CH	*Church History*
CSEL	Corpus Scriptorum Ecclesiasticorum Latinorum
Dok.	Hanns Christof Brennecke, Uta Heil, Annette von Stockhausen, and Angelika Wintjes, eds. 2007. *Athanasius Werke: Dokumente zur Geschichte des arianischen Streites.* Vol. 3, pt. 1. *Lieferung 3: Bis zur Ekthesis Makrostichos.* Berlin: De Gruyter
	Hanns Christof Brennecke, Annette von Stockhausen, Christian Müller, Uta Heil, and Angelika Wintjes, eds. 2014. *Athanasius Werke: Dokumente zur Geschichte des arianischen Streites.* Vol. 3, pt. 1. *Lieferung 4: Bis zur Synode von Alexandrien 362.* Berlin: De Gruyter
DOP	*Dumbarton Oaks Papers*
FC	The Fathers of the Church
GCS	Die griechischen christlichen Schriftsteller der ersten drei Jahrhunderte

GRBS	*Greek, Roman, and Byzantine Studies*
HTR	*Harvard Theological Review*
JAEMA	*Journal of the Australian Early Medieval Association*
JECS	*Journal of Early Christian Studies*
JEH	*Journal of Ecclesiastical History*
JLA	*Journal of Late Antiquity*
JRS	*Journal of Roman Studies*
JTS	*Journal of Theological Studies*
Lampe 1961	Lampe, G. W. H. 1961. *A Patristic Greek Lexicon.* Oxford: Oxford University Press.
LCL	Loeb Classical Library
NBA	Nuova Biblioteca Agostiniana
NPNF	A Select Library of Nicene and Post-Nicene Fathers
PG	Patrologia Graeca
PL	Patrologia Latina
PLRE	Prosopography of the Later Roman Empire
RAC	*Reallexikon für Antike und Christentum*
RHE	*Revue d'historie ecclésiastique*
SC	Sources chrétiennes
StPatr	*Studia Patristica*
TTH	Translated Texts for Historians
Urk.	Hans-Georg Opitz, ed. 1934. *Athanasius Werke III.1, Lieferung 1–2: Urkunden zur Geschichte des arianischen Streites, 318–328.* Berlin: De Gruyter
VC	*Vigiliae Christianae*
ZAC	*Zeitschrift für antikes Christentum*
ZKG	*Zeitschrift für Kirchengeschichte*

1   Introduction

YOUNG RICHARD KIM

THE COUNCIL OF NICAEA AS CONSPIRACY

A little over an hour into Ron Howard's cinematic adaptation of *The Da Vinci Code*, for the first time in a major Hollywood film we see a portrayal of the Council of Nicaea. The brief scene takes place in an expansive, ornately decorated basilica, ending in an apse whose vault is decorated with an anachronistic image of an enthroned Christ, who presides over the proceedings (figure 1.1).

The great hall is filled with scribes sitting at a long table and taking notes, as a motley crew of attendants, clerics, and bishops, garbed in decorative robes and capped with lofty miters, gesture wildly at one another, yelling across the aisle and apparently debating the particulars of the future of Christianity. As the camera pans across the basilica to the center of the nave, we see Roman soldiers, equipped with spears, shields, and helmets with fancy feather plumes and stationed on elevated platforms along the colonnades of the venue, ominously standing guard over the proceedings. It appears (as far as I can tell) that Constantine is standing in the center of the basilica, next to the notary's table, somewhat bewildered at the ferocity of the debate surrounding him.[1]

The character Leigh Teabing, portrayed in the movie by Sir Ian McKellen – with a smoky, grandfatherly, and rather pedantic voice – has just explained how the lifelong pagan emperor Constantine decided to unify his disintegrating empire by imposing a single religion. In Brown's novel, Teabing describes Constantine as a shrewd businessman, placing his bets on the "winning horse" that was Christianity. He elucidates the rationale for the Council in this way:

---

[1] In cinematic history, Constantine does appear in a few films, for example, *In hoc signo vinces* (1913) and *Constantine and the Cross* (1961), originally titled *Constantino il grande*. List in Solomon 2001, 329. As the titles indicate, the thematic concern in these films was Constantine's conversion to Christianity. See Carlà-Uhink 2017. On Constantine in additional modern media, see Goltz 2008.

1

FIGURE I.I From The Da Vinci Code (© 2006 Columbia Pictures Industries Inc.). All Rights Reserved. Courtesy of Columbia Pictures.

> "Indeed," Teabing said. "Stay with me. During this fusion of religions, Constantine needed to strengthen the new Christian tradition, and held a famous ecumenical gathering known as the Council of Nicaea." [...] "At this gathering," Teabing said, "many aspects of Christianity were debated and voted upon – the date of Easter, the role of the bishops, the administration of sacraments, and of course, the *divinity* of Jesus."

Up to this point in history, we read, many of the followers of Jesus viewed him as a "mortal prophet ... a great and powerful man, but a *man* nonetheless. A mortal," and thus the Council of Nicaea was a conspiratorial event, where a majority vote decided that the man Jesus was now the Son of God. Why, we may ask? Teabing explains:

> By officially endorsing Jesus as the Son of God, Constantine turned Jesus into a divinity who existed beyond the scope of the human world, an entity whose power was unchallengeable. This not only precluded further pagan challenges to Christianity, but now the followers of Christ were able to redeem themselves *only* via the established sacred channel – the Roman Catholic Church.[2]

Dan Brown's fanciful novel (and its cinematic adaptation), of course, is entertaining fiction, but the lines between story and history can be extremely blurry and even a single page can divulge a whole series of outlandish claims, as we have just seen above, and a single scene can be

---

[2]   All quotations from Brown 2003, 232–33.

chock-full of anachronisms.[3] But perhaps in an unexpected way *The Da Vinci Code* brought the Council of Nicaea to public awareness, even if only for a brief moment, as readers and moviegoers learned that some kind of debate over the status of Jesus Christ unfolded there. The aftermath of the book's publication witnessed a proliferation of talking-head documentaries on cable television channels, countless online musings for and against Brown's conspiracy theories, and books by a mix of scholars, "experts," pastors, and laypeople. Many of these publications now sit in stacks in discount bookstores, gathering dust after a short-lived boon, particularly for the Christian publishing industry. But still, there is a lingering afterlife to the momentary craze that the novel and film generated. For example, interested professors and students can even reenact the debates in a role-playing game in which members of the "Alexandrian Faction" and the "Arian Faction" try to persuade undecided delegates to vote for their respective theological positions, all the while as the emperor Constantine oversees the gathering.[4] Such is in no small part a reflection of a broader public interest in the history of Christianity that is keen on the developmental, deliberative, and some might say deceptive aspects of the faith, with a dash of conspiracy, secret societies, and an all-powerful Magisterium for added intrigue.

THE COUNCIL OF NICAEA AS CONFIRMATION

But for many, many Christians all over the world, the story of the Council of Nicaea was and is something entirely different. While most have only vague notions of the historical event and its specific circumstances, they are certainly familiar with its eponymous creed, which many recite on a weekly basis. In doing so, they knowingly (or not) proclaim Nicaea as part of the heritage of their faith and church communities.[5] In describing the creed, the *Catechism of the Catholic*

---

[3] See Ehrman 2004. Ine Jacobs's chapter in this volume discusses the venue in which the council took place, below 82–86.

[4] Henderson and Kirkpatrick 2016, which is part of the "Reacting to the Past" game series developed at Barnard College. For a very interesting review of the game in practice, see www.ancientjewreview.com/articles/2015/3/18/re-enacting-nicaea [accessed April 28, 2018].

[5] For example, on the website of the Episcopal Church describes the Apostles' Creed and the Nicene Creed in this way: "We will always have questions, but in the two foundational statements of faith – the Apostles' Creed used at baptism, and the Nicene Creed used at communion – we join Christians throughout the ages in affirming our faith in the one God who created us, redeemed us, and sanctifies us" (www.episcopalchurch.org/page/creeds [accessed April 28, 2018]). The (translated) text of the Nicene Creed as found on the website and in most other citations of the creed is

Church says, "195: The Niceno-Constantinopolitan or Nicene Creed draws its great authority from the fact that it stems from the first two ecumenical councils (in 325 and 381). It remains common to all the great Churches of both East and West to this day."[6] This catechetical instruction offers a hopeful lesson on how the creed is shared and held in common by Christians, as it conveys a sense of continuity from antiquity to the present, rooted in councils that were *ecumenical*.[7] The Coptic Orthodox Church of Alexandria identifies the creed as one of the pillars of faith.[8] And even for a decidedly non-creedal tradition, as expressed by the United Methodist Church, the perspective of the Nicene Creed is still positive: "The Nicene Creed set forth the key affirmations concerning the Christian faith and served as a guide in combating heretical or false teaching."[9]

Those with a bit more knowledge about the history of Christianity understand that the Council of Nicaea was a crucial moment when the leaders of the church, contesting the teaching of Arius, "resolved" the theological debate about the Son in relation to God the Father. For example, the Presbyterian Church (USA) teaches:

> The new emperor [Constantine] soon discovered that "one faith and one church" were fractured by theological disputes, especially conflicting understandings of the nature of Christ, long a point of controversy. Arius, a priest of the church in Alexandria, asserted that the divine Christ, the Word through whom all things have their existence, was *created* by God before the beginning of time. Therefore, the divinity of Christ was similar to the divinity of God, but not of the same essence. Arius was opposed by the bishop,

not the original Nicene Creed, but the so-called Niceno-Constantinopolitan Creed, which combines content connected to the councils of Nicaea and Constantinople, a topic that is discussed in several chapters in this volume.

6   Catholic Church 1994, 53.
7   There is no comment, however, on the procession of the Holy Spirit "from the Father *and the Son*," the latter of which is a source of contention with the eastern Orthodox, Coptic, and other churches. This is an old dispute over the Latin phrase *Filioque*, which is addressed in this volume by Paul Gavrilyuk and Geoffrey Dunn.
8   http://lacopts.org/orthodoxy/coptic-orthodox-church/ [accessed May 10, 2018].
9   www.umc.org/what-we-believe/glossary-nicene-creed, accessed May 10, 2018. An interesting contrast is offered by the teaching of the Church of Jesus Christ of Latter-Day Saints: "Mormons do not believe in the Trinity concept because it is not supported by scripture. It was not until the councils of Nicaea (AD 325) and Chalcedon (AD 451) that the doctrine of the Trinity was defined. The formal doctrine of the Trinity is not found in the New Testament because *the idea was only introduced hundreds of years later*" (emphasis mine); see www.mormon.org/blog/do-mormons-believe-in-the-trinity [accessed May 11, 2018].

Alexander, together with his associate and successor Athanasius. They affirmed that the divinity of Christ, the Son, is of the same substance as the divinity of God, the Father. To hold otherwise, they said, was open to the possibility of polytheism, and to imply that knowledge of God in Christ was not final knowledge of God.

To counter a widening rift within the church, Constantine convened a council in Nicaea in A.D. 325. A creed reflecting the position of Alexander and Athanasius was written and signed by a majority of the bishops. Nevertheless, the two parties continued to battle each other. In 381, a second council met in Constantinople. It adopted a revised and expanded form of the A.D. 325 creed, now known as the Nicene Creed.[10]

Although the Presbyterian Church (USA)'s description uses phrases like "of the same substance," it is not entirely clear from the narrative above what this "substance" entails, and perhaps the denomination leaves it to its pastors to clarify, or not, as it were. Christians who have delved even deeper into the subject may know that the Greek word, *homoousios* (ὁμοούσιος) was the term in the creed that described the "same substance" or "consubstantial" relationship between Father and Son.[11] While they may not be able to explain the finer, sophisticated theological and philosophical meaning and implications of the language of the creed, they trust that the Council *affirmed* what the Church already had received and believed, implicitly or otherwise, about Christ (from the beginning of the faith), and *rejected* the incorrect teachings espoused by those who would ultimately be condemned as heretics. In other words, in this account of the Council and Creed of Nicaea, we also see a deliberative element as we did above, but the difference in this case is that the participants at the Council were defending and defining more precisely what they already understood or believed to be true rather than deciding (for the first time) that Christ was divine.[12]

[10] Presbyterian Church (U.S.A.) 2016, 2. Furthermore, it also recognizes the ecclesiastical unity of Christian churches based on the council and creed: "The Nicene Creed is the most ecumenical of creeds. The Presbyterian Church (U.S.A.) joins with Eastern Orthodox, Roman Catholic, and most Protestant churches in affirming it."

[11] *Homoousios* is often translated into English as "consubstantial" or "of the same substance," but of course there is always the risk that something can be "lost in translation."

[12] Although consider in contrast the teaching of the Jehovah's Witnesses: "Constantine asked the bishops, who may have numbered in the hundreds, to come to a unanimous accord, but his request was in vain. He then proposed that the council adopt the ambiguous notion that Jesus was 'of one substance' (*homoousios*) with the Father. This unbiblical Greek philosophical term laid the foundation for the Trinity doctrine

Perhaps it is too much a cliché to say so, but there is a certain degree of resonance to the notion that history is written by the powerful. The same applies to the disputes of ancient Christianity. Laying exclusive claim to the moniker "orthodox," the winners ultimately were able to control the narrative over the manifold arguments and controversies that emerged over the books of scripture, theology, ecclesiastical organization and leadership, and liturgical practice, among other subjects of disagreement. Furthermore, the orthodox at times suppressed the writings and points of view expressed by the losers, branding them "heretics" and imputing upon them all manner of devious and diabolical motivations to deceive their followers with their false teachings.[13] Such is the case with Arius, the polarizing figure who initiated the theological quarrel that ultimately led to the Council of Nicaea. Those who opposed him in antiquity, of course, thoroughly demonized him as a blasphemer who denigrated the divine Christ. For example, a heresiological writer in the late fourth century offered the following description of Arius: "He was very tall in stature and wore a downcast expression – counterfeited like a guileful serpent, he was well able to deceive every innocent heart through his cunning outer display. For he always wore a short cloak and a sleeveless tunic. He was pleasant in speech, and people found him persuasive and flattering."[14] The mellifluous Arius dressed like a monk, but beneath the seemingly pious outer display was a deceptive snake. The manner of Arius's death – essentially excreting his guts into a latrine in Constantinople – is even more illustrative of how his ancient opponents vilified him.[15] For them, how he died – like the traitor Judas Iscariot – was proof positive of his depraved character, the falsity of his beliefs, and his condemnation by God. Such a perspective of an ill-intentioned Arius persists to this day, such that the Greek Orthodox Archdiocese of America teaches:

> Arius was a protopresbyter of the Church of Alexandria, and in 315, he began to blaspheme against the Son of God saying that He was not the true God, consubstantial with the Father, but rather a work or creation of God and different from the essence and glory of the

as later set forth in the church creeds"; seewww.jw.org/en/publications/magazines/g201308/trinity [accessed May 11, 2018].

13   This impulse gave rise to the production of anti-heretical writings, collectively identified by modern scholars as "heresiology" or "heresiography." On this subject, see Le Boulluec 1985; Henderson 1998; Smith 2015.
14   Epiphanius, *Panarion* 69.3.1.
15   Athanasius, *Epistulae* 54; cf. Epiph., *Pan.* 69.10.3. On this, see Leroy-Molinghen 1968; Brennecke 2010; Muehlberger 2015.

Father [. . .] Arius continued with his heretical teachings, creating controversy and division in the churches of other cities, which led to a theological and ecclesiastical crisis throughout the Christian church.[16]

While the language of this portrayal is measured, descriptors like "blasphemy" and "heretical teachings" make clear how Arius has been received in this tradition. But is it possible to think of Arius otherwise? Can we question the traditional narrative of him as a blasphemer and one who sought to malign Christ? Could we imagine for a moment that Arius believed he was a true Christian and that he desired to honor and worship the God he believed in? Perhaps not without some difficulty. Old impressions, shaped by the powerful, die hard.

The other historical figure who is inextricably linked to the Council of Nicaea is of course the emperor Constantine, who also generates equally vexing interpretative questions. As a subject of academic but also public interest, he is never lacking for scholarly attention, and in the last two decades a steady stream of publications has continued to reevaluate the first Christian emperor.[17] His role in convoking and presiding over the Council is well known, but lively debate continues as to his motivations and desired results. He certainly had embraced some form of Christianity and favored it, but scholars wrestle with questions of how deep an understanding he had, how sincere his beliefs were, and how interested he was in promulgating a particular version of the faith over and against others. This last question is also why Constantine's relationship to the Council of Nicaea is so complicated. Were his motives theological? Political? Pragmatic? Without a doubt, Constantine was one of the "winners" in history, and yet by strictly "Nicene" standards one might hesitate to count him among the orthodox, since he was baptized before his death by Eusebius of Nicomedia, a decidedly non-Nicene bishop. Yet the same Greek Orthodox Archdiocese of America that condemns Arius unequivocally recognizes Constantine (and his mother Helena) as a saint "Equal-to-the-Apostles," who "in 325 gathered the First Ecumenical Council in Nicaea, which he himself personally addressed."[18] The Episcopal Church affirms that "Constantine was

---

[16] www.goarch.org/en/fathers-first-ecumenical-council [accessed May 1, 2018].
[17] See, for example, Lenski 2006; Van Dam 2007; Stephenson 2009; Girardet 2010; Leithart 2010; Barnes 2011; Potter 2013; Lenski 2016.
[18] www.goarch.org/chapel/saints?contentid=62 [accessed May 10, 2018]. It is worth noting, however, that the perspective on Constantine by different Christian traditions is quite varied. For example, the Anabaptists were deeply critical; see Klaassen 1981, for a brief summary. See also Roth 2013.

a strong supporter of Christianity and sought to build a Christian empire."[19]

And so even in this cursory examination of the reception of Nicaea in a variety of Christian traditions, we are left with the impression that the council was one of the most important moments in the history of the church, a point at which its leaders affirmed one of the fundamental beliefs of the faith, the divinity of Jesus. Furthermore, we see that it is appropriate to condemn Arius as one of the "losers," a "heretic," but to count Constantine among the righteous. But as much as Dan Brown's version of the first Christian emperor begs credulity, the same might be said of the easy confirmation of Constantine on the "right side" at Nicaea. These disparate pictures should give us pause, and we ought to consider if we also have received and implicitly accepted the narrative of the winners. These kinds of questions will serve as a starting point for a reflection on the goals of this volume.

YET ANOTHER STUDY?

The two perspectives we described above lie at opposite ends of a spectrum – the Council of Nicaea as conspiracy or the Council of Nicaea as confirmation – but much of the interstitial space is where scholars have done their most significant work.[20] Perhaps one could make the argument that different disciplinary frameworks and approaches tend to indicate to some degree where along the spectrum a given scholar's interpretation might be found. Historians, especially those with interest in the politics of religion, might view the Council as an event driven by the dynamics of power and authority, whereas theologians could see it as the beginnings or a continuation of a sincere effort to define (and protect) the parameters of right belief. Such an endeavor by fourth-century Christians necessarily resulted in the marginalization and condemnation of certain thinkers, such as Arius, as heretics. Scholars of religious studies, anthropology, psychology, and other disciplines have offered and continue to develop additional perspectives. In any case, there is a capacious, at times contested, yet consistently revisited, tradition of scholarly inquiry on the Council and its implications in the

---

[19] www.episcopalchurch.org/library/glossary/constantine-i [accessed May 10, 2018].
[20] The bibliography is as voluminous as it is varied, and I omit here any discussion of the seminal works of the nineteenth and early twentieth centuries; see Williams 2001, 1-25, for a useful survey. Rebecca Lyman also discusses in her chapter some of the major studies on Arius. A good overall starting point is the massive, now classic work, Hanson 1988. For a survey of events before the Council of Nicaea, see Löhr 2006a.

fourth century and beyond.[21] The new millennium has seen the production of even more excellent studies of Nicaea and its aftermath, and we
fortunately have no shortage of scholarly investigations and fodder for
deep thought and dispute.[22]

So perhaps it is worth asking why yet another volume, no less
a *Cambridge Companion*, on a subject that has received so much attention over the past two centuries? But as we approach a milestone anniversary (1,700 years), we can hope that the council and creed will return
again to the public sphere and that the chapters in this volume together
will offer a reassessment of the Council of Nicaea on its own (potentially
unstable) terms.[23] We know well the degree to which the council and its
creed did *not* resolve the theological (and political) issues raised initially
by and associated with Arius, but rather initiated several different and
often competing theological and ecclesiological trajectories that led to
a proliferation of councils and synods, many of which produced additional creeds and confessional statements. Perhaps lost amid the many
detailed studies of the fourth-century debates over the Trinity is the
Council of Nicaea itself, and we have taken for granted our understanding of the event, its historical and ecclesiastical context, its purpose and
intended outcomes, its initial uncertain future implications and impact,
and of course its main players. Therefore a fresh examination can prove
to be very beneficial.

The deep theological interest characteristic of nineteenth- and early
twentieth-century scholarship on the council and the creed, and for these
earlier writers (many of them theologians) their status as markers of
orthodoxy, exposes a set of historiographic challenges that necessarily
come with any interpretation of Nicaea. First, when we examine in
hindsight the council and what unfolded in the ensuing decades, we
can fall into the trap of reading back into the beginning the end result,
that the correlative divinity of the Son (and eventually, the Holy Spirit) in
relation to the Father and to the Godhead was a foregone conclusion and
the inevitable outcome of the theological debates of the fourth century.
As we noted earlier, we simply cannot conceive of a Saint Arius of
Alexandria, let alone the heresiarch Alexander or Athanasius the heretic.

---

[21]   Several influential monographs and edited volumes that were published at the end of
       the last millennium: Simonetti 1975; Kopecek 1979; Brennecke 1988; Barnes and
       Williams 1993; Lienhard 1999; Vaggione 2000.
[22]   See Ayres 2004; Behr 2004; Parvis 2006; Gwynn 2007; Anatolios 2011;
       Galvão-Sobrinho 2013.
[23]   Surprisingly, there are few studies that concentrate on just the council itself and its
       circumstances. See for example, Luibhéid 1982. A more recent examination is offered
       by Pietras 2016, albeit with a very pessimistic perspective.

We are also compelled to make the logic of the seemingly illogical Trinity work and to ascertain the reasons why the subordinating perspective(s) that were held by almost all Christians in one form or another before the fourth century "lost" in the end.[24] In other words, how did the initially minority view become the majority?

Second, the notion of "ecumenical council" retroactively imagines a sequence of conciliar gatherings whose results were decided by a fairly unified group of leaders and thinkers and ratified by all of Christendom. But again, recent scholarship has demonstrated just how muddy the picture was, especially in the years between the councils of Nicaea and Constantinople in 381, the first two so-called ecumenical councils.[25] We recognize our almost complete dependence on the Athanasian narrative, and for better or for worse, how difficult it is to imagine those he vilified as anything other than conspirators with malicious intentions and deceptive tactics.[26] The perspective of Athanasius was taken up by later writers, including Epiphanius, Theodoret, Socrates, and Sozomen, and so the available sources function as a sort of feedback loop, mutually reinforcing the original Athanasian account.[27] What we can reconstruct of the ecclesiastical history of the non-Nicene Philostorgius provides some counterbalance, but with limitations due to the fragmentary survival of his work.[28] We are also well informed to what extent Athanasius himself, a young attendee, did not appeal to the council and creed as the standards of orthodoxy until over a decade (or more) *after* 325. Therefore a reexamination of the context and outcomes of the events in 325, looking forward, will allow us to view subsequent developments from the vantage point of the "starting line" (with its uncertain future) of the debates to ascertain first the possible intentions of the council itself and second to explore the question of why the council was not from the beginning the universally accepted (and ecclesiastically binding) moment that it became in subsequent centuries. All of these circumstances and developments take us to the events of 325, which will serve as the pivot point in this volume.

WHAT THIS VOLUME IS ... AND IS NOT

First, let me begin by reflecting on what this *Cambridge Companion* is not. It is not designed or intended to provide the reader with

[24] Although Behr 2001 offers a thoughtful narrative of the ante-Nicene tradition.
[25] A concise summary can be found in Smith 2018, 7–34.
[26] Gwynn 2007. Also see Barnes 1993.
[27] On these receptions and others, see Lim 1995, 182–216.
[28] Amidon 2007.

a comprehensive, diachronic narrative of the time before, during, and after the council, and all of its associated events, people, places, and dates. Nor will it dive into the intricacies of ongoing debates about the sources, their dates of composition and authorship, their authenticity, their transmission, and their reliability. Such can be found in already published works, especially the massive study by Richard Hanson, and studies by Lewis Ayres, John Behr, and Khaled Anatolios.[29] For the related documents, the classic collection by Opitz and recent updates by Brennecke, von Stockhausen, and others, are excellent resources.[30] Rather, the essays collected here offer several possibilities. Some revisit old debates and discussions, others ask new questions, and still more provide different viewpoints on the people, context, and consequences linked to the Council of Nicaea. My hope is that there is something for everyone interested in the Council of Nicaea, from the public to the professional, from the student to the senior scholar, and that the sum total of the chapters provides perspectives that will enhance the reader's thinking about the monumental event, the lead-up to it, and its long afterlife. As is true of any edited volume focused on a particular topic, there will be some overlap among the various contributions, and, I am pleased to say, there are instances of different and even conflicting interpretations of particular historical or theological problems. But these only enhance the critical value of the volume, as the chapters function dialectically as conversation and debate partners with each other, as they also do with the reader. There will also be noticeable gaps or subjects not covered. There simply are not enough pages or acceptable word counts that would make this possible. In some sense, the bibliography itself of this volume mirrors this potential criticism. While on the one hand it is lengthy and contains many (and in some cases) "canon" entries, it is not comprehensive. My ultimate goal is that the contributions of all of the expert writers in this volume will stimulate thought, provoke unexpected reactions, and ultimately inspire renewed interested in one of the most important – albeit often misunderstood – moments in the history of Christianity.

THE CONTRIBUTIONS

Part I of this *Cambridge Companion* will explore the "contexts" leading up to the Council of Nicaea, with examinations of the political, social,

---

[29]   Hanson 1988. In addition, Ayres 2004b and Behr 2004 each offer concise summaries.
[30]   See Opitz 1934, Brennecke et al. 2007 and 2014.

ecclesiastical, and theological developments that informed and influenced the gathering and its deliberations. **Raymond Van Dam** offers a "prelude," which investigates a series of questions related to the political and social context in the lead-up to Nicaea. Eschewing a teleological perspective that assumes the inevitability of the theology of Nicaea, he explores how the symbols and language of religion are reflections of social and cultural concerns. Van Dam pays special attention to the Tetrarchic framework that in turn led to the rise of Constantine, and how the ambiguities inherent in his complex rise to power and conversion were very much reflected in the theological debates that emerged about the Son's relationship to the Father. **Rebecca Lyman** studies the uncertain and contested origins of the theological dispute between Alexander of Alexandria and Arius, in particular the social, cultural, and political developments of the years 312–24, which set the stage for the escalation of the conflict and the convocation of the council. After surveying previous scholarly interpretations, which are varied and debated rigorously, she argues that the political, social, and religious tensions resulting from the empire of Constantine and Licinius and the development of ascetic ideals and practices in the post-Diocletianic, post-persecution dispensation set the context in which the theological dispute between Arius and Alexander unfolded.

In Part II, **Ine Jacobs** uses her expertise in late antique and Byzantine archaeology to analyze the material considerations of the council. She first reflects on the change in locale, from Ancyra to Nicaea, and what may have motivated it, and then she examines the available remains of Nicaea (modern Iznik) to ascertain the suitability of the city to host such a gathering, including practical concerns such as where the imperial court and officials were housed, where the meeting space was in the overall landscape of the city, and how and where the delegates were hosted. Finally, she discusses the broader Constantinian building program reflected in other locales and how developments in Christian architecture resulted from changing liturgical and conciliar needs. **David Gwynn** explores the council and what we know about its convocation, participants, and proceedings from a broad perspective. His discussion includes reflections on the difficulties presented by the conflicting sources, and in his reconstruction of the events he draws on later, more secure conciliar documents to tease out insights into what may have transpired at Nicaea. In addition, he tries as much as possible to recover the voices and perspectives of the "humble individuals." **Hal Drake** reflects on the "elephant in the room," namely, the emperor Constantine, whose presence at the council was an unprecedented development. Drake explores what motivated Constantine to be so intimately involved with the council, shifting attention away from the usual theological interpretations and back to the political motivations of the emperor. He considers the significance of Constantine's earlier dealings with the Donatists, which gave him a framework for how to approach the Arian controversy. While Constantine sought unity and harmony in his empire, the internal dynamics of Christianity itself ultimately made this an impossibility.

In Part III, on the outcomes of the council, **Mark Edwards** offers a detailed study of the creed itself. His assessment begins with the evidence for earlier creeds and creed-making and then analyzes the one produced at Nicaea, its language, biblical foundations, and theological implications, including a close look at the history and origin of the term *homoousios*. He also examines the anathemas and their allegations. Finally, Edwards discusses the promulgation and reception of the creed in the immediate aftermath of the council. **Andreas Weckwerth** studies the canons by first considering their textual transmission and their translation into several languages, and second discussing their purpose and content. He then shifts to an analysis of their reception and function in later tradition, in particular how other councils and churchmen understood, adapted, and applied the Nicene canons in subsequent centuries. **Daniel Mc Carthy** investigates the debate at the council regarding the calculation for when to celebrate the Pasch, that is, Easter. He provides an overview of the Paschal Controversy before and after the fourth century, and he discusses if and how the issue was resolved at the council and received by later traditions. **Aaron Johnson** writes on the council specifically from the perspective of Eusebius of Caesarea, examining the theological, ecclesiastical, and political vision of arguably the most important eyewitness to the council and its aftermath. Eusebius has left us with several immeasurably important texts, and this chapter surveys the scholarly debates resulting from various interpretative issues. Finally, Johnson challenges traditional and perhaps uncritical arguments about the famous ecclesiastical historian, that he was a dishonest Arian sympathizer who signed the creed out of cowardice or that he did so because he was awestruck in the presence of the emperor. Eusebius was, in fact, an original thinker with a coherent vision that was deeply influential for later writers.

Part IV examines the aftermath of the council, up to the end of the fourth century, with careful attention on the theological trajectories initiated by Nicaea. **Sara Parvis** argues against recent scholarly assessments that eschew the development of discrete parties, for or against

Arius, and correspondingly for or against the Council of Nicaea and its creed. With close analysis of the evidence, she traces the extent to which politics, theology, friendships and enmities, and the talent, ambitions, and charisma of prominent individuals all influenced the decades-long dispute until the Council of Constantinople in 381. In particular, she identifies Athanasius as the key player. **Mark DelCogliano** discusses the various theological strands in the aftermath that eventually culminated in the so-called pro-Nicene position, championed at first by Athanasius and refined by the Cappadocian fathers: Basil of Caesarea, Gregory of Nazianzus, and Gregory of Nyssa. He argues that this pro-Nicene alliance was ultimately a consensus-building movement that borrowed from tactics employed by earlier theologians, but that it espoused a particular interpretation of the Nicene Creed that positioned their theology as a middle ground between the extremes of the theology of Arius and Marcellus of Ancyra. **Kelley Spoerl** studies the term *homoousios* and its implications for Christology, viewed primarily through the teaching attributed to Apollinarius of Laodicea, but also in anticipation of the Christological disputes that unfolded at the end of the fourth century and through the fifth century. The Council of Nicaea, and the fourth century in general, are often (mistakenly) described as only trinitarian in focus, so this chapter offers a valuable corrective to the overly simplistic binary between the trinitarian fourth and Christological fifth centuries. **Dan Williams** examines the fourth-century developments in the western half of the Roman empire, tracing the pro-Nicene theological trajectory initiated among others by Hilary of Poitiers and Marius Victorinus and gradually solidified by prominent western bishops like Ambrose and Augustine. He demonstrates how the eventual affirmation of a "neo-Nicene" trinitarian doctrine was achieved sometime in the 380s, after a protracted struggle against the Homoian doctrine, which rejected any "substance"-related terminologies.

Finally, in Part V, the contributions investigate the "long" reception of the council and creed by two Christian traditions. **Paul Gavrilyuk** considers Nicaea from the perspective of the Orthodox tradition and traces the importance of the council and creed first in the work of Cyril of Alexandria and then in Byzantine liturgy in the sixth century. He introduces the idea of the "hermeneutic of conciliar authority" as evident in later councils, all of which made Nicaea a crucial reference point, and his chapter concludes with reflections on the council in light of the pan-Orthodox council, held in Crete,

June 2016. **Geoffrey Dunn** begins with an examination of the reception of the council in the churches of the West up to 1054 and then specifically by the Roman Catholic Church in the centuries following. He explores broadly the reception of the creed, including the controversy of the *Filioque*, and the Canons and their function in church discipline. Dunn also pays special attention to the modern Catholic reception of Nicaea.

Together, these chapters together provide a picture of the immediate, the middle, and the long-term impact of the Council of Nicaea, and they will inspire new questions and research trajectories, provoke debate and disagreement, and ultimately contribute to an ongoing conversation that in reality began as soon as the gathering ended. Seventeen hundred years is a long time in which to discuss anything, but for the nature of the Godhead, ecclesiastical leadership and organization, orthodoxy and heresy, among other related subjects, perhaps such a span of time is only the beginning. The *Cambridge Companion to the Council of Nicaea* pays respect to its forebears but also looks ahead to continued dialogue, discussion, and debate about the people and their actions, the events and their outcomes, and the ideas and their lasting legacy in the history of Christianity.

NOTE TO THE READER

The chapters in this volume are each followed by a "Select References" list, rather than a complete bibliography. These lists include fifteen scholarly works chosen by each author, which are relevant to the individual chapter's contents. All works cited in the contributions can be found in the Bibliography at the end of the volume.

SELECT REFERENCES

Anatolios, Khaled. 2011. *Retrieving Nicaea: The Development and Meaning of Trinitarian Doctrine*. Grand Rapids: Baker Academic.

Ayres, Lewis. 2004. *Nicaea and Its Legacy: An Approach to Fourth-Century Trinitarian Theology*. Oxford: Oxford University Press.

Behr, John. 2004. *The Nicene Faith*, Formation of Christian Theology 2. Crestwood, NY: St Vladimir's Seminary Press.

Brown, Dan. 2003. *The Da Vinci Code*. New York: Doubleday.

Carlà-Uhink, Filippo. 2017. "Thinking through the Ancient World: 'Late Antique Movies' as a Mirror of Shifting Attitudes towards Christian Religion." In

A Companion to Ancient Greece and Rome on Screen, ed. Arthur J. Pomeroy, 307–28. Malden, MA: Wiley-Blackwell.

Ehrman, Bart. 2004. *Truth and Fiction in the Da Vinci Code: A Historian Reveals What We Really Know about Jesus, Mary Magdalene, and Constantine.* Oxford: Oxford University Press.

Galvão-Sobrinho, Carlos R. 2013. *Doctrine and Power: Theological Controversy and Christian Leadership in the Later Roman Empire.* Transformation of the Classical Heritage 51. Berkeley: University of California Press.

Goltz, Andreas. 2008. "Der 'mediale' Konstantin: Zur Rezeption des ersten christlichen Kaisers in den modernen Medien." In *Konstantin der Große: Das Bild des Kaisers im Wandel der Zeiten*, ed. Andreas Goltz and Heinrich Schlange-Schöningen, 277–308. Cologne: Böhlau.

Hanson, R. P. C. 1988. *The Search for the Christian Doctrine of God: The Arian Controversy, 318–81.* Edinburgh: T&T Clark.

Henderson David E., and Frank Kirkpatrick. 2016. *Constantine and the Council of Nicaea: Defining Orthodoxy and Heresy in Christianity, 325 C.E.* Chapel Hill, NC: Reacting Consortium Press.

Lenski, Noel. 2016. *Constantine and the Cities: Imperial Authority and Civic Politics.* Philadelphia: University of Pennsylvania Press.

Löhr, Winrich. 2006a. "Arius Reconsidered (Part 1)." *ZAC* 9(3): 524–60.

Smith, Mark S. 2018. *The Idea of Nicaea in the Early Church Councils, ad 431–51.* Oxford Early Christian Studies. Oxford: Oxford University Press.

Solomon, Jon. 2001. *The Ancient World in the Cinema.* New Haven: Yale University Press.

Williams, Rowan. (1987) 2001. *Arius: Heresy and Tradition, rev. ed.* Grand Rapids: Eerdmans.

Part I
Contexts

2 Imperial Fathers and Their Sons
Licinius, Constantine, and the Council of Nicaea

RAYMOND VAN DAM

After the retirement of the emperors Diocletian and Maximian, the grand experiment of four concurrent emperors known as the Tetrarchy disintegrated in a series of usurpations and civil wars. Before one battle against a rival, an emperor had a vision of "an angel of God," and he taught his troops to recite a prayer (Lactantius [Lact.], *De mortibus persecutorum* [*DMP*] 46.3–6). That divinely inspired emperor was Licinius, who defeated Maximinus in 313. After his victory Licinius ruled over the eastern provinces until 324. During this same long decade the controversy over the priest Arius and his theology intensified in Egypt and expanded to other eastern provinces. Our fascination with the emperor Constantine makes it easy to forget that Licinius was the emperor who presided over the initial stages of the search for the Christian doctrine of God.

Interpreting the significance of the Council of Nicaea raises similar challenges about proper contextualization. One problematic issue is indeed the involvement of Constantine. In the early fourth century Tetrarchic emperors had initiated persecutions of Christians. But now, because Constantine had summoned and hosted this council, its convocation might seem to have initiated a new era of harmony between bishops and emperors, and between church and state. Such an optimistic presumption overlooks the disruptive impact of this collaboration. Constantine was a Christian emperor, not merely an emperor who tolerated Christianity, and a Christian emperor was such a novelty that bishops were still figuring out how he was to coexist with the ecclesiastical hierarchy. Were they to stand when he entered the council chamber? Should he wait for their permission before sitting on his gold throne?[1] Because theologians had not yet developed a Christian political philosophy for imagining an emperor as another representative of their

---

[1] According to Eusebius of Caesarea, who attended the council, the answer to both questions was yes (Eusebius [Eus.], *Vita Constantini* [*VC*] 3.10).

God on earth, the dominating presence of the emperor at this council would become an awkward precedent.

A related issue is the inadvertent distortion introduced by our own perspectives. Because the Council of Nicaea appeared to be a strictly Christian event, modern interpretations often reflect devotional, even pietistic, perspectives. Christianity is treated, sometimes unconsciously, as *sui generis*, a unique way for people to configure their lives around specific beliefs and practices; this assumption seemingly allows modern scholarship to discuss early Christianity in isolation from other aspects of society. In fact, Christianity was one among many cults in the Roman world, and religion in general competed with other symbolic idioms that enabled people to find meaning and identity in their daily lives and represent themselves within their communities. In this more expansive perspective, theology becomes a medium certainly for thinking about the Christian God, but also for thinking with God as another symbolic category, similar to Jupiter, the supreme deity in the pantheon of traditional Roman cults. As a result, direct disagreements about theology were also implicit arguments about social norms, political authority, and cultural structures.

Two pointed questions intrude. Of all the doctrinal disputes among early Christians in previous centuries, why did the council discuss these particular topics? And why did these topics blow up into a major dispute at this specific moment? An historical account of the Council of Nicaea would stress the contingency of the outcome, as notions of both "orthodoxy" and "heresy" were in flux. It would also emphasize the larger context, including the non-Christian and even non-religious circumstances. Defining Christianity as one among various strategies for constructing meaning and identity allows us to relate the topics discussed at the Council of Nicaea to contemporary political and social issues.

Emperors had always been grand patrons who were expected to respond favorably to petitions; now those petitioners included Christians (see below, section 1). At the same time emperors had been experimenting with new ways of defining imperial rule and projecting their authority. Most notably, the recognition of four legitimate emperors created a tension between the unity of empire and the multiplicity of imperial rule. This political tension intersected with doctrinal disputes. Because the controversy over Arius and his theology had a limited impact in the western provinces, Constantine's information before his victory over Licinius in 324 was restricted. But even though he knew little about the specific doctrines, he was familiar with the issues. When Constantine attended the Council of Nicaea, he had already been thinking for years about fathers and sons (section 2), the shape of the calendar year (section 3), and the divinity of rulers (section 4). These were as much imperial matters as religious concerns.

Constantine's personal experiences contributed to the discussions at the council; at the same time those discussions influenced his ideas about his family (section 5). After the council he also reformulated his own autobiography in stories about his earlier victories (section 6). As a result, the Council of Nicaea was a crucible for the formation of both a theology of God and a political philosophy of a Christian emperor.

1. EMPEROR LICINIUS, BISHOP EUSEBIUS OF NICOMEDIA, AND THE CONTROVERSY OVER ARIUS

Diocletian became emperor in late 284 after a military coup, and in the following year he selected Maximian to become his colleague. In 293 the two senior emperors (known as Augusti) promoted Constantius and Galerius as junior emperors (known as Caesars) to form a Tetrarchy, a college of four emperors. In 305 Diocletian and Maximian retired, while Constantius and Galerius became the Augusti and Severus and Maximinus the new Caesars.[2]

But the orderly relationships among the official emperors soon crumbled. After the death of Constantius in 306, the army in Britain elevated his son Constantine, and at Rome the praetorian guard hailed Maxentius as emperor. Maxentius soon summoned his father, Maximian, out of retirement. Galerius, who was now the preeminent emperor, recognized Constantine as a Caesar, but in 307 he had Severus invade Italy to depose Maxentius. After Severus's failure and execution, Galerius himself led another futile invasion. He also turned against Constantine for having accepted promotion as an Augustus from Maximian. When Diocletian finally emerged from retirement, he supported Galerius's attempt to reinstate a proper Tetrarchic hierarchy of four official emperors. In 308 Licinius was promoted to join Galerius as another Augustus, and Constantine and Maximinus were the Caesars; but Diocletian and Maximian, even though sidelined, each retained the formal title of "elder Augustus." The outcome in fact created more confusion, because rather than being revived, the Tetrarchy had become a Hexarchy. As a contemporary observer concluded, now there were "six emperors at one time" (Lact., *DMP* 29.2).[3]

[2] Narrative surveys: Barnes 1981; Bowman 2005; Lenski 2006; Barnes 2011.
[3] Digeser 2000, on Lactantius.

Licinius's primary qualification to become emperor was his friend-ship with Galerius. After Galerius's death in 311, Licinius's jurisdiction included the Balkan provinces and mainland Greece, while Maximinus, who had been administering Egypt, Palestine, and Syria already for sev-eral years, seized Asia Minor. In late 312 Constantine defeated Maxentius, and in 313 Licinius defeated Maximinus. Although nomin-ally the two victorious emperors shared imperial rule, in reality they divided jurisdiction, with Licinius governing an eastern empire that extended from the Balkans to Egypt. After a short civil war, in 317 Licinius was forced to cede almost all of his European regions to Constantine. Thereafter his empire included the arc of eastern provinces from Thrace through Asia Minor, Syria, and Palestine to Egypt.

In the western provinces Constantine's engagement with ecclesias-tical controversies was limited. Soon after seizing control over Italy and North Africa in late 312, he responded to appeals from Caecilianus, the bishop of Carthage, by offering financial support and exemptions for clerics. In his letters Constantine identified Caecilianus as the leader of "the catholic church" (Eus., *Historia ecclesiastica* [*HE*] 10.6–7). In fact, Caecilianus's leadership was not universally acknowledged in North Africa, and a rival faction associated with Donatus, an alternative bishop of Carthage, also appealed for the emperor's patronage. In 314 Constantine may have attended a council of bishops at Arles. The bishops formed a microcosm of Constantine's empire at the time, repre-senting Britain, Gaul, Spain, Italy, Sicily, Africa, and even Dalmatia on the eastern coast of the Adriatic Sea. Their decisions covered the ongoing dispute in North Africa, as well as the consecration of bishops, the treatment of converts, and the celebration of Easter. Constantine appar-ently enjoyed himself: "he was eager to attend their debates and to sit together with the bishops" (Eus., *VC* 1.44.2).

But the outcome of this council was inconclusive, and Constantine was dismayed that the partisans of Donatus continued to appeal their negative verdict. They also attacked the emperor personally. "They demand judgment for me; I myself anticipate the judgment of Christ" (Optatus, Appendix 5.32b). Eventually he had to concede his ineffective-ness. "The reasoning of our policy was not able to subdue the force of that innate wickedness" (Optatus, Appendix 9.35a). Participation in the ecclesiastical disputes of North Africa had been a lesson in the limits of imperial power.[4]

---

[4]   Excellent recent scholarship on the Donatist controversy includes Shaw 2011 and
      Miles 2016.

In the eastern provinces Licinius campaigned against the Persians before returning to the Balkan regions. In his jurisdiction he was immersed in typical administrative and military activities. He fought battles against the Goths; he consolidated provinces into dioceses administered by vicars; and he issued legislation about prisoners, marriage, burials, and the collection of taxes (Eus., *HE* 10.8.11–12, *VC* 1.55.1). Through his "sacred command" he authorized repairs for a bridge outside Cyzikus.[5] As a result, Licinius acquired a favorable reputation. A famous sophist at Antioch would remember him for invigorating cities and their councils, while blaming Constantine for their subsequent decline (Libanius, *Orationes* 30.6, 49.2).

But after his defeat by Constantine in 324, Licinius's reputation was condemned and distorted, twice over. The usual degradation of the loser in a civil war combined with the vicious infighting among bishops over theology to transform him into both an illegitimate "tyrant" and a merciless "persecutor." Eusebius of Caesarea could barely restrain himself. In the narrative of his *Ecclesiastical History* he inserted snide comments about Licinius's madness; then he downgraded Licinius as a "monster." In his opinion the emperor's legislation had been an affront to both Christianity and "the ancient laws of the Romans" (Eus., *HE* 9.9.12, 10.8–9, *VC* 1.49.1). This extravagant condemnation has warped our perspective on Licinius's interactions with Christianity, as well as our recognition of Eusebius's own collaboration with the emperor. In early 313 Licinius and Constantine had formulated a joint resolution supporting religious toleration, and as he advanced in his campaign against Maximinus, Licinius had sent the resolution to provincial governors. Christians would now serve among Licinius's courtiers, provincial administrators, and military officers (Eus., *HE* 10.8.10, *VC* 1.52, 54.1). Because Licinius continued to engage positively with Christianity, it is likely that Christians in the East petitioned for his favor, just as Christians in the West appealed for Constantine's support.

One bishop who certainly maneuvered at Licinius's court was Eusebius of Nicomedia. As bishop of Beirut, Eusebius may have met Licinius during his visit to the eastern frontier; soon afterward Eusebius transferred to Nicomedia, which would become a primary residence for Licinius after being pushed out of the Balkan regions. The top official in Licinius's administration was Julius Julianus, who had been serving as his praetorian prefect since at least 315. As prefect Julius Julianus would have been responsible for appointing the provincial

---

[5] Sünskes 1983.

governors and other high-ranking officials in the imperial administration, and his connections may also have provided access to the ecclesiastical hierarchy of bishops. Eusebius was a relative of Julius Julianus; and once he assumed his new episcopacy at Nicomedia, he became an adviser to the emperor's wife (Socrates [Socr.], *Historia ecclesiastica* [HE] 1.25; Sozomen [Soz.], *Historia ecclesiastica* [HE] 2.27; Philostorgius, *Historia ecclesiastica* 1.9) and a confidant of the prefect's daughter (Athanasius, *Historia Arianorum ad monachos* 5.1). Eusebius of Nicomedia, a central player in the networks of eastern bishops and other churchmen, came from the same family as Julius Julianus, the top official in Licinius's imperial administration.[6]

Eusebius of Nicomedia championed the priest Arius against Bishop Alexander of Alexandria. In a statement of his theology Eusebius argued that there was only one "unbegotten" God and that the "begotten" Son, who was "created and fashioned," did not share in his "essence" (*Urk.* 8).[7] After Arius may have visited Eusebius (Epiphanius, *Panarion* 69.5.2), Alexander circulated a letter to the eastern bishops in which he criticized Eusebius as a carpetbagger (for his improper move from Beirut to Nicomedia) and a self-promoter (*Urk.* 4b.4–5). Eusebius and his supporters convened a council in Bithynia and afterward requested Alexander to readmit Arius (*Urk.* 5).

Another supporter of Arius was bishop Eusebius of Caesarea. In a letter to Eusebius of Nicomedia, Arius cited Eusebius of Caesarea as confirmation for his subordinationist doctrine that "God exists before the Son without a beginning. [...] Before the Son was begotten, created, determined, or established, he was not. He was not unbegotten" (*Urk.* 1, 6). Sometime in the early 320s Eusebius of Caesarea travelled to central Asia Minor, where he preached sermons at Laodicea and Ancyra (Eus., *Contra Marcellum* 1.4.42, 45–46). Since the theology of Eusebius of Caesarea seemed to align with the doctrines of Eusebius of Nicomedia, he too presumably enjoyed imperial patronage. In fact, passing comments in his historical narratives hinted at Licinius's support. In *Ecclesiastical History* he noted that after Maximinus's death "letters from the emperor, honors, and gifts of money arrived for individual bishops" (Eus., *HE* 10.2.2). In *Life of Constantine* he claimed that before disputes over doctrine had flared up in Egypt, "the people of God flourished, embellished by the actions of the emperor" (Eus., *VC* 2.61.3). In

---

[6]   Van Dam 2018.
[7]   See Gwynn 2007, 211–18, for an overview of the theology of Eusebius of Nicomedia.

the context of Eusebius's almost exclusive interest in eastern affairs, that helpful emperor should be Licinius.

In his retrospective denigration of Licinius, however, Eusebius complained that the emperor had issued a law restricting bishops from meeting in councils (Eus., *VC* 1.51.1, 2.66). He also accused Licinius of having conspired against bishops and even allowing some to be executed by imperial officials (Eus., *HE* 10.8.14–18). This alleged hostility was not necessarily proof that Licinius had initiated a general persecution of Christianity. Instead, as he responded to the disputes among bishops and clerics by granting or withholding his support, he could not avoid being seen by some churchmen as an adversary. In the western provinces Constantine was likewise choosing which petitioners to support, and the churchmen who failed to receive his patronage, such as the supporters of Donatus in North Africa, were angry enough to remember his officials as persecutors, even "executioners" (Council of Carthage in 411, *Gesta* 3.258). Constantine and Licinius were both typical emperors who had to make decisions about the distribution of their patronage.

Eusebius also claimed that Licinius was upset because he thought Christians in the East were praying on behalf of Constantine (Eus., *HE* 10.8.16). Some eastern churchmen may indeed have been reaching out to the western emperor, in particular as he gradually became an eastern emperor too. After Constantine's jurisdiction expanded to include the Balkan regions, he started hearing directly about the doctrinal conflicts in the eastern provinces. Eventually he revealed that one surprising source of information had been Eusebius of Nicomedia. As the relationship between the emperors deteriorated during the early 320s and war seemed likely, Eusebius of Nicomedia "secretly sent various envoys to flatter me on his behalf, and he requested my assistance" (*Urk.* 27.14). After defeating Licinius, Constantine visited Nicomedia. The news about ecclesiastical discord was "stunning," and he "grieved in his soul" (Eus., *VC* 2.61.2, 63). In late 324 the emperor composed a letter addressed nominally to Arius and Alexander. Although much of the letter was a vague recommendation for unity, he did mention some specific details: "I understand that this is the origin of the current dispute" (Eus., *VC* 2.69.1). The source of this information was perhaps again Eusebius of Nicomedia, who presumably slanted the account in his favor. But for the moment Constantine seemed to be trying to learn from his experiences in the West by not taking sides.

After the Council of Nicaea, Eusebius of Nicomedia continued to support the disgraced Arius (*Urk.* 31). Constantine concluded that Eusebius had sent his earlier envoys only as spies, and he banished him into exile. But the council had already decided in favor of forgiveness, and one canon extended penance to those who had sinned because of necessity, danger, or other hardships "that happened during the tyranny of Licinius" (canon 11). Magnanimity was also good pragmatic policy. Eventually Constantine had one of his half-brothers marry the daughter of Julius Julianus, Licinius's prefect, and he allowed Eusebius of Nicomedia to return. In order to oversee his newly acquired eastern provinces and their Christian congregations, Constantine acknowledged that he needed the support of Licinius's former supporters.

The controversies about the making of theology had hence intersected with two larger political and social trends. One was the potential emergence of a distinctly Greek Roman empire in the eastern provinces. After 313 the eastern provinces coalesced into the jurisdiction of only one emperor, and it was possible to imagine an autonomous eastern empire. The disputes among bishops were a preview of future conflicts about the possible orientations of an eastern Roman empire. Egypt had once been the heartland of the old Ptolemaic kingdom, it produced a large surplus of grain that supplied Rome, and Alexandria was one of the great cosmopolitan cities in the eastern Mediterranean. Syria was the major staging area for campaigns against the Persian empire on the eastern frontier, and Antioch was another large multicultural city. The Balkans were the buttress for the long Danube frontier, and recent emperors had resided at Sirmium and Serdica. Another possible core region centered on Thrace and Bithynia. In Bithynia, Diocletian had already developed Nicomedia as an imperial residence, and Eusebius of Nicomedia had made his see into an important ecclesiastical node. Between Bithynia and Thrace, the Bosphorus marked the junction between Europe and Asia, and Licinius had sometimes resided at Byzantium. In 325 Constantine claimed that he had moved the upcoming ecumenical council from Ancyra because the weather was better in Nicaea (*Urk.* 20). As a result, by meeting at Nicaea the council previewed the future focus of the Byzantine empire at Constantinople (formerly Byzantium), on the Bosphorus.[8]

The other developing trend was uncertainty over the role of a sympathetic emperor in Christian affairs. The reign of Constantine may have brought the problem to a boil, but in the eastern provinces it had been the reign of Licinius that had precipitated the tension. During their quarrels bishops had certainly appealed for the emperor's patronage, and supporters of Arius such as Eusebius of Nicomedia had

---

[8]   Van Dam 2010, 47–80; Grig and Kelly 2012; Van Dam 2014.

benefitted from Licinius's assistance. Although he had had to backpedal rapidly after Constantine's victory over Licinius, Eusebius of Nicomedia would successfully revive his ecclesiastical career, and eventually he would transfer once more to become bishop of Constantinople. As the climax of his rehabilitation, in 337 he would baptize Constantine.

2. THE POLITICS OF IMPERIAL FATHERS AND SONS

A discourse about fathers and sons, about making and begetting, about sameness and difference, and about subordination and coordination was not unique to Christianity, or even to religion in general. The establishment of the Tetrarchy had raised concerns about the rule of concurrent emperors, their relative ranks and titles, their identification with deities, and the vagaries of dynastic succession. A Tetrarchy of emperors was something like a Trinity of divinities: collective but distinct, equal but hierarchical, somehow divine and human simultaneously. Often it was difficult to distinguish among the persons of the Tetrarchy, because even though emperors had different ranks, technically they all shared the same essence of imperial rule, as well as some names and titles. As a Christian rhetorician described the harmony of the emperors, they shared "one intelligence, the same opinion, a similar conviction, and the same viewpoint" (Lact., *DMP* 8.1). This political statement sounded like a theological statement. As a result, Tetrarchic emperors and Christian theologians were arguing about similar issues at the same time.[9]

As long as Diocletian presided as the foremost emperor, differences within the Tetrarchy were suppressed. In 305 the changeover to a new regime was remarkably smooth. The two Augusti retired, the two Caesars became the Augusti, and two new Caesars were selected. The retirements may have been unprecedented, because imperial rule had always been a lifetime job, the dual promotions and dual appointments were different, but the transition seemed to promise stability for imperial succession. Retirements and replacements could become predictable, and in the future Augusti could retire, Caesars could advance, and new Caesars would be selected repeatedly.

In fact, the structure of multiple emperors was inherently fragile. In the early empire dynastic succession from father to son (or sons), as defined by birth or by adoption, had stabilized imperial rule, while civil wars had marked the end of imperial families and a transition to new

[9] Kolb 2001, on the "theology" of the Tetrarchy.

dynasties. The Tetrarchic system inverted these expectations. Now natural sons were not considered the expected heirs, and their dynastic advancement could even trigger civil wars.[10]

Family dynamics hence raised several important issues about the nature of imperial rule. One was the selection of new emperors. The original Tetrarchy had not included relatives by birth. In 285 Diocletian selected Maximian as his fellow emperor; in 293 they selected as junior emperors Constantius and Galerius. The common bonds among these emperors was their military service and their origins in the frontier zones of the Balkans. This new preference for non-family succession was readily apparent when Diocletian and Maximian retired. Adult sons with considerable credentials were available for advancement. Constantine, Constantius's oldest son, was in his early thirties and had military experience; Maxentius, Maximian's son, was in his early twenties, and he was already married to Galerius's daughter. But neither was selected for promotion. New emperors were to be made, not begotten.

As a result, one oddity is the appearance of imperial sons who did not become emperors. Some sons died or were killed while still young. But in 305 Constantine was literally pushed aside so that Galerius could instead introduce Maximinus as a new emperor (Lact., *DMP* 19.4), and at the same time Maxentius was living outside Rome as a private citizen with the rank of a senator. In 306 when Constantius died, his troops were thought to have rejected his "legitimate sons" in favor of Constantine, his "first son" (Zosimus, *Historia nova* 2.9.1; *Panegyrici latini* [*Paneg. lat.*] 6(7).4.2). Constantine's half-brothers were apparently the first imperial sons to reach adulthood but never become emperors.[11]

A second issue was the ideological overlay of family relationships on this assortment of unrelated emperors. Diocletian and Maximian represented themselves as "brothers" and the junior emperors as "sons." Constantius and Galerius were already the sons-in-law of Maximian and Diocletian respectively, and the senior emperors furthermore adopted the junior emperors. The imposition of these contrived relationships was so powerful that they might even affect thinking about succession. When Galerius started scheming about the future, he hoped eventually to promote Licinius directly as a fellow senior emperor. In that case he could avoid having to call his friend "son" and instead designate him "brother" (Lact., *DMP* 20.3).

---

[10]   Hekster 2015, on imperial succession.
[11]   Van Dam 2018; excellent commentaries on the Latin panegyrics in Nixon and Rodgers 1994.

Fraternal harmony highlighted the equality between the senior emperors, while paternal hierarchy reinforced the differences in rank and authority between Augusti and Caesars. Not surprisingly, the junior emperors complained. Already as a Caesar, Galerius had been especially disruptive: he "never sang in harmony with the melody of four notes" (Julian, *Caesares* 315c). Diocletian once forced his impertinent junior emperor, while still dressed in purple, to march beside his carriage as penance for a defeat (Ammianus Marcellinus, *Res gestae* 14.11.10). This humiliation had little effect, because on a triumphal arch at Thessalonica Galerius would hype his own victories over the Persians. As an Augustus, Galerius faced grumbling from the junior emperor Maximinus, who was upset at being overlooked for promotion. "Galerius begged him to show respect for his age and his grey hair" (Lact., *DMP* 32.2). Then he agreed to bestow a new formal title on the Caesars: "sons of the Augusti."[12] Constantine, the other Caesar who was already using the title of Augustus, simply ignored this new title, and soon Maximinus's troops hailed him as an Augustus too. Equality trumped hierarchy, and Galerius finally had to agree that all four emperors would be Augusti. Overnight "sons" became "brothers."

The final issue was the role of fathers. Arrogance and annoyance were not the only challenges to the idea of a Tetrarchy. Despite the ideology, emperors were always scheming to promote their own sons. Galerius was already dreaming about advancing his own son when the boy was only nine years old (Lact., *DMP* 20.4). Constantius requested that Constantine, a longtime officer at Diocletian's court, return to his side; when Constantius died in York, his troops hailed his son as emperor. Maximian returned from retirement to support his son, Maxentius, as emperor at Rome; in turn, Maxentius held consulships with his young son.

As long as Diocletian had been the dominant emperor, no natural sons were willingly invited to join the Tetrarchy. Although Constantine may have compelled recognition from Galerius through his military coup, Galerius declined to acknowledge Maxentius: "he could not make a third Caesar" (Lact., *DMP* 26.4). In one respect the refusal of hereditary succession reflected a peculiar circumstance, because Diocletian was the only Tetrarchic emperor who did not have a son. But the pull of hereditary succession remained undeniable. Once Constantine and Licinius had eliminated their rivals, they soon

---

[12]   Stefan 2005a; Stefan 2005b.

promoted their sons as Caesars. Thereafter emperors would again be begotten, not made.[13]

In their theological treatises churchmen struggled to find the appropriate vocabulary to describe Jesus Christ the Son as a manifestation of God the Father.[14] Their nuanced terminology included "Second God," "Son-Father," and "legitimate son."[15] In formulating these analogies perhaps the theologians drew upon their own experiences as sons; some of their doctrinal comments almost beg for modern psychoanalysis. At the Council of Nicaea Constantine could contribute to the discussions by sharing his own many permutations of sonship: first (but possibly illegitimate) son of Constantius, son of a deified emperor, grandson of Maximian by adoption, son-in-law of Maximian, son of the Augusti, brother of imperial sons who did not become emperors. But in contrast to the bishops, Constantine had an additional unique qualification from his life. He could also share his experiences as a father. At the Council of Nicaea he presided as a "son-father."

3. KEEPING TIME

In the world of late antiquity the abstract notion of "time" was a multivalent philosophical concept. It was also a disputed theological concept. Arius had argued that because God was unique, he was "alone eternal, alone without beginning," and that "there was a time when God was not a Father." "The Son was begotten by the Father outside time [...] He was not everlasting." Alexander of Alexandria had insisted that God did not precede the Son: "Always God, always Son; at once God, at once Son" (*Urk.* 1, 4b, 6, often summarizing the other's doctrines). The anathemas appended to the creed of the Council of Nicaea tried to resolve this issue of the eternal existence of the Son: "the catholic church condemns those who say 'there was [a time] when he was not,' and 'he did not exist before he was begotten.'"

In daily life "time" might likewise seem to be a somewhat static monotony, because for most people the steady repetition of agrarian life imposed a dreary uniformity. In northern Italy, for instance, an old

---

[13]   Van Dam 2007, 79–129.
[14]   On the theological controversies, see the chapter by Rebecca Lyman in this volume.
[15]   Second God, attributed to bishop Narcissus of Neronias: *Urk.* 19. Son-Father, as taught by Sabellius: *Urk.* 6.3. Legitimate son, as asserted by Alexander of Alexandria: *Urk.* 14.33. See Gregg and Groh 1981, 43–76, for an excellent discussion of the implications of doctrines of sonship for schemes of salvation, in a chapter entitled "The Son: One of Many Brothers."

farmer "calculated the passage of the years not from the name of the consul but from the alternating harvests" (Claudian, *Carmina minora* 20.11). Agrarian time was invariable. Even as the years passed, every year seemed to remain the same.

Because the passage of the seasons and the demands of working the land imposed an annual tempo, cities and religious cults often piggy-backed on those rhythms, and the tenures of municipal magistrates and the celebration of festivals were recurring cycles. Official timekeeping for the imperial administration also followed annual cycles. For centuries the standard format for designating each year had been the names of the two ordinary consuls, who had typically been distinguished senators and sometimes emperors.

During the late third and early fourth centuries the times changed – literally so. Under the Tetrarchs and Constantine the ordinary consuls were often emperors. Diocletian was consul ten times, Maximian nine times, Galerius and Constantine eight times each. Increasingly each official year was an imperial year. This emphasis on emperors also appeared in annual calendars of holidays. At Rome a calendar assembled in the mid-fourth century listed the festivals for each month. Some of the festivals were religious or political holidays, such as the anniversary of the foundation of the city on April 21, but in almost every month there was at least one festival celebrating something about Constantine, such as his birthday on February 27, the beginning of his reign on July 25, his victories over Licinius on July 3 and Maxentius on October 28, and his formal arrivals at the capital on July 18, July 21, and October 29.[16] At Rome the official calendar would be not just imperial, but Constantinian.

The Tetrarchic emperors also introduced another cycle of administrative time. Every five years a census was conducted throughout the empire for compiling registers of citizens and their property and calculating their taxes. In order to support a larger army and a larger administration, government officials now organized people's lives around the collection of taxes and the enlistment of new recruits. A contemporary protested that the new census was "a public calamity and a shared sorrow" (Lact., *DMP* 23.1). In addition, although the extraction of taxes was onerous enough, some emperors also associated fiscal policy with religious correctness. In Palestine soldiers tried to enforce an imperial order to sacrifice to pagan gods by summoning everyone by name from

[16] Salzman 1990.

a census register (Eus., *De martyribus Palaestinae*, recensio brevior 4.8). Time-keeping was a powerful means for projecting imperial authority.

Christians had already moved away from imperial time by organizing their annual cycle of festivals around events in the life of Jesus, in particular his crucifixion and resurrection at Easter as the culmination of the Lenten season. But Easter was not celebrated on the same date each year, and the determination of its date involved proprietary calculations based on different chronological cycles that resulted in discrepancies in timing among various regions.[17] At the Council of Nicaea the participants hoped to establish a liturgical schedule that would be standard throughout the empire. One canon declared that provincial councils should meet twice each year, once before Lent, and again "at about the time of late autumn" (canon 5). The council also announced that it had concurred on a common criterion for calculating the date of Easter (*Urk.* 23.12).

Eusebius of Caesarea credited Constantine with encouraging everyone to agree "on the same time for the festival of salvation" (Eus., *VC* 3.14). The emperor apparently thought highly of the agreement, and in a general letter to the churches he summarized the outcome of the council by discussing almost exclusively the concord over timekeeping. In his perspective, a common day of Easter was a reflection of a unified church. But Constantine also implied that this agreement had wider implications about the unity of the empire by listing the regions in both West and East that would accept "one and the same day": the city of Rome, Africa, Egypt, Spain, Gaul, Britain, Libya, Greece, and Asia Minor (Eus., *VC* 3.19.2). Having only recently reunified the empire after a civil war and emerged as the sole Augustus, now the emperor wanted ecclesiastical harmony too.[18] Christian standard time could become imperial standard time. Constantine seems to have concluded that a harmonized Christian calendar could reinforce his imperial authority: one orthodoxy, one Easter, one empire, one Augustus.

4. DIVINE EMPERORS

Over the centuries many emperors had been deified after their deaths. In 306 Constantius, Constantine's father, was added to the pantheon as another *divus*, the first of the original Tetrarchs to be deified; subsequently Diocletian, Maximian, and Galerius would be deified. So would

---

[17]   On the calculation of Easter, see the chapter by Daniel Mc Carthy in this volume.
[18]   On Constantine's intentions, see the chapter by Hal Drake, 116–19.

be Constantine: the first Christian emperor was also one of the last deified emperors.

But one telling feature of the Tetrarchic emperors was that already during their reigns they were explicitly represented as deities. By adding the name *Jovius* or *Herculius* to their standard titulature, they openly identified themselves with Jupiter, "the ruler of heaven," and Hercules, "the pacifier of the earth" (*Paneg. lat.* 10(2).11.6). According to a panegyrist, Jupiter had been the "creator of Diocletian" (*Paneg. lat.* 11(3).3.3). Not surprisingly, when Diocletian retired in 305, he removed his purple robe in the presence of a statue of Jupiter (Lact., *DMP* 19.2).

Diocletian had become emperor in 284 after a coup. Numerianus, the previous emperor, was found dead in dubious circumstances, and military officers and soldiers quickly acclaimed Diocletian. Although the new emperor hoped to shift suspicion by immediately murdering Numerianus's prefect, and although he would share imperial rule with fellow emperors, during his long reign the loyalty of the army and the challenge of regional usurpers remained problematic. Because Diocletian and the other Tetrarchs could not claim imperial ancestors, their legitimacy was a constant concern.

Instead, identification with gods created an alternative dynastic legitimacy. Diocletian apparently had people greet him as "Lord" in public, and he "allowed himself to be worshipped and addressed as a god" (Aurelius Victor, *De Caesaribus* 39.4). A dedication from Epirus described Diocletian and Maximian as "begotten of the gods and creators of gods."[19] This formulation implied that as descendants of gods, the emperors could transfer their divinity to new emperors, who in turn could create more divine emperors. At Panamara in Caria two priests serving at the Temple of Zeus hailed Maximinus as a Jovian emperor and thanked him for eradicating local bandits through his "divinity."[20] Even senators were expected "to adore the emperors' sacred faces" (*Paneg. lat.* 11(3).11.1). The divinity of emperors made their rule independent of confirmation by the senate at Rome, the fickle allegiance of the army, and even the approval of their subjects.

Initially Constantine was likewise identified with pagan deities. His imperial titles included the name *Herculius*; in a temple in Gaul he claimed to have recognized himself as Apollo offering the promise of victory (*Paneg. lat.* 6(7).21.4–5); a dedication in Italy honored him as

[19]   *Inscriptiones Latinae Selectae* 1:141, no. 629, from Dyrrhachium (modern Durrës in Albania).

[20]   Şahin 1981, 170–71, no. 310, dated to 312/13.

"begotten of the gods."[21] Then this heir of Tetrarchic emperorship presided over sessions of a council of bishops. Nicaea was itself a city with
Tetrarchic associations. It claimed Hercules as its legendary founder, and
during the council the bishops met in a large room of an imperial palace
that had been constructed perhaps by a Tetrarchic emperor (Eus., *VC*
3.10.1).[22] Churchmen now argued Christian theology in the shadow of
the Tetrarchic theology of imperial rule.

One participant was Eusebius of Caesarea, who subsequently
became an occasional acquaintance of the emperor.[23] He also began to
develop a distinctive Christian theology of imperial rule. In 336 Eusebius
attended another council at Constantinople. Since Constantine again
presided, the decision of the council to reinstate Arius seemed to
acknowledge the emperor's own interest in, perhaps even preference
for, the sort of theology that Eusebius also favored. Eusebius remained
at the capital in order to celebrate the thirtieth anniversary of the
emperor's accession in late July, and during the festivities he delivered
a panegyric in honor of Constantine.[24] In his panegyric Eusebius praised
three rulers. One was the "Great Emperor," God the Father. Another was
the Logos, the Word, who commanded the armies of heaven. Although
Eusebius emphasized that the Logos was "the only-begotten Son," he
also insisted that the Logos was "distinguished with second place in his
Father's kingdom." The third ruler was Constantine, "the friend of
God," who commanded the armies that had defeated barbarians and
pagan demons. Eusebius furthermore essentially equated the standing
of the Logos and the emperor by comparing each to "a prefect of the Great
Emperor" (Eus., *De laudibus Constantini* 1.1, 6; 3.5–6; 7.13).

Modern scholarship can deal with the identification of emperors as
pagan deities by interpreting the religious language as a symbolic
medium for articulating the distribution of power. Because there are no
modern cults of Jupiter and Hercules, there are no vested interests. But
the equation of an emperor with the Son of God is more difficult to
appreciate, because so much scholarship on early Christianity still
reflects confessional concerns. Instead, by classifying Christian theological terminology as another symbolic language, it is possible to conclude that representations of God and of emperors could be used to
imagine the other. In this panegyric Eusebius had constructed an image

---

[21]   Grünewald 1990, 222, no. 272, dated to 312/15.
[22]   On the venue of the council, see the chapter by Ine Jacobs, below 82–86.
[23]   On the procedures of the council see the chapter by David Gwynn in this volume; on
       Eusebius's account of the council see Chapter 10 by Aaron Johnson.
[24]   Drake 1976, for commentary on Eusebius's panegyric.

of Constantine that supported his particular theology, because by equating the emperor with the Logos, Eusebius was again promoting his subordinationist doctrines. In the triad of rulers he honored, the coordination of the emperor and the Logos implied that both were subordinate to God the Father. A panegyric about the emperor was also theology about God.[25]

In the early fourth century controversies over theology evaluated God, gods, and emperors. The coincidence of concepts was striking, and modern analyses of Christian theology should also consider the terminology of panegyrics and dedications for emperors. Tetrarchic political ideology highlighted Four divine emperors sharing One undivided rulership. Christian theology argued about Three divine persons sharing One essence. Eusebius's comments in his panegyric implied that Constantine was a divine emperor similar to Jesus Christ, who was likewise both divine and human. This overlapping indicates that the arguments at the Council of Nicaea had been as much about imagining a Christian emperor as about defining God.

5. FAMILIES

After the triumphant campaign against Licinius in 324, the reputation of another emperor was also ascending. During the campaign Crispus, Constantine's oldest son, had commanded a fleet that seized the Hellespont and blockaded Byzantium. To describe this victory Eusebius of Caesarea used a theological analogy. In his estimation the father and the son owed their success to an alliance with "God, the emperor over all, and the Son of God, the savior of all." During the battles Crispus had been a "most generous emperor," who had "extended his right hand of salvation to all people who were being defeated." While Constantine may have emerged as the "greatest victor," his son Crispus was "the most beloved of God" and hence "similar to the father in all respects" (Eus., *HE* 10.9.4–6). The imperial duo of father and son mimicked the divine duo of Father and Son.

Eusebius included this encomium of Constantine's victory as the conclusion of the narrative of his *Ecclesiastical History*, which he apparently finished shortly before the Council of Nicaea. Because the laudatory language was characteristic of a formal panegyric, it hinted at apologetic objectives. Perhaps Eusebius was burying his own previous association with Licinius's regime in the hope of earning the support of

[25]   Van Dam 2007, 290–93.

the new emperor. Perhaps also, by deploying the idea of a "similarity" between father and son, he was subtly previewing and promoting his own doctrines about the relationship between Father and Son.

Eusebius's theology was certainly contentious, and the transition to a new emperor opened new opportunities for his opponents. In early 325 a council at Antioch supported the theology of Alexander of Alexandria and pointedly condemned Eusebius as a supporter of Arius's doctrines (*Urk.* 18). A few months later Eusebius met Constantine for the first time at the Council of Nicaea. Subsequently he claimed that the emperor had accepted his doctrinal creed. Supposedly Constantine "was the first to admit that this creed included the most correct statements," and "he urged everyone there to agree and subscribe to these doctrines" (*Urk.* 22.7). As a result, while Eusebius of Nicomedia was sent into exile, Eusebius of Caesarea could claim that his doctrines corresponded to the creed issued by the council. Nominally at least, he was a Nicene bishop.

More importantly, he had now caught the emperor's ear. In July, immediately after the Council of Nicaea, Constantine celebrated the beginning of the twentieth year of his reign by hosting a banquet for bishops, which was held in Nicomedia. Perhaps it was at this banquet that Eusebius of Caesarea "took the stage at the council of God's ministers" to deliver a panegyric about Constantine's anniversary (Eus., *VC* 1.1.1). In his oration he probably drew from his laudatory comments about the emperor in his recently completed *Ecclesiastical History*.

One year later Constantine returned to Rome to celebrate the end of the twentieth year of his reign. But by then his family had changed dramatically, because in mysterious circumstances he had been responsible for the deaths of both his wife and Crispus. This turmoil was a challenge to his own authority and the succession of his surviving sons, and Constantine responded by redefining his family's outreach. In the past his own marriage and the marriages of his half-siblings had been designed to form links with other imperial dynasties and senatorial families; now his sons and daughters almost always married their cousins.[26] Instead, the one outside "family" with which he did form a bond was itself another blended configuration: God, his Son Jesus Christ, and Jesus's virgin mother, Mary.

The primary liaison was the emperor's mother, Helena. After the Council of Nicaea, Helena went on a tour of the eastern provinces, where she cared for the poor and imprisoned and distributed gifts to cities and

[26] Van Dam 2018.

churches. In particular, her contributions supported the new Church of the Nativity at Bethlehem, where "the most pious empress adorned the pregnancy of [Mary,] the 'God-Bearer,' with marvelous memorials," and the new Church of the Ascension at the Mount of Olives (Eus., *VC* 3.41.1–43.3). Her generosity also effectively provided an innovative understanding of the Constantinian dynasty by establishing parallels with the career of Jesus Christ. As a patron she lavished her munificence on the two sites associated with the beginning and the end of Jesus's life on earth; as a mother she represented the birth of the emperor and the handover to his future successors, her grandsons. Helena too had been the mother of an "only-begotten son," as Eusebius would claim in his *Life of Constantine* (Eus., *VC* 3.46.1), and through her generosity the imperial family was to be linked to the divine family.

The renewed interest in the sites associated with Jesus's life on earth should be interpreted as another outcome of the Council of Nicaea. At the council churchmen had argued about the divinity of Father and Son; afterward Constantine had become interested in Jesus's humanity. Perhaps Jesus's life could become a model for his life. In his final years he even hoped to travel to Palestine to be baptized in the Jordan river (Eus., *VC* 4.62.2). Subsequent pilgrims travelled to Palestine with the same expectations, to learn about Jesus's life and to transform their own lives. While arguments about theology could seem abstract and timeless, visiting the Holy Land and walking in Jesus's footprints offered contact with his immediate presence.[27]

6. CONSTANTINE'S POST-NICENE STORY

The Council of Nicaea marked a culmination and an introduction. For eastern bishops the council was supposed to be a resolution of doctrinal controversies; but for Constantine it was an initial direct encounter with these bishops and their controversies. Their conversations certainly influenced his own thinking.

Soon after his victory over Licinius in late 324 he had introduced himself to the provincials in the East. In one letter he remedied various injustices, in another he contrasted his wish for peace with his predecessors' persecution of Christians. The inspiration for his new guidelines was a God he described as "greatest," "saviour," and "lord of all." Although he once referred to "your Son," he never mentioned Jesus Christ by name (Eus., *VC* 2.24–42, 48–60). Even in the letter he sent to

[27]   Frank 2000.

Arius and bishop Alexander scolding them for their squabble, he did not
mention Jesus.

Then Constantine attended the Council of Nicaea and participated
in the debates, which were all about Jesus Christ. Eusebius of Caesarea
asserted that the emperor himself had suggested using the adjective
homoousios, "of the same essence," to describe Jesus Christ in his
relationship with God the Father (*Urk.* 22.7). Afterward Constantine
sent a letter to the eastern churches in which he praised the adoption
of a common day for the celebration of Easter. He also funded the
construction of a new Church of the Holy Sepulchre at Jerusalem (Eus.,
VC 3.25–40). The cross, Jesus's passion, and his resurrection were now on
the emperor's mind.

Constantine's new awareness was particularly apparent in what has
become the most famous story he told. The emperor claimed that before
a battle he had had a vision of a cross in the sky, accompanied by
a caption, "conquer in this." At the time, he continued, he did not
understand the significance of the vision. But during the evening he
saw, in a dream, "the Christ of God," and soon experts identified this
God as "the only-begotten Son of the one and only God" (Eus., *VC*
1.28–32).

In the narrative of his *Life of Constantine* Eusebius of Caesarea
inserted Constantine's story about his vision and his dream before the
emperor's battle against Maxentius in 312. But that was not when
Constantine told the story. Eusebius explicitly noted that he had heard
the story from Constantine himself: "a long time afterward the victorious emperor himself narrated [this story] to me, the author of this
account, when I was honored with his acquaintance and his conversations" (Eus., *VC* 1.28.1). Eusebius first met Constantine at the Council of
Nicaea. During the remaining twelve years of his reign they met again
only infrequently, at the banquet celebrating the twentieth anniversary
of the emperor's reign immediately after the Council of Nicaea, perhaps
at a council in Nicomedia in 327, and at Constantinople in 335, and again
for the thirtieth anniversary of the emperor's reign in 336. Whenever
Constantine told his story to Eusebius and other bishops, it was sometime after the Council of Nicaea, either soon afterward or toward the end
of his reign.[28]

This story about the emperor's vision of a cross and his dream of
Jesus Christ neatly encapsulated the important topics discussed at the
Council of Nicaea: God and his only-begotten Son, the cross and its

[28]   Van Dam 2011, 56–81, on Constantine's stories.

celebration at Easter. After the council Constantine seems to have developed a "post-Nicene" autobiography in which he attributed his earlier victories to his direct relationship with Jesus Christ. His association with Jesus Christ became the key for a consistent retrospective interpretation of his entire reign as a Christian emperor. The Council of Nicaea changed the emperor's life; or rather, it changed his story about his life.

Constantine memorialized his new life's story at Constantinople, his innovative capital city in the eastern empire. For the new Church of the Holy Sepulchre at Jerusalem the emperor had presented the twelve columns that encircled the apse and commemorated the twelve apostles (Eus., *VC* 3.38). At Constantinople he constructed a shrine, either a mausoleum or a church, to serve as his funerary memorial, in which the niche for his sarcophagus was surrounded by twelve cenotaphs that represented, and possibly were inscribed with the names of, the twelve apostles (Eus., *VC* 4.58–60). Constantine was furthermore thought to have placed a fragment of Jesus's cross in a giant statue of himself (Socr., *HE* 1.17). The emperor and Jesus each seemed to be an analogue of the other. As a result, Constantinople was also a memorial to the life of Jesus, and "Constantine's city" might be known as "Christ's city" (Soz., *HE* 2.3.8).

The Council of Nicaea became famous for its creed, its canons, and its anathemas. Its influence also generated Constantine's story about his vision of a cross in the sky, his appropriation of a relic of the True Cross, and the placement of his sarcophagus. Eusebius of Caesarea thought that the emperor had appeared at the council "like a heavenly angel of God" (Eus., *VC* 3.10.3). This was not simply a literary conceit, because afterward Constantine seems to have agreed. His buildings, his monuments, and his own story about his life were constant reminders that a Christian emperor was imagined as Christ-like and Jesus Christ as emperor-like.

Timeline

284 November	Diocletian becomes Augustus
285 July	Maximian selected as emperor
286 April	Maximian becomes Augustus
293 March	Constantius and Galerius promoted as Caesars
305 May	Diocletian and Maximian retire; Constantius and Galerius become Augusti; Severus and Maximinus become Caesars

(cont.)

306 July	death of Constantius; proclamation of his son Constantine, recognized as Caesar by Galerius
306 October	proclamation of Maxentius as emperor at Rome; he recalls his father, Maximian
307	death of Severus
308 November	Licinius selected as Augustus with Galerius; Maximinus and Constantine recognized as Caesars; Diocletian and Maximian recognized as "elder Augusti"
310	Maximinus and Constantine recognized as Augusti
311 spring	death of Galerius
312 October	Constantine's victory over Maxentius outside Rome
313	joint proclamation of religious toleration issued by Constantine and Licinius; Licinius's victory over Maximinus
313 summer	death of Maximinus
316–317	inconclusive war between Constantine and Licinius
317 March	promotion of Constantine's sons Crispus and Constantine II and of Licinius's son Licinius II as Caesars
324	Constantine's victory over Licinius; deaths of Licinius and Licinius II
324 November	promotion of Constantine's son Constantius II as Caesar
325 winter or spring	council at Antioch
325 summer	**Council of Nicaea**
325 July	celebration at Nicomedia of 20th anniversary of Constantine's accession
326	death of Crispus; visit of Constantine at Rome
later 320s	pilgrimage of Helena, Constantine's mother, to Palestine; subsequent imperial patronage for Church of the Nativity at Bethlehem and Church of the Ascension at the Mount of Olives
330 May	dedication of Constantinople
333 December	promotion of Constantine's son Constans as Caesar
335 September	promotion of Constantine's nephew Dalmatius as Caesar; dedication of Church of the Holy Sepulchre at Jerusalem
336	council at Constantinople
336 July	celebration of 30th anniversary of Constantine's accession, and panegyric by Eusebius of Caesarea

(cont.)

337 May	death of Constantine
337 summer	execution of Dalmatius and other members of Constantine's family
337 September	succession of Constantine II, Constantius II, and Constans as Augusti

SELECT REFERENCES

Barnes, Timothy D. 1981. *Constantine and Eusebius*. Cambridge, MA: Harvard University Press.

Barnes, Timothy D. 2011. *Constantine: Dynasty, Religion and Power in the Later Roman Empire*. Chichester: Wiley Blackwell.

Bowman, Alan K. 2005. "Diocletian and the First Tetrarchy, A.D. 284–305." In *The Cambridge Ancient History, Second Edition, Volume XII: The Crisis of Empire, A.D. 193–337*, edited by Alan K. Bowman, Averil Cameron, and Peter Garnsey, 67–89. Cambridge: Cambridge University Press.

Drake, H. A., trans. 1976. *In Praise of Constantine: A Historical Study and New Translation of Eusebius' Tricennial Orations*. Berkeley: University of California Press.

Frank, Georgia. 2000. *The Memory of the Eyes: Pilgrims to Living Saints in Christian Late Antiquity*. Transformation of the Classical Heritage 30. Berkeley: University of California Press.

Gregg, Robert C., and Dennis Groh. 1981. *Early Arianism: A View of Salvation*. Philadelphia: Fortress Press.

Gwynn, David M. 2007. *The Eusebians: The Polemic of Athanasius of Alexandria and the Construction of the "Arian Controversy."* Oxford Theology and Religion Monographs. Oxford: Oxford University Press.

Hekster, Olivier. 2015. *Emperors and Ancestors: Roman Rulers and the Constraints of Tradition*. Oxford Studies in Ancient Culture and Representation. Oxford: Oxford University Press.

Kolb, Frank. 2001. *Herrscherideologie in der Spätantike*. Berlin: Akademie Verlag.

Lenski, Noel, ed. 2006. *The Cambridge Companion to the Age of Constantine*. Cambridge: Cambridge University Press.

Miles, Richard, ed. 2016. *The Donatist Schism: Controversy and Contexts*. TTH, Contexts 2. Liverpool: Liverpool University Press.

Salzman, Michele Renee. 1990. *On Roman Time: The Codex-Calendar of 354 and the Rhythms of Urban Life in Late Antiquity*. Transformation of the Classical Heritage 17. Berkeley: University of California Press.

Van Dam, Raymond. 2007. *The Roman Revolution of Constantine*. Cambridge: Cambridge University Press.

Van Dam, Raymond. 2010. *Rome and Constantinople: Rewriting Roman History during Late Antiquity*. Waco, TX: Baylor University Press.

Van Dam, Raymond. 2011. *Remembering Constantine at the Milvian Bridge.* Cambridge: Cambridge University Press.

Van Dam, Raymond. 2018. "Eastern Aristocracies and Imperial Courts: Constantine's Half-Brother, Licinius's Prefect, and Egyptian Grain." *Dumbarton Oaks Papers* 72:1–24.

3 Arius and Arianism
The Origins of the Alexandrian Controversy
REBECCA LYMAN

The bitter division in Alexandria began as a theological dispute between Alexander, the bishop of Alexandria, and a significant number of his clergy, including a presbyter Arius, but quickly overflowed into a feud among eastern bishops, and famously continued well into the next century in spite of imperial intervention. Constructed later to serve as the archetypal counterpoint to Nicene orthodoxy, "Arianism" was assumed by scholars and theologians to be a coherent set of heretical teachings embraced by a succession of followers: Arius was an unwary intellectual, who relied too much on philosophical categories, but was caught out by his bishop Alexander, and defeated theologically and spiritually by the tenacious Athanasius.[1] However, attempts by scholars to link him to specific philosophers or indeed to earlier Christians such as Origen or Lucian of Antioch have never been wholly convincing. To date no reading or assembling of the few extant fragments has succeeded in portraying a convincing reason why Arius argued, in the words of Rowan Williams, such an "obstinate, consistent, and radical agnosticism" or why such a seemingly idiosyncratic or academic Christianity should create such a lasting furor with outside episcopal and imperial intervention and local popular support.[2] In the past forty years scholars have shifted from sifting the problematic and limited evidence of the origins of the controversy to examining the continuing debates after the Council of Nicaea. In place of well-formed theological parties, they have mapped sets of alliances which may agree on certain theological points, and disagree on many others.[3] Athanasius's lifelong use of Arius and the original controversy in Alexandria to ensure the success of later, and often endangered, Nicene orthodoxy was a masterful rhetorical and political move; his version of "Arianism," however, can no longer be

---

[1] On the construction of "Arianism" as a heresiological school and its place in doctrinal history, see Wiles 1996; Parvis 2006, 180–85; Gwynn 2007.

[2] Williams 1987, 166; Vaggione 1989.

[3] See Vaggione 2000; Ayres 2004; Parvis 2006.

trusted as the basis for historical research. In this new context Arius has become, in the helpful phrase of Lewis Ayres, not the founder of a sect, but the catalyst of a wider theological controversy around the Mediterranean.[4]

This separation of Arius from later "Arianism," together with the continuing critical revision of the textual evidence, encourages a fresh look at the initial controversy, that is, an "Alexandrian controversy" rather than "the Arian controversy." Since the extensive theological and exegetical polemics of "Arianism" were developed well after Nicaea, the issues and motivations in the initial local conflict in Egypt are not necessarily the same as those in later debates. In this chapter I will review the current state of the textual evidence, the various interpretations of the origins of the controversy in Alexandria, and offer some suggestions as to how the initial controversy may be reframed in light of recent scholarship about religion and society in the early fourth century. By restoring our historical peripheral vision a bit beyond the traditional theological genealogies, we can set the original and fierce debate on divine generation into contemporary, and perhaps more intelligible, cultural, and religious categories.

EVIDENCE AND CHRONOLOGIES

The paucity of textual material combined with the abundance of heresiological distortions has made the reconstruction of the initial conflict and a consensus on its origins extremely difficult, if not impossible. The few extant primary sources are letters or public statements that encouraged performances of self-justification as well as pithy theological arguments, usually wrapped in polemical rhetoric.[5] Constantine ordered the destruction of the works of Arius, but whether or not this actually happened, there are in fact no extant titles of any theological works or commentaries, but only one piece, the so-called *Thalia*, which seems to have been composed as a theological apology during the later stages of the controversy. The extant literature on Alexander is also limited.[6] In

---

[4]   Ayres 2004, 12, n. 3.
[5]   On letters as conventional expressions of individual identity in Graeco-Roman culture, see Poster 2007, 24–28. See comments by Ayres 2004, 13–16. Parvis 2006, 38–68, speculates that Alexander and Eusebius of Nicomedia may have been in conflict before, and places the events within arguments of the early fourth century, outlining theological allies of Arius and Alexander. For Philostorgius on Arius and Alexander as rivals for bishop, see Vaggione 2000, 48, n. 97; Williams 1987, 40–42.
[6]   Also noted by Hanson 1988, 6: "It may be doubted, in view of this total dearth, whether Arius ever wrote any but the most ephemeral works."

other words the slight literary evidence strongly suggests that this was a local clerical dispute rather than a clash of theological traditions or schools.

The first modern collection of the literary evidence was assembled from various ancient historians and theologians by Hans-Georg Opitz in 1934 as the third volume of his *Athanasius Werke*; it has since been re-edited with some slight changes in the order as well as the inclusion of other documents which extend the collection to 344.[7] The few primary documents from Arius himself consist of a letter to Eusebius of Nicomedia, a letter to Alexander from all dissenting clergy, the apologetic piece called the *Thalia*, a brief conciliatory letter after Nicaea, and testimonia from a letter which is contained in a later letter of Constantine.[8] The traditional interpretative framework for these fragments has been largely drawn from the two polemical letters of Alexander; the second of these is now generally attributed to Athanasius.[9] We also have additional letters and conciliar pronouncements before Nicaea.[10] After Nicaea we have a range of documents including the works of Athanasius that contained further church declarations, conciliar proceedings, and his own account of the controversy. Later ancient heresiologists and historians continued to add their own interpretations and alleged evidence.[11] The ongoing critical editing of these few texts continues to reduce the reliable evidence, so that many polemical constructions in Alexander and Athanasius, formerly used as evidence of the initial conflict, must now be used with greater care or simply disregarded. Mark DelCogliano, for example, has helpfully sifted through the blending of Arius and the later work of Asterius.[12] As outlined by David Gwynn, Athanasius, who has been one of the most mined sources for the history and theology of the dispute, created his own version of his early opponent, "Athanasian Arianism," which

[7] See the complete list of documents with English translations at www.fourthcentury.com/documents-of-the-early-arian-controversy.
The documents concerning Eusebius of Nicomedia were moved to later in the controversy; Constantine's letters about Arius were moved to just after Nicaea. See Brennecke et al. 2007.

[8] Löhr 2006b, 124–51, discusses the letters and recent scholarship; on the *Thalia*, see the essential article DelCogliano 2018.

[9] See Gwynn 2007, 59–69.

[10] Hanson 1988, 129–38, outlines this material.

[11] For a review of Athanasian material, see Gwynn 2007, 69–100; Löhr 2006a, 525–27, discusses the evidence of Epiphanius, perhaps from Egypt; on Sozomen, Socrates, and Epiphanius, 533–45.

[12] Two recent and essential articles, DelCogliano 2015 and DelCogliano 2018, critically review the literature and evidence.

included the selective editing and paraphrasing of texts as well as here-siological exaggerations.[13]

The chronology of these early events in Alexandria must also be reconstructed from the few extant documents that pertain to the dispute and have been assembled in different orders by various scholars.[14] The first chronology was proposed by Opitz; it has since been re-edited with some slight changes in the order, but suggesting the conflict began in 318.[15] Rowan Williams suggested that the conflict was shorter, beginning in 321.[16] Sara Parvis argued that the conflict began in 322, and that many documents were impossible to order, having been issued as a flurry of defensive correspondence.[17] The general sequence of events includes a growing disagreement between Alexander and his clergy over formulas concerning the generation and nature of the Son, which resulted in a separation within the community. Alexander convened a synod of Egyptian and Libyan bishops to condemn Arius and his allies. Arius then wrote for support to the powerful bishop of Nicomedia, Eusebius, evoking a shared connection through the famous martyr and bishop, Lucian of Antioch. Eusebius began a letter campaign among other bishops against Alexander and his theology, which included Eusebius of Caesarea. The dissenting Egyptian clergy wrote a statement of faith challenging Alexander and his theology of eternal generation. Alexander then issued encyclical letters, signed by bishops in Libya and Egypt, which outlined the disobedience and heretical theology of his opponents. A council in Antioch in 324 provisionally excommunicated Eusebius of Caesarea, Theodotus of Laodicea, and Narcissus of Neronias as allies of the dissenters, and issued a statement of faith supporting Alexander. With the victory of Constantine over Licinius in late 324, a larger council was called in Ancyra, which later shifted to Nicaea, to settle the matter. As a result of the council, Constantine ordered the writings of Arius to be burned. Arius, along with several others, was exiled, but later restored after submitting a statement of faith that Constantine accepted. Arius returned to Alexandria, though Athanasius, now bishop, refused to admit him to communion. Arius died suddenly, perhaps poisoned, on the streets of Constantinople around 336. If the theological opinions of

---

[13]   Gwynn 2007, 177–202.
[14]   A helpful chart and overview of these issues may be found at www.fourthcentury.com /index.php/urkunden-chronology-issues/.
[15]   Brennecke et al. 2007.
[16]   Williams 2001, 58–59, 67–81. Williams reversed the traditional order of Alexander's letters.
[17]   Parvis 2006, 72–83, 100–1.

Arius and his colleagues were short lived, his name as founding heresiarch was attached to the varied oppositions to Nicene orthodoxy that continued in both the eastern and western parts of the empire.[18]

INTERPRETATIONS OF THE ALEXANDRIAN CONTROVERSY

The extant textual evidence offers only a few glimpses into a controversy already under way, and in our documents the definitions and distortions on both sides on divine nature and generation are certainly intertwined. To begin from a minimalist reading of the fragments, the theological positions particular to Arius that were discarded by his later allies and explicitly condemned in the initial stages of the conflict included an apophatic theology that denied the knowledge and limited the vision of the Son of the Father, *creatio ex nihilo* with regard to the creation or begetting of the Son with the result of denying the traditional biblical names (Wisdom, Word, Image) that indicated shared or eternal nature, and the unchanged/changeable nature of the Son.[19] Recent studies have also emphasized the innovations of Alexander in his formulation of eternal generation and his understanding of the Son as eternal image.[20] The criticisms of Alexander in the letter from his dissenting clergy include a defense of traditional and biblical monotheism and the singular nature of generative divinity; they appear to believe that his theology is fatally compromised by implications of materiality and linked to similar mistakes by other contemporary Christians, including Manichees and the ascetic Hieracas. The response of Alexander and his deacon Athanasius was to accuse their opponents of defining the Son as a creature since he did not share the same nature as the Father, and therefore to teach the heresy of adoptionism. Both sides discuss problems of sequence and time, proper language for creation and generation, appropriate worship of Father and Son, the problem of suffering and divine nature, and the problem of the changeability of the Son as created. This cluster of issues around generation reveals significant conflict with regard to definitions of monotheism and the shape of revelation and mediation.

---

[18] This outline follows Parvis 2006, 72–93; see also Hanson 1988, 129–51, 172–78, 264–65. On later non-Nicene theology, see Vaggione 2000. On the death of Arius, see Muehlberger 2015; Brennecke 2010.

[19] Gwynn 2007, 189–220, helpfully contrasts the lists of charges used by Alexander and Athanasius to recent evidence and discussions; see Vaggione 2000, 377.

[20] On Alexander see Ayres 2004, 43–52; DelCogliano 2006.

Several major revisions of the controversy over the past forty years have offered new insights into this bitter theological standoff. The lack of consensus on the origins of the controversy has to do with the limited textual evidence, but also with conflicting assumptions as to how and why ancient theologians argued, especially in light of the continuing authority of Nicene definitions in the Christian tradition.[21] Making dogmatic or spiritual sense of Arius's problematic and popular, if short-lived, priorities thus remains a challenge for the historical imaginations of scholars in spite of the acknowledged diversities of ancient Christian beliefs and practices. As an Alexandrian presbyter, why would Arius so tenaciously defend the creation of the Son rather than accept Alexander's seemingly Origenist account of eternal generation? Shifting the focus to incarnation as well as generation, Robert Gregg and Dennis Groh, Richard Hanson, and Rudolf Lorenz broke new ground in outlining the variety of Christian views in the early fourth century. The exhaustive historical and philosophical investigation by Rowan Williams also allowed the controversy to be reframed through proposing new philosophical readings of Arius's life and work.[22]

The most controversial attempt at reframing the fragments was Gregg and Groh's thesis that the descriptions of "self-determination" (autexousios) and accusations of adoptionism revealed a biblical soteriology of advancement which portrayed the created and consequently mutable Son as "first of many brothers"; he was an exemplar of moral freedom within a cosmology of divine and human will that led to union with God.[23] Their exploration of competing spiritualities in the monastic Life of Antony also proposed the possibility of multiple forms of Christian asceticism in Egypt.[24] This focus on biblical exegesis and spiritual practices to ensure salvation was an intentional move to expand the theological interpretation beyond philosophical or dogmatic formulas, and to make sense of his broad support in the community.

This construction was criticized for being based uncritically on the polemical reports of Alexander and Athanasius. The language about freedom and advancement contradicted the two extant fragments of Arius in which the Son is defined as unchangeable; the descriptions of

---

[21] On the constructions of "Arianism" as reflecting the bias of the author or the historical context, see Wiles 1996; Vaggione 1989, 77–78, examined Williams's use of Barth; Gregg and Groh's characterization of free will is seen as "Western post-Augustinian" by Anatolios 2011, 48.

[22] This is summarized in Löhr 2006a and 2006b; Lyman 2008.

[23] Gregg and Groh 1981; Gregg 1985.

[24] Gregg and Groh 1981; Brakke 1995.

the election or grace given to the Son in Athanasius were then simply *reductio ad haeresim* to characterize his opponents falsely as adoptionists.[25] The definition of the created Son as *autexousios* by Arius should be understood only as part of the traditional response to fatalism; like Origen, Arius needed to portray moral freedom as part of the incarnate Son's human faithfulness, but this was not a central affirmation of changeability and advancement.[26] The odd focus on changeability in fact may have been the fault of his enthusiastic and populist supporters that was exploited polemically by Alexander and Athanasius and not in accordance with Arius's own extant and more philosophical views.[27] Gregg and Groh in their reconstruction did incorporate polemical statements by Alexander and Athanasius; they also drew together opinions of Arius with Asterius and Eusebius of Nicomedia as "early Arians," which would now be distinguished and indeed separated from the early dispute.[28]

After surveying possible apocalyptic and Jewish influences on Arius's strict defense of monotheism, Rudolf Lorenz argued that the structure of Arius's Logos theology appeared to be based on Origen's description of the changeable and created soul of Jesus, but modified through a Lucianist understanding of a single transcendent deity. The created Logos therefore functioned as the subject of the soulless incarnate Christ.[29] This thesis was criticized as more speculative than convincing, especially given the mixed reports concerning the presence of the human soul in incarnational theology of the early fourth century, the admitted difficulties of linking Arius directly to Origen, and the fragmentary evidence of Lucian of Antioch. An exemplary Christology again appeared to be unlikely or modern.[30] In an exhaustive survey of the conflicts of the fourth century in both East and West, Richard Hanson

[25] Stead 1994, 31: "most unlikely Arius thought in exclusively exemplarist terms"; Williams 2001, 258; Gwynn 2007, 189–202.

[26] Stead 1983.

[27] Williams 1987, 10; Williams 2001, 258: "If it [advancement] is so central, novel and distinctive a feature of Arius' thought, it is odd that it figures only in passing in what has to be recognized as a somewhat unreliable report. Compared with the strongly contested issues like the Son's eternity or mutability or knowledge of the Father, it is very elusive." Gwynn 2007, 189–202, summarizes the criticisms of Gregg and Groh on mutability.

[28] While their work broke important ground on the important themes of will in God and humanity, certain points were overstated: discussion of Athanasius (Ath.), *Orationes tres adversus Arianos* (*Ar.*) 3.24 in Gregg and Groh 1981, 6; see 50–52, on common sonship by adoption as all others.

[29] Lorenz 1979; Lorenz 1983.

[30] See comments by Stead 1982; Stead 1994.

attempted to define "Arianism" as a broad theological movement which emphasized the mediating incarnation of a subordinate son as a response to the problem of suffering and divine transcendence. The separation of the essence of the Father and the Son was necessary in order to affirm the reality of the suffering of the Son.[31]

Rowan Williams outlined and analyzed the life, theological antecedents, and theology of Arius most thoroughly after these controversial works. He suggested that new developments in later Platonic thought might lie behind Arius's unusual and unyielding defense of apophatic theology and a created Son.[32] In order to maintain the utter transcendence of the uncreated and one god, Arius used the doctrine of will in both creation and revelation. This resulted in the intellectual necessity of a substantial difference between Father and Son as well as the ignorance of the Son apart from the gift of the gracious divine will.[33] Arius was a spiritual teacher with conservative theological instincts and progressive philosophical concepts, who criticized his bishop's woolly and materialist attempts to explain eternal generation. It is difficult, however, to confirm any textual links between his theological fragments and Plotinus or Porphyry. Christopher Stead argued that in fact Arius was a Middle Platonist, that there was no compelling evidence to link him to contemporary Neoplatonic formulas, and therefore it was unlikely that he drew on the work of Plotinus. Arius as a serious Christian thinker did not wish to demote the Son, but rather to preserve the attributes of the Father, so that the Son was directly hypostasized by the Father's will.[34] Friedo Ricken had earlier wished to see Nicaea as an argument concerning transitions in Platonism, but Arius does not consciously discuss or reject these ideas in his extant letters.[35] As admitted by Williams, Arius's apophatic focus on divine will as the model of relation and action simply did not fit any existing philosophical models. As elegantly summed up by Winrich Löhr: "It implies the abrogation of the intellectualist agenda of much of late antique religious philosophy – both pagan and Christian [...] The emphasis is on praising and glorifying [...] divine transcendence is democratized."[36]

---

[31] "The Rationale of Arianism" in Hanson 1988, 99–128.
[32] Williams 1987 and 2001, in two editions with a response to critics in the second edition. Williams 1997.
[33] Williams 2001, 226–27.
[34] Stead 1997; Rowett 2012.
[35] Ricken 1969; Löhr 2006b, 132.
[36] Löhr 2006b, 149.

In addition to these theological studies, the active presence of the Manichees in late third-century and early fourth-century Egypt has also been a persistent, if curiously neglected, theme; the letter of the dissenting Alexandrian clergy had cited their errors in their letter to Alexander.[37] Manichee missionaries were active in Egypt in the third century, earning a letter of condemnation from Bishop Theonas of Alexandria. Their cosmology of two co-existent principles attracted philosophical as well as theological refutation, one of the earliest being a Neoplatonist, and perhaps former Christian, in Lycopolis, Alexander. Hieracas, the leader of another dualistic ascetic group, was also named in the letter to Alexander as having a controversial description of divine generation.[38]

Sociological or political categories have also been proposed as explanations for the irreconcilable division in Alexandria. Rowan Williams and David Brakke have offered a portrayal of Arius as a spiritual and intellectual teacher who was in conflict with the rising episcopal authority of Alexander.[39] The controversy then reflected the shift in the early fourth century from earlier independent study groups toward a public and eventually imperial episcopal orthodoxy. Since it is Epiphanius, a later heresiologist, not Alexander, who makes this accusation from his own ready arsenal of heresiological characterizations, and Arius is without a doubt a presbyter in a parish and part of a schism of clergy and laity which extends beyond Alexandria to include allies who are predominately bishops, this attractive interpretation remains difficult to maintain historically. The binary comparison of the authority of "bishops and teachers" in fact masks, as it was invented to do in ancient polemics, the many conflicts, theologies, and authorities of ancient Christianity. This included in Alexandria the Melitians as well as the emerging ascetic and theological challenges of Hieracas and the Manichees mentioned specifically by the dissenting clergy.[40] The exact nature of Arius as a "populist" in opposition to his bishop must also remain obscure due to the hostile sources which portray him and his followers in negative stereotypes as disorderly, public, and socially inconsequential, that is, artisans, young men, and women. In fact the evidence of the popular support most likely indicates the breadth of the break within the church of Alexandria, that is, one third of the presbyters were at one point in opposition to Alexander.[41] Rather than a conflict of

[37]   Lyman 1989; Heil 2002; Williams 2001, 260, rejected Manichaean material.
[38]   Knight 2012; on Athanasius and Hieracas, Brakke 1995, 44–53.
[39]   Williams 2001, 41–47; Brakke 1995, 57–61.
[40]   On this point see Lyman 2008, 241–42.
[41]   For a different view see Galvão-Sobrinho 2013.

bishops and ascetic intellectuals or a populist theological uprising, this local debate seems to fit the usual characteristics of ancient Christian urban conflicts, which have been increasingly recovered as less binary as well as more polyfocal and dialogical within the broad theological interests of varied clerical and lay constituencies.[42]

Finally, the broad and rapid spread of the controversy beyond Alexandria as well as its persistence after Nicaea has led to the supposition that the initial conflict was part of ongoing arguments in the eastern church. Following the genealogies sketched out by the participants, Manlio Simonetti outlined various wings of exegetical traditions and beliefs linked to the earlier conflicts over Origen.[43] Sara Parvis has discussed the early support of Marcellus and Eustathius of Antioch over against Arius, and she has suggested an underlying conflict between Eusebius of Nicomedia and Alexander, perhaps linked to the aspirations of Arius to the episcopacy.[44] The most recent discussions of Arius by Winrich Löhr and Khaled Anatolios have focused on his devotion to monotheism as a determinative principle, which may not be linked directly to philosophy, but may reflect ancient liturgical and devotional Christian themes.[45] The function and definitions of changeability, however, remain problematic with respect to Arius and the early controversy, even if scholars affirm its necessity to an authentic model of incarnation. The conflict in Alexandria may be linked to contemporary shifts concerning human nature and therefore new models of incarnation.[46]

RETHINKING ARIUS

Given the continuing lack of consensus with regard to the discernible influences of theological genealogies or philosophical models, the events of the Alexandrian controversy may be illuminated by placing the central issues of monotheism, apophatic theology, and the lingering problem of changeability in the legacies of the Great Persecution. The physical and literary conflicts between Christianity and traditional religion and philosophy provoked extensive theological and spiritual

---

[42] The new reflections of Brown 2015, xxiii, concerning the emergence of the cult of the saints.
[43] Simonetti 1975; on exegesis, see also Kannengiesser 1982.
[44] Parvis 2006, 38–68.
[45] Löhr 2006b, 156–57; Anatolios 2011, 42–52.
[46] Anatolios 2011, 51; on image and soul in the early fourth-century anthropologies, see Cartwright 2015.

literature on the nature of Christian monotheism as well as arguments about revelation and appropriate images of God. The Christian refutations of philosophical defenses of traditional material representations of the gods offered in place a "living image," that is, the human person as the only true image of the one transcendent God, and this image was usually located in the soul. The centrality of such apologetic arguments among various protagonists of the initial controversy strongly suggests that social issues around religious identity as well as contrasting theologies of God and representation could have escalated a local clerical debate into a larger crisis of Christian practice and belief. Around the time of the conflict between Arius and Alexander in Alexandria, the uneasy alliance between Constantine and Licinius was reaching a breaking point. The "Edict of Milan" did not ensure the end of traditional Graeco-Roman religion nor the uncontested rise of Christianity, especially in the first decades of the fourth century.[47] Christians, who practiced non-conformity to many traditional religious practices, were still vulnerable by choice as well as through shifting imperial policies.[48]

In February 303 Diocletian and Galerius ordered the burning of scripture and churches as well as the dismissal of Christians from imperial posts. In the East, in Alexandria as in other urban areas such as Nicomedia, Antioch, and Tyre, the persecution was episodic from 303, and then increasing in severity from 311 to 312. A series of edicts increased the pressure by imprisoning clergy and requiring them to sacrifice, then a general requirement for all inhabitants of cities, including, men women, and children. Christian responses included those who refused to comply, and those who negotiated in various ways.[49] These different responses to persecution and martyrdom created the significant schisms of the Donatists in North Africa and the Melitians in Egypt: both groups challenged the legitimacy of clergy linked to communities who had reconciled with those who had sacrificed. Although Epiphanius recorded that Melitius and Alexander reconciled, the Melitian movement in fact expanded during the course of his episcopacy: by 327 after the contested election of Athanasius, the Melitians numbered half the churches in Egypt and were active in monasticism as well as claiming to be "the church of the martyrs," a title later adopted by the Egyptian church as a whole.[50]

---

[47] Watts 2015; Lenski 2017.
[48] Recently summarized in Gaddis 2005, 29–45; MacMullen 2014.
[49] Luijendijk 2008.
[50] The complaints of Melitians against Alexander in Ath., *Apologia secunda contra Arianos* (*Apol. sec.*), 11; *Epistula ad episcopos Aegypti et Libyae* 23. According to Ath., *Apol. sec.* 71; Hauben 1998, 340.

Licinius had, in the words of T. D. Barnes, an ambivalent attitude toward the transitional religious policies after Constantine.[51] He had tolerated Christians in 313 and had received a vision with a universal monotheistic prayer; at his imperial court in Nicomedia, he maintained close ties with the Neoplatonic philosophers in Apamea.[52] Through his Christian wife, Constantia, Licinius also was in contact with Eusebius of Nicomedia, pupil of the famous martyr, Lucian of Antioch.[53] Licinius, however, later expelled Christians from the palace; he required the army to sacrifice to a statue of Sol, and this was sometimes extended to other citizens. He created a series of measures to limit and regulate Christian activity, perhaps in response to the divisions in Alexandria, including men and women worshipping together and assemblies having to be held outside the city gates.[54] Eventually, Constantine would move against Licinius in 324, in part, he opportunistically claimed, as a means of protecting Christians.

Arius's adult experience with many of his theological peers was profoundly shaped by the loss of public legitimacy including the death and torture of their communities. "Apologetics" has often been dismissed as an unoriginal and repetitive genre, yet recent studies argue for its critical significance with regard to theological and social legitimacy in the early fourth century. The numerous works of Eusebius present a Christian account of the authenticity and authority of religious and philosophical knowledge, including a sustained debate with contemporary Jewish and Hellenistic thought about the names, nature, and mediation of God. Sébastian Morlet has argued that these works were more constructive and less focused against Porphyry than traditionally thought, and created a new genre in which the science of theology was created.[55] The authors of these contemporary philosophical and religious treatises included several participants of the early controversy who held distinct doctrines of God and definitions of divine image: Eusebius of Caesarea and his encyclopedic works, the *Apology* of Marcellus, and in Alexandria the young Athanasius's *Contra gentes*.[56] These works

---

[51]   Barnes 1981, 70.

[52]   Barnes 1981, 70–72; Scholars date Iamblichus's *On the Mysteries* anywhere from 300 to 325. See Shaw 2014.

[53]   Eusebius appeared related to Julius Julianus, who was the praetorian prefect. Eusebius brokered the escape of Licinius which left him initially at odds with Constantine.

[54]   On the legislation of Licinius and possible connection to events in Alexandria, see Barnes 1981, 71.

[55]   Morlet 2009, 283, on the birth of science of theology; on the question of Porphyry, 17–20.

[56]   Pouderon 2009. This work by pseudo-Justin has now been attributed to Marcellus.

exploited the contemporary Neoplatonic rejections of dualism and their defense of the proper connections between traditional polytheism and philosophy to present a Christian cosmology.[57]

Accompanying these literary arguments on correct religious practice and theology was the spiritual groundswell of the veneration of martyrs and confessors in the early fourth century, which is sometimes overshadowed by the contemporaneous ascetic movement. The later conflict, and perhaps the initial dispute, undoubtedly involved the ideals of the emerging ascetic movement.[58] However, the legacy of the martyrs in the fourth century became enormous, including impacts on asceticism, ecclesiastical building, liturgy, calendar, and pilgrimage.[59] As in most aspects of ancient Christian practice, there was no single theology of martyrdom, but each expressed spiritual beliefs on the nature of the body and divine being. In Egypt the experiences of persecution and suffering were translated into theology and practice in various communities from the preservation of physical bodies by rural Millenarians, to the psalms of praise and remembrance by the Manichees, to the intercessory power of ascetics, who like martyrs continue to defeat demons who lurk in idols.[60] As recently discussed by Candida Moss and Stephanie Cobb, ancient martyr accounts preserve a variety of spiritual themes that have not always been noted in genealogical or dogmatic histories of theology. The portrayal of the deaths of martyrs were powerful texts of *ekphrasis*, constructed to convey visualized narratives of the relations between divine and human life.[61] Martyrs were living models for Christians to contemplate and imitate through their virtues of courage and endurance as a means of being assimilated to Christ.[62] In different ways these authors argue that scholars have often misread these accounts, which are based on later theological principles. The importance of *mimesis* in

[57]   Burns 2014.
[58]   On the question of ascetic women in Alexandria, see Brakke 1995; Elm 1994, 331–72; Burrus 2000, 36–80; on the legacies of martyrdom, see below.
[59]   Recently summarized in Leemans et al. 2003, 3–52; the unfortunate legacy of violent language and struggle in Gaddis 2005, 68–102; Young 2001.
[60]   Frankfurter 1994, 38: "Of course the third century in Egypt saw the diversification of Christianity into many sects from the Alexandrian 'orthodoxy' of Dionysius and Peter to their urban Gnostic competition to the various Syrian and Manichaean missionaries to the chora, to the amorphous rural millennialist cults [...] Each sect in its literature addressed martyrdom, martyrs, and in the fourth century the cult of the martyrs [...] a product of its area, culture, and socio-economic context." Brakke 2006, 23–47; Moss 2012.
[61]   Cobb 2016, 2–8.
[62]   Moss 2010, 21, 46; for later concerns and the deliberate distinction between mimesis and *theōsis*, see 164–71.

antiquity underscores the soteriological importance of the martyrs as a means to unite spiritually with Christ as co-sufferers and co-heirs.[63] Cobb argues that modern interpreters have mistakenly focused on the physical anguish of the martyrs, when in fact the narratives point toward God's sheer power in the world, testifying to freedom from pain through divine deliverance.[64] Through the martyrs' divinely sustained endurance, the persecutors' intentions and expectations are subverted; the verbs focus on endurance rather than suffering.[65] Thus they endure and conquer as Jesus did; confession and faithfulness as well as athletic metaphors illustrate their common divine victory.[66] The martyr, like Christ, in spite of relentless torture, remains unmoved, revealing the transformed human soul in imitation of Christ's own endurance. Christ's *hupomenō* is within them.[67]

Equally important is the unity of the earthly and spiritual spectacle: as the hearers fixed their eyes on the martyrs, so the martyrs fixed their eyes on Christ.[68] The revelation of the transcendent Christian God pervades this endurance and visions of the martyrs: "For the invisible God is revealed in our brothers we see."[69] The martyrs were the visible images of the spiritual and physical victory of Christians as co-sufferers and children of God.[70] These dramatic narratives present an *ekphrasis* of the transcendent Christian God as revealed through power and deliverance as well as a shared status with Christ through titles such as sons, brothers, and co-heirs of God.[71] These literary spectacles of spiritual transformation were joined by devotion to the physical remains of martyrs. Portrait panels of the liminal dead have been argued to be early precursors of icons, and part of the "material turn" in late antiquity.[72] The continuation of this visible witness to spiritual power in material

[63] Moss 2010, 157. On the development of mimesis as ethical and spiritual in Christianity, see below.
[64] Cobb 2016, 11–12.
[65] Cobb 2016, 21–28
[66] Cobb 2016, 29–30, 59; Moss 2010, 109.
[67] Cobb 2016, 70–73, 75.
[68] Cobb 2016, 77–79.
[69] Moss 2010, 159.
[70] 6.1, 6.5, 7.11, 8.10, in Moss 2010, 116; on their close connection to Christ, 5.1, 5.2, 6.41, 8.7, at 178; Frankfurter 2009, 233.
[71] Moss 2010, 164: "For those in the fourth century and beyond, schooled in and sensitive to Christological debate and Trinitarian theology, language of the martyr's exaltation is significant, but does not suggest shared status. For those unaware of or uninterested in ontological categories or invested in adoptionist Christology, the exaltation of the martyr may have been understood as indicative of shared status." On different portraits of Christ, 174; and on early evidence of different theories of salvation, 175.
[72] Most recently argued by Mathews and Muller 2016; Cox Miller 2009; Francis 2009.

witness was of course the ascetics. Methodius deliberately inter-twined the struggles of martyrs and virgins in the arena of the world as a larger invitation to a "performance of Christology."[73] In this context of suffering and unity with Christ, narratives of endur-ance expressed apocalyptic as well as mystical and devotional themes of divine power.

Within this political and spiritual context, a theological argument over monotheism in a community already divided by persecution had potentially deep emotional resonances.[74] The often noted plurality of language among the early combatants about the Son as the image of the transcendent Father could be particularly volatile precisely in relation to fears about divine materiality and religious identity.[75] Apologetic litera-ture in response to suspected materialism and polytheism offers signifi-cant parallels to the curious apophatic theology of Arius. Eusebius credited the "Hebrews," his depicted ancestors of Christians distinct from Jews, with the true and original radically transcendent monotheism:

> These are the teachings which we received from the Hebrews, which we preferred to the polytheism and deceptive daimons of the Greeks [...] confessing only God and worshipping only him [...] for even the only begotten god and first born of all, the beginning of all, commands us to believe his Father alone is true God and to worship him alone.[76]

The "Hebrews" were then as Christians now, according to Eusebius, the first people devoted to the pure and correct worship of the unseen and invisible god, who is unbegotten and unchanging, whose name could not be uttered or conceived; the name of God is only the one which he has given himself in Exodus 3:14; and he cannot be seen by the flesh.[77] This was also central in the apology of Marcellus: the only name of God is Exodus 3:14, which God has called himself.[78] In testimonia by Alexander and Athanasius, Exodus 3:14 is attributed to Arius in the initial conflict as a designation of God, which Eusebius defended to Alexander.[79]

---

[73] Hughes 2016.

[74] Vaggione 1989, commented that scholars have yet to connect the seemingly arcane discussions to the populist and emotional reaction it engendered.

[75] Williams 2001, 166; pluralist *eikōn* theology in Behr 2004, 32; see the outline of possible theologies in DelCogliano 2006.

[76] Eusebius (Eus.), *Praeparatio Evangelica* (*PE*) 7.15 (327c); my translation.

[77] Eus., *PE* 7.11 (520a).

[78] Pouderon 2009, 51–53, on the theology of Marcellus.

[79] *Urk.* 3; the designation of God is repeated in Ath., *Ar.* 1.22.

Scholars have noted in Eusebius the critical importance of the ancient Hebrews and martyrs as illustrations or icons whose narratives point toward the transcendent divine power.[80]

Arius also addressed the definition of God as invisible (*aoratos*) to all things that were made through the Son and to the Son. Yet, the invisible may be seen by the Son, by the decision of God to reveal himself: "by that power by which God is able to see, each according to his measure, the Son endures (*hupomenei*) to see the Father, as is allowed." These terse phrases seem to evoke a "seeing" of the invisible as part of a relational and spiritual process. Origen and Eusebius had noted that God saw not the physical being, but saw spiritually, that is, the inward person or soul; Origen in fact claimed that Jesus taught us to see how God sees, that is, to the heart.[81] Affirming the unique power of divine will, this passage conveys that the Son, however unique in direct begetting or relation, may see the invisible God in the same spiritual way that all may one day achieve the vision of the face of God (2 Cor 3:18), perhaps through endurance: he kept his eyes on the one who is invisible (Hebrews 11:27). This emphatic emphasis on divine will is similar to the economy and language of Irenaeus in which the unknowable Father is gained through obedience and love, and whose final goal is immortality through the gift of the vision of God.[82] The point of such descriptions is of course the gift of self-revelation only by the will of the singular Father, who is the source of all existence. These examples illustrate the defense of monotheism through the singularity of divine nature, power, and will in contrast to contemporary polytheism.

The discussion about monotheism and images in Eusebius and Athanasius in response to Porphyry may be helpful to understanding the tortured evidence concerning changeability in the teaching of Arius. Athanasius repeats several testimonia attributed to "the Arians" that the Son is not wood or stone, that he as *autexouios* can change; this common definition implied both animation and moral freedom in

---

[80] Johnson 2004; Verdoner 2011, 114–15.

[81] Origen (Or.), *De principiis* (*De princ.*) 1.1.8: the Son can know God, but not see him as "the image of the invisible god"; Or., *Contra Celsum* (*Cels.*) 7.33: power of the soul to see God in proportion to their spiritual rather than sensual eyes; Or., *Cels.* 8.18, God revealed to pious: "In each who do all in their power to imitate him in this way, there is an image (*agalma*) after the image (*eikōn*) of the Creator which they make by looking to God with a pure heart, being imitators of God."

[82] Irenaeus, *Adversus haereses* 4.20.1: "The Father remains unknown, for he cannot be measure, yet through obedience we begin to understand the existence of God"; 4.20.5: "For man does not see God by his own power, but when he pleases he is seen by men, who whom he wills and when"; in 5.16.2, this vision is immortality.

ancient culture, but for Christians this was used to assert a living, that is, human, image of God as a regular rebuttal of material divine images.[83] These testimonia from the early controversy then echo the apologetic rebuttals of idolatry, suggesting that the definition of the Son as *autexousios* is linked to the disputed definition of the Son as image who reveals the Father. Eusebius in Caesarea and Athanasius in Alexandria had responded to Porphyry's work on images by making a similar contrast, and asserting that the only true image of God was not material, but the soul of a human being.[84] Given that Athanasius is the hostile source of the testimonia, Arius may not have asserted that the Son changed, but rather only as a living being was he capable of it, and was therefore both the revealer of the divine image and the archetypal Son or second Adam. The construction of advancement or adoptionism could then be the polemical rebuttal of this voluntarist definition of incarnate image. The uncreated Father therefore is not seen or known apart from his direct action of revelation through the Son, who does not share his eternal essence.

In contrast Alexander describes the Son as living but underlines repeatedly that the Son is unchanging (*atrepton*) and unchangeable (*analloiōton*), eternal and in some sense necessary, and therefore the complete and the exact image of the Father, who is seen and known through the Son.[85] This lengthy and contrasting description of the living, exact, and unchangeable image who reveals the Father strongly suggests that image and changeability are part of a contested definition of the Son in the early debate. Notably, the Council of Antioch in 324 will explicitly condemn a definition of image as unchangeable by will.[86] Constantine

---

[83] See Or., *De princ.* 3.1.1, for general use with regard to the soul. These repeated testimonia in Ath., *Ar.*, are slightly different in wording (1.22, 1.35, 2.18), and undoubtedly contain Athanasian tampering. At the very least they reflect the definition of the Son as *autexousios*, which in these reports may have been altered to reflect actual or necessary change. In *Henos Sōmatos*, Athanasius reported an alleged conversation, in which they admitted the Son could change (*Urk.* 4b.10). I disagree with Stead 1983, that Ath., *Ar.* 1.5, is authentic. An emphasis on progress and advancement could well be part of a construction of adoptionism to avoid questions about a docetic incarnate image in Alexander. Defining the Son as *atrepton* and *analloiōton* as a perfect creature would not exclude *autexousios* (*Urk.* 6.3) nor his exemplary faithfulness as the image of the invisible God.

[84] For Porphyry's argument, see Miles 2015. Eusebius quotes a fragment from "On the Images" in *PE* 3.7–10; Athanasius addresses the same argument in *Contra gentes* 19–21.

[85] *Urk.* 14.27, 29, 38, 39, 47, 48. DelCogliano 2006, 465–70, on the epistemological meaning of *aparallaktos eikōn* in Alexander and Athanasius.

[86] In the Letter of the Council of Antioch (*Urk.* 18), we read that there is one unchangeable and unalterable God and his Lord Jesus Christ who exists eternally as God's

will later report that Arius claims that to give God a form or an image is an outrage.[87] Eustathius of Antioch complained that Arius had placed the Son into the flesh to do the work of the soul.[88]

Placing the language of Arius into the context of contemporary apologetics rather than theological genealogies suggests the reasons for his avoidance of any suggestion of eternal principles or materialism as well as his rejection of Alexander's new definition of eternal image which conveyed direct knowledge or sight of the transcendent God. By defining the image of the incorporeal God as *autexousios*, Arius attempted to place revelation within the place of the soul, that is, the spiritual rather than material being, and the analogical rather than visually literal sense of the body.[89] The uniquely created/begotten Son then becomes the one who reveals, worships and glorifies the transcendent God as the means of revelation. While defining an exemplarist Christology in Arius has been roundly criticized, I think this construction allows us to see these issues a bit differently in their ancient context. The Son as changeable image reveals the invisible God through actions which include a mimetic path within divine will; the incorporeal God alone then grants the vision and immortality to his creatures.[90] Methodius's cosmology with its emphasis on divine will is often cited with regard to Arius, yet his ascetic and exemplary Christology is oddly not included; however, his model included the centrality of Jesus, the arch virgin, created as the "second incarnation" to restore relation and immortality with

image, and as truly begotten, he is unchangeable and inalterable, and not like anything else. He is the image not of the will or anything else but of the *hypostasis* of the Father. The anathema is therefore against "those who teach he is unchangeable by his will. He is the Father's image and does not change." Williams 2001 attributed this to their acceptance of the polemics of Alexander.

[87] Constantine criticized his theology in *Urk.* 34 with another theological pun by accusing Arius of making a *plasma* of him who condemned the *plasmata* of the heathen (30). Arius stated that "Christ suffered for us" (32), and affirmed that he was sent in the form of a body (*morphē sōmatos*). "Truly, but it is necessary that we seem not to make him less in any respect" (32). Significantly, Constantine went on to lecture Arius that the world is itself a form (*morphē*), and stars have images (*charaktēres*), and a circle is a figure (*eidos*). Yet, God is present everywhere so how are such forms "outrages"? Is it then a sin that God is present in Christ? (33). This seems to imply that for Arius any form of God would be an "outrage," and may link back to his rejection of *eikōn* as an essential title in the *Thalia*.

[88] See now Cartwright 2015, 72–73, 149–52.

[89] On Eustathius's theology of the image in body and soul, including Adam as statue (*agalma*), see Cartwright 2015, 149–63.

[90] Athanasius denied mimesis to the Son in *De decretis Nicaenae synodi* 20.3. On the ethical and spiritual uses of mimesis in Christianity and Platonism, see Stefaniw 2016; Motia 2017.

God.[91] Image in this sense as revealer and archetype is not merely moral exemplar, but rather the distinctive Christian representation of the transcendent God in human form. The historical context of the intense refutation of polytheism not only by theologians, but in the actions of the martyrs and ascetics, and the resulting spiritual unity with Christ, outlines why this might have been an attractive spiritual path in the early fourth century. *Autexousios* here is then not solely part of the analytical and anthropological necessities of a two-nature Christology, but rather the lynchpin of a mimetic Christology which defended a transcendent, gracious, but apophatic theology. This definition would also convey the contemporary epistemic practices of obedience and endurance as outlined and pictured in the martyr narratives. These theological structures may narrate, however imperfectly, the motions and images of lived religion in ancient Christianity. Defined by the divine will of the one God, the created world, however, no longer has a symbolic or representational relation to God nor can there be a necessarily existent image of the singular incorporeal God.[92]

Athanasius in *De incarnatione* is often credited with an original synthesis of embodied image and incarnation in response to the cosmology of *creatio ex nihilo*, but I suggest that he cut his teeth on precisely these problems in the early controversy between Arius and Alexander.[93] His focus on the revelatory function of the human body of the Logos, and in significant contrast to Eusebius's work *Theophany*, continues the contemporary argument concerning revelation and representation. John Behr commented that Arius's "Christ reveals a God beyond whereas Alexander's Christ reveals God himself and eternal relation to Christ," and this may be exactly the point of the original debate concerning monotheism in Alexandria: how can the one transcendent creator be revealed?[94] How in the world of material images may the Son be uniquely defined as the image of God? Arius attempted to protect the singularity of the Christian deity from the materiality of emanation or revelation and the duality of co-existent principles through an original,

[91] Bracht 1999.

[92] On the very different shifts in Porphyry and Iamblichus, including theurgy, see Struck 2004, 214–80.

[93] According to Young 2013, 163: "Athanasius integrated three strands of biblical material: the commandment to make no images, the affirmation that human beings are created in God's image and the confession of Christ as the true image into creative systematic relationship."

[94] Behr 2004, 149; Anatolios 2011, 50: "the son is the supreme negative theology in person."

but short-lived, apophatic and perhaps mimetic theology, perhaps only formed in opposition to Alexander's theology of eternal Son and Image. In the ensuing controversies, the relation of the Son and the Father as well as the definition of incarnation, including the language of body and soul, was only gradually resolved as local theologians continued to have multiple definitions of humanity as well as conflicting Christologies.[95] The Alexandrian controversy was thus a conflict about social identity and divine representation as well as the means of generation and salvation.

SELECT REFERENCES

Anatolios, Khaled. 2011. *Retrieving Nicaea: The Development and Meaning of Trinitarian Doctrine*. Grand Rapids: Baker Academic.

Ayres, Lewis. 2004. *Nicaea and its Legacy: An Approach to Fourth Century Trinitarian Theology*. Oxford: Oxford University Press.

Behr, John. 2004. *The Nicene Faith*, Formation of Christian Theology 2. Crestwood, NY: St Vladimir's Seminary Press.

DelCogliano, Mark. 2006. "Eusebian Theologies of the Son as the Image of God before 341." *JECS* 14(4): 458–84.

DelCogliano, Mark. 2015. "Asterius in Athanasius' Catalogue of Arian Views." *JTS*, n.s., 66(2): 625–50.

DelCogliano, Mark. 2018. "How Did Arius Learn from Asterius? On the Relationship between the Thalia and the Syntagmation." *JEH* 69(3): 477–92.

Galvão-Sobrinho, Carlos R. 2013. *Doctrine and Power: Theological Controversy and Christian Leadership in the Later Roman Empire*. Transformation of the Classical World 51. Berkeley: University of California Press.

Gregg, Robert C., and Dennis Groh. 1981. *Early Arianism: A View of Salvation*. Philadelphia: Fortress Press.

Gwynn, David M. 2007. *The Eusebians: The Polemic of Athanasius and the Construction of the Arian Controversy*. Oxford: Oxford University Press.

Hanson, R. P. C. 1988. *The Search for the Doctrine of God: The Arian Controversy, 318–381*. Edinburgh: T&T Clark.

Löhr, Winrich. 2006a. "Arius Reconsidered (Part 1)." *ZAC* 9(3): 524–60.

Löhr, Winrich. 2006b. "Arius Reconsidered (Part 2)." *ZAC* 10(1): 121–57.

Lorenz, Rudolf. 1979. *Arius judaizans? Untersuchungen zur dogmengeschichtlichen Einordnung des Arius*. Forschungen zur Kirchen- und Dogmengeschichte 31. Göttingen: Vandenhoeck & Ruprecht.

Parvis, Sara. 2006. *Marcellus of Ancyra and the Lost Years of the Arian Controversy 325–345*. Oxford: Oxford University Press.

Williams, Rowan D. 1987. *Arius: Heresy and Tradition*. London: Darton, Longman and Todd. Rev. ed. 2001. Grand Rapids: Eerdmans.

---

[95]   See the chapter in this volume by Kelley McCarthy Spoerl.

Part II
The Council

4 Hosting the Council in Nicaea
Material Needs and Solutions
INE JACOBS

INTRODUCTION

Despite all that is written on the content, impact, and importance of the Council of Nicaea, we know very little about the actual physical circumstances in which it took place, the appearance of the city of Nicaea at the time of the council, the travel and lodging of its participants, and the location where it was held, the so-called palace. There is also uncertainty about the number of participants as well as the start and end dates of the proceedings. The last two issues are explored by David Gwynn in chapter 5, whereas I will focus on the surroundings and circumstances in which the council took place. In the first part, I will summarise what we know of the city of Nicaea, what it looked like in the early fourth century, and if it had the necessary infrastructure to host a large gathering, before asking why the council was moved here. As will become clear, this question needs to be split into two: why was the council transferred from Ancyra to Nicaea and why was Nicaea chosen over Nicomedia? The second part of this chapter considers the palace of Nicaea and physical form of the council hall. It will explore both the possibility of the council taking place in a large basilica-like setting and an alternative of the bishops convening inside a rotunda. Finally, I briefly compare the setting of the Nicaean Council to that of contemporary Christian meeting places.

A BRIEF INTRODUCTION TO THE CITY OF NICAEA

Nicaea was a wealthy city, located on the eastern shore of Lake Askania, modern-day Lake Iznik, in western Bithynia (Figs. 4.1–4.2). It was situated in a wide and fertile valley, surrounded by mountains. The settlement was connected to the nearby Sea of Marmara via the main highway leading from the Balkans to central Anatolia and extending to the southeast toward Syria. Nicaea was founded around the year 300 BC and has remained continuously occupied since then. Consequently, despite its

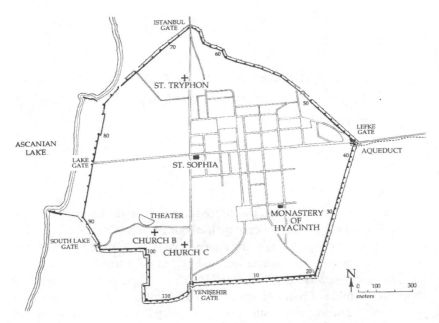

FIGURE 4.1 Plan of Roman Nicaea, from Foss 1996a, Fig. 1 (© Holy Cross
Orthodox Press). Used with permission.

very rich history and abundant material remains, modern-day occupation makes archaeological research very difficult. In the last few years,
however, new research projects aiming to examine the ancient street grid
and ancient monuments by means of geophysical prospection and a
thorough investigation of reused building material have expanded our
knowledge of the city's monuments.[1] Much of our information on the
city of Nicaea comes from literary sources, including a brief description
from Strabo, a passage in the *Expositio totius mundi et gentium*, a
section in the hagiography of Neophytus, and various inscriptions.[2]

   The first monument that visitors, including all bishops participating
in the council, to the city of Nicaea would have seen was its state-of-the-
art defensive system.[3] These walls were the second defensive system

[1]   See, for instance, Rabbel et al. 2015; the project "Micro-Identities of Bithynia during the
      Hellenistic and Roman Imperial Times: Archaeological Survey in Nicaea (Iznik/
      Turkey)" of the Ruhr-Universität Bochum. Peschlow 2017, gives a recent overview of
      the material remains from antique and Byzantine times discovered at Nicaea.
[2]   Şahin 1979–87; Abbasoğlu and Delemen 2003; Şahin 2003.
[3]   These walls have been studied in detail in Schneider and Karnapp 1938; Foss and
      Winfield 1986.

FIGURE 4.2 Aerial view of Nicaea [GoogleEarth, accessed October 1, 2018]. Used under the terms of fair usage as per the rightsholders terms and conditions.

with which the city had been equipped. The first wall circuit, built around 300 BC and described by the geographer Strabo as being 16 stadia or *c.* 2960 m long, fell into disuse and disappeared during Roman times.[4] Rather than by continuous walls, the new and larger city area was indicated by freestanding Roman triumphal arches built under Vespasian at the ends of the city's main streets.[5] One of them, the Lefke Gate (east), furthermore bears testimony to Hadrian's rebuilding of the city after an earthquake.[6]

When the Goths crossed the Black Sea and devastated northwest Asia Minor in AD 258, Nicaea as well as the other rich cities of the region were entirely defenceless. The Nicaeans fled their home and returned only after the Goths had withdrawn, having burned the city. Wall construction started soon afterwards.[7] The city's coins minted under Gallienus (253–68) and the usurpers Macrianus and Quietus (260–61)

---

4 Strabo, *Geography* 12.4.7.
5 Schneider and Karnapp 1938, 45, nos. 11–12 (Lefke Gate), 48, nos. 24–25 (Istanbul Gate); Foss 2003, 249; Şahin 2003, 18–20.
6 Schneider and Karnapp 1938, 45, no. 12.
7 Foss 1996a, 5; Foss 2003, 250.

indicate that construction began almost immediately and continued for some twenty years. The monument was finally dedicated in the reign of Claudius Gothicus (268–70), as attested by two dedicatory inscriptions on the new city walls, one on the Yenişehir Gate and one on the Lake Gate.[8] The new circuit was 5 km long and enclosed an area of some 210 ha. The walls were 4 m thick and rose to a height of 9 m. They consisted of a mortared rubble core, faced with coursed rubble and interspersed by bands of four layers of brick, and the circuit was accompanied by a moat. Every 60–70 m a brick-faced tower was inserted.[9] The existing triumphal arches were provided with square towers and reused as the four main city gates: the Istanbul Gate (north), the Lefke Gate (east), the Yenişehir Gate (south) and the Lake Gate (west). There was one smaller gate in the southwest.[10] These new walls followed a type that so far had only been applied in military contexts.[11] They represented the newest, most advanced system of fortification that would also inspire the builders at Nicomedia when the capital of Bithynia was provided with new walls a few decades later under Diocletian (284–305).[12] The third-century walls remained standing virtually untouched until the year 727 and were maintained and restored throughout the Byzantine period.

From its foundation, Nicaea had an orthogonal north–south and east–west oriented street system, which is still largely preserved in the layout of modern-day Iznik (Fig. 4.2). In the middle of the fourth century, the author of the *Expositio totius mundi et gentium* commented that:

> it is difficult to find elsewhere a city plan like that of Nicaea; one would think it a model set for all cities on account of its regularity and beauty, which are such that the tops of all its buildings, adorned with equal symmetry, appear to offer a splendid view to the beholder. It is decorated and harmonious in every respect.[13]

The main streets that connected the city gates were colonnaded. They met in the centre of the city at a crossroads that may have been marked by a tetrapylon. At least, the presence of such a monument somewhere within the walls is indicated by an inscription.[14] Beyond the east gate,

---

[8]   Schneider and Karnapp 1938, 43, nos. 1 and 50, no. 32.
[9]   Foss and Winfield 1986, 79–117; Crow 2001, 90.
[10] Foss 2003, 250; Şahin 2003, 17.
[11] Crow 2001, 90–91.
[12] Foss and Winfield 1986, 129–30; Crow 2001, 90–91; Foss 2003, 251.
[13] *Expositio totius mundi et gentium* 19, cited and translated by Foss 1996a, 9.
[14] Şahin 1979–87, 1:135, no. 173.

traces of an aqueduct have been noted. The theatre of Nicaea has been located and excavated in the southwest of the city, whereas a monumental gate, thought to belong to the gymnasium, still stands in the centre near the St. Sophia Church Mosque.[15] Literary sources and coins moreover testify to the presence of a temple dedicated to Rome and Caesar and temples dedicated to Apollo, Asclepius, Dionysus, and Tyche,[16] all of which must still have been standing at the time of the council. Finally, Nicaea may also have housed a treasury where tax revenue, in the form of goods, gold, and bullion, was deposited.[17] If so, it would have had to cooperate closely with the mint that was located in Nicomedia.

By contrast, there is no indication at all that the city at the time of the council already possessed a church building.[18] The evidence for the Christian community at Nicaea in the first quarter of the fourth century overall is scattered; in contrast, the presence of an educated pagan elite is much better attested.[19] The city had its own early Christian martyrs, the earliest of which, Tryphon, supposedly died for this faith under the persecutions of Decius (249–51), whereas Neophytos the Martyr, and possibly also Eustathios, Theodote, Antonia, and Bassos, fell victim to the Great Persecution under Diocletian and Galerius (303).[20] The earliest material remains are Christian tombstones,[21] whereas the oldest architectural evidence is a brightly painted chamber tomb (hypogaeum) in the necropolis to the northwest of the city, probably from the mid-fourth century, whose decoration includes peacocks, flowers, and a Christogram.[22] The existence of a cathedral as well as an extra-urban church dedicated to Saint Diomedes is suggested in literary sources by the reign of Valens.[23] St. Sophia, the best known late antique basilica at Nicaea and the setting of the second Ecumenical council in 787, was constructed as late as the second half of the fifth century.[24] Two meters underneath the surface of Lake Iznik, about 20 m away from the shore, lie the typical remains of another late antique basilica surrounded by tombs, possibly a memorial church for Neophytos the Martyr.[25] The building,

[15] Abbasoğlu and Delemen 2003, 191–92.
[16] Abbasoğlu and Delemen 2003, 192.
[17] Foss 1996a, 10.
[18] Peschlow 2003.
[19] Foss 1996a, 8–9.
[20] Foss 1996a, 5–7.
[21] Şahin 1979–87, 1:265–67, nos. 516–18.
[22] Fıratlı 1974.
[23] Foss 1996a, 16, n. 24.
[24] Schneider 1943, 10–17; Möllers 1994, 39–48.
[25] The building was discovered in 2014: http://arkeolojihaber.net/2014/02/26/1600-yil lik-bazilikanin-sirri-cozuluyor/ [accessed 26 June 2018]. Underwater excavations

which may have been built on the location of an older Roman temple, has been tentatively dated to the late fourth century.

WHY ORGANIZE A CHURCH COUNCIL AT NICAEA?

The question why the council was organised in Nicaea can be split into two separate queries: first, why was the council not held in Ancyra, as was originally planned? And second, why was the council moved to Nicaea specifically, and not, for instance, to nearby Nicomedia, where Constantine is known to have resided regularly?

Ancyra was a logical choice for a church council. The city was the centre of the province of Galatia; it was also the most important road junction in central Asia Minor; its bishop, the metropolitan bishop of Galatia, was highly ranked in the ecclesiastical hierarchy; and Ancyra had already hosted a synod in 314, which had dealt with matters arising from behaviour shown during the persecutions.[26] Transfers of councils are known to have happened at other (later) occasions in ecclesiastical history, but in such cases the reasons for the transfer are quite obvious. In 358, the Roman emperor Constantius II ordered two councils to be held on the topic of the Arian controversy, one of the western bishops at Ariminum and one of the eastern bishops at Nicomedia. An earthquake struck Nicomedia though, killing the bishop Cecropius. A transfer to Nicaea was briefly anticipated, but due to the proximity of Nicaea to Nicomedia, it was not considered a safe venue either. Eventually, the eastern council only took place on 27 September 359 in Seleucia, on the south coast of Turkey.[27]

In contrast, the reason or reasons to move the council of 325 from Ancyra to Nicaea has been the topic of some debate. According to a Greek document only preserved in a Syriac translation, Constantine himself gave three grounds, all of them pragmatic. He first referred to the more wholesome climate of Nicaea. He also pointed out that the city was conveniently located, easy to reach for the bishops from Italy and Europe who would be attending. Finally, the proximity to the imperial court at Nicomedia was given as a factor.[28] To the contrary, it has been argued in modern literature that the reasons for moving the council were

---

were begun in 2015: http://arkeofili.com/iznik-golunun-altindaki-1500-yillik-bazi lika-ziyarete-aciliyor/ and www.livescience.com/63498-ancient-church-hidden-in-t urkey-lake.html [accessed 12 October 2018]. See also Peschlow 2017, 209.

[26]   Foss 1977, 36–37.

[27]   Socrates (Socr.), *Historia ecclesiastica* (*HE*) 2.39.

[28]   Opitz 1934 (*Urk.* 20).

political rather than practical. According to Drake, Constantine took into account the objections raised by Eusebius of Nicomedia on holding the council in a locale that was overseen by a staunch opponent of Arianism, bishop Marcellus of Ancyra. Constantine had already learned the hard way that the bishop who would be given the prerogative of presiding over the council could strongly influence the outcome and apparently wished to avoid this from happening.[29]

Be that as it may, there is no denying that Nicaea was a much more convenient location than Ancyra for what not only became the first ecumenical council, attended by bishops from both east and west, but also the first council in which the emperor himself participated. The second reason given by Constantine himself therefore certainly is a solid one. Synods had generally been held at a location that was opportune for all their participants. Thus, the bishops of the African church met in Carthage, or, more exceptionally, in Hippo.[30] Both cities had good harbours and were located centrally on the densely inhabited North African coastline. Even though for most bishops the journey could largely be made overseas, it was still considered an onerous undertaking and also meant they had to be away from their sees for a lengthy period of time. The Synod of Carthage in 407 eventually stipulated that it was not necessary to meet on a yearly basis but that synods should only be held when necessary for the entire African territory and, moreover, in locations that were most convenient for the purpose.[31]

The Council of Nicaea greatly surpassed its predecessors in terms of the number of attending bishops.[32] The previous synod of Ancyra had been attended by about a dozen bishops, nowhere near the size of the council called in late 324 or 325. Moreover, most of these bishops no doubt had come from within Asia Minor. The Synod of Elvira, held around 305–6 in modern-day Granada in Hispania Baetica, had an attendance of nineteen bishops and twenty-six presbyters, most of them in charge of sees within the province itself.[33] The Synod of Arles, called by Constantine in 314, had at least twenty-five and at most forty-four attendants.[34] From this point of view, the decision to move a council to which bishops from all over the empire had been invited to participate to a coastal location was very sensible. For delegate bishops from around

[29]   Drake 2006, 125.
[30]   Beaver 1936, 173–75.
[31]   Beaver 1936, 176–77.
[32]   David Gwynn discusses the numbers more specifically in chapter 5.
[33]   For a recent overview of the Council of Elvira, see Streeter 2006.
[34]   Munier 1963, 14–22.

the Mediterranean, the travel distance to Nicaea would have been considerably shorter than that to Ancyra, as they did not have to travel an additional ten days overland after disembarking at Nicomedia. For instance, according to *ORBIS: The Stanford Geospatial Network Model of the Roman World*, Alexander would have been able to make the journey from Alexandria over the sea in April in sixteen days, seventeen if he waited a bit longer to commence his journey, but it would have taken him twenty-six or twenty-seven days to get to Ancyra. Likewise, it would have taken the Arabian bishop Pamphilus, potentially residing in Anasartha,[35] ten fewer days to get to Nicaea than to Ancyra. Conversely, many of the bishops of inland Asia Minor – and more than a hundred bishops came from Asia Minor – were suddenly confronted with a longer travel time.[36]

Constantine's third reason to bring the council to Nicaea, its proximity to Nicomedia, was a very sound one as well. Even though the Council of Rome in 313 as well as the Council of Arles in 314 had taken place on Constantine's instigation, he had not physically been present.[37] Initially, Constantine may not have been involved in the decision to organise a great council at Ancyra to decide on the fate of Arianism or have had the intention to participate in such a council. The decision appears to have been made at a synod of Alexandria, where Ossius, the emperor's representative, was present, but not the emperor himself.[38] From the moment Constantine decided to be directly involved in the fate of Christianity by attending and even presiding over the council, that decision was crucial for finalising the council's location.[39] Despite his frequent travels, Constantine ruled from Nicomedia, at least until the formal dedication of Constantinople. Nicomedia had been upgraded to the status of imperial capital under Diocletian because of its central and strategic location on both land and sea routes. Constantinople would share these characteristics. Conversely, Ancyra may have been located strategically within the region of Asia Minor, but it was twelve days away from the nearest Aegean harbour, some eight days from Heraclea Pontica, the nearest Black Sea harbour, and some sixteen days removed from Tarsus on the south coast of Asia Minor.[40] In

---

[35]   Shahîd 1984, 337–39.
[36]   Honigmann 1942–43.
[37]   Girardet 1993, 331–32. See also the discussion by Hal Drake in chapter 6, 113–16.
[38]   Barnes 1981, 213.
[39]   Girardet 1993, argues that Constantine not only attended but also presided over the Council of Nicaea.
[40]   http://orbis.stanford.edu/ [accessed 1 October 2018].

view of the recent turbulent history of the empire and the frequent problems along the Danube border, it would have been unwise for an emperor to be removed so far away from a strategic base with good access to both the eastern and northern frontier for too long. It must have been pretty clear from the beginning that a council with an agenda as long and important as that of, eventually, Nicaea would not be over in a matter of days. Nicaea certainly was much closer to Nicomedia than to Ancyra. *ORBIS* indicates a travel distance of 58 km, easily covered in two days of travel, between Nicomedia and Nicaea.[41]

From the moment emperors started attending church councils, ecumenical and others, it is apparent that the meetings frequently took place at locations where they resided or that were convenient to them. For instance, Constantius, who had a residence in Sirmium, convened the first council of Sirmium in 347. Three more would follow there, in 351, 357, and 358. Milan, the western imperial capital for most of the fourth century, can be regarded as a western counterpart to Sirmium, with three synods between 345 and 389. In 451, the ecumenical council that was initially planned to take place at Nicaea for obvious symbolic reasons was moved to Chalcedon for the convenience of the emperor Marcian.[42] These council locations were therefore a consequence of the personal involvement of emperors who did not have the time in between all other matters of state to travel long distances to attend to ecclesiastical matters.

As to the first reason recorded in antiquity, the more pleasant climate of Nicomedia, the northwest of Turkey also today in summer certainly is much more bearable than the Anatolian plateau, even though Strabo commented that the town was not very salubrious in summer.[43]

If Constantine thought it opportune to bring the council to him, for political and/or practical reasons, why did he bring it to Nicaea instead of Nicomedia? We know that Constantine was in Nicomedia in February 325 and again from the end of July to mid-September.[44] Delegates coming from overseas would have disembarked in Nicomedia and, like Constantine himself, still needed to travel two more days south to reach their final destination.

Nicaea was the second largest city in the province of Bithynia, after the capital Nicomedia, although its rural territory may have been the largest. In Byzantine times, the importance of Nicaea would grow, first

---

[41]   In comparison, the distance between Nicomedia and Ancyra was 358 km or twelve days.

[42]   Theodore the Reader, *Historia ecclesiastica* 1.3.4. (PG 86:168).

[43]   Strabo, *Geography* 12.4.7.

[44]   Barnes 1982, 76.

when the city became the capital of the Opsician theme in the eighth
century and thus a central military base controlling access to
Constantinople, and eventually in the early thirteenth century, after the
fall of Constantinople, when the city became the residence of the Laskarid
"Empire of Nicaea" (1204–61).[45] In Roman and late Roman times,
however, Nicaea remained overshadowed in size and importance by
Nicomedia. This did not stop Nicaea from relentlessly contesting
Nicomedia's primacy.[46] The conflict appeared to have ended when
Nicaea, having given its support to Pescennius Niger, was stripped of
its titles by Septimius Severus (probably in early 194).[47] It would, however, resurface in late antiquity, when the Nicaeans appealed to the
emperor Valentinian to have the title of metropolis returned to them.[48]
In addition, in 368, the bishop of Nicaea was granted metropolitan status
and thus raised to the same rank as the bishop of Nicomedia.[49] The
bishop of Nicaea started to interfere in matters that were within the
jurisdiction of the bishop of Nicomedia. At the Council of Chalcedon, an
entire day was spent on the matter, and Nicaea was forced to acknowledge that its metropolitan designation was purely honorific.[50]

  Nicomedia's location was vastly superior to that of Nicaea.[51] Like
Nicaea, it was positioned in a fertile territory, on the military road
leading from Chalcedon to Ancyra in inland Anatolia. However, as
Nicomedia overlooked the Gulf of Attacus in the east of the Propontis
(Sea of Marmara), it developed into a major commercial and military
port, housing the imperial fleet.[52] For this reason, Nicomedia had been
favoured by emperors already in the third century.[53] With Diocletian,
Nicomedia rose to prominence as one of the Tetrarchic capitals, officially dedicated in 304.[54] As part of its new status, it was provided with a

---

[45] Foss 1996a, 17, 57–77; Peschlow 2017.
[46] Robert 1977.
[47] Şahin 1979–87, 1:19–21, nos. 25–26, 25–27, nos. 29–30, 49, nos. 53–54; Şahin 2003, 11.
[48] Şahin 1979–87, 4:31–32, T23 and 4:37–41, T26; Şahin 2003, 12.
[49] Şahin 2003, 12.
[50] Foss 1996a, 12–13.
[51] Foss 1996b, 1. For an overview of the archaeological research carried out at Nicomedia,
      see Karababa 2008, 70–75. Our knowledge of Roman Nicomedia, like Roman Nicaea,
      is rather patchy and mainly based on literary sources, since Nicomedia, modern-day
      Izmit, has also been permanently occupied since antiquity, which prevents systematic
      excavations.
[52] Karababa 2008, 67.
[53] For a detailed overview of the importance of the city to emperors, see Karababa 2008,
      8–12.
[54] This is proven in the most spectacular fashion in the series of relief panels depicting an
      adventus scene of the co-emperors Diocletian and Maximian (Ağtürk 2018).

wall circuit, which, as said above, took inspiration from the walls of Nicaea, as well as several new building complexes, including a palace, an arms factory, a mint, a circus, and a basilica.[55] We know of one Christian church in Nicomedia, as Lactantius notes that this building, which was located in a residential area, was plundered and destroyed by imperial troops in the Great Persecution of 303. The building was replaced under Constantine.[56] As in Nicaea, there is not much other evidence for the presence of a sizeable or important Christian population in Nicomedia,[57] even though the prestige gained when the city became an imperial capital would make its bishop's position a highly influential and thus desirable one.

Nicomedia remained important in later centuries as well, and regular mention was made of emperors and their families residing here.[58] As already said, Constantine resided in Nicomedia on at least two occasions in 325 and generally treated the city as his capital between 324 and 330. The emperor's presence was attested again at the end of July 327; he was present at the church council of Nicomedia from December 327 to January 328; and he visited in early March of the same year. After the dedication of Constantinople on 11 May 330, he returned to the city only twice more, in 331 and in 334, both times for brief visits.[59] Constantine no doubt stayed in the palace built for Diocletian, which he probably had renovated, as Eusebius claims it had burned down during the reign of Diocletian.[60] Later emperors known to have spent time in Nicomedia include Arcadius and Theodosius II, who each stayed at least a month in the city.[61]

From the summary above, it is clear that there was not much practical advantage in moving the council to Nicaea rather than to Nicomedia. For the bishops who had already gathered in Ancyra, it would have only meant a minor time gain, as they would have reached Nicaea two days earlier travelling over the highway in the direction of

---

[55] Lactantius (Lact.), *De mortibus persecutorum (DMP)* 7.8–10, cited by Humphrey 1986, 581–82; Karababa 2008, 10. The imperial palace at Nicomedia has been located, but it is badly understood. Excavations in Diocletian's palace have begun in earnest in 2016 under the supervision of the Kocaeli Museum.

[56] Lact., *DMP* 11.7–8; Eusebius (Eus.), *De vita Constantini (VC)* 3.50 (*Oratio ad Sanctos* 25). Discussed in Johnson 1984, 123–24, who rightfully concludes that there is no reason to assume this church was remarkable or spectacular in any way.

[57] Johnson 1984, 124.

[58] Karababa 2008, 11.

[59] Barnes 1982, 77–79.

[60] Eus., *Historia ecclesiastica (HE)* 8.6.6.

[61] *Codex Theodosianus* 6.4.32 (397), 12.12.16 (426), 8.7.21–23 (426); *Codex Justinianus* 11.62.9 (398), cited by Foss 1996a, 10, n. 58.

Chalcedon. Conversely, for Constantine and all bishops still arriving from overseas, Nicomedia would have been a far more convenient venue. Therefore, the reasons for not doing so in this case must have been entirely political and can be connected to Nicomedia's ambitious bishop Eusebius. Having exchanged in a brilliant career move his first see in Berytus for the much more high-end imperial capital of Nicomedia,[62] Eusebius held a special status in the early fourth-century church and became remarkably influential as he, literally, was close to the emperor.[63] The ultimate confirmation of his high standing is the fact that, despite Eusebius's temporary deposition between 325 and 328, he became an ecclesiastical advisor to Constantine and was the bishop who administered the emperor's baptism in 337.[64]

In the years leading up to the Council of Nicaea, however, Eusebius showed himself a staunch supporter of the Arian cause and, moreover, used his perceived authority to convene a synod of his own to force Alexander to reinstate Arius to communion. Eusebius appears in the sources as an extremely influential, arrogant, and calculating ecclesiastical ruler, whose impact needed to be curtailed. Constantine may have responded to Eusebius's objections against holding the council in Ancyra, but apparently was not planning to add to the bishop's prestige by giving him the right to preside over what would become by far the biggest council in Christian history thus far. The move to Nicaea can be considered a clear statement on the part of Constantine in terms of who was in charge. Theognis, the contemporary bishop of Nicaea and also an Arian supporter, was of an entirely different rank, as Nicaea did not hold the same prestige in the ecclesiastical hierarchy, simply because it was not the imperial capital. Both Theognis and Eusebius would be deposed at the Council of Nicaea as they refused to recognise Arius's dismissal.[65] They were restored three years later, in 328, at a council that was held, more conveniently, at Nicomedia.

When it was time to celebrate the emperor's *vicennalia*, the entire imperial retinue and bishops gathered in Nicomedia. Eusebius describes how all bishops who partook in the council were invited to take part in the *vicennalia* celebrations inside the imperial palace on 25 July 325, at which time "soldiers ringed the entrance to the palace, guarding it with drawn swords, and between these the men of God passed fearlessly, and

---

[62] Johnson 1984, 117.
[63] Socr., *HE* 1.6, discusses Eusebius's career. See also the chapter by Sara Parvis in this volume, 229–32, 239–42.
[64] Barnes 1981, 226.
[65] Barnes 1981, 225–29.

entered the innermost royal courts."[66] The text in the *Vita Constantini* is unclear as to which palace this passage pertains, an ambiguity that some secondary literature has copied. Jerome is more explicit and places the celebrations in Nicomedia, not Nicaea.[67] It would indeed be very surprising to learn that the emperor started his *vicennalia* celebrations in a city other than his regular residence.

TRAVEL TO AND LODGING AT NICAEA

Before we move on to the physical setting of the council, some brief words on the travel, accommodation, and subsistence of the bishops whilst at Nicaea. All costs were apparently covered by the state treasury, including travel expenses, lodging, and meals.[68] Bishops travelling to Nicaea could make use either of state-provided pack-animals or of the *cursus publicus*, the imperial postal service.[69] With these services, Constantine repeated a prerogative granted for the first time to the bishops attending the Council of Arles in 314.[70] It would be repeated for later councils as well.[71] Travelling was an expensive undertaking. The costs, on top of the prospect of a prolonged absence from their sees, no doubt deterred bishops from attending councils. This munificence therefore no doubt ensured a greater attendance and encouraged bishops from far-away sees such as Persia and Spain to make the journey to the northwest of Asia Minor.

There is no information on where the bishops and their retinue stayed during their three months at Nicaea. Perhaps a select few of them stayed inside the so-called palace at Nicaea, which will be discussed in the next section. We know for instance that several dozen participants in the Council of Serdica in 343 were lodged in the imperial palace.[72] However, considering the number of bishops, to which the members of their entourage need to be added – each bishop had permission to travel with a small retinue of two priests and three deacons, so that the total number of ecclesiastical visitors to Nicaea may been somewhere between 1,200 and 1,900 – it is more likely that they were lodged in private houses all over the city.

[66] Eus., *VC* 3.15.2.
[67] Jerome, *Chronicon* 231^e.
[68] Eus., *VC* 3.9.
[69] Eus., *VC* 3.6.1.
[70] Eus., *HE* 10.5.21–24.
[71] In later centuries as well, it was possible for bishops to travel to church councils for free (Ammianus Marcellinus, *Res gestae* 21.16.18), discussed in Arce 2016, 150–51.
[72] Athanasius, *Historia Arianorum ad monachos* 15.5. Discussed in De Sena 2014.

THE IMPERIAL PALACE AT NICAEA

As mentioned in the introduction to this volume, the Hollywood depiction of the setting of the council is full of anachronisms. One such anachronism is the portrayal of the council taking place inside a Christian basilica. As with the content of the council, we risk falling into the trap of projecting the end result back in time, assuming that important church events and gatherings must have taken place in churches. Yet, literary sources leave no doubt that the council gathered not in one of the Christian basilicas of Nicaea, which as described above probably did not yet exist in this time, but inside the palace itself. According to Eusebius, the council gathered in "the very innermost hall of the palace, which appeared to exceed the rest in size."[73] Gregory, a presbyter of the church of Caesarea in Cappadocia, similarly described the setting as a huge hall, detached from the palace, in his *Laudation of the 318 Fathers*, a text that probably dates to the first half of the eighth century.[74]

First of all, it is useful to inquire what an imperial palace in the early fourth century would have entailed. The term "palace" (*palatium, basileion*) in antiquity was very ambiguous and by itself tells us very little about the appearance or the extent of the complex.[75] It was used to denote every lodging where the emperor on his travels took up residence.[76] Thus Julian described his mud and wood lodgings at Batnae during his campaign against the Sassanids as a *basileia*.[77] In most cases, however, a mansion, villa, town house, or *praetorium* can be surmised, since the emperor generally travelled with a large retinue, all members of which needed to be provided with accommodation and food, and presumably needed to be nearby when called upon.[78] Some authors have doubted the presence of a building complex reserved solely for the emperor at Nicaea. There indeed is no evidence for or mention of an imperial residence before it became the location of the council according to Eusebius. There would also not have been time to build a palace once the decision to move the council to Nicaea was made.[79] The characterization of the building as a palace in any case stuck, and it turned up in later sources as well. Ammianus Marcellinus recounted how in 364,

---

[73] Eus., *VC* 3.10.1 (trans. Cameron and Hall 1999, 125).
[74] Mango 2005, nn. 24–25 for further references, 30–32 for a discussion of its date.
[75] Arce 1997, 302; Wilson 2014.
[76] Millar 1977, 41; Arce 2016, 153.
[77] Julian, *Epistulae* 98, discussed in Arce 2016, 153.
[78] MacMullen 1976, 35.
[79] Peschlow 2003, 201.

Valentinian addressed the army in a camp presumably outside the walls, after which he was escorted to the palace.[80] We know from Procopius that there was still a palace in the time of Justinian, who had it restored as it was in disrepair and apparently partially collapsed.[81]

Moreover, there is reason to suspect that the imperial palace in Nicaea was more than the house of a prominent local citizen or high-ranking public servant occasionally turned into an imperial residence. There are some indications that Nicaea already had attracted imperial attention before the fourth century. If Nicaea was indeed the location of an imperial treasury, it obviously played an important role in the imperial administration. Moreover, an imperial interest in the city of Nicaea is chiefly suggested by its wall circuit described above. Its novel military architecture, together with two imperial inscriptions and two fragments of relief sculpture that probably derive from a monument for the Tetrarchs and were built into the wall at a later date, offer further support.[82] Imperial capitals from the Tetrarchic period onwards, including not only Nicomedia, but also Thessalonica, Antioch, and Constantinople, were given very similar fortification systems, inspired by the circuit at Nicaea. The investment of central resources in the Nicaea defensive system has even led Crow to suggest that the walls were built in order to prepare Nicaea to be an imperial centre.[83] Therefore, even if the palace grew out of an already existing structure, by the early fourth century it must have been substantial enough for the emperor not only to reside there himself at least intermittently during the duration of the council, but also to accommodate an assembly of bishops, some of them with their advisors, amounting probably to more than 300 people. It is certainly not unusual for imperial palaces to incorporate and extend older private villas. For instance, the residential area in Galerius's palace at Thessalonica grew out of an existing luxurious elite house of the second and third centuries AD.

The location of the palace of Nicaea remains unknown; but if we accept that the council hall was turned into the Church of the Holy Fathers that is mentioned on several occasions in later sources, it can be surmised that it was located in the northern sector of the city, not too far removed from the Istanbul Gate and the city walls. Indeed, the ninth-century Chronicle of Theophanes suggests that the church was located in proximity to a section of the city wall destroyed by the

[80]   Amm., *Res gestae* 26.1.3–5, 26.2.
[81]   Procopius, *De aedificiis* 5.3.3.
[82]   Crow 2001; Crow 2017, 409. The relief sculpture is discussed in Laubscher 1975.
[83]   Crow 2001, 91.

Arabs in 727.[84] The area near the Istanbul Gate especially was so badly damaged that it needed to be rebuilt,[85] hence it is not unreasonable to assume the presence of both the church and the palace in this area.

In order to get a better idea of what the palace in which the council took place potentially looked like, it is worthwhile briefly discussing what we know of nearly contemporary residences of emperors elsewhere and how they related to other luxurious private houses.

Earlier emperors had villas outside of Rome, but permanent imperial residences only multiplied with Diocletian and the Tetrarchy. A range of literary and archaeological evidence confirms palaces occupied by reigning emperors in the early fourth century at Milan, Trier, Sirmium, Serdica, Thessalonica, and Antioch, as well as at Nicomedia.[86] Of all these, only the internal plan of the palace at Thessalonica is relatively well known (Fig. 4.3).[87] The imperial complex of Galerius took up the southeastern section of the city. It was located next to the eastern city walls and stretched from the famous Rotunda in the north, originally intended to be either a temple or a mausoleum, to the harbour area in the south. Visitors to the palace would have been led through the Arch of Galerius and a vestibule, over a monumental marble staircase, into a porticoed square. From here, one could gain access to the hippodrome to

---

[84]   Theophanes, *Chronographia* 624B (AM 6218) (de Boor 1883, 405–6); Foss 1996b, 114; Mango 2005, 31–32.

[85]   The rebuilding of the walls by Leo III (717–41) is commemorated in an inscription. Schneider 1943, 1–2; Foss 2003, 252.

[86]   Spalato/Split and Felix Romuliana/Gamzigrad are not taken into consideration, as they were inhabited by "retired" emperors, Diocletian and Galerius respectively.

[87]   http://galeriuspalace.culture.gr/en/ [accessed 1 October 2018]. Of the size or layout of the palace in Nicomedia, nothing is known. The same is true for the palace of Milan, which is thought to have been located in the western part of the city, near the circus (Duval 1978, 137–38). The palace in Sirmium has little to distinguish it from an elite villa, and Noel Duval has disputed that the building excavated to the south of the city's hippodrome was indeed the location where the emperor resided (Duval 1978, 129–30). The palace at Serdica is believed to have occupied an area of at least 150 by 150 m in the southeastern area of "Old Serdica," where currently the Church of St. George still stands (Kirin 2000, 269–333; De Sena 2014). Although the presence of several "palatial features," including a bath complex and a basilica dated to the time of Constantine, makes it possible that this was the palace of Galerius and later Constantine who resided here intermittently between 316 and 323 and again between 328 and 330, as at Sirmium, concluding evidence has not yet been unearthed. The palace at Antioch was located on an island in the river Orontes, but its internal layout again remains unknown (Saliou 2000; Dey 2015, 34–38). Of the palatial complex of Trier, built for Constantius Chlorus (293–306) and used by Constantine between his coronation in 306 and 316, certain components are known, including an imperial bath house in the south, a circus in the southeast and a well-known basilica, the brick-built audience hall, in the north (Dey 2015, 45). The location of the residential quarters, adjoining the basilica, is known, but their internal layout and rooms are not.

FIGURE 4.3 The Galerian complex at Thessaloniki (reconstruction) (©
Ephorate of Antiquities of Thessaloniki City). Used with permission.

the west or continue southwards into the imperial premises. The most northern element of the palace proper was an apsidal building, possibly a triclinium, which opened up to another porticoed courtyard with the basilical audience hall at its other end. West of the basilica, the oldest part of the complex was located. This so-called Central Building Complex, which had at its core remains of luxurious houses dating to the second and third centuries AD, measured 30 by 40 m, consisted of a squarish courtyard with a fountain in the middle and [flanking] rooms on three sides. These rooms were surrounded by a mosaic-decorated corridor that connected this residential area to the basilica in the east, the "Octagon" and palace baths and presumably also the main entrance into the complex from the sea in the south, and the "Centrally Planned Building" in the north. Constantine is known to have resided in this palace for two years, in 323–4, and to have been involved in local projects.[88]

Although in the past it has been questioned if other imperial residences possessed the same elements, and even though the extent of our knowledge on palaces elsewhere remains limited, there is now general consensus that a set of "palatial" features was present in all of them. These include large dimensions, the arrangement of palace components along a central axis, and the presence of multiple apsidal spaces, including reception halls and dining rooms, as well as a central peristyle courtyard.[89] That being said, luxurious private houses that did not serve as imperial residences but belonged to extremely wealthy landowners, the leading elite of cities, or magistrates in the imperial administration, possessed many of the same features, including impressive entrances, grand reception rooms, and dining halls provided with apses, a central peristyle, luxurious decoration, and multiple fountain features.[90] Admittedly, the scale of most of these complexes was less impressive than that of imperial residences, but the ongoing discussion about whether or not the villas in Serdica and Sirmium were used by the emperor or not already indicates that scale was not always indicative.[91]

THE COUNCIL HALL: A BASILICA OR ROTUNDA?

There have not been many attempts to reconstruct the shape of the hall in which the council eventually took place as there is not much information

---

[88]   Athanasiou et al. 2013, 11.

[89]   Uytterhoeven 2007a, 33.

[90]   The vast literature on this topic has been assembled in Uytterhoeven 2007a and 2007b. See also Özgenel 2007.

[91]   Uytterhoeven 2007a, 34, for other complexes where it is not clear whether or not they belonged to an emperor.

FIGURE 4.4 The so-called throne room in Trier (Wikimedia Commons, author: Pudelek (Marcin Szala)).

to go on. Eusebius only indicated the location of the space but did not explicitly comment on practical aspects such as shape or size. Scholars have generally assumed that the council met in a rectangular hall, presumably based on the seat arrangement as described by Eusebius: "Many tiers of seating had been set along either side of the hall," so that the emperor "walked along between them [the assembled bishops]," and "When he reached the upper end of the rows of seats and stood in the middle, a small chair made of gold having been set out."[92] The situation imagined is that of half of the bishops along one long end of a hall, the other half seated opposite them and the emperor at the end, opposite the entrance.

Such an arrangement in a rectangular hall is certainly possible. All imperial palaces, as well as other luxurious residences, possessed a basilical reception hall intended to receive foreign delegations, guests, and clients (Fig. 4.4). These reception halls often were the most sizeable spaces within a complex. Of those with known locations, most are situated close to the main entrance and thus the street, so that they were easily accessible to outsiders who were not permitted to see the rest of the residence.[93] At first sight, this does not coincide with Eusebius's comment that the hall was the "very innermost hall of the palace." However, as mentioned above, when the bishops were invited to Constantine's palace in Nicomedia, here also the bishops were allowed

92 Eus., VC 3.10.1–5 (trans. Cameron and Hall 1999, 125).
93 Özgenel 2007, 252–53.

into the "innermost" courtyards, after having passed the guards at the entrance. It is very possible that Eusebius's usage of "innermost" did not mean more than simply "inside the imperial complex."

The second possibility, argued at length by Cyril Mango, is that the council took place not in a rectangular hall, but in a centrally planned space. His interpretation follows from the assumption that the meeting hall was turned into a church dedicated to the Holy Fathers.[94] The church was in existence by the eighth century at the latest, as it was visited by the Anglo-Saxon pilgrim Willibald at some point between 727 and 729, and it is mentioned again in the ninth-century Chronicle of Theophanes.[95] This church collapsed during the earthquake that struck Nicaea in 1065,[96] but was rebuilt and converted into a monastery,[97] which may have been the setting of another ecclesiastical council in 1232. A church dedicated to the Holy Fathers was shown to a Latin delegation in 1234. Finally, a thirteenth-century epigraphic description of the monastery mentions that the complex, which housed forty-two monks, twelve priests, and twenty-four deacons, occupied a plot of land of about 25 by 45 m (or 1125 m²).[98]

This Church of the Holy Fathers, and hence also the original meeting hall, appears to have been centrally planned. This can be concluded based on one reading of Willibald's comparison between the Church of the Holy Fathers at Nicaea and the Church of the Ascension in Jerusalem that he had previously visited.[99] His description makes it possible to imagine either a domed octagon or rotunda with an oculus in the centre. Alternatively, it has been suggested that the rotunda described by Willibald was only part of a larger complex, functioning maybe as a baptistery, a martyr's tomb, or a memorial attached to a basilica that had hosted the council.[100]

Centrally planned halls were not common within private villas, although they are not entirely unknown either.[101] The imperial residence at Thessalonica had two centrally planned halls. The first, the "Centrally Planned Building," was located to the north of the imperial apartments. Only its foundations have been recovered, but they indicate

[94]   Foss 1996a, 111–14.
[95]   Mango 2005, 28–29.
[96]   Foss 1996a, 112.
[97]   Mango 1994, 354–56.
[98]   Foss 1996a, 111–13; Mango 2005, 33.
[99]   Foss 1996a, 111–14; Mango 2005, 27–28.
[100] Foss 1996a, 113–14.
[101] For instance, the villa at Centcelles (Hispania Tarraconensis) possessed two rooms with a square exterior plan but round interior. The famous Centcelles mosaic covered the dome of a room with exterior dimensions of 15.24 by 15.24 m (Puche and López 2017, 173).

FIGURE 4.5 The Octagon in the Galerian complex at Thessaloniki (axonometric section, graphic reconstruction) (© Ephorate of Antiquities of Thessaloniki City). Used with permission.

a circular structure with a diameter of *c.* 29 m (=660 m²), situated in the centre of a courtyard. The position of this structure indicates it was probably accessible from the courtyard in between the apsidal building and the basilical audience hall. In other words, it was located in the innermost area of the complex, separated from the imperial apartments, though still accessible from them. Its function, however, remains unknown. The second centrally planned hall at Thessalonica, the "Octagon," is better preserved (Fig. 4.5).[102] Its form, location, and decoration have led scholars to presume that this was another audience hall or a throne room. The structure was begun under Galerius, but construction continued when Constantine resided in Thessalonica. The marble floor and wall decoration were probably only installed by the end of the fourth century. It possessed seven semi-circular niches, with the largest one, where presumably the emperor took his place, located opposite the entrance in the south. The hall itself was fronted by a monumental vestibule and a spacious peristyle courtyard, from which one could probably access the sea front. In other words, this hall was far removed from the main palace entrance used by visitors coming from the centre of

[102] http://galeriuspalace.culture.gr/en/monuments/oktagono/ [accessed 1 October 2018].

Thessalonica, but easily accessible for visitors arriving by water. Interestingly, this Octagon eventually was also converted into a Christian church, possibly in the second half of the fifth century. Overall though, centrally planned structures were used more often for mausolea than as actual living spaces.

In the end, the theory of a centrally planned council hall is based on a combination of two assumptions: the conversion of the hall into the Church of the Fathers and the description of Willibald as pertaining to the Church itself and not to one of its annexes. The only contemporary source is Eusebius's description, which remains more difficult to reconcile with a round seating plan than with a rectangular one.

As with the original shape, the size of the council hall also remains unknown, but we can try to reconstruct the minimal square meters necessary to accommodate an assembly of Nicaea's size. There are no guidelines as to what constituted a comfortable seating arrangement, but if we assume that some 400 ecclesiastics attended, which is a generous estimate, each of them occupying a space of minimum 0.50 and maximum 0.70 m, in rows that were separated by a comfortable distance of 1 m, the rows on each side of the hall separated by a central of aisle of 4 m, and leaving ample space (2 m) between the rows and the short walls, we would end up with an interior space of 24 by 14 to 32 by 14 m (336 to 448 m²).[103] In comparison, the imperial basilica in Thessalonica measured 24 by 67 m on the exterior (1608 m²), and that in Trier was very similar in size, 26 by 67 m (1742 m²).[104] Both were thus far larger than what would have been needed. The projected size of the council hall is more comparable to the basilical hall in a luxurious residence such as Piazza Armerina, which was about 12 by 30 m (360 m²). The basilical halls in other, more standard private residences were somewhat smaller, with lengths nearer to 10 m and occupying often about half of the surface.[105]

In the second scenario, that of a centrally planned council location, we would need a space with a diameter of some 21 to 24 m to end up with a usable floor surface comparable in size. At Thessalonica, both central halls were large enough to host several hundred people at the same time. The dome of the Octagon has a diameter of 23 m, and the second circular hall had a diameter of 29 m. Both the projected rectangular hall and the

[103]   To compare: Vitruvius, *De architectura* 5.6.3, recommends a seat depth of 0.6–0.7m. Rose 2005, on the basis of markings on the seats of the theatre at Arles as well as a study of modern stadia, arrived at an average seat width of only 0.4 m.

[104]   Athanasiou et al. 2013, 40.

[105]   Özgenel 2007, 252–53.

rotunda would have fit within the monastic compound that housed seventy-eight people as mentioned in the thirteenth-century inscription.

CHRISTIAN MEETING PLACES IN CONSTANTINIAN TIMES

From the previous discussion, it has become clear that the Nicene council hall had no direct relation to contemporary church architecture.[106] The conversion of the palace hall, basilical or centrally planned, into a church happened only after the actual event, at a date that remains unknown. The first attestation of the church only dates back to the eighth century. The simplest explanation for Constantine's decision to convene the council in the palace is that there were no public churches in Nicaea at the time, or at least none that were suited to accommodate a party of several hundred. As mentioned, the evidence for a Christian community at Nicaea is very limited.[107] The signs for church construction under the reign of Constantine and his sons in the region of Asia Minor overall are thin, and most of the evidence comes from literary sources.[108] Constantine is said to have restored the cathedral church in Nicomedia,[109] whereas we do not know of any similar interventions in Nicaea.

Instead, the organisation of the council inside a private residence, imperial or not, was very much in line with the initial gatherings of Christians in houses with the house owner presiding over the meeting.[110] We do not know much about the very earliest of these meeting places, as they are undistinguishable in the archaeological record. From the third century onwards, the designated spaces were physically altered into domus ecclesiae, rectangular halls probably with a dais at one end, large enough to host growing Christian communities. Such spaces must have existed in all cities of the Roman empire. The most famous example of a domus ecclesiae is that of Dura Europos, established c. 240–41 at the very eastern border of the empire. The adaptation of the Lullingstone villa

---

[106] See for instance Ward Perkins 1954; Krautheimer 1979; White 2017, on the development of church architecture in the Constantinian period.

[107] The city had its own bishop, but in this period a bishop's presence does not say anything about the existence of public Christian architecture. Rapp 2005, 24–55, discusses the role of bishops in the first centuries of Christianity.

[108] The number of Constantinian churches in Asia Minor attested by archaeological evidence can be counted on one hand, although this low figure may be a consequence of the fact that excavations have stayed limited to city centres, whereas the earliest churches may have been built in the cemeteries or necropoleis (Niewöhner 2016, 300).

[109] See n. 56.

[110] White 1996–97; Adams 2015.

(England) for Christian services dates to the second half of the fourth century. Both halls were large enough to host a few dozen faithful.

CONCLUSION

In conclusion, the Council of Nicaea opened a new era in the history of Christianity, but many details of its physical organisation come across as improvised and impractical. Constantine himself appears to have been responsible for most of this, as his personal involvement caused the transfer from Ancyra to the northwest of Asia Minor and determined the setting of the event in a private residence. Christianity's newly found position and prestige under Constantine created new needs for which novel architectural solutions would eventually be found. But for the time being, both Christian architecture and church hierarchy were still developing. The setting of the council was not novel at all, but very much in line with both existing imperial protocol and the traditional settings of Christian gatherings.

SELECT REFERENCES

Akbaygil, Isýl, et al., eds. 2003. *İznik throughout History*. Istanbul: Türkiye İş Bankası Kültür Yayınları.

Crow, James. 2001. "Fortifications and Urbanism in Late Antiquity: Thessaloniki and Other Eastern Cities." In *Recent Research in Late-Antique Urbanism*, ed. Luke Lavan, 91–107. Journal of Roman Archaeology Supplementary Series 42. Portsmouth, RI: Journal of Roman Archaeology.

Fıratlı, Nezih. 1974. "An Early Byzantine Hypogaeum Discovered at Iznik." In *Mélanges Mansel*, 919–32. Ankara: Türk Tarih Kurumu Basımevi.

Foss, Clive. 1996a. *Nicaea: A Byzantine Capital and Its Praises: With the Speeches of Theodore Laskaris, "In Praise of the Great City of Nicaea," and Theodore Metochites, "Nicene Oration."* Archbishop Iakovos Library of Ecclesiastical and Historical Sources 21. Brookline, MA: Hellenic College Press.

Foss, Clive. 1996b. *Survey of Medieval Castles in Anatolia II. Nicomedia*. London: The British Institute of Archaeology at Ankara.

Krautheimer, Richard. 1979. *Early Christian and Byzantine Architecture*, 3rd ed. New York: Penguin.

Mango, Cyril. 2005. "The Meeting Place of the First Ecumenical Council and the Church of the Holy Fathers at Nicaea." *Deltion* 26: 27–34.

Niewöhner, Philipp. 2016. "Church Building in Anatolia during the Reign of Constantine and His Dynasty." In *Costantino e i Costantinidi: l'innovazione costantiniana, le sue radici e i suoi sviluppi, Pars I (Acta XVI congressus internationalis archaeologiae christianae (Romae 22–28.9.2013)*, ed. Olof Brandt, Vincenzo Fiocchi Nicolai, Gabriele Castiglia, 295–308. Studi di

Antichità Cristiana 66. Città del Vaticano: Pontifico Istituto di Archeologia Cristiana.

Peschlow, Urs. 2017. "Nicaea." In *The Archaeology of Byzantine Anatolia: From the End of Late Antiquity until the Coming of the Turks*, ed. Philipp Niewöhner, 203–16. New York: Oxford University Press.

Robert, Louis. 1977. "Le titulature de Nicée et de Nicomédie: la gloire et la haine." *Harvard Studies in Classical Philology* 81: 1–19.

Şahin, Sencer. 1979–87. *Katalog der antiken Inschriften des Museums von Iznik (Nikaia)*, 4 vols. Inschriften griechischer Städte aus Kleinasien 9–10.3. Bonn: Habelt.

Schneider, Alfons M. 1943. *Die römischen und byzantinischen Denkmäler von Iznik*. Istanbuler Forschungen 16. Berlin: Archäologisches Institut des Deutschen Reiches.

Schneider, Alfons M., and Walter Karnapp. 1938. *Die Stadtmauer von Iznik (Nicaea)*. Istanbuler Forschungen 9. Berlin: Archäologisches Institut des Deutschen Reiches.

White, L. Michael. 2017. "Early Christian Architecture: The First Five Centuries." In *The Early Christian World*, ed. Philip Francis Esler, 2nd ed., 673–716. London: Routledge.

5 Reconstructing the Council of Nicaea

DAVID M. GWYNN

The Council of Nicaea was a landmark event in the history of both the Christian Church and the Roman empire. Yet uncertainty surrounds almost every aspect of the council and its proceedings. The organisation of the council's meetings and the identities and motivations of those who participated remain controversial, and modern reconstructions in turn have varied widely.[1] Rather than add another hypothetical reconstruction to those already in circulation, the aim of this chapter is to reconsider the different interpretations made possible by our limited evidence and the particular questions that have divided scholarly opinion. Who attended the Council of Nicaea? Who took the leading roles in the council's deliberations? And who proposed and supported the crucial decisions, such as the inclusion of the contested term *homoousios* into the Nicene Creed? Not only are such questions essential to understanding the council and its legacy, but our search for answers offers the opportunity to look beyond the emperor Constantine and the most famous episcopal protagonists, and consider the significance of Nicaea for some of the less prominent figures who contributed to the drama. While their voices are difficult to hear, these more humble individuals had their own parts to play and shared the contemporary awe at a spectacle that symbolised the changing status of Christianity within the fourth-century Roman empire.

The challenges posed by our sources for the council are examined in detail elsewhere in this volume, so only a few preliminary remarks are necessary here. No *Acts* survive, if any were ever written, recording the debates that preceded the adoption of the original Nicene Creed and canons. It is therefore necessary to some extent for any reconstruction to work backwards from the decisions finally reached, an approach that

---

[1] The bibliography is vast, as is reflected throughout this volume. Older works that demonstrate the shifting tides of scholarly interpretation in the English-speaking world include Burn 1925; Person 1978; Barnes 1981, 212–19; Luibhéid 1982; Hanson 1988, 152–78; and, from a rather different perspective, Rubenstein 1999, 48–89.

imposes an excessively linear progression upon the council's discussions and obscures the diversity of opinions that must have been expressed. Moreover, at least two major decisions reached at Nicaea, regarding the date of Easter and the Melitian Schism, do not appear in the disciplinary canons and instead are known from letters circulated at the council's conclusion by either the assembled bishops or Constantine. The extant signatory lists are incomplete, and the eyewitness accounts left by Eusebius of Caesarea, Eustathius of Antioch, and Athanasius of Alexandria are highly selective and differ significantly in the details that they describe and the motives that they attribute to the participants. A number of episodes said to have taken place at the council are also reported in subsequent sources, especially the fifth-century ecclesiastical historians Socrates, Sozomen, and Philostorgius, in stories that illustrate vividly the complex relationship between historical memory and later legend.

In light of this paucity of evidence, reconstructing what transpired at Nicaea inevitably involves a degree of calculated guesswork. Scholars have examined the conventions followed at other late antique assemblies that might serve as models for the Nicene council. The late Roman senate and imperial consistory were often cited as potential archetypes in older research, although these comparisons have sometimes been imposed too rigidly and threaten to exaggerate the emperor's role.[2] Church councils were also influenced by the practices of contemporary law courts, particularly for the prosecution of those accused of heresy or schism.[3] Perhaps the most important models are provided by later ecumenical councils whose proceedings are better documented, notably the extensive *Acts* from the Council of Chalcedon in 451.[4] It should be remembered, however, that the level of conciliar organisation attested at Chalcedon did not necessarily exist in 325, and the Council of Nicaea was undoubtedly rather less clearly ordered than our modern reconstructions tend to imply.

THE PRELIMINARY ARRANGEMENTS

The earliest reference to the impending gathering of the Church occurs in the Syriac synodal letter of the Council of Antioch that met in late 324

[2] For a classic statement of this argument, see Dvornik 1951. A more balanced interpretation appears in Drake 2000, 225–28.
[3] Humfress 2007, 205–11.
[4] Translation and commentary in Price and Gaddis 2005, with further analysis in Price and Whitby 2009.

or early 325. Presided over by Ossius of Cordova, this council supported Alexander of Alexandria in his condemnation of Arius and issued a creed opposing Arius's teachings. Three bishops who objected to that creed – Theodotus of Laodicea, Narcissus of Neronias and Eusebius of Caesarea – were offered the chance for repentance at "the great and priestly synod at Ancyra." We do not know who originally proposed that this great synod should be summoned, but we know it was Constantine who then moved the council from Ancyra to Nicaea. His letter of explanation, again preserved only in Syriac, cited Nicaea's ease of access for western travellers, superior climate, and the location that would allow the emperor to attend in person, with the last of those motives usually interpreted as the most important.[5]

Ine Jacobs has discussed earlier in this volume the careful preparation that the transportation and accommodation of so many clergy demanded. Constantine permitted the bishops to use the imperial post, just as he had done in the West for the Council of Arles in 314. This must have placed heavy strain on the postal system, a charge that Ammianus Marcellinus would later bring against Constantius II.[6] Nevertheless, the movement of numerous bishops across Asia Minor must have impressed the wider population as the episcopal entourages passed by towards Nicaea.[7] The sight reaffirmed the new prestige of the Christian Church and its representatives, and was a sign to all that a momentous event was about to occur.

WHO ATTENDED THE COUNCIL OF NICAEA?

According to tradition, 318 bishops came to Nicaea in the presence of the emperor to attend the first "ecumenical" council of the Church. The figure of 318, as is well known, is the number of Abraham's servants (Genesis 14:14) and was only attributed to the council some decades after the event.[8] In our contemporary sources, Constantine asserted that there were at least 300 bishops (*Letter to the Alexandrian Church*, in Socrates, *Ecclesiastical History* 1.9), Eustathius of Antioch estimated around 270 (in Theodoret, *Ecclesiastical History* 1.8), and Eusebius of Caesarea

---

[5]   The change of venue in theory also strengthened the influence of the local metropolitan Eusebius of Nicomedia over that of his rival Marcellus of Ancyra. On the negotiations this may have involved, see Drake 2000, 251–2. But also see above, 75–77.

[6]   Ammianus Marcellinus, *Res Gestae* 21.16.

[7]   One man who was reportedly influenced by the spectacle was Gregory the Elder, as reported by his son Gregory of Nazianzus (Gr. Naz.), *Orationes* (*Orat.*) 18.12.

[8]   Aubineau 1966.

indicated more than 250 (*Life of Constantine* 3.8). The overwhelming majority of those bishops were from the Greek-speaking East. The bishop of Rome was represented by two presbyters; otherwise there was just a single bishop from each of Italy, Spain, Gaul and North Africa. One came from Persia, another from Scythia. The Council of Nicaea was not therefore truly ecumenical (literally "world-wide" and actually meaning across the Roman empire), but was still a remarkable event and arguably the most representative Christian gathering since the apostolic Council of Jerusalem.

The identification of those who attended at Nicaea is made significantly more complex by the fragmented state of our evidence. A considerable number of manuscripts preserve what claim to be signature lists of the Nicene fathers. These lists, which vary widely from each other and survive in diverse languages (including Greek, Latin, Syriac, Coptic, Arabic and Armenian), were edited by Gelzer, Hilgenfeld and Cuntz in 1898 and re-examined with reference to subsequent scholarship by Honigmann in 1939.[9] Honigmann argued that all the lists derived from a single source which organised the bishops' names geographically by province.[10] The most accurate witness to that original source was preserved in Latin (manuscript class Lambda V) and recorded approximately 200 names. This list was then expanded into a collection of around 220 names contained in the Antiochene *Corpus canonum*, which in turn became the basis for the numerous manuscript variants, several of which were revised to bring the total of signatories to 318.[11]

Honigmann's reconstruction has proved highly influential, and underlies most modern estimates of 200–50 bishops at Nicaea.[12] The first bishop to sign would seem to have been Ossius of Cordova, reinforcing the argument that Ossius presided over the council debates. He was followed by Vitus and Vincentius, the two presbyters who signed on behalf of the absent Silvester of Rome. The other bishops then signed by geographical region, usually led by their provincial metropolitan. The

---

[9] Gelzer, Hilgenfeld, and Cuntz 1898; Honigmann 1939.

[10] See Honigmann 1939, 44–48, for his reconstructed list. Honigmann considers the possibility that a still earlier original source existed that was not arranged with such geographic precision, noting the much looser catalogue of the regions represented at the council given by Eusebius (Eus.), *Vita Constantini* (*VC*) 3.7, but acknowledges that there is insufficient evidence for any certain judgement.

[11] In one legendary version, two bishops named Chrysanthus and Musonius who passed away during the council miraculously added their names after their deaths to complete the 318 signatures. See the anonymous Byzantine *Life of Constantine* 27, in Lieu and Montserrat 1996, 130–32.

[12] See Appendix 1 at the end of this volume.

reconstructed list still raises certain unresolved questions. In the entry
for Palestine, the signatures are headed by Macarius of Jerusalem with
the metropolitan, Eusebius of Caesarea, down in fifth. This may reflect
Eusebius's undoubted concerns regarding the decisions reached at the
council, as well as the rivalry between the two sees as Jerusalem gained
in prestige under a Christian emperor. In the Galatian entry, the name of
Marcellus is absent, with the see of Ancyra represented by the otherwise
unknown Pancharius. It is possible that Marcellus was absent or ill, and
that Pancharius was the presbyter or deacon who signed in his stead.[13]
Several entries for less prominent bishops may have been omitted or
corrupted, while attendance at Nicaea must have fluctuated across the
two months in which the council was in session. The Nicene signature
lists thus remain open to ongoing revision and provide a basis for discussion rather than numerical accuracy.

A swift glance at the signature lists also highlights immediately one
of the great challenges facing modern interpretations of the council. The
organisation of the entries emphasises the importance of regional metropolitans, and without question men like Alexander of Alexandria,
Eustathius of Antioch and Eusebius of Nicomedia were highly influential. Many of the other provincial bishops, on the other hand, are little
more than names to us. There are obvious exceptions, such as the scarred
Egyptian confessor Paphnutius or the sole North African representative,
Caecilian of Carthage. But the majority of the attending bishops are
faceless and voiceless, easily dismissed in some scholarly accounts as
simple pastors who could not understand the intellectual scope of the
theological debates and were more interested in witnessing the spectacle
and beholding their new Christian ruler.[14] There is no doubt a degree of
truth behind that judgement, particularly for bishops who had travelled
from as far afield as Gaul or Persia.[15] Yet the evidence from the Council
of Chalcedon suggests that even within a crowded gathering individuality could still be expressed. In the fourth session of that council, the

[13] Honigmann 1939, 35, rejected the suggestion that Pancharius's name was a later
      invention to replace that of the controversial Marcellus. It has also been suggested
      that Marcellus signed the canons but not the creed, as his name does appear in some of
      the expanded signature lists, although it is unclear if there ever were separate signa-
      ture lists for the creed and the canons which were then later combined. See Parvis
      2006, 91–92.

[14] On the "ordinary bishop" in the early Church councils, see the original and wide-
      ranging work of MacMullen 2006.

[15] Eus., VC 3.6.2, himself stated that the bishops "were drawn by the hope of good things,
      the opportunity to share in the peace, and the desire to behold something new and
      strange in the person of so admirable an emperor." All translations of the VC are my
      own, adapted from NPNF 2.1 and Cameron and Hall 1999.

bishops were asked to confirm the harmony of Leo's *Tome* with the original Nicene Creed of 325 and the Niceno-Constantinopolitan Creed of 381 (*Acts of Chalcedon* IV.8–9). One hundred and sixty bishops each responded in turn, and while the majority followed a consistent formula there were several who took the opportunity to omit the contested creed of 381 from their acclamations or even doubted the validity of the comparison.[16] Although the sparse evidence from Nicaea does not permit such in-depth analysis, we should at least be cautious with the generalisations that we impose upon those bishops who actually participated in the debates that we are trying to reconstruct.

How many people were really present at the council? The approximately 220 bishops who attended the formal sessions had not made the journey to Nicaea alone. Every bishop required an entourage, as too did the emperor. A significant number of imperial officials and servants must have been present, but one of the only individuals identified is the *magister* Philumenus who supervised the signing of the creed.[17] The size of an episcopal entourage presumably varied with the status of the see and its occupant, but we gain an approximation from Constantine's letter to Chrestus of Syracuse (quoted in Eusebius, *Ecclesiastical History* 10.5) before the Council of Arles. Chrestus was instructed to select two presbyters and three servants to accompany him on the public post to Arles, a relatively modest escort equally appropriate for many of the bishops at Nicaea. These supporting characters are almost entirely faceless and indeed nameless. The one great exception, of course, is Athanasius, who attended Nicaea as a deacon assisting Alexander of Alexandria. Later writers attributed Athanasius with a leading role, reflecting his eventual legacy as the champion of the Nicene Creed. In reality, Athanasius was only a young priest in 325, and even in his later writings on Nicaea he makes no reference to direct involvement. He did no doubt listen closely to the debates and discussed the issues with Alexander, but only after Athanasius's death did the claim appear that "he held the first rank among the members of the council."[18] Given the limitations of our evidence, a precise tally of all those in attendance during the council's proceedings will never be possible. As a very approximate estimate, a figure of 2,000 is perhaps not far off the

---

[16] Notably Seleucus of Amaseia (4.9.12), Theodore of Damascus (4.9.14), Polychronius of Cilician Epiphaneia (4.9.117), and Romanus of Lycian Myra (4.9.131). See further Gwynn 2009, 16–19.

[17] Philostorgius, *Historia ecclesiastica* 1.9a. Philumenus was possibly *magister officiorum*. PLRE 1:699.

[18] Gr. Naz., *Orat.* 21.14.

mark and bears witness once more to the unprecedented scale of the
Nicene synod.

THE OPENING CEREMONY

Modern reconstructions of the Nicene council have varied widely on
many points of interpretation and detail, but descriptions of the formal
ceremony that opened the council have remained strikingly
consistent.[19] We owe this uniformity to Eusebius of Caesarea, whose
vivid eyewitness account is recorded in the *Life of Constantine*. The
bishops assembled in the great hall of the imperial palace at Nicaea,
with tiers of seating set along each side. After every bishop had taken
his assigned place, silence fell. The first members of the emperor's
entourage appeared, without the usual bodyguards.

> Now, all rose at a signal, which announced the emperor's entrance,
> and at last he himself proceeded through the midst of the assembly,
> like some heavenly angel of God, clothed in raiment which glit-
> tered as it were with rays of light, reflecting the glowing radiance of
> a purple robe, and adorned with the dazzling brilliance of gold and
> precious stones.[20]

Despite the splendour of his dress, Constantine displayed his reverence
for God through his downcast eyes and the dignity of his behaviour.
A small golden chair was set out for him, level with the first seats in
each row, yet only when the bishops gave their assent did the emperor sit
and then the bishops did likewise. Once all were settled, "the bishop who
was first in the row on the right" gave a short speech of thanks and
welcome.[21] Constantine then made a formal speech in Latin rejoicing
in the gathering and urging the need for harmony to secure divine favour.
An interpreter presented a Greek translation of his words, and the
emperor "made way for the leaders of the council to speak."[22]

Eusebius does not indicate the specific day on which the opening
ceremony took place. The traditional date is 20 May 325, which Socrates
states that he copied from the record of the council.[23] It has been argued,

---

[19]   A rare contrary interpretation is offered by Galvão-Sobrinho 2013, 86–89, who places
        this ceremony near the end of the council after the major theological debates had
        already occurred.
[20]   Eus., *VC* 3.10.3.
[21]   Eus., *VC* 3.11.1.
[22]   Eus., *VC* 3.13.1.
[23]   Socrates (Socr.), *Historia ecclesiastica* (*HE*) 1.13.

however, that Socrates misread that notation and that the council actually began in early June.[24] The implications of such a re-dating are not particularly significant, beyond shortening slightly the duration of the Nicene deliberations. The identity of the bishop who gave the speech of welcome has also been disputed. Sozomen believed it was Eusebius of Caesarea himself, while Theodoret proposed Eustathius of Antioch.[25] The most probable candidate is Eusebius of Nicomedia, who was the bishop of the current imperial residence and the local metropolitan. Should that identification be correct, then the opening ceremony arguably marked the high point of the council from the orator's perspective, for the Nicomedian bishop would find little to cheer in the debates that followed.

In its essential character, the account given in the *Life of Constantine* is highly compelling. The impact that the spectacle had upon the watching Eusebius is clear, and the description sets the tone for his wider depiction of the council and the role played by the emperor. Constantine had abandoned court protocol in dispensing with his bodyguards and awaiting the permission of the bishops before taking his seat, actions which distinguished the Church synod from a meeting of the senate or consistory. The speech that Eusebius attributed to the emperor expressed the same themes of peace and unity that recur in all of Constantine's statements concerning Nicaea, and the relationship between imperial and episcopal authority that Eusebius presents is one of mutual respect.[26] Nevertheless, the emperor was not the president at Nicaea, or at any other council.[27] Upon the conclusion of his speech, Constantine stayed in his seat and allowed the "leaders" (*proedroi*) to begin the official proceedings.

THE NICENE CREED

Few subjects in the history of early Christianity have received greater scholarly attention than the theological debates that took place at Nicaea, and those debates receive detailed discussion in several other contributions to this volume. The following remarks do not address the doctrinal questions at stake, but instead focus more narrowly on how the

[24] Schwartz 1959, 79–82, adapted by Barnes 1981, 215.
[25] Sozomen (Soz.), *Historia ecclesiastica* (*HE*) 1.19; Theodoret (Thdt.), *Historia ecclesiastica* (*HE*) 1.7.
[26] On the importance of Constantine's speech for revealing his motives and methods, see Drake 2000, 252–54.
[27] Rightly emphasised by Barnes 1993, 168–69.

debates may have unfolded and how the original Nicene Creed came to
be composed and signed. Under the influence of hindsight, it is all too
easy from a modern perspective to assume that the creed eventually
agreed was the only possible conclusion. Yet there was a wide spectrum
of theological beliefs represented at Nicaea, and few if any of those in
attendance could have foreseen the course that their deliberations would
follow. This very uncertainty must have contributed to the atmosphere
of the council and helped make possible the introduction of ideas with
which the majority of the bishops were by no means comfortable. Even
when the creed was agreed, no single interpretation was imposed, and the
controversies continued for more than half a century.

Some later ecumenical councils were organised in clearly designated
sessions, as we see in the *Acts of Chalcedon*. The proceedings at Nicaea
cannot be reconstructed so neatly. Our eyewitness reports condense
several weeks of extensive dialogue into short summaries, and their
accounts are difficult to reconcile and biased by apologetic and polemical
motives. Older scholarship expended great effort on attempting to define
the different ecclesiastical factions believed to have existed at the council: "Arians," "Eusebians," "Origenists," "Conservatives" and others.[28]
In reality, the situation was much more fluid and the fragmented evidence may be reassembled in a variety of different ways, a challenge
reflected in the diversity of more recent interpretations.

On one important point, modern scholars are now largely unanimous. The president who chaired the sessions was Ossius of
Cordova.[29] While this is never made explicit in the contemporary
accounts, Ossius was Constantine's representative and his name appears
at the head of the signature lists. The emperor was certainly present,
intervening in the discussions in Greek as Eusebius emphasises (*Life of
Constantine* 3.13.2), and his insistence on unity and conciliation must
have influenced the progress of the debates. But Constantine was not
a voting member of the synod, and in his letters he expressed his admir-
ation for the authority of bishops gathered in council.[30] It fell to Ossius to
set the agenda and guide the at times contentious exchanges to a final

---

[28]   Conveniently summarised in Person 1978, 44–51.
[29]   On Ossius's long and distinguished career, De Clercq 1954 remains a valuable if at times
       out-of-date guide. On Ossius's presidency at Nicaea, see also Barnes 1978, 56–57.
[30]   "They demand my judgment, when I myself await the judgment of Christ. For I tell
       you, as is the truth, that the judgment of the priests should be regarded as if God
       Himself were in the judge's seat" (Constantine, *Letter to the Catholic Bishops*, quoted
       in Optatus, *Against the Donatists*, Appendix 5, written to the Council of Arles in 314;
       translation from Edwards 1997, 190).

consensus, a feat that he managed with remarkable success whatever the long-term implications of the council's decisions.

As we do not possess the agenda that Ossius adopted, the precise order of business can only tentatively be reconstructed. The first question discussed may have been the status of Theodotus of Laodicea, Narcissus of Neronias and Eusebius of Caesarea, the three bishops provisionally condemned at the preceding council in Antioch. These bishops needed to be approved to take their seats in the assembly before the debates could begin, just as the legitimacy of Dioscorus of Alexandria became the focus of the opening session of Chalcedon. And it was this need for approval, as has been widely recognised, that provides the immediate context for Eusebius's account of the council in his *Letter to the Church of Caesarea* (quoted in Socrates, *Ecclesiastical History* 1.8). Eusebius presented the creed of Caesarea to prove his faith and insists that Constantine, before anyone else spoke, affirmed the creed's orthodoxy. The emperor, however, required the addition of the term *homoousios*, and this was then included in the creed issued by the council.

A rather different account was given by Eustathius of Antioch, preserved by Theodoret (*Ecclesiastical History* 1.8). According to Eustathius, when the bishops began to debate the faith, "the formulary of Eusebius was brought forward, which contained undisguised evidence of his blasphemy." The document was torn up in the sight of all, but further condemnation was prevented due to silence being imposed "under the pretence of preserving peace." If Eustathius and Eusebius of Caesarea are describing the same episode, then one of the two narratives must be grossly misleading. Alternatively, the Eusebius in Eustathius's account may not be the bishop of Caesarea but his more influential namesake Eusebius of Nicomedia. Several decades later, Ambrose of Milan (*On the Christian Faith* 3.15) asserted that a letter by the Nicomedian bishop was read out at Nicaea.[31] This letter, which is otherwise unknown (it is not Eusebius's extant *Letter to Paulinus of Tyre*), condemned any description of the Son as *homoousios* with the Father and so encouraged Eusebius's opponents to incorporate that term into the creed.[32] Taken together, the reports of Eustathius and Ambrose

[31]   Tetz 1993, proposed, without any conclusive evidence, that the fragment which Ambrose attributed to Eusebius of Nicomedia should actually be assigned to Eusebius of Caesarea.

[32]   Socr., *HE* 1.8, likewise reports that Eusebius spoke against *homoousios* at Nicaea. Eusebius's *Letter to Paulinus* (quoted in Thdt., *HE* 1.6) rejects any description of the Son as "from the *ousia*" of the Father, but does not mention the term *homoousios*.

suggest that Eusebius of Nicomedia made an initial bid to rally support for his theological position and was rejected, even if Eustathius may perhaps overstate the hostile response.[33]

We therefore have a potential glimpse of two early episodes in the council's proceedings: Eusebius of Caesarea securing recognition of his orthodoxy and his namesake of Nicomedia failing in a bid for theological leadership. Our third testimony by an eyewitness, written almost thirty years after the event, appears in Athanasius's *On the Council of Nicaea* 18–20.[34] The scene that Athanasius describes seems to reflect a later stage in the debates, with those who had previously defended Arius clearly on the back foot. Athanasius's highly polemical narrative depicts the council polarised into two factions, the "Nicene fathers" and the "Eusebians" (*hoi peri Eusebiōn*) led by Eusebius of Nicomedia.[35] The assembled bishops sought to express the orthodox faith in scriptural terms, but under cross-examination the "Eusebians" were constantly able to interpret those terms along "Arian" lines. The bishops were thus forced to invoke language from outside the scriptures, and so affirmed the Son as "from the *ousia* of God" and *homoousios* with the Father.

Of all the questions that still surround the Council of Nicaea, the inspiration behind the inclusion of the term *homoousios* in the Nicene Creed remains the most disputed.[36] The three eyewitness accounts offer varying explanations, including imperial patronage, the proven hostility of suspected "Arians" towards the term and the need to prevent heretical misinterpretation. While Constantine does not exhibit any deep theological knowledge in his extant writings, his overriding aim was unity rather than doctrinal precision, and he may have recognised or been persuaded that such language might offer an acceptable compromise. The opposition of Arius to describing Father and Son as *homoousios* was already known from his *Letter to Alexander* in 320/1, and Philostorgius (*Ecclesiastical History* 1.7) in the fifth century claimed that Ossius and Alexander met before the council began to agree upon the use of the term.[37] Athanasius's narrative suggests that *homoousios*

---

[33] A more negative interpretation of Eusebius of Nicomedia's position, arguing that he was already on the defensive when his writing was read out, is presented by Person 1978, 60–66.

[34] Athanasius repeated this account in slightly revised form in his later *Epistula ad Afros episcopos* (*Ep. Afr.*) 5–6.

[35] See Gwynn 2007, especially 239–44, and the chapter by Sara Parvis in this volume.

[36] Older scholarship is concisely surveyed in Hanson 1988, 190–202, and Ayres 2004, 92–98. Also see the chapter by Mark Edwards, below 145–49.

[37] The significance of this reported meeting, and the possible influence of Alexander on the creed, are discussed in detail in Skarsaune 1987 and Edwards 2012.

was instead only brought forward as a last resort when all scriptural options had failed, although this does not preclude preliminary discussions. Given that no one in the decades that followed seems to have endorsed the language employed at Nicaea, it may be true that the term was brought forward as an expedient compromise that excluded extreme "Arian" teachings and which the vast majority of the bishops could at least tolerate.

Homoousios is the most famous word associated with the first ecumenical council, yet it is only one word in the original Nicene Creed. So how did that creed, with its concluding anti-"Arian" anathemas, come to be composed? Eusebius's *Letter to the Church of Caesarea* was once believed to indicate that the Nicene Creed was based upon the creed of Caesarea which Eusebius presented to the council. Careful comparison of the two creeds demonstrated that this could not be correct, for the differences between them are far greater than merely the addition of a few anti-"Arian" formulas.[38] The Nicene Creed was therefore composed at the council itself, perhaps by a small committee who used existing creedal statements (possibly from Syria or Jerusalem) as a model for their work.[39] We cannot identify the individuals responsible with certainty, although Ossius and Alexander were presumably influential and a Cappadocian priest named Hermogenes is reported to have transcribed the final document.[40] This creed was then brought forward to the wider council. The ensuing debate is best attested in Eusebius's *Letter*, with each clause of the creed and anathemas weighed and accepted. The tone of that *Letter* is apologetic, and Eusebius's interpretation of the creed was very different from that of Alexander or Athanasius. But no single interpretation was insisted upon at Nicaea, and Eusebius may indeed be correct that Constantine played a key role in permitting a fluid definition that allowed almost everyone present to accept the creed with a clear conscience.

The assembled bishops were then asked to sign their affirmations. Two Libyan bishops refused, Secundus of Ptolemais and Theonas of

[38] Kelly 1972, 217–30.

[39] At the fourth ecumenical council, the Chalcedonian Definition was drafted in this manner by a committee whose work was then debated by the assembled bishops and revised before acceptance (Price and Gaddis 2005, 2:183–243).

[40] Athanasius (*Historia Arianorum ad monachos* 42) claimed that Ossius put forward the Nicene Creed, while the council's synodal letter to the churches of Egypt declared that Alexander "had the principal direction" in everything transacted. Hermogenes is said to have written "the great and invincible creed" by Basil of Caesarea, *Epistulae* 81, although whether Hermogenes contributed to composing the creed or merely copied down the text remains uncertain.

Marmarica, and were sent into exile. The rest complied. A later legend claimed that Eusebius of Nicomedia and his ally Theognis of Nicaea amended their text to read *homoiousios* rather than *homoousios* (Philostorgius, *Ecclesiastical History* 1.9 c). In their own testimony written two years after the council, however, Eusebius and Theognis stated that they subscribed to the creed but not to the anathemas, on the grounds that Arius's teaching had been misrepresented.[41] Arius himself was condemned and exiled. Intriguingly, this is almost the only reference to Arius in the proceedings at Nicaea. None of our eye-witness accounts discuss his presence, and there is no record of any formal examination of the man or his doctrines.[42] By the council's end, the theological issues at stake were already leaving Arius behind, with new debates emerging to divide the Church across the next half-century.

THE DATE OF EASTER

The second major decision associated with the Council of Nicaea concerned the Easter celebration.[43] No extant formal decree records the verdict reached at the council, but the subject is touched upon in the synod's letter to the Egyptian church and emphasised particularly in Constantine's letter after the council (quoted in Eusebius's *Life of Constantine* 3.17–20). It is usually assumed, not unreasonably, that Easter was the next item on the council's agenda after the theological debates, although the state of our evidence once again makes certainty on such matters of schedule impossible. The council insisted that Christians everywhere must celebrate Easter on the same day, and that the calculation of that date must not derive from the Jewish dating of the Passover. The customs followed by the churches of Rome and Alexandria, which were already shared by most eastern and western churches, were now to be adopted by all.

As a number of modern commentators have argued, the inspiration behind this decision may well have derived from the emperor himself. Constantine had already encountered differences in the observance of Easter at the Council of Arles in 314, and the first canon of that council

---

[41] Eusebius and Theognis were condemned not long after the council concluded, apparently for receiving friends of Arius. Their so-called *Letter of Recantation*, written to secure their return from exile, is quoted in Socr., *HE* 1.14, and Soz., *HE* 2.16.

[42] Person 1978, 59–60. The earliest reference to Arius being repeatedly summoned and interrogated at the council appears in Rufinus, *Historia ecclesiastica* 10.5.

[43] See the chapter by Daniel Mc Carthy in this volume. See also Di Berardino 1992 and L'Huillier 1996, 19–26. On the wider early Christian debates over Easter and its dating, see Mosshammer 2008.

declared that the Lord's Pasch should be commemorated "throughout the whole world on one day and at one time." The desire for unity that shaped Constantine's approach to the theological debates also underlay his vision of Christian practice, and his letter to the churches endorsing the Nicene ruling repeatedly upheld the need for uniformity in the celebration of so great a festival. All Christians should reflect, "how grievous and scandalous it is that on the same days some should be engaged in fasting and others in festive enjoyment; and again, that after the days of Easter some should be attending banquets and amusements while others are fulfilling the appointed fasts" (*Life of Constantine* 3.18.6).[44] Constantine's letter is also known for its vehement denunciation of the Jews, who are parricides and Lord-killers, and with whom Christians should have nothing in common. The extent to which Constantine here expressed views shared by others present at Nicaea cannot be determined with any accuracy, but similar statements do appear in other fourth-century works concerning Easter, notably Eusebius of Caesarea's *On Easter* (see below) and the *Festal Letters* of Athanasius.[45]

In his letter, Constantine offers no explanation of how the Nicene decision was reached and gives no hint that anyone dissented from the final verdict. We gain a slightly greater insight from our other major source on this ruling: Eusebius's *On Easter* (*De Sollemnitate Paschali*).[46] Writing at an unknown date not long after the council, Eusebius endorsed the judgement reached at Nicaea and may in fact have been commissioned by Constantine to do so against ongoing opposition.[47] According to Eusebius, Constantine sat in the midst of the assembled bishops while "a lively debate ensued" (*On Easter* 8). The unanimity of the representatives from north, south, and west prevailed over the eastern minority, who defended their own ancient custom but finally yielded. It was particularly the churches of Syria and Mesopotamia which had to abandon their previous traditions,[48] hence

---

[44] This concern that all Christians should celebrate Easter at the same time and in the same manner is likewise a recurring theme of Athanasius's *Festal Letters*.
[45] Gwynn 2012, 131–46.
[46] English translation in Barnes 2011, Appendix D.
[47] DelCogliano 2011b. Barnes 2011, 124, argues that Eusebius wrote more to justify his own acceptance of the Nicene decisions.
[48] There is a slight confusion over the exact regions affected. Constantine in his letter only listed the regions already in agreement rather than those which differed (Eus., *VC* 3.19.1), with Syria-Palestine the obvious omission. Several decades later, Athanasius (*Ep. Afr.* 2) wrote that the churches of Syria, Cilicia and Mesopotamia "kept the feast at the same time as the Jews," but as Constantine had included Cilicia in his catalogue of those in agreement the situation in that region remains uncertain.

the importance of the decision for Eusebius personally, and the composition of *On Easter* suggests that disagreements continued despite the recurring appeals for unity.

THE MELITIAN RECONCILIATION

The Melitian Schism in Egypt, like the better-known Donatist Schism in North Africa, emerged as a consequence of the Great Persecution.[49] Angered by the lenient treatment of lapsed Christians by Peter of Alexandria, the bishop and confessor Melitius of Lycopolis rallied those who shared his own more rigorous views into a parallel "Church of the Martyrs." Melitius's following posed a genuine threat to the authority of the Alexandrian see, and the division was sufficiently serious to receive close attention at Nicaea. The council's synodal letter to the churches of Egypt declared that Melitius and his clergy should retain their positions, although inferior in status to the equivalent clergy of the majority Egyptian Church led by Alexander of Alexandria, and that properly elected Melitian bishops could succeed Catholic bishops when the contested sees became vacant. As an attempted reconciliation, this compromise failed after Athanasius succeeded Alexander in 328. Melitian accusations of violence contributed to Athanasius's first exile in 335, while Athanasius denounced the Melitians for allying with the "Arians" against him, a conflict which continued across Athanasius's episcopate.[50]

No account exists to reveal how the Nicene council reached its Melitian verdict. The tone of the synodal letter strongly condemns Melitius, who has received clemency that he did not deserve, and emphasises that Melitian clergy have no authority to act without approval from their Catholic counterparts. Nevertheless, the relative leniency of the Melitian reconciliation may not have pleased Alexander, and was certainly regretted later by Athanasius (*Defense against the Arians* 59, 71). A cynical interpretation might attribute the leniency in part to Alexander's opponents, as the schism weakened the Alexandrian Church and the Melitians were later accused of allying with the "Arians."[51] But it would seem more probable that Constantine encouraged the charitable verdict, which was in accordance with his wider desire for unity and may have reflected the lessons that the emperor had learned from his unsuccessful efforts to suppress the North African Donatists.

---

[49]   For an overview on the Melitians, including their treatment at Nicaea, see the various articles collected in Hauben 2012.

[50]   Barnes 1993; Gwynn 2012.

[51]   On that polemical charge see Williams 1986; Gwynn 2007, 129–31.

THE CANONS

By 325, the custom for episcopal assemblies to issue canons on matters of church order was already firmly established. The procedure by which such canons were agreed and transcribed is less clear, however, even for councils with far more extensive surviving records than Nicaea. In a few rare instances we are informed which bishop proposed a specific canon, as is the case with the western Council of Serdica in 343 where a number of canons were formally attributed to Ossius of Cordova.[52] Sadly, no comparable evidence exists for the Nicene canons, nor do we know exactly how the canons came to be compiled. It is often assumed that a special session took place at which the canons were agreed, but while entirely plausible this hypothesised session cannot be confirmed.[53] The difficulties involved in reconstructing the composition of such canonical collections are well demonstrated by the canons attributed to Chalcedon in 451. Despite the extensive *Acts* preserved from that council, the twenty-seven Chalcedonian canons are recorded without any annotation, date of discussion or list of signatories. They may in fact never have been approved at a formal session of the council at all, but rather issued subsequently by Anatolius of Constantinople in Chalcedon's name.[54]

Any analysis of the twenty canons of Nicaea therefore depends almost exclusively on their individual content.[55] The canons cover a wide range of disciplinary issues, influenced by both the end of persecution and the growing organisation of the Church, and only in a few cases can more personal motives be tentatively proposed. Canon 6 reaffirmed Alexandrian authority over Egypt, Libya, and Pentapolis, which Alexander may have requested in light of the proposed reconciliation with the Melitians and the ongoing Libyan support for Arius. A possible dispute between Eusebius of Caesarea and Macarius of Jerusalem may in turn underlie canon 7, which sought to balance the honour owed to the bishop of Aelia (i.e. Jerusalem) with the authority of Caesarea as the metropolitan see for that region. There must also have been some discussion regarding canon 15 with its ban on translating any bishop,

---

[52] On the Serdican canons, see Hess 2002 and now Stephens 2015.

[53] Similarly, while there were several bishops present with previous experience in drawing up canon collections (including not only Ossius from the earlier Council of Elvira but also Marcellus, as rightly emphasised by Parvis 2006, 94), we cannot assign a dominant role to any one individual.

[54] Price and Gaddis 2005, 3:92–103. The so-called 28th canon of Chalcedon, on the authority of the see of Constantinople, was read out and debated separately.

[55] See L'Huillier 1996, and the chapter by Andreas Weckwerth, below 161–73.

presbyter or deacon from one city to another. This ban was not made retroactive, but those assembled at Nicaea could hardly have ignored the presence of Eusebius of Nicomedia and Eustathius of Antioch, both of whom had been translated from less prestigious sees (Berytus and Beroea respectively).[56] Finally, two canons refer to dissenting groups, the Novatianists (canon 8) and the followers of Paul of Samosata (canon 19). It is interesting that the Melitians were not handled in the same manner, and the judgement on their reconciliation only appears in the council's synodal letter to Egypt, not in the canons. The verdict on the Novatianists parallels to a considerable degree that concerning the Melitians, while the Paulianists are judged more severely as heretics and required to undergo rebaptism for admission to the Catholic Church.

The other Nicene canons are harder to interpret with reference to specific people or events.[57] Several of the rulings reflect widespread Christian attitudes of the time, notably concerning the treatment of those who lapsed during the persecutions. Later tradition also reported that one motion was defeated, a proposal that married clergy must separate from their wives. The scarred confessor Paphnutius maintained that marriage was an honourable state and that forced separation placed too great a strain on human frailty, and the council deferred to his esteemed judgement.[58] Overall, there was little contained in the canons to trouble the majority of the bishops at Nicaea. The Libyans Secundus of Ptolemais and Theonas of Marmarica may have disliked the support for Alexandrian authority in the sixth canon,[59] while the seventh canon only served to escalate the tensions between Jerusalem and Caesarea. Yet most of the canons probably passed with little debate, and were far less contentious than the other decisions reached at the council.

OTHER BUSINESS

As the prestige of the Nicene council increased across the fourth century, a number of stories circulated of varying degrees of historical veracity. Many of these stories are recorded by the fifth-century ecclesiastical historians,[60] and cannot always be pinned down to specific points in

---

[56] Eusebius of Nicomedia would of course be translated again more than a decade later, to the new imperial see of Constantinople.

[57] Canon 18 regarding the roles appropriate for deacons opens with the statement "it has come to the knowledge of the holy synod," but no explanation is given for how that knowledge was received.

[58] Socr., *HE* 1.11. L'Huillier 1996, 36, rejects this anecdote as a later eastern legend.

[59] See further Chadwick 1960.

[60] On the fifth-century reconstructions of Nicaea, see Lim 1995, 182–216.

the conciliar proceedings. One well-known instance depicts Constantine receiving petitions from rival clergy bringing charges against each other, which he publicly burned as a statement of unity (Rufinus, *Ecclesiastical History* 10.2; Socrates, *Ecclesiastical History* 1.8; Sozomen, *Ecclesiastical History* 1.17; Theodoret, *Ecclesiastical History* 1.11). Eusebius refers to mutual recriminations and to Constantine's efforts to bring those in dispute together, which he sets immediately after the emperor's opening speech (*Life of Constantine* 3.13.1). But he makes no reference to the burning of petitions, which appears to be a later embellishment.

Another and more plausible episode concerns Constantine's encounter with the schismatic Novatianist bishop Acesius. Our source for this story is Socrates (*Ecclesiastical History* 1.10, 1.13), who in turn was told by an aged Novatianist presbyter named Auxanon who in his youth accompanied his bishop to Nicaea.[61] Acesius had been summoned to the council by Constantine directly, and affirmed to the emperor that the Novatianists endorsed both the Nicene Creed and the ruling on Easter. When asked by Constantine why the Novatianists nevertheless separated themselves from the wider Church, Acesius repeated his conviction that those who lapsed under persecution could not be readmitted to the sacraments, provoking the memorable response: "Place a ladder, Acesius, and climb into heaven alone." Constantine's respect for the Novatianists probably influenced their relatively mild treatment in Nicaea's eighth canon, although that respect may not have lasted long. In an edict quoted by Eusebius (*Life of Constantine* 3.64–5), the emperor included the Novatianists along with other minor schismatic and heretical groups who are condemned as "opponents of truth, enemies of life and counsellors of ruin." While the exact date of the edict is not given, Eusebius clearly places the text later than the Council of Nicaea, which if correct suggests a hardening imperial attitude.

The story of Acesius offers a tantalising glimpse of one of the many "lesser" figures who played their own parts in the Nicene drama. Constantine was said to have particularly honoured the confessors who were in attendance, such as Paphnutius whose empty eye socket the emperor kissed (Rufinus, *Ecclesiastical History* 10.4). We are also told that pagan philosophers and dialecticians were present and displayed their arts in disputation, one of whom was converted to Christianity by the simple faith of an unnamed confessor (Rufinus, *Ecclesiastical History* 10.3). Stories such as these shed as much light on Nicaea's

---

[61] Urbainczyk 1997, 26–28, assesses Socrates's relationship with the Novatianists.

later reputation as on the historical council, and they leave many intriguing questions still unanswered. Did Caecilian of Carthage receive official recognition against his Donatist rivals, or was his attendance and the signing of the creed sufficient to justify his long journey from North Africa to Asia Minor? How was the sole Persian bishop received, and what report did he take back to his church? Similar uncertainty surrounds the personal concerns of the vast majority of the council's participants, ensuring that any reconstruction of Nicaea and its aftermath must always be incomplete.

THE FINAL CELEBRATION

The official proceedings of the council concluded in the first weeks of July 325. Encyclical letters were circulated to announce the decisions to all churches, and the emperor composed his own letters reaffirming imperial support for the Nicene decrees. Constantine, however, had planned a special celebration to reward the assembled bishops. His *vicennalia* commemoration began on 25 July, and the ministers of God were invited to feast with the emperor.

> Not one of the bishops was missing from the imperial banquet, the circumstances of which were splendid beyond description. Detachments of the bodyguard and other soldiers surrounded the entrance to the palace with drawn swords, and through their midst the men of God proceeded fearlessly into the innermost imperial apartments, where some were the emperor's own companions at table while others reclined on couches arranged on either side. One might have thought that it was an imaginary representation of the kingdom of Christ. (Eusebius, *Life of Constantine* 3.15)

This well-known passage in the *Life of Constantine* follows on directly from the account of the council, and Eusebius gives no indication of any change of location. Nevertheless, the famous banquet may have taken place not in Nicaea but in the imperial palace in nearby Nicomedia, to which the bishops would have travelled *en masse*.[62] Constantine was now accompanied by his bodyguard, unlike the Nicene opening ceremony, and to walk past the soldiers was a powerful experience for the many bishops like Eusebius who were survivors of the Great Persecution. The banquet may also have been the setting at which

---

[62] Stephenson 2009, 268. The celebration of Constantine's *vicennalia* in Nicomedia in 325 is recorded in Jerome's translation of Eusebius's *Chronicle*.

Eusebius heard Constantine's description of his vision of the solar cross in 312 (*Life of Constantine* 1.28), and likewise of the emperor's notoriously ambiguous statement that "You are bishops of those within the Church, but I am perhaps a bishop appointed by God over those outside" (*Life of Constantine* 4.24).

In his farewell address to the bishops, Constantine once again returned to the theme of harmony and tolerance (*Life of Constantine* 3.21–22). He bestowed all with gifts appropriate to their rank, and sent monetary contributions in addition to those who had not been able to attend. The unanimity that the emperor acclaimed may at times have been a little forced, and under the surface the unease regarding the Nicene Creed continued to simmer. Yet for all those in attendance, the Council of Nicaea was an event that could never be forgotten. When he recalled the glory of the final banquet, Eusebius must have spoken for many. It had indeed been "an imaginary representation of the kingdom of Christ."

SELECT REFERENCES

Aubineau, Michel. 1966. "Les 318 serviteurs d'Abraham (Gen., XIV, 14) et le nombre des pères au concile de Nicée (325)." *RHE* 61:5–43.

Barnes, Timothy D. 1978. "Emperors and Bishops, AD 324–344: Some Problems." *American Journal of Ancient History* 3:53–75.

Chadwick, Henry. 1960. "Faith and Order at the Council of Nicaea: A Note on the Background of the Sixth Canon." *HTR* 53:171–95.

De Clercq, Victor C. 1954. *Ossius of Cordova: A Contribution to the History of the Constantinian Period*. Studies in Christian Antiquity 13. Washington, DC: Catholic University of America Press.

DelCogliano, Mark. 2011b. "The Promotion of the Constantinian Agenda in Eusebius of Caesarea's *On the Feast of Pascha*." In *Reconsidering Eusebius: Collected Papers on Literary, Historical, and Theological Issues*, ed. S. Inowlocki and C. Zamagni, 39–68. Supplements to *Vigiliae Christianae* 107. Leiden: Brill.

Gelzer, Heinrich, Heinrich Hilgenfeld and Otto Cuntz, eds. 1898. *Patrum Nicaenorum nomina Latine Graece Coptice Syriace Arabice Armeniace sociata opera*. Leipzig: Teubner.

Gwynn, David M. 2009. "The Council of Chalcedon and the Definition of Christian Tradition." In *Chalcedon in Context: Church Councils 400–700*, ed. Richard Price and Mary Whitby, 7–26. TTH, Contexts 1. Liverpool: Liverpool University Press.

Gwynn, David M. 2012. *Athanasius of Alexandria: Bishop, Theologian, Ascetic, Father*. Christian Theology in Context. Oxford: Oxford University Press.

Hauben, Hans. 2012. *Studies on the Melitian Schism in Egypt (AD 306–335)*, ed. Peter Van Nuffelen. Farnham: Ashgate.

Honigmann, Ernst. 1939. "La liste originale des pères de Nicée: à propos de l'Évêché de 'Sodoma' en Arabie." *Byzantion* 14(1): 17–76.

Kelly, J. N. D. 1972. *Early Christian Creeds*, 3rd ed. London: Longmans.

Lim, Richard. 1995. *Public Disputation, Power, and Social Order in Late Antiquity*. Transformation of the Classical Heritage 23. Berkeley: University of California Press.

MacMullen, Ramsay. 2006. *Voting About God in Early Church Councils*. New Haven: Yale University Press.

Person, Ralph E. 1978. *The Mode of Theological Decision Making at the Early Ecumenical Councils: An Inquiry into the Function of Scripture and Tradition at the Councils of Nicaea and Ephesus*. Theologische Dissertationen 14. Basel: F. Reinhardt.

Price, Richard, and Michael Gaddis, eds. 2005. *The Acts of the Council of Chalcedon*. 3 vols. TTH 45. Liverpool: Liverpool University Press.

6 The Elephant in the Room
Constantine at the Council
H. A. DRAKE

It is impossible to discuss, or even think about, the first ecumenical council without considering the role played by the emperor, Constantine the Great (r. 306–37). It was Constantine who summoned the council, Constantine who decided its setting and (probably) its agenda, and Constantine who enforced its decisions. Yet too often he sits in the synod like the proverbial "elephant in the room" – an object of considerable weight that, for one reason or another, no one wishes to acknowledge. Part of the reason for this discomfort is theological: even though Constantine was for centuries held up as a model for future Christian emperors, honored with the title *Isapostolos* ("equal to the Apostles"), and even revered as a saint, leaders of the Protestant Reformation demonized him as the man who robbed the early church of its purity.[1] From this viewpoint, his participation taints the proceedings.

Our modern concept of the separation of church and state is also partly to blame, since the emperor clearly represents the state, and therefore his participation in the affairs of the church amounts to sticking his nose where it did not belong – a practice now condemned as "Caesaropapism," a modern term coined to define situations where the secular power ("Caesar") acts as a religious leader ("Pope").[2] Such thinking assumes that our concept of such separation applies to the ancient world. It does not. Every ancient state was also a religious institution, and it was the primary duty of every official, not just the priests, to maintain good relations with those divine forces whose support was needed for victory in war and bountiful harvests in peacetime. This duty was particularly pronounced for the Roman emperor, who was not just the highest religious official in the empire but also thought to be

---

[1] On Constantine's legacy, see Cowdrey 1997; Lieu and Montserrat 1998; Marcone 2002; Di Marco 2014; Bjornlie 2017. For *Isapostolos*: Meier 2003, 139.

[2] Dagron 2003, 283–84; McGuckin 2003, 251.

personally sacrosanct – not a god, but closer to the gods than the rest of us.[3] So the real question is not whether Constantine had any right to intervene at Nicaea but how he would exercise that right.

When Constantine took control of the western empire in 312, Christianity's troubled relationship with the imperial government – rooted in the crucifixion of their god by Roman authorities and marked by periodic pogroms thereafter – meant that neither he nor the bishops who made decisions about church doctrine had clear guidelines about the role an emperor of their faith should play. Such precedents as did exist suggested, at best, a policy of "benign neglect." In 260, the emperor Gallienus (r. 253–68) had ended persecution and recognized the corporate rights of the church to own property, but there is no surviving record of efforts by this emperor to assert his religious authority over Christians in any other way. Then, in 270, Christian bishops themselves asked the emperor Aurelian (r. 270–75) to intervene in a dispute with bishop Paul of Samosata, who had refused to surrender the church of the great eastern metropolis of Antioch after being deposed by a council. Aurelian agreed, but instead of intervening himself he turned the case over to the bishop of Rome and promised to abide by his decision.[4]

Closer to home, Constantine's brother-in-law, Maxentius, had adopted a more activist stance, intervening in the affairs of the Roman church to keep the peace during the six years he was in control of that city.[5] But Maxentius had the misfortune to stand in the way of Constantine's sense of mission, leading to his defeat and death at the Battle of the Milvian Bridge on October 28, 312 – the event that came to be associated with Constantine's Vision of the Cross and conversion to Christianity. As a ruler quickly labeled a persecutor, Maxentius was at best a dubious precedent for his successor to follow.[6] By the time Nicaea rolled around, however, Constantine had found an answer.

---

[3] As Isis told her son Horus in a Hermetic tract, the king is "last of gods but first of men." *Corpus Hermeticum* 24.3, edited by Scarpi 2009–11, 1:356–57.

[4] For Gallienus's edict: Eusebius (Eus.), *Historia ecclesiastica* (*HE*) 7.3. For Aurelian, Eus., *HE* 7.30.19. On the issues, see Millar 1971. The phrase "benign neglect" was coined by Daniel Patrick Moynihan in 1969 to characterize President Richard Nixon's shift away from the more activist role his predecessors had played in enforcing civil rights.

[5] Eus., *HE* 7.30.19.

[6] In his pioneering *Ecclesiastical History* (*HE* 8.14), Eusebius took note of Maxentius's favorable actions, which he quickly labeled as "pretended." For a spirited defense of Maxentius, see De Decker 1968. More recently, Leppin and Ziemsen 2007; Humphries 2008; Donciu 2012; Bleckmann 2015, 323.

DISSENT IN NORTH AFRICA

Within weeks of his victory over Maxentius, Constantine was con-fronted with a conflict in the church of North Africa that wound up establishing important precedents. The issue was a schism that trad-itionally has been called "Donatism" after the name of the man who emerged as its most vigorous proponent, Donatus of Casae Nigrae, though scholars now prefer a more neutral term, such as "dissidents."[7] The dissidents insisted, among other things, that sacraments adminis-tered by clergy who had succumbed during the recently concluded Great Persecution were invalid and needed to be performed anew.

Constantine seems to have been unaware of this controversy – cer-tainly of its depth and extent – when, shortly after his victory over Maxentius, he sent a letter to the governor of his new province of Africa (roughly, modern Tunisia), instructing him to restore property seized from Christians during the persecution to its rightful owners. About the same time, he wrote to the bishop of Carthage, Caecilian, granting him a sizeable sum of funding and assuring him that he need not fear those of "unsound mind" (μὴ καθεστώσης διανοίας) who were causing trouble.[8] The emperor soon learned otherwise. In April, 313, the gov-ernor, Annulinus, wrote that his office had been mobbed by dissidents, and he forwarded their request for a panel of bishops from Gaul, which had largely been spared the effects of the persecution, to hear their case.[9]

At this point, Constantine was already back in Gaul. He responded to the dissidents' appeal by asking the bishop of Rome, Miltiades, to hear their case.[10] To this extent, Constantine followed the precedent set by Aurelian almost half a century earlier. Yet even at this point, Constantine showed that he was taking an active interest. As he informed Miltiades, he had also appointed three bishops from Gaul to

---

[7] The label "Donatism" was slapped on the dissidents by their opponents, who called themselves "Catholics," even though the dissidents were probably the majority church in North Africa for most of the century. Modern scholars prefer "dissidents" or, out of fairness, labeling their opponents "Caecilianists," after the bishop of Carthage who was a target for dissidents. Many key documents in the controversy were assembled about half a century later by a Catholic bishop, Optatus of Milevis: edited with a French translation by Maier 1987–89; English translation by Edwards 1997. See further Frend 1952; Shaw 2011; Miles 2016. On the practice of naming dissident groups after a leader as a rhetorical device, see Robertson 2018.

[8] Eus., *HE* 10.5.15–17; 10.6. Maier 1987–89, 1:138–42 (documents 11, 12) dated both letters to the end of 312 or start of 313.

[9] Maier 1987–89, 1:142–48 (documents 13–15). For the events of this year, see Drake 2013.

[10] Constantine's letter to Miltiades is in Eus., *HE* 10.18. See Maier 1987–89, 1:138–50 (document 16).

hear the case with him and had already provided them with the same documentation he was sending to Miltiades. Effectively, Constantine had given the dissidents everything they wanted, except the venue.

It would be fascinating to speculate how the relationship between Constantine and the church might have worked out had Miltiades adhered to the emperor's plan. But it was not to be. Bishops of Rome were always jealous of their prerogatives, and Miltiades demonstrated his own by using the latitude Constantine gave him in his letter to turn the proceedings into a full-blown trial, adding fifteen bishops from Italy who, presumably, he found more reliable than strangers from Gaul. Miltiades was on solid ground at this point, since Aurelian had turned the earlier case over to the bishops of Rome and Italy. But when the council met, he innovated. Instead of the informal arbitration process that Constantine seems to have envisioned, Miltiades insisted that the strict rules of Roman legal procedure be followed. When the unprepared dissidents were unable to introduce sworn documents to support their claims, the bishop dismissed all of them. Miltiades might have assumed that Constantine, far off in Gaul, would accept a *fait accompli*. If so, he badly misjudged his new emperor.

THE COUNCIL OF ARLES (314)

Although Constantine gave Miltiades a great deal of leeway for resolving the dispute, this outcome was not what he envisioned. It is clear from the letter he sent the bishop that he had had in mind a more informal procedure, something more akin to an arbitration process than a court trial. His goal was not vindication but reconciliation, as he made clear with his final words, writing, "I do not wish you to leave schism or division of any kind anywhere."[11]

A sign of Constantine's unhappiness with the result lies in another letter, this one to the bishop of Syracuse in Sicily, in which he repeats a complaint that Miltiades had rendered a hasty judgment without due process.[12] This charge had been made by the dissidents, who had appealed to Constantine about the treatment they had received. We do not need to guess how seriously the emperor took their complaints, because in this same letter we learn that he had taken the unprecedented step of summoning a council on his own authority, to be made up of

---

[11]   Eus., *HE* 10.5.29, trans. Williamson 1965.
[12]   Eus., *HE* 10.5.22. Van Nuffelen 2017, 76, uses the claims made by dissident bishops in 411 to reconstruct what their predecessors would have argued in 313.

bishops from all the provinces under his control. In this letter, he not only informed the Syracusan bishop of these proceedings but also authorized him to travel via the imperial post, another unprecedented action, akin to providing first-class passage on a supersonic transport today. Effectively, Constantine had thrown out the judgment of the Council of Rome and taken matters into his own hands. To underscore the fact, he chose Arles as the site, physically moving the proceedings to Gaul, as the dissidents had originally asked. It was also a location close enough for him to monitor the proceedings, and even attend if necessary.

The Council of Arles, which met in August, 314, also ruled against the Donatists. Its judgment hardly settled the schism, which roiled the North African church for another century. But it is important here not as much for what it did as for what it taught Constantine. Whereas the limited and localized Council of Rome in the preceding year had given him precious little authority for dealing with the dissidents, the consensus reached at Arles by bishops representing the entirety of his domain allowed him to neutralize the dissidents' claim that they had been mistreated and instead depict them as trouble-makers who were out of touch with the broader Christian community.

Scholars rarely take notice of the important precedents set by this council, for the obvious reason that the bishops at Arles ultimately confirmed and reasserted the decision reached in Rome, making the whole procedure seem a bit anti-climactic. But when we consider the relationship Constantine was working out with the Christian hierarchy, it is important not just because it is the first council summoned directly by an emperor, but even more because it shows that Constantine had learned the right rhetoric for dealing with a Christian constituency. He consistently portrayed himself as a servant of Christ, proclaimed the sanctity of episcopal decision-making, and complained loudly about the audacity of the dissidents in appealing to him, exclaiming at one point, "They demand my judgment, but I myself await Christ's judgment." Amid such fireworks, the fact that Constantine granted the dissidents' requests easily escapes notice.[13]

This was something new. It had become standard for emperors to rely on their majesty and the awesome power it represented when issuing law; compliance, at least theoretically, was a foregone conclusion. The Great Persecution, launched by the emperors Diocletian and Maximian in 303, showed that such assumptions did not apply to Christians.

---

[13] *Meum iudicium postulant, qui ipse iudicium Christi exspecto!* Letter to Bishops at Arles: Maier 1987–89, 1:167–69 (document 21).

Diocletian's successor, the emperor Galerius, admitted as much in 311, when he reversed course and ruled that Christians could pray to their own god instead of performing the traditional rite of sacrifice.[14] Constantine himself briefly forgot that lesson. Evidently thinking that his profession of Christianity authorized him to compel the African dissidents to obey his will, in 315 he wrote a blustering letter threatening to come personally to Africa to teach them a lesson.[15] He even resorted briefly to military action, but when that blew up in his face he quickly reversed course and added the Christian notion of patient suffering to his repertoire, counseling the Caecilianist party to leave punishment to God.[16]

His decision to summon a council on his own authority shows that Constantine was not going to assume a passive role in Christian governance, and his letters show that he had found a way to sugar-coat what amounted to an unprecedented interference in episcopal affairs. In return, he had found a way to gain the moral high ground when dealing with Christian dissidents. His decision a dozen years later to move the council to Nicaea shows that Constantine had not forgotten that lesson.

AGENDAS

For scholars, the important lesson from Constantine's involvement in the North African schism is to recognize that his flattering rhetoric can mask a strikingly different agenda. A case in point is his frequent call for concord and unity. As Ramsay MacMullen pointed out long ago, Constantine's use of terms like *homonoia* in Greek or *concordia* in Latin "is the key to his whole Church policy."[17] But it can be seen as well as part of a broader policy, for in the religious atmosphere of late antiquity it was axiomatic that an emperor could only be successful in conducting affairs if he had the unanimous support of the people. Hence the frequent legend of *consensus omnium* ("everybody agrees") on coins. Concern that Christians were preventing this consensus by refusing to perform the traditional act of sacrifice underlay the empire-wide persecutions that began in the mid-third century and culminated in the Great Persecution of the early fourth. One way to understand Constantine's

---

[14]   For the edict, see Lactantius, *De mortibus persecutorum* 34, edited and translated by
       Creed 1984; Eus., *HE* 8.17. On its significance see Humfress 2008, 129–30; Digeser
       2014; Van Nuffelen 2017, 50.
[15]   Maier 1987–89, 1:194–95 (document 26).
[16]   Maier 1987–89, 1:239–42 (document 30).
[17]   MacMullen 1969, 165.

religious policy is to see him seeking a way to achieve this consensus by harmonizing Christianity with all other religious sentiments in the empire.

Bishop Eusebius of Caesarea, the author of an important *Life of Constantine* (*De vita Constantini*, hereafter *VC*),[18] shows us that Constantine's desire to find a common religious platform remained in force down to the very end of his long rule. In a speech delivered in 336, on the occasion of the emperor's thirtieth anniversary and less than a year before his death, Eusebius asserts that "the entire species of mankind in general, people of every race, shape, and tongue, all in common alike and individually, though divided in their opinions on other matters, agree on this alone, calling on the One and Only God with an inbred logic, a self-taught and self-learned knowledge." He concludes the speech with the same image of a harmonious chorus of subjects, all committed "to pursue the pious life under the same set of customs and laws; to praise one God who is over all; to acknowledge one Only Begotten Savior, the cause of all good things; and to recognize also one sovereign, rector of the earth, and his sons beloved of God."[19]

Eusebius was always given to exaggerate the breadth and depth of Christian numbers and influence, so he assuredly was thinking of Christians when he spoke these words. Even so, a bishop ordinarily would not speak of Christians coming to the faith through "an inbred logic, a self-taught and self-learned knowledge," rather than through catechetical training, and even Eusebius might hesitate before trying to claim that his religion comprised "the entire species of mankind." Since this speech was delivered on an official occasion, it is safe to assume that Eusebius chose words that he thought would be most pleasing to his imperial audience.[20] These words in fact encapsulate Constantine's priorities: a united judgment of all Romans that Constantine was the chosen ruler of a single Supreme God with whom he had a special relationship, combined with prayers to that God for the safety of the empire and Constantine's own dynasty (not necessarily in that order).

It is a virtual certainty that the vast majority of bishops who attended the Council of Nicaea shared Constantine's concern for harmony and

[18] Unless otherwise indicated, all translations of this work are by Cameron and Hall 1999.

[19] Eus., *De laudibus Constantini* 1.3, 10.6. English translation Drake 1976, 83–102; French trans. Maraval 2001; Italian trans. Amerise 2005. On the political theology of this speech, see Calderone 1988; Singh 2013; Singh 2015.

[20] On the role of panegyrics, See Whitby 1988, esp. ch. 1; MacCormack 1981. For an ancient handbook, see Russell and Wilson 1981.

unity in the church. Disagreement would come over the means of achieving this goal: Constantine thought in traditional terms of a body politic that needed to be treated and restored to health. Thus he began his first attempt to deal with the theological crisis in the east by referring to his "twofold purpose" in the recently concluded war: "My first concern was that the attitude towards the Divinity of all the provinces should be united in one consistent view," he wrote, "and my second that I might restore and heal the body of the republic which lay severely wounded."[21] Bishops, on the other hand, thought in terms not of healing, but of purity. As Jesus taught, "If your hand causes you to stumble, cut it off; it is better for you to enter life maimed than to have two hands and to go to hell, to the unquenchable fire."[22] Whereas Constantine saw unity as an end in itself, to bishops unity was only to be achieved by enforcing correct belief (ortho-doxa) – not by binding wounds but by removing the diseased limb.

This difference in agendas is the key to understanding Constantine's first response to the Arian crisis, a letter that Eusebius of Caesarea says the emperor sent shortly after seizing control of the eastern empire from his brother-in-law, Licinius, in 324. It was addressed to the two principal antagonists in the theological controversy that would lead to the Council of Nicaea, but probably sent to a wider audience.[23] In it, the emperor makes light of their conflict, repeatedly dismissing it as "worthless" (2.68; 2.71), "petty and a complete waste of time" (2.68), "really silly" (2.71), "trivial and entirely unimportant" (2.71) because, as he points out with a thoroughly Roman sense of the matter, their dispute did not involve any point of law (2.69.2).[24]

Given the central importance of these issues to Christian belief, it is hardly surprising that Constantine has been ridiculed for the ignorance and naiveté he seemingly displays. It provoked one of Gibbon's funniest footnotes.[25] Yet other parts of the same letter show that the emperor was aware of the complexity of the issues involved, for he points out that they are too subtle to be understood by the laity, which would only be

[21] Eus., VC 2.65.1.
[22] Mark 9:43 (NRSV). Cf. Matt. 5:30.
[23] Eus., VC 2.64–72. Hall 1998 argues that the letter was sent to the bishops meeting at Antioch. See Parvis 2006, 77. For an account of the controversy's origins, see the chapter by Rebecca Lyman in this volume.
[24] MacMullen 2006, 28, observes this difference in education between the eastern and western empires, that the Latin West emphasized legal training, while the Greek East stressed philosophy.
[25] "The principles of toleration and religious indifference, contained in this epistle, have given great offence to Baronius, Tillemont, &c. who suppose that the emperor had some evil counsellor, either Satan or Eusebius, at his elbow." Gibbon 1909–14, 2:376 (ch. 21, n. 77).

confused by them. Far more important, to him, was the threat their dispute posed to public order. Alluding to the way it had divided congregations and even been taken into the streets, he characterizes such activities as "hasty" and "ill-advised," likely to result in either "blasphemy or schism" (2.69).[26]

The bishops who assembled at Nicaea surely shared the emperor's concern for unity and harmony, but a higher priority – at least for those most heavily embroiled in the Arian controversy – would have been to settle the theological issues raised by the Arian controversy. Constantine's dismissive comments suggest that, in his case, the opposite was true. So, what the letter really tells us is that (to borrow the language of the theological controversy) it is better to think that the agendas of the bishops and the emperor were *similar* (*homoiousios*), rather than *identical* (*homoousios*). *Homoousios* became the dominant term theologically, but to study the politics of the council *homoiousios* is the better guide. Constantine had his own agenda, one that was similar to but also distinctly different from that of the bishops.

It is important to think about agendas for two reasons. First, because it lets us see that, however much Constantine's own agenda may have overlapped with that of the bishops, it would nevertheless be a mistake to use theological priorities to understand his thoughts and actions. Second, because meetings the size of the Council of Nicaea – approximately 200 bishops with attendants and advisors that would easily have tripled that number – required advance planning to get anything done.[27] With the activist bent he had already shown, Constantine was certain to be involved at this stage.

PRE-NICENE MANEUVERING

Constantine sent his letter to Alexander and Arius via a person Eusebius of Caesarea identifies as a Christian in the emperor's retinue, one "whom he well knew to be approved for the sobriety and genuineness of his faith, and who had before this time distinguished himself by the boldness of his religious profession" (*VC* 2.63). In all likelihood this was Bishop Ossius of Cordoba, who had served Constantine in this capacity in the west.[28]

[26] On the role of popular actions, see Stead 1978; Hall 1985; Galvão-Sobrinho 2013.
[27] MacMullen 2006, 83. The canonical number of bishops in attendance became 318, but modern scholars put the number as low as 200. See MacMullen 2006, 41. Eus., *VC* 3.8, gives the number as 250. Also see above, 92–96.
[28] Ossius had been a confessor in the persecution. He carried Constantine's letters to North Africa in his first effort to resolve the Donatist crisis: Eus., *HE* 10.6.2. See Vilella

There is not full agreement among scholars about the exact sequence of subsequent events. Since the discovery in 1905 of a letter in Syriac purporting to be the decisions of a council in the eastern metropolis of Antioch, a majority of scholars has held that Ossius brought Constantine's letter to Antioch, perhaps after first travelling to Alexandria, where yet another council was held. According to this letter, the Council of Antioch provisionally excommunicated Eusebius of Caesarea and two other bishops, pending the decision of a great council to be held in the spring in Ancyra (the modern Turkish capital of Ankara).[29] As Aaron Johnson observes in Chapter 10, there is reason to doubt the genuineness of this letter. There are also time constraints imposed by the rigors of winter travel, but these are not as absolute as supposed, especially if (as the letter seems to suggest) plans had already been made for a council in Ancyra, either in Nicomedia or at the Council of Alexandria.[30]

In any case, if Constantine had hoped his letter would smooth over the controversy, he must have been disappointed by this turn of events, all too reminiscent of the Council of Rome a dozen years earlier. This time he did not wait to see what would happen in Ancyra. Acting on his own authority, Constantine changed the site of the upcoming meeting to Nicaea, some 300 kilometers (186 miles) to the northwest. As Ine Jacobs discusses in Chapter 4, there were plausible reasons for the change: the weather was, indeed, milder, and being near the coast Nicaea would be more accessible to bishops coming from other parts of the empire. The emperor had already planned a meeting at Nicaea for the purpose of celebrating the twentieth anniversary of his rule, so the shift might not have been as abrupt as it now seems.[31] And it goes without saying that

---

2014. Since this event occurred only months (if not weeks) after Constantine's victory over Maxentius, it suggests that Ossius had already been known to and trusted by the emperor. Warmington 1985, suggested that the letter to Alexander and Arius was not carried by Ossius but by the notary Marianos.

[29]   See Ayres 2004, 18.

[30]   Pietras 2016, 148, assumes the sea would have been closed to travel between mid-September 324 and late May 325. Travel by land certainly would have been slow. ORBIS, the Stanford Geospatial Network Model of the Roman World (www .orbis.stanford.edu) calculates approximately 73 days for land travel at that time of year between Nicomedia and Alexandria and another 38 days for the trip from Alexandria to Antioch. Such a length of time makes it more likely that, as Hall 1998 suggested, Ossius went directly to Antioch, a trip of about 35 days from Nicomedia. However, ORBIS does not rule out sea travel in this period, which would have cut travel time from Nicomedia to Alexandria to about 9 days, with another 8 days to go from Alexandria to Antioch. A direct sail to Antioch would have taken about 11 days. For the letter of the Council of Antioch, see *Urk.* 20.

[31]   Pietras 2016, 147. For Constantine's *vicennalia*, see Eus., *VC* 3.15.

Nicaea would be more accessible to Constantine himself, since the *de facto* eastern capital of Nicomedia was only a stone's throw away.

But, plausible as it was, there are grounds for thinking the reason Constantine gave was only a pretext. A fiery letter he wrote in the aftermath of the council leaves some faint tracks that could lead to a different interpretation.[32] Constantine addressed this letter to the Christians of Nicomedia, and his aim was to explain why he had exiled their masterful bishop, Eusebius of Nicomedia. Eusebius had emerged as the most forceful champion of the embattled Arius, and until his death in 341 he dominated church politics in the east, easily frustrating even the wily Athanasius, Alexander's successor as bishop of Alexandria.[33] In a rare misstep, Eusebius evidently had shared communion with allies of Arius at some point after the conclusion of the council, and Constantine took this action as a betrayal. His indignation is highly suggestive; it provides an opening into the emperor's thinking and actions in the run-up to Nicaea. Prior to the council, Constantine writes:

> He [Eusebius] secretly sent various worthies to me to make intercession on his behalf, that I should make some alliance with him, fearing that because of his shameful transgressions he would be expelled from his honorable estate. As God himself, may he ever be well-disposed to you and me, is my witness, because that man deceived me and inappropriately undermined me and kept hidden his evil designs, as you too will learn, everything was done at that time exactly as he himself wished.[34]

Loaded (and clearly retrospective) language aside, a course of pre-Nicene maneuvering emerges from these lines. Facing the prospect of a synod dominated by bishops aligned with Alexander of Alexandria, Eusebius made use of his proximity to the emperor, who had taken up residence in Nicomedia. This was a delicate matter, requiring the use of intermediaries, because in the recently concluded war Nicomedia had been the capital of Constantine's now-defeated brother-in-law, the emperor Licinius, and Eusebius had evidently maintained good relations with him (earlier in the letter, Constantine accuses the bishop of being Licinius's "bloodiest collaborator").[35] Predictably, subsequent to his defeat Licinius came to be portrayed as a persecutor, even though the evidence for this charge is slim. But he did institute a ban on church

---

[32] *Urk.* 27.
[33] Gwynn 1999; De Decker 2005; Gwynn 2007; Gwynn 2010.
[34] *Urk.* 27 (Opitz 1934, 61), trans. Stevenson 1957, 373–74.
[35] ὠμότητος συμμύστης: *Urk.* 27 (Opitz 1934, 60.9). See above, 21–27.

councils, probably to impose a cooling-off period on the burgeoning theological controversy. If so, he very likely acted on the advice of Eusebius of Nicomedia, whom Sozomen describes as "a man of considerable learning and held in high repute at the palace."[36] This closeness would have made the bishop, in Constantine's eyes, a traitor.

But Eusebius also seems to have been close to Licinius's wife, Constantine's half-sister Constantia, so it is a good bet that Constantia served as Eusebius's peacemaker, just as she had in the past for her husband.[37] When the two finally met, Eusebius evidently won Constantine's support by saying things that in retrospect the emperor decided were lies. A theological discussion should not be ruled out as the basis of these "lies," since this likely would have been the first time Constantine heard anything positive about Arius's position. But gauging from his letter to Alexander and Arius, in which he had gone so far as to promise that he would not snoop into whatever beliefs the two held in private,[38] a sobered Constantine is less likely to have felt betrayed by anything Eusebius said about theology than by more pragmatic commitments that the bishop made. Constantine's abrupt shift of venue for the great council is a good indication of what those commitments were.

Eusebius is the one most likely to have called Constantine's attention to the problem posed by Ancyra as a site for the council, since its bishop, Marcellus, was so vehement in his condemnation of Arius that Eusebius could plausibly have doubted that a council presided over by such a bishop would provide a fair hearing for either Arius or the bishops provisionally excommunicated at Antioch.[39] This is precisely the kind of charge to which Constantine would have been most sensitive, and even though he chose to characterize it in his letter to the Nicomedians as nothing more than Eusebius's pitiful fear of losing his office, it is fair to assume that, at the time, Eusebius warned that the party that supported Alexander was out for blood. Constantine's decision to convene the Council of Arles in the aftermath of the Council of Rome a dozen years earlier was made in reaction to just such a claim. This time he acted swiftly: even before the council planned for Ancyra could meet, Constantine announced the switch to Nicaea, where bishops already had been invited to celebrate the twentieth

---

[36]   Sozomen (Soz.), *Historia ecclesiastica* (*HE*) 1.15 (translation in NPNF 2.2).
[37]   Hanson 1988, 38.
[38]   Eus., *VC* 2.71.6.
[39]   For an indictment of Marcellus, see Eusebius of Caesarea, *Contra Marcellum*, in Klostermann 1991, 1–58. See further Logan 1989; Lienhard 1999; Parvis 2006; Robertson 2007.

anniversary of his reign.[40] In addition to its other advantages, Nicaea had as its bishop Theognis, a close ally of Eusebius.

Constantine drew on his prior experience with the Council of Arles in another way. Just as he had summoned bishops from all the western provinces to that council, now that he controlled the east as well he ordered this one to include bishops from everywhere, making it the first "ecumenical," or worldwide, session.[41] By moving the council to Nicaea, the emperor could himself be present, to insure not just that extremists would be kept under control, but even more that the outcome would represent a consensus position. It was an easy commitment to make, since his experience had taught him that a decision made by consensus among the broadest array of bishops was the best way to isolate dissenters.

In such negotiations, there is always a *quid pro quo*. In return for accommodating Eusebius's concerns in this way, Constantine must have gotten from the bishop a promise to abide by the decision of the council, so long as due process was observed. That would explain why, when Eusebius subsequently shared communion with clerics who had remained firm in their commitment to Arius, Constantine believed he had been hoodwinked. A *quid pro quo* would also be necessary to get the bishops ranged against Arius to agree to give up the advantages that Ancyra afforded them, and in this case it would have to have been Constantine who provided it. This conclusion is speculative, to be sure. But positing a commitment on his part to insure that no decision would be made that did not meet with their approval best accords with the proceedings and their outcome. Perhaps without his fully realizing it, this was also a commitment that effectively gave Alexander's side a veto over any creed that violated its theological position, virtually assuring that one way or another Arius would be condemned.

Thus was the stage set for the proceedings at Nicaea.

THE POLITICS OF THE COUNCIL

In his *Life of Constantine*, the other Eusebius (of Caesarea), gives the impression that, from beginning to end, Constantine was in charge at Nicaea.[42] There is no sign of hesitation or pre-synod maneuvering in his

---

[40] See n. 31 above, but also 75–77, 91–92.

[41] In actuality, almost all of those we know to have attended were from eastern provinces, but there was a smattering from the West, and Eus., *VC* 3.7, says that a bishop from Persia was also present.

[42] Eus., *VC* 3.6–16.

telling: as soon as Constantine called, bishops came running (3.6); the emperor provided transportation (3.6) and meals (3.9), and the great hall of the palace itself for the sessions (3.10). The assemblage was completely captivated by the pomp and circumstance of a late Roman court, which included an honor guard with drawn swords (3.15). The emperor endeared himself to them by his modest behavior, eschewing his usual bodyguards and demurely waiting for permission before taking his seat (3.10), and he set a tone for the proceedings by giving patient attention even to the fiercest speakers and guiding the debate with mild comments of approval and encouragement (3.13).

However inadvertently, Eusebius's account of the proceedings lets us see how the emperor worked the council, from its opening moments:

> When the whole council had with proper ceremony taken their seats, silence fell upon them all, as they awaited the Emperor's arrival. One of the Emperor's company came in, then a second, then a third. Yet others led the way, not some of the usual soldiers and guards, but only of his faithful friends. All rose at a signal, which announced the Emperor's entrance; and he finally walked along between them, like some heavenly angel of God, his bright mantle shedding lustre like beams of light, shining with the fiery radiance of a purple robe, and decorated with the dazzling brilliance of gold and precious stones.[43]

The scene evokes a late Roman court in all its ceremonial splendor. Admirably stage-managed, Constantine's entrance was preceded by the kind of activity that is meant to silence an audience and focus its attention. When all were settled, a signal (probably a trumpet cadence) brought everyone to their feet, prepared to be dazzled by his bejeweled and purple-clad majesty.

Eusebius emphasizes the emperor's affability and modesty: he came into the room without his usual military retinue; and when a gilded chair was brought in, he refused to sit until given permission by the bishops themselves.[44] All the more reason, then, to call attention to what Constantine did not do: he did not enter an unsettled room, and when he spoke it was not in the colloquial Greek that he was perfectly capable of using but the distant tones of Latin, the language of law and power.[45]

---

[43]   Eus., *VC* 3.10.

[44]   On the imagery in Eusebius's account, and its emphasis on harmony, see Torres Guerra 2017, 88.

[45]   Eus., *VC* 3.13, says that Constantine spoke in Greek when participating in the discussions.

The overall message was clear: Constantine was favorably disposed, but was in the room to insure that his own priorities of unity and harmony were not ignored.

Similarly, when Eusebius goes on to describe the way Constantine participated in the proceedings – he "took up what was said by each side in turn, and gently brought together those whose attitudes conflicted" (*VC* 3.13) – we should not think of the emperor raising his hand from the sidelines and waiting to be recognized. Church councils had long ago adopted the Roman Senate as their model,[46] which meant that the presiding officer chose what questions would (and would not) be put to the assembly, and called on speakers in accordance with a strictly hier- archical list of seniority. If Constantine did not preside himself, he certainly sat next to the official who did and spoke whenever he wished. In terms of the dynamics of the debate, his frequent responses, as Eusebius describes them, had the effect of making the next speaker think twice about what he was going to say.

Eusebius has been roundly criticized for this account, since more careful analysis minimizes the emperor's role. Furthermore, the scant attention Eusebius pays to the theological issues at stake, especially in light of the way he dwells on the ceremonial aspects of the council, seems disingenuous, to say the least.[47] But after decades of neglect, scholars have rediscovered the importance of ceremony as a representation of power,[48] and there were participants other than Eusebius who felt the weight of Constantine's presence. Bishop Eustathius of Antioch, who spearheaded an attack on Eusebius of Nicomedia at the council, wrote bitterly in its aftermath of "some people" who used the pretext of "reconciliation" to allow those bishops

---

[46] MacMullen 2006, 18.

[47] Duchesne 1908–10, 2:191 characterized the *VC* as "the triumph of reticence and circumlocution." As early as the fifth century, the church historian Socrates read Eusebius's silence as "a determination on his part not to give his sanction to the proceedings at Nicaea." Socrates (Socr.), *Historia ecclesiastica* (*HE*) 1.23 (translation in NPNF 2.2).

[48] Writing under an eighteenth-century monarch, Gibbon 1909–14, 1:413, readily under- stood the importance of display: "Like the modesty affected by Augustus, the state maintained by Diocletian was a theatrical representation [. . .] It was the aim of the one to disguise and the object of the other to display, the unbounded power which the emperors possessed over the Roman world." For an appreciation of the attention paid to ceremony by earlier scholars, see Mathews 1993, 12–19. MacCormack 1981, rekin- dled modern interest. For more recent studies, see Wienand 2015. Earle 1997, 149, defines "ideology" in a way that recognizes its ceremonial role: "a system of beliefs and ideas presented publicly in ceremonies and other occasions. It is created and manipulated strategically by social segments, most importantly the ruling elite, to establish and maintain positions of social power."

who, he thought, were really on Arius's side to wiggle off the hook. With Eusebius of Caesarea as a guide, it is not difficult to see Constantine's fine hand working to deny Eustathius the blood he sought. As Sara Parvis has pointed out, Alexander's side "had the overwhelming superiority of numbers" at the council, and they had intended to use it in precisely the way Eusebius of Nicomedia had feared. Frustrated in this effort, these hardliners regarded Nicaea as "not a triumph but a failure."[49]

Eustathius's outrage thus shows that Constantine held up his side of the bargain with Eusebius of Nicomedia. But a letter of Athanasius of Alexandria indicates that he was equally firm in his commitment to the other side.[50] More focused than Eustathius on the tactics of the decision, Athanasius observes that every time language defining the relationship of Son to Father was proposed, "the Eusebians" would decide by signals to each other that the wording was acceptable. "But the bishops," he writes, "saw through their evil design and impious artifice," and in turn offered "a clearer elucidation" until they hit on a term that the Eusebians found unacceptable: *homoousios*. Not only did Constantine not interrupt this coordinated effort to isolate the Eusebians, but according to Eusebius of Caesarea he introduced the deal-breaking word himself.[51]

Yet in the end even Athanasius was frustrated, because all but a few of the opposing side ultimately agreed to the creed, an outcome that points us back toward Constantine's own agenda. As the emperor had made clear in his letter to Alexander and Arius, as well as in other writings at the time, a correct understanding of the faith was important, but the precise terminology was of far less concern to him than arriving at a consensus that would produce unity and lead to peace. This objective is what makes Eusebius of Caesarea correct to have concentrated on the ceremonial aspects of the council.

CONSTANTINE'S CHARM OFFENSIVE

Constantine continued to push his own agenda after the council concluded. In a closing banquet, he loaded the bishops with gifts and once again praised them for the moderation they had shown.[52] It might have

---

[49]   Parvis 2006, 5.

[50]   For both letters, see Theodoret, *Historia ecclesiastica* 1.7

[51]   *Urk.* 22.7. This is the letter Eusebius sent to his congregation in Caesarea to justify his actions, so it was in his self-interest to invoke the emperor's authority for his decision. But his statement indicates at the very least that Constantine was involved in discussion of the term, even if he did not introduce it himself.

[52]   Eus., *VC* 3.15–16.

been at this dinner where, Eusebius tells us, Constantine "let slip the remark that he was perhaps himself a bishop too, using some such words as these in our hearing: 'You are bishops of those within the Church, but I am perhaps a bishop appointed by God over those outside.'"[53] Eusebius does not situate this occasion chronologically, but since he himself was present the two most likely times are banquets Constantine hosted for his twentieth and thirtieth anniversary celebrations,[54] and whether spoken at Nicaea or later, the remark is consistent with Constantine's behavior after Nicaea. In any case, Eusebius evidently approved of this characterization, for in the first book of the *Life* he himself refers to Constantine as "a universal bishop appointed by God."[55]

Constantine's remark has been much parsed. If by "those" he meant "those *people*" outside the church, i.e., non-Christians, he would be assigning himself a missionary role, akin to the one Paul had taken with respect to the gentiles. If he meant "those *matters*," then he was thinking of himself as more of an overseer (the original meaning of the word for bishop, *episkopos*) and thereby beginning the long process of a separation of powers that would result in our own concept of separate spheres for church and state.[56]

But one obvious further implication should not be overlooked. By describing himself as one of their own, Constantine effectively raised the status of these Christian overseers to a par with himself, the most powerful and sacrosanct person in their world. Small wonder that Eusebius (and, presumably, other bishops) approved. But this is a concession that should raise more eyebrows than it has. Ever since his victory at the Milvian Bridge in 312, if not earlier, Constantine had been carving out a role for himself as a ruler chosen by God to govern the Christian church. He was, after all, no ordinary Christian, but one who (in his own telling) had been chosen directly by God, by means of a miraculous intervention. Eusebius is the source for the most well-known version of this event, which he also relates in the first book of the *Life*:

> About the time of the midday sun, when day was just turning, he said he saw with his own eyes, up in the sky and resting over the sun, a cross-shaped trophy formed from light, and a text attached to it which said, "By this conquer". Amazement at the spectacle

---

[53] Eus., *VC* 4.24.

[54] A long-standing assumption that Eusebius was in frequent contact with the emperor was overturned by Barnes 1981, 266. For the banquet following Nicaea, see Eus., *VC* 3.12.

[55] Eus., *VC* 1.44: οἷά τις κοινὸς ἐπίσκοπος ἐκ θεοῦ καθεσταμένος.

[56] Rapp 1998; Angelov 2014.

seized both him and the whole company of soldiers which was then accompanying him on a campaign he was conducting somewhere, and witnessed the miracle.[57]

Prior to telling this story, Eusebius explains just how miraculous the event was:

> If someone else had reported it, it would perhaps not be easy to accept; but since the victorious Emperor himself told the story to the present writer a long while after, when I was privileged with his acquaintance and company, and confirmed it with oaths, who could hesitate to believe the account, especially when the time which followed provided evidence for the truth of what he said?[58]

An important part of this account is Eusebius's specific claim that he heard it from the emperor's own lips, for it shows that Constantine was actively involved in promoting this story. Too much should not be made of this effort; it was not, for instance, due to megalomania or a rash power grab. Roman imperial ideology already assigned to the emperor a role with regard to the gods of the state religion that was not simply titular but also charismatic: beginning with the first in the line, Augustus, Roman emperors were believed to be closer to the gods, holier than the rest of us. The miracle narrative shows how a Christian Constantine applied this traditional understanding to his changed circumstances.[59] In writing to Christians, he frequently referred to himself as the "man of God" or the "servant of God," emphasizing the direct and personal connection that late Roman imperial ideology demanded of its rulers.[60] The importance he placed on this unique bond makes his choice of a terminology ("bishop of those outside") that potentially diminished his own majesty all the more puzzling.

Once again, Constantine's earlier experience with the dissidents in North Africa points to an answer. When the dissidents continued to resist after the decision reached at Arles, Constantine's first response was outrage. Christians had demonstrated their willingness to resist persecuting emperors, but Constantine apparently was surprised to learn that the dissidents could ignore a Christian emperor just as easily,

---

[57]   Eus., *VC* 1.28.2.
[58]   Eus., *VC* 1.28.1.
[59]   The literature on Constantine's vision is immense. Weiss 2003, has garnered much support, but has not gone uncontested. See Harris 2005, and for historiography Van Dam 2011. On emperor as "last of gods, first of men," see n. 3 above.
[60]   See his letter to Arius (*Urk.* 34), where Constantine twice refers to himself as "the man of God" (ὁ τοῦ θεοῦ ἄνθρωπος and πρός θεοῦ ἄνθρωπον). See further, Drake 2016.

even one hand-picked by God to lead them. This was a sober awakening. Because of this experience, Constantine learned not only to renounce force but also to share responsibility for governing this new constituency with the bishops.

In other words, Constantine's claim to be a bishop himself shows that he had learned to play the game of empire. Just as emperors in an earlier era had chosen to portray themselves as simply extraordinary officers of the Roman Senate, a move that reinforced the prestige of a body that not only supplied the skilled administrators they needed to run the empire but also the seal of authority that legitimated their rule, so now Constantine began to define a relationship between two entities that we think of as "church and state" by identifying himself with the core group that could help him and his successors run a Christian Roman empire.[61]

Eusebius's vignette shows something more: a relaxed and confident emperor. Following Nicaea, he had every reason to be. With the hard-liners mollified, only the few exiles needed to be reconciled for his cherished unity agenda to be realized, and Constantine seems to have believed that he had a free hand to tie up these loose ends himself. His optimism may seem foolhardy in retrospect, but it becomes more plausible if, as scholars now conclude, the creed established by this council was not, at the time, considered an immutable touchstone for orthodoxy, but rather a work in progress.[62] Eusebius of Caesarea provides us with a good sense of the state of the emperor's thinking in a report on the council that he sent to his congregation. When Constantine himself introduced the word *homoousios*, Eusebius writes, he effectively said it could be understood in a number of ways.[63] Hence it should come as no surprise that, when Constantine set about reconciling exiles to the creed, he did not make use of *homoousios* a sticking point. His priorities remained unity and concord, not theological niceties.

One of the first beneficiaries of this charm offensive was none other than Arius himself, who won Constantine's favor with a profession of faith that conveyed his desire to be part of a unified church while completely ignoring the issue that had separated him.[64] Perhaps even more surprising, given the ferocity of Constantine's letter to the Christians of

---

[61] On the Principate, see Wallace-Hadrill 1982. For the "game of empire," see Drake 2000, ch. 1.

[62] Ayres 2004. See also Gwynn 2007 and Paul Gavrilyuk's chapter in this volume.

[63] *Urk.* 22. Earlier in this letter, Eusebius describes how he had introduced the traditional creed of Caesarea and how the emperor himself pronounced it orthodox.

[64] Arius's letter: Socr., *HE* 1.26 (= *Urk.* 30). Translation in NPNF 2.2.

Nicomedia, was the return of their bishop to the emperor's good graces. In his petition for restoration, Eusebius of Nicomedia explained that his opposition had never been to the creed but only to the condemnation of Arius; now that the emperor himself had found the priest's confession acceptable, Eusebius wrote, there was no reason for him or his colleague Theognis to remain in exile.[65] Eusebius succeeded in winning Constantine's favor to such an extent that it was he who in 337 baptized the emperor on his deathbed.[66]

CONCLUSION: TAMING THE ELEPHANT

The elephant in this room no longer needs to be a source of either embarrassment or amusement. Given the religious foundation of the ancient state and the emperor's acknowledged primacy in maintaining relations with divinity, Constantine's participation in the council was neither an unwarranted intrusion nor a hostile takeover by a secular ruler; it was innovative, but only in the sense that, as a Christian ruler, he was the first to extend his traditional role to the unique requirements of his new faith.

At Nicaea, Constantine was arguably at the height of his power over the church, still new enough in the East to be enjoying what today would be called his "honeymoon," the time when the goodwill a new leader enjoys gives him maximum leverage, and he adroitly made use of that goodwill to advance an agenda of unity and consensus. Honeymoons end when the power brokers who provide this respite get the measure of their new leader and decide they have to push back against his plans. In Constantine's case, this pushback began in the aftermath of the council, when the inherent conflict between his own definition of unity and that of the bishops became increasingly apparent. Nowhere was it more obvious than in the reaction of each party to the profession of faith sent by Arius and his fellow exile Euzoïus. After repeating their baptismal vows and generic belief in the Trinity, the pair wrote that all they wished was to be "reunited to our mother, the Church, all superfluous questions and disputings being avoided." This being done, they added, "we and the whole church being at peace, may in common offer our accustomed

---

[65] *Urk.* 31. Eusebius's letter is in Soz., *HE* 2.16: "but we did not subscribe to the anathema, not because we impugned the creed, but because we did not believe the accused to be what he was represented to us" (translation in NPNF 2.2). See further Sara Parvis's chapter, below 229–33.

[66] Gwynn 2010, 293–94, calls attention to the "personal bond" that developed between the two. See also Norderval 1988.

prayers for your tranquil reign, and on behalf of your whole family."[67] These words harmonized completely with the emperor's own priorities, and he immediately pushed for Arius's return to the church in Alexandria. But first Alexander and then his successor, Athanasius, resisted, since Arius had said nothing about the central theological issue of *homoousios*.

Whereas Constantine's right to participate at Nicaea may be taken for granted, the impact of that participation is harder to evaluate. Just as the first council he summoned at Arles in 314 did not end the schism in North Africa, so the second at Nicaea in 325 failed to bring theological harmony to the east, and the tension between emperors who focused on unity and churchmen who demanded conformity continued long into the future. But much of this failure was due to the internal dynamics of the Christian community, and the example Constantine set of imperial initiative became a hallmark for future rulers. The sorry history of church and state in the west is grounds for taking a jaundiced view of his initiative, but in the east a case can be made that these ties helped the empire survive for another thousand years.[68]

SELECT REFERENCES

Bjornlie, M. Shane, ed. 2017. *The Life and Legacy of Constantine: Traditions Through the Ages*. London: Routledge.

Cameron, Averil, and Stuart G. Hall. 1999. *Eusebius: Life of Constantine*. Oxford: Clarendon Press.

Drake, H. A., trans. 1976. *In Praise of Constantine: A Historical Study and New Translation of Eusebius' Tricennial Orations*. Berkeley: University of California Press.

Drake, H. A. 2000. *Constantine and the Bishops: The Politics of Intolerance*. Baltimore: Johns Hopkins University Press.

Gwynn, David M. 2007. *The Eusebians: The Polemics of Athanasius of Alexandria and the Construction of the "Arian Controversy."* Oxford Theology and Religion Monographs. Oxford: Oxford University Press.

Lieu, Samuel N. C., and Dominic Montserrat, eds. 1998. *Constantine: History, Historiography and Legend*. London: Routledge.

MacCormack, Sabine. 1981. *Art and Ceremony in Late Antiquity*. Transformation of the Classical Heritage 1. Berkeley: University of California Press.

---

[67] For Arius's letter: Socr., *HE* 1.26 (*Urk.* 30). Translation in NPNF 2.2.

[68] For Constantine's influence on subsequent rulers, see Magdalino 1994; Bellen 1997. Gaddis 2005, x, called attention to the ongoing tension between extremists' demands for violent solutions and the court's "desire to maintain order and harmony at all costs." Frend 1972 argued for monks as a cohesive force in the east.

MacMullen, Ramsay. 2006. *Voting About God in Early Church Councils*. New Haven: Yale University Press.

Pietras, Henryk. 2016. *Council of Nicaea (325): Religious and Political Context, Documents, Commentaries*. Rome: Gregorian and Biblical Press.

Singh, Devin. 2013. "Disciplining Eusebius: Discursive Power and Representation of the Court Theologian." *StPatr* 62: 89–101.

Singh, Devin. 2015. "Eusebius as Political Theologian: The Legend Continues." *HTR* 108(1): 129–54.

Torres Guerra, José B. 2017. "Image and Word in Eusebius of Caesarea (*VC* 3.4–24): Constantine in Nicaea." In *Rhetorical Strategies in Late Antique Literature: Images, Metatexts and Interpretation*, ed. Alberto J. Quiroga Puertas, 73–89. *Mnemosyne*, Supplements 406. Leiden: Brill.

Weiss, Peter. 2003. "The Vision of Constantine." Trans. A. R. Birley. *Journal of Roman Archaeology* 16: 237–59.

Whitby, Mary, ed. 1988. *The Propaganda of Power: The Role of Panegyric in Late Antiquity*. *Mnemosyne*, Supplements 183. Leiden: Brill.

Wienand, Johannes, ed. 2015. *Contested Monarchy: Integrating the Roman Empire in the Fourth Century AD*. Oxford: Oxford University Press.

Part III
Outcomes

7 The Creed

MARK J. EDWARDS

We might guess from Eusebius's *Life of Constantine* that the principal achievement of the first oecumenical council was to fix the date of Easter. Perhaps against his will, it is best remembered for its unprecedented framing of a creed in which Jesus Christ, as Son of God, is said to be *homoousios*, or consubstantial, with the Father. We should not exaggerate the significance of this pronouncement – there is strictly no Nicene doctrine of the Trinity after all – yet it is no small thing that after half a century of ecclesiastical conflict, in which creeds were as thick as councils, it emerged as the oecumenical pattern of Christian orthodoxy. Its authorship, of course has been the subject of much inquiry, but the simple answers returned by ancient witnesses are manifestly false. Basil of Cappadocian Caesarea, for example, seems to ascribe it to his countryman Hermogenes (Letter 81); but whether he means by the participle *grapsas* that Hermogenes wrote it or merely that he signed it, no Cappadocian see was represented by a prelate of that name at the Nicene council. According to Eusebius of Palestinian Caesarea, the formula of 325 differs only in this one word, *homoousion*, from that of his native city; he too will be found, however, to have handled the truth with a freedom scarcely becoming in a bishop. This truth in fact cannot be reduced to a single appellation, for the Nicene Creed is the work of many hands, and not only those of the 250 bishops who subscribed it. They themselves were aware of creeds already in use, and also of many private attempts to condense the norms of Christian teaching into brief memoranda, which had become increasingly uniform in phrasing and arrangement. We shall begin this study, therefore, with a history of the incremental hardening of confessions into creeds, and will then proceed to a closer examination of the novel elements in the Nicene Creed in the hope of finding clues to the process and purpose of its composition. Our study will not be complete until we have also taken note of certain familiar yet half-forgotten doubts concerning the content of the original proclamation and its efficacy as a unifying canon of belief.

ANTECEDENTS

It has long been customary to distinguish between the declaratory creed, in which the faith is reduced to its principal tents for the purpose of exposition or subscription, from the liturgical creed prescribed for recitation by the clergy and the laity together in the course of worship or the performance of a particular rite. The declaratory creeds fall commonly under two descriptions, some being promulgated at ecclesiastical councils, others being published or recited by individuals (almost invariably bishops) whose orthodoxy had come under suspicion. We may add that a conciliar pronouncement had two related purposes, to publish the belief of the majority (which was apt to be represented as the tradition of the fathers) and to isolate the dissident minority, who might then suffer the penalty of excommunication or deposition. Where its only function was to show that the council's decrees were grounded in pious and orthodox principles, it was not thought necessary to give expression to every article of faith, or to seek a form of words that lent itself to transmission through the centuries without change. If, on the other hand, there was any intention of establishing a formula for liturgical use (as there may have been at Constantinople in 381), glosses and anathemas would be equally foreign to the intended purpose, and the form of words would be such as to present, in the most economic manner, the sum of those beliefs that were necessary to salvation. The majority of liturgical creeds do not in fact appear to have issued from councils, whether local or oecumenical; in addition to their regular use in congregational worship, they were also recited at baptism by the one undergoing the rite. It has been proposed, but cannot be proved, that even before Nicaea the confession of faith was sometimes elicited from the neophyte by a series of interrogations. Whatever the verbal process, the words which framed the doctrine of the church would remain unchanged in any one place from one generation to another. Notwithstanding the all but perfect unity of the episcopate before Nicaea, however, absolute uniformity between the liturgical creeds of different bishoprics had not yet been achieved, and its absence, so far as our knowledge goes, was not lamented.

That the creed of 325 is a declaratory rather than a dogmatic utterance is obvious from the presence of six anathemas which, as has been said, would have had no place in a corporate affirmation of faith by the laity at prayer. In examining its likely antecedents, we must also bear in mind that in addition to the declaratory and liturgical creeds, early Christian writers sometimes seem to enunciate the common deposit of faith in language of their own choosing, though the content remains traditional and the idiom formulaic. J. N. D. Kelly, following Irenaeus and Tertullian, speaks of these as personal expressions of a common rule of faith, in which the author tempers his words to the argument of his text and the circumstances of composition.[1] One of the earliest specimens is perhaps 1 Timothy 3:16, which declares that God, or the mystery of godliness, "was manifest in the flesh, justified in the spirit, seen of angels, preached to the nations, believed on in the world and received up into glory." We may see the nucleus of a dogmatic creed in Ignatius of Antioch's protestation that "there is one physician, in flesh and in spirit, generate and ingenerate, God come to be in flesh [or in man], in death true life, Son of Mary and Son of God, first passible, then impassible, Jesus Christ our lord" (Ephesians 7:2).

Justin Martyr, writing about half a century after Ignatius, explodes the Roman charge of atheism by declaring that the church reveres the true God, his Son who came from him, and the prophetic Spirit (First Apology 6.2); that the church prays to the Father of the universe through the name of his Son and of the Holy Spirit (65.3); that the same Father is the maker of all through Jesus Christ his Son and the Holy Spirit (67.2), and most effusively that the church has reason to honour not only the Father as creator but the Son as the one who revealed and who suffered crucifixion under Pilate, holding the second rank while the third is allotted to the prophetic Spirit (13). Kelly detects a credal norm which mentions only the Father and the Son.[2] Thus First Apology 21.2 proclaims that the Word, begotten without carnal intercourse, was crucified, died, rose again and ascended to heaven. First Apology 31.1 is all but identical in substance, with a prefatory assertion that all these works were foretold by the prophets; First Apology 42.4 adds that he reigns in the heaven to which he ascended; First Apology 46.5 repeats the same articles of belief, as does Dialogue with Trypho 63.1. At Dialogue 85.2 the crucifixion is ascribed to Pontius Pilate, and the glorification of Christ after suffering is the evidence of his power to drive out demons. His coming again is the peroration to similar pronouncements at Dialogue 126.1 and 132.1. By contrast the account of his trial, with perfect verisimilitude, attributes to him a simple "binitarian" confession of God the Father as creator and of Jesus Christ as his redeeming Son.[3]

---

[1]   Kelly 1972, 70–99.
[2]   Kelly 1972, 73–75.
[3]   Musurillo 1972, 79.

Around 180 Justin's admirer Irenaeus declares in his *Apostolic Demonstration* that the church baptizes not only in the name of God the Father but in that of his Son Jesus Christ, who was incarnate, died and rose again, and also in the name of the Holy Spirit (of whom, as so often, nothing more is said). Not everyone will agree with Kelly in seeing a "clear implication" that the candidate for baptism was successively asked to affirm belief in the Father, the Son and the Spirit. On the other hand, the structure of future creeds is evident when, in chapter 6, Irenaeus lays down, as a rule of faith, that God the Father is maker of all things seen and unseen, that his Son, Jesus Christ our Lord, was manifested to the prophets before he took flesh in the latter days for our salvation, and that the Holy Spirit, through whom the fathers prophesied, has been poured out upon humankind in the wake of the Incarnation, restoring us to God. In his masterpiece *Against Heresies*, Irenaeus anticipates the content of the Nicene Creed, proclaiming the faith of the church in

> one God, maker of heaven and earth and all that are in them, through Jesus Christ the Son of God who on account of his sublime love for his creation underwent birth from a virgin, uniting humanity to God in himself, and suffered under Pontius Pilate, then rose again, was received up in majesty and will come again in glory to save the redeemed and judge the reprobate. (3.4.2)[4]

At 3.16.6, Kelly observes, Irenaeus restricts himself to two articles, the Fatherhood of God and the Lordship of Jesus Christ his Son who died and rose for us, no doubt taking as his model the dictum of Paul, "to us there is one God and one Lord Jesus Christ."[5]

It is reasonable to suppose, though he does not say so, that Irenaeus regards these affirmations as constituents of the rule of faith which has been transmitted without change by the bishops of all the major sees since the time of the apostles. The apostles themselves are the notional authors of another document, which inculcates belief in the Father as ruler of the cosmos, in Christ as Redeemer, in the Holy Spirit, the Holy Church and the remission of sins. Tertullian, writing early in the third century, expressly invokes a rule of faith which teaches that the one God created the world in the beginning through his Word, that this same Word after speaking in every age through the prophets, entered the womb of Mary the Virgin, that he came forth as Jesus Christ to preach

[4] All translations are mine unless otherwise stated.
[5] Kelly 1972, 80.

the kingdom and perform mighty works, that he died on the Cross but rose again and ascended into heaven, and that he sent the Holy Spirit to take his place until he comes again in glory (*On the Castigation of Heretics* 13). This confession, although it implies a Trinity, is binitarian in structure,[6] as is the laconic asseveration in the same work (ch. 36) that the church acknowledges God the Father as creator, the Son as creator "from the Virgin Mary," and the general resurrection of the flesh. While this formula may be designed to refute a particular heresy, its author liked it well enough to repeat it with amplification in the first chapter of his tract *On the Veiling of Virgins*, where the articles of the rule of faith are said to be the One God, almighty Creator of the universe and his Son Jesus Christ, who was born from the Virgin Mary and crucified under Pontius Pilate, to rise again on the third day and ascend into heaven, where he sits at the right hand of the Father until his coming again to judge the dead and the living through the resurrection of the flesh.

Tertullian anticipates much of the Nicene Creed when he sets out the teaching of the church against Praxeas:

> We believe in one God, but under this order of things, which we call the economy, that of this sole God there is also a Son, his own Word who has proceeded from him, through whom all things came to be and without whom nothing came to be. This one was sent from the Father into a virgin and was born from her as man and God, as Son of Man and Son of God, and was given the name Jesus Christ. This is the one who suffered, died and was buried in accordance with the scriptures, who was also restored to life by the Father and after being taken up into heaven sits at the Father's right hand, and will come to judge the living and the dead. For there he has sent, according to his own promise, the Holy Spirit as a paraclete from the Father, the sanctifier of the faith of those who believe in the Father and the Son and the Holy Spirit.[7]

The final clause recalls the baptismal formula of Matthew 28:19, which may be regarded as the germ of all liturgical formulae. At the same time this summary embraces many other verses from the New Testament: John 1:3–4 on the creation of all through the Word; Paul's appeal to the scriptures at 1 Corinthians 15:3 and 15:4; John 14:16 and 15:26 on the sending of the Paraclete; and a battery of texts (Matthew 26:64, Mark

---

[6] The oblique reference to the Holy Spirit should not be allowed to disguise this obvious fact, *pace* Kelly 1972, 85.

[7] Tertullian (Tert.), *Adversus Praxean* (*Prax.*) 2.1.

14:62, Acts 7:56, Romans 8:34, Hebrews 1:3, etc.) on the session of Christ at the right hand of the Father. At the head, as at the head of every subsequent creed, is the Shema (Deuteronomy 6:4), which Christ himself recalls at Mark 12:29: "Hear, O Israel, the Lord our God, the Lord is one."

The parenthetic qualification "under this order of things, which we call the economy" suggests that this is the author's own synthesis of biblical matter. This survey of Tertullian and his precursors has revealed evidence, not of a statutory creed that was employed without variation in all the churches – or for that matter in a single congregation – but of a widespread codification of certain articles of belief. An author was permitted to digest some or all of these into a lapidary profession of the Christian faith, with increments and elaborations at his own discretion, always providing that he bore witness to the birth, death and salvific resurrection of Jesus Christ the Son of God. The first article to be added in any lengthening of this formulary was the acclamation of almighty God as sole creator and the Father of Christ, thus unchurching both the polytheist and the Gnostic for whom creation was the work of a lesser agent. It is always the Spirit who succeeds the Son in any expansion of these binitarian statements, though there appears to be no convention that an epitome of doctrine should mirror the trinitarian litanies that were now in regular use. Any appended clauses would pertain to the church or the end for which it existed, the resurrection of the saints.

Origen too is aware of a deposit of revelation from the apostles, the cardinal tenets of which, as he sketches them in his *On First Principles*, are firstly, that the Creator of the world is one, the God of all the righteous from Abel onward, and the Father of Jesus Christ; secondly, that Christ his Son, through whom he created the world, became incarnate of the Virgin Mary, not only assuming our flesh but undergoing a real death, after which he rose and conversed again with the apostles before ascending into heaven; and thirdly, that the Holy Spirit is associated in honour and dignity with the other two and that he has inspired the prophets (*On First Principles*, proem 4). The manner of his origin, however, is undetermined; so too, while the church maintains that the soul will receive its deserts after death, it has not decided whether it is corporeal or incorporeal in substance (proem 5). It leaves us a similar latitude of belief regarding the natures of angels and demons, though it is certain of their existence; it maintains the temporality of the material world, without resolving whether any other worlds receded or will succeed it; and it trusts in the infallible inspiration of the scriptures (proem 6–8). Tradition credits Origen's pupil Gregory Thaumaturgus with a personal confession which, if genuine, is one of the latest formularies of this kind to survive from the ante-Nicene era.[8]

Arius himself, in his letter to Alexander of Alexandria, purports to have received from this "blessed Pope" the teaching of their common fathers, that there is one God alone, ingenerate, eternal, without beginning, the only true, the only good, the only wise, the sole judge, sovereign, governor and provider, who is just and good without change or alteration, and who begot his unique (monogenēs) Son before the ages and created the universe from him, begetting him not in appearance but in reality and sustaining him without change or alteration by his will (Athanasius, On Synods 16). Although its phrasing is for the most part biblical, this formula is not of a piece with those which we have culled from previous doctors of the church, and is unlikely to contain either the germ or an echo of any liturgical confession. It is equally hard to posit an occasion for the invention or recital of a brief elaboration of Romans 11:36, asserting that is from the Father, through the Son and in the Holy Spirit, which is held up in opposition to the Nicene Creed by the "Arian" Eunomius and said by Basil the Great to have been espoused by certain "fathers" (meaning probably bishops of the Nicene age) in the simplicity of their hearts.

CREEDS BEFORE NICAEA

Have we any example of the kneading of such phrases into a common ecclesiastical manifesto before Nicaea? The first specimen that is undoubtedly liturgical occurs in the *Apostolic Tradition* attributed to Hippolytus, which is commonly understood to represent the practice of at least one faction in Rome in the early decades of the third century. It takes the form of an interrogation of the candidate for baptism, which in its Latin version runs as follows:[9]

> Do you believe in God the Father almighty?
> Do you believe in Jesus Christ the Son of God, who was crucified under Pontius Pilate, [buried] and rose again on the third day from the dead and ascended into the heavens, sits at the right hand of the Father, and will come to judge the living and the dead?

---

[8] But see Abramowski 1992b.
[9] On the Codex Veronensis, the most important document in this reconstruction, and on the possibility that it served as a prototype for the Old Roman Creed, see Kinzig 1999, especially 78–85. For criticism see Westra 2002, 49–62.

> Do you believe in the Holy Spirit, the holy church and the
> resurrection of the flesh?[10]

This catechetical sequence can be turned into a declarative one, which
puts the burden of affirmation on the candidate rather than the celebrant,
by the mere substitution of the indicative for the interrogative. It is
widely held that the falsely named "Apostles' Creed," which attained
almost its present form in the commentary by Rufinus from the late
years of the fourth century, is an amplified version of a Latin prototype
which was current in Rome by the middle of the third century.[11] This
creed is not in use in the eastern churches, and the most primitive Latin
form of it, recovered by the seventeenth-century scholars Isaac Vossius
and James Ussher, runs as follows:[12]

> I believe in God the Father Almighty, and in Christ Jesus, his only
> son, Our Lord, who was born of the Holy Spirit and the Virgin
> Mary, who was crucified under Pontius Pilate and buried, rose
> again on the third day from the dead, ascended to the heavens,
> and sits at the right hand of the father, whence he will come to
> judge the living and the dead; and in the Holy Spirit, the holy
> church, the remission of sins and the resurrection of the flesh.

It has never been proved beyond doubt, however, that this creed ante-
dates the fourth century or that it was indigenous to Rome. The strongest
evidence for both positions, as most would argue, is Marcellus of
Ancyra's recitation of a similar formulary in 341 before Julius of Rome
as a demonstration of his orthodoxy.[13] Evidently nothing could have
served his purpose better than a text which was already a Roman shibboleth, and this alone would explain his decision not to invoke a creed that
was already current in the east. Markus Vinzent and Wolfram Kinzig
propose that, on the contrary, Marcellus was the author of this creed,
which was then adopted in the west.[14] We may, however, doubt the
probability of such universal deference to a man who was widely
regarded as a heretic in the West as in the East. Liuwe Westra points
out that we know of no instance of the transformation of a private creed

---

[10] Translating the Latin version given by Kelly 1972, 91. For comments on the text see
      Stewart-Sykes 2001, 114–16.
[11] See Westra 2002, 15–98.
[12] Kelly 1972, 102–3.
[13] Kelly 1972, 103–4. The omission of the title Father in the first clause and the addition
      of eternal life as the final article are the most notable deviations. The source is
      Athanasius (Ath.), *Apologia contra Arianos* 32.
[14] Kinzig and Vinzent 1999.

into a liturgical creed, and that the Latin variants differ from Marcellus in a manner that suggests an acquaintance with some prototype.[15]

No such doubts can be raised with regard to the statement of belief submitted to the Nicene council by Eusebius of Caesarea. This was the baptismal creed of his own flock, as he assures them in his letter after the council, which is the subject of another contribution to this volume. Since he repeats it in full, we are able to judge his own presentation of it as a first impression of the Nicene formula:[16]

> We believe in one God, Father, all-ruler, the maker of all things seen and unseen; and in one Lord Jesus Christ, the *Logos* of the Father, God from God, light from light, life from light, unique [or only-begotten: *monogenēs*] Son, firstborn of creation, begotten from the Father before all the ages, through whom also all things have come into being, the one who for our salvation has taken flesh and conversed among humans,[17] who has suffered and risen again on the third day, and has gone up [or back] to the Father, and will come again in glory to judge the living and the dead. And we believe also in the Holy Spirit.

Two features of this text set it apart from any declaratory creed, conciliar or personal, and also from any other liturgical creed that has come down to us from antiquity. The first is the appellation *Logos*, a two-edged sword as the scripture says, for while it implied to some, like Alexander of Alexandria, that the Son is related as intimately to the Father as a word is related to the one who utters it, there were others, like Arius, who followed Origen in holding that it betokens the Son's relation to the world as the architect of rational order. To the second party it seemed that the first denied the substantiality of the *Logos*; to the first it appeared that the second was casting doubt on the community of nature between the Father and the Son. The creed of Caesarea, by juxtaposing the term with the affirmation of Christ's sonship, mirrors the teaching of Alexander. In a document submitted to Constantine after Nicaea, Arius couples it instead with the statement that Christ is the one

---

[15] Westra 2002, 33–37.

[16] Kelly 1972, 182, substituting "we believe" for the "I believe" of Theodoret (Thdt.), *Historia ecclesiastica* (*HE*)I.12.4 in agreement with the Latin text. Eusebius is reciting the creed at this point as a personal confession, but lapses into the first-person plural in the later clauses. With Kelly I omit the justificatory epilogue, which is irrelevant to the present discussion. See below, 208–12.

[17] Baruch 3:18, a text which was regarded as canonical even by those who, with Ath., *Epistula festivalis* 39, adopted an approximation to the Hebrew scriptures as their Old Testament. Cf. Hippolytus (Hipp.), *Contra haeresin Noëti* (*Noët.*) 2.5 and 5.5.

through whom all came to be.[18] Although the word *Logos* is biblical, we
need not be surprised that the Council of Nicaea shunned the choice that
the adoption of it would have forced upon them.

The Nicene Creed, as we shall see, concurs with that of Caesarea in
attaching the Johannine epithet *monogenēs* to the Son,[19] in proclaiming
him God from God and light from light and in maintaining his existence
before all ages. These are augmentations to the rule of faith, as we meet it
in Tertullian, and to any known version of the Apostles' Creed. They are
not, however, original to the creed of Caesarea, for Hippolytus had styled
the Son a light from a light in his treatise *Against Noetus*.[20] We shall also
find that even where the two coincide, the Nicene Creed says more than
the Bishop of Caesarea could trace to the confession of his own church.

THE TEXT OF THE NICENE CREED

Eusebius himself is our oldest source for the content of the Nicene Creed,
which is represented in his letter as the immediate result of the addition of
the word *homoousion* to the Caesarean creed at the behest of Constantine.
Had this been so, he would not have used the pronoun "they" in speaking
of those who laid it before the council, and he would not have subjected
their handiwork to such close examination. The reasons for his misgivings
will be apparent from the following translation of the Greek text as
Athanasius reproduces it in the transcript of the letter to Caesarea
which he appended to his treatise *On the Decrees of the Nicene Synod*.
Towards the end of my commentary I shall have occasion to speak of the
important omission in the other version of the same letter which we owe
to Theodoret (*Ecclesiastical History* 1.12.8). The matter which is not
found in the creed of Eusebius is italicised:[21]

> We believe in one God, Father, all-ruler, maker of all things seen
> and unseen, and in one Lord Jesus Christ, the Son of God, *begotten
> from the Father* monogenēs, *that is from the substance of the
> Father*, God from God, light from light, *true God from true God*,
> begotten not made (poiēthenta), homoousios *with the Father*,
> through whom all came to be, both things in the heavens and
> those on earth; the one who on account of us humans and our

---

[18]   Origen (Or.), *Commentarii in Johannem* (*Jo.*) 1.24.151; Socrates (Socr.), *Historia eccle-
       siastica* (*HE*) 1.26.
[19]   Cf. John 1:14, 1:18, 3:16.
[20]   Hipp., *Noët.* 11.1; the extant text, however, is almost certainly adulterated.
[21]   Modifying the translation by Edwards 2006, 561. For the fullest textual study of both
       this and the Constantinopolitan Creed see Dossetti 1967.

salvation came down and took flesh, becoming man, suffering and rising again on the third day and going up [or "back"] to the heavens, and who is coming again to judge living and dead.

But those who say "there was when he was not," and "before he was begotten he was not," and "he came to be from what is not," or assert that the Son of God is from another *hypostasis* or *ousia*, or alterable or changeable, these the church catholic anathematizes.

One sees at a glance that the Caesarean creed was not the template for this proclamation, which retains not one of its distinctive features. The absence of the title *Logos* calls for little comment, as it figures neither in the Apostles' Creed nor in that of Hippolytus. Any motion to include it at Nicaea would have foundered on the ambiguities which have already been noted in this chapter. Again the Nicene Creed would seem to concur with the Christian world outside Nicaea in omitting the Pauline phrase "firstborn of creation"; once again, the question will have been where it ought to stand if it were included, for some would have referred the term "firstborn" to the begetting of Christ before all ages, others to his nativity as man. The epithet *monogenēs* is now placed in a position which forestalls any possibility of referring it to the incarnate rather than the eternal sonship.[22] Most striking, as it appears to be without precedent, is the reinforcement of the accolade "God from God" with "true God from true God." This is a fusion of two Johannine verses, in the first of which (John 17:3) the Son addresses the Father as the "one true God", while the second (1 John 5:20) is syntactically ambiguous, and could be understood as plausibly of the Father as of the Son.

OUSIA AND HOMOOUSIOTĒS

Of far more consequence is the introduction of terms pertaining to the *ousia* of the Father. The first of these innovations (a transient one, which was not retained in 381) is the parenthesis which explains that the word *monogenēs* means "from the substance (*ousia*) of the Father." Tertullian wrote that the Son is from the *substantia* of the Father, and Pamphilus (in the Latin of Rufinus) attributes the same proposition to Origen after quoting from his commentary on Hebrews 1:3, where the Greek word denoting substance is *hypostasis*.[23] *Hypostasis* is certainly the term

---

[22]   See Skarsaune 1987, arguing for the preponderantly Alexandrian provenance of the formula.

[23]   Tert., *Prax.* 7.9; Pamphilus (Pamph.), *Apologia Origenis* (*Ap. Orig.*) 100. Pamphilus, if the text is sound, purports to be explaining Origen's use of the term *homoousios*, not

employed in the declaration of the synod in Antioch which preceded the Nicene council by a few months.[24] The expression "from the *ousia* of the Father" was anticipated only by Theognostus, an Alexandrian teacher quoted by Athanasius in defence of the Nicene wording (*On the Decrees* 25), but otherwise held to be of questionable orthodoxy. Although Theognostus is often described as a follower of Origen, the latter concludes in his *Commentary on John* that the Son proceeds not from the *ousia* but from the *dunamis* or power of the Father.[25] Eusebius of Nicomedia, the patron of Arius, is also said by Theodoret to have denounced the view that the Son is "from the *ousia*" of the Father (*Ecclesiastical History* 1.6.7). Whether the Nicene council was aware of his position we cannot say, as not only the date but the authenticity of his letter to Paulinus are in dispute.[26] On the other hand, we can say with confidence that one of the anathemas which this Eusebius refused to sign reinforces the text of the creed by excluding "any other *ousia* or hypostasis" as the origin of the Son. This rules out his derivation from matter or from nothing; it does not determine whether *ousia* and *hypostasis* are synonyms or complementary terms of which the first guarantees the unity of essence and the second the sole dependence of the Son upon the Father. It should not be forgotten that the teaching of Arius was advanced as an antidote to gnostic errors, and that one of these was the doctrine that the Spirit is the mother of the Son.

Since Eusebius of Caesarea offers no apology for the gloss "from the *ousia* of the Father," we may guess that for him it was semantically equivalent to the adjective *homoousios*, on which he feels obliged to dwell at length. He had excellent reasons for challenging it, though he never alludes to them either in his letter to Caesarea or in the seventh book of his *Ecclesiastical History*, completed before the council, in which he records the proceedings of the Council of Antioch in 269 and quotes abundantly from the letters of its intended president Dionysius of Alexandria. It is only from the champions of Nicaea, some decades later, that we learn of the denunciation of the term *homoousios* at Antioch and of the scruples which prevented Dionysius of Alexandria from making

---

directly of the relation between the Father and the Son but analogically of the relation between an ointment and the vapour that it exhales. See further Edwards 1998.

24 For the declaration of Antioch see Pietras 2016, 142: "we confess him to have been begotten of the unbegotten Father, God the Word, true light, righteousness, Lord and saviour of all. For he is the image, not of the will or of anything else but of his Father's very substance (*hypostasis*)."

25 Or., *Jo.* 13.25.153, appealing to Hebrews 1:3.

26 See now Löhr 2006a, 554.

this term his own.[27] Whatever he knew of these matters in 325, Eusebius was certainly not ignorant of the letter to Alexander of Alexandria in which Arius intimated that to think of the Son as a *homoousion meros*, a "consubstantial part" of the Father, would be to fall into the heresy of the Manichees, for whom God was a physical continuum (Athanasius, *On Synods* 16). It would seem that for Eusebius these facts count for nothing against the will of Constantine, the king raised up by God whom he portrays elsewhere as Christ's vicegerent in the present world.

In Theodoret's version of the letter we read that Constantine went on to maintain that Christ existed potentially in the Father before he evolved from him as a new *hypostasis* (*Ecclesiastical History* 1.12.7). This is not the explicit doctrine of the emperor in any extant writing (though it may be implied by the letter in which he fulminates against Arius as a - Porphyrian[28]); on the other hand, it is not the doctrine of Eusebius and bears so close a resemblance to that of his adversary Marcellus that he would not have any reason to fabricate the intervention. He elicited from the authors of the creed the more satisfactory explanation that the term *homoousios* signifies only the Son's transcendence of the created order. Athanasius, while he refrains from an open accusation of dishonesty, upholds a much stronger reading of the word as an affirmation of the natural affinity between the Son and the Father. The juxtaposition of the *homoousion* with "true God from true God" supports his reading; for all that, it is Eusebius who writes as a witness to the pronouncements of his fellow-bishops, and the contents of a public letter, written with impunity so soon after the event, will surely have fallen within the acceptable latitude of interpretation. The bishops did not define the term *homoousios*, and we may guess that their reticence was calculated, as there were many who argued, even after the council, that the term was applicable only to material entities.[29] It was tainted by the patronage of at least one Gnostic sect, the Valentinians,[30] and perhaps by its recent occurrence in the theosophic corpus which became known as the Hermetica.[31] It was even possible, on the eve of the council, for Eusebius of Nicomedia to say in a letter against Alexander that if the latter were right, the Son would be

---

[27] See Ath., *De synodis Arimini et Seleuciae* 45 and Hilary of Poitiers, *De synodis* 88, for the Council of Antioch; Ath., *De sententia Dionysii* (*De sent. Dion.*), with Abramowski 1992c.

[28] See Edwards 2013.

[29] Sozomen (Soz.), *Historia ecclesiastica* (*HE*) 3.18. The term *homoousios* probably lends itself to every sense that we can give to the statement "X is the same as Y." See Stead 1961.

[30] See Stead 1977, 190–202.

[31] Beatrice 2002, contending that the council borrowed the term from this source and putting aside with a high hand any evidence that suggests the contrary.

homoousios with the Father. The rhetorical implication, of course, is that not even Alexander would suppose this to be true.

It was this very letter, says Ambrose of Milan, that induced Alexander to import the word *homoousios* into the creed and thus disarm him with his own sword (*On the Faith* 3.15.15). He has been described as a questionable witness, but his statement that the letter of Eusebius was read out at the Nicene council to universal execration is corroborated by Theodoret (*Ecclesiastical History* 1.8.1). Moreover we have one circumstantial account which assigns the responsibility jointly to Alexander and the Spanish bishop Hosius of Cordova, the two men whom we might have expected to wield the greatest influence at the council: "[Philostorgius] asserts that before the Nicene council, Alexander, having encountered Hosius and his fellow-bishops after his arrival in Nicomedia, arranged by a synodical agreement to confess the Son *homoousios* with the Father and secure the banishment of Arius" (Photius, *Bibliotheca* 40 = Philostorgius, *Ecclesiastical History* 1.7). Philostorgius is the least trusted of historians, and with reason: he has put his pen at the service of the vanquished, yet for the most part he has no detectable sources beyond the narrative already written by the victors. In this case, however, his testimony is supported and embellished by an anonymous life of Constantine:[32]

> When the Sunday arrived, and they convened, each maintaining his own opinion, the Emperor was in the midst but waiting for their common decision. Those around Hosius of Cordova and Alexander prepared the book which all were to sign, which was composed in the very words that follow: 'In Nicaea the metropolis of Bithynia it seemed good to the victorious Constantine Augustus to hold a synod of the holy bishops of the holy catholic and apostolic church. *We believe in one God, Father, all-ruler, maker of heaven and earth, of all things seen and unseen, etc.* And next: *Those who say "there was when he was not," or "before he was begotten he was not," and that "he came to be from what was not," or assert that he is from another ousia or hypostasis, or that the Son of God is created or changeable or mutable, these the holy catholic and apostolic church anathematizes.*'

Any document in which Nicaea is named as the metropolis of Bithynia is most likely to be a product of that city, as elsewhere the pretensions of its rival Nicomedia were seldom challenged.[33] We have already seen that

---

[32]   Best consulted in Bidez 1913, 9–10.
[33]   Robert 1977.

Eusebius credits Constantine with the introduction of the word *homoousios* into the creed, and there was no other prelate more likely to have prompted this intervention than the Latin-speaking Hosius. While few scholars now entertain the view that the *homoousion* is a calque on the Latin *unius substantiae*, it is probable enough that the supposed equivalence would have been advanced as an argument on its behalf by the Spanish bishop.[34] If Alexander's patronage of the *homoousion* can be traced to more honourable motives, we can accept the story in Sozomen that before the Nicene council he had already convened a synod in which, having listened to advocates pleading for and against the term, he inclined to the former party, expelling Arius and his allies when they continued to demur.[35]

THE ANATHEMAS

The anathemas are new, and were peculiarly contentious: Eusebius of Nicomedia's refusal to endorse them is alleged to have been the cause of his deposition. They do not go so far as to substitute the eternity of the Son for the begetting before all ages which was asserted in the creed of Caesarea; yet surely nothing less than this is implied by the anathema against those who say "before he was begotten he was not," and "there was when he was not." The first proposition occurs in the letter of Arius to Eusebius of Nicomedia, while the second, though not attested in his letters, is all the more likely to be authentic because it does not posit any *time* before his birth.[36] Arius himself declares the origin of the Son to be timeless, albeit not eternal. The first might also have been ascribed to Marcellus of Ancyra, if we take the verb to connote existence as a distinct *hypostasis* and the birth to be not the origin of the Word but the nativity in Bethlehem. Again, it could have been uttered by Athanasius if it meant simply that there was no time before the eternal generation of the Son. The second could be attributed to Marcellus on the same premises, but never to Athanasius; of all the putative tenets of Arianism, it is the one that most plainly contradicts the teaching of Origen.[37]

Eusebius does not deny that Arius is the object of the anathema, and he endorses the condemnation of the words "from that which was not," which are acknowledged by the Alexandrian presbyter in his letter to Eusebius of Nicomedia (Theodoret, *Ecclesiastical History* 1.5). The reasoning of Arius

---

[34] And it is so translated by Rufinus at Pamph., *Apol. Orig.* 99.
[35] Soz., *HE* 1.15. On the ambiguity of Alexander's position see Pietras 2016, 19.
[36] Thdt., *HE* 1.5.5.
[37] See Or., *De principiis* 4.4.1 (28), perhaps indebted to Alexander of Aphrodisias, *in Aristotelis Metaphysica commentaria* (Hayduck 1891, 449, 818).

was that if, as was commonly held, all things must come from God or from matter or out of nothing,[38] only the third can be said of the Son without implying either that the substance of the Godhead is divisible or that one member of the Trinity is subject to corruption. The creed, of course, replies that the Son is from God; Eusebius prefers to reject this tenet, without endorsing an alternative, on the grounds that it is not warranted by the scriptures. For him Isaiah's question, "his generation who can declare?," was a bar to profitless speculation, not (as Athanasius thought) a hint that the origin of the Son was inexpressible because it was eternal.[39] The anathemas on the words "changeable" and "alterable" are no doubt designed to prohibit the inference, drawn on behalf of Arius by others if not by himself, that if the Son is unchangeable by the Father's will he must be changeable by nature.[40] Eusebius, however, insinuates that the heresy reprimanded here is the one which asserts that the Son underwent a change in becoming man. A recognised error since Tertullian's day, it was espoused by no-one in the early fourth century but Marcellus of Ancyra, if indeed he has been correctly represented by Eusebius himself.[41]

The anathema on the participle *ktiston* ("created") appears in the Athanasian transcription of the letter of Eusebius and in the *Ecclesiastical History* of Socrates, who is clearly following Athanasius.[42] It is absent, however, not only from Theodoret's transcription, but from the texts of the Nicene Creed transmitted by Ambrose, Basil of Caesarea, and Cyril of Alexandria, all authors who held both Athanasius and the Nicene council in high esteem.[43] This is more than a trivial point, because the doctrine that the Word is created appears to be authorised by Proverbs 8:22, where Wisdom, in the Septuagintal rendering, proclaims "the Lord created me in the beginning of his ways." The term proscribed in the body of the creed is not "created" but "made" (*poiēthenta*), which so far as is known was never espoused by Arius, though it had been condoned for a time (to his later regret) by Dionysius of Alexandria.[44] In subsequent polemics it is customary to characterize an Arian as one who holds that the Son was created, yet it

---

[38] Tert., *Aduersus Hermogenem* 2.1. See further Stead 1998.
[39] Isaiah 53:8 LXX.
[40] Socr., *HE* 1.6.6–12.
[41] On Marcellus and Nicaea see Parvis 2006, 29–95.
[42] Ath., appendix to *De decretis Nicaenae synodi*; Socr., *HE* 1.8.4. At 4.12, Socrates reproduces a letter by Eustathius of Antioch, in which the creed is transcribed without the anathemas.
[43] See Ambrose, *De fide* 1.20; Basil, *Epistulae* 125.2; Cyril of Alexandria, *Epistula ad Nestorium* 3.3; Thdt., *HE* 1.12.8.
[44] By implication at least in his simile of ship and shipwright (Ath., *De sent. Dion.* 24), notwithstanding the disclaimers at Ath., *De sent. Dion.* 21.

cannot be proved that this had been defined as a heretical position. Many scholars now hold that the council pronounced no anathema on the adjective *ktiston*, and some suspect Athanasius of deceit.[45]

I have argued elsewhere that we need not do so if we can trust the account which Philostorgius gives of the drafting of the creed.[46] As we have seen, he reports that it was submitted to Constantine by Alexander of Alexandria and Hosius of Cordova with the intention of embarrassing Eusebius of Nicomedia. The version which he quotes ends with the anathema on *ktiston*, which otherwise appears only (as we have seen) in the transcription of Athanasius and his admirers, of whom Philostorgius certainly was not one. Let us suppose that the draft which was submitted to the emperor was in large part the creation not of Alexander himself but of his deacon and lieutenant – by no means a reckless proposal when we consider that Athanasius is thought to have been the author of one of Alexander's two surviving letters.[47] If this were the case, Athanasius (who was not a signatory to the creed when promulgated) may have subsequently forgotten, if he was ever aware, that the final redaction was not in all respects identical with the original draft.

SUBSEQUENT VARIATIONS

The citations of the creed by Basil, Cyril, and Ambrose indicate that copies of the creed were preserved at least in the major sees. The form, as we see, remained rigid except for the persistence of the anathema on *ktiston* in those versions which are derived from Athanasius. Notwithstanding its currency, however, the Nicene symbol (as we call this creed to distinguish it from subsequent variations) does not appear to have been a universal shibboleth, even for the Greek clergy. Although a canon attached to the Dedication Council of Antioch in 341 extols Nicaea itself as a great and holy council, none of the five creeds which would appear to have been examined or promulgated at this gathering includes the term *homoousion* or agrees with the symbol of 325 in all other particulars. The creed of the church in Jerusalem at the time of Bishop Cyril names the Virgin but omits the *homoousion*.[48] Had it been identical in substance with that of Nicaea, it would scarcely have been possible to keep it a secret, as Cyril himself enjoined. One of the most

45 See especially Wiles 1993.
46 Edwards 2012, 498.
47 Stead 1988.
48 Heurtley 1911, 12–13. It also asserts that Christ's kingdom will have no end and that the Spirit has spoken through the prophets.

pugnacious champions of the *homoousion*, Epiphanius of Salamis, assumed that he was at liberty to vary the text of 325, his boldest interpolation being a clause which asserts, against Apollinarius of Laodicea, that Christ incarnate possessed a rational soul in addition to the animal soul and his body.[49] The creed appended to the current text of his *Ancoratus*, which many scholars believe to be a substitute for a more accurate citation of the Nicene symbol, approximates to the Nicene Creed that is now recited in churches.[50] To scholars this is known as the Niceno-Constantinopolitan Creed in deference to the Chalcedonian fathers of 451 who, as a warrant for their own publication of a new decree on the natures of Christ, alleged that the Council of Constantinople in 381 had recognised the necessity of amplifications in the original wording in order to meet new heresies. As the italics indicate, new clauses have been added and the anathemas removed:[51]

> We believe in one God, Father, all-ruler, maker of heaven and earth, of all things seen and unseen; and in one Lord Jesus Christ, the one Son of God unique [or only-begotten],[52] the one begotten from the Father before all the ages,[53] light from light, true God from true God, begotten not made, consubstantial with the Father, through whom all things came into being, the one who for us humans and for our salvation has descended from the heavens and taken flesh *from the Holy Spirit and the Virgin Mary*, who also has been made man and was crucified for our sake *under Pontius Pilate*, who has suffered and been buried, and risen again on the third day in accordance with the scriptures, and has gone up [or back] to the heavens, is seated at the right hand of the Father, and will come again with glory to judge the living and dead; *of whose kingdom there will be no end*.[54]
>
> And in the Spirit that is holy, *the Lord and life-giving one, the one proceeding from the Father, the one co-worshipped and co-glorified with the Father and the Son, the one who has spoken through the prophets; in one holy catholic and apostolic church. We confess one baptism for the remission of sins. We look forward*

---

[49]   Kelly 1972, 319–20; Heurtley 1911, 16–18.
[50]   Kelly 1972, 318; Heurtley 1911, 14–16. In fact it encompasses both the articles of the Niceno-Constantinopolitan Creed and the Nicene gloss on *monogenēs*.
[51]   Kelly 1972, 297–98.
[52]   The gloss "from the substance of the Father" is now absent.
[53]   Note the absence of "God from God," which is strictly redundant.
[54]   Adducing Luke 1:33 against the interpretation of 1 Corinthians 15:28 which was attributed to Marcellus of Ancyra. See Lienhard 1983.

*to the resurrection of the dead and the life of the coming age.
Amen.*

Between 381 and 451 we hear nothing of this document, and some regard it as a fabrication of the fifth century.[55] Since the decisions of Constantinople were not ratified immediately in Rome, it would not be surprising that the status of any creed that it promulgated should remain uncertain until it received the sanction of a new council. But perhaps we are not entirely bereft of evidence for its use before Chalcedon. Nestorius, for example, implies in a letter to Cyril that the Nicene Creed had spoken of Christ's birth from the Virgin Mary.[56] This is true of the creed that the Chalcedonian Fathers ascribe to Constantinople, but not of the original proclamation of 325. Again, when Leo I of Rome charged Eutyches with ignorance of the creed, he repeats two of its clauses – one affirming that Christ was born of Mary and the other that he is God from God – which are not found in conjunction either in the Apostles' Creed or in the creed of 325.[57] When Cyril informed Nestorius that the Nicene Fathers already honoured Mary as the Theotokos, or bearer of God, he may have intended only to say that Alexander, Eusebius, and Athanasius all make use of this title in their other writings, but his argument would be more to the purpose if he were recalling a version of the Nicene formula which named the mother of Christ.[58] It is possible then that the creed of Constantinople had displaced the creed of 325 in the memory of these disputants, and that only when they were driven back to the archives were they able to reproduce the very words of the original promulgation.

Yet even the archives may have been subject to interpolation. When the Council of Chalcedon undertook to prove that they were not devising a new creed but expounding that of Nicaea in imitation of the Constantinopolitan fathers, they reproduced what they took to be the creed of 325. In the version which is regarded as most authentic by the recent translators Price and Gaddis, however, the opening sentence contains some additional matter but omits the gloss on the word *monogenēs*:[59]

---

[55] Hort 1876, 72–97, argues that its prototype is the creed of Jerusalem, as attested by Cyril of Jerusalem and Epiphanius.

[56] Loofs 1905, 167. For a different view see Hort 1876, 111–16.

[57] Leo, *Tomus ad Flavianum* 2, at Bindley 1899, 196 and 206–7.

[58] Bindley 1899, 107 and 113–15.

[59] Price and Gaddis 2005, 2:191.

> We believe in one God, Almighty, maker of heaven and earth, of all things visible and invisible, and in one Lord Jesus Christ, the only-begotten Son of God, who was begotten from the Father before all ages, true God from true God.

Other versions add clauses stating that Jesus was born of Mary and the Spirit and that he was crucified under Pontius Pilate. It is possible that these were interpolations made by later scribes who were less familiar with the original creed than with its liturgical adaptation; it is equally possible that these interpolations were accepted at Chalcedon and later deleted in the interests of historical accuracy. If the creed of 381 was not a new promulgation but a ratification of changes which had already taken place in certain quarters, Cyril and Leo may have been acknowledging not the contested authority of Constantinople, but the right of the church as a whole to strengthen its phylacteries in the light of new temptations. If this is so, Epiphanius may have been one of the principal sponsors of innovation, and the text of the *Ancoratus* as we know it may be sound.

Of one thing we may be certain: variation abounded even where the creed was held in the greatest reverence. When the Armenian church repudiated the Chalcedonian Definition, three successive assemblies were held to confirm the Nicene Creed, which was then republished in the form that was thought to be primitive. The inserted matter is here italicised:[60]

> We believe in one God, almighty Father, creator of heaven and earth, of things visible and invisible. And in one Lord Jesus Christ, Son of God, only-begotten born of the Father, that is from the being of the Father, God from God, light from light, true God from true God, born and not created. The same nature of the Father, through whom everything visible and invisible was made in heaven and earth.[61] Who for the sake of us men and for our salvation, descended, was incarnate, was made man, *was born completely from the holy virgin Mary from the Holy Spirit. He took soul and body and mind and everything which pertains to man, truly and not seemingly. He was tormented, that is* crucified, was buried and rose on the third day. He ascended into heaven, *with the same body* he sat at the right hand of the Father. He will

---

[60] Translation Thomson and Howard-Johnston 1999, 125–26.
[61] The punctuation of Thomson and Howard-Johnston 1999 suggests that the Father, not the Son, is here acclaimed for a second time as the creator.

come *with the same body, and with the glory of the father*, to judge the living and the dead; *of whose kingdom there is no end.*

We believe also in the Holy Spirit, *uncreated and perfect, who spoke in the law and the prophets and the gospels, who descended to the Jordan, preached in the apostles, and dwelt in the saints. We also believe in one holy catholic church, in one baptism, in repentance and forgiveness of sins, in the resurrection of the dead, in the eternal judgment of souls and bodies, in the kingdom of heaven and life everlasting.*

As for those who say, there was once when the Son was not, or there was once when the Holy Spirit was not, or that they were created from nothing, or that the Son *and the Holy Spirit* were from a different being or existence, or are mutable and changeable, *such persons we anathematize, because* the catholic apostolic church also anathematizes them.

So let us glorify [the one] who is before eternity, worshipping the holy Trinity and the consubstantial divinity of the Father, the Son and the Holy Spirit, now and always and for ages of ages. Amen.

This is a contamination of the creed of 381 with matter peculiar to the Armenian church. When the Visigothic church of the late sixth century modified the Constantinopolitan Creed to say that the Spirit proceeds not only from the Father but from the Son also, unwittingly it laid itself open to the Armenian anathema on those who derive the Son or the Spirit from any other *ousia*. In all, their innovations were more modest but more momentous, once the Filioque was taken up by the Franks and at last received the seal of authority when the bishop of Rome condoned its use at the crowning of the Holy Roman Emperor Henry II.[62] As is well known, this unilateral claim to hegemony played a greater role than the Filioque itself in the gradual estrangement of the eastern and western churches. The patriarch and polymath Photius hinted in the tenth century that the error arose from the poverty of the Latin language rather than perversity of thought.[63] It was hardly conceivable that the haughty Michael Cerularius would submit to the admonitions of a dead Pope in 1054, and yet at the Council of Florence in 1438, after almost four centuries of plunder and humiliation, the Greek church was prepared to accommodate the Latin doctrine with the formula that the Spirit proceeds from the Father through the Son.[64] This reconciliation was

---

[62] Kelly 1972, 358–67.
[63] Hoegenroether 1869, 63 (article 1 of *Opusculum contra Francos*).
[64] Siecienski 2010, 151–72.

subverted by the laity of the Byzantine world, who preferred to keep faith
with their ancestors in servitude to the Turks than to betray them for the
sake of a Roman alliance. The lesson of history is that words, for all that
poets say of their durability, are more subject to change and chance than
the institutions which purport to be founded on them. In an age before
the printing press they cannot be read unless there is someone to copy
them, and they cannot maintain their primitive form more rigidly than
the transitory materials on which they are inscribed.

APPENDIX: THE NICENE CREED

Πιστεύομεν εἰς ἕνα θεὸν, πατέρα, παντοκράτορα, πάντων ὁρατῶν τε καὶ ἀοράτων
ποιητήν·

και εἰς ἕνα κύριον Ἰησοῦν Χριστὸν, τὸν υἱὸν τοῦ θεοῦ, γεννηθέντα ἐκ τοῦ
πατρὸς, μονογενῆ, τουτέστιν ἐκ τῆς οὐσίας τοῦ πατρός, θεὸν ἐκ θεοῦ, φῶς ἐκ
φωτός, θεὸν ἀληθινὸν ἐκ θεοῦ ἀληθινοῦ, γεννηθέντα οὐ ποιηθέντα, ὁμοούσιον τῷ
πατρί, δι' οὗ τὰ πάντα ἐγένετο τά τε ἐν τῷ οὐρανῷ καὶ τὰ ἐν τῇ γῇ, τὸν δι' ἡμᾶς τοὺς
ἀνθρώπους καὶ διὰ τὴν ἡμετέραν σωτηρίαν κατελθόντα καὶ σαρκωθέντα,
ἐνανθρωπήσαντα, παθόντα καὶ ἀναστάντα τῇ τρίτῃ ἡμέρᾳ, ἀνελθόντα εἰς τοὺς
οὐρανοὺς ἐρχόμενον κρῖναι ζῶντας καὶ νεκρούς· καὶ εἰς τὸ ἅγιον πνεῦμα.

τοὺς δὲ λέγοντας· ἦν ποτε, ὅτε οὐκ ἦν καὶ· Πρὶν γεννηθῆναι οὐκ ἦν, καὶ ὅτι ἐξ
οὐκ ὄντων ἐγένετο ἢ ἐξ ἑτέρας ὑποστάσεως ἢ οὐσίας φάσκοντας εἶναι [ἢ κτιστὸν] ἢ
τρεπτὸν ἢ ἀλλοιωτὸν τὸν υἱὸν θεοῦ, τούτους ἀναθεματίζει ἡ καθολικὴ καὶ
ἀποστολικὴ ἐκκλησία.

We believe in one God, the Father Almighty, Maker of all things both
visible and invisible; and in one Lord Jesus Christ, the Son of God,
begotten from the Father, only-begotten, that is, from the substance of
the Father; God from God, Light from Light, true God from true God,
begotten, not made, consubstantial with the Father; "through whom all
things came into being" [John 1:3; 1 Cor 8:6], both things in heaven and
things on earth; who for us humans and for our salvation descended,
became incarnate, was made human, suffered, on the third day rose
again, ascended into the heavens, will come "to judge the living and
the dead" [2 Tim 4:1, 1 Pet 4:5]; and in the Holy Spirit.

The catholic and apostolic Church anathematizes those who say,
"There was when he was not," and, "He was not before he was begotten," and that he came to be from nothing, or those who claim that the
Son of God is from another hypostasis or substance, (or created,) or
alterable, or mutable.[65]

---

[65] Kinzig 2017, 290–91.

SELECT REFERENCES

Beatrice, Pier Franco. 2002. "The Word *'Homoousios'* from Hellenism to Christianity." *CH* 71(2): 243–72.

Bidez, J., ed. 1913. *Philostorgius, Kirchengeschichte.* GCS 21. Leipzig: Hinrichs.

Bindley, Thomas Herbert. 1899. *The Oecumenical Documents of the Faith.* London: Methuen.

Dossetti, Giuseppe. 1967. *Il simbolo di Nicea e di Constantinopoli: Edizione critica.* Rome: Herder.

Edwards Mark J. 2012. "Alexander of Alexandria and the *Homoousion.*" *VC* 66(5): 482–502.

Heurtley, Charles Able. 1911. *De Fide et Symbolo.* Oxford: Parker.

Hort, Fenton J. A. 1876. *Two Dissertations.* Cambridge: Macmillan.

Kelly, J. N. D. 1972. *Early Christian Creeds.* 3rd ed. London: Longmans.

Pietras, Henryk. 2016. *Council of Nicaea (325): Religious and Political Context, Documents, Commentaries.* Rome: Gregorian and Biblical Press.

Price, Richard, and Michael Gaddis. 2005. *The Acts of the Council of Chalcedon.* TTH 45. Liverpool: Liverpool University Press.

Siecienski, A. Edward. 2010. *The Filioque: History of a Doctrinal Controversy.* Oxford Studies in Historical Theology. New York: Oxford University Press.

Skarsaune, Oskar. 1987. "A Neglected Detail in the Creed of Nicaea (325)." *VC* 41 (1): 34–54.

Stead, G. Christopher. 1961. "The Significance of the *Homoousios.*" *StPatr* 3: 397–412.

Stead, G. Christopher. 1998. "The Word 'From Nothing'." *JTS*, n.s., 49(2): 671–84.

Thomson, Robert, and James Howard-Johnston, trans. 1999. *The Armenian History Attributed to Sebeos.* TTH 31. Liverpool: Liverpool University Press.

Wiles, Maurice F. 1993. "A Textual Variant in the Creed of the Council of Nicaea." *StPatr* 26: 428–33.

8 The Twenty Canons of the Council of Nicaea

ANDREAS WECKWERTH

INTRODUCTION

While most students of ancient Christianity may be familiar with the famous Nicene Creed and the Arian controversy, only a few of them are probably aware of the twenty Nicene canons, which were not only esteemed in the early Church and often quoted by other councils and bishops, but also still form an important part of current Orthodox canon law.[1] But before proceeding with an explanation of the Nicene canons, we must sketch out the genre "canons" among the various types of documents preserved in synodal acts. Some of these documents deal with doctrinal issues, such as creeds (*symbola fidei*), which as exactly as possible express and define important *dogmata* of the Christian faith, or anathemas, which reject a heterodox doctrinal position and usually condemn the person who was propagating it. But to what kind of synodal discussions do the so-called "canons" belong?[2] They comprise synodal decisions on various disciplinary issues and were therefore the result of episcopal deliberations on canonical problems which the bishops probably encountered in their dioceses.[3] In some cases, the canons are the only document of a synod that has been handed down to us.[4] On the other hand, many councils, especially in the eastern part of the Roman empire, did not issue any disciplinary

---

[1] In contrast to the Roman Catholic tradition, the Orthodox churches have never codified their canon law. Therefore, the synodal canons of the first millennium are still considered as a primary source of Orthodox canon law. See Potz, Synek, and Troianos 2007, 211–13, 228–32.
   For an English translation of the canons, see www.earlychurchtexts.com/public/nicaea_canons.htm (from NPNF 2.14). On the number of canons, see Hefele and Leclercq 1907, 503–28.

[2] On the ancient terminology, see Ohme 1998, 570–82; Ohme 2004, 19–25.

[3] Weckwerth 2010, 151–55.

[4] For example, the canons of the councils of Ancyra (314), Neocaesarea (315/19), Antioch (330), but also canons promulgated by many western councils otherwise unknown, such as the councils of Elvira (305?), Valence (374), Saragossa (380), and Nîmes (396).

canons.[5] Nevertheless, their literary form resembles imperial edicts and Roman laws.[6] Some of them depend on verbs of deciding (such as ἔδοξεν), while others use forms of the imperative or other grammatical constructions. The extensive use of conditional and relative clauses seems to be typical of synodal canons, because the bishops wanted to formulate disciplinary decisions as precisely as possible.

It may be surprising that no allusions to the Arian controversy can be found in the Nicene canons, but it is quite common that canons promulgated by a council differ from the cause of its convocation. For example, the Council of Chalcedon was convened in order to discuss the doctrine of Eutyches and to resolve the Christological controversy, while its canons dealt with many disciplinary problems. Obviously, the bishops who came together at synods liked to use the opportunity for deliberating upon questions concerning ecclesiastical law.

My following remarks on the canons of Nicaea will be divided into four sections. To begin, I would like to give a brief outline of the textual transmission of the Nicene canons. Then after dividing them into various thematic groups, I will briefly explain each canon in order to provide a short overview of its purpose and content. The third part will deal with the reception of the canons in the early church by councils, bishops, and ecclesiastical writers and what importance was attributed to the Nicene canons. Finally, I will briefly present some possible *desiderata* for future research.

THE TRANSMISSION OF THE CANONS OF NICAEA

The ancient and medieval canonical collections are of primary importance for the transmission of the ancient disciplinary canons in the West and East. We can distinguish between two types: historical collections arranged according to the chronological order of the councils, and systematic collections, in which the canons have been separated from their historical context and organized according to various aspects of canon law.[7]

The Greek text of the twenty Nicene canons has been handed down to us mainly by the following two collections: the *Collection of Fifty Titles* (Συναγωγή κανόνων ἐκκλησιαστικῶν εἰς ν᾿ τίτλους

---

[5] Famous examples are the fifth and sixth ecumenical councils, held at Constantinople in 553 and 680/1. Therefore, the council of Constantinople *in Trullo* (691/2) had to fill this gap, so that it is also called *Quinisextum* (fifth-sixth).

[6] Weckwerth 2004, 70–81.

[7] See Maassen 1870, 3–7.

διηρημένη)[8] and the *Syntagma of Fourteen Titles*.[9] The former was compiled and systematically arranged by John Scholastikos, patriarch of Constantinople (565–77), in the middle of the sixth century,[10] while the latter, which is sometimes attributed to the patriarchs of Constantinople Eutychos and John IV Nesteutes, emerged during the last decades of the sixth century and is something between a systematic and chronological collection.[11] Its text has been preserved only by the *Nomokanon of Fourteen Titles*. An anonymous ancient church historian, falsely identified as Gelasius of Cyzicus,[12] inserted the Greek text of the Nicene canons in his *Historia ecclesiastica*, "without varying from the content or sequence of what is found in Greek canonical collections."[13]

Furthermore, the Nicene canons were translated into various ancient languages, usually together with the canons of other Greek councils. There were many Latin translations produced from the fourth to the seventh centuries that have mostly been preserved in western canonical collections.[14] Among them, the so-called *versio Caeciliani* seems to be the oldest, which Caecilianus, bishop of Carthage, who was present at the Council of Nicaea, probably brought directly from there to North Africa. Rufinus of Aquileia inserted an abbreviation of the Nicene canons in his translation of the *Ecclesiastical History* written by Eusebius of Caesarea.[15] From the fourth and fifth centuries onward, when the languages of the Christian Orient were becoming increasingly more and more important, the Nicene canons were also translated into Syriac, Coptic, Arabic, Ethiopian, Armenian, Georgian, and Ancient Slavonic.[16]

[8] Critical edition: Beneševič 1937.
[9] Critical edition: Beneševič (1906), 1974.
[10] See Troianos 2012, 118–20.
[11] Troianos 2012, 20: "It was divided into fourteen titles, and every title was subdivided into chapters. In every chapter, related canons are mentioned by their number according to synod, etc., without however the inclusion of their text. The texts, listed according to their source [...] were gathered in a special collection."
[12] See Röwekamp 2003. Gelasius of Cyzicus, *Historia ecclesiastica* 2.32
[13] Ohme 2012, 36–37. Gelasius of Cyzicus, *Historia ecclesiastica* 2.32 (Loeschke and Heinemann 1918, 112–13).
[14] See Maassen 1870, 8–50. Critical edition: Turner 1904, 112–273.
[15] Eusebius (Eus.), *Historia ecclesiastica* (*HE*), 10.6.
[16] *Clavis Patrum Graecorum* (*CPG*), 8520–27.

Critical editions of the Greek text	• Beneševič 1937, passim (see the index on page 258).
	• Beneševič (1906) 1974, 83–93.
Ancient versions	• See *Clavis Patrum Graecorum* 8520–27.
Modern translations	• **English**: Tanner 1990, 6–19; L'Huillier 1996, 31–100.
	• **German**: Wohlmuth 1998, 6–19.
	• **French**: Joannou 1962, 23–41.
	• **Italian**: Alberigo and Jedin 1991, 6–16.

ISSUES ADDRESSED BY THE NICENE CANONS

If we consider the twenty Nicene canons, we recognize that they have no continuous systematic order. Thus, we can suppose that the preserved order of the canons mirrors the thematic sequence of the topics discussed by the bishops at the Council of Nicaea. We do not have much information about the procedure the bishops used for their disciplinary deliberations. According to some North African synodal proceedings and the acts of the Council of Serdica, one bishop proposed a canonical problem that was discussed and decided by the synod.[17] It seems that bishops did not make any subsequent procedural systematization.

For the following explanation of the Nicene canons, it is very useful to divide them into various groups in order to be able to identify tendencies in the legislative action of the bishops. We will follow the proposal given by Heinz Ohme:[18]

Discipline and hierarchical order of the clergy	Canons 1, 2, 3, 9, 10, 17, 18
Organisation of ecclesiastical leadership and administration	Canons 4, 5, 6, 7, 15, 16
Regulations of public penance	Canons 11, 12, 13, 14
Reconciliation of members of heterodox groups	Canons 8, 19
Liturgy	Canon 20

[17]   Weckwerth 2010, 151–55.
[18]   Ohme 2012, 36–38.

Discipline and the Hierarchical Order of the Clergy

Most canons of this first group established rules for admission to the clergy by defining some impediments or irregularities and also governed what was to be done if persons marked with them had already been ordained. The bishops wanted to prohibit people admitted to the clergy who were unworthy of this honour due to any moral blemish in their previous life as expressed in canon 9: "The Catholic Church vindicates only what is above reproach" (τὸ γὰρ ἀνεπίληπτον ἐκδικεῖ ἡ καθολικὴ ἐκκλησία).

Canon 1 excluded all persons from the clergy who had castrated themselves. Such persons were not be promoted to the clergy; or if they had already become clerics, they had to be suspended. This canon seems to have been directed against some forms of hyper-asceticism which sometimes included self-castration.[19] Thus, all cases of castration that were not self-inflicted, but by physicians for necessary medical reasons or by barbarians during captivity, did not necessarily lead to exclusion from the clergy.[20] Canon 2 forbade neophytes – persons who had recently been baptised – from immediately being ordained bishops or presbyters (ἅμα τῷ βαπτισθῆναι προάγειν εἰς ἐπισκοπὴν ἢ εἰς πρεσβυτερεῖον).[21] It was reasoned that this practice contradicted the Apostolic word (ἀποστολικὸν γράμμα) given in 1 Tim 3:6–7, which was quoted verbatim in the canon. There was no provision that clerics ordained as neophytes before this decision were generally to be excluded from the clergy, unless they had been convicted by two or three witnesses of having committed a presumed carnal sin (ψυχικὸν[22] ἁμάρτημα). The bishops aimed to prevent candidates from being admitted to the clergy who had not undergone a longer time of examination and probation.

Canon 9 also required a detailed inquiry for future presbyters. But if this had been neglected and the candidates confessed grave sins after an investigation and were ordained despite their confession, they were not allowed to function as presbyters. The canon sought to ensure the moral

---

[19] A famous example is the self-castration of Origen, reported by Eus., *HE* 6.8.1–2. See Muth 2004, 318–19. The *Canones Apostolorum* (*Can. App.*) 22 (Metzger 1987, 280), called someone who castrated himself a suicide (αὐτοφονευτής) and an enemy of God's creation (τῆς τοῦ Θεοῦ δημιουργίας ἐχθρός).

[20] Muth 2004, 298–301, 326–27. *Can. App.* 21, makes a rule very similar to the Nicene one.

[21] Lafontaine 1963, 244–48. Cf. *Can. App.* 80; Council of Laodicea, can. 3 (Beneševič 1937, 107).

[22] See Lampe 1961, s.v. "ψυχικός," 1553: "natural, carnal." See, however, L'Huillier 1996, 33: "[…] it must mean serious sin that a cleric commits in the exercise of his functions by pride or lack of sound judgement."

integrity of the clerics. One's life before consecration was taken into account and examined, and serious sins were considered an obstacle to ordination.[23] Canon 10 excluded from the clergy the so-called lapsed (παραπεπτωκότες) – Christians who had denied the faith in times of persecution.[24] If such persons had already become clerics "through the ignorance of their promoters or even with their connivance" (κατὰ ἄγνοιαν ἢ καὶ παρειδότων τῶν προχειρισαμένων), they had to be deposed.

Two canons dealt with the clerical way of life: canon 3 forbade all clerics from living together with women called suneisaktoi (συνείσακτοι; Latin: virgines subintroductae), except their closest female relatives, such as their mothers, sisters, or aunts. Considering the use of the term συνείσακτος, we can conclude that this canon was directed against the cohabitation of a celibate clergyman with a female ascetic in the guise of a spiritual marriage without sexual contact.[25] There are some other sources that rejected this practice as an offence against the ecclesiastical order.[26] Obviously, the bishops feared that illicit sexual relationships could arise as a consequence of such cohabitation. Canon 17 deposed all clerics who practiced usury.[27] The quest for profit was considered incompatible with the moral integrity of the clergy, and Psalm 14:5 was quoted as scriptural evidence of the prohibition of usury. The names of such clerics were to be deleted from the κανών, that is, a list of all persons who had an ecclesiastical function and therefore received support from the church.[28]

Finally, canon 18 stressed the hierarchical order of the ordo maior by prohibiting the practice of deacons giving the body of Christ to presbyters

[23]   See L'Huillier 1996, 63: "From the origins of Christianity, there has been consensus on the fact that serious sin, such as apostasy, murder, fornication and adultery, constituted insurmountable obstacles to becoming a cleric."

[24]   With regard to canons 11, 12 and 14, it seems probable that the anti-Christian measures under Licinius were behind them.

[25]   The wives of clerics were not mentioned among the women with whom a cleric might legitimately live together. Since there were married clerics in the ancient Church, we can conclude that this Nicene canon implied unmarried clerics living together as ascetics. See L'Huillier 1996, 36.

        See Ferguson 1997. Cf. Cyprian, Epistulae 4.4.1–2; Eus., HE 7.30.2–14; Council in Trullo (691/92) can. 5 (ACO 2.2.4, Ohme 2013, 27).

[26]   See Dockter 2015, 19.

[27]   Dockter 2015, 77–82; L'Huillier 1996, 76. Cf. Council of Elvira, can. 20 (Martínez Díez and Rodríguez 1984, 248–49: Si quis clericorum detectus fuerit usuras accipere, placuit eum degredari et abstineri; Council of Arles (314), can. 13 (12) (Munier 1963, 11). On the view of usury in the ancient church, see Bogaert 1976.

[28]   On this connotation of κανών, see Ohme 1998, 368, and Gryson 1972, 86: "[...] the list of individuals who fulfilled a function within the internal structures determined by ecclesiastical legislation and who, as such, received a subsidy from the Church."

or receiving the Eucharist even before the bishops. Moreover, deacons should not sit among the presbyters. It was emphasized that they were the ministers of the bishop (τοῦ ἐπισκόπου ὑπηρέται) and subordinate to the presbyters (τῶν δὲ πρεσβυτέρων ἐλάττους τυγχάνουσιν). As in the western church, especially in Rome,[29] some deacons probably wanted to extend their liturgical status because of their influential position in the administration of the church. In contrast to the *presbyterium*, which had a larger number of members, there were often only seven deacons in a city, according to Acts 6:5.[30] Since the deacons had close contact with the bishop, they might sometimes have seen themselves as superior to the presbyters. Therefore, the Council of Nicaea exhorted deacons not to exceed the limits imposed by their hierarchical rank and reminded them that they participated in the ministry (*ministerium*), but not in the priesthood (*sacerdotium*). The problem, however, seems to have persisted, and the so-called Council of Laodicea,[31] and the Quinisextum,[32] still exhorted deacons to observe the hierarchical order.

Organisation of Ecclesiastical Leadership and Administration

The main topic of this section was the implementation of an ecclesiastical organisation that was oriented on the division of provinces carried out by Diocletian and Constantine.[33] The metropolitan bishop (μετροπολίτης), at the head of an (ecclesiastical) province (ἐπαρχία), became an institution that superseded the juridical authority of all individual local bishops.[34] In addition, larger organizational structures that went beyond the level of ecclesiastical provinces were also addressed by the bishops at Nicaea.

Canon 4 gave rules for the designation and ordination (καθίστασθαι[35]) of a bishop, who had to be appointed by all bishops of an ecclesiastical province. If this was not possible, at least three bishops should come

---

[29] Cf. Council of Arles (314), can. 18 (Munier 1963, 13): *De diaconibus Urbicis: Ut non sibi tantum praesumant, sed honorem presbyteris reservent, ut sine conscientia ipsorum nihil tale faciant.* See Domagalski 1980. Compare with Klauser 1957, 899.

[30] On the Roman clergy of the third century, see Eus., *HE* 6.43.11. But later on, this numerical limitation was no longer maintained despite the decision of the Council of Neocaesarea (319) in can. 14 (15) (Beneševič 1937, 81). See Klauser 1957, 898–99.

[31] C Laod., can. 20 (Beneševič 1937, 107). Most likely, however, it was not a council, but a collection of synodal decisions. See Ohme 1998, 402–3.

[32] C Trull. (691/92), can. 7 (*ACO* 2.2.4, Ohme 2013, 27–28).

[33] Gaudemet 1958, 379–80; Lübeck 1901, 52–98.

[34] See Gaudemet 1958, 380–82.

[35] L'Huillier 1996, 36: "This verb has reference to the whole procedure for becoming a bishop: the election, the sacramental consecration and the installation."

together in order to ordain him; the absent bishops had to give their consent by sending a letter.[36] The metropolitan bishop had to confirm the election of a new bishop in his province. In the second part of canon 6, the role of the metropolitan in the election of bishops was emphasized once again. No one was to become a bishop without his consent (χωρὶς γνώμης τοῦ μετροπολίτου). In general, bishops seemed to have discussed and voted on an election beforehand; however, if two or three bishops of the province were opposed to the majority opinion, this objection could be neglected and the majority was to be followed. Personal rivalry (φιλονεικία) is explicitly cited as the reason for such a deviation. Canon 5 established a provincial synod to be held twice a year (δὶς τοῦ ἐνιαυτοῦ), which should offer laymen as well as clerics excommunicated by their local bishop the possibility of appeal against their sentences. In other words, the provincial synod retained the function of an ecclesiastical court.[37] On the one hand, this canon wanted to ensure the effectiveness of an excommunication – no bishop should accept (προσίεσθαι) a person excommunicated by another bishop – but on the other hand it also wanted to guarantee the appropriateness of such a judgment through the possibility of an examination.

The famous first part of canon 6 dealt with the primacy of the episcopal sees of Alexandria and Antioch.[38] The oversight of these bishoprics crossed the boundaries of provinces: Alexandria's authority (ἐξουσία) over Egypt, Libya, and the Pentapolis,[39] called an ancient custom (ἀρχαῖα ἔθη), was confirmed by the Council of Nicaea and compared to Rome's.[40] The expression ἐξουσία meant in this context that the Alexandrian bishop could confirm or refuse not only the elections of metropolitans of his area, but probably also the elections of their

---

[36]   The canon explicitly gives two reasons: a pressing necessity (διὰ κατεπείγουσαν ἀνάγκην) and the length of the distance to be travelled (διὰ μῆκος ὁδοῦ).

[37]   Cf. also Council of Antioch (330), can. 20 (Beneševič 1937, 150).

[38]   L'Huillier 1996, 45, 48, adopts another syntactic incision by drawing the words ὁμοίως δὲ καὶ κατὰ τὴν Ἀντιόχειαν to the previous ones: "[...] since for the bishop of Rome there is a similar practice and the same thing concerning Antioch; and in other provinces, let the prerogatives of the churches (of the capitals) be safeguarded." For L'Huillier, the canon focuses only on the episcopal see of Alexandria; its sphere of influence is merely compared with that of Rome and Antioch, so that their areas of influence are not mentioned.

[39]   This is the territory of the later civil diocese of Egypt, which was founded between 365 and 386 and included five provinces. Cf. Notitia dignitatum 2.24–29 (Seeck 1876, 6): "(diocesis) Aegypti quinque: Libya superior, Libya inferior, Thebais, Aegyptus, Arcadia." See Lübeck 1901, 116–34.

[40]   The Bishop of Rome exercised jurisdiction over the civil diocese of Italia suburbicaria, which included central and southern Italy as well as Sicily, Corsica, and Sardinia. See Pack 1998, 1166–70.

suffragan bishops. Furthermore, he had the authority to convoke synods and to arbitrate appeals throughout his whole territory.[41] Thus, his authority was obviously superior even to that of metropolitans, which was limited to one province. Similarly, the prerogatives (τὰ πρεσβεῖα) of Antioch (κατὰ τὴν Ἀντιόχειαν) should be preserved. In contrast to Alexandria, however, the bishop of Antioch's sphere of influence was not outlined.[42] Finally, privileges "in the other provinces" (ἐν ταῖς ἄλλαις ἐπαρχίαις) were also confirmed, although the meaning of these controversial words has been debated by modern scholars.[43] In this canon, we can recognize the beginnings of the later patriarchal system, which was finally formed in the sixth century into the so-called Pentarchy (Rome, Constantinople, Alexandria, Antioch, and Jerusalem).[44] Canon 7 affirmed that the episcopal see of Jerusalem, called Aelia (Αἰλία),[45] should be honoured (τιμᾶσθαι) and the consequence of this honour (ἀκολουθία τῆς τιμῆς) should also be given to it.[46] What exactly this ἀκολουθία τῆς τιμῆς means was not explained.[47] However, the canon emphasized that the rights of the metropolitan see of Caesarea Maritima to which Jerusalem

---

[41] See Hinschius 1869, 540; Linck 1908, 39, 46; Lübeck 1901, 110–11.

[42] Lübeck 1901, 134–40. Hinschius 1869, 540, assumes that the bishop of Antioch's sphere of influence essentially extended over the area of the later diocese of the East, founded between 365 and 386, above all the Syro-Palestinian and Mesopotamian regions. Cf. Notitia dignitatum 2.8–23 (Seeck 1876, 5–6). L'Huillier 1996, 48: "It seems probable, therefore, that the bishops of Antioch, by virtue of ancient customs, confirmed the elections of bishops of a certain number of sees beyond the limits of Coelosyria."

[43] Linck 1908, 41, applies these words to the metropolitan sees of individual, not specified provinces whose privileges were confirmed. In contrast, Maassen 1853, 48–63, supposes that the civil dioceses of Asia, Pontus, and Thracia were implicated with their metropolitan sees of Ephesus, Cappadocian Caesarea, and Heraclea. Maassen assumes this against the background of canon 2 of the Council of Constantinople (381), where these areas were explicitly named. See also Lübeck 1901, 140–48. But in view of the wording of the Nicene canon, the first solution seems to be the more likely one. The term ἐπαρχία is used in the canons of Nicaea exclusively in the sense of a province, but not of a (civil) diocese. In this way, L'Huillier 1996, 49–50, also understands these words with reference to Latin translations.

[44] On the historical development of the Pentarchy, see Gaudemet 1958, 389–96.

[45] After the destruction of Jerusalem following the Bar Kokhba revolt, the city was rebuilt under the name Aelia Capitolina.

[46] Lübeck 1901, 148–58.

[47] See Hinschius 1869, 544. The expression ἀκολουθία τῆς τιμῆς here probably means a precedence over other bishops, similar to that of the bishops of Rome, Alexandria, and Antioch, which in contrast to them had no jurisdictional effects due to the addition of τῆς τιμῆς (of honour). L'Huillier 1996, 55, however, assumes that the bishop of Jerusalem only took precedence over the bishops of his own province, with the exception of the Metropolitan of Caesarea. See Daley 1993, 536: "Despite its vagueness, this canon seems to imply more than the purely ceremonial rank some have seen in it; if the 'consequences of rank' confirmed here were not of some practical import in

belonged were not infringed upon (τῇ μετροπόλει σῳζουμένου τοῦ οἰκείου ἀξιώματος).

In addition to these regulations for larger ecclesiastical organizational structures, canons 15 and 16 focused on the level of the ecclesiastical diocese (παροικία). Especially bishops, presbyters, and deacons, but also all people listed in the κανών (ὅλως ἐν τῷ κανόνι ἐξεταζόμενοι) were forbidden to leave their diocese permanently on their own initiative and to go to another. They should return or be excommunicated. The bishops were specifically urged not to accept any clergymen from foreign dioceses, unless they had the consent of their home bishop. Obviously, it had happened more often that clergymen departed from their dioceses in order to be accepted into the clergy of another, perhaps because they wanted to join a larger and richer diocese or had quarrels with their own bishop.[48] The Council of Nicaea thus underlined the bond through which every clergyman was connected to his diocese by virtue of his consecration, which must not be dissolved on his own initiative.

Regulations of Public Penance

The anti-Christian measures under the "tyranny of Licinius" (ἐπὶ τῆς τυραννίδος Λικινίου) in the eastern part of Roman empire had ended a short time before the Council of Nicaea.[49] It is therefore not surprising that some Nicene canons dealt with the question of handling Christians who had denied their faith in a time of persecution. Already in the middle of the third century, due to the Decian persecution, this severe problem had triggered a fierce dispute, at the end of which the practice of allowing a one-time repentance to the so-called *lapsi* had become established.[50] In this tradition, canon 11 granted the possibility of public penitence to all those who had apostatized (περὶ τῶν παραβάντων[51]) under persecution (for

the life of the Palestinian churches, there would be no need to stress the continuing 'dignity' of Caesaraea as well."

[48] Weckwerth 2004, 164–69.

[49] Eus., *HE* 10.8.10–17, reports of various measures against Christians in Licinius's part of the Roman empire. The credibility of this report is disputed. Bleckmann 2010, 144–45, sees a strong influence of Constantinian propaganda. The actual extent of Licinius's anti-Christian measures is hardly discernible. Such pro-Constantine propaganda could be related to the formulation ἐπὶ τῆς τυραννίδος Λικινίου, especially since the Council of Nicaea was dominated by Constantine. Novak 2001, 166, suspects that the anti-Christian reactions can be explained by the opposition of Licinius to Constantine. Licinius was probably aware that the Christians were on Constantine's side in the civil war.

[50] Poschmann 1951, 28–32.

[51] Lampe 1961, 1007, s.v. "παραβαίνω": 5. lapse from the faith.

example, by Licinius) without any external compulsion.[52] It was stressed that the bishops wanted to show leniency (φιλανθρωπία[53]) towards them, even if the lapsed were unworthy. They were to stay among the hearers (ἐν ἀκροωμένοις) for three years and seven years among the prostrators ("they shall fall down" [ὑποπεσοῦνται]). Then they were allowed to participate only in prayers (κοινωνήσουσι τῷ λαῷ τῶν προσευχῶν), for two years, but not in the offering (χωρὶς προσφορᾶς). The total time of repentance was twelve years, twice as long as the Council of Ancyra (314) had decreed.[54]

This canon and the following ones cannot be understood without knowledge of the various orders of penitents, which were characteristic for the East, but not for the West. We can distinguish four levels:[55] the first stage, not mentioned in the Nicene canons, were the "Mourners," who were placed in front of the entrance to the church, lamenting and crying for the prayers of the faithful. The next order, called the "Hearers," was permitted to listen to the Scriptures read and the sermon, "but were obliged to depart, before any of the common prayer began."[56] The "Prostrators," "were allowed to stay and join in certain prayers particularly made for them whilst they were kneeling upon their knees."[57] The last level, the "Repenters," was allowed to be present throughout the Eucharistic celebration and could participate in prayers, but without receiving communion or making their own oblations.[58] In other sources, they were called "Co-standers" (συνιστάμενοι).[59] Canon 14 applied a reduced penance to catechumens who had lapsed during persecution. They were to belong to the Hearers (αὐτοὺς ἀκροασαμένους) for three years and could then take part in prayer (εὔχεσθαι) together with the other catechumens. The Council of Nicaea thus distinguished among the lapsed between full Christians and catechumens, and it probably

---

[52] Examples mentioned are the confiscation of property (ἀφαίρεσις ὑπαρχόντων) and, in general, a dangerous situation (κίνδυνος). The canon, however, does not say how to deal with people who have denied their faith because of such threats.

[53] Hornung 2016, 191: The term φιλανθρωπία refers to the care of a ruler towards his subjects and can be associated with a reduction in punishment.

[54] Council of Ancyra (314), can. 6 (Beneševič 1937, 120). See Hornung 2016, 183–84.

[55] Bingham 1840, 445–51; Poschmann 1954; Schwartz 1911, 44–52.

[56] Bingham 1840, 448.

[57] Bingham 1840, 448.

[58] Cf. C Anc. (314), can. 4 (Beneševič 1937, 120): "[...] εὐχῆς δὲ μόνης κοινωνῆσαι δύο ἔτη [...]".

[59] Bingham 1840, 450: "The last order of penitents were the συνιστάμενοι, 'Consistentes' or Co-standers, so called from their having liberty (after the other penitents, energumens, and catechumens, were dismissed) to stand with the Faithful at the altar, and join in the common prayers, and see the oblation offered; but yet they might neither make their own oblations, nor partake of the eucharist with them."

granted the latter a shorter period of repentance because they had not yet been baptized.[60]

Canon 12 dealt with those who had quit military service (ἀποθέμενοι τὰς ζώνας[61]) after their conversion, but then tried to return to it again.[62] Perhaps this canon can also be understood against the background of the anti-Christian measures of Licinius.[63] Eusebius of Caesarea reported that Licinius forced soldiers to make pagan sacrifices to prove their loyalty.[64] It is conceivable that some Christians withdrew from the military because of this, but may later have asked to be reinstated, which could then be interpreted as apostasy. According to the canon, they should be among the Hearers for three years and then ten years among the Prostrators. However, the seriousness and intensity of their penance should be examined by the bishop. If such was discernible through fear (φόβῳ), tears (δάκρυσιν), perseverance (ὑπομονῇ), and the good works (ἀγαθοεργίαις) of the penitents, the bishop could shorten their penance and, after three years of being among the Hearers, allow them to participate in prayer. But those whose penitential zeal was deemed rather low, thinking that the outward form (σχῆμα) of penitence was already sufficient to be reintegrated in the church, had to complete their term to the full.

Canon 13 confirmed the old canonical rule (ὁ παλαιὸς καὶ κανονικὸς νόμος) that all those who were near death (τῶν ἐξοδευόντων) should receive the *viaticum* (ἐφόδιον[65]). But if someone, for whose salvation one had given up hope (ἀπογνωσθείς[66]), had received the *viaticum* and became healthy again, he should only be allowed to participate in prayer "until the term fixed by this great ecumenical synod has been completed."[67] He was therefore assigned to the last order of penitence. In general, the bishop should give communion to all who were close to death, after an examination.

Reconciliation of Members of Heterodox Groups

In two canons, the Council of Nicaea dealt with the readmission of members of two separated groups who wished to return to the Church.

---

60   Hornung 2016, 191.
61   Literally: "who have taken off their military belts."
62   On the view of military service in pre-Constantinian Christianity, see Brennecke 1997.
63   L'Huillier 1996, 67–68.
64   Eus., *HE* 10.8.10.
65   Lampe 1961, 588 s.v. "ἐφόδιον."
66   Lampe 1961, 190 s.v. "ἀπογινώσκω": despair, give up hope (of salvation).
67   L'Huillier 1996, 69, suspects that this clause is a later addition (*scholion*), that is, not from the Council of Nicaea itself.

Canon 8 was dedicated to the Novatianists, who also called themselves καθαροί (the "pure ones").[68] They were formed in the middle of the third century, when the Roman presbyter Novatian and his followers refused to give the Christians who had lapsed from the faith in the Decian persecution any possibility of penance.[69] This led to a fierce dispute with the Roman bishop Cornelius, such that Novatian and his followers were excommunicated.[70] Under Novatian's leadership, a separate church with its own clergy emerged, which, although rigorous on moral issues, otherwise shared the doctrine of the wider Church.[71] The Council of Nicaea gave rules for Novatian clerics (but not for the laity) who wanted to join the Catholic Church. Former members of the Novatian clergy were to receive an imposition of hands, which very probably implied a re-ordination, and were then accepted into the clergy.[72] However, they first had to declare in written form (ἐγγράφως) that they would follow all of the teachings of the "Catholic and Apostolic Church" (τῆς καθολικῆς καὶ ἀποστολικῆς ἐκκλησίας). In particular, they were required to be willing to have communion with those who had remarried after the death of their spouse (δίγαμοι),[73] as well as with the *lapsi* (τοῖς ἐν τῷ διωγμῷ παραπεπτωκόσιν), who were received again after a period of penance. They should remain in the same clerical rank which they also held with the Novatianists. In areas where only Novatian clergymen

[68] This self-designation, mentioned in canon 8, is also documented by inscriptions on graves. See Wallraff 1997, 254, n. 8.

[69] Mattei 2013.

[70] Mattei 2013, 1149.

[71] Wallraff 1997, 251–79.

[72] The expression χειροθετουμένους αὐτούς has been discussed intensively. Vogt 1968, 192, considers this imposition of hands as a "gesture of reconciliation," while Wallraff 1997, 258, n. 25, identifies it with the re-ordination of the Novatian clerics and translates it as follows: The synod decides that "when the hand is laid on them for ordination, they may remain in the clergy." Wallraff confirms his view by pointing out that ancient readers and translators of the Nicene canons had already applied the passage to an ordination. Cf. Rufinus, *Historia ecclesiastica* 10.6 (GCS 9.2, 967): *clericos in ordine quidem suscipi debere, sed ordinatione data*. L'Huillier 1996, 59–60, also assumes a re-ordination.

[73] Cereti 1991 understands δίγαμοι to be divorced and remarried people, which does not convince, however, due to the ancient sources concerning the practice of the Novatianists. See Crouzel 1978. The rejection of a second marriage after the death of the spouse was a typical characteristic of the eastern Novatianists, although there were differences. Socrates (Socr.), *Historia ecclesiastica* (*HE*) 5.22.60, mentioned that the Novatians in Phrygia excluded δίγαμοι, while the Novatians in Constantinople were undecided on this issue. According to Epiphanius, *Panarion* 59.4.1–3, the Novatians transferred to all laypeople the provision of 1 Tim. 3:2, 8, which applies to bishops and deacons, that they should be a man of one woman. See Wallraff 1997, 259, n. 28. Also in the Church such a second marriage, especially in the East, was often judged at least negatively, sometimes even punished with penance. See Kötting 1957.

existed, this practice was uncomplicated.[74] But difficulties could arise in the case of Novatian bishops, when there was also a Catholic bishop in a given city at the same time. Then, the Novatian bishops should receive the rank of a presbyter or chorbishop.[75] However, the bishop who received him had the possibility of granting him the honour of the title (τῆς τιμῆς τοῦ ὀνόματος). This obviously meant that a former Novatian bishop might retain the title but without having any episcopal jurisdiction. It should be avoided under all circumstances that there be two bishops in one city (ἵνα μὴ ἐν τῇ πόλει δύο ἐπίσκοποι ὦσιν).[76] Since the differences between the Catholic and Novatian churches were purely disciplinary and not doctrinal,[77] a rebaptism of the Novatianists willing to return was not required by the fathers of the Nicene council.[78]

The situation was quite different with the admission of the so-called Paulianists, which was regulated in canon 19. These were the followers and disciples of Paul of Samosata,[79] bishop of Antioch, who was deposed by an Antiochene council (268) and was regarded as a propagator of a heretical doctrine of the Son.[80] The Council of Nicaea decreed that Paulianists had to be rebaptized if they wanted to be admitted into the Catholic Church. In contrast to the Novatianists, the baptism of the Paulianists was not recognized as valid, since in the

---

[74] The canon explicitly says that there were villages and cities where only a Novatian cleric existed (ἔνθα μὲν οὖν πάντες εἴτε ἐν κώμαις εἴτε ἐν πόλεσιν αὐτοὶ μόνον εὑρίσκοιντο χειροτονηθέντες).

[75] Kirsten 1954; McHugh 1997, 242: "Bishop responsible for the care of people living in rural districts." The syllable *chor-* is taken from Greek ἡ χώρα (country). The intention of the Nicene canon is therefore to make a Novatian bishop "an auxiliary for a rural area administratively dependent on the city" (L'Huillier 1996, 60).

[76] In the background is the principle "one city-one bishop," which is widely testified in the ancient Church. See L'Huillier 1996, 61.

[77] Socr., HE 1.10, reported on the Novatian Bishop Acesius, who was summoned by Constantine to the Council of Nicaea and declared that he had no difficulties in accepting the Nicene Creed or the decision regarding Easter. The only divisive issue he mentioned was the question of the reconciliation of the lapsed.

[78] It is true, as Wallraff 1997, 259, points out, that the question of recognition of Novatian baptism was not explicitly solved in the Nicene canon. However, a comparison with canon 19 suggests that the lack of mention of this problem can be understood as an implicit recognition. C Laod., can. 6 (Beneševič 1937, 115), requires those who wished to convert from the Novatianists and other heterodox movements to the Catholic Church to condemn their old beliefs and accept the Catholic profession of faith. Afterwards, they should receive an anointing with chrism and were accepted into the church. Indeed, a rebaptism was not demanded.

[79] Vössing 2015.

[80] Fischer and Lumpe 1997, 357–64. The Christology of Paul of Samosata is hardly recognizable anymore. In the fourth and fifth centuries he was branded as a forerunner of Arius and was regularly counted among the heretics. See Vössing 2015, 1262.

eyes of the Nicene bishops the latter had adhered to a heterodox view of the Son in relation to the Father. Paulinian clerics were to be tested for their suitability and then either removed or rebaptized and consecrated. The canon maintained that a similar approach was to be taken with deaconesses and all those listed in the κανών. With regard to deaconesses, it specifically stipulated that they had to be counted among the laity due to the lack of an imposition of hands. Why this was specifically emphasized by the bishops is the subject of controversial discussion among scholars. According to Martimort and others, the lack of imposition of hands and its consequence on the occasion of a possible assumption of deaconesses in the large Church should only be recalled, but a rejection of a perhaps divergent practice of the Paulianists was not necessarily to be assumed.[81]

Liturgy

Canon 20 forbade kneeling on Sundays and during Easter time (ἐν ταῖς τῆς πεντηκοστῆς ἡμέραις) at church services. Prayers should be offered standing instead. The aim of the regulation was the uniformity of liturgical practice in all dioceses (ἐν πάσῃ παροικίᾳ). However, there was no explanation for this rule given in the canon, although one might be found in some remarks of Christian authors.[82] Sunday as the day of resurrection is a day of joy (χαρμοσύνης ἡμέρα),[83] and was considered an image of the future eternity (τοῦ προσδοκωμένου αἰῶνος εἰκών),[84] and, as well as the whole of Easter time,[85] a symbol of resurrection.[86] The gesture of

---

81 Martimort 1982, 101–2: "The precision given by the council on the subject of deaconesses was not intended on this point to set in opposition the use of the Paulinianists to that of the Church, but perhaps to make understood what this institution of deaconesses was, little known and not widespread beyond the eastern regions." See also L'Huillier 1996, 82: "Consequently, we cannot affirm that the phrase 'We have mentioned the deaconesses [...]' is uniquely related to the Paulianists. If this phrase concerns deaconesses in general, maybe the fathers of Nicea wanted to remind people that this type of ministry did not have a priestly character properly speaking."

82 Alexopoulos 2017, 368.

83 Peter of Alexandria, *De Paschate ad Tricentium*, frg. (Joannou 1963, 58): Τὴν γὰρ κυριακὴν χαρμοσύνης ἡμέραν ἄγομεν διὰ τὸν ἀναστάντα ἐν αὐτῇ, ἐν ᾗ οὐδὲ γόνατα κλίνειν παρειλήφαμεν. This fragment has been handed down in the canonical tradition as canon 15 of Peter of Alexander and probably comes from his writing *De Paschate ad Tricentium*. See CPG 1640.

84 Basil (Bas.), *Liber de spiritu sancto* (*Spir.*) 27.66.

85 Bas., *Spir.* 27.66 (Pruche 1947, 486): Καὶ πᾶσα δὲ ἡ πεντηκοστὴ τῆς ἐν τῷ αἰῶνι προσδοκωμένης ἀναστάσεώς ἐστιν ὑπόμνημα. Cf. Tertullian, *De corona* 3.4.

86 Theodoret, *Quaestiones et responsiones ad orthodoxos* 126 (Papadopoulos-Kerameus 1895, 117–18: [...] τὸ δὲ ἐν τῇ κυριακῇ μὴ κλίνειν γόνυ σύμβολόν ἐστι τῆς ἀναστάσεως [...]

kneeling, which was understood as a reference to repentance over sin, was seemingly incompatible with the joy of Christ's resurrection.[87]

SOME ASPECTS OF THE ANCIENT RECEPTION OF THE NICENE CANONS

The importance of the Council of Nicaea grew continually due to the fact that after the troubles of the fourth century caused by the controversy over the famous term *homoousios*, the pro-Nicenes had finally emerged victorious. Thus, the initial focus, of course, was on the *fides Nicaena*. Hermann Joseph Sieben traced in detail this process of a continuous increase of its authority in the course of the fourth century.[88] The disciplinary canons seem to have benefited from the prominent significance of the Council of Nicaea, since in comparison to other Greek canons they have hardly any special content.

The high appreciation attached to the Nicene canons can be seen in the fact that they usually directly follow the Apostolic canons in canonical collections and are thus at the head of all synodical canons, even before earlier councils such as Ancyra (314) or Neocaesarea (315/19). This order is also found in the second canon of the Quinisextum, which lists the canonical sources binding on the eastern Church.[89] In some western collections, the Nicene canons are preluded by a short poem written in elegiac distiches which probably originated at the turn of the fifth to the sixth centuries. The canons are called the "summits of venerable law" (*venerandi culmina iuris*). They are reins (*frena*) through which the clergy is guided in a just manner (*iusto moderamine*). The bishops (*pontifices summi*) followed the orders of the ancients (*veterum praecepta*) and explained them in their admonitions (*planius haec monitis exposuere suis*).[90]

In western and in eastern canonical texts one can observe quite a few explicit as well as implicit references to the Nicene canons. For instance, the fathers of the Council of Toledo (400) declared that the consecration of clerics should be based above all on the decisions of the Council of Nicaea. Anyone who acted against them must be considered excommunicated.[91] Other western synods also allude to the canons of

---

[87] Cf. Bas., *Spir.* 27.66 (Pruche 1947, 486): Καὶ καθ᾽ ἑκάστην δὲ γονυκλισίαν καὶ διανάστασιν, ἔργῳ δείκνυμεν, ὅτι διὰ τῆς ἁμαρτίας εἰς γῆν κατερρύημεν, καὶ διὰ τῆς φιλανθρωπίας τοῦ κτίσαντος ἡμᾶς εἰς οὐρανὸν ἀνεκλήθημεν.

[88] See Sieben 1979, 198–230. See also Ulrich 1994.

[89] C Trull. (691/92) can. 2 (*ACO* 2.2.4, Ohme 2013, 24).

[90] Turner 1904, 1.2.105; see Maassen 1870, 45–46.

[91] Council of Toledo (400), prol. (Martínez Díez and Rodríguez 1984, 326–28).

Nicaea.[92] In addition, the letters of the Roman bishops often contain citations and allusions to them.[93] Leo the Great specifically emphasized the importance of the Nicene canons: they have been enacted by the Holy Spirit (*illa Nicaenorum canonum per Spiritum vere sanctum ordinate conditio*) and have their validity until the end of the world (*in finem mundi*). Everything that contradicts them has to be suspended without hesitation (*sine cunctatione cassatur*).[94] Some eastern examples of references to the Nicene canons can be found in letters written by bishops,[95] and also in later synodal texts.[96] The canons of Nicaea were also received in the Persian Church as the decisions of the Synod of Seleukia-Ktesiphon (410) clearly show.[97] The high authority of the Council of Nicaea has even led to the creation of pseudepigraphic Nicene canons. In particular, eighty-four canons have been handed down in Arabic and Ethiopian, some of which find their counterparts in the seventy-three Syrian pseudo-Nicene canons contained in a treatise on the Council of Nicaea attributed to Marutha from Maipherkat.[98]

An insightful episode can be found in the acts of the Carthaginian synod of the year 419.[99] Apiarius of Sicca, a North African presbyter, had been excommunicated by his bishop and had appealed to the Roman bishop Zosimus, who accepted the petition of Apiarius.[100] The legitimacy of this approach was questioned by the North African bishops who generally rejected *appellationes transmarinae*, that is, appeals going beyond North Africa to Rome. Zosimus had justified this practice in a *commonitorium*,[101] by referring his right of appeal to canons which he falsely attributed to the Council of Nicaea (although they were in fact Serdican canons).[102] The North African bishops assembled in Carthage

[92] Cf. Council of Valence (374), can. 3 (Munier 1963, 39); Council of Riez (439), can. 3 (Munier 1963, 66).
[93] Thus, see Siricius, *Epistulae* 1.1 (Zechiel-Eckes 2013, 86; 1.12 (Zechiel-Eckes 2013, 108); 5.2.2 (PL 13:1158A); Innocent, *Epistulae* 5 (PL 20:495A). See also Speigl 1975.
[94] Leo the Great, *Epistulae* 106.2.4 (PL 54, 1005B).
[95] See Bas., *Epistulae* 55; Theophilus of Alexandria, *Epistula ad Aphyngium* (Joannou 1963, 271).
[96] Cf. Council of Constantinople (381), can. 2 (Beneševič 1937, 32–33); Second Council of Nicaea (787), can. 3 (*ACO* 2.3.3, Lamberz 2016, 900–2); can. 6 (*ACO* 2.3.3, Lamberz 2016, 906).
[97] Bruns 2000.
[98] Graf 1944, 586–593. See also *CPG* 8521.5; 8523.3.4.
[99] Munier 1963, 89–155.
[100] See Marschall 1971, 161–73. Also see the discussion by Geoffrey Dunn, below 361–63.
[101] See Munier 1963, 90–91.
[102] Apparently, in some manuscripts the canons of Serdica are connected with those of Nicaea. See Maassen 1870, 52–63.

did not immediately follow the argumentation of the Roman bishop, since they could not find the corresponding canon among those of Nicaea, but they assured him that they would exactly observe the decisions of Nicaea. Therefore, the bishops decided to ask their colleagues in Antioch, Alexandria, and Constantinople for the *exemplaria verissima* of the Nicene canons in order to examine the claim of Zosimus. Until then, the African bishops wanted to observe the canons in question. In the meantime Apiarius had been excommunicated again and appealed to the Roman bishop Celestine, the successor of Zosimus, who had taken Apiarius back into the ecclesiastical community. The Carthaginian synod of 424/25 addressed Celestine in a letter and objected to his behaviour. On the one hand, they pointed out that the canons quoted by his predecessor Zosimus in no way came from the Council of Nicaea,[103] and on the other hand they referred to canon 5 of Nicaea, which forbade a bishop from accepting a person excommunicated by another bishop.[104] This dispute over the legality of transmarine appeals was practically based on alleged and genuine Nicene canons, which underlines the high esteem and authority of the Nicene canons in such discussions.

DESIDERATA

The canons of Nicaea have already been widely discussed in research because of their importance in ecclesiastical law. However, there is still no comprehensive critical edition of their text, which takes into account all textual witnesses, both the Greek text tradition and the various translations or paraphrases, such as those of Rufinus of Aquileia or Gelasius of Cyzicus. Based on such an *editio maior*, a detailed historical-philological commentary could be written, which bundles the many individual investigations and lays a solid and useful foundation for an occupation with the Nicene canons. Finally, another interesting field of research would be to investigate the history of their reception from late antiquity to late Byzantine times.

---

[103] Council of Carthage (424/25) (Munier 1974, 171–72): *Nam ut aliqui tamquam a tua sanctitatis latere mittantur, in nullo invenimus partum synodo constitutum; quia illud quod pridem per eumdem coepiscopum nostrum Faustinum tamquam ex parte Nicaeni concilii exinde transmisisti, in codicibus verioribus [...] tale aliquid non potuimus repperire.*

[104] C Carth (424/25) (Munier 1974, 170): *Impendio deprecamur ut deinceps ad vestras aures hinc venientes non facilius admittatis, nec a nobis excommunicatos in communione ultra velitis excipere; quia hoc etiam Nicaeno concilio definitum facile advertat venerabilitas tua.*

SELECT REFERENCES

Alberigo, Giuseppe, and Hubert Jedin, eds. 1991. *Conciliorum oecumenicorum decreta*. Bologna: Edizione Dehoniane.

Beneševič, Vladimir. 1937. *Ioannis Scholastici Synagoga L titulorum ceteraque eiusdem opera iuridica*. Abhandlungen der Bayerischen Akademie der Wissenschaften: Philosophisch-Historische Abteilung, Neue Folge 14. Munich: Verlag der Bayerischen Akademie der Wissenschaften.

Beneševič, Vladimir. (1906) 1974. *Drevne-slavjanskaja kormcaja XIV titulov bez tolkovanij (Syntagma XIV titulorum sine scholiis secundum versionem Palaeo-Slovenicam, adjecto textu Graeco e vetustissimis codicibus manuscriptis exarato*. St. Petersburg, 1906. Reprinted Leipzig: Zentralantiquariat der Deutschen Demokratischen Republik.

Hefele, Carl Joseph von, and Henri Leclercq. 1907. *Histoire des conciles d'après les documents originaux*, 1.1. Paris: Letouzey et Ané.

Joannou, Périclès-Pierre, ed. 1963. *Discipline générale antique (IVe–IXe s.)*, vol. 2: *Les canons des Pères Grecs*. Fonti: Pontificia commissione per la redazione del codice di diritto canonico orientale ser. 1, 9.2. Grottaferrata (Roma): Tipografia Italo-Orientale "S. Nilo."

Lafontaine, Paul-Henri. 1963. *Les conditions positives de l'Accession aux Ordres dans la première legislation ecclésiastique (300–492)*. Ottawa: Éditions de l'Université d'Ottawa.

L'Huillier, Peter. 1996. *The Church of the Ancient Councils: The Disciplinary Work of the First Four Ecumenical Councils*. Crestwood, NY: St Vladimir's Seminary Press.

Linck, Heinrich. 1908. *Zur Übersetzung und Erläuterung der Kanones IV, VI und VII des Konzils von Nicaea*. Gießen: Münchow'sche Hof- und Universitäts-Druckerei.

Lübeck, Konrad. 1901. *Reichseinteilung und kirchliche Hierarchie des Ostens bis zum Ausgange des vierten Jahrhunderts: Ein Beitrag zur Rechts- und Verfassungsgeschichte der Kirche*. Kirchengeschichtliche Studien 5.4. Münster: Schöningh.

Ohme, Heinz. 1998. *Kanon ekklesiastikos: Die Bedeutung des altkirchlichen Kanonsbegriff*. Arbeiten zur Kirchengeschichte 67. Berlin: De Gruyter.

Ohme, Heinz. 2012. "Greek Canon Law to 691/2." In *The History of Byzantine and Eastern Canon Law to 1500*, ed. Wilfried Hartmann and Kenneth Pennington, 24–114. Washington, DC: The Catholic University of America Press.

Poschmann, Bernhard. 1954. "Bußstufen (Bußstationen)." In *RAC* 2: 814–16.

Tanner, S. J., Norman P., ed. 1990. *Decrees of the Ecumenical Councils*, vol. 1. London: Sheed & Ward.

Ulrich, Jörg. 1994. *Die Anfänge der abendländischen Rezeption des Nizänums*. Patristische Texten und Studien 39. Berlin: De Gruyter.

Weckwerth, Andreas. 2010. *Ablauf, Organisation und Selbstverständnis westlicher antiker Synoden im Spiegel ihrer Akten*. Jahrbuch für Antike und Christentum: Ergänzungsband Kleine Reihe 5. Münster: Aschendorff Verlag.

Wohlmuth, Josef, ed. 1998. *Dekrete der ökumenischen Konzilien*, vol 1. Paderborn: Ferdinand Schöningh.

9 The Council of Nicaea and the Celebration of the Christian Pasch

DANIEL P. MC CARTHY

INTRODUCTION

In AD 525 in Rome Dionysius Exiguus (d. *c.* 550) sent his continuation of the Alexandrian Paschal (Easter) table for 532–626 to an otherwise unknown bishop Petronius, accompanied by a letter in which he asserted that the Council of Nicaea had established the nineteen-year cycle of Paschal full moons to be used for Paschal calculation. Ever since the time of the astronomer Meton in the fifth century BC, the Greek scientific world possessed a good numerical approximation to the movements of the sun and moon. Meton equated nineteen solar years of about 365¼ days each, with 235 lunar months of length either 29 or 30 days. These months were synchronized so that the fourteenth day (luna 14) of each lunar month corresponded fairly closely with the actual occurrence of the full moon. Christians came eventually to use a version of this 19-year cycle to choose a springtime full moon as their Paschal full moon. Dionysius further declared that this cycle had subsequently been maintained by the Alexandrian bishops Athanasius (d. 373), Theophilus (d. 412) and Cyril (d. 444).[1] This table schedules Pasch on the Sunday which falls between luna 15 and luna 21 inclusive, and after 21 March, the date assumed for the spring equinox; I shall refer to this as the Alexandrian Paschal tradition.

It was Dionysius's table which eventually came to determine the Paschal celebration for the entire western Christian church and, consequently, up until the early eighteenth century the Council of Nicaea was repeatedly cited as the primary authority for this celebration. Dionysius's table listed for the ninety-five years, AD 532–626, the date of the Paschal luna 14, the date of the Pasch, and the age of the moon on that day, together with related chronological criteria. However, in 1718 Johann Wilhelm Jan challenged Dionysius's claim that the council had

---

[1] Krusch 1938, 63–68, for the letter to Petronius, 69–74, for Paschal table. For Meton's 19-year cycle, see Toomer 1998, 12.

authorized a 19-year lunar cycle.[2] In 1770 Christian Walch comprehensively reviewed the early and medieval literature and concluded that the council had not made any ruling concerning either a lunar cycle or observation of the equinox.[3] Subsequently some scholars endorsed these conclusions, while others disputed the matter.[4] Recently Alden Mosshammer, in the most wide-ranging study ever published in English of the Christian Paschal computus, offered the opinion that this "denial to Nicaea of any Paschal rule may have gone too far," and suggested that "the Council 'apparently' or 'implicitly' endorsed the rule of the equinox, even if it published no rule as such."[5]

In this chapter I shall consider the matter by: first examining the Gospel accounts of Jesus's Passion and resurrection which provide the basis for the Christian celebration of the Pasch; then reviewing the Christian Paschal practice prior to the Council of Nicaea in order to understand the circumstances for the council's deliberations upon the Paschal celebration; then considering contemporaneous documents that mention the council's discussion of the Pasch; finally, examining the question of the inception of the Alexandrian Paschal tradition.

SCRIPTURAL BASIS FOR THE CHRISTIAN PASCHAL CELEBRATION

By the middle of the second century the Gospels were established as the authoritative account of the life of Jesus, and all four give a closely corresponding version of Jesus's final days in Jerusalem. They all relate a sequence commencing with his Last Supper, seizure by the Jews, judgement and condemnation by Pontius Pilate, crucifixion, entombment, and resurrection. Comparison of the temporal references associated with these events shows that each Evangelist has the same relative chronology for them extending over three nights. These commence with the Last Supper on the evening of the first night, followed by Jesus's entombment at the beginning of the second night, and finally the discovery of Jesus's resurrection by his followers around dawn at the end of the third night. All Evangelists also agree that the resurrection was revealed

[2] Jan 1718, 458–60 (reprinted in PL 67:453–83).
[3] Walch 1770, 53–60.
[4] Endorsed: Ideler 1825–26, 2:206; Schmid 1905, 110; Daunoy 1925, 436. Disputed: von Hefele 1871–96, 1:325; Duchesne 1880, at 5, 21–26; Jones 1943, 22.
[5] Mosshammer 2008, 52. Other important studies of computus are: Ideler 1825–26; Krusch 1880; Schwartz 1905; Krusch 1938; Jones 1943, 3–129; Strobel 1984; Warntjes 2010, xv–ccvi.

to Jesus's followers about dawn "on the first day of the week," that is on Sunday.[6] Consequently, because all Gospels give the same relative chronology from Last Supper to resurrection, all implicitly place these events on the same Jewish weekdays, namely Last Supper on the fifth day, crucifixion on the sixth day, Tomb on the Sabbath, and resurrection on the first day.

Regarding the time of these events within the solar year, all Evangelists locate them by reference to the Passover, the Jewish annual celebration of God's protection for their exodus from Egypt described in Exodus 12:1–8. Here God prescribed to Moses and Aaron that the congregation of Israel should kill and eat a lamb on the fourteenth day of the first month of the year, which fell about the time of spring. However, the Evangelists do not agree on the relationship between Passover and the crucifixion, with John placing it on the day of the Passover, while the Synoptic Gospels all place it on the day after the Passover.[7] Thus there immediately arises conflict between the Johannine and Synoptic accounts of the crucifixion and the fourteenth day of the first month. John's account of the crucifixion places it at about the time that the Jews were sacrificing their Passover lamb, while the Synoptics place it on the following day. It is the case therefore that John's Gospel uniquely associates the crucifixion with luna 14 and the sacrifice of the Passover lamb, while the Synoptic Gospels associate the crucifixion with luna 15, so that the Passover lamb and luna 14 play no role in their account of the crucifixion. Given this inherent Gospel conflict it was inevitable that luna 14 would eventually become a divisive issue amongst Christians.

A further complication for early Christians was that the two crucial events of crucifixion and resurrection occurred on two separate days, so in their celebration how were these to be acknowledged? Those who considered that it was Jesus's sacrifice on the cross that had obtained their redemption might emphasize the crucifixion, while those who considered that it was his resurrection that demonstrated his divinity and triumph over death might emphasize the resurrection. In order to respect the Gospel accounts, Christians needed to agree upon both a lunar and solar calendar and also criteria by which to identify the first lunar month of the spring. As we shall see, Christians came to

---

[6] Last Supper: Matt. 26:17–20, Mark 14:12–18, Luke 22:7–14, John 13:1–29; crucifixion: Matt. 27:45–50, Mark 15:33–37, Luke 23:44–46, John 19:14–16; Tomb: Matt. 27:57, Mark 15:42–43, Luke 23:50–54, John 19:31–38; resurrection: Matt. 28:1–6, Mark 16:2–7, Luke 24:1–5, John 20:1–18.

[7] Johannine–Synoptic conflict: Jones 1943, 7; Mosshammer 2008, 45; Nothaft 2012, 23–25.

choose the spring equinox as the criterion for the first lunar month, but here further ambiguity arose. The Roman calendar placed the spring equinox on 25 March, whereas the Alexandrian polymath Claudius Ptolemy (d. c. 175), in his authoritative astronomical compilation, the *Mathematical systematic treatise* (μαθηματικὴ σύνταξις), placed it on 22 March for the year 140. Moreover, Ptolemy stated that it would advance by approximately one day in 300 years, implying that it must eventually advance to 21 March.[8] We shall see that this one-day shift was to play an important role in the evolution of Christian Paschal celebration.

While decisions upon the lunar calendar and the first month were sufficient for those who celebrated on luna 14, which tradition came to be designated by its opponents as "Quartodecimanism," on the other hand those who wished their feast to fall on feria 1, Sunday, had further to agree on a range of seven lunar days to accommodate this. The Latin word *feria* followed by a number between one and seven inclusive was used by Christians from the third century on to identify the weekdays, where Sunday = feria 1, [...], Saturday = feria 7.[9] This question also proved problematic and divisive, and instances of celebration on luna 14–20, luna 15–21 and luna 16–22 are all attested. When one contemplates the situation that confronted the Christians of the second century it is apparent that they faced difficult questions in determining both how and when they should celebrate these events. With no scriptural authority to guide them through most of these questions, diverse results were unavoidable.

CELEBRATION OF THE CHRISTIAN PASCH PRIOR TO NICAEA

I now consider sources that refer to the Christian celebration of Pasch prior to the Council of Nicaea and begin with the *Ecclesiastical History* (*Historia Ecclesiastica* [*HE*]) of Eusebius of Caesarea (d. 339), his final edition completed before the council, drawing upon his earlier *Chronological Canons*.[10] The final edition of these *Canons*, extending year by year from

---

[8]   Toomer 1998, 137–8, for spring equinox on 22 March in AD 140 and the slow equinoctial advance of this date by one day in about 300 years.

[9]   The earlier Latin usage was plural, *feriae* (festivals), but the Christian usage of the singular, *feria* with an integer 1–7, dates at least from Tertullian (d. c. 240). See Mosshammer 2008, 81.

[10] Compilation dates of the *Chronological Canons* and *Ecclesiastical History*: Barnes 1981, 111–13; Burgess 1997, at 482, 486, 496, 501.

the birth of Abraham eventually to 325, demonstrates Eusebius's interest in chronology, while his nine references to Pasch in *HE* indicate his interest in this matter. The further fact that Eusebius attended the council and subsequently compiled two works that refer to the council's decisions on Pasch, namely his *On Easter* and *Life of Constantine*, make his documents essential reading for any student of the council's deliberations on Pasch.

Eusebius's first reference to Pasch in *HE* recounts a meeting in Rome *c.* 155 between Anicetus of Rome (d. *c.* 160) and Polycarp of Smyrna (d. *c.* 155), at which they discussed "a certain question relating to the day of the Pascha."[11] Thus from the very outset Eusebius identifies Paschal conflict. Then, Eusebius quotes the work of Melito of Sardis (d. *c.* 190), "On the Pascha" (composed *c.* 166), telling that "there arose a great discussion in Laodicea concerning the Pascha."[12] Next, *c.* 190, under the heading "The Paschal Controversy," Eusebius relates that:

> For the communities of the whole of Asia, relying on a tradition of great antiquity, thought they ought to observe the fourteenth day of the moon – the day on which the Jews were ordered to sacrifice the lamb – as the day for the festival of the Saviour's Pascha [...] no matter on what day of the week it should fall. But it was not the custom for the churches throughout all the rest of the world thus to celebrate it, preserving as they did by an apostolic tradition the custom which had obtained hitherto, that it was not proper to end the fast on any other day than on the day of the resurrection of our Saviour.[13]

Thus this account, Eusebius's earliest actual description of Christian Paschal conflict, explicitly identifies that the Asian dioceses had adopted the "fourteenth day of the moon" as the key datum for their celebration, whereas elsewhere celebration on Sunday (feria 1) prevailed. As a result episcopal synods were convened and, according to Eusebius, these "unanimously drew up in letters an ecclesiastical decree for the faithful everywhere, to the effect that the mystery of the Lord's resurrection from the dead should never be celebrated on any other but the Lord's day, and that on that day alone we should observe the close of the paschal fast."[14] For their part the Asian bishops defended their luna 14 custom by referring to their early Christian tradition, and Eusebius continues by quoting

[11] Eusebius (Eus.), *Historia ecclesiastica* (*HE*) 4.14.1. Schwartz and Mommsen, 1903–9; translated by Lawler and Oulton 1928, 1:115.
[12] Eus., *HE* 4.26.2–3; Lawler and Oulton 1928, 1:131–32.
[13] Eus., *HE* 5.23.1–2; Lawler and Oulton 1928, 1:168,
[14] Eus., *HE* 5.23.2.

a letter from Polycrates of Ephesus (d. *c.* 196), writing to Victor of Rome (d. 198): "For indeed in Asia great luminaries have fallen asleep, such as shall rise again on the day of the Lord's appearing [...] Philip, one of the twelve apostles [...] John too, he who leant back on the Lord's breast [...] Polycarp too [...] and Thraseas [...] These all observed the fourteenth day for the Pascha according to the Gospel."[15] Here Polycrates's reliance on "the Gospel" can only refer to John's Gospel for the "fourteenth day," as does his reference to John who leant "on the Lord's breast." Polycrates's statement shows that the Asian churches' choice of the fourteenth moon for Pasch rested upon the authority of John's Gospel, not on the Jewish tradition of Passover as Eusebius's account suggests.

Eusebius then recounts that Victor proclaimed the excommunication of all the Asian communities on the ground of unorthodoxy, but this did have the support of other bishops. In particular, Irenaeus of Lyon (d. *c.* 202) counselled moderation, writing that "this variety of observance did not originate in our time, but much further back, in the times of those before us." Irenaeus also affirmed the importance of the disciple John to the Asian tradition, writing that Polycarp "had always observed with John the disciple of our Lord and the other apostles with whom he consorted," and he pointed out how Anicetus and Polycarp had accommodated each other's practices and "they held communion with one another."[16]

Next, Eusebius writing of events of *c.* 196 states that bishops from Palestine, Tyre, and Ptolomais assembled in Palestinian Caesarea and "treated at length of the tradition concerning the Pascha that had come down to them." They composed a letter in which they declared "that they in Alexandria do also hold it on the same day as do we. For they receive letters from us, and us from them, to the end that we may keep the holy day in concord and at the same time."[17] From the foregoing we can see that by the end of the second century serious antagonism had developed in Rome towards the Asian churches, and a concordance had been established between the Palestinian and Alexandrian churches on the need to synchronize their Sunday Paschal celebration. This they accomplished by distributing an announcement by letter, which would clearly imply that there did not then exist any agreed method capable of reliably scheduling the date in advance. Their scheme presented some obvious difficulties: the matter of first obtaining Palestinian–Alexandrian

---

[15]   Eus., *HE* 5.24.2–6; Lawler and Oulton 1928, 1:169.
[16]   Eus., *HE* 5.24.13, 16–17; Lawler and Oulton 1928, 1:170.
[17]   Eus., *HE* 5.25; Lawler and Oulton 1928, 1:171.

agreement on the date, and then the reliable distribution of this over a wide area. Finally, Eusebius describes the works of Clement of Alexandria (d. c. 215), including his book *On the Pascha*, where he recorded early authoritative oral traditions.[18]

It is in the opening decades of the third century that Eusebius first remarks on the appearance of scheduling techniques when he states that the Roman theologian Hippolytus (d. c. 236), had "composed the treatise On the Pascha, in which he sets forth a register of the times and puts forward a certain canon of a sixteen-year [cycle] for the Pascha, using the first year of the Emperor Alexander as a terminus," that is the year 222.[19] Independent confirmation of this cycle exists in the form of tables inscribed on the base of a statue found in Rome about 1550. On one side, under a heading identifying the first year of Alexander, are listed the dates of sixteen Paschal full moons (luna 14) and the feria of these dates for the 112 years 222–333, arranged in seven columns of sixteen years. On the other side is a similar arrangement of a 112-year table of dates of the Paschal Sunday for 222–333.[20] The sixteen-year table of Paschal full moons actually consists of an eight-year lunar cycle repeated twice, and the Paschal dates imply celebration of Pasch on Sunday falling on luna 16–22 between 20 March and 21 April inclusive. This earliest date of 20 March implies that no known equinoctial date was used to determine the Roman Paschal moon.

Further accounts of celebration on luna 16–22 from a Roman context are found in accounts of two 84-year cycles, the Ambrosian table and the table described in the Cologne prologue. Both tables implicitly commence in the late third century and so prior to the Council of Nicaea.[21] Then, within a couple of decades Eusebius states that Dionysius of Alexandria (d. c. 264), wrote "festal letters [...] with reference to the festival of the Pascha." In one of these letters Dionysius "sets forth a canon based on a cycle of eight years, proving that it is not proper to celebrate the festival of the Pascha at any other time than after the vernal equinox."[22] This is Eusebius's earliest explicit reference to the equinox in relation to the celebration of Pasch, and he indicates the use of an eight-year cycle by both Roman and Alexandrian churches. However, it

[18]   Eus., *HE* 6.13; Lawler and Oulton 1928, 1:188.
[19]   Eus., *HE* 6.22.1. Lawler and Oulton 1928, 1:195.
[20]   Hippolytus and his tables: Schwartz 1905, 34–35; Mosshammer 2008, 116–25.
[21]   Jones 1943, 26–28 for Roman Paschal limits; Krusch 1880, 227–35 for the Cologne prologue; 236–40 for the Ambrosian table; cf. Mosshammer 2008, 206–9.
[22]   Eus., *HE* 7.20.1; Lawler and Oulton 1928, 1:231–32.

is the case that the eight-year lunar cycle exhibits poor synchronism with the real moon, gaining about one day every six years.[23]

Regarding the origin of this eight-year lunar cycle, Mosshammer reviews considerable evidence from tenth-century and twelfth or thirteenth-century Coptic sources that attribute its construction to Demetrius of Alexandria (d. c. 231). The later of these sources state that Victor had convened a council which "accepted the formula of Demetrius and established the standard regulations for fasting and for Easter," thus suggesting that Demetrius may have been the source of the eight-year lunar cycle used by both Hippolytus and Dionysius.[24]

Eusebius's last reference to the Pasch is his most complex and controversial. He commences with a detailed account of Anatolius of Laodicea (d. c. 282), emphasizing his secular scholarly achievements in arithmetic, geometry, astronomy, logic, physics, and rhetoric in his native Alexandria. Anatolius was subsequently consecrated bishop in Palestinian Caesarea and then engaged as the bishop of Laodicea. Eusebius adverts to Anatolius's written works, acknowledging his eloquence and erudition, adding, "In these he presents, especially, his opinions with reference to Pascha; from which it may be necessary on the present occasion to give the following passage."[25] This diffident introduction is followed by the heading, "From the Canons of Anatolius on the Pascha," and the ensuing passage begins by stating that the first month of the first year of the 19-year cycle has a new moon on 22 March when the sun is passing through the fourth day in the first sign of the zodiac. This is followed by a protracted sequence of mutually inconsistent statements concerning zodiacal and equinoctial signs and their relation to Passover, citing Jewish authorities and concluding emphatically that all "ought to sacrifice the Passover after the vernal equinox." These statements are given in the first-person plural, but at their conclusion a voice, suddenly writing in the first-person singular, repeatedly expresses doubt about the relationship between the equinox and Passover, stating:

> I know many other statements of theirs, some of them probable, others advanced as absolute proofs, by which they attempt to establish that the Feast of the Passover and of unleavened bread ought without exception be held after the equinox. But I refrain from demanding proofs thus composed from those for whom the

[23] Schwartz 1905, 30, for the eight-year lunar cycle inaccuracy.
[24] Mosshammer 2008, 111.
[25] Eus., HE 7.32.14; Lawler and Oulton 1928, 1:248.

veil upon the law of Moses has been taken away, and for whom it now remains with unveiled face ever to behold as in a mirror Christ and the things of Christ, both what He learned and what He suffered. But that the first month with the Hebrews lies around the equinox is shown also by the teachings in the Book of Enoch.[26]

These words, which have been represented by modern editors as taken from Anatolius's Canons, are in fact the voice of Eusebius. They are an instance of the phenomenon identified by Timothy Barnes when examining the *Ecclesiastical History*:

> A close inspection of the text and a comparison of the History with the documents and writers employed as sources immediately discloses several grave deficiencies. When Eusebius paraphrases, he feels free to rewrite, to omit or to expand passages, just as if he had composed his paraphrase from memory [...] As a result, he sometimes misrepresents his authority [...] The quotations, moreover, are often preceded by introductions or paraphrases which partially contradict or are contradicted by their contents [...] In any event, it is unwise to rely on Eusebius' reports as reproducing exactly the precise tenor, or even main purport, of lost evidence.[27]

The only difference with *HE* 7.32.14–19 is that Eusebius's contradiction follows, rather than precedes, the supposed quotation. Both Robert Grant and Vincent Twomey have published similar conclusions regarding the unreliability of Eusebius's quotations.[28]

Further evidence that Eusebius's quotation of Anatolius is untrustworthy comes from Rufinus's Latin translation of the *Ecclesiastical History* compiled *c.* 402. Rufinus's Latin does not translate Eusebius's Greek, but instead provides a consistent account of the zodiacal and equinoctial signs. Moreover, when Rufinus came to Eusebius's concluding denial cited above, he contradicted it, writing. "I have read in their books also many other things expounded concerning these most valid assertions, which should show evidently that the solemnity of Easter is to be celebrated in every race after the equinox."[29] Furthermore, the Latin citation of Anatolius given by Rufinus is found almost verbatim

---

[26] Eus., *HE* 7.32.19; Lawler and Oulton 1928, 1:249. See Mc Carthy and Breen 2003, 129–34, for a detailed analysis of the inconsistencies in Eus., *HE* 7.32.14–18, versus the consistency of *DRP* §2; see 136–37, for Eusebius's authorship of *HE* 7.32.19.

[27] Barnes 1981, 140–41.

[28] Grant 1972; Twomey 1982, 19–20; cf. Mc Carthy and Breen 2003, 128–29.

[29] Rufinus, *Historia ecclesiastica* 7.32.19; I gratefully acknowledge the assistance of Dr David Howlett with this translation. Schwartz and Mommsen 1903–9, 2:725.

as part of a complete Paschal tract ascribed to Anatolius. This tract is found in eight manuscripts dating from the eighth to the eleventh centuries, the headings of five of which attribute it to Anatolius.[30] For example, the heading of Cologne, MS Dombibliothek 83^{ii} f. 188^r is *Liber Anatholii de ratione paschali*, and this is customarily shortened to *De ratione paschali (DRP)* to serve as a title for the tract. This tract was known to Sulpicius Severus in southern Gaul in *c.* 410, who used its lunar and Paschal principles as the basis for his 84-year Paschal table. Within about two decades Sulpicius's table was established in some churches of the British Isles, where it flourished for about three centuries.[31]

Consequently *DRP* was known and referenced by Insular authors such as Columbanus (d. 615) and Bede (d. 735), and in works such as Cummian's *De controversia paschali* of *c.* 633 and the anonymous Irish computistical text-book *De ratione conputandi* of *c.* 719.[32] However, from the later seventh century, as the Alexandrian Paschal tradition transmitted by Dionysius's table prevailed in the British Isles, so interest in and references to *DRP* waned. In 1633 Aegidius Bucherius published an edition of the tract from the Sirmond manuscript, supposing that Rufinus himself had made the translation.[33] In 1733 Johannes van der Hagen repeatedly referred to *DRP* as *Pseudo-Anatolii Canonem Paschalem*, without offering any justification for this designation. In 1736 he published a brief discussion of some technical details of Bucherius's edition, comparing them critically with the Alexandrian Paschal tradition, and finding difficulties with them, declared the tract to be a forgery by a seventh-century author pretending to be Anatolius. He again named this author "pseudo-Anatolius" and located him in the British Isles, most likely Scotland or Ireland.[34] Over the ensuing

---

[30] Mc Carthy and Breen 2003, 25–30 for MSS; 45 for MS headings.

[31] Sulpicius's 84-year Paschal table: Mc Carthy 1993; Mc Carthy 1994.

[32] Walsh and Ó Cróinín 1988.

[33] Bucherius 1633, 433–66; the Sirmond manuscript was identified by Charles Jones in 1937 as Oxford, Bodleian Library, Bodley 309.

[34] van der Hagen 1733, 332, 336, 339 for "Pseudo Anatolii" references; van der Hagen 1736, 118–19, where he lists seven objections to *DRP*; 123: "Haec, meo judicio, sufficere poterunt, ad probandum, quod Canon ille Latinus, a Bucherio editus, sit opus spurium, & Anatolio ab impostore suppositum" (These, by my judgement, could suffice to prove that Latin canon edited by Bucherius is a spurious work, imposed by the impostor upon Anatolius); 140: "hunc Pseudo-Anatolii Libellum conscriptum esse in seculi 7mi parte priore" (this little work of Pseudo-Anatolius was written in the early part of the seventh century) and "Unde probabilis conjectura nascitur hunc Pseudo-Anatolium Anglum, vel potius Scotum aut Hibernum fuisse" (Whence is prompted the probable conjecture that this Pseudo-Anatolius was English, or rather was Scottish or Irish).

250 years this remained the dominant scholarly view of the tract, except that the alleged forger was located specifically in Ireland and his supposed *floruit* advanced to the sixth century.[35] However, the perspective on *DRP* changed significantly in 1985 when Dáibhí Ó Cróinín discovered in Padua Biblioteca Antoniana, MS I.27 ff. 76ʳ–77ᵛ, a full copy of the 84-year Paschal table of Sulpicius Severus. Examination of its structural details showed that these derived from *DRP*, with the exception only of the length of its lunar cycle, so it became clear that the claims by Insular Christians who followed the 84-year table to be maintaining Anatolius's Paschal tradition were justified. As a result Aidan Breen and I examined all eight manuscripts of *DRP* and in 2003 published a critical edition with the conclusion that *DRP* represents an accurate translation of Anatolius's Paschal tract, a section of which Eusebius had paraphrased and distorted in *HE* 7.32.14–18.[36]

This conclusion has significant implications for our understanding of Paschal practice prior to the Council of Nicaea. On the one hand, the reconstructions of Anatolius's 19-year cycle by Schwartz and Mosshammer, which exhibit significant correlation with the Alexandrian cycle but rely on Eusebius's paraphrase of Anatolius's specification of the equinox, cannot stand, as shall be discussed further below. On the other hand, *DRP* reveals that Anatolius's Paschal table did not share any significant features with the subsequent Alexandrian Paschal tradition. Specifically it employed:

(a) The equinox defined as the four-day interval 22–25 March.
(b) Pasch celebrated on Sunday falling within luna 14–20 inclusive, and after 25 March.
(c) Full lunar months with 30 days and hollow lunar months with 29 days, each aligned respectively with the Julian 31-day and 30-day months.
(d) Only two bissextile years in the 19-year cycle.

This demonstrates that the earliest known reference to the Christian use of the 19-year lunar cycle does not relate to the origin of the Alexandrian table.[37] Moreover, it shows that Anatolius's compilation was highly

---

[35] Mc Carthy and Breen 2003, 19–23 for scholars' judgments on *DRP* from 1766 to 2000.

[36] Mc Carthy and Breen 2003, 44–53, for edition; 142–43, for conclusion. For an independent and alternative confirmation of the third-century origin of the 19-year lunar and Paschal tables of *DRP* see Zuidhoek 2017, 75–92. Using the NASA catalogue of third-century lunisolar conjunctions, Zuidhoek demonstrates that the Paschal lunae 14 of *DRP* correspond very closely with the spring full moons observed from Alexandria for 271–89; see 79, Figure 1, 86, Figure 4.

[37] Zuidhoek 2017, 90: "The classical Alexandrian cycle must have been constructed on the basis of new principles, not by manipulating the dates of the Anatolian PFM [Paschal full moon]."

speculative and synthetic, acknowledging both the Ptolemaic and Roman dates for the equinox and accommodating both the Asian preference for celebration on luna 14 and the insistence elsewhere that celebration be on Sunday. As we shall see, any such accommodation of Paschal celebration on luna 14 was subsequently prohibited by the council's decision in 325.

Anatolius's tract also furnishes considerable details of Paschal practice and events from all around the Mediterranean, referring specifically to:

(a) Hippolytus's 16-year cycle, and other unidentified 25-year, 30-year, and 84-year cycles "never arriving at the true method of calculating Pasch."

(b) That on luna 21 or luna 22 "it is impossible to offer up the true Pasch," and those who "say that the Pasch can be celebrated in this phase of the moon not only cannot corroborate that by the authority of holy scripture, but also incur the charge of sacrilege and contumacy, and endanger their souls."

(c) Certain "computists of the region of Gaul" who accept celebration on luna 21, and who "added three days before the equinox, in which they hold that the Pasch can be celebrated."

(d) That the conflict between Polycrates, insisting on luna 14 alone, and Victor, insisting on Sunday, was "settled in a peaceful manner by Irenaeus."

(e) The Asian followers of John who insinuated that "we cannot celebrate the bright beginning of Pasch after luna 14" are dismissed.

(f) The "African Novatianists, who have composed longer cycles," wherein celebration included luna 21 and was confined between 22 March and 21 April inclusive, are vehemently rejected.[38]

Collectively all the references discussed above show that before the Council of Nicaea there were very widely divergent Paschal customs spread around the Mediterranean: lunar cycles of length 8, 19, 25, 30, and 84-years; equinoctial dates of 22 and 25 March and the interval 22–25 March; Paschal lunars of luna 14–20, 15–21, and 16–22, as well as the Asian luna 14. On the other hand, we have no evidence from any source attesting to the Alexandrian church employing a 19-year cycle or choosing equinox on 21 March. These references also show that the Asian churches had adopted the Johannine luna 14 chronology for their Paschal celebration, explaining this choice by the presence of the

[38]   Mc Carthy and Breen 2003: (a) 63, *DRP* §1, (b) 65, *DRP* §4, (c) 65–66, *DRP* §5–6, (d) 66, *DRP* §7, (e) 67, *DRP* §8, (f) 69, *DRP* §12.

traditions of John and other early Christian "luminaries" in their province. Outside of Asia other churches preferred the Synoptic crucifixion chronology and chose to celebrate Pasch on Sunday. Inevitably conflict developed and in time intensified, particularly between the Roman and Asian churches, and it was this conflict that the emperor Constantine (d. 337) sought to resolve at the council he convened in Nicaea.

DOCUMENTS CONTEMPORANEOUS WITH THE COUNCIL REFERRING TO PASCH

I now consider documents composed by persons who attended the Council of Nicaea and which refer to the Pasch, commencing with a letter addressed to the "church of the Alexandrians" included by Socrates Scholasticus (d. 450) in his *Ecclesiastical History*.[39] The author of this letter considered it "indispensably necessary that a letter should be written to you on the part of the sacred Synod; in order that you may know what subjects were brought under consideration and examined, and what was eventually determined on and decreed." Socrates does not identify the author but since he twice refers to Alexander of Alexandria (d. 328), as "our most-honored fellow-minister," who has been "present with us," and who "has been a participator in whatever is transacted, and has had the principal direction of it," it is clear that the author had worked very closely with Alexander at the council. In these circumstances it seems likely that the author was Athanasius, secretary to Alexander at the council. Athanasius succeeded as bishop of Alexandria following Alexander's death on 17 April 328. The letter's account of the council's decisions concludes as follows:

> We have also gratifying intelligence to communicate to you relative to unity of judgement on the subject of the most holy feast of Easter: for this point also has been happily settled through your prayers; so that all the brethren in the East who have heretofore kept this festival when the Jews did, will henceforth conform to the Romans and to us, and to all who from the earliest time have observed our period of celebrating Easter.[40]

---

[39] Socrates (Socr.), *Historia ecclesiastica* (*HE*) 1.9. Hansen 1995; NPNF 2.2, at 12–13 (modified).

[40] Socr., *HE* 1.8; NPNF 2.2, 9, for Athanasius and Alexander; 12–13. Socr., *HE* 1.9; NPNF 2.2, 12–13, for letter. See Barnes 1981, 206: "Alexander of Alexandria was aided during his struggle with Arius by his secretary Athanasius [...] Athanasius was Alexander's protégé from an early age"; at 215: "The bishop of Alexandria received advice throughout the proceedings from his deacon Athanasius"; at 230, Alexander's date of death.

This statement clearly identifies that the resolution consisted of the acceptance by the "brethren in the East" to abandon their celebration on luna 14 and instead to celebrate with the Romans and Alexandrians on Sunday. Had the council made any further decree in favour specifically of the Alexandrian church's current Paschal tradition, it is here one would expect to find mention of it.

I turn next to Eusebius's tract *On Easter*, written *c.* 335, a Latin translation of which he sent to Constantine.[41] In this Eusebius gives a substantial account of the evolution of the Christian Pasch from the Hebrew Passover, insisting that "we celebrate the festival of our own Passover every week on the Lord's day, the day of our salvation." He then recalls that at the council the result of the debate concerning the Pasch was that:

> the party of three-quarters of the whole inhabited world prevailed by the large number of their bishops as they opposed the <bishops> of the East. For the nations of the north, of the south and of the setting sun together, gaining strength by agreeing with one another, brought forward a custom opposite to the ancient one which the bishops of the East defended. Finally, the easterners yielded the argument, and thus a single festival of Christ came about.[42]

For the remainder Eusebius cites the Synoptic Gospels in order to maintain that it was "on the fifteenth day of the lunar month, on which [. . .] our Savior was being tried by Pilate." Thus Eusebius's account of the outcome of the council's debate on the Pasch agrees with the above-mentioned letter to Alexandria, and he himself emphatically maintains the Synoptic chronology for the crucifixion and that the celebration should be held on Sunday.

Finally, I consider the references to Pasch in Eusebius's *Life of Constantine*. Eusebius suggests that Constantine's second reason for calling the Council of Nicaea was because "some claimed that one ought to follow the practice of the Jews, and some that it was right to observe the exact time of the season."[43] Regarding the outcome of this conflict he states that, "Faith prevailed in a unanimous form, and the same timing for the Festival of the Saviour was agreed on all sides."[44]

---

[41]   Cameron and Hall 1999, 326, for the date of *On Easter*.

[42]   Edition PG 24:693–706; trans. Barnes 2011, 185–91, "Appendix D: Eusebius, *On Easter* (*De Sollemnitate Paschali*)"; at 189, on the council's decision.

[43]   Eus., *De vita Constantini* (*VC*) 3.5. Cameron and Hall 1999, 123.

[44]   Eus., *VC* 3.14; Cameron and Hall 1999, 127.

Additionally, Eusebius includes a letter from Constantine to the churches in which Constantine asserts that, "on the subject of the most holy day of Easter, it was unanimously decided that it would be best for everyone to celebrate it on the same day."[45] More specifically he adds that "it was decreed unworthy to observe that most holy festival in accordance with the practice of the Jews," and Constantine concludes with a reiteration that, "to put the most important point concisely, by unanimous verdict it was determined that the most holy feast of Easter should be celebrated on one and the same day."[46] It seems clear that the references here and elsewhere to Christians celebrating according to "the practice of the Jews" were deliberately intended to denigrate the Johannine authority for the Asian luna 14 Paschal tradition. The tradition was subsequently identified by opponents with the derisory term "Quartodecimanism."

In summary these statements from participants in the council agree in identifying that the decision there on Pasch was to impose celebration on Sunday and to exclude the Asian celebration on luna 14. There is no indication whatsoever that the council made any decree concerning the matters of a lunar cycle or the equinox. Moreover, when one contemplates the wide diversity and dispersal of the then existing traditions celebrating Pasch on Sunday, the practical difficulty of arbitrating amongst them is obvious. To have endeavoured to do so would have threatened their unified opposition to the Asian luna 14 tradition.

THE INCEPTION OF THE ALEXANDRIAN PASCHAL TRADITION

All the foregoing sources except *DRP* have been examined by scholars seeking to establish the Council of Nicaea's decisions regarding Pasch. While some of these arrived at a similar conclusion to that stated above, there have been some important dissenters, as remarked in the introduction. The principal reason for this has been the estimates made concerning the inception of the 19-year lunar cycle and equinoctial date employed in the Alexandrian Paschal tradition. For if it should be demonstrated that these predated the council, then the claim made by Dionysius Exiguus regarding the origin of his table appears plausible, notwithstanding the silence of the contemporaneous sources. As stated above the reconstructions by both Schwartz and Mosshammer of

---

[45] Eus., *VC* 3.18; Cameron and Hall 1999, 128.
[46] Eus., *VC* 3.19; Cameron and Hall 1999, 129.

Anatolius's 19-year cycle have both concluded that these show that essential elements of the Alexandrian Paschal tradition did indeed pre-date the council.

In 1905 Schwartz published his very substantial study of Christian and Jewish Paschal tables, commencing with the Alexandrian cycle.[47] For this Schwartz took as his sources Eusebius's quotation of Anatolius in *HE* 7.32.14–18 and the Index prefixed to the Athanasian Paschal epistles. Athanasius's Paschal epistles present either his brief notifica-tions to the Egyptian presbyters and deacons of the date of the Pasch of the forthcoming year written around the time of the preceding Pasch – see his notification for 346 cited below – or his *Festal Letters*, which are prolonged spiritual reflections on the Pasch written shortly before the imminent Lenten fast, which also include the date of the Pasch. Their textual history has been studied intensively since the recovery of the Syriac translation in 1842, and the scholarship to 1993 is comprehen-sively reviewed by Timothy Barnes. All of the notifications and Festal letters are undated, and the only chronological data that they present is that relating to the Alexandrian calendrical date of the Pasch. Following Athanasius's death, the notifications and Festal letters preserved in Alexandria were arranged into a chronological sequence based upon these Paschal dates, and then enumerated serially 1–45 to identify them with the forty-five years of Athanasius's episcopacy from 329 to 373. The author then used these serial numbers to construct an index for these years, giving for each year the date of Pasch to which he added extensive chronological data and brief accounts of Athanasius's activ-ities, noting ten years in which Athanasius had not written a letter. From his extensive study of Athanasius's Festal letters and notifications, Alberto Camplani concluded that the Index was prefixed to these in Alexandria in *c.* 400.[48]

Schwartz took the Paschal dates of this Index as his starting point and commenced his introduction with the statement:

> Following a usage first attested for the "great" Dionysius [Feltoe, p. 64 ff.], the Alexandrian patriarchs indicated to the bishops of their parishes the yearly date of Easter through a Ἐπιστολὴ ἑορταστική [Festal letter]. Thus, through the Festal letters of

---

[47] Schwartz 1905, 3–18, Der alexandrinische Cyclus.
[48] Camplani 2003, 215–558, for notifications and letters, and 559–88, for Index; trans. Robertson 1892, 503–53, for Index and letters; Camplani 1989, 115–29, 190–93, for transmission of letters and Index. See Barnes 1993, 183–91, for a review of Festal letter scholarship.

Athanasius, Theophilus, Cyril, a great number of Alexandrian Easter dates are preserved. In addition, however, an official list was kept in the Patriarchate of the celebrated Easter celebrations; for the Index of the Athanasian Easter letters record the Festal dates also for the years in which Athanasius could not have written a letter or for which they were lost.[49]

Here, from the Paschal dates of the Index, Schwartz hypothesized an "official list" kept in the Alexandrian Patriarchate. He then continued, asserting:

> Ever since the Alexandrian Enneakaidekaeteris [19-year cycle] had taken its firm form, the Bureau of the Patriarchate of course had tables from which the festival could be calculated for each year. From such tables is borrowed the information added for each date of Easter in the Index and the headings appended to the letters of Athanasius.

Schwartz's reasoning here is circular, first inferring from the Index "an official list" (eine offizielle Liste) kept in the Patriarchate, and then inferring that the Index derived its additional chronological information from this hypothetical list, now expanded to "tables" (Tabellen). He did not consider the possibility that some of the Index's additional Paschal data might be retrospective, projected back onto the episcopacy of Athanasius. But critical examination of the Index and collation of it with the notifications and Festal letters suggest that the Paschal lunar data was indeed a retrospective compilation, dating from the time of the compilation of the Index.

First, if as Schwartz assumed, the Alexandrian Patriarchate was using a 19-year lunar cycle to schedule Pasch, there would have been no need for Athanasius to send notifications to Egypt one year in advance of the forthcoming Pasch. Indeed, to have done so would have invited conflict of authority should the dates differ. Since some of his notifications between 340 and 364 survive, it is implicit that Athanasius was determining the date of Pasch up until at least 364. Second, the timing of Athanasius's notifications written about the time of Paschal celebration suggests that he was using the Paschal moon of the present celebration to judge that for the following year and hence determine a Paschal date. These year-to-year notifications implicitly excluded the use of a predictable lunar cycle for scheduling purposes. Third, in all his

49   Schwartz 1905, 3; I gratefully acknowledge the assistance of Prof. Immo Warntjes with translations from Schwartz and access to other German source material.

surviving notifications and letters Athanasius never makes any reference
to the lunar age in relation to Pasch. Moreover, his distrustful attitude
towards both astronomical observations and tables, and those who made
them, is explicit in his letter for 367:

> They have fabricated books which they call books of tables, in
> which they show stars, to which they give the names of Saints.
> And therein of a truth they have inflicted on themselves a double
> reproach: those who have written such books, because they have
> perfected themselves in a lying and contemptible science; and as to
> the ignorant and simple, they have led them astray by evil thoughts
> concerning the right faith established in all truth and upright in the
> presence of God.[50]

Furthermore, in his letter for 333, having cited Psalm 1:1–2 warning
against accepting the "counsel of the ungodly," Athanasius, referring
to the Lord, added: "For it is not the sun, or the moon, or the host of those
other stars which illumines him, but he glitters with the high effulgence
of God over all."[51] This dismissive attitude towards all celestial objects,
and the moon in particular, is in accordance with Athanasius's presentation of the date of Pasch in his notifications and Festal letters, where he
never once adverts to the age of the Paschal moon.

Fourth, the only justification for a Paschal date offered by
Athanasius is in his notification for the year 346, where he wrote:

> Therefore, after the conclusion of this feast, which is now drawing
> to its close, on the twelfth of the month Pharmuthi, which is on the
> vii Id. Apr., Easter-day will be on the iii Kal, April; the fourth of
> Pharmuthi, according to the Alexandrians. When therefore the
> feast is finished, give notice again in these districts, according to
> early custom, thus: Easter Sunday is on the iii Kal. April, which is
> the fourth of Pharmuthi, according to the Alexandrian reckoning.
> And let no man hesitate concerning the day, neither let any one
> contend, saying, It is requisite that Easter should be held on the
> twenty-seventh of the month Phamenoth; for it was discussed in
> the holy Synod, and all there settled it to be on the iii Kal. April.
> I say then that it is on the fourth of the month Pharmuthi; for the
> week before this is much too early.[52]

---

[50]   Athanasius (Ath.), *Epistula festivalis* (*Ep. fest.*) 39; Robertson 1892, 551–52 (modified).
[51]   Ath., *Ep. fest.* 5; Robertson 1892, 517.
[52]   Ath., *Ep. fest.* 18; Robertson 1892, 544; 501, tabulates the Alexandrian months versus
       the Julian months.

Here, having first emphatically stated his own date for the Pasch of the following year, he only references the discussion at the anonymous "holy Synod" in order to endorse his own choice. Moreover, the only other justification he offers for his date is that the alternative is vaguely "much too early." Furthermore, the date on which Athanasius here insists is in fact one week later than the Alexandrian lunar cycle would schedule.

In summary, there is no evidence in either his notifications or Festal letters that Athanasius was employing a lunar cycle to schedule Pasch, and consequently there is no basis on which to assume that the Paschal lunar data of the Index originated with Athanasius.

The author of the Index, on the other hand, systematically introduces each year with the words, "In this year, Easter-day was on [...]," followed by the date of the Pasch, followed by the age of the Paschal moon, immediately followed in most instances by the age of the moon on 22 March, the lunar epact, and the feria on 24 March. The epact and feria are the essential data required to compute the Paschal date and moon. These systematic Paschal, epactal, and ferial data, continued for forty-five years, bear all the hallmarks of retrospective compilation.

Schwartz, believing the Index Paschal lunar data to originate from tables kept by the "Bureau of the Patriarchate," sought evidence to identify when "the Alexandrian Enneakaidekaeteris [19-year cycle] had taken its firm form." Observing that in 338 the Index gave Pasch on 26 March with luna 19, which then implied the acceptance on 21 March of the Paschal luna 14, he stated: "one must further conclude that in the year 338 Easter was scheduled for the first time after the full moon of 25 Phamenoth [21 March]: the canonical Enneakaidekaeteris can therefore be introduced at the earliest in 320."[53] In this way Schwartz inferred that the Bureau of the Patriarchate was using equinox on 21 March by 338, and so he advanced by eighteen years the possible starting year of their tables to 320, five years before the Council of Nicaea. But Schwartz's deduction here rests completely upon the Index Paschal datum of luna 19 which was supplied after Athanasius's death by the author of the Index. Rather, all Athanasius's notifications and Festal letters suggest that he took no interest whatsoever in the lunar age on his Paschal dates.

Schwartz, however, in order to explore what may have been the situation before his deduced starting year of 320, turned to Eusebius's quotation of Anatolius in *HE* 7.32.14–18, which he considered identified

<hr>

[53] Schwartz 1905, 3, 18.

the "precursor" (*Vorstufe*) of the Alexandrian table.[54] His reconstruction started from Eusebius's statement of a new moon (luna 1) on 22 March, from which he computed nineteen successive luna 14 dates. He tabulated these for the years 258–76 against luna 14 of the Alexandrian cycle, which demonstrated that seven dates were identical, eleven were one day in arrears, and one with a 30-day difference. This 30-day difference arose when the Alexandrian table placed Paschal luna 14 on its equinox of 21 March, whereas Schwartz's assumption of equinox on 22 March obliged him to locate his Paschal luna 14 on 20 April. Schwartz's tabulation of his reconstruction for 258–76 suggested that at least fifty years before the council, a 19-year Paschal cycle resembling the Alexandrian cycle had existed. To achieve complete correspondence this reconstruction required only the adoption of equinox on 21 March and an eleven-year advance of the saltus, which is the omission of one day from the lunar year made every nineteen years. Each of Schwartz's deductions in relation to the time of origin of the Alexandrian Paschal cycle, 320 from the Index and c. 258 from *HE* 7.32.14–18, rests upon a single, unreliable lunisolar date.

In 2008 Mosshammer, characterizing Eusebius's quotation from Anatolius as "testimony," reconsidered and revised Schwartz's reconstruction. He assumed that Anatolius had actually employed equinox on 21 March, and he advanced Schwartz's position for the saltus by eight years. Mosshammer's equinox assumption removed the only instance of a 30-day difference in Schwartz's reconstruction, while his advance of the saltus reduced the count of the one-day differences from eleven to three.[55] Like Schwartz, Mosshammer tabulated his reconstruction beside the Alexandrian cycle for 258–76, and their evident correspondence suggested that a 19-year cycle very closely related to the Alexandrian cycle and employing equinox on 21 March had existed by the middle of the third century.[56]

---

[54] Schwartz 1905, 15: "der Vorstufe der kanonischen Enneakaidekaeteris, wie sie bei Anatolius vorliegt" (the precursor to the canonical nineteen-year cycle, as was set forth by Anatolius).

[55] Mosshammer 2008, 148: "we must accept the testimony of Eusebius"; 148–50, for Schwartz's reconstruction; 156–57, for the assumption of 21 March equinox; 161, for Mosshammer's reconstruction. Zuidhoek 2017, 89, Figure 6, demonstrates that the full moons of both these reconstructions are between one and three days in advance of the observed full moon, whereas fifteen *DRP* full moons correspond precisely with the observed full moon, and the remaining four are just one day in advance.

[56] Subsequently Mosshammer 2017, 7–8, critically reconsidered the matter of Anatolius's Paschal cycle and the inferences that could be drawn from Eusebius's citation of Anatolius in *HE* 7.32.14. He wrote, "Unfortunately the fragment lacks

Mosshammer then gave a detailed account of the Index, asserting that it "contains data culled from a Paschal table," and that "its author must have used a full-fledged Paschal table," in neither instance identifying a time or place for this Paschal source table. Nevertheless, he concluded that "The Index to the Paschal letters of Athanasius is a crucially important document for the history of Paschal calculations." He then tabulated the Index's Paschal data over 328–73 beside the Alexandrian Paschal table, demonstrating that the Index data observed equinox on 21 March and Paschal lunars of luna 15–21. The Index epacts, however, differ over three years repeated after nineteen years, from which he concluded that the Index "represents an intermediate stage in the development of the [Alexandrian] cycle"; that is, he saw the Index as representing a development from his own reconstruction of Anatolius towards the Alexandrian cycle. Mosshammer, even while dating the Index "probably" to the 380s, did not consider the possibility that its lunar data may be a retrospective compilation from that time.[57] Moreover, since Egyptian astronomers considered their day commenced at midnight his assumption that Anatolius employed equinox on 21 March by 276 cannot be reconciled with Ptolemy's account of the equinoctial advance which implies that by 276 the equinox had advanced only to about 2 a.m. on 22 March.

It is clear from the foregoing discussion that the equinoctial date of 21 March played a crucial role in both the evolution of the Christian celebration of Pasch and modern scholarship concerning the history of the Alexandrian Paschal tradition. The adoption of this date may seem a trivial one-day advance from Ptolemy's date of 22 March for the year 140, but it required very substantial development: first, a well-educated, numerate Christian to read and understand Ptolemy's intricate deduction of the approximate one-day equinoctial advance in about three hundred years; second, a judgement as to how many years from 140 were needed for the equinoctial date to have advanced definitely to

---

sufficient precision and detail to permit reconstruction of the cycle," and stated specifically that, "we do not know where Anatolius positioned the saltus, what date he recognized as the vernal equinox, whether he meant literally that the Passover moon must follow the equinox or only that it must not precede it, and what rules he followed with respect to permissible dates for Easter Sunday." Finally, he described his own reconstruction of 2008 as "a novel proposal." Mosshammer's observations here on Eusebius's citation of Anatolius raise serious doubts regarding all reconstructions depending upon it, and in particular both Schwartz's and his own.

[57] Mosshammer 2008, 61, 165–66, 182, for citations; 166, on the date of the Index; 179, on tabulation for 328–73 where the Index epacts for 342–5 and 361–3 differ from the Alexandrian epacts.

21 March; third, to persuade the Christian spiritual leadership to accept this judgement. All of these steps were complex and there is no evidence that they were all accomplished until the time of Theophilus, appointed bishop of Alexandria in 385.[58]

Between his consecration as bishop and the death of Theodosius I in 395, Theophilus sent to the emperor a 100-year table of dates of the Paschal luna 14 and the Pasch, commencing at the year 380. To his table Theophilus prefixed a prologue and included a letter to Theodosius which have both survived. In the letter Theophilus stated that "many people urged us earnestly to reflect on a number of questions about the date of Easter." Consequently Theophilus undertook "to compile a table of the dates of the most blessed holy Pascha in your most blessed times from the first consulate of your God-loving name, O most blessed emperor, to a hundred years hence." He concluded by stating that it was necessary "in your most blessed times for the reliable date of the divine Pascha to be established by diligent examination in the Alexandrian Church." Thus, Theophilus claimed the table to be the result of contemporaneous research in the Alexandrian church and his own compilation, not a continuation.[59]

Then, in his prologue Theophilus stated that many people mistake the last month of winter for the first month of the year, adding:

> They do this in ignorance of the fact that spring begins on 12 kalends April, which is Phamenoth 25, and among the Syrians of Antioch and the Macedonians Dystros 21, in the solar calendar. This is the date that must be marked very carefully, lest anyone should erroneously place the fourteenth of the moon earlier and be mistaken about the Pascha, thinking that this full moon is the full moon of the first month.[60]

---

[58] Zuidhoek 2019, 72–74, has published the hypotheses based upon the NASA catalog of lunar phases that the lost archetype of the Alexandrian 19-year lunar cycle, respecting the equinox on 21 March, was compiled between 300 and 324, and that the position of the saltus of this cycle was modified after Athanasius' death by the Indexer, Theophilus, and finally Cyril. Whatever may be the final judgement of scholarship on these hypotheses it remains that Theophilus is the earliest known ecclesiastical authority to insist that 21 March is the terminus for the Paschal luna 14.

[59] Krusch 1880, 220–26, for editions of Theophilus's letter and prologue; Russell 2007, 81–84, for translations of the letter and prologue, and 81–82, for citations; Mosshammer 2017, 46–79, for editions and translations of the letter and prologue.

[60] Russell 2007, 83. Mosshammer 2017, 58, gives four recensions of this passage, one Greek and three Latin, all of which emphatically assert 12 kalends April to be the spring equinox. Russell 2007, 80, 189, n. 4, points out that an imperial rescript of 7 August 389 made Easter a legal holiday when courts would not sit, the

This is the earliest known authoritative Christian statement that 21 March marks the beginning of spring and the earliest permissible date for the Paschal luna 14. By *c.* 387 Ambrose (d. 397), bishop of Milan, was citing equinox on 21 March "according to those who are skilled in such matters."[61] This late fourth-century emergence of Christian reliance on an equinoctial date of 21 March in Alexandria and Milan, together with the contemporaneous Index evidence that a 19-year Paschal table closely approximating the Alexandrian Paschal tradition also existed in the late fourth century, suggest that Dionysius Exiguus was correct to trace the origin of the Alexandrian Paschal tradition back as far as Theophilus. But Dionysius's continuation of the tradition on through Athanasius back to Nicaea is not in accordance with our available evidence.

CONCLUSIONS

The contemporaneous statements referring to the decision taken at Nicaea on the Pasch show that this matter formed an important agenda item for the bishops at the council. Their decision that Pasch be celebrated only on Sunday reflects the unanimity of all four Gospels on the chronology of the resurrection and avoided the complication of the conflicting Johannine and Synoptic chronologies for the crucifixion. Their decision also emphatically differentiated the Christian Pasch from the Jewish Passover, as the repeated derisory references to the Asian churches celebrating according to "the practice of the Jews" underline. In 325, as Constantine was formally accepting Christianity as an imperially approved religion, these were clearly essential features for him.

It will be clear from the foregoing discussion of Paschal celebration before the council that *DRP* plays an important role in establishing the details of Anatolius's Paschal contribution. This valuable witness was ignored by mainstream scholarship for 250 years as a consequence of van der Hagen's dismissal of the tract as a "forgery," relying on an edition based upon a single manuscript. He similarly dismissed two further Paschal tracts, the *Acta Synodi Caesareae* and *Tractatus Athanasii*, as forgeries. Here, by dismissing three Paschal tracts whose numerical

administration of which would certainly require the widespread availability of Easter dates well in advance.

[61] Mosshammer 2008, 154–55, for Ambrose's citation; 69–70, for Theophilus's and Ambrose's use of equinox on 21 March. Jones 1943, 29: "Theophilus (AD 385–412) created the first direct progenitor of Bede's Easter-tables."

criteria he could not rationalize, van der Hagen established a convenient but hazardous precedent followed by successors. In 1880 Bruno Krusch followed suit, endorsing van der Hagen's three dismissals and adding two of his own, the *Prologus Cyrilli* and *Epistola Cyrilli*, and in 1901 Bartholomew Mac Carthy added the *Epistola Moriani* to the list.[62] These tracts, summarily dismissed, all relate to events or persons considered to have made significant contributions to the evolution of the Christian Pasch.

There is an important lesson to be learned here. While all texts are susceptible to corruption in transmission, tracts relating to Paschal celebration are particularly vulnerable for two reasons. First, because Paschal celebration was subject to conflict and controversy from at least the second century, their content had always the potential to challenge the Paschal preferences of a reader. Second, tracts dealing with calendar dates and lunar ages inevitably contain a significant numerical component which plays a crucial role in their discussion, and in transmission these numbers are especially prone to corruption, whether deliberate or accidental. In these circumstances it is essential that scholars critically examine every available witness to such tracts and their numerical structure. If this is done, there is the real possibility of gaining new insight into Christian Paschal history.

SELECT REFERENCES

Barnes, Timothy D. 1981. *Constantine and Eusebius.* Cambridge, MA: Harvard University Press.

Cameron, Averil, and Stuart G. Hall, trans. 1999. *Eusebius: Life of Constantine.* Oxford: Clarendon Press.

Jones, Charles. 1943. *Bedae opera de temporibus.* Cambridge, MA: Medieval Academy of America.

Krusch, Bruno. 1880. *Studien zur christlich-mittelalterlichen Chronologie: Der 84jährige Ostercyclus und seine Quellen.* Leipzig: Veit.

Krusch, Bruno. 1938. *Studien zur christlich-mittelalterlichen Chronologie: Die Entstehung unserer heutigen Zeitrechnung.* Abhandlungen der Preussischen Akademie der Wissenschaften 8. Berlin: Verlag der Akademie der Wissenschaften.

Mc Carthy, Daniel. 1993. "Easter Principles and a Fifth-Century Lunar Cycle Used in the British Isles." *Journal for the History of Astronomy* 24: 204–24.

[62]   van der Hagen 1733, 329–36, dismissing *DRP, Acta Synodi* and *Tractatus Athanasii;* Krusch 1880, 98, 108, dismissing *Prologus Cyrilli* and *Epistola Cyrilli;* 304, 312, 328, endorsing van der Hagen; Mac Carthy 1901, cxl, dismissing *Epistola Moriani.* See Mc Carthy 2011, 51–57, reviewing the alleged Paschal "forgeries."

Mc Carthy, Daniel. 2011. "On the Arrival of the *Latercus* in Ireland." In *The Easter Controversy of Late Antiquity and the Early Middle Ages*, ed. Immo Warntjes and Dáibhí Ó Cróinín, 48–75. Turnhout: Brepols.

Mc Carthy, Daniel and Aidan Breen, eds. 2003. *The Ante-Nicene Christian Pasch "De ratione paschali": The Paschal Tract of Anatolius, Bishop of Laodicea.* Dublin: Four Courts.

Mosshammer, Alden. 2008. *The Easter Computus and the Origins of the Christian Era.* Oxford: Oxford University Press.

Mosshammer, Alden, ed. 2017. *The Prologues on Easter of Theophilus of Alexandria and [Cyril].* Oxford: Oxford University Press.

Robertson, Archibald, trans. 1892. *Athanasius: Select Works and Letters.* NPNF 2.4. Edinburgh: T. & T. Clark.

Schwartz, Eduard. 1905. *Christliche und jüdische Ostertafeln.* Abhandlungen der Königlichen Gesellschaft der Wissenschaften zu Göttingen, philologisch-historische Klasse, Neue Folge, vol. 8, no. 6. Berlin: Weidmann.

Schwartz Eduard and Theodor Mommsen, eds. 1903–9. *Eusebius Werke II.1–3. Die Kirchengeschichte.* GCS 9.1–3. Leipzig: J. C. Hinrichs.

van der Hagen, Johannes. 1733. *Observationes in Prosperi Aquitani Chronicon* [. . .] Amsterdam: Johannem Boom.

Walch, Christian. 1770. "Decreti Nicaeni de Paschate Explicatio." *Novum Commentarium Societatis Regiae Scientiarum Goettingensis, commentationes historicae et philologicae* 1: 10–65. Göttingen.

10 Narrating the Council
Eusebius on Nicaea
AARON P. JOHNSON

Eusebius of Caesarea became involved in the Arian controversy from the first moments it expanded beyond the Alexandrian sphere, and he remained involved throughout its first two decades of exponential growth, in terms of both geographical spread and lasting theological and political impact, until the deaths of Arius and then Constantine. Eusebius is the only bishop directly involved in the early years of the controversy to have been an already recognized polymath and heavy-hitter in the development of a distinctively Christian intellectual culture in late antiquity. Probably already in his sixties when Arius first sought his aid, Eusebius was a central contributor to the fields of history, world chronology, apologetics, theology, and biblical scholarship.[1] He would continue to make contributions to most of these areas of academic inquiry until his death in 339. Furthermore, not only did he engage in theological polemics with some of the key players of Nicaea, but he was also the author of a highly significant letter describing some of the theological dynamics of the council (his *Epistle to the Caesareans*) as well as the single most important eye-witness narrative of the council (contained in his *Life of Constantine*). These accounts are both tantalizing and frustrating – for his composite portrait of the council is both more

---

[1] See briefly, Perrone 1996; see also, Barnes 1981; Drake 2000, 355–92; Johnson 2014. I have used the following abbreviations and editions:

PE = *Praeparatio Evangelica* in Mras 1954.
DE = *Demonstratio Evangelica* in Heikel 1913.
HE = *Historia Ecclesiastica* in Schwartz and Mommsen 1903–9.
Marcell. = *Contra Marcellum* in Klostermann 1906, 1–58.
De ecc. th. = *De ecclesiastica theologia* in Klostermann 1906, 60–182.
VC = *De vita Constantini* in Heikel 1902, 3–148.
Ep. Euphrat. = *Epistula ad Euphrationem* (*Urk.* 3) in Opitz 1934, 4–6 (*Dok.* 10) in Brennecke et al. 2007, 86–87.
Ep. Alex. = *Epistula ad Alexandrum Alexandrinum* (*Urk.* 7) in Opitz 1934, 14–15, (*Dok.* 9) in Brennecke et al. 2007, 85–86.
Ep. Caes. = *Epistula ad Caesarienses* (*Urk.* 22) in Opitz 1934, 42–47 (*Dok.* 24) in Brennecke et al. 2007, 105–8.

and less than we would expect based on what later sources tell us. If we privilege such later material, Eusebius appears disturbing in his silences and suspect of subterfuge.

The following examination of Eusebius's accounts of the council will first couch them within what we can discern of his theological position and involvement in ecclesiastical politics before the council. It will secondly remark on his first account of the council in his *Letter to the Caesareans* before turning, thirdly, to appreciate his narrative in the *Life of Constantine* as a piece of Eusebius's literary craftsmanship. Such an approach to his narrative of Nicaea hopes to illumine his portrayal of the council in ways natural to the bishop of Caesarea (even if exasperating to modern readers).

EUSEBIUS'S THEOLOGICAL ENTANGLEMENTS

Eusebius was already a person of known intellectual abilities and theological commitments when he became bishop of Caesarea in Palestine in c. 313, having already composed the painstaking *Chronicon* (a masterpiece reference tool of world chronology), the *General Elementary Introduction* (the remains of which argue for a Christian hermeneutic of the Hebrew Scriptures), and probably the *Against Porphyry* (a now-lost response to one of antiquity's greatest critics of Christianity), as well as other works, such as the *Onomasticon* (a reference tool on places mentioned in the Bible).[2] The following years up to Constantine's seizure of the eastern half of the empire and the quickly transpiring ecclesiastical events leading up to the Council of Nicaea appear on surviving evidence to be Eusebius's most intellectually and literarily productive period. In the decade from 314 to 324 (in other words, the years of the emperor Licinius's control of the East), Eusebius penned the massive two-part apologetic defense of the faith, the *Preparation for the Gospel* (*Praeparatio Evangelica*) and the *Demonstration for the Gospel* (*Demonstratio Evangelica*), together originally totaling thirty-five books. During the same years he also wrote what many consider to be his most significant contribution to Christian literature, the *Ecclesiastical History*, which canvassed the history of Christianity up to the time of Constantine. Appended to this work was a short treatise *On the Martyrs of Palestine*. He also composed and delivered an *Oration on the Church at Tyre* and possibly two works of *Gospel Questions* (dealing with differences in the Gospels' narratives of

---

[2] For brief discussion of these and the other works mentioned below, with additional bibliography, see Johnson 2014.

Christ's birth and death). From his writings up to the outbreak of the Arian controversy, there are well over 2,000 pages of almost unrivalled intellectual industry still extant for our study today.

When Arius solicited Eusebius's aid in his dispute with Alexander (sometime just after 318?), he was bringing an august luminary of Christian intellectual culture into the fray and heightening the ecclesiastical drama significantly.[3] Eusebius joined the epistolary firefight that was quickly erupting as letters began to crisscross the eastern Mediterranean in opposing efforts to confirm alliances based on social-ecclesial networks and theological sensibilities that are still being explored by scholars. Unfortunately, only two letters survive from Eusebius's hand during this period (both only in part), but there were certainly others. He wrote directly to Alexander claiming that the Alexandrian bishop misunderstood Arius's position (*Urk.* 7);[4] and he sent a letter to Euphration of Balanea in order to clarify the importance of the Father's unbegottenness and the Son's begottenness (*Urk.* 3).[5]

The fact that he was confronted for his defense of Arius and placed on a sort of theological probation at a synod held in Antioch just months before the council is known only from a belatedly discovered Syriac translation of a letter from members of that synod in March 325 (*Urk.* 18).[6] The letter remarks that he and two other associates (Narcissus of Neronias and Theodotus of Laodicea, the latter of whom had been the recipient of his *Praeparatio* and *Demonstratio Evangelica*) were to be given the time until the "great and holy council" that was soon to be held in Ancyra (later moved to Nicaea by Constantine) to reconsider their theological stance. Naturally, Eusebius was a bit taciturn on his uncomfortable status leading up to the council: there is not a single hint anywhere in his corpus of the existence of the synod, his presence there, or the unfortunate outcome of the synod for his ecclesiastical standing and reputation.

Indeed, there is no reference to the synod anywhere else in ancient literature, and all attempts to explain this silence seem to fall flat. From the year of the synodal letter's first discovery in 1905 up until this last decade, the few attempts to argue that the letter is a forgery in whole or in part and that there was no synod, or at least that any synod that might have been held in Antioch that year did not provisionally excommunicate Eusebius, have each time been met swiftly with often detailed and

---

[3]   For a reassessment of the chronology, see Brennecke et al. 2017, xix–xxxviii.
[4]   On the letter to Alexander, see Strutwolf 1999, 29–31.
[5]   On Euphration, see Strutwolf 1999, 27, n. 25; on Eusebius's letter to him, 27–29.
[6]   See Cross 1939; translation of the letter from Schwartz's Greek is at 71–76.

perceptive defenses of the letter's authenticity.[7] In the wake of such scholarly defense it is probably best not to dismiss the letter just yet – even while we should acknowledge the acute problems it raises if authentic. Aside from the total silence about such a synod condemning Eusebius in all other sources, especially by those sources who would have been most apt to cite it if they knew of its existence, it does not explain the tone or nature of Eusebius's *Letter to the Caesareans* (discussed below), the description by Eustathius of Eusebius's behavior at Nicaea,[8] Eusebius's overwhelmingly positive portrait of Nicaea in his *Life of Constantine* (discussed below), or his positive reference there to Ossius (the apparent presider over the alleged synod at Antioch).[9]

In any case, even if the condemnation of Eusebius at Antioch just months before the Council of Nicaea could be disproven, we must still recognize that Alexander of Alexandria had already rejected Eusebius as "anathema"[10] and must ask what Eusebius's theological position on the Father and Son might have been when he gave his initial support to Arius. His letters to Alexander and Euphration survive only in piecemeal fashion and cannot provide a sufficient answer; the few paragraphs of each were selected for their unorthodox expressions by the Second Council of Nicaea (787) and should not be taken as representative of the original tone and scope of the two letters.[11] There is significant material, however, from which to discern Eusebius's general theological views before the synod at Antioch and the Council of Nicaea within his earlier works, especially the *Demonstratio Evangelica*.[12]

---

[7]   Most recently, see Brennecke and Heil 2012.

[8]   Quoted at Theodoret (Thdt.), *Historia ecclesiastica* (*HE*) 1.8.1–3.

[9]   *VC* 3.7.1; additionally, 2.63, 73 probably refer to Ossius (although Warmington 1985, sees these as references to the notary Marianus). All the manuscripts of the synodal letter name a certain Eusebius as the presider at Antioch, except for a modern copy of an apparently tenth-century manuscript, which gives Ossius instead; see Chadwick 1958. Unfortunately, this modern copy bears a hint of suspicion, as its tenth-century exemplar is missing and it was made in the very year that Brilliantov was suggesting that the named Eusebius be emended to Ossius in the first discovered manuscript (on Brilliantov's suggestion, see Chadwick 1958, 295–97 [there spelled Brillantov]).

[10] Arius, *Epistula ad Eusebium Nicomediensem*, Urk. 1.3; cf. Alexander of Alexandria, *Epistula ad Alexandrum Thess.*, Urk. 14.37.

[11] And yet, even what we do have of these two letters shows significant points of agreement with what we know of Alexander's theological position, as well as points of divergence from what we know of Arius's position; see Strutwolf 1999, 27–31.

[12] Admittedly, the *DE* can only be dated to a pre-Nicene period by an argument *e silentio* (it nowhere refers to Arius or the Arian controversy); see Morlet 2009, 87. A pre-Nicene context remains probable, however, since it seems unlikely that, if it were post-Nicene, there should be no hint of defensiveness with regard to his theological formulations (aside from the defensiveness against the focal criticisms of Christianity as well as against polytheism in general) nor any attempt to make explicit his

Briefly put, Eusebius exhibited a consistent and pervasive concern – from his apologetic writings to his biblical commentaries and his theological polemic – to protect the integrity of the persons of the Trinity, especially the Father and the Son. The notion that Eusebius was unduly influenced by pagan philosophers and thus over-emphasized the transcendence of the Father at the expense of the Son's full deity is misleading caricature (and has equally been used to explain Arius's theological proclivities). Instead, Eusebius defended the hypostatic distinctiveness of each member of the Trinity in ways that resonate with, and indeed were influential upon, later orthodox developments.[13] He was careful to maintain the unique nature of the Father's unbegottenness and the Son's begottenness.[14]

As many have noted, a primary mechanism for this was his application of the image conception of the Son.[15] This allowed for an ineffably intimate relation of Father and Son, which could be explored through a number of metaphors from nature (especially that of a light and its ray, which was already made available to him from Hebrews 1:3).[16] At the same time, he rigorously employed a method of removing any physicalist assumptions with respect to their relationship. So, for instance, while the light and its ray shared between themselves *hypostasis* and *hyparxis* (two significant terms which seem in Eusebius to be synonymous for "individual existence" or "subsistence") since the light "was completed by its ray," the Father and Son, on the other hand, did not share their *hypostasis* and *hyparxis* since the Father stood in need of no such completion.[17] While he thus maintained the individual integrity of the Father and Son, Eusebius was no theological egalitarian: the Father "subsisted in priority," *proüparchei* and *proüphestēken* (a priority which most likely was for him logical and hierarchical not chronological, since the Son was begotten before

---

avoidance of other Christian theological parsings of the nature of the Father and Son and their relationship to each other, towards which he would be greatly sensitized following his experiences at the synod at Antioch and the Council of Nicaea.

[13] Because of the lack of attention given to properly formulating the status of the Holy Spirit (except at the end of one of his latest works, the *De ecc.th.*), Eusebius has sometimes been called more of a binitarian than a trinitarian; see Drecoll 2013.

[14] See esp. *DE* 4.2–4, which must be read in the Greek as the single available English translation by Ferrar 1981, can often mislead. For general discussion of the *DE*'s contribution, see Lyman 1993, 82–123.

[15] See DelCogliano 2006; Strutwolf 1999, 164–79.

[16] He seems also to have been indebted to Philo, *De aeternitate mundi* 91.

[17] *DE* 4.3.5, 147d: καὶ πάλιν ἡ μὲν αὐγὴ συνυπάρχει τῷ φωτί, συμπληρωτική τις οὖσα αὐτοῦ (ἄνευ γὰρ αὐγῆς οὐκ ἂν ὑποσταίη φῶς), ὁμοῦ τε καὶ καθ' ἑαυτὸ συνυφέστηκεν· ὁ δὲ πατὴρ προϋπάρχει τοῦ υἱοῦ καὶ τῆς γενέσεως αὐτοῦ προϋφέστηκεν, ᾗ μόνος ἀγέννητος ἦν.

time).[18] Eusebius was careful in his distinctive use of these terms and does not seem to allow them to be simply equated with *ousia* (being or substance) as was common in contemporary philosophical and theological usage (including Nicaea's anathemas, as we shall see below).[19] In fact, the Father and Son share their being (*sunōn*).[20]

Throughout his theological formulations there was an attempt to avoid falling into the Sabellian error. Both in his earlier *Demonstratio* and in his later attacks against Marcellus, where he explicitly named the heretic Sabellius as Marcellus's theological predecessor,[21] he displayed a concern over the recurrence of what he saw as a conceptual depletion of the hypostatic distinctiveness and identity of each member of the Trinity into a simplistic singularity.[22] Significantly, Arius had advertised Alexander as proclaiming that the Son "shared the *hyparxis*" (*sunuparchei*) of the Father, precisely what Eusebius had already been at pains to reject in the *Demonstratio*. Aside from possible social networks and the possibility that Eusebius may have seen Arius's struggles with Alexander as analogous to Origen's earlier struggles with his bishop (wherein Caesarea provided support for the intellectual who had discomfited his hometown episcopal establishment), Eusebius appears, therefore, to have also had serious theological reasons for being suspicious of Alexander's theology.

Eusebius's subordinationist formulation might strike against the finely tuned sensibilities of later post-Nicene language[23] (and, in fact, earned him later glosses baldly stating "Arianism!" in the margins of manuscripts of the *Demonstratio* and the anti-Marcellan

---

[18] Cf. *DE* 5.1, 215c; *Ep. Euphrat.* 1 (*Urk.* 3). Notice that he could use an *ousia* cognate in order to distinguish God from creation (*proontos*; *DE* 4.1.7, 145d2), but did not use it in distinguishing the Father from the Son.

[19] Most appositely, see Iamblichus, *De mysteriis* 1.7[22].6–9. For greater complexity in contemporary Platonism, see, Smith 1994.

[20] *DE* 5.4, 226d2. One is unduly confused by the only English translation of the *DE*, which had earlier rendered Eusebius's *oude anarchōs sunuphestēken* as "nor was He eternally co-existent with the Father" (Ferrar 1981, 234); more literally, the phrase should read "nor does the Son have His individual existence without a source/beginning" (the latter being a reference to the Son being "in the beginning," *archē*, with God at John 1:1, or Wisdom's being "created the beginning of His ways" or being "founded in the beginning" at Prov. 8:22–23).

[21] *De ecc. th.* 1.5. On his earlier description of Sabellius at *HE* 7.6, see Willing 2008, 341–44.

[22] On his critique of Marcellus, see Lienhard 1999; Johnson 2014, 113–42; Spoerl and Vinzent 2017, 33–60.

[23] Without naming Eusebius, Athanasius would belittle those who thought the *sunuparchein* of Father and Son would destroy the Trinity; see, e.g., Athanasius, *Orationes tres adversus Arianos* 1.32.4.

writings[24]); but it was precise enough to prevent us from seeing his later acceptance of "consubstantial" (*homoousios*) at Nicaea as a disingenuous move contradicting his earlier thought.[25] His consistent theological outlook allowed him to offer preliminary support to what he thought might be Arius's concerns as well as later to give assent to the Nicene Creed (properly interpreted), as we shall see. What made the creed so exquisite and useful was its adaptability to a wider spectrum of trinitarian thinking than we often suppose, from Eusebius on one side to Marcellus of Ancyra on the other. To label either one as non-Nicene (or somehow less Nicene) misses this point.

THE IMMEDIATE RESPONSE TO THE COUNCIL

Immediately following the Council of Nicaea, Eusebius penned another letter to his home congregation at Caesarea, offering a very brief account of his role at the council and his decision to accept the creed there formulated, with an interpretation of those elements that might have offended his fellow Caesareans' theological sensibilities (*Urk.* 22).[26] The letter is frequently taken as proof of Eusebius's theological duplicity: at first an ardent supporter of Arius, Eusebius quickly adapted under pressure and changed his colors like an imperializing chameleon. His letter has been characterized as an attempt at "rehabilitation" of his episcopal standing after the synod in Antioch,[27] or even "a document of despair."[28] The letter deserves closer scrutiny,[29] however, since in general, as just remarked, Eusebius evinced similar theological proclivities from his earliest to his latest writings and, while it is defensive in tone, it was not such as one would expect if he was the victim of a preliminary excommunication but as one whose home congregation expected him to maintain his (and purportedly their) creed without undue alteration in the face of powerful personalities at the council.

In fact, the letter is the earliest account of Nicaea to survive, since it was written directly following the decisions of the council. At the outset, he explained that although the Caesareans may certainly have heard

---

[24] See the GCS apparatus criticus for each, passim.

[25] Ferrar 1981, xxviii–xxix; Edwards 2015, 286–87; and especially, Strutwolf 1999, 24–61.

[26] For discussion, see variously, Stevenson 1929, 97–102; Williams 2001, 69–70; Kelly 1972, 220–26; Strutwolf 1999, 46–60.

[27] Stevenson 1929, 98.

[28] Abramowski 1975.

[29] Such as has been performed notably by Strutwolf 1999, 46–60.

rumors of what transpired at the council, they needed to be provided with an accurate account of Eusebius's conduct there: he had reported the symbol of faith as handed down by the church at Caesarea to the assembly and had received the confirmation of Constantine himself that there was nothing out of place in Eusebius's creed. Herein was stated the belief in "one God the Father" and "one Lord Jesus Christ, the Word of God, God from God [. . .] only begotten Son, first-born of all creation, before all the ages begotten from the Father."[30] An affirmation of the personal depth of these convictions and of the consistency with which he had always held such convictions followed the quotation of the creed. "The most pious emperor," Eusebius averred, "testified that it was most orthodox."[31]

The emperor furthermore avowed that Eusebius's Caesarean creed represented his own faith and, according to Eusebius, recommended it to the bishops of the synod, "with the insertion of the single word consubstantial" (homoousios), which, he was quick to add, did not imply bodily affection, separation, or division in the ineffable relation of Father and Son.[32] Eusebius next provided the creed adopted by the bishops of Nicaea with its distinctive language departing significantly, for many modern readers, from that of Eusebius's creed:[33] "We believe in [. . .] one Lord Jesus Christ, the Son of God, begotten of the Father, only-begotten, that is, from the substance of the Father, God from God [. . .] very God from very God, begotten not made, consubstantial with the Father."[34] Given his report of Constantine's assertion that such language implied no somatic connotations, which would have been precisely the issue in his resistance to such language, Eusebius had already provided the proper set-up for accepting the creed of the bishops. "Consubstantial" became acceptable because it had been shorn of any hint of physical substance (and, in any case, did not contradict his earlier formulations in the Demonstratio). It had been rendered innocuous by removal of any materialist sense and by its recommendation from a pious emperor.

Of course, it seems rather unlikely that Constantine's recommendation of the shibboleth "consubstantial" arose from the emperor's own

[30] Ep. Caes. 4; trans. Stevenson 1929, sect. 3. It should be noted here that Stevenson's translation adopts different sections numbers than Opitz's Urkunde (the latter of which I have kept).

[31] Ep. Caes. 7; trans. Stevenson 1929, sect. 4.

[32] Ep. Caes. 7.

[33] E.g., Kelly 1972, 217–20. For a reminder of similarities, see Strutwolf 1999, 48–53.

[34] Ep. Caes. 8; trans. Stevenson 1929, sect. 4. See above, 143–45.

theological convictions (given what we can discern of them from his previously delivered Good Friday sermon, or *Oration to the Saints*, and his later attempts to accept Arius's personal creedal statements, which continued to avoid the term).[35] Instead, it seems more likely that Eusebius's singular reference to Constantine as the recommender of this key word was meant rhetorically to assuage any fears on the part of his epistolary recipients that he had been bullied by the other bishops, in the midst of whom he should have been an equal (or even a first among equals), or that the term had arisen from an unsavory source (like Alexander of Alexandria, Eustathius of Antioch, or worse, Marcellus of Ancyra).

Following the creed proper were the anathemas against those who say, "There was when he was not," and "Before his generation he was not," and "he came to be from nothing," or he was "of another *hypostasis* or *ousia*," or he was created, alterable, or mutable.[36] These anathemas unmistakably targeted Arius; but Eusebius leaves this point implicit and, in fact, never names Arius (or any other individual besides Constantine) in the entirety of the letter. More striking was his acceptance of the anathema against the difference of the Son's "*hypostasis* or *ousia*," given the fact that he unequivocally asserted the hypostatic difference of Father and Son throughout his episcopal career. Because the creed was here adopting the ambiguity of *hypostasis* that was general at the time and treating it as a mere synonym of *ousia*, he was only accepting the anathema insofar as these terms were treated as uncritically synonymous. The letter still allowed for the possibility of affirming the Son's distinct *hypostasis* if one used the term in a more technical sense, as he himself did in his theological writings. His acceptance of this anathema did not therefore signal a contradiction on Eusebius's part.

The remainder of the letter was taken up with Eusebius's report of his careful inquiry of those elements that he (and apparently his Caesarean readers) found most troubling and the reasons for nonetheless accepting them: "of the substance of the Father" was not to be understood in a material partitive sense but only that the Son "really was of the

---

[35] Edwards 1995, is correct to deny any presumed "Arianism" in the oration; but on any account, the author of the oration seems unlikely to have quickly become an advocate for *homoousios* without external pressure or motivations. For a broader approach to the oration's purposes, see Drake 2000, 292–305.

[36] *Ep. Caes.* 8. On the Nicene Creed and the anathemas, see the discussion by Mark Edwards in this volume, above 144–51.

Father";[37] "begotten not made" was meant only to emphasize that the Son was not like the works that had been made "through him";[38] the term "consubstantial" merely meant that the Son was unlike the creatures and was entirely like the Father and that "he is not from some other *hypostasis* and *ousia* but from the Father."[39]

As to the anathemas, since the offending phrases were not found in Scripture as such, it was best to follow the bishops at Nicaea and avoid this language, and, in any case, "it had not been our custom hitherto to use these terms."[40] Furthermore, since nobody doubted the Son's existence before the Incarnation, it was fitting to accept the anathematizing of "before his generation he was not" (an assertion already rejected in his *Demonstratio*).[41] Even the emperor in a speech had declared the Son to exist, he added, if not yet "in actuality" before his being begotten, at least "in potentiality" in an ingenerate manner.[42]

At key points, Eusebius seems to applaud the spirit of true inquiry that governed the council: "questions and explanations took place, and the discussion tested the meaning of these phrases";[43] "all of us assented, not without inquiry, but according to the specific meanings";[44] and Eusebius himself "resisted even to the last minute" variant statements, "but received without contention" those which could be understood "on a candid examination of the sense of the words."[45] The aim of peace was combined with the "fear of deviating from the correct meaning."[46] Throughout his explanations of his acceptance of the troubling components of the creed, he displayed a concern not only for ecclesiastical concord among the gathered bishops, but also for the creed's compatibility with key theological truths (such as the ineffable and immaterial nature of the deity), the resonance with scriptural language, and the coherence with his own Caesarean theological tradition. While the letter tells us too little of other details that would greatly benefit the historian

---

[37] *Ep. Caes.* 9; trans. Stevenson 1929, sect. 5.
[38] *Ep. Caes.* 11; no doubt Eusebius's concern here arose from the import to his mind of Col 1:15, namely that Christ was the "first-born of creation," included in his own creed.
[39] *Ep. Caes.* 13.
[40] *Ep. Caes.* 15; trans. Stevenson 1929, sect. 8.
[41] *Ep. Caes.* 16; trans. Stevenson 1929, sect. 9; see Strutwolf 1999, 57–58.
[42] *Ep. Caes.* 16; trans. Stevenson 1929, sect. 10. The emperor's reasoning is contradicted by Eusebius's claims in earlier and later writings; for an attempt at resolving this conundrum, see Strutwolf 1999, 58–60.
[43] *Ep. Caes.* 9; trans. Stevenson 1929, sect. 5.
[44] *Ep. Caes.* 14; trans. Stevenson 1929, sect. 8.
[45] *Ep. Caes.* 17; trans. Stevenson 1929, sect. 11.
[46] *Ep. Caes.* 10; trans. Stevenson 1929, sect. 5.

or the theologian in filling out our understanding of the dynamics of the council's proceedings, it nonetheless reveals consistent themes of Eusebius's literary, theological and historical-political sensibilities, as we shall see.

NARRATING THE COUNCIL

Over a decade would pass after Eusebius's involvement in the council and his epistolary report of that involvement to his home congregation before he would return to a narration of the council. In that period, he would remain a central figure in ecclesiastical politics in the eastern empire: he was active at synods at Antioch (327, in which Eustathius was deposed) and Tyre (335, in which Athanasius was condemned) and made a visit to Constantinople in order to assure Marcellus's removal from the episcopal chair at Ancyra.[47] The common assertion that these depositions marked the execution of Eusebius's personal vendetta against those who were behind his theological probation before Nicaea or those who subsequently defended Nicaea rests upon assumptions that overstep our very limited evidence for his motivations and involvement at these gatherings. In fact, this activity could even be seen as his defense of Nicaea (as he understood it).

In this period, he would also remain active as an author. He composed two massive commentaries on the Psalms and the prophet Isaiah, reworked significant material from his *Demonstratio Evangelica* for a different focus in his *Theophania* (a five-book apologetic centered on the Incarnation of Christ), repurposed some motifs of his *Praeparatio Evangelica* in an apologetic oration given the title *In Praise of Constantine*, defended the emperor's construction of the Church of the Holy Sepulcher in Jerusalem, and penned two works of theological polemic against Marcellus of Ancyra (who espoused a position in which the oneness of the Trinity was suspected by Eusebius of collapsing altogether into a revived Sabellianism). Eusebius had thus matured and developed as an author and theologian; yet his theological proclivities, biblical hermeneutical foci, and ecclesiological sensibilities maintained a high degree of steadiness throughout these very different literary forms. In fact, what seems most distinctive of his later narrative of the council are the facts that the ecclesiastical-theological context had changed in the intervening years and the genre for the narrative itself was radically different from his earlier letter's exposition. The later account in his *Life*

---

[47] See Barnes 1981, 224–44; Morlet and Perronne 2012, 9–12.

of Constantine, to which we now turn, was rife with several concerns and motifs that Eusebius had exhibited earlier and had become hallmarks of his thinking.

Narrating Synods before Nicaea

It is best to approach the narrative of the council in the *Life of Constantine* in terms of what it presents for our literary viewing and what it keeps out of sight or opaque. To do this, we should read the account against the backdrop of his narrations of councils in his earlier *Ecclesiastical History*. There we discover that the Council of Nicaea, described later in the *Life* as a "new work produced by God,"[48] was in fact not such a new thing after all. In particular, Eusebius had given special attention to councils in the second and third centuries, one of which had even induced imperial involvement. Most notable are those accounts of synods of the second-century Paschal controversy,[49] the synod at Rome dealing with Novatus,[50] and the synod at Antioch dealing with Paul of Samosata.[51]

The first passage reports on what appear to have been no less than five synods (in Palestine, Rome, Pontus, Gaul, and Osrhoene)[52] addressing the practice by the Christians in the province of Asia of following the Jewish reckoning in their determinations of when to celebrate the Easter eucharist. "Synods and marshaling (*sunodoi kai sunkrotēseis*)[53] of bishops arose on the same issue," Eusebius wrote, "and all issued the ecclesiastical dogma with one mind by means of letters."[54] A consultation of those letters, according to Eusebius, revealed that they were all "of the same opinion and judgment" and gave "the same verdict" so that "there was one rule" (*horos heis*) of Christian practice.[55] Fascinatingly, Eusebius allowed this picture of unity to be tempered by quotations from a letter of Irenaeus recommending peace and love within a diversity of Christian practices and liturgical calendars, for "the diversity (*diaphōnia*) of [times of] fasting establishes the oneness of mind (*homonoia*) of the faith."[56] His

---

[48] *VC* 3.2.1.
[49] *HE* 5.23–25. On the controversy and subsequent developments, see the chapter by Daniel Mc Carthy in this volume.
[50] *HE* 6.43.
[51] *HE* 7.27–30.
[52] *HE* 5.23.2.
[53] See Dainese 2011, for Eusebius's complex relationship to second-century synodal thinking and usage of these terms.
[54] *HE* 5.23.2.
[55] *HE* 5.23.4.
[56] *HE* 5.24.13.

appeal to epistolary proof of unity thus opened up a more richly textured reality of diversity and "unity (henōseōs) among neighbors."[57]

The second significant synodal narration describes how the church in Rome responded to Novatus and his followers, who, because of their "brother-hating and misanthropic mind," adopted an exclusivist position against those who had lapsed. "A great synod was marshalled (sunodou megistēs sunkrotētheisēs) at Rome," numbering sixty bishops, "and still many more presbyters and deacons,"[58] and letters could display the geographical range of unity in response to the Novatian schism, the need for grace towards the fallen, and the dangers of Novatus's ecclesial practices.[59] While the terminology of synodal gathering (sunodos, sunkrotēsis) marks what begins to look like Eusebius's formulaic manner of describing an episcopal assembly for the purposes of dealing with a problematic person, unique to his narration of the synod at Rome is his report of the number of bishops who had attended; before this, Eusebius's discussions of synodal gatherings remarked on their universality in general terms, usually expressed only as a gathering "of the faithful."[60]

The third passage is found within an account of the history of the church in "our generation"[61] and, after a statement on Paul of Samosata's low view of Christ, the synod convened at Antioch to deal with Paul is introduced rather abruptly into the text.[62] Eusebius did not provide his readers with an account of how events unfolded before the synod, only the haste with which a number of important bishops made their way to Antioch.[63] He failed to give the number, though he remarks "someone counting them would not be at a loss [in recognizing] a great many others, along with presbyters and deacons, marshalled (sunkrotēthentas) for the same reason."[64] There is some ambiguity about the order of proceedings, since Eusebius next added that they "frequently all came together at different times" while the two sides sought to conceal or expose Paul's heterodoxia.[65] Following some chronological notes, he

---

57   HE 5.24.10.
58   HE 6.43.2.
59   HE 6.43.3–4; see Willing 2008, 323–34.
60   E.g., HE 5.16.10 (= an anonymous anti-Montanist letter). See Dainese 2011, 888, on Eusebius's earlier references to synods of the faithful.
61   HE 7.26.3; on the importance of this for his sources on heresy, see Willing 2008, 354–56, 365.
62   HE 7.27.2.
63   HE 7.27.2–7.28.1.
64   HE 7.28.1.
65   HE 7.28.2. On Eusebius's avoidance of the term heterodoxia in his later accounts of synods, see Dainese 2011, 902, 911.

narrated that there was a "final synod" of a great many bishops at which Paul was "excommunicated from the universal church under heaven."[66] Proof of the purported unanimity of the assembled bishops came through quotations of "a single letter (mian [...] epistolēn) that the shepherds who were marshalled (sunkekrotēmenoi) for the same purpose drafted out of a common mindset" (koinēs gnōmēs),[67] to prove Paul's hetero-doxia, the arguments and questions addressed to him, and his whole lifestyle. After quotations from the synodical letter[68] and Eusebius's summative remarks on how Paul fell from both his episcopate as well as orthodoxia,[69] we are told that Paul's refusal to leave the "house of the church" at Antioch prompted his opponents to petition the emperor Aurelian,[70] who "justly ordered" the assignment of the church to those to whom the bishops in Italy and the city of Rome should write; thus, Paul was shamed by the worldly power.[71] This narrative contains more formulaic items: the "marshalling" of bishops, their singularity of mind, the heterodoxy of the one condemned by the synod, the quotation of a letter to convey the synodal decision. Unique here is the appeal to an emperor and his intervention as a confirmation of the synod's verdict.

Narrating Nicaea

Unlike Eusebius's Epistle to the Caesareans, with its focus upon doctri-nal issues, the narrative in the Life of Constantine continued and expanded motifs within the Ecclesiastical History's synodal episodes. Consistent with his earlier synodal narratives, his account of Nicaea adopted the language of marshalling, unity, singularity of mind, and the epistolary transmission of that unity. Bishops were marshaled (sunk-rotein) to a synod,[72] the decisions of which would be broadcast immedi-ately following the council in a letter of Constantine.[73] This letter was quoted by Eusebius after his description of the council so as to mirror his quotation of Constantine's letter to Alexander and Arius before the council (which had requested that they grant mutual pardon to each other).[74] Most pointedly, throughout the description of the council the

---

[66] HE 7.29.1.
[67] HE 7.30.1.
[68] HE 7.30.2–17; see Willing 2008, 356–58.
[69] HE 7.30.18.
[70] Only later would Aurelian be tempted to persecute the church, we are told, at HE 7.30.20–21.
[71] HE 7.30.19.
[72] VC 3.6.1.
[73] VC 3.16–20.
[74] VC 2.64–72.

reader of the *Life* encounters the emphatically reiterated theme of unity: those separated geographically and doctrinally were brought together to one city,[75] one house of prayer received priests from the continents of Europe, Africa and Asia,[76] and one emperor wove them together in unity;[77] they "shared in" the emperor's hospitality,[78] while he in turn hoped for "one singled-minded judgment shared (*koinēs*) by all"[79] and "one common (*koinēn*) peaceful harmony;"[80] true to his wishes, the faith prevailed "in unison" and was agreed upon "by all";[81] the bishops departed joyfully "in one harmonious mind" (*mia gnōmē* [...] *sumphōnētheisa*),[82] having been joined in "one body."[83]

All of this expanded and enlivened formulaic components of his earlier synodal descriptions in the *Ecclesiastical History*. From this perspective, the Council of Nicaea was only the most recent instantiation of the ongoing maintenance of peace and unity in the universal church. It highlighted the success of episcopal traditions in cleaning up the partisan variance that could arise at different times in the life of the church. Yet, at the same time, there are a number of features in Eusebius's narration of Nicaea in the *Life of Constantine* that make it a singular synod. His account,[84] which fills roughly twenty-four pages in the critical edition of the Greek text, may be divided into five sections: a first preface providing the background to the council,[85] a second preface providing a different angle on the background to the council,[86] the calling of the council,[87] the proceedings of the council itself,[88] and the aftermath of the council.[89] Interwoven throughout these five sections are a series of unique features that set this synodal narration apart from all others in Eusebius's corpus. By attending to each briefly, we arrive at a fuller appreciation of what Eusebius wanted his readers to see in the drama of this particular Council.

[75] *VC* 3.6.2.
[76] *VC* 3.7.1.
[77] *VC* 3.7.2.
[78] *VC* 3.1.5.
[79] *VC* 3.12.1.
[80] *VC* 3.12.4.
[81] *VC* 3.14.
[82] On the importance of *sumphōnia* in Eusebius's thought, see now Morlet 2019.
[83] *VC* 3.21.4.
[84] *VC* 2.61.2–3.24.2.
[85] *VC* 2.61.2–2.73.
[86] *VC* 3.1–5.
[87] *VC* 3.6–9.
[88] *VC* 3.10–14.
[89] *VC* 3.15–24.

First, a minor but noteworthy point involves slight modification to his traditional usage of letters and language. Eusebius's quotations from letters is limited to the emperor's open letters (the first addressed to Alexander and Arius but with signs of a larger intended audience, the second addressed "to the churches" following the council); but unlike epistolary quotations in the *Ecclesiastical History*, which were quoted only selectively, these two letters, which literarily frame the Council of Nicaea in the *Life*, appear to be quoted *in extenso*. Yet, both seem to be carefully chosen to do significant work for Eusebius: they both highlight the emperor's concern for unity, whether doctrinally (as in the first letter) or liturgically (as in the second). Interestingly, Eusebius may have allowed his own language to be influenced by that of Constantine, though this was limited to "divisive banter" (*ereschelia*), a term unique in Eusebius's corpus to the *Life of Constantine*,[90] and "discord" (*stasis*).[91]

Even more substantially, a second unique element of his narration of Nicaea lies in his understanding of the cause of the controversy: at the forefront of what I have demarcated as the first and second prefaces to the council, Eusebius narrated the activity of a central, albeit phantasmic, character in the daemon Envy (*Phthonos*) "who hates what is good."[92] While Eusebius had quoted sources that blamed daemons or evil spirits for earlier division among Christians,[93] nowhere else had he been so emphatic about the daemonic character of discord and the distinctive character of the daemon (namely, envy) as he was in the Nicaea episode. The closest earlier parallel occurs in his account of the outbreak of the so-called Great Persecution in the eighth book of the *Ecclesiastical History*, where Christian leaders were described as falling into slander and envy (*diaphthonoumenōn*) of each other because of their prosperity and peaceful standing in the empire.[94] Christians apparently were seen

---

[90]   ἐρεσχελία before Nicaea: *VC* 2.63; 2.69.2 (= Constantine's letter to Alexander and Arius); ἐρεσχελία before Tyre: *VC* 4.41.1, 3.

[91]   *VC* 3.12.2. Compare also Eusebius's *tarachas emphulious* (*VC* 2.61.3) to Constantine's *emphulios stasis* (*VC* 3.12.2). The classical *stasis* language for civil discord is largely limited to Jewish urban unrest in the *Ecclesiastical History* (drawing on quotations of Josephus) and almost never designates intra-Christian disagreement; the only exception appears to be at *HE* 8.1.7 where congregations are said to be "in discord against" (*katastasiazontōn*) other congregations; see below.

[92]   *VC* 2.61.3; 3.1.1. See Cameron and Hall 1999, note at 2.61.3. On Eusebius's demonology, see Johannessen 2016, especially 58–64, 168–69.

[93]   E.g., the Montanist controversy at *HE* 5.16.8–9, 17; see Willing 2008, 436–44.

[94]   *HE* 8.1.7. The description of "leaders striking against leaders and congregations in discord against congregations" (*HE* 8.1.7) is echoed by "bishops striking against bishops and peoples attacking peoples" (*VC* 3.4).

as unable to handle the comforts of freedom under the empire, a situation
described as being "without envy (*phthonos*) or any wicked daemon" to
harass the church externally.[95] The *Life*'s account significantly demonized the *phthonos* and made it jealous of the church's prosperity; rather
than prosperity being the cause of envy (as in the *HE*), it was here the
object of envy's attack. Eusebius had clearly made his peace with prosperity and externalized envy as the cause of ecclesiastical disharmony.

Even if a daemon was to blame for the disagreement, it remained
a source of acute embarrassment to the church and sadness to the
emperor. This was highlighted by the third crucial aspect of the Nicaea
narrative that makes it stand out as distinct among Eusebius's synodal
narrations: Nicaea is marked by a higher concern with visuality. This
becomes obvious in different ways in the two prefaces as well as in the
description of the proceedings of the council itself. In the first preface,
Eusebius declared that:

> it was possible to see not only the leaders of the churches sparring
> with words, but the multitudes also fragmented, some inclining to
> one side, some to the other. The spectacle (*thea*) of these events
> reached such absurdity that sacred points of divine doctrine were
> now subjected to disgraceful public mockery in the theaters (*thea-
> trois*) of the unbelievers.[96]

The shameful spectacle was not left to stand on its own, however, as
Eusebius deftly introduced others so that his narrative becomes something of a collage of images.

The spectacle of embittered bishops and congregations loses much of
its initially striking power when the second preface provides lengthier
descriptions of the God-loving emperor's production of more edifying
images. In spite of the fact that the emperor's virtue was a work of God
and a "new thing" as "had been known to no ear and seen by no eye,"[97]
Eusebius painted a verbal portrait of the visual pictures commissioned by
the emperor (for instance a painting of the emperor piercing with
a javelin the fallen dragon, representing Satan[98]), which "by divine
inspiration portrayed what the words of the prophets had
proclaimed"[99] in a way that "was a marvel (*thauma*) to me."[100] And,

---

95 *HE* 8.1.6.
96 *VC* 2.61.5; trans. Cameron and Hall 1999; cf. Thdt., *HE* 1.6.10.
97 *VC* 3.2.1.
98 *VC* 3.3.2.
99 Eusebius cites Isaiah 27:1.
100 *VC* 3.3.3.

even more, Eusebius verbally painted an image of the "spectacle (*thea*) of the strange marvel (*xenou thaumatos*)"[101] that all the bishops hoped to see: a Christian emperor adorned not only with dazzling regalia but with the Christian virtues. More significant even than the stately court ceremonial of Constantine's entrance into the council-chamber[102] was Eusebius's description of the emperor's physiognomy, in which the outward appearance revealed the inward qualities of the man.[103] "As for his soul, he was clearly adorned with fear and reverence for God," which was displayed in humility expressed in his eyes, the blush of his face, and his gait.[104] Mingled with the nobility and gentleness of his character, these outward physical markers "put on display better than any word his supernatural understanding."[105]

In his address to the assembled bishops, in turn, Eusebius had the emperor declare his wish to gaze at the spectacle (*theasasthai*) of their unanimity.[106] Indeed, they had presented a marvelous spectacle, according to Eusebius: the gathering of priests were like a "wreath of a great diversity of flowers in bloom,"[107] or "an image of the apostolic choir" (a parallel that prompts him to quote from the description of peoples gathered at Pentecost in Acts 2:9–11),[108] or even more, "an image of the kingdom of Christ" (which prompts him to quote Homer: "though it was a dream not a waking vision of what happened," *Odyssey* 19.547).[109] The increased attention to visuality in Eusebius's narration of Nicaea's bishops and its emperor aligned well with a concern throughout the *Life of Constantine* to paint an enduring picture with his thousand words;[110] it also complemented his sustained application of biblical images and words to events and figures within his own world in an act of what amounts to an "enscripturation" of the present.[111] While unique in comparison to his earlier descriptions of synods, his portrayal of Nicaea was a coherent piece of this larger verbal tapestry in the *Life*.

The final distinctive feature of Eusebius's narrative of the council is likewise a well-known particularity of his biography of Constantine,

---

[101] *VC* 3.6.2.
[102] *VC* 3.10.1–3; see Hal Drake's discussion, above 96–97, 123–26.
[103] On the importance of physiognomy, see Swain 2006; for its significance in early Christianity, see Parsons 2006.
[104] *VC* 3.10.4.
[105] *VC* 3.10.4.
[106] *VC* 3.12.1.
[107] *VC* 3.6.2.
[108] *VC* 3.7.2.
[109] *VC* 3.15.2.
[110] See Van Nuffelen 2013; Johnson 2004.
[111] See Williams 2008, 1–16, 25–57; Johnson 2014, 159–62.

namely his meticulously crafted characterization of the emperor himself. As already noted, his physiognomy was taken as expressive of
Constantine's exemplary moral state, which was expressed throughout
the entirety of Eusebius's Nicaea episode. The first preface contained the
letter of Constantine to Alexander and Arius, which allowed Eusebius's
readers to glimpse the emperor's self-representation as one imbued with
a godly distress at whatever tore at the unity and peace of the church, an
upholder of ecclesiastical concord, and a healer of spiritual disease.[112]
The emperor's goodness is then exemplified in the second preface, which
alluded to urban violence in Alexandria involving the destruction of the
emperor's statues and to which Constantine responded not with anger
but with sadness.[113]

Aside from the physiognomic assessment of the emperor in
Eusebius's description of the proceedings of the council itself, probably
the most striking imperial portrayal within the episode is a powerful
comparison (sunkrisis) of Constantine and the previous emperors ("tyr-
ants") that contains a lengthy series of antitheses: while they promoted
worship of non-existent gods, he promoted the worship of the truly
existing God; while they blasphemed Christ, he esteemed Christ's passion; they deprived godly people of their homes, he restored them to their
homes; they humiliated the godly, he honored them; and so on. Most
importantly, Eusebius reminds his readers that, whereas the persecuting
emperors prohibited synods, Constantine "marshaled (sunekrotei) them
from all nations."[114]

Although the need for a synod was otherwise a "spectacle" of
shame,[115] this new way of framing the synod, as a generous gift of
imperial piety after tyrannical restriction of assembly, put the council
in a positive light. The gathering was not merely a result of discord but
was a vivid and exhilarating display of God's new work in the late
Roman empire. The severity of unthinking persecutors could not be
more sharply contrasted than by comparison with an emperor who
responded to stubborn and angry bishops with mildness and gentle
persuasion.[116]

---

[112]   VC 2.64–72.
[113]   VC 3.4.
[114]   VC 3.1.5.
[115]   VC 2.61.5.
[116]   Constantine showed "pleasant flexibility" (VC 3.13.1) and maintained a "pleasant
and agreeable" demeanor (3.13.2), trans. Cameron and Hall, 1999; see Drake 2000,
252–54.

CONCLUSION

As has often been noted, there is much that Eusebius obscures in his account of Nicaea: we learn nothing of the tensions between Caesarea and Jerusalem (where Macarius quickly supported the anti-Arian position and then at the council pushed for greater recognition of Jerusalem);[117] Eusebius's own initial support for Arius is entirely omitted from all Eusebius's writings and, aside from Constantine's letter, Arius is not even named in the *Life of Constantine*; likewise, Eusebius's past censure at Antioch – if true – is entirely (and understandably) omitted; and finally, there is no indication of Eusebius's own theological position itself.

What we do see, however, are many hallmarks of Eusebius's character as an author. The narrative of Nicaea continued and elaborated earlier attitudes and descriptive proclivities. At the same time, it is marked by several of the central themes peculiar to his experimental imperial biography. Frustrating as it is to historians, the *Life* is a masterpiece on many levels. Within its pages, Eusebius artfully deconstructed the boundaries between verbal and visual art forms. He developed a distinctively Christian vision of a Christian emperor in ways that diverge carefully from the expectations of imperial panegyric (a fact often not appreciated by modern readers ensconced within anti-monarchic contexts with their own democratic interpretive lenses).[118] Eusebius pursued a thoroughgoing enscripturation, which saw emperors and synods in terms of biblical types and language. His quotational methodology likewise shaped his account of Nicaea, with its two imperial letters, which allowed for the detection of threads of literary play not only with the *Life*'s other quoted letters, but also with different modes of quotation in his earlier *Ecclesiastical History*.

The narrative of Nicaea lies at the nexus of these literary explorations and, in some sense, encapsulates them. Combined with a theologically and morally charged desire for peace within diversity, Eusebius's final portrait of Nicaea firmly resists our modern attempts to parse doctrinal particularities, assign blame, or determine reliability based on objectivist assumptions. He instead offers us the clarity forged of personal involvement and hope, grounded within his own inescapably contextual vision. His narration of Nicaea shows Eusebius to be a master of his literary art.

---

[117] See Irshai 2011.
[118] See Johnson 2014, 143–69.

SELECT REFERENCES

Barnes, Timothy D. 1981. *Constantine and Eusebius*. Cambridge, MA: Harvard University Press.

Cameron, Averil, and Stuart G. Hall, trans. 1999. *Eusebius: Life of Constantine*. Oxford: Clarendon Press.

Dainese, Davide. 2011. "Συνέρχομαι – συγρότησις – σύνοδος. Tre diversi usi della denominazione." *Cristianesimo nella storia* 32: 875–943.

DelCogliano, Mark. 2006. "Eusebian Theologies of the Son as the Image of God before 341." *JECS* 14 (4): 458–84.

Drake, H. A. 2000. *Constantine and the Bishops: The Politics of Intolerance*. Baltimore: Johns Hopkins University Press.

Drecoll, Volker Henning. 2013. "How Binitarian/Trinitarian Was Eusebius?" In *Eusebius of Caesarea: Tradition and Innovations*, ed. Aaron P. Johnson and Jeremy Schott, 289–305. Washington, DC: Center for Hellenic Studies Press.

Irshai, Oded. 2011. "Fourth Century Christian Palestinian Politics." In *Reconsidering Eusebius: Collected Papers on Literary, Historical, and Theological Issues*, ed. Sabrina Inowlocki and Claudio Zamagni, 25–38. Supplements to Vigiliae Christianae 107. Leiden: Brill.

Johannessen, Hazel. 2016. *The Demonic in the Political Thought of Eusebius of Caesarea*. Oxford Early Christian Studies. Oxford: Oxford University Press.

Johnson, Aaron P. 2014. *Eusebius*. London: I. B. Tauris.

Lyman, Rebecca. 1993. *Christology and Cosmology: Models of Divine Activity in Origen, Eusebius and Athanasius*. Oxford Theology and Religion Monographs. Oxford: Oxford University Press.

Morlet, Sébastien. 2009. *La* Démonstration évangélique *d'Eusèbe de Césarée: Étude sur l'apologétique chrétienne à l'époque de Constantin*. Collection des Études augustiniennes, Série Antiquité 187. Turnhout: Brepols.

Spoerl, Kelley McCarthy and Markus Vinzent, trans. 2017. *Eusebius of Caesarea: Against Marcellus and On Ecclesiastical Theology*. FC 135. Washington, DC: Catholic University of America Press.

Strutwolf, Holger. 1999. *Die Trinitätstheologie und Christologie des Euseb von Caesarea*. Forschungen zur Kirchen- und Dogmengeschichte 72. Gottingen: Vandenhoeck & Ruprecht.

Van Nuffelen, Peter. 2013. "Eusebius and Images of Truth in the *Life of Constantine*." In *Eusebius of Caesarea: Tradition and Innovations*, ed. Aaron P. Johnson and Jeremy Schott 133–49. Washington, DC: Center for Hellenic Studies Press.

Williams, Michael Stuart. 2008. *Authorized Lives in Early Christian Biography: Between Eusebius and Augustine*. Cambridge: Cambridge University Press.

Part IV
The Aftermath

11 The Reception of Nicaea and *Homoousios* to 360

SARA PARVIS

Although scholarly interpretations vary concerning the ecclesiastical events of the years from Nicaea to 360, and some chronological details remain in dispute, if we focus on the reception of the Council of Nicaea, the progress of events is fairly clear.[1] The key acts of the council were all one by one reversed over these years. Arius's exile was revoked in the autumn of 327 by Constantine, and his condemnation was as far as possible reversed in the East by the time of his death in 336.[2] During the lifetime of Constantine, the canons of Nicaea, particularly canon 15 forbidding the translation of bishops, were held to be operative; after Constantine's death in 337, they were set aside.[3] Alternative creeds began to be issued by councils from 328 onwards.[4] The Nicene Creed, including the term *homoousios*, was first sidelined, and then, from 357 to 360, officially replaced across the whole empire, with public use of *homoousios* specifically banned in 360.[5] Anathemas verbally similar to those issued by Nicaea against Arius's theology were appended to some

---

[1]   The finer points of the relevant chronology for this period, particularly for the activities and writings of Athanasius of Alexandria, are discussed in detail by Barnes 1993. In my own reconstruction of the ecclesiastical politics of the years 325–45 (Parvis 2006), I proposed different readings of the evidence on a few points, which will be noted where relevant.

[2]   *Urk.* 29 (*Dok.* 33); for the date of Arius's death, see Barnes 1978.

[3]   For the Greek and Latin texts of the creed and the canons of Nicaea, see Alberigo 2006, 19–34; English translation in Tanner 1990. Although it has long been argued that the Nicene canons in general were marginalised from shortly after Nicaea until 379, it is only in the case of canon 15 that we have clear evidence for the date at which they were sidelined. For Constantine's praise of Eusebius of Caesarea for upholding canon 15, though without explicit reference to Nicaea, see Eusebius (Eus.), *Vita Constantini* (*VC*) 3.61.1. Canon 15 was set aside by Constantius in at least two appointments of major significance, both to the see of Constantinople: Eusebius of Nicomedia in 337, and Eudoxius of Antioch in 360.

[4]   For the Greek and/or Latin texts of all the creeds discussed here, see Kinzig 2017, vol. 1. Although this work also includes English translations, I have generally used my own.

[5]   On these developments, see also the chapters by Mark DelCogliano, Kelly McCarthy Spoerl, and Daniel Williams in this volume.

of the creeds of the 340s, but in forms which no longer ruled out any of his theological tenets other than ἐξ οὐκ ὄντων ("out of non-being").[6] The name of the Council of Nicaea continued to be held in honour throughout the reign of Constantine, but by the 350s the main honour paid in official policy to Nicaea was the series of attempts to hold a new council either there or somewhere else with a similar name.[7]

How do we explain all of this? Why was the Creed of Nicaea officially replaced and all discussion of the term *homoousios* (and, indeed, *ousia* language in general) banned in 360, only to be reaffirmed at the Council of Constantinople of 381? Do the answers lie in imperial politics, in theological debate, in friendship networks, in the talents and ambitions of individual bishops, or in popular support for charismatic individuals and appropriation of their theology?

The short answer is all of these. As I have argued elsewhere for the earlier part of the period and will set out more briefly for the whole of it here, the ecclesiastical events of 325–60 were caused and controlled by two alliances which had formed for and against certain aspects of the theology of Arius in the years before Nicaea and continued to renew themselves by uniting in attack and defence against one another in the years afterwards.[8] One was much more closely bound in friendship, theology, and common purpose than the other, which was largely formed in reaction to the actions of the first. Both alliances included talented individuals, who were shored up by popular local support in many cases, but two stand out: Eusebius of Nicomedia, related by marriage to Constantine's half-brother Julius Constantius, and Athanasius, Alexander's low-born, highly effective successor in the see of Alexandria.[9]

What we may initially call the "Eusebian alliance," and afterwards the "anti-Athanasian alliance," was led until their deaths in late 341 and 339 respectively by Eusebius of Nicomedia/Constantinople and Eusebius of Caesarea. Although the theological differences between

---

[6] See e.g. the original anathemas to the so-called Fourth Creed of Antioch (Kinzig 2017, 1:347).

[7] Eus., *VC* 4.47; Kinzig 2017, 1:420–23.

[8] See Parvis 2006, especially 39–68, 134–78. After 359, the two alliances become three parties, and after Jovian five parties.

[9] This reading of events runs against the grain of much scholarship in English from Hanson 1988 onwards, including Gwynn 2007, who argues that claims by Athanasius of an opposition organised by "those around Eusebius" against him and other anti-Arian bishops are not sustainable. In my view, the prosopographical evidence for a widespread clearance of non-Arian-supporting Nicene bishops by 343 refutes these arguments.

them were not negligible, and the bishop of Caesarea was somewhat wary of his namesake, both acted decisively to support Arius before and after Nicaea, even though both abandoned him to his fate during the council itself.[10] Each brought a knot of friends and geographically close colleagues to the alliance, which included at least another fifteen bishops in the initial stages, as well as the learned lay theologian Asterius the Sophist.[11] Eusebius of Nicomedia argued that the Son was different in *ousia* from the Father, terminology alien to Eusebius of Caesarea, but both continued to support Arius in arguing against the eternity of the Son.[12] From 342 onwards, as we shall see, the party, whose theology now covered a wide spectrum but was united by lasting opposition to the episcopal tenure of Athanasius, was led by Eusebius's successor Acacius of Caesarea and Marcellus's replacement Basil of Ancyra, and continued to act in concert against Athanasius, his allies, and the use of Nicene terminology and anathemas. Only the Council of Constantinople of 360, at which Basil was deposed, put a definitive end to the remains of the Eusebian alliance: by 365, its surviving erstwhile members had dispersed in four different theological directions, including in some cases reluctant support for Nicaea.

The other, anti-Arian alliance which formed before Nicaea was led by Alexander of Alexandria, with theological support initially from Philogonius of Antioch, Macarius of Jerusalem, and Hellanicus of Tripolis.[13] After the death of Philogonius in December 323, his place was enthusiastically taken by Eustathius, who was recognised as bishop of Antioch in late 324 by Ossius of Corduba, acting with the authority of Constantine.[14] Another staunch opponent of Arius's theology at Nicaea was Marcellus of Ancyra, though it is not clear how closely he worked with Alexander.[15] Alexander was also supported at Nicaea by the presbyters representing Sylvester, bishop of Rome; the stance of successive bishops of Rome would continue to be crucial to the survival of the authority of the Council of Nicaea.

---

[10] On the theology of the two Eusebii and other leading figures of the Eusebian alliance, see Ayres 2004, 52–61.

[11] For a more detailed analysis of the prosopography of the Eusebian alliance, see Parvis 2006, 39–50.

[12] See Anatolios 2011, 60–61.

[13] For discussion of the evidence for the membership, views and degrees of commitment of the initial anti-Arian alliance, see Parvis 2006, 50–68. On the differing theological traditions on which this alliance drew, see Ayres 2004, 43–52, 62–75.

[14] See P. Parvis 2006. On Ossius's career in general, see De Clercq 1954.

[15] On Marcellus's actions at Nicaea, see the *Letter of Julius* in Athanasius (Ath.), *Apologia (secunda) contra Arianos (Ap. sec.)* 32.2.

The main theological works of this party during the immediate post-Nicene period survive only in fragments. Its key theologians, Eustathius and Marcellus, were self-consciously anti-Origenist and miahypostatic, attacking positions dear to the pro-Nicene party of the 370s and 380s.[16] Both attacked Eusebius of Caesarea in particular, whose defence was a key goal of his successor Gelasius of Caesarea's continuation of Eusebius's *Ecclesiastical History*, which underlies the fifth-century pro-Nicene histories.[17] The pro-Nicene tradition eventually was able to canonise Eustathius and preserve those parts of his thought which well suited Antiochene Christology, but Marcellus was adopted by the Meletian party as a shibboleth in the politics over appropriating the Nicene tradition in the 370s. Only the combined efforts of Athanasius and successive bishops of Rome preserved him uncondemned in the West.[18]

All the leading eastern opponents of Arius before or during Nicaea, including Alexander's successor Athanasius, had died or been deposed by the summer of 336. The anti-Arian alliance was reconstituted by Athanasius on Constantine's death in 337, only to be dismantled almost immediately by the Eusebian alliance with the support of Constantius II.[19] Over the next twenty-one years, only Athanasius would manage to return to the East and hold his see for any length of time, but the resurgence of the former supporters of Eustathius in Antioch and Marcellus in Ancyra after 361 shows that some popular support for the old anti-Arian alliance must have continued beyond Egypt as well.

Constantius's regions went their own theological and political way at the Council of Antioch of 341, signalling to Julius, bishop of Rome, that they were not prepared to stand by Nicaea's condemnation of Arius, or to engage with western support for Athanasius. By the time of the would-be "ecumenical" Council of Serdica of 343, there were only two bishops in the eastern party who had been present and signed at Nicaea who are not known to have been supporters of Arius.[20] But the "western" council, led by Ossius and Protogenes of Serdica, also played its part in sidelining Nicaea by producing a new theological statement, leaving Athanasius (reinstated to his see on his replacement's death in 345) in

---

[16] On the fourth-century categories of miahypostatic and trihypostatic theology, see Lienhard 1987.

[17] For the identifiable fragments of Gelasius's continuation of Eusebius's *Ecclesiastical History*, see Wallraff et al. 2018.

[18] See John Chrysostom's homily on Eustathius (PG 50:515–20); Lienhard 1993.

[19] Parvis 2006, 139–48.

[20] Parvis 2006, 218–21.

something of a dilemma. He had offered a brief theological defence of *homoousios* in the early 340s, but it was only in 353, when Constantius secured his grip on the whole empire, that Athanasius circulated a full theological defence of Nicaea.[21] Official moves to dislodge Athanasius and ban *homoousios* ensued, ending with his flight in 356 and the forbidding of all discussion of *ousia* terminology by the Council of Constantinople of 360. But by this time, the Nicene Creed had become the banner of anti-Constantian resistance in the West, and its formal acceptance would be a *sine qua non* for anyone expecting recognition from Rome after Constantius's death in 361.[22]

Despite the tendency of much English-speaking scholarship since Hanson to play down the evidence for a systematic empire-wide struggle over the reception of Nicaea throughout 325–60, we show here that the battle to suppress Nicaea's condemnation of the theology of Arius on the part of one ecclesiastical party, and to keep that condemnation alive on the part of the other, never ceased to be determinedly fought during this period. But for much of the period, the case for Nicaea was held together above all by one man, Athanasius of Alexandria. He had many allies, but none were committed to Nicaea's precise terminology in the way that he increasingly was. Without Athanasius's political and theological under-standing of the importance of that first "great and holy Council," and his rhetorical skill in communicating it, the Creed of Nicaea and the term *homoousios* alike would almost certainly have sunk with very little trace long before 381.

325–328: EUSEBIUS'S FALL AND RISE, ARIUS'S RECALL, THE FALL OF EUSTATHIUS OF ANTIOCH AND THE COUNCIL OF NICOMEDIA

Constantine's ecclesiastical policy took several different tacks in the three years after his defeat of Licinius in September 324, before more or less setting a clear course in one direction. Ossius committed Constantine to recognising Eustathius as bishop of Antioch at the coun-cil there in late 324, which effectively tied imperial policy to supporting Alexander's party in the controversy over Arius's theology in the initial instance. Thereafter, however, Constantine attempted to dampen or silence the theological debates as far as possible.[23] Petitioned to allow

---

[21]   Ath., *Ap. sec.* 1.9; *De decretis Nicaenae synodi* (*De decr.*). For the context and dating, see Barnes 1993, Appendix 4.
[22]   Socrates (Socr.), *Historia ecclesiastica* (*HE*) 4.12.
[23]   Eus., *VC* 3.5–14.

an ecclesiastical council to take place at Ancyra, he moved it to the
imperial palace at Nicaea under his own eye, urging peace on the participants and silence on the most argumentative.[24] Although he accepted
that Arius himself was bound to be condemned, the bishops who had
previously supported Arius were pressured or cajoled into signing the
Nicene Creed: only Secundus of Ptolemais and Theonas of Marmarica
refused to sign and were exiled by Constantine in consequence.[25] But
three months after the council, Constantine changed tack again and also
exiled Eusebius of Nicomedia and Theognis of Nicaea.[26] Both had chosen
to regard Nicaea's condemnation of Arius in minimalist terms, welcom-
ing Arius's associates into communion immediately after the council;
kind friends informed Constantine, raising his ire against them and
leading to their banishment.[27]

Constantine returned to Rome in summer 326, amid what must
have been considerable speculation concerning his intended future
arrangements for governing the empire. If his eldest son, the Caesar
Crispus, was expected to be promoted to Augustus, with his next
sons Constantinus and Constantius continuing as Caesars according
to the recent norms of the Tetrarchy, Constantine put an end to such
speculation by executing Crispus, followed by his own wife Fausta.
Ossius seems to have left the imperial court around this point.[28] On
Constantine's return to the East the following year with his mother
Helena, he changed his ecclesiastical policy completely. He recalled
Arius from exile and began to work to have Arius's ecclesiastical
condemnation reversed, allowing Eusebius and Theognis also to
return shortly afterwards.[29] At the same time (or just before), he
turned against the leading bishops of the anti-Arian side at Nicaea,
in particular Eustathius of Antioch, whom he gave orders to have
deposed.[30]

The reasons for this decisive change of policy must remain speculative. However, they may reflect *inter alia* a greater prominence at court
of Constantine's half-brothers, Flavius Dalmatius and Julius
Constantius, as a consequence of the death of Crispus (Constantinus

---

[24]   *Urk.* 20 (*Dok.* 22); Theodoret (Thdt.), *Historia ecclesiastica* (*HE*) 1.8.1–5.
[25]   *Urk.* 23 (*Dok.* 25).
[26]   *Urk.* 27 (*Dok.* 31); Thdt., *HE* 1.20.11.
[27]   Constantine's letter (see previous note) implies that someone had also reminded him
       of Eusebius's earlier attempt to plead for Licinius's life. Whether the intervention
       came from Ossius or some other figure at court is unknown.
[28]   See De Clercq 1954, 282ff.
[29]   Socr., *HE* 1.25.7, 1.14.2–6.
[30]   Thdt., *HE* 1.21.

and Constantius were only eleven and ten at the time).[31] As both the
uncle of Julius Constantius's wife, Basilina, and the friend of his sister
and Constantine's half-sister Constantia, Eusebius of Nicomedia had
two excellent routes to imperial clemency.[32] In any case, Eusebius
remained in imperial favour thereafter, baptising Constantine on his
deathbed ten years later.[33]

Eustathius was replaced as bishop of Antioch with Paulinus of
Tyre.[34] The ecclesiastical side of Eustathius's sentence was carried out
in a council at Antioch in autumn 327, in the context of Helena's visit to
the Holy Land that year. The complete secrecy of the operation meant
that the reasons for the deposition were and remained unclear to
Eustathius's friends and enemies alike: some reports claimed he was
deposed for fornication, others for "Sabellianism," while Athanasius
claimed Eustathius was deposed for offending Helena in some unspeci-
fied manner.[35]

Shortly after the return of Eusebius and Theognis to their sees,
according to the fragments of Philostorgius's Eunomian *Ecclesiastical
History*, a large council took place at Nicomedia. It issued and circulated
widely an alternative creed to that of Nicaea, and condemned Alexander
of Alexandria for using the term *homoousios* and Eustathius for
fornication.[36] Eusebius of Caesarea's *Life of Constantine* confirms that
some such gathering did indeed take place, but he was clearly less than
comfortable about its actions and downplayed its significance.[37] This
council is never included in the lists of "orthodox" councils in surviving

[31] It is notable that Julius Constantius was named ordinary consul for the year 335,
      the year of the Council of Tyre.
[32] For Eusebius's relationship to Basilina's father Iulius Iulianus, see Ammianus
      Marcellinus, *Res gestae* 22.9.4.
[33] Jerome, *Chronicon*, a. 337.
[34] Thdt., *HE* 1.21. On the chronology of bishops of Antioch before and after Eustathius,
      see P. Parvis 2006.
[35] The ecclesiastical charge against Eustathius was indeed likely to have been fornica-
      tion, real or trumped-up. A secret deposition of the bishop of Antioch for heresy in 327
      is unlikely for a number of reasons: see the discussion in Parvis 2006, 101–7.
[36] Philostorgius (Phil.), *Historia ecclesiastica* (*HE*) 2.7. He seems to have said that the
      πλήρωμα of this council was 250, but this is unlikely to mean it was attended by 250
      bishops, given that it made so little impression on the later record otherwise, includ-
      ing among Eusebius's allies. The 250 probably included other clerical ranks (as with
      the signatories of the Council of Arles in 314).
[37] Eusebius of Caesarea makes clear that he did not consider this council as in any way in
      the same league as Nicaea and Tyre/Jerusalem: cf. Eus., *VC* 3.23, 4.47. See Hanson
      1988, 174–76, for a discussion of the evidence for a second session of Nicaea, and
      Parvis 2006, 111–12, for a refutation (though note that I was wrong to say that
      Constantine was in Trier at the time of the synod: he went there in autumn 328).

documents from eastern councils of the 340s and 350s (e.g. those in the easterners' letter of Serdica or the letter of the Council of Ancyra of 358); only the Eunomian historiographical tradition records it and celebrates its actions, and the fragment of Philostorgius's discussion of it is tantalisingly brief. Nonetheless, if we accept the basic details of his account, we have here the first of many attempts from 328 to 360 to replace the Nicene Creed with an alternative, to condemn or at least sideline the term *homoousios*, and to oust major bishops who were supporters of the creed. We do not know which creed was issued at Nicomedia, but two plausible candidates are Arius's rehabilitation creed and the Lucianic Creed (Dedication Creed).[38] This synod may also have been the locus of Arius's official theological rehabilitation after his recall from exile.[39]

Constantine was in Nicomedia at this point and could well have been present, but we cannot tell how far he backed the actions of the council with legal force.[40] Nonetheless, he had already moved against Eustathius, and he put pressure on Alexander to receive Arius back into communion at around the same time as the Council of Nicomedia.[41] Alexander was summoned to Nicomedia to explain his refusal to accede to Constantine's request but was too ill to come (he died on 17 April 328).[42] He despatched his deacon Athanasius (who had been at Nicaea and knew the arguments well) in his stead. At the news of Alexander's death, Athanasius rushed back to Alexandria and was chosen and consecrated his successor on 8 June 328 by a group of six or seven bishops.[43]

---

[38] Arius's rehabilitation creed is given in Socr., *HE* 1.26.2 (*Urk.* 30; *Dok.* 34); for the argument for the Dedication Creed on the basis of Asterius's writing in defence of Eusebius of Nicomedia, see below.

[39] Constantine asked Alexander to receive Arius back before Alexander's death in April 328 (see below); it is likely, though not certain, that this was on the basis of Arius's rehabilitation at the Council of Nicomedia rather than simply his own authority as emperor.

[40] Photius, epitomising Philostorgius's account, calls the synod παράνομος, "lawless," which may mean simply that Constantine did not ratify its acts, or not all of them (Phil., *HE* 2.7.2). Most of the religious laws of Constantine from this period were not included in the Theodosian Code.

[41] Barnes 1993, 18.

[42] Cf. Eus., *VC* 3.23; *Syriac Index to the Festal Letters of Athanasius* (Martin and Albert 1985, 226, lines 4–5).

[43] See Barnes 1993, 18–20, for a discussion of the circumstances. The endless scholarly pearl-clutching of the twentieth century over "the behaviour of Athanasius" (e.g. Hanson 1988, ch. 9) is now beginning to seem rather quaint in the face of more recent scholarly recognition that violence was endemic in fourth-century religious government, imperial and episcopal. Although scholars in recent years (including Barnes)

Eusebius of Caesarea, meanwhile, was himself offered the see of Antioch in summer 328 by a group of Arius's supporters led by Theodotus of Laodicea, following the deaths of Paulinus and his successor Eulalius.[44] He referred the matter to Constantine, wary of infringing Nicaea's canon against the transfer of bishops, particularly in the wake of what had clearly been major riots in Antioch. The emperor commended his integrity and proposed two other candidates, one ordained by Alexander of Alexandria (George of Arethusa) and the one who was chosen, Euphronius.

328–336: EARLY POST-NICENE DEBATES ON OUSIA AND THE PUSH FOR THE REHABILITATION OF ARIUS

Some discussion of the theological terms of the Creed of Nicaea had already happened by 328. We are told that Eustathius of Antioch and Eusebius of Caesarea exchanged treatises debating the term *homoousios* in the period immediately after the council.[45] Eustathius accused Eusebius of interpreting the term in an unorthodox manner, and Eusebius in reply accused Eustathius of following the heresy of Sabellius.

Sophie Cartwright has argued that much of the substance of Eustathius's treatise against Eusebius is to be found in the fragments ascribed to Eustathius by José Declerck of a work he entitles *Contra Ariomanitas et de Anima*, though they do not include explicit discussion of the term *homoousios* itself (which none of Eustathius's other extant works does either; it was clearly not a term he was drawn to).[46] As Marcellus was to do again a few years later, Eustathius wrote against the theology not just of Eusebius of Caesarea but of a whole party: not yet the "Arians" in his terminology, but the "Ariomaniacs" (a play on warmongers, *Areomanitai*: those maddened by and mad for not the war-god Ares, but Arius). One of Eustathius's main concerns was to rule out the notion that the Eternal Son is mutable, which he sought to do with medical

---

have often followed the Eusebian alliance in considering Athanasius's election dubious, there was no real canonical problem with it by the standards of the day (which is why those charges did not stick), and there was no canonical reason why either the Melitians or anyone outside Egypt should have been involved in the election in the first place.

[44] Eus., *VC* 3.59–62. This assumes that the sees of the bishops addressed by Constantine can be supplied as those of Theodotus of Laodicea, Theodore of Tarsus, Narcissus of Neronias, Aetius of Lydda, and Alphaeus of Apameia. See Parvis 2006, 107–10, and Appendix Table 3 for more extensive discussion of this council.

[45] Socr., *HE*, 1.23.6–8; Sozomen (Soz.), *Historia ecclesiastica* (*HE*) 2.18.3–4.

[46] Eustathius, *Fragmenta* 1–61 (Declerck 2002, 63–130); Cartwright 2015, 57–66.

terminology by insisting on the human soul in Christ as the subject of Christ's passions, but he was also keen to rule out all forms of docetism, which he again saw as a logical conclusion of Eusebius's thought.[47]

More explicit discussion of *ousia* language would soon follow. Shortly after the Council of Nicomedia, after the death of Paulinus of Tyre and probably in the context of Eusebius of Nicomedia's rehabilitation, Asterius the Sophist wrote a theological defence of Eusebius of Nicomedia's pre-Nicene *Letter to Paulinus* (a document which is a strong candidate for the "blasphemy of Eusebius" which was "torn up" at Nicaea).[48] Eusebius had written:

> For neither have we heard of two Unbegottens, nor have we been taught or put our trust in one divided in two, nor something which suffered bodily, Lord Paulinus; but the Unbegotten is one thing, and that which was brought into being by it is another, truly brought into being and not from its essence [οὐσία], not partaking at all of the nature of the Unbegotten, or being from its essence, but brought into being absolutely other in nature and in power, having been brought into a perfect likeness of disposition and power of the one who made it.[49]

Eusebius then robustly defended his claim that the one "brought into being" was not from the Father's essence, on the basis of a close exegesis of Proverbs 8:22. Asterius, in defending Eusebius, softened his language from two impersonal neuters (ἓν μέν, ἓν δέ) to masculine personal subjects (the Father and the Logos) and explained his meaning in terms of image Christology, drawing extensively on terminology close to that of the Dedication Creed.[50]

> For the Father who begot (γεννήσας) from himself the only-begotten Word and first-born of all creation is ἄλλος μὲν [one of two contrasting masculine subjects], One [begetting] One, Perfect [begetting] Perfect, King [begetting] King, Lord [begetting] Lord, God [begetting] God, an unvarying image of both *ousia* and will, and glory and

---

47 See also Spoerl 2016, and Parvis 2006, 58.

48 The length of Asterius's work is unknown. For the fragments of Asterius, see Vinzent 1993. Eustathius's account of the "blasphemy of Eusebius" appears in Thdt., *HE* 1.8.1–5. The *Letter to Paulinus* is discussed in Ayres 2004, 52–53. For discussion of the literary interdependence of Eusebius's *Letter to Paulinus*, Asterius's *In Defence of Eusebius*, Marcellus's *Against Asterius*, and Athanasius's *Orations Against the Arians*, see Parvis 2008.

49 *Urk.* 8 (*Dok.* 4).

50 See Vinzent 1993, 164–66; Parvis 2006, 112–16. For the text of the Dedication Creed, see Kinzig 2017, 1:342–45.

power. But the one who was begotten from him is another (ἄλλος δὲ), who is the image of the invisible God.

Asterius here turned Eusebius's explicit and forceful denial that the Son was from the Father's essence into an affirmation that Eusebius understood him to be the unvarying image of the Father's essence. This was fleshed out with extensive Scriptural exegesis, with which Marcellus would later engage. Asterius sought in this way to build a bridge between Eusebius of Nicomedia's position and that of more classical Origenists. Athanasius would work very hard over the next thirty years to attempt to break that bridge.[51]

One of Athanasius's most significant theological works, the double treatise *Against the Pagans and On the Incarnation*, can be dated to around this time.[52] Khaled Anatolios has argued that it represents a covert attack on the theology of Arius, Asterius, and Eusebius of Caesarea.[53] Athanasius made no use of *ousia* language in this text, but engaged with ongoing debates by referring to the Word of God as image simply of the Father (rather than of the Father's *ousia*), and the Father's own Word (ἴδιος λόγος). He would develop this theology in terms of *ousia* in the *Orations Against the Arians* of the early 340s.

The first theologian to attack Asterius's work explicitly, however, was Marcellus of Ancyra, in a treatise generally given the name *Contra Asterium (Against Asterius)*, in which he also argued against the theology of Eusebius of Nicomedia, Eusebius of Caesarea, Paulinus of Tyre, and Narcissus of Neronias.[54] Marcellus's use or avoidance of the term *homoousios* itself cannot be fully reconstructed: his work survives only in fragments quoted by Eusebius and Acacius of Caesarea, and both were clearly keen to avoid discussing this term. He seems, however, to have

[51] Athanasius argues against Asterius's version of image theology in the *Orations Against the Arians* and in *On the Decrees of Nicaea* and for his own, different understanding of the term. See the discussion below and in Anatolios 2011, 53–59, 104–33.

[52] This work has been variously dated to 318, 325–28, 328–33, 335–37, 339–45, and 356–62 (see Anatolios 2011, 26–30). I have argued for 325–28, accepting Barnes 1993, 12–13. If Anatolios is correct that the work targets Asterius specifically (which I do not think it is possible to demonstrate), his dating of 328–33 would be preferred to the slightly earlier date. The arguments for a date before the *Orations* seem to me unanswerable.

[53] Anatolios 2011, 100–8.

[54] About one-sixth of Marcellus's work survives in citations in writings against him by Eusebius and Acacius of Caesarea (Klostermann 1991). The most recent critical edition of the fragments (in effectively the order proposed by Seibt 1994) is Vinzent 1997, though I am preparing a critical edition in a new order. English translations are my own.

accused first Asterius and then all the others of believing in two (or three) *ousiai*, and hence in two or three gods:

> For since [Asterius] had dared to divide the Word from God and to name the Word another God, separated from the Father by essence and by power, it is possible clearly and easily to learn the great blasphemy into which he fell from the very words which he himself wrote. And he wrote thus in these words: "The image indeed, and that of which it is the image, are understood not to be one and the same thing, but two essences and two realities and two powers, as so many appellations."[55]

Marcellus allows that the use of image terminology specifically excludes the idea that what is imaged is the same sort of thing as the image, and he draws the conclusion (which he also ascribes to Asterius) that what is the image of God's essence is no longer God's essence.[56]

> So [Asterius] intends [the Word of God] to be none of the things which he said before; for he says that he is image of all these things. So then, if he is image of essence, he is no longer able to be essence itself; and if he is image of will, he is no longer able to be will itself; and if image of power, no longer power, and if image of glory, no longer glory. For the image is not image of itself, but of something else.

For Marcellus, the whole point of an image (which he interprets in the sense of "statue," like the great images of the imperial family) is that it makes the invisible visible, and thus is different from what it represents:

> For images are demonstrative of those things of which they are images, even when they are absent, so that that even the one who is absent seems to be made manifest through them. But if it should be the case, God being invisible, that the Word also is invisible, how is the Word of himself able to be image of the invisible God, he also

---

[55] P(arvis), frag. 75; S(eibt)/V(inzent), frag. 117; K(lostermann), frag. 82: οὐ δήπου δὲ ἡ εἰκὼν καὶ τὸ οὗ ἐστιν ἡ εἰκὼν ἓν καὶ ταὐτὸν ἐπινοεῖται, ἀλλὰ δύο μὲν οὐσίαι καὶ δύο πράγματα καὶ δύο δυνάμεις, ὡς καὶ τοσαῦται προσηγορίαι. See further his citation of Eusebius of Caesarea referring to two *ousiai*: "For truly was [St Paul] in labour with a keen and bitter labour, because he knew the Galatians did not hold an opinion concerning Godly piety like [Eusebius of Caesarea's], nor did they say there were two essences and realities and powers and Gods." P 78 S/V 117 K 82. See also P 79 S/V 121 K 40 on Paulinus; P 62 S/V 116 K 81 (= *Urk.* 19 [*Dok.* 21]) on Narcissus.
[56] Marcellus, frag. P 60 S/V 114 K 97.

being invisible? For it is impossible that what is not seen should ever be made manifest through the invisible.[57]

Marcellus might conceivably have been accusing Asterius of denying that the Word is *homoousios* with God (because an image is not *homoousios* with what it is an image of), but if so, neither Eusebius nor Acacius noted the fact. The "image of the invisible God" of Colossians 1:15 is the incarnate Christ, for Marcellus, not the pre-incarnate Logos:

> Now, clearly, did he become true image of the invisible God, at the time when he assumed the flesh which had come to be according to the image of God. For if through this image we were made worthy to know the Word of God, we ought to believe the Word himself saying through the image "I and the Father are one." For it is not possible for anyone to know either the Word or the Father of the Word apart from this image.[58]

Marcellus's exegesis of Proverbs 8:22, that what was "created" by the Lord "as the beginning of his ways for his works," was the humanity of Christ (flesh, soul or both), would be widely picked up in the later pro-Nicene tradition, since it is the only possible interpretation of the passage compatible with Nicaea if it is read Christologically. But his interpretation of Colossians 1:15 was largely avoided by the rest of the anti-Arian alliance, and Athanasius in particular. The eternal Word as "image of the Father" remains for Athanasius an enduring guarantee of the newly unbreakable hold on a world beyond change which the Incarnation has conferred on humanity.[59]

Constantine pressured Athanasius as he had Alexander to receive Arius back into communion in the name of peace, and like Alexander, Athanasius refused. In 331/2 and 334, Athanasius successfully fended off attempts to have Constantine depose him, but in 335, he was less successful (the fact that Eusebius of Nicomedia's nephew-in-law, Julius Constantius, was consul that year may not be irrelevant).[60] Constantine called a great liturgy of reconciliation for the dedication of the Church of the Holy Sepulchre at Jerusalem and in honour of his own *tricennalia*, at which Arius was to be restored.[61] All the important

---

[57] P 55 S/V 54 K 93.
[58] P 56 S/V 55 K 94. On Marcellus's image theology, see Parvis 2006, 32–36.
[59] Anatolios 2011, 107–8.
[60] Barnes 1993, 20–22.
[61] For the proceedings of the Council of Tyre and Jerusalem, see Barnes 1993, 22–23; Parvis 2006, 123–27.

bishops of the East were expected to attend.[62] A council took place beforehand at Tyre to try Athanasius for various charges of violence, but the investigative commission to Egypt took so long to report that the bishops had to leave for Jerusalem before it was completed. Athanasius headed off instead to Constantinople to petition Constantine himself. Marcellus, meanwhile, refused to participate in the Jerusalem liturgy with Arius.[63] The council reconvened at Tyre, condemned Athanasius, and now also raised charges against Marcellus, who appealed to Constantine in turn.[64] The two Eusebii, Theognis of Nicaea, Patrophilus of Scythopolis, Ursacius of Singidunum, and Valens of Mursa hastily travelled to Constantinople to pursue the cases against Athanasius and Marcellus.

Constantine exiled Athanasius to Trier (though probably on different charges from the ones brought at Tyre), and called a council to try Marcellus before his closing *tricennalia* celebrations at Constantinople in July 336.[65] Constantine himself was present, and the expert witness against Marcellus was Eusebius of Caesarea.[66] Eusebius argued that Marcellus had disturbed the theological peace by attacking so many bishops, that he had taught that the Son of God first had a beginning from Mary, and that Christ's kingdom would have an end (accusations which were all justifiable in a literal sense).[67] Marcellus was condemned and exiled. He was replaced by Basil of Ancyra, who would be one of the leading eastern theologians from 336 to 359.

Arius was scheduled to be involved in the great *tricennalia* liturgy in Constantinople. According to Athanasius, Alexander, bishop of Constantinople, unwilling to receive Arius into communion, prayed out loud that either he or Arius might die before it took place.[68] Arius did die, possibly on the day of the ceremony itself, in a public lavatory. His friends believed he had been poisoned.[69]

---

[62] Eus., *VC* 4.42.3–4; on the guest-list, see Parvis 2006, 124–27.
[63] Soz., *HE* 2.33.2–3.
[64] See Parvis 2006, 118–23, on the timing of the various charges against Marcellus and his appeal to Constantine.
[65] Barnes 1978, 64–65 ; Barnes 1993, 24.
[66] Vinzent 1997, xix.
[67] See Parvis 2006, 127–32.
[68] Ath., *De morte Arii* 2.
[69] Soz., *HE* 2.29.5.

337–350: DIVIDED EMPERORS, DIVIDED VIEWS ON NICAEA

Constantine died on 22 May 337. His second surviving son, Constantius II, was the first of the four Caesars on the scene and had the fourth Caesar, his half-cousin Dalmatius, killed, together with Flavius Dalmatius, Julius Constantius, and all the other male descendants of Constantius I's second wife, Theodora, except Julius Constantius's younger sons Gallus and Julian.[70] He met the other two Caesars, his brothers Constantine II and Constans, in Pannonia with Dalmatius's army behind him later in the summer, and by 9 September they eventually agreed to a new division of the empire in which they were all proclaimed Augustus. All three were under twenty-one years of age.

Constantine II had already sent Athanasius back from the court in Trier to Alexandria with an official letter cancelling his exile.[71] He may also have cancelled the exiles of some of Athanasius's allies, including Asclepas of Gaza, Marcellus of Ancyra, and Lucius of Adrianople.[72] Athanasius took immediate steps in the chaos of that summer to rebuild a new anti-Eusebian alliance. As he took the long land route back through Constantinople, Asia Minor, Syria, Phoenicia, and Palestine, he restored condemned bishops, consecrated new ones, and deposed others (presumably in Egypt in the last case).[73] His most potentially significant new ally was Paul, who had just been elected to replace the recently dead Alexander as bishop of Constantinople, and in whose consecration Athanasius took part when he passed through the city.[74] At this point (which must have been before 9 September), Constantinople may not yet have been decisively under Constantius's control: it had been in the territory of Dalmatius. But once Constantius II came to Constantinople as its new territorial emperor in autumn 337, he removed Paul and replaced him with Eusebius of Nicomedia.[75]

The council which consecrated Eusebius included (indeed, may have been confined to) Eusebius himself, Maris of Chalcedon, Theodore of

---

[70] On the imperial settlement following the death of Constantine, see Burgess 2008; almost all of his narrative is here assumed.

[71] Athanasius gives the text of Constantine II's letter in *Ap. sec.* 87.4–7. It was dated 17 June 337.

[72] These three bishops returned to their sees after Constantine's death (Hilary of Poitiers [Hilar.], *Fragmenta Historica* [FH] A 4.1.8.3); Wickham 1997, 26), but it is not known on whose authority.

[73] Hilar., *FH* A 4.1.8.2 (Wickham 1997, 25–26).

[74] This meant that Paul would have found it difficult to join in any attempts to depose Athanasius without impugning his own ordination.

[75] On Paul of Constantinople, see Barnes 1993, Appendix 8.

Heraclea, Theognis of Nicaea, Ursacius, and Valens.[76] They seem also to have reaffirmed the condemnations of Athanasius, Marcellus, and Asclepas, elected a certain Pistus as Bishop of Alexandria, and sent letters reporting the acts of their council to Julius of Rome and to all three emperors.[77] All this would already have happened before Athanasius returned to Alexandria on 23 November 337.[78]

The status of Nicaea moved to the forefront of diplomatic exchanges between Constantinople, Antioch, Alexandria, and Rome during the four years following Constantine's death. Eusebius of Constantinople continued to make clear by his actions that he regarded Nicaea as a dead letter, particularly now that Arius was deceased.[79] Flacillus, bishop of Antioch, had presided over the Council of Tyre; we must assume that he had therefore communicated with Arius at the Council of Jerusalem, and so was thereby also committed to the view that Nicaea's main acts had been definitively reversed.[80]

But this was not the view taken in Rome, where Arius's rehabilitation had never been accepted.[81] The presbyters Vitus and Vincent, Rome's legates at Nicaea, were still alive and had clear views on what had happened there.[82] Athanasius sent envoys to Rome in spring 338, carrying the letter of a council in Alexandria which had exonerated him from all charges immediately after his return.[83] They there met the envoys from Constantinople with the letters announcing the deposition of Athanasius, the appointment of Pistus, and the election and consecration of Eusebius as bishop of Constantinople. These letters evidently claimed communion with the bishop of Rome according to the usual custom.[84]

After listening to and questioning both sets of ambassadors, Julius wrote back to Eusebius and the others.[85] He clearly recognised Eusebius

---

[76] For the names, see Hilar., *FH* B 2.1.2.1 (Wickham 1997, 42).

[77] See Parvis 2006, 150–57, for these events all taking place at a synod in Constantinople in late 337.

[78] *Festal index* (Martin and Albert 1985, 236, lines 4–6, with 286, note 30).

[79] Eusebius of Caesarea was still prepared to honour Nicaea in name, though giving a higher status to the Council of Jerusalem of 335 (at which Arius had been received back into communion). See Eus., *VC* 4.47.

[80] Ath., *Ap. sec.* 8; *De synodis* (*De syn.*) 21; Eus., *VC* 4.43.

[81] The diplomatic moves made at Rome in 338 must be deduced from references to them in a later letter from Julius to Eusebius and others, which was sent in 341. See Ath., *Ap. sec.* 22.

[82] Ath., *Ap. sec.* 32.

[83] Barnes 1993, 37; Parvis 2006, 147.

[84] This is implied by the statement in Ath., *Ap. sec.* 34 that Julius has preferred Athanasius's communion to that of Eusebius and his friends.

[85] Ath., *Ap. sec.* 22, 26.

as bishop of Constantinople and accepted communion with him, though making it clear that he disapproved of Eusebius's translation from Nicomedia in contradiction to Nicaea canon 15.[86] But he refused to accept either the deposition of Athanasius or the election of Pistus. As Athanasius's envoys pointed out, Pistus had been consecrated by Secundus, who had been deposed at Nicaea for supporting Arius, and so was invalidly ordained from the point of view of a Church which believed Nicaea's condemnation of Arius still stood.[87] As regards Athanasius, Julius noted that many bishops from Egypt and elsewhere had written letters declaring his innocence. Julius made it clear that he wanted to hear the case against Athanasius himself, for which he called on all parties to come to Rome.[88]

That Rome was in a different imperial jurisdiction from Constantinople and Alexandria was of course crucial to Julius's ability to reject ecclesiastical actions sponsored by Constantius. Although Julius's letters to Eusebius and his allies were polite, to judge by the one that survives, it is unlikely that he needed Athanasius's *Encyclical Letter* of 339 to persuade him that their motives for deposing Athanasius and his allies were theologically questionable. Vitus and Vincent had clearly already told him as much on the basis of their experiences at Nicaea.[89]

Though Julius had first invited Eusebius of Constantinople and the others in 338 to come to Rome for a council to reconsider the case of Athanasius, his hand was strengthened in this regard two years later, when Constans came to Rome as emperor of the whole West.[90] Constantine II had invaded his brother's territory and been killed. Athanasius and Marcellus had in the meantime been expelled from their sees again and had come to Rome in the hopes of having their cases reviewed.[91] Around the time of Constans's *adventus* in summer 340, Julius despatched envoys to the East with instructions to bring back representatives from Constantius's regions for a council in Rome the following spring (which he claimed that they had originally requested), apparently confident that they would come.

[86]   Ath., *Ap. sec.* 21, 25.
[87]   Barnes 1993, 40.
[88]   Ath., *Ap. sec.* 22.
[89]   Ath., *Ap. sec.* 32
[90]   Barnes 1993, 225.
[91]   Parvis 2006, 150–60.

Instead, Constantius hosted a council in Antioch for the dedication
of the Golden Basilica, which finished on 6 January 341.[92] He detained
Julius's envoys, and then sent them back with nothing but an insolent
letter refusing to send any representatives. The Dedication Council,
attended by ninety-seven bishops, was Constantius's first attempt at
a major council. It endorsed three creeds, one of which, the Dedication
Creed, would be considered a better alternative to the Creed of Nicaea by
most of the bishops of the East at the Council of Seleucia in 359.[93] It
renewed the condemnations of Athanasius and Marcellus, and declared,
"We have not been followers of Arius – for how could bishops, such as we
are, follow a presbyter? [...] but after taking on ourselves to examine and
to verify his faith, we have admitted him rather than followed him."
Marcellus was the particular target of this council's opprobrium, at the
hands of Eusebius of Caesarea's successor, Acacius, who yielded nothing
to Athanasius in his talent for invective unmitigated by nuance.[94]

Julius responded by accusing the council leaders of abandoning
Nicaea, which he believed had had the sanction of 300 bishops.[95]
Marcellus defended himself to the assembling Roman council with
a new creed of his own based on the Roman tradition.[96] Athanasius,
meanwhile, went on the theological offensive, rewriting Marcellus's
original attack on Asterius and Eusebius of Nicomedia as his own three
Orations Against the Arians, silently correcting the parts which had
attracted Eusebius of Caesarea's condemnation and omitting all attacks
on the now dead Eusebius of Caesarea himself, as well as briefly but
explicitly defending the term *homoousios* ("True God, *homoousios* with
the true Father").[97]

For almost everyone other than Athanasius, however, Nicaea faded
into the background. After Eusebius of Constantinople's death in the
winter following the Dedication Council, the bishops of Constantius's
regions, now led by Acacius of Caesarea and Basil of Ancyra, held firmly
to the status quo: all attempts to reverse the depositions of Athanasius
and the others were strenuously resisted, while one alternative after
another to the Nicene Creed was drawn up and issued for discussion.[98]
Some months after the Dedication Council, a "Fourth Creed of

[92]   Parvis 2006, 160–78.
[93]   For the texts of all of these, see Kinzig 2017, 1:341–46.
[94]   On Acacius, see Lienhard 1989.
[95]   Ath., *Ap. sec.* 23.
[96]   Kinzig 2017, 2:222–25. See Parvis 2006, 181–85.
[97]   Ath., *Orationes tres adversus Arianos* 1.9. See Parvis 2008; Anatolios 2011, 108–26.
[98]   For the evidence that Acacius led the eastern party at Serdica, or at least wrote their
       encyclical letter, see Parvis 2006, 221–23.

Antioch," close in some of its formulations to the Creed of Nicaea but with no *ousia* language, was taken to Constans's court at Trier, where the envoys who brought it were ignored.[99] This creed would be reproduced with various annotations and anathemas on a number of occasions over the next decade.[100]

With further pressure from Constans, an ecumenical council was convoked in the name of both emperors to assemble at Serdica, near the border between their territories, in 343.[101] The bishops from Constantius's regions successfully employed wrecking tactics of various sorts, and the council never met as one body; instead, both groups met separately and issued letters denouncing one another. However, the western council produced a new exposition of faith (while the easterners reproduced the Fourth Creed of Antioch with new anathemas); it was closer to the theology of Marcellus of Ancyra than that of Athanasius.[102] The new statement specified that there is one hypostasis of the Father and of the Son and of the Holy Spirit, and it also employed some of Marcellus's characteristic exegetical moves.[103]

From this moment, we see a breach developing between Athanasius and Marcellus which was only healed towards the end of their lives, in 371.[104] According to Hilary of Poitiers, the break was caused by the Christology of Marcellus's former deacon Photinus, now bishop of Sirmium (a strategically vital city on the main military route between East and West, situated between the sees of the two prominent western Eusebians, Ursacius and Valens).[105] Photinus, who was held to teach that the Son of God was a "mere man," was condemned by a council in Milan in 345 with the acquiescence of Athanasius and Julius. As Constans did not respond to the condemnation by removing him from his see, at this stage it simply represented a withdrawal of communion by prominent western bishops.[106] Meanwhile, the eastern party produced a lengthy supplement to the old "Fourth Creed of Antioch," lampooned by Athanasius as *Makrostichos* (long-winded), which grappled to find

[99]   Barnes 1993, 68–69.
[100] Kinzig 2017, 1:346–48.
[101] Parvis, 2006, 210–45.
[102] Kinzig 2017, 1:349–54 (eastern) and 354–62 (western) for the text.
[103] E.g. picking up the "only-begotten and first-born" pairing of the Dedication Creed and assigning one to the Word and the other to the humanity: "We confess that he is only-begotten and first-born, but the Word is only-begotten since he always was and is in the Father, but the term 'first-born' refers to the humanity." Parvis 2006, 236–46.
[104] Lienhard 1993.
[105] Hilar., *FH* B 2.9.1.2–3 (Wickham 1997, 56–57).
[106] On the politics of the Council of Milan of 345, see Barnes 1993, 88–89; on the theology of Photinus, see Hanson 1988, 235–58.

a way of expressing some kind of unity between Father and Son without using *ousia* language.[107]

Despite the debacle of Serdica, Constans insisted on the restoration of Athanasius and Paul of Constantinople to their sees in 345–46, threatening his brother with war.[108] Athanasius was much more careful with the politics of his return than Paul, with the result that, though both were condemned by further councils in 349, when Constans's grip was visibly weakening, Paul was deposed that year and executed in 350, while Athanasius managed to cling on.[109] But when Constans was killed by the usurper Magnentius in 350, Athanasius's removal was only a matter of time.

Athanasius never seems to have accepted the Western Creed of Serdica, though he cites Serdica's exoneration of him in his *Apology Against the Arians*, mainly written in 349.[110] I have argued elsewhere that he seems to have taken steps to have the Western Creed excised from Serdica's official records by Julius.[111] It is not clear whether Athanasius was more troubled by the theology of the Western Creed, or concerned at the ecclesiastical-political *faux pas* it represented: it supplemented the creed agreed by bishops from across the empire with a regional anti-Origenist statement of interpretation, thereby implying that Nicaea's faith was inadequate. In the *Apology*, however, he let Julius's letter of 341 in reply to the Dedication Council do the work of citing Nicaea as authoritative, presumably not wishing to undermine Constans's attempt at a replacement ecumenical council while he was still living.[112] Nonetheless, Athanasius was about to turn more strongly than ever to the theological defence of Nicaea.

350–356: DISLODGING ATHANASIUS

A council in Sirmium in 351 deposed Photinus (this time in practice as well as in theory, now that the city was controlled by Constantius), and also condemned Athanasius and Marcellus once again, with Basil of Ancyra serving as expert witness.[113] Its rulings were sent to Julius, in

[107]   Ayres 2004, 127–29.
[108]   Soz., *HE* 3.20.1. On the genuineness of Constans's threat of war, see Parvis 2006, 200.
[109]   Barnes 1993, 214–17.
[110]   Ath., *Ap. sec.* 1.
[111]   Parvis 2006, 236–39.
[112]   Ath., *Ap. sec.* 20–35.
[113]   On the theological significance of this council, which engaged explicitly and at length with *ousia* language, see Ayres 2004, 133–35.

territory now disputed between Constantius and Magnentius. But since Constantius did not gain clear control of Rome until September 352, Julius, who died on 12 April 352, was never obliged to respond.[114] Once Constantius had established his rule there, Julius's successor Liberius had at least to pretend to address the situation, which he did by writing to all parties to ask for another council. The most significant of Athanasius's works discussing the Council of Nicaea was produced in this context.[115]

The date of Athanasius's *On the Decrees of Nicaea* is disputed, placed at various points in the decade 350–60.[116] Hanns Brennecke insisted that it must be dated after 357, on the grounds that Nicaea was only explicitly attacked after that point, but Barnes rightly rejected his argument, reiterating Schwartz's case that the work implies threatened but not yet actual violence against Athanasius and pointing out that the range of citations from third-century theological works in Greek implies access to the library of the see of Alexandria.[117] Barnes dates the work to 352/3, but 352 is in fact unlikely: Liberius would have known it was unnecessary and perhaps impolitic to address Sirmium's condemnation of Athanasius while Magnentius still controlled the routes to Italy, and so he would not have needed to write to Athanasius until after September, and there was no need for Athanasius to reply until it was clear that Constantius would be the ultimate victor. Once Magnentius had been decisively dealt with, however, Athanasius had every reason to expect that Constantius would consolidate the moves he had already made to sideline Nicaea. Barnes argues that Athanasius, in sending envoys with a gift for Constantius in May 353, sent with them his initial version of the *Defence before Constantius*.[118] It is likely that he sent *On the Decrees of Nicaea* to Rome at the same time.

The strongest evidence for Athanasius having disseminated *On the Decrees of Nicaea* in the early rather than the late 350s is how quickly the West went from being a region where Nicaea was to some extent honoured in name, but no one knew its creed, to one where the text of the Nicene Creed was in wide circulation, and the terms *homoousios* and *ousia* were being hotly debated (which in turn renewed debate about these terms in the East). Hilary of Poitiers is our main informant. He

[114] Barnes 1993, 110.
[115] Anatolios 2011, 127–33.
[116] Anatolios 2011, 127, dates the work to immediately after the Council of Sirmium of 351; Hanson 1988, 419, dates it to 356 or 357.
[117] Barnes 1993, 198–99, Appendix 4.
[118] Barnes 1993, 112.

claims to have heard the Nicene Creed for the first time shortly before his own exile in 356, which Barnes argues must mean the occasion of the Council of Milan in 355.[119] According to Hilary, at this council Eusebius of Vercelli produced a copy of the Nicene Creed and asked those in attendance to sign it before considering the case of Athanasius, which Valens of Mursa prevented anyone doing.[120] Although this might give the impression of being a mere ruse to try to prevent Athanasius's condemnation, there is a striking change from a similar episode in the same city a decade earlier.[121] In Milan in 345, four bishops had walked out of a council rather than anathematise Arius; by 355, it was not the name of Arius but the text of the Nicene Creed which halted the council.

On the Decrees argues that there is no Christological "middle way" (as Basil of Ancyra had been attempting to argue at Sirmium): "Whoever does not agree with Arius must necessarily hold and embrace the decisions of the Council."[122] The Son of God is either Son by nature or Son by adoption. Athanasius addresses the charge that homoousios and "from the ousia of the Father" (ἐκ τῆς οὐσίας τοῦ πατρός) should be rejected as unscriptural. Scripture everywhere makes clear, Athanasius argues, that the Son is proper and true Son of God. But Nicaea used the two philosophical terms because there was no other way of ruling out the interpretations offered by Arius and his supporters of Scriptural terms such as "wisdom of God," "power of God," and even "image of God." He also points out that the supporters of Arius themselves relied on the unscriptural term "unbegotten" (ἀγέννητον) to describe God. Finally, he appended the letter of Eusebius of Caesarea to his church, arguing that Acacius was being disloyal to his predecessor, who showed that the Nicene Creed might reasonably be signed even by those who had concerns about some of its language. It was his most powerful defence of Nicaea, and its effects in the West, at least, are palpable. For the first time since Nicaea itself, the text of the Nicene Creed was now at the centre of ecclesiastical politics.

Constantius moved strategically to isolate Athanasius, requiring bishops in the West in councils and as individuals to subscribe to the condemnation of Photinus, Marcellus, and Athanasius of Sirmium 351.[123] He had bishops of Gaul do so at a council in Arles in the winter of 353/4, at which Paulinus of Trier was deposed for refusing to accept

[119] Barnes 1993, 118.
[120] Hilar., FH A 1.9.3 (Wickham 1997, 69).
[121] Hilar., FH A 2.3.7 (Wickham 1997, 73); for the dating, see Barnes 1993, 88–89.
[122] Ath., De decr. 20.
[123] Barnes 1993, 115–17.

the condemnation of Athanasius. He had bishops of North Italy do so in Milan in 355, where Dionysius of Milan, Lucifer of Cagliari, and Eusebius of Vercelli were deposed, and Dionysius was replaced by Auxentius, who would be a mainstay of non-Nicene theology in the West until he died in 374.[124] In autumn 355, Liberius, having refused to sign the condemnation of Athanasius, was arrested and brought to Milan, persisted in his resistance, and was exiled to Beroea in Thrace.[125] Increasing force and intimidation seem to have been used in these and other cases. Finally, on 8/9 February 356 Constantius dislodged Athanasius, who fled into hiding. In spring 357, in order to win a return from exile, Liberius acceded to the condemnation of Athanasius: the Roman condemnation that Eusebius of Constantinople had sought twenty years earlier was now finally achieved.[126]

356–360: DISLODGING NICAEA

At the Council of Milan in 355, Eusebius of Vercelli had tried to persuade the council to sign up to the Nicene Creed before discussing the case of Athanasius. Dionysius of Milan had begun to append his name when the paper was snatched out of his hand by Valens of Mursa.[127] In summer 357, Ossius of Corduba, who had presided at the Council of Nicaea and had also been intended to preside at the abortive ecumenical Council of Serdica, was persuaded to sign a statement at Sirmium in the presence of Ursacius and Valens banning the use of *ousia* and *homoousios*, the key terms of the Creed of Nicaea, on the grounds that they were unscriptural:

> But since some, or rather many, persons were worried by *substantia*, which in Greek is called *ousia*, that is, that it be understood more expressly, *homoousios*, or what is called *homoiousios*, there ought to be no mention of this at all, nor ought it to be preached, for this cause and reason, because it is not contained in the divine Scriptures.[128]

To ban these terms was effectively to ban the Nicene Creed. The symbolic repudiation of Nicaea by its president was a powerful step on the way to its complete replacement, which would be achieved three years later.

---

[124]   See chapter 14 by Daniel Williams.
[125]   Ath., *Historia Arianorum ad monachos* 41.
[126]   Barnes 1993, 119, 138.
[127]   Hilar., *FH* A 1.9.3 (Wickham 1997, 69).
[128]   Text in Kinzig 2017, 1:404–8, translation altered. On Sirmium, see below, 306–10.

Eudoxius of Germanicia, who had accompanied Constantius on his
adventus in Rome in May 357, had impressed the emperor, whose com-
mendation facilitated his election to the see of Antioch when it fell
vacant that summer.[129] Constantius then spent most of the next two
years in Sirmium and on campaigns nearby.[130] The influence of Ursacius
and Valens can be seen in various of his decisions during that period, but
so can that of Basil of Ancyra, who was never far from the court during
these years.

Basil invited a number of bishops to Ancyra in early 358 to celebrate
the dedication of a new church there.[131] George of Laodicea, who had not
been invited to the council that had elected Eudoxius, wrote to Basil,
complaining that Eudoxius was openly teaching that the Son is unlike
the Father in *ousia*, and had received back Aetius, a radical non-Nicene
who openly taught the Son's unlikeness to the Father in *ousia*, to his
position as deacon in Antioch.[132] Basil, in the name of those gathered at
Ancyra, self-consciously attempted to steer a middle course between
Nicaea and the teaching of Eudoxius and defied the statement at
Sirmium by continuing to use *ousia* language.[133] He issued a long letter
setting out which councils and creeds he and his associates accepted (and
by implication did not), making use of *ousia* terminology as the only way
of ruling out Eudoxius's assumed support for "other in being"
(ἑτεροούσιος).[134] Basil recognised the Council of Constantinople of 336
(which made him bishop), the Dedication Creed of 341, the Creed of
(Eastern) Serdica, the Council of Sirmium of 351, and the Macrostich
Creed of 344.[135] The letter argued that the Son must be considered to be
like the Father "with regard to essence" (κατ᾽ οὐσίαν), though not *homoousios*. He did not use the term *homoiousios*.

Spring 358 was the high watermark of the influence of Basil and his
associates. He, Eleusius of Cyzicus, and Eustathius of Sebaste presented
themselves at court and persuaded Constantius to sign up to the term
"like in essence" (ὅμοιος κατ᾽ οὐσίαν) in relation to the Father and the
Son.[136] They also persuaded him to denounce Aetius and to accuse
Eudoxius of misusing imperial authority to get himself elected to the
see of Antioch. They further successfully petitioned Constantius to hold

[129] Socr., *HE* 2.37.7–9; Soz., *HE* 4.12.3–5.
[130] Barnes 1993, 222–23.
[131] Epiphanius (Epiph.), *Panarion* (*Pan.*) 73.2–11.
[132] Soz., *HE* 4.13.1–3.
[133] Ayres 2004, 150–52, 158–60.
[134] For the claim that Eudoxius was a heterousian, see Phil., *HE* 4.4.
[135] Kinzig 2017, 1:408–11.
[136] Soz., *HE* 4.14.

another ecumenical council (which he may well have been intending to do in any case).

Constantius had wanted to hold the council at Nicaea, but Basil – so it was claimed – persuaded him to hold it in Nicomedia instead.[137] However, on 24 August, Nicomedia was almost wiped out by a terrible earthquake and fire. Cecropius, its bishop, an associate of Basil's and signatory to the Council of Ancyra, was killed.[138] Constantius abruptly lost interest in ὅμοιος κατ' οὐσίαν, but retained hope for a new creed; however, it was decided to hold separate councils in the East and West. In autumn 358, the eastern council was expected to meet at Ancyra; it was moved to Nicaea, then Tarsus, then finally Seleucia. The western council was called to Ariminum on the east coast of Italy.

Hilary of Poitiers, who had been deposed in 356 and exiled to Phrygia, became persuaded in 358 that the best hope in the East for restoring orthodoxy as he understood it, since there now seemed to be virtually no Nicene orthodoxy in the East at all outside Egypt, was the party to which Eleusius of Cyzicus belonged, that of Basil of Ancyra and Macedonius of Constantinople.[139] In autumn 358, he wrote to the bishops of Gaul and Britain defending to some extent the list of synods of the Council of Ancyra and arguing that the term its leaders had been prepared to countenance, *homoiousios*, effectively meant the same as *homoousios*.[140] Hilary was reacting in particular to the embassy of Basil, Eleusius, and Eustathius of Sebasteia to Sirmium, which he saw as having saved the emperor from heresy and outwitted the designs of Ursacius, Valens, and Germinius, Photinus's replacement in Sirmium.

A copy or a summary of Hilary's work clearly made its way to Athanasius's hiding-place in Egypt. He demurred, in a carefully constructed document designed to engage appreciatively with Hilary's case, but to argue that no alternative to the Nicene Creed would be effective in reversing the designs of those who had made Ossius sign the repudiation of *homoousios* in Sirmium in 357.[141] He was not as ready as Hilary to forgive Basil of Ancyra (despite some apparently warm language), to forget that the Council of Antioch of 341 had targeted Athanasius as well as Marcellus, or to show any sympathy to the eastern party at Serdica. As far as he was concerned, all bishops attempting to

[137]   Soz., *HE* 4.16.1–13.
[138]   Barnes 1993, 140.
[139]   Hilar., *De synodis* 63.
[140]   Barnes 1993, 142.
[141]   See Ayres 2004, 171–73, on Athanasius's *On the Synods of Ariminum and Seleucia* (*De syn.*) as riposte to the theology of Basil of Ancyra.

produce or embrace an alternative to Nicaea were at best ecclesiastical Prodigal Sons, who needed to come to their senses, realise how far they were from home, and make the journey back to the faith of their Nicene fathers.[142]

In May 359, a group of bishops met once again at Sirmium, to produce a creed which could be offered to the two councils for ratification. They were silently at war, though outwardly working together on account of the presence of Constantius. They consisted of Mark of Arethusa (who had drafted the creed), Ursacius, Valens, Germinius, Basil, George of Alexandria, Pancratius of Pelusium, and possibly Hypatian of Heraclea.[143] This creed, nicknamed the "Dated Creed" because, as an official document, it was headed with the consular year, returned to the policy of the 357 statement of Sirmium banning all discussion of *ousia* language:

> Since the term *ousia* was adopted by the fathers rather naively, and, not being known by the people, causes scandal because the Scriptures do not contain it, it seemed good that it should be removed, and henceforth there be absolutely no mention of *ousia* in the case of God, because of the fact that the divine Scriptures do not at all mention *ousia* concerning the Father and the Son.[144]

So far, Basil had lost the argument, but he insisted on a final clause which he hoped would protect the theology of ὅμοιος κατ' οὐσίαν. It stipulated that the Son is "like the Father in all things, as also the Holy Scriptures both declare and teach" (ὅμοιον [...] τῷ Πατρὶ κατὰ πάντα, ὡς καὶ αἱ ἅγιαι γραφαὶ λέγουσί τε καὶ διδάσκουσι).[145] "All things," for Basil, must include *ousia*.

The Dated Creed was given to both councils for discussion. The Council of Ariminum rejected it in favour of the Nicene Creed, while the Council of Seleucia, for the most part, took its stand on the Dedication Creed.[146] A minority party demurred at both councils: in

---

[142]   Ath., *De syn.* 32.
[143]   Barnes 1993, 144.
[144]   Kinzig 2017, 1:413–15 (modified). See also the discussion below, 310–12.
[145]   Ath., *De syn.* 8.7; Epiph., *Pan.* 73.22.6–7.
[146]   On the twin councils of Ariminum and Seleucia, see Barnes 1993, ch. 16, and Socr., *HE* 2.39–40. The proceedings of the Council of Seleucia are better documented than those of any other fourth-century council, and give a good flavour of the general discussion. Of the 160 bishops who attended, Hilary of Poitiers (*Against Constantius* 12) tells us that 105 supported the theology of the Homoiousian party, which was in favour of the Dedication Creed, while the Egyptian bishops mainly supported *homoousios* (presumably in the form of the Nicene Creed). Forty-three supported Acacius

Ariminum, Ursacius, Valens, Germinius, and others preferred the Dated Creed, while at Seleucia, Acacius of Caesarea composed a new one. Basil was on trial for kidnapping and other nefarious activities, and his associates were not inclined to stand by the creed he had signed. Four delegations of bishops, a majority and a minority delegation from each council, made their way to court.

Constantius, however, had no intention of allowing either the Creed of Nicaea or the Dedication Creed to be adopted, despite the fact that the latter had been endorsed earlier in his own regime. He welcomed the minority party of Ariminum and made it clear to the other western bishops that they were expected to accept the Dated Creed. The delegates of the majority party accepted a form of the Dated Creed revised at Nikē in Thrace, from which "in all things" had now been removed.[147] This was the version which would legally become known as the "Creed of Ariminum" in the West, and the "Creed of Constantinople" in the East.

Constantius kept the majority eastern delegation in Constantinople until its bishops also signed the revised creed, persuading its last remaining members to give in on the night before his consular ceremonies on 1 January 360.[148] There followed a chaotic series of episcopal gatherings commonly designated the Council of Constantinople of 360.[149] Macedonius, the bishop of Constantinople, who had been accused of various acts of violence against his enemies, was deposed, and on 27 January Eudoxius of Antioch was consecrated in his stead.[150] Over the period between then and the dedication of Constantius's new basilica on 14 February, and afterwards, more than half the metropolitan bishops of the East were also deposed, including Basil of Ancyra, Eleusius of Cyzicus, Eustathius of Sebasteia, and most of their party. The Creed of Nikē was re-promulgated as the Creed of Constantinople, Aetius was condemned, but his pupil Eunomius was made Bishop of Cyzicus to replace the deposed Eleusius.[151]

It is important to recognise that the Creed of Nikē/Constantinople not only banned the Creed of Nicaea, but also the Dedication Creed, which used *ousia* language. In noting that "the term *ousia* was adopted by the fathers rather naively," the Creed of Constantinople deliberately

---

of Caesarea's new *ousia*-free creed (Epiph., *Pan.* 73.26; for the text, see Kinzig 2017, 1:416–17). On Ariminum, see the chapter below by Daniel Williams.

[147]   Kinzig 2017, 1:420–23.
[148]   Soz., *HE* 4.23.8.
[149]   For the gathering which consecrated Eudoxius, see the *Chronicon Paschale* 543–4. On the council's other actions, see Phil., *HE* 4.12; Socr., *HE* 2.41–3; Soz., *HE* 4.24–5.
[150]   On Macedonius, see Dagron 1974.
[151]   On Aetius and Eunomius, see Vaggione 2000.

did not specify whether it was speaking of the bishops of Nicaea, or those of Antioch 341. In either case, however, it treated the "fathers" with scant reverence. The generation of martyrs and confessors was set aside in favour of the small cabal who had drawn the new document up (a point which had already been made at the Council of Seleucia).[152] The creed made no attempt to engage with recent tradition and wasted no words in ascribing good intentions to previous councils. It simply set out to wipe the theological slate clean and begin again, banning all discussion of the key terms.

The Creed of 360, for all its apparent universality, was therefore only attractive to those without particular reverence for Nicaea or the Dedication Creed, who in 359 were a clear minority among the politically active bishops of the East. In order to promulgate it, Constantius had to accept the deposition of more than half the leading bishops of the East, to add to the previous round of bishops he had deposed at the beginning of his reign. Those who see the Creed of 360 as some kind of well-meant compromise can only do so at the price of ignoring all the politics surrounding it. It was in fact a thoroughly sectarian document.

The defeat of Nicaea and the erasure of the term *homoousios* were apparently complete. But Constantius died the following year, and by 365 a repentant Liberius had persuaded most of the bishops of the West and a good number of those of the East to sign up to Nicaea again. After further vicissitudes, Theodosius I eventually restored the original Nicene Creed by law in 381 and lived long enough to see off further attempts to overturn it.

CONCLUSION: ATTACKING AND DEFENDING NICAEA FROM 325 TO 360 AND BEYOND

When we focus squarely on the reception of Nicaea in its different aspects, a number of things fall clearly into place. First, accepting Nicaea always involved rejecting Arius, and initially the two were almost synonymous. Constantine's recall of Arius in 327 led to an ecclesiastical battle across the whole East over Arius's ongoing ecclesiastical status, which lasted not only up until Arius's death in 336, but well beyond. After the 341 Council of Antioch confirmed to Julius of Rome that it had received Arius as orthodox, Julius set all that council's acts aside as contrary to the decisions of Nicaea. Athanasius was also thereby

---

[152] Socr., *HE* 2.39–40.

enabled to continue to designate the post-Eusebian anti-Athanasian alliance as "Arians" up to the late 350s and beyond.

Secondly, Constantine, nonetheless, honoured the name and the canons of Nicaea, particularly canon 15 forbidding the transfer of bishops from one see to another. His son Constantius, however, began his reign by allowing the transfer of Eusebius from Nicomedia to Constantinople, and toward the end facilitated Eudoxius of Germanicia's move first to Antioch and then to Constantinople. Neither Constantius nor his brother Constans showed any particular reverence for Nicaea; instead, both sought to replace it by new councils.

Thirdly, the pre-Nicene debates over the relationship of the Son's *ousia* to that of the Father continued unabated after Nicaea, only ever briefly interrupted by attempts to avoid *ousia* language altogether. Eusebius of Caesarea, Eustathius of Antioch, Asterius the Sophist, and Marcellus of Ancyra all discussed correct and incorrect uses of the term in the years immediately following Nicaea. Athanasius, having written his first treatise against the theology of Arius and his supporters without using *ousia* language, began to engage extensively with it from the early 340s. Though *ousia* language was mainly absent from the eastern creeds of the 340s (except, of course, the Dedication Creed), Basil of Ancyra turned to arguing directly against the term *homoousios* in 351, and Athanasius responded in 353 with a robust defence of Nicaea's terminology. Ossius of Corduba was brought to ban the term *homoousios* in 357, but Basil continued to express himself with *ousia* language, and the majority of eastern bishops present at Seleucia in 359 embraced the Dedication Creed's theology of the Only-Begotten Son as image of the Father's *ousia* in preference to the *ousia*-free language of the Dated Creed.

Although all theological use of *ousia* language was banned in 360, the ban lapsed as soon as Constantius died in late 361. The Council of Alexandria of 362 returned to discussing the extent to which *homoiousios* could be considered compatible with *homoousios*, Meletius of Antioch and Acacius of Caesarea clarified the sense in which they were prepared to accept *homoousios* in Jovian's reign, and discussion of the subject continued throughout the reigns of Valentinian and Valens. In the end, though *homoousios* had all the attached philosophical difficulties one would expect from any attempt to speak about the "essence of God," the Council of Constantinople of 381 decided that there was only one thing worse than affirming that the Son was *homoousios* with the Father, and that was not affirming it.

Fourthly, we must recognise that it was in the long run Athanasius who kept the name of Nicaea and the text of its creed alive, almost single-handedly at certain points. Athanasius's envoys and then his presence steeled Julius of Rome to insist on the enduring validity of the acts of Nicaea. When the westerners at Serdica in 343 added a new exposition of faith to the Nicene Creed, Athanasius worked hard to prevent it from being contained in the *acta* of that council. He defended the term *homoousios* in the early 340s, insisted on Nicaea's deposition of Arius in his works of the late 340s, and circulated widely the text of the Nicene Creed with a defence of its theology in the mid-350s. In 359 Athanasius strongly resisted the well-meaning attempts of Hilary to argue that the Dedication Creed was nearly as good as Nicaea, insisting that the Nicene Creed was the only true bulwark against the theology of Arius. In 362 he once again insisted in the *Tome to the Antiochenes* that those who wanted to be in communion with him and his allies had to subscribe to the Nicene Creed. He also continued until his death to protect the groups loyal to the original Nicene confessors, the Eustathian community of Paulinus at Antioch and the Marcellan community of Eugenius the Deacon, from attempts by the Meletian party to have them sidelined.

Athanasius's death in 373 emboldened a new generation, led by Basil of Caesarea and his brother Gregory of Nyssa, to risk deposition or worse for the sake of the Nicene Creed, and there were enough staunch supporters of Nicaea in key positions by 380 for Theodosius to be able to legally restore the (original) Nicene Creed in 381.[153] Imperial politics had done its best and worst, as had serious and sustained theological debate, moving through ever wider circles as the century progressed. The task of cementing Nicaea into popular consciousness now passed to the church historians, and some (particularly Sabinus of Heraclea and Philostorgius) continued to keep criticism of both Nicaea and Athanasius alive. But critical or adulatory, to a considerable degree the histories of Nicaea and Athanasius merged, and with good reason. In almost every year from 328 to 373 (with the possible exceptions of 362–64), the odds were against the survival of the term *homoousios*. Its theological and political endurance depended above all on a man who was simultaneously brilliant theologian, consummate politician, and storyteller extraordinaire.

---

[153] The Constantinopolitan Creed, commonly called the "Nicene Creed" today, though it was drawn up at the 381 Council, was first officially promulgated at the Council of Chalcedon in 451. See the next chapter by Mark DelCogliano.

SELECT REFERENCES

Anatolios, Khaled. 1998. *Athanasius: The Coherence of His Thought*. London and New York: Routledge.

Anatolios, Khaled. 2011. *Retrieving Nicaea: The Development and Meaning of Trinitarian Doctrine*. Grand Rapids: Baker Academic.

Ayres, Lewis. 2004. *Nicaea and Its Legacy: An Approach to Fourth-Century Trinitarian Theology*. Oxford: Oxford University Press.

Barnes, Timothy D. 1993. *Athanasius and Constantius: Theology and Politics in the Constantinian Empire*. Cambridge, MA: Harvard University Press.

Burgess, R. W. 2008. "The Summer of Blood: The 'Great Massacre' of 337 and the Promotion of the Sons of Constantine." *DOP* 62:5–51.

Cartwright, Sophie. 2015. *The Theological Anthropology of Eustathius of Antioch*. Oxford Early Christian Studies. Oxford: Oxford University Press.

Hanson, R. P. C. 1988. *The Search for the Christian Doctrine of God: The Arian Controversy, 318–381*. Edinburgh: T&T Clark.

Kinzig, Wolfram, ed. 2017. *Faith in Formulae: A Collection of Early Christian Creeds and Creed-related Texts*, 4 vols. Oxford: Oxford University Press.

Lienhard, S. J., Joseph T. 1987. "The 'Arian' Controversy: Some Categories Reconsidered." *Theological Studies* 48:415–37.

Lienhard, Joseph T. 1993. "Did Athanasius Reject Marcellus?" In *Arianism after Arius: Essays on the Development of the Fourth Century Trinitarian Conflicts*, ed. Michel R. Barnes and Daniel H. Williams, 65–80. Edinburgh: T&T Clark.

Parvis, Paul. 2006. "Constantine's Letter to Arius and Alexander?" *StPat* 39: 89–95.

Parvis, Sara. 2006. *Marcellus of Ancyra and the Lost Years of the Arian Controversy, 325–345*. Oxford Early Christian Studies. Oxford: Oxford University Press.

Parvis, Sara. 2008. "'Τὰ τίνων ἄρα ῥήματα θεολογεῖ;': The Exegetical Relationship between Athanasius' *Orationes contra Arianos* I–III and Marcellus of Ancyra's *Contra Asterium*." In *The Reception and Interpretation of the Bible in Late Antiquity: Proceedings of the Montréal Colloquium in Honour of Charles Kannengiesser, 11–13 October 2006*, ed. Lorenzo DiTommaso and Lucian Turcescu, 121–48. The Bible in Ancient Christianity 6. Leiden: Brill.

Parvis, Sara. 2010. "Joseph Lienhard, Marcellus of Ancyra, and Marcellus' Rule of Faith." In *Tradition and the Rule of Faith in the Early Church: Essays in Honor of Joseph T. Lienhard, S.J.*, ed. Ronnie J. Rombs and Alexander Y. Hwang, 89–108. Washington, DC: Catholic University of America Press.

Spoerl, Kelley McCarthy. 2016. "Eustathius on Jesus' Digestion." *St Pat* 74: 147–58.

12 The Emergence of the Pro-Nicene Alliance
MARK DELCOGLIANO

The pro-Nicene alliance was a consensus-building movement in the fourth-century trinitarian controversies centered on the confession of the Nicene Creed as interpreted according to a trinitarian logic and doctrine articulated by its chief proponents. While the roots of the movement can be traced back to the early 350s, it emerged as a force in the theological debates of the era in the early 360s in reaction to a series of catalyzing events in the years 357–61. It gained momentum in the 370s through the support of key bishops and achieved lasting ascendency in the 380s through its endorsement at the Council of Constantinople as well as through imperial patronage and legislation. Pro-Nicene trinitarian theology remains today a touchstone for all Christian traditions that confess the Nicene-Constantinopolitan Creed.

This chapter narrates the emergence of the pro-Nicene alliance first by tracing the history of other consensus-building movements in the fractured theological landscape of the years 325–61, in order to demonstrate both that pro-Nicenes adopted the tactics of previous consensus-building efforts and that the impetus for the alliance itself was dissatisfaction with, or the failure of, these previous efforts. It then turns to shifts in thinking that occurred in the early 360s that made consensus between former opponents possible before narrating the consolidation and ascendency of the pro-Nicene alliance in the late 370s and early 380s.[1]

PRECEDENTS AND IMPETUS

As a consensus-building movement, the pro-Nicene alliance was nothing new in the fourth-century trinitarian controversies. Prior to its

---

[1] Good surveys of the fourth-century trinitarian controversies include: Simonetti 1975; Hanson 1988; Ayres 2004; Behr 2004; and Anatolios 2011. See also the essays in Barnes and Williams 1993.

emergence there had been other attempts to build consensus and other creeds had been composed for this purpose. It is helpful to trace their history because several tactics for consensus-building arose in these earlier attempts, the most effective of which were in turn adopted by the pro-Nicene movement. The pro-Nicene alliance was thus not very different from earlier endeavors in terms of its strategy and tactics, but it succeeded at least in part because it managed to avoid previous problems in the execution of these tactics.

In the theological debates during years 325–60 four effective tactics can be seen in consensus-building strategies.[2] First, a consensus-building creed needed to affirm a center and to eliminate one or more extremes. As originally formulated, the Nicene Creed was designed to exclude the theology of Arius as a viable option and did not present itself as the middle ground between extremes. A key approach after Nicaea, however, was to identify viewpoints at both ends of the theological spectrum and to present one's own position as centrist in opposition to the extremes. Second, a consensus-building creed needed to be as minimalist as it could be yet not so ambiguous that it was liable to misinterpretation. Drafters of such creeds had to avoid formulations that some might find objectionable or that were so over-determined as to exclude desired allies, but they also had to include substantive language that was taken to convey true Christian belief. A creed that said too much or too little risked rejection. The proper balance had to be found. The third tactic was a result of the second: a consensus-building creed needed supplementation. This was a tacit admission that a creed's meaning was not self-evident. Some sort of additional material was needed to insure its interpretation in the correct manner (however that was understood). Fourth, a consensus-building creed needed to have imperial patronage in addition to (or more cynically, in order to secure) widespread episcopal support. In this period the idea of an ecumenical council that was authoritative for the entire church had not yet been developed, and no existing

---

[2]   The term "consensus-building" describes a conflict resolution-process used to settle multiparty disputes. Its goal is typically understood to be unanimity on the part of all stakeholders, or at least overwhelming agreement. My use of this term to describe fourth-century movements comes with an important proviso: no theological alliance of the era sought to achieve unanimity or even overwhelming agreement. Rather, the goal was to enable as many as possible to subscribe to what was taken to be an orthodox definition of the faith while excluding those whose views were deemed inimical to that faith. Accordingly, these movements were as much "consensus-building" as they were "boundary-marking," in the sense that they attempted to bring together as many as possible of those whose theological opinions were at least compatible without being identical, while excluding many whose views were outside the bounds of orthodoxy as defined by the architects of the movement.

ecclesiastical structure was tasked with governing the whole church. Accordingly, only the emperor had the clout to oversee attempts at consensus-building – and indeed to enforce consensus.

In the first fifteen years or so after Nicaea, there were no consensus-building efforts but rather growing theological and ecclesio-political divisions. In the years immediately after the Council of Nicaea the focus of controversy shifted from Arius to Eustathius of Antioch and Marcellus of Ancyra.[3] Both had been opposed to Arius at Nicaea, but in the council's aftermath each became embroiled in theological debate with Eusebius of Caesarea, one of the figureheads, along with Eusebius of Nicomedia, of a loose but powerful alliance of bishops and theologians some now call "the Eusebians."[4] While Eusebius's argument with Eustathius seems to have been at least partially over the meaning of the *homoousion*, the dispute between Eusebius and Marcellus makes no significant reference to the Nicene council or its creed. Eusebius of Caesarea accused both bishops of Sabellianism and orchestrated their deposition and exile: Eustathius in 327 and Marcellus in 336.[5] Debate over Marcellus in fact lasted throughout the fourth century because his theology, animated by the singular concern to preserve the unity of God at all costs, was viewed by many to have veered into Sabellianism and thus become an undesirable interpretation of the Nicene faith.

Another target of Eusebian accusations was Athanasius of Alexandria.[6] He was convicted for malfeasance in 335, which made him suspect in the eyes of many eastern bishops for the rest of his career. In the early 340s, Athanasius began to conceive of his ecclesio-political struggles with the Eusebians as a quest for orthodoxy against the Arianism of his opponents. In his manifesto *Orations against the Arians*, Athanasius set out to refute the tenets of Arianism supposedly

---

[3] On these figures, see Parvis 2006 and Cartwright 2015. On the anti-Marcellan tradition, see Lienhard 1999.

[4] I use "Eusebian" in contrast to the Athanasian usage deconstructed by Gwynn 2007, and in line with Lienhard 1999, 34–35, and Ayres 2004, 52, to name the *ad hoc* alliance of eastern bishops and theologians initially formed around the figures of Eusebius of Nicomedia and Eusebius of Caesarea. The alliance emerged when several eastern bishops rallied around Arius in common cause against what they deemed to be Alexander of Alexandria's doctrinal innovations and his mistreatment of Arius. But they did not agree with Arius's theology in every detail, and there were theological differences among them. Cf. above, 226–27.

[5] Named after the early third-century Sabellius, who espoused the monarchian belief that the Father, Son, and Holy Spirit were three manifestations of the single God or three modes in which the one God appeared or was revealed to humanity in salvation history.

[6] On Athanasius, see Barnes 1993 and Morales 2006. For the following, see above, 239–52.

taught by his Eusebian enemies. In this early text he provided no defense of the Nicene Creed; he did not use it as a touchstone for his own trinitarian theology; he did not appeal to it as the standard of orthodoxy. Athanasius was concerned, like Marcellus, not to compromise the divine unity, but also taught that the Father and Son are distinct, though he did not employ any technical terminology for distinguishing them as the Eusebians did. Some Eusebian opponents of Athanasius believed that he failed to distinguish the Father and Son adequately and so had fallen into the error of Sabellianism as had Marcellus.

Western bishops led by Julius of Rome continued to support Marcellus and Athanasius, in spite of their deposition by eastern synods – a decision inexplicable to most eastern bishops, who thus came to view their western counterparts as willing to tolerate Sabellianism. At the same time, many western bishops, having accepted Athanasius's polemic, viewed the eastern bishops as Arians. We see here, then, a widening gulf between western and eastern churches, a breach that continued to plague efforts at consensus for decades.[7]

The first attempt at consensus-building came at the Dedication Council of Antioch in 341.[8] Here the Eusebians presented themselves as upholders of the mainstream tradition of theological orthodoxy in the East that avoided the extremes of Arianism and Sabellianism. The Dedication Council produced a creed (the so-called "second creed") now recognized as a watershed restatement of Eusebian theology.[9] Twenty years after it was written, the pro-Nicene Hilary of Poitiers considered it compatible with Nicene theology, though Athanasius still viewed it as Arian.[10] Shortly after the council, an abridgement of the second creed (the so-called "fourth creed") was produced and brought to the West as the basis of doctrinal agreement.[11] This creed, minimalist in approach and ambiguous in its formulations, lacked specifically Nicene language but ended by repeating an edited selection of the ana-themas appended to the Nicene Creed. An ongoing legacy of the Eusebians, first seen in these Dedication creeds, would be to position theological orthodoxy as the center between the extremes of Arianism and Sabellianism (i.e. Marcellus's views), and to express this theological

---

[7]   On post-Nicene developments in the west, see the chapter in this volume by Daniel Williams.

[8]   Many relevant documents from this period are helpfully collected in Brennecke et al. 2007 and 2014 (= Dok.).

[9]   Dok. 41.4.

[10] Athanasius, *De synodis Arimini et Seleuciae* 23; Hilary (Hilar.), *De synodis* (*De syn.*) 32–33.

[11] Dok. 42.

center with a minimalist creed designed for consensus-building. While the fourth creed failed to achieve its immediate aim, for nearly twenty years in the East it was the basis for other consensus-building creeds.

At the Council of Serdica in 343, the eastern bishops cited the "fourth creed" as their statement of faith (with a few additional anathemas).[12] In 344 the same creed was adapted in the Macrostich Creed, but with the additional anathemas of the eastern bishops at Serdica. An extensive explanation was appended as well.[13] It was presented to western bishops at a council in Milan in 345 for purposes of reconciliation but was rejected. After the Council of Sirmium in 351 deposed the local bishop, Photinus, whose views were associated with those of Marcellus, it issued a creed, a replica of the fourth creed of Antioch but with many additional anathemas, some of which function as brief theological explanations.[14] Here for the first time a worry was expressed about whether using *ousia* language for God had materialistic implications, a concern that some scholars have interpreted as anti-Nicene. So then, the trend in these early attempts at consensus-building in the 340s was to put forward a minimalist anti-Arian, anti-Marcellan, anti-Photinian creed that would be acceptable to as many as possible but to supplement that creed with an explanatory apparatus (such as anathemas, often quite detailed; appended explanations, etc.) that would insure its interpretation in a particular (anti-Arian, anti-Marcellan, anti-Photinian) manner.[15]

A new phase in consensus-building began in 353 when Constantius became the sole ruler of the Roman empire and thus was able to pursue religious unity between East and West in a way that no emperor had been able to do since the death of Constantine in 337. Constantius came to adopt the stance of the heirs to the Eusebians in the East, that Athanasius's theology represented a minority position out-of-step with their brand of anti-Arian, anti-Marcellan, anti-Photinian consensus-building and was thus an obstacle to reconciliation between East and West. Accordingly, Constantius worked to get western bishops to

---

[12] *Dok.* 43.12.
[13] *Dok.* 44.
[14] *Dok.* 47.
[15] The long explanation appended to the Macrostich Creed ends with this justification (*Dok.* 44): "We have been compelled to elaborate these points in fuller detail, along with the faith that is expounded briefly, not for excessive ostentation but to clear away all suspicions about our own opinions on the part of others who are ignorant of our affairs, so that the westerners may know both the shamelessness of the slander of the heterodox and the easterners' ecclesiastical mindset in the Lord" (Brennecke et al. 2007, 287). My translation.

denounce Athanasius, as happened at councils at Arles in 353 and Milan in 355. But these efforts spearheaded by the emperor that were based on the minimalistic fourth creed of Antioch supplemented by an explanatory apparatus began to unravel in 357 when a small council of bishops met in Sirmium and issued a confession of faith that condemned all use of *ousia* language for God (absolutizing the concerns in the Sirmium Creed of 351) and explicitly prohibited, for the first time, the terms *homoousios* and *homoiousios*.[16] This Sirmium Confession was not a document aimed at rapprochement, but it advanced a stark subordinationist agenda that by implication rejected the centrist approach of the fourth creed of Antioch. Unsurprisingly, it came to be viewed as irredeemably Arian not only by western bishops but also by many eastern bishops who were heirs of the Eusebian tradition. The Sirmium Confession of 357 catalyzed all participants in the trinitarian debates to formulate responses.

But even prior to this, Constantius's campaign against Athanasius and his heavy-handedness in promoting his imperially endorsed creed had generated opposition in the West. Western bishops such as Liberius of Rome (Julius's successor), Lucifer of Cagliari, and Eusebius of Vercelli expressed support for Athanasius, a stance that led to their exile. Some western bishops even suggested that the Nicene Creed be used as the basis for consensus instead of the imperially endorsed creed, as did Eusebius at the Council of Milan in 355.[17] In reaction to the Sirmium Confession, Phoebadius of Agen composed his *Contra Arianos* in which he defended the Nicene position, though without appeal to the creed's key formulas. These initial western appeals to the Nicene Creed were probably not motivated by prior acceptance of it but by dissatisfaction with Constantius. Westerners were seeking an alternative. Athanasius was doing something similar around the same time when, more than twenty-five years after the Council of Nicaea, he produced his first explicit defense of its creed. In the *De decretis*, written in the years 353–56, Athanasius attempted to refute objections to the key Nicene phrases ἐκ τῆς οὐσίας τοῦ Πατρός and ὁμοούσιον τῷ Πατρί, phrases which he saw as necessary supplements to scriptural language about God that preserve the fundamental scriptural sense of God. Accordingly, the ἐκ τῆς οὐσίας and ὁμοούσιον functioned primarily as "grammatical rules" for interpreting scriptural language about God, insuring that it was not

---

[16] *Dok.* 51. See the discussion below, 306–10.

[17] At this same council Hilary of Poitiers claims to have heard the Nicene Creed recited in public (i.e. as an authoritative statement of faith) for the first time; see Hilar., *De syn.* 91.

interpreted in an Arian manner. These efforts by some western bishops and Athanasius were the initial steps in the formation of the pro-Nicene alliance.

Soon after the Sirmium Confession was issued, Eudoxius of Antioch signaled his support of it and brought the theologian Aetius to his see, a proponent of what is today called "Heteroousian" theology because it emphasized that the Son was "different in substance" (heteroousios) from the Father.[18] For many churchmen at that time, Heteroousian teaching would have appeared the logical conclusion of the theology endorsed by the Sirmium Confession. The reticence of the imperially endorsed theology of the late 350s – which we may label as broadly "Homoian," that is, ambiguously affirming that the Father and Son are "alike" (homoios) without much further specification – allowed for various and divergent interpretations of it. Alarmed by Eudoxius's actions, in early 358 Basil of Ancyra (Marcellus's replacement) presided over a council in Ancyra that responded to the teachings of Aetius and produced a long doctrinal statement that constitutes the initial statement of what is today called "Homoiousian" theology.[19] Homoiousians preferred to say that the Son was "like the Father in substance" (ὅμοιον τὸν υἱὸν τῷ πατρὶ κατ' οὐσίαν). The synodal letter of Ancyra began by affirming its continuity with the creed of the Dedication Council of Antioch in 341 (probably the second creed), that of the eastern bishops at Serdica in 343, the Macrostich Creed of 345, and that of the Council of Sirmium in 351. This was a rhetorical move that tacitly acknowledged that these creeds were in themselves no longer sufficient and needed a supplementary explanation to insure their correct interpretation. The Homoiousians followed a program of theological consensus that meant to exclude the extreme Sabellian views of Marcellus and Photinus on the one side (following the longstanding approach of the Eusebians and their heirs) and the newer Heteroousian theology of Aetius and his supporters on the other side.

Basil of Ancyra then choreographed the deposition and banishment of Eudoxius, Aetius, and Aetius's pupil Eunomius, and he convinced Constantius to give imperial endorsement to Homoiousian theology. The emperor then arranged for a meeting to be held in Sirmium in early 359 to compose a statement of faith that could achieve lasting theological consensus. This document came to be called the "Dated Creed" because the date of its promulgation was preserved in its

---

[18]   On the Heteroousians, see Kopecek 1979 and Vaggione 2000.
[19]   Dok. 55.

preamble, 22 May 359.[20] At this point Constantius seems to have abandoned the minimalistic approach found in the fourth creed of Antioch in favor of more specificity. The Dated Creed seems intended to be a document that would find acceptance among Homoiousians and Homoians, but exclude Heteroousian and Homoousian theologies. But the Dated Creed affirmed that the Son was "like the Father in all respects" (ὅμοιον τὸν υἱὸν τῷ πατρὶ κατὰ πάντα), not "like in substance" (ὅμοιον κατ' οὐσίαν), and also condemned the use of all "substance" (οὐσία) language. For these reasons the creed undermined the Homoiousian position. Soon afterward, George of Laodicea together with Basil of Ancyra composed a defense of Homoiousian theology against Heteroousian theology, which was presented as a competing and mistaken way of interpreting the Homoian theology of the Dated Creed.[21] At this juncture Constantius began to orchestrate councils in the East and West to effect religious unity on the basis of the Dated Creed, believing that theological consensus could be achieved if the Homoiousians and Homoians could agree.

The western council was held in Ariminum in Italy in late May 359. The majority of western bishops refused to adopt any new creed, claiming the Nicene Creed sufficient. The council then sent delegates from each side to Nikē in Thrace and under imperial pressure signed a version of the Dated Creed, sometimes called the Creed of Nikē, which omitted the phrase "in all respects" (κατὰ πάντα), an omission that precluded the very possibility of its Homoiousian interpretation. Like the Sirmium Confession and the Dated Creed, the Creed of Nikē also proscribed all ousia language.[22] The eastern Council of Seleucia met in September 359.[23] Initially, though there was some support among Homoiousians for the Nicene Creed as the basis for consensus (provided the homoousion was removed), the Dedication Creed of 341 (the second creed) garnered the most support. But the Homoians led by Acacius of Caesarea would not subscribe to it because of their continued opposition to all ousia language for God (including homoousios and homoiousios) and proposed another creed much like the Dated Creed. At an impasse, each side then sent embassies to Constantius at Constantinople, where through coercion both the Homoians and Homoiousians agreed to subscribe to the Creed of Nikē. Another council was held in Constantinople in January, 360, to ratify the decisions of the twin councils of Ariminum and Seleucia. The

---

[20] Dok. 57.2. See the discussion by Williams below, 310–12.
[21] Dok. 58.
[22] Dok. 59.9.
[23] Dok. 60.2.

imperially backed Homoians, under the leadership of Acacius of Caesarea, deposed their opponents, not only the leading Homoiousians but also Aetius.[24] And thus did Constantius achieve theological consensus in the Roman empire on the basis of the Creed of Nikē, a status it would officially hold for nearly two decades.

The events of 357–61 instigated by Constantius and the Homoians marked a departure from the anti-Arian, anti-Sabellian, anti-Photinian efforts of the Eusebians and their heirs from the early 340s onward to build consensus on the basis of the minimalist fourth creed of Antioch, a tradition still upheld by the Homoiousians. The Creed of Nikē achieved the status that it did only because of its imperial patronage, and often bishops subscribed to it only under threats of deposition or exile. In all other ways it was flawed: it did not present itself as centrist between incontestable extremes; it was not viably minimalist; and its supplementary apparatus was inadequate. The Creed of Nikē by design precluded Homoousian or Homoiousian theology, neither of which were widely recognized extremes like Sabellianism or Arianism (which of course were also ruled out). Instead of finding a way to accommodate differences between Homoians and Homoiousians, the Creed of Nikē exacerbated them. Furthermore, the creed's ambiguity allowed Homoian theology to be interpreted in a Heteroousian direction. This was one of the factors that led to its ultimate undoing because opposition to Heteroousian theology ballooned in the following years. The creedal supplement that prohibited *ousia* language (which itself would prove problematic) did nothing to forestall such an interpretation.

THE BIRTH OF A MOVEMENT

Constantius died in 361 and was succeeded by the anti-Christian Julian, who actively promoted dissension among Christians until his death in 363. Had Constantius lived longer, he might have been able to consolidate the position of the Creed of Nikē by sidelining its opponents through deposition and exile. But as it turned out, efforts to dislodge it from its newly acquired position after January 360 only accelerated in the absence of Constantius and in the chaos under Julian. Many bishops forced to sign the Creed of Nikē reneged as soon as Constantius was out of the picture. In this period a number of small dissenting councils met that rejected the Creed of Nikē, supported *ousia* language, and endorsed the *homoousion* and other Nicene formulations, or sometimes

---

[24] Dok. 62.

even the Nicene Creed itself as an alternative: for example, at Paris in 360 or 361, at Alexandria in 362, at Antioch in 363,[25] at Lampsacus between 364 and 366, and at Tyana in 367. While the Nicene Creed had first been promoted by Athanasius and some western bishops as an alternative to Constantius's consensus-building creeds of the late 350s, it was the events in the year 357–61, culminating in the hated Creed of Nikē, that coalesced these previous disparate expressions of preference for the Nicene Creed into a cohesive movement. The pro-Nicene alliance was born in reaction to the events of 357–61 and extreme dissatisfaction with the Creed of Nikē.

There were two developments in the aftermath of January 360 that made a pro-Nicene alliance possible in the long run. The first development took place among those who had previously supported the Nicene Creed or had seen it as an alternative to Constantius's creeds of the late 350s and especially the Creed of Nikē. Some of these figures came to realize that some of their opponents held to a theology which was sufficiently close to their own, such that their opponents might be convinced that it was possible to accept the Nicene Creed *in toto* without abandoning their own theology in the essentials. The second development involved those who had been ambivalent to or even suspicious of the Nicene Creed or at least some of its key phrases. Some of these people came to realize that their theology was sufficiently close to that of those who endorsed the Nicene Creed or that the specific formulations of the Nicene Creed guaranteed their theology more adequately than any other creed and thus that they could accept the Nicene Creed without abandoning their theology in the essentials. The most important representatives of each shift in thinking were Athanasius of Alexandria and Basil of Caesarea.

Athanasius wrote a response to the councils of Ariminum and Seleucia, *De synodis*. In the first two-thirds of this document he presented the Creed of Nikē as nothing but the latest in a long line of Arian creeds and expressions of faith, and he indicted the Homoian leaders at Seleucia as nothing more than Arians. But in the last third of *De synodis* Athanasius adopted a more irenic tone, that is, toward the Homoiousians. He attempted to demonstrate that Homoiousian theology was consistent with the Nicene Creed and in fact that Nicene formulations expressed Homoiousian theology with greater precision and with more security against misinterpretation. In making this argument

---

[25] The Homoian leader Acacius of Caesarea was in attendance and supported the council's statement.

Athanasius attempted to remove Homoiousian objections to *homoousios*, in particular the charge that it had material overtones and was not used in Scripture. In fact, he made a virtue out of the latter, suggesting that *homoousios* was necessary, in the face of Arianism, to preserve the scriptural doctrine of God. Athanasius was able to discern that the Homoiousians, like himself, saw *ousia* language as necessary for articulating an orthodox understanding of the Trinity, and he exploited this foothold as the basis for making common cause with them against the imperial Homoianism of the Creed of Nikē.

This new irenic approach of Athanasius was also evident in the so-called "Antiochene Tome" penned by Athanasius and others in connection with the Council of Alexandria in 362.[26] This was a letter sent to the Christians of Antioch to help reconcile two factions there with longstanding differences and rival bishops. The first group was the "Meletians," supporters of Meletius, who was consecrated bishop of Antioch in 361 with the support of Eudoxius, who by this point was bishop of Constantinople. Meletius had had some association with the imperially backed Homoianism of the late 350s but by 361 was seen as Homoiousian-leaning – the public expression of which views got him exiled soon after his consecration. The other group was the "Eustathians," Nicene supporters of the long-dead Eustathius, who as mentioned above had been deposed as bishop of Antioch in 327. The leader of the Eustathians in the 360s was Paulinus, who was consecrated as bishop of Antioch by the westerner Lucifer of Cagliari in 361. Paulinus was supported by the bishop of Rome – and Athanasius himself – as the rightful bishop. Accordingly, the Antiochene Tome was addressed to the Meletians, whom Athanasius viewed as once tainted by Arianism but, as Homoians leaning toward Homoiousianism, potential allies for the Nicene cause. In order for the Meletians and any Arians who wished to reestablish communion with Paulinus, four conditions had to be met: they had to (1) "anathematize the Arian heresy," (2) "confess the faith confessed by the fathers at Nicaea," (3) "anathematize those who claim the Holy Spirit is a creature and separate from the substance of Christ," and (4) also anathematize various other heresies including Sabellianism.[27] One of the barriers to communion between Meletians and Eustathians was the term *hypostasis*. The Meletians, following a tradition that went back to the earliest Eusebians (and in fact is found in Arius himself), preferred to speak of three divine hypostases, language also used by Homoians and Homoiousians, whereas

---

[26]   *Dok.* 69.2.
[27]   *Tomus ad Antiochenos* 3; *Dok.* 69.2.

the Eustathians spoke of only one hypostasis in God, language also used by Marcellus. This different usage of hypostasis contributed much to the Meletians and Eustathians viewing each other as Arians and Sabellians, respectively. In the Tome, Athanasius explained that three-hypostases language could be used in an orthodox, non-Arian manner; likewise, one-hypostasis language could be used in an orthodox, non-Sabellian manner. In his remarks about the compatibility of one-hypostasis and three-hypostases language, Athanasius was one of the witnesses in the period 357–62 to growing distinction between the terms *ousia* and *hypostasis*, a semantic development that would prove to be of the utmost importance for pro-Nicene theology.[28]

Athanasius's approach in the Tome, while it marked a shift *for him*, was nothing new: a minimalist creed was put forward for communion between parties at odds; extremes were ruled out by means of anathematisms; and the creed was supplemented with some sort of theological explanation. He was adopting elements of the consensus-building approach developed by the Eusebians and their heirs. What was new was that the consensus-building creed put forward was the Nicene Creed, and his promotion of this creed as a minimum condition for communion had widespread influence.[29] Among the creed's other virtues, at least in Athanasius's mind, was its explicit *ousia* language: given the theological landscape of the late 350s and early 360s, Athanasius held that *ousia* language was necessary for guaranteeing an orthodox understanding of God, and he believed that the Nicene Creed met this need better than any other available option. Yet he seemed to realize that the Nicene Creed was not enough, as he provided a supplement on the essential theological harmony of one-hypostasis and three-hypostases language. It was in this supplement that Athanasius really broke new ground. He suggested that seemingly opposed terminologies could actually express compatible theologies. He did not require Meletians to abandon their three-hypostases language, nor the Eustathians to abandon theirs. What mattered was how one explained one's faith, not the adoption of specific, precise terminology.

Basil of Caesarea attended the Council of Constantinople in January 360 as a minor cleric.[30] At this council Eunomius delivered

---

[28]   The others who witness to the distinction in this period are Apollinarius of Laodicea (see the chapter in this volume by Kelley McCarthy Spoerl), George of Laodicea, Marius Victorinus, and possibly the anonymous *Against Arius and Sabellius*; see Ayres 2004, 202–4.

[29]   Ayres 2004, 175.

[30]   On Basil, see Rousseau 1994; Hildebrand 2007.

a speech to demonstrate his agreement with the imperially endorsed Homoian theology in order to avoid the fate of his teacher, Aetius. When it was published in 360 or 361 as the *Apologia*, it must have confirmed what many feared when Eudoxius endorsed the Sirmium Confession of 357 and promoted Aetius: the imperially backed Homoian theology enshrined in the Creed of Nikē was so ambiguous that it could legitimately be interpreted in as extreme a fashion as the Heteroousians were doing. In 364 or 365, Basil published his *Contra Eunomium*, the first of many anti-Eunomian, anti-Heteroousian treatises that would be produced in the subsequent decades by pro-Nicenes.[31] Basil's focus in this treatise was the refutation of the Heteroousian theology as expressed in the *Apologia*; it was not directed against the Creed of Nikē or Homoian theology in general. In fact, it did not promote any creed, including the Nicene Creed. In refuting Eunomius, Basil communicated a theology of God's unitary substance and the distinctive features that characterize the Father, Son, and Holy Spirit. He did not formulate an explicitly Nicene position, and though he used *homoousios* once it was not central to his argument.[32] Rather, his trinitarian theology in this early treatise could be described as broadly Homoiousian-inspired. Basil's anti-Heteroousian stance would in time become a key component of the pro-Nicene position.

Basil's single use of *homoousios* in *Contra Eunomium* was a milestone on a journey that took him from his initial Homoiousian-inspired suspicion of the term to his mature promotion of the Nicene Creed as the standard of faith. The evolution in his thinking can be traced by comparing his letters from the early 360s to those from the 370s. In his early letter to Apollinarius, which if genuine predated the *Contra Eunomium*, Basil presented himself as open to *homoousios* but reluctant to adopt it because of its material connotations. In other letters Basil noted that some oppose the term because it could be taken in a Sabellian or Marcellan sense and was rejected by the third-century bishops who condemned Paul of Samosata.[33] There were three unsound, materialistic interpretations of *homoousios* that Basil recognized as early as his letter to Apollinarius but consistently rejected, that the Father and Son were "brothers" derived from "a common overlying class" (γένος κοινὸν ὑπερκείμενον) or "an underlying pre-existing

---

[31]   On this seminal text, see DelCogliano and Radde-Gallwitz 2011.

[32]   *Contra Eunomium* (*Eun.*) 1.20. Interestingly, Basil used *homoousios* to interpret Heb 1:3, implicitly suggesting, much as Athanasius did, that the term helped guarantee the proper understanding of scriptural language about God.

[33]   *Epistulae* (*Ep.*) 9, 52, 125.

material" (ὑλικὸν ὑποκείμενον προϋπάρχον) or that the Son was a portion divided off from the Father (ἀπομερισμὸς τοῦ προτέρου εἰς τὸ δεύτερον).[34]

In his earliest letters Basil conceptualized the relation between the *ousia* of the Father and that of the Son to be that the *ousia* of the Son must be understood to be whatever the *ousia* of the Father was understood to be.[35] Between the Father and Son there was no "difference of substance" (οὐσίας διαφορὰν), "inferiority of power" (δυνάμεως ὕφεσιν), or "distinction in glory" (δόξης παραλλαγήν).[36] Given the liability of *homoousios* to materialistic misinterpretations, Basil initially thought that "exactly and indistinguishably alike according to substance" (ὅμοιον κατ' οὐσίαν ἀκριβῶς καὶ ἀπαραλλάκτως) was a more accurate way of expressing his understanding of the relation between the *ousiai* of the Father and the Son.[37] Yet we have a remarkable letter from Basil in which he registered his shift from a strong version of Homoiousianism to the *homoousios* itself:

> But as for me, if I must express my own opinion, I accept the expression "like according to substance" but only if "indistinguishably" is added to it, seeing that this refers to the same thing as "same-in-substance" (*homoousios*) according to the interpretation of the phrase "same-in-substance" that is clearly sound. It was precisely for this reason that those at Nicaea, who addressed the Only-Begotten as "Light from Light" and "true God from true God" and suchlike, had the idea to introduce the "same-in-substance" following upon these statements. So then, it is impossible to conceive of any variation either between light and light, or ever between truth and truth, or between the substance of the Only-Begotten and that of the Father. So then, if anyone understands the term in the way that I have outlined, I approve it. But if anyone eliminates the indistinguishability of the "like," just like those at Constantinople have done, I am suspicious of the word, seeing that the glory of the Only-Begotten is belittled. After all, we frequently use the term "like" for similarities that are faint and utterly inferior to the archetypes. So then, since I think "same-in-substance" is less liable to distortion, I too adopt this term.[38]

---

[34] *Ep.* 52, 226, 361.
[35] *Ep.* 361.
[36] *Ep.* 9.
[37] *Ep.* 361.
[38] *Ep.* 9.3 (Courtonne 1957–66, I :39). My translation.

Basil feared that it was too easy for "indistinguishably" to be dropped
when "like according to substance" was used to describe the relationship
between the *ousiai* of the Father and the Son, much as had been done at
the Council of Constantinople in January 360, to which he referred.
Thus, Basil came to view *homoousios* as the better term to guarantee
his theology in spite of its materialistic connotations.

In his letters, Basil argued that his understanding of *homoousios* was
that intended by the council fathers. As in the quotation above, his
argument was exegetical: it was no accident, thought Basil, that the
term appeared *after* what Michel Barnes calls the X from X language.[39]
According to Basil, this X from X language revealed the διάνοιαν of the
Nicene fathers – their intention, their meaning, their interpretation –
and how they "interpreted" (ἡρμήνευσαν) the term.[40] This language
encoded a specific understanding of the relationship between the *ousiai*
of the Father and the Son that was encapsulated by the term *homoousios*:

> For after they said "Light from Light" and that the Son "was
> begotten, not made," "from the substance of the Father," they
> introduced in addition to these words "same-in-substance" (*homo-
> ousios*) thereby indicating that whatever formula (*logos*) of light is
> assigned to the Father, the same formula will also apply to the Son.
> For there is no distinction at all between "true light" and "true
> light" according to the same notion of light. So then, since the
> Father is beginningless light, and the Son begotten light, and the
> one a light and the other a light, it was right of them to say "same-
> in-substance" in order to communicate the equal honor of their
> nature. After all, things which are brothers to one another are not
> called "same-in-substance," which is what some have supposed.
> But whenever both the cause and that which has existence from
> that cause are of the same nature, they are called "same-in-
> substance."[41]

Basil's remarks here echoed the *Contra Eunomium*, even if he did not use
homoousios there. In this treatise, he taught that those terms predicated
in common of the Father and Son had the same signification, and that
they named what he called "the commonality of the substance" (τὸ κοινὸν
τῆς οὐσίας).[42] A term predicated in common of Father and Son signified
a property of the common nature or substance shared by Father and Son.

---

[39] Barnes 2001.
[40] *Ep.* 52.2, 226.3.
[41] *Ep.* 52.2. See also *Ep.* 125.1, 159.1, 226.3.
[42] *Eun.* 1.19.

"Light," no matter how one understood or defined it (i.e. no matter what its "formula" is), was thus one of those terms said in common of the Father and the Son; it meant the same thing when applied to each; and it referred to their commonality of substance. According to Basil, then, the Nicene fathers inserted *homoousios* to preclude the Arian idea that the Son was a *creatio ex nihilo*. Similarly, the term eliminated Sabellianism, as nothing could be *homoousios* with itself; thus, *homoousios* "differentiates the individuality of their hypostases and communicates the indistinguishability of their nature."[43]

Once Basil came to prefer *homoousios* to other ways of expressing the relationship between the *ousiai* of the Father and Son, in the 370s as bishop he ceaselessly promoted confession of the Nicene Creed as the means to unity.[44] In this he appears to have been influenced by Athanasius, from whom Basil received a letter in which the Alexandrian bishop said that Arians only need to confess the Nicene Creed to be received back into communion.[45] In one letter Basil spelled out three groups for whom confession of the Nicene Creed was necessary: (1) heretics wishing for communion with the orthodox; (2) novices being instructed in the faith; and (3) anyone suspected of unsound doctrine.[46] So Basil was going beyond Athanasius: it was not only former heretics who were required to confess the creed. Basil also thought that it could be used as a test for suspected heretics. This was precisely what Basil did in the case of Eustathius of Sebasteia. If a suspected heretic should confess the Nicene Creed, he either corrected his hidden heresy or became responsible for his deception. Basil noted that confession of "the words" (τὰ ῥήματα) of the creed was not enough; one must also understand it "according to the sound interpretation manifest by those words" (κατὰ τὴν ὑγιῶς ὑπὸ τῶν ῥημάτων τούτων ἐμφαινομένην διάνοιαν).[47] This was a frank admission on the part of Basil that the Nicene Creed itself was insufficient and required some form of supplementation to insure that it was understood in the correct way.

Basil also held that the Nicene Creed required supplementation in another way. In addition to confessing the Nicene Creed, one also had to refuse to call the Holy Spirit a creature and anathematize those who did, who separated the Spirit from the Father and the Son, who deprived the Spirit of the divine nature.[48] In this Basil may also have been influenced

[43] *Ep.* 52.3.
[44] *Ep.* 92, 113, 114, 128, 140.
[45] *Ep.* 204.
[46] *Ep.* 125.
[47] *Ep.* 125.1.
[48] *Ep.* 113, 114, 125, 128, 140, 159, 258.

by Athanasius, who required a similar anathema in the Antiochene Tome. At any rate both were dealing with an issue that had come to the fore in the late 350s and early 360s when diverse groups, sometimes called Pneumatomachians, or "fighters against the Spirit," denied the divinity of the Holy Spirit (one of whom was the above-mentioned Eustathius of Sebasteia). Athanasius's *Letters to Serapion* from 359–61, Didymus the Blind's *On the Holy Spirit* (possibly written around the same time), Basil's *On the Holy Spirit* from around 375, and Gregory of Nyssa's *On the Holy Spirit against the Macedonians* from the early 380s represent some of the earliest attempts to argue systematically for the full divinity of the Spirit. Through these efforts, affirmation of the Holy Spirit's divinity became a key element of pro-Nicene theology. Basil's explanation for the Nicene Creed's deficiency on the Holy Spirit was that at the time of the Council of Nicaea no controversy had yet arisen over the Holy Spirit.[49] He insisted that these supplementations in regard to the Holy Spirit were in no way innovations but rather part of the Nicene faith he had received and consistent with Scripture, even if not explicitly stated in the Nicene Creed.[50]

Even though Basil contended that the confession of the Nicene Creed needed these additional affirmations and anathematisms, he never advocated altering the Nicene Creed itself, as it had been expounded by "the holy fathers," and he claimed the tradition he inherited held it in the highest honor.[51] Furthermore, he considered his opponents' practice of revising creeds according to the occasion as evidence that they did not share the "one Lord, one faith, one baptism."[52] Accordingly, the Nicene Creed was for Basil the creedal expression of that "one faith" that had the authority of tradition behind it. At the same time, he seems to have been comfortable using the language of "adding" to the creed in reference to those additional affirmations.[53] And yet Basil was reluctant to add to the Nicene Creed in response to the controversies over the Incarnation that erupted in the later 370s.[54] It may well be the

---

[49]   *Ep.* 140, 159, 258.
[50]   See *Ep.* 159.2, 226.3.
[51]   *Ep.* 125, 159; see also *Ep.* 52.
[52]   *Ep.* 226.3, with reference to Ephesians 4:5.
[53]   "even if there should be need for some greater addition (προστεθῆναι) for clarification" (*Ep.* 113); "we are adding (προστίθεμεν) the statement about [the Holy Spirit] in a way consistent with the sense of the scripture" (*Ep.* 159.2); and "as for us, we can add (προστιθέναι) nothing to the faith at Nicaea, not even the slightest thing, except the glorification for the Holy Spirit" (*Ep.* 258.2).
[54]   *Ep.* 258.

case that had he lived Basil would not have supported the restatement of the Nicene faith at the Council of Constantinople in 381.

Basil's efforts to build a pro-Nicene alliance between eastern and western bishops based upon a shared commitment to the Nicene Creed were frustrated by the protracted theological and ecclesio-political divisions in Antioch.[55] Western bishops such as Damasus of Rome and Athanasius (and after 373, Athanasius's successor, Peter) supported Paulinus, whereas Basil and most other eastern bishops supported Meletius, even though both rival bishops were Nicene. Basil correctly saw the contested episcopacy in Antioch as a roadblock to any pro-Nicene alliance between eastern and western bishops and so strove without success to win western support for Meletius – particularly from Damasus. Believing that Paulinus was inclined toward the views of Marcellus, Basil tried to get Damasus to condemn Marcellus, showing the persistence of eastern suspicion over western support for Marcellus. Damasus never did, likely interpreting Basil's request as a cover for an insufficiently Nicene theology.[56] In the end, even though Basil and Damasus professed the Nicene Creed, their support for different bishops in Antioch caused each to suspect the orthodoxy of the other. In a letter to western bishops written toward the end of his life, Basil suggested that the only way to resolve the current theological differences and the breaches in communion caused by the Arians, Eustathius, Paulinus, and Apollinarius was for eastern bishops to hold a common council with western bishops.[57] But immediately he admitted that the times would not permit it. Basil died in late 378, probably without any sense of how soon his hopes for an ecumenical council and a lasting pro-Nicene alliance would be realized.

VICTORY

The accession of Theodosius as eastern emperor marked a turning point in the fortunes of the pro-Nicene alliance. We cannot be certain to what extent his pro-Nicene sympathies were known prior to his being named co-emperor in early 379, as different groups maneuvered to gain the favor of the new emperor. Between late 378 and the early 380s, Eunomius, after a long period of silence, issued his *Apologia apologiae* in response to Basil's *Contra Eunomium*. This contributed to something of a resurgence of

---

[55] Hanson 1988, 797–805; Rousseau 1994, 288–313.
[56] Ayres 2004, 227–28.
[57] *Ep.* 263.5.

Heteroousian theology. Basil's brother, Gregory of Nyssa, circulated his own *Contra Eunomium*, a refutation of this new apology of Eunomius, between 380 and 383.[58] In the summer of 379 Meletius presided over a council in Antioch at which a pro-Nicene statement was issued, possibly in agreement with a statement sent east by Damasus, and this was sent to Theodosius, perhaps to signal the eastern bishops' hope for the direction that the new emperor's religious policy should take (if they were not already aware of it). In any event, the pro-Nicene leanings of Theodosius soon became manifest to all.

It was probably this same Council of Antioch that summoned Gregory of Nazianzus to Constantinople to build up support for the small pro-Nicene community there.[59] Though a disgruntled pawn in Basil's machinations to build a pro-Nicene alliance in Asia Minor, by this time Gregory had long been recognized as a champion of the pro-Nicene cause and his unparalleled skills in rhetoric were ideally suited for the task to which he had been summoned. Many of the orations he preached in Constantinople are extant but none are more important and none more famous, and justly so, than the so-called "five theological orations" delivered in the summer of 380. In these Gregory boldly articulated an anti-Arian, anti-Eunomian, anti-Marcellan, and anti-Pneumatomachian, pro-Nicene theology of Father, Son, and Holy Spirit that emphasized the paradox of divine unity and multiplicity. As he had previously, he even went so far as to call the Holy Spirit "God" and to extend the ὁμοούσιον τῷ Πατρί to the Holy Spirit as well as to the Son. Insisting thus that the Holy Spirit was from the substance of the Father as much as the Son was, Gregory was also responsible for solidifying the terminological distinction between the Son's and the Spirit's manner of "being from" the Father – the Son via "begetting" and the Spirit via "procession."[60] When Theodosius finally entered Constantinople in November 380, he exiled its "Arian" bishop Demophilus because he would not affirm the Nicene faith and, no doubt in response to the success of Gregory's mission there, made Gregory the *de facto* archbishop of the imperial see.

Soon Theodosius launched plans to hold a council in Constantinople under the presidency of Meletius of Antioch. Held between May and July of 381, its purpose was to affirm the pro-Nicene faith and settle the affairs of the eastern church, particularly reconciling certain "Macedonians"

---

58 On Gregory of Nyssa, see Radde-Gallwitz 2018.
59 On Gregory of Nazianzus, see McGuckin 2001 and Beeley 2008.
60 For a survey of the orations, see McGuckin 2001, 277–310.

(former Homoiousians with Pneumatomachian views). At the first session Gregory of Nazianzus was formally confirmed as bishop of Constantinople, and when Meletius suddenly died the presidency fell to him. Efforts to bring about a reconciliation between pro-Nicenes and Macedonians broke down because Gregory refused to compromise. In the attempts to sort out of the episcopal succession in Antioch, Gregory made enemies by backing Paulinus (Flavian would be consecrated bishop of Antioch after the council), and then some Egyptian bishops questioned the legitimacy of Gregory's election as bishop. It seems that eventually Gregory lost the support of Theodosius and then resigned both the presidency and episcopacy. It is not clear at which point the council issued a creed, now known as the Nicene-Constantinopolitan Creed. Though commonly seen as a revision of the original Nicene Creed, it was intended to be, not a replacement, but a restatement of the Nicene faith in new circumstances in which a fuller affirmation of the Spirit's divinity was necessary. There is considerable scholarly debate over the creed's article on the Spirit. Some see it as the tepid language of compromise designed to be acceptable to Macedonians. Some see it as a rejection of Gregory of Nazianzus's unequivocal affirmation of the Spirit's divinity, in which the terms "God" and *homoousios* were applied to the Spirit, in favor of Basil's cautious reticence of insisting that the Spirit be worshipped as equal to the Father and Son in glory and honor. Some see it channeling the "subtle pragmatism" of Gregory of Nyssa's approach to the pneumatological debates.[61] However one interprets the Nicene-Constantinopolitan Creed's article on the Holy Spirit, it was a realization of Basil's contention that the original Nicene Creed needed supplementation, though done so in a way that seems counter to Basil's own inclinations.

The Council of Constantinople also produced a detailed statement of faith that does not survive. But a letter from a smaller council in Constantinople in 382 with many of the same players provides a definition of the trinitarian theology encapsulated in the Nicene-Constantinopolitan Creed approved the previous year:

> [The Nicene faith] teaches us to believe in the name of the Father, and of the Son, and of the Holy Spirit. It is believed that there is one divinity, power, and substance of the Father, and of the Son, and of the Holy Spirit; the dignity [of each] is equally honored, and the kingship [of each] is co-eternal; they exist in three perfect subsistences (*hypostaseis*), that is, in three perfect persons. Accordingly,

[61] Ayres 2004, 257–58.

there is no room for the madness of Sabellius that confuses the subsistences in such a way that the distinguishing marks [of each] are destroyed. And the blasphemy of the Eunomians, the Arians, and the Pneumatomachians is weakened, in which the substance or nature or divinity is cut apart, and a nature that is generated later or created or different-in-substance is introduced into the uncreated, same-in-substance, and co-eternal Trinity.[62]

The focus of this supplementary text is the logic of the nature–person distinction that should govern how one interprets the Nicene-Constantinopolitan Creed. It also makes the centrist nature of this creed clear by identifying the extreme positions that it rules out.

The ascendancy of the pro-Nicene alliance would not have been possible without the patronage of Theodosius. In addition to his superintendence of the Council of Constantinople, in a series of imperial edicts from even before this council until the end of his reign in 394 he made pro-Nicene orthodoxy the official religion of the Roman empire. This was done by mandating an empire-wide adherence to the pro-Nicene faith, by instituting various coercive measures against heretics (legally defined as those who do not subscribe to the pro-Nicene faith), and by outlawing pagan sacrifices and worship.[63] In 383 Theodosius even convened a "council of heresies" in a last-ditch attempt to bring dissident groups into the orthodox fold. Representatives of the various heresies submitted a statement of faith to see whether they should be admitted to communion. Only one statement met with approval, that of the Novatianists. Now that the heretical groups had been legally identified, Theodosius released a flurry of legislation against them. Coercive measures were most frequently directed against Arians, Manichaeans, Eunomians, Macedonians, and Apollinarians: they had their property rights revoked, were liable to confiscation of their property, and could neither inherit property nor bequeath it via wills; they were expelled from orthodox churches, forbidden the right to assemble for worship, to build churches, and to teach their doctrines; eventually they were banned from cities and even subject to capital punishment if their dissent disturbed the peace of the church.[64] Unlike Constantius, Theodosius lived long enough to secure the status of the consensus-

---

[62] Theodoret, *Historia ecclesiastica* 5.9.11. My translation.
[63] See *Codex Theodosianus* 16.10.7, 16.10.8, 16.10.10, 16.10.11.
[64] See *Codex Theodosianus* 16.1.2, 16.5.6, 16.5.7, 16.5.8, 16.5.9, 16.7.3, 16.5.10, 16.5.11, 16.5.12, 16.4.1, 16.5.14, 16.5.15, 16.5.16, 16.5.17, 16.5.18, 16.5.20, 16.5.21, 16.5.22, 16.5.23, 16.5.24.

building creed he endorsed through legislation that effectively eliminated dissent. Furthermore, his successors continued his religious
policies.

But these edicts of Theodosius were also supplements to the Nicene-
Constantinopolitan Creed that insured its proper interpretation – legal
supplements expressing the imperial will and thus privileged documents
for understanding the pro-Nicene faith. None of the edicts provided
a detailed account of the pro-Nicene faith but instead summarized the
trinitarian logic according to which the creed should be understood.
Cunctos populos (February 380) summed up the pro-Nicene faith as
follows: "we shall believe in the single deity of the Father, the Son, and
the Holy Spirit, under the concept of equal majesty and of the Holy
Trinity."[65] In *Nullis haereticis* (January 380) a defender of the Nicene
faith was described as one

> who confesses that Almighty God and Christ the Son of God are
> One in name, God of God, Light of Light, who does not violate by
> denial the Holy Spirit which we hope for and receive from the
> Supreme Author of things; that [one] who esteems, with the per-
> ception of inviolate faith, the undivided substance of the incorrupt
> Trinity, that substance which those of the orthodox faith call,
> employing a Greek word, *ousia*.[66]

Here language of the Nicene Creed was borrowed but redeployed in an
expression of the pro-Nicene understanding of the Son's and Spirit's
indivisible unity with the Father. *Episcopis tradi* (July 381) stipulated
that all churches should be surrendered

> to those bishops who confess that the Father, the Son, and the Holy
> Spirit are of one majesty and power, of the same glory, and of one
> splendor; to those bishops who produce no dissonance by unholy
> distinction, but who affirm the concept of the Trinity by the
> assertion of three Persons and the unity of the Divinity.[67]

None of these edicts put forth the *homoousion* as a key marker of pro-
Nicene orthodoxy; rather, the emphasis was on formulas that articulated
"the logic of three divine persons within the unitary Godhead" without
any insistence on particular technical terminology.[68]

[65] *Codex Theodosianus* 16.1.2; translation by Pharr 1952, 440.
[66] *Codex Theodosianus* 16.5.6; translation by Pharr 1952, 451.
[67] *Codex Theodosianus* 16.1.3; translation by Pharr 1952, 440 (slightly modified).
[68] Ayres 2004, 251–53.

Cunctos populos and particularly *Episcopis tradi* were important for another reason: they named bishops with whom any bishop must be in communion to demonstrate their pro-Nicene bona fides. *Cunctos populos* named Damasus of Rome and Peter of Alexandria, but *Episcopis tradi* listed twelve bishops including Nectarius of Constantinople (Gregory's successor), Timothy of Alexandria (Peter's successor), Pelagius of Laodicea, Diodore of Tarsus, Amphilochius of Iconium (a cousin of Gregory of Nazianzus and a trusted colleague of Basil), Helladius of Caesarea (Basil's successor), and Gregory of Nyssa. These bishops were thus held up as paragons of pro-Nicene orthodoxy. By implication these bishops were given imperial approbation as teachers and transmitters of the fundamental logic and principles as well as the contours and details of the pro-Nicene faith. This imperial recognition of certain bishops as singularly representative of the pro-Nicene orthodoxy went hand in hand with the ecclesiastical recognition that there were certain bishops whose writings were exemplary of the pro-Nicene faith. In other words, the writings of certain bishops involved in the trinitarian debates of the era constituted essential supplements for interpreting the Nicene-Constantinopolitan Creed and thus the pro-Nicene faith. The writings of the so-called Cappadocian Fathers above all fell into this category: Basil of Caesarea, Gregory of Nazianzus, and Gregory of Nyssa. The five theological orations of Gregory of Nazianzus were perhaps the best example. In the estimation of John McGuckin,

> in the subsequent history of the ancient church, these five Orations were never surpassed for their Trinitarian doctrine and were, in fact, adopted as the ultimate statement of Trinitarian orthodoxy despite what the conciliar creed of 381 had to say. It is a providential irony that the creed, which was itself a clear and explicit rebuke of Gregory's boldness in teaching the consubstantiality of the Spirit, has come in the subsequent history of theology to be so strictly interpreted in terms of Gregory's Orations.[69]

Even if one does not agree with McGuckin that the Nicene-Constantinopolitan Creed rebuffed Gregory's pneumatology, it cannot be denied that these five orations have from the 380s functioned as a key matrix for understanding the Nicene-Constantinopolitan Creed. Other Cappadocian texts that similarly functioned as supplements were Basil's *Contra Eunomium* and *On the Holy Spirit* and Gregory of Nyssa's *Contra Eunomium* and *Catechetical Oration*. To this list one can add

[69]   McGuckin 2001, 277.

a variety of texts from western and eastern authors. Conciliar documents have never been and should never be interpreted without the supplements provided by the tradition.

CONCLUSION

As a consensus-building movement, the pro-Nicene alliance borrowed tactics employed by previous consensus-building movements, but it was the unique and perceptive manner in which they were executed that made all the difference. First, the pro-Nicene alliance consistently defined itself as the center between the extreme positions of the day as represented by Marcellus (Sabellianism), by the Pneumatomachians (including Macedonians), and by the Arians and Heteroousians (Eunomians). Here they drew upon a framing of their consensus-building initiative that was started by the Eusebians (anti-Arian, anti-Marcellan) and continued by the Homoiousians (anti-Arian, anti-Marcellan, anti-Heteroousian). The new element was the anti-Pneumatomachian stance of the pro-Nicenes. Second, like its predecessors the pro-Nicene alliance promoted a minimalist creed. But the Nicene-Constantinopolitan Creed they promoted as minimalist as could be at the same time included language deemed necessary to eliminate any ambiguities that could be exploited for undesired interpretations. A key insight of the pro-Nicene alliance was that *ousia* language and the *homoousion* in particular, even if not scriptural, were essential for articulating the orthodox doctrine of the Trinity and ruling out the extreme positions it hoped to avoid. The same was true for the expanded article on the Holy Spirit. Thus, the Nicene-Constantinopolitan Creed seems to have been viewed as striking that proper balance between saying too little and saying too much – it said precisely what was viewed as needing to be said in a substantive way without being over-determined. Third, the pro-Nicene alliance, like previous consensus-building movements acknowledging that the meaning of a creed was not self-evident, produced a wealth of supplementary material to insure its correct interpretation. This included not only the brief expressions of pro-Nicene trinitarian logic found in the letter of the 382 council in Constantinople and the Theodosian edicts, but also the fuller accounts of pro-Nicene trinitarian theology communicated in the writings of its main proponents such as the Cappadocian Fathers. Finally, the success of the pro-Nicene alliance was due in no small part to the patronage of Theodosius and to the fact that he lived long enough to secure its position through coercive legislation. But this imperial muscle should not blind us to the fact that the pro-Nicene alliance also succeeded because it perceptively read "the signs of the times" in the theological landscape of the era and responded in a way that made sense to the majority of the stakeholders. Its anti-Marcellan, anti-Pneumatomachian, anti-Arian, anti-Heteroousian stance, its advocacy of *ousia* language and the *homoousion* as essential, its promotion of the restatement of the Nicene faith in the Nicene-Constantinopolitan Creed, its efforts to provide supplements for correctly understanding that creed, resonated with so many bishops, theologians, and church people in general at the time that lasting consensus was achieved.

SELECT REFERENCES

Anatolios, Khaled. 2011. *Retrieving Nicaea: The Development and Meaning of Trinitarian Doctrine*. Grand Rapids: Baker Academic.

Ayres, Lewis. 2004. *Nicaea and Its Legacy: An Approach to Fourth-Century Trinitarian Theology*. Oxford: Oxford University Press.

Barnes, Michel René. 2001. *The Power of God: Δύναμις in Gregory of Nyssa's Trinitarian Theology*. Washington, DC: Catholic University of America Press.

Barnes, Michel René, and Daniel H. Williams, eds. 1993. *Arianism after Arius: Essays on the Development of the Fourth Century Trinitarian Conflicts*. Edinburgh: T&T Clark.

Barnes, Timothy D. 1993. *Athanasius and Constantius: Theology and Politics in the Constantinian Empire*. Cambridge, MA: Harvard University Press.

Behr, John. 2004. *The Nicene Faith*, Formation of Christian Theology 2. Crestwood, NY: St Vladimir's Seminary Press.

Brennecke, Hanns Christof, Uta Heil, Annette von Stockhausen, and Angelika Wintjes, eds. 2007. *Athanasius Werke: Dokumente zur Geschichte des arianischen Streites*. Vol. 3, pt. 1. *Lieferung 3: Bis zur Ekthesis Makrostichos*. Berlin: De Gruyter.

Brennecke, Hanns Christof, Annette von Stockhausen, Christian Müller, Uta Heil, and Angelika Wintjes, eds. 2014. *Athanasius Werke: Dokumente zur Geschichte des arianischen Streites*. Vol. 3, pt. 1. *Lieferung 4: Bis zur Synode von Alexandrien 362*. Berlin: De Gruyter.

DelCogliano, Mark, and Andrew Radde-Gallwitz, trans. 2011. *St. Basil of Caesarea: Against Eunomius*. FC 122. Washington, DC: Catholic University of America Press.

Hanson, R. P. C. 1988. *The Search for the Christian Doctrine of God: The Arian Controversy, 318–381*. Edinburgh: T&T Clark.

Kopecek, Thomas. 1979. *A History of Neo-Arianism*. 2 vols. Cambridge, MA: Philadelphia Patristic Foundation.

Lienhard, Joseph. 1999. Contra Marcellum: *Marcellus of Ancyra and Fourth-Century Theology*. Washington, DC: Catholic University of America Press.

Morales, Xavier. 2006. *La théologie trinitaire d'Athanase d'Alexandrie.* Études Augustiniennes, Série Antiquité 180. Paris: Institut d'Études Augustiniennes.

Radde-Gallwitz, Andrew. 2018. *Gregory of Nyssa's Doctrinal Works: A Literary Study.* Oxford Early Christian Studies. Oxford: Oxford University Press.

Vaggione, Richard. 2000. *Eunomius of Cyzicus and the Nicene Revolution.* Oxford: Oxford University Press.

13 Apollinarius and the Nicene *Homoousion*

KELLEY MCCARTHY SPOERL

INTRODUCTION

Apollinarius was a cleric in the Syrian city of Laodicea, in orders since the late 320s or early 330s.[1] He worked as a teacher of rhetoric but in time also became an energetic Christian intellectual, lecturing on the Bible in Antioch and composing numerous treatises against pagan philosophers and a variety of fourth-century Christian heresies. He was elected bishop likely in the late autumn of 359 or early 360 after the death of his predecessor George,[2] and by this time he endorsed the Nicene *homoousion*, possibly even counseling Basil of Caesarea on how the term should be understood.[3] His authority as bishop, however, was undermined shortly after his election by the imperial appointment of Pelagius to the see at the instigation of Homoian theologians, who rejected both Homoousian and Homoiousian approaches to trinitarian theology in favor of the more ambiguous assertion that the Son was "like" the Father.[4] Thereafter, Apollinarius seems to have ministered to that part of the Laodicea community that supported the Nicene *homoousion*. He had been allied with Athanasius of Alexandria since their initial meeting in 346,[5] sent monks from his diocese to the Council of Alexandria in

---

[1]   For recent overviews of the history of Apollinarius and the Apollinarian schism, readers may consult Orton 2015, 3–27, and Carter 2011, 400–21.

[2]   Spoerl 2015.

[3]   There is a letter exchange attributed to Basil and Apollinarius in Basil's corpus (letters 361–64). Prestige 1956, argues for the authenticity of the exchange and many scholars accept this. Prestige dates the exchange between 359 and 362 (at 1–14).

[4]   Spoerl 2015, 25–32. For Pelagius's links to the Homoian party, see Philostorgius, *Historia ecclesiastica* 5.1.

[5]   Sozomen (Soz.), *Historia ecclesiastica* (*HE*) 6.25. The close relationship that ensued is confirmed by Apollinarius's disciple Timothy of Berytus according to Leontius of Byzantium (Leont.), *Deprehensio et Triumphus super Nestorianos* 41 in Daley 2017, 438–39; Epiphanius (Epiph.), *Panarion* (*Pan.*) 77.2 (who says that Apollinarius was always beloved by Athanasius); and by Apollinarius's own profession in *Epistula ad Diocaesarienses* 1.255.24–25 to have followed Athanasius's lead in all things. All

362,[6] and until the early 370s had a sterling reputation for his support of the pro-Nicene position on the Trinity.

Such was Apollinarius's renown for sound theology that when news of his Christological views emerged in the early 370s, many writers expressed surprise or regret to know that this paragon of trinitarian orthodoxy could have gone so wrong in understanding the Incarnation.[7] Apollinarius's Christology became an explicit topic of discussion around 373, when his name became embroiled in a controversy between Basil of Caesarea and Eustathius of Sebasteia.[8] The spotlight on Apollinarius's Christology became more intense around 376, when Apollinarius appointed his disciple Vitalis to the see of Antioch, aggravating a schism that had been troubling the city for decades. Sometime in this period (either before or after his consecration), Vitalis went to Rome to seek the support of Pope Damasus, who initially seemed favorable, but later wrote a letter condemning Apollinarius's Christological views. Leontius of Byzantium reports that another bishop appointed by Apollinarius, Timothy of Berytus, also went to Rome seeking approval of his views, but his second trip in 377 resulted in reiterated condemnation and deposition from office for both Apollinarius and Timothy.[9] This and other conciliar condemnations in 379 (Antioch),[10] 381 (Constantinople),[11] and 382 (Constantinople and Rome)[12] did not stop Apollinarius from writing or appointing his disciples to other sees in the Greek East, and we have records from at least one synod held by Apollinarian bishops.[13] Apollinarius himself probably died around 390,

references to texts by Apollinarius and his disciples here are from the edition of Lietzmann 1970, citing by chapter, page, and line number.

[6] Athanasius (Ath.), *Tomus ad Antiochenos* (*Tom.*) 9.
[7] For example, Epiph., *Pan.* 77.2, and Basil of Caesarea (Bas.), *Epistulae* (*Ep.*) 129 to Meletius of Antioch.
[8] I address the conflict in some depth in my dissertation, Spoerl 1991, 32–39.
[9] Spoerl 1991, 39–46. We hear about Damasus's condemnation of Apollinarius's doctrine in a letter preserved in Theodoret (Thdt.), *Historia ecclesiastica* (*HE*) 5.10. Leont., *Adversus fraudes Apollinaristarum* (*Apoll.*) 6 (Daley 2017, 570–71) confirms that the Roman condemnation in 377 involved deposition from episcopal office.
[10] Mentioned in the synodal letter of the Council of Constantinople 382 in Thdt., *HE* 5.9. See also NPNF 2.14, 188–90.
[11] Canon 1 in Joannou 1962, 45–48. See also NPNF 2.14, 172.
[12] In Constantinople in Thdt., *HE* 5.9, and Rome (Ambrose, *Epistulae* 14; Jerome, *Aduersus Rufinum libri III* 2.20, Soz., *HE* 7.11, and Thdt., *HE* 5.8). See also *Codex Theodosianus* 16.5.12–13 for laws passed in 383 and 384 denying the right of meetings and clerical ordination to Apollinarians.
[13] The *Tomus synodikos* in Lietzmann 1970, 262–64. See further on this, Lietzmann 1970, 149.

though the schismatic movement he launched may have continued into the fifth century.[14]

What marked Apollinarius's Christology was the assertion that the incarnate Word lacked a rational human soul, hence a human mind or *nous*, with emotions and decision-making capabilities. In its place was the divine Word itself, who directed Christ's saving activities on earth in a sinless and unwavering way. Apollinarius is not consistent on this: sometimes he suggests that Christ lacked a human soul (*psychē*) altogether, and that the indwelling Word provided not just Christ's emotional and intellectual capabilities, but also was the principle of life animating the body that the divine Word assumed.[15] The negative reaction to Apollinarius's teaching in this domain was quick to assert itself. The swiftness of the condemnation of his Christology is in marked contrast, for example, with the protracted debate that Arius's trinitarian theology triggered earlier in the century. Even more intriguing is that Apollinarius's Christology was then correlated with "Arian" Christology of the Heteroousian variety that was emerging in the late 350s and still current in the 370s when Apollinarius's Christology became the focus of concern, especially among his pro-Nicene colleagues such as Basil of Caesarea and Epiphanius of Salamis.[16] Heteroousians believed that the first and second persons of the Trinity possessed different substances in a way that compromised the divinity of Christ. However, despite the accusations, we have no evidence that any "Arian" of the late fourth century articulated a Christological model resembling Apollinarius's. It seems to have been an accusation made by his opponents to augment his perfidy.

We observe this technique of accusing a newly emergent heresy of implying an older heresy, and specifically with regard to defective Christologies, earlier in the fourth century. We have fragments of a text allegedly written against the Arians by the one-time bishop of Antioch and Nicene supporter, Eustathius of Antioch.[17] This text likely dates from the late 320s, before Eustathius's deposition from office *c.* 327.[18] In

---

[14]   See Bergjan 2015, especially 229–32.

[15]   These two different Christological models, the "dichotomous" (body/soul) versus "trichotomous" (body/soul/spirit) are discussed in Rufinus, *Historia ecclesiastica* 2.20 and have been the source of much scholarly discussion. On this see Orton 2015, 8–11. The theory has been more favorably assessed recently by Carter 2011.

[16]   On the Heteroousians, see the chapter in this volume by Mark DelCogliano.

[17]   *Contra Ariomanitas* in Declerck 2002, 63–130. All references to Eustathius's work here will be to this edition, citing by fragment, page, and line number.

[18]   Declerck 2002, cccc–cccci. For the date of Eustathius's deposition, see Parvis 2006, 101–7.

it, Eustathius accuses his opponents of denying that Christ had a human soul, so that they could attribute all indications of weakness, vulnerability, or change in the gospels to the indwelling Word and thus have proof of the inferior divinity of the second person of the Trinity, as taught by Arius himself in his extant fragments.[19] Two things to note about Eustathius's response to this claim: first, he asserts that to deny that Christ had a human soul is to deny the completeness of the Incarnation and thus to endorse Docetism,[20] a theological claim that had already been rejected in the New Testament and explicitly in the writings of Ignatius of Antioch. Secondly, Eustathius is at pains in the extant fragments of this anti-Arian work to assert that Christ *did* have a human soul, and that that soul was the subject operating in any given passage of Scripture wherein Christ exhibited human vulnerability (the Agony in Gethsemane the premier example).[21]

One scholar has questioned the authenticity of the fragments and Eustathius's charge (repeated by Apollinarius's opponents later in the century) that "Arians" denied that Christ had a human soul.[22] However, support for the fragments' attribution and their reliability at least in representing his Christology appears in statements in the anti-Marcellan works of Eusebius of Caesarea, who by one report was instrumental in securing Eustathius's deposition.[23] Written in the late 330s, both texts, *Against Marcellus* and *On Ecclesiastical Theology*, assert that Christ had no human soul, and to claim that he did leads to the adoptionism of Paul of Samosata, an Antiochene bishop deposed in 268.[24] This is another instance of condemnation by association in the history of Christology. Eusebius was closely allied with bishop Theodotus of Laodicea,[25] and it is possible that Eustathius in his anti-

---

[19] For example, Eustathius of Antioch (Eust.), Fr. 6.67.1–14; Fr. 19.81.21–26, and Fr. 74.145.14–146.18.

[20] There are references to Docetism in Eust., Fr. 9 (70.9), 12 (72.11), 19 (80.3, 11, 13, 14), and to Gnostic teachers who espoused Docetic views: Marcion and Marcionites Fr. 13 (73.2), 19 (80.2), and 23 (87.1), and to Valentinus in Fr. 44 (118.32).

[21] Eust., Fr. 6.67.1–13. For more on Eustathius's Christology, see Cartwright 2015.

[22] Brennecke 2015.

[23] Thdt., *HE* 1.21.

[24] Eusebius of Caesarea (Eus.), *Contra Marcellum* 2.4.24 and *De ecclesiastica theologia* (*De ecc. th.*) 1.20.6 in Klostermann 1991, 57 and 87. For more on this, see Spoerl and Vinzent 2017, 50–55. For the key reference to Paul of Samosata and his supposition that Christ "is a mere man, *composed of body and soul*, in no way different from the common nature of human beings" (my italics), see Eus., *De ecc. th.* 1.20.43 in Klostermann 1991, 88.

[25] See DelCogliano 2008.

Arian work articulated some aspects of his Christological model with a view to the medical expertise of Theodotus, who was a doctor.[26] Though it is not clear that Marcellus of Ancyra, who is the explicit target in Eusebius's final works and another of the opponents of Arius at Nicaea along with Eustathius of Antioch, endorsed a human soul in Christ, his Christology exhibited certain features that suggest he could have.[27]

If we accept the authenticity of the Eustathian anti-Arian fragments and see Eusebius's Christological statements as in part a reaction against them, we can say that the issue of Christ's human soul and human mind had received some attention prior to the emergence of Christological views specifically attributed to Apollinarius in the early 370s. Moreover, given the significant influence of the Eusebius-inspired anti-Marcellan tradition on Apollinarius's trinitarian theology, evident in his text, the *Kata Meros Pistis* (*The Detailed Confession of the Faith*; hereafter = *KMP*),[28] it is likely that Eusebius was also an important influence on Apollinarius's Christology and had been from early in his career, in the 340s and 350s.[29] Yet the Eusebian/Apollinarian Christological model did not attract much notice until later in the period. Apollinarius articulates it explicitly in his *KMP* from the late 350s or early 360s,[30] and a similar Christological model seems to be discussed – and condemned – at the Council of Alexandria in 362.[31] The source of such a claim is not identified in the *Tomus ad Antiochenos* (*Tome to the Antiochenes*) and Apollinarius's monks seemed to have agreed with the council's statement on the subject.

Athanasius's own stance on the issue of the human soul of Christ has prompted a lot of scholarship, which earlier claimed that while Athanasius asserts the existence of a human soul in Christ in his late works, it has no soteriological significance in his theology. That view has been challenged in more recent assessments.[32] We can say that when Athanasius does make explicit claims about the human soul of Christ, beginning *c.* 370 in his late letters, his remarks reflect a state of

---

[26] Spoerl 2016.

[27] Spoerl 2008, especially 136.

[28] Spoerl 1994.

[29] Gregory of Nazianzus (Gr. Naz.), *Epistulae* (*Ep.*) 102 (*c.* 382), says that Apollinarius had been developing his unique Christology for thirty years, which places its development at least in the early 350s, though the model is there in Eusebius of Caesarea's anti-Marcellan works from the late 330s and could have been influential on Apollinarius in the previous decade.

[30] For example, at *KMP* 11, 30–31.

[31] Ath., *Tom.* 7.

[32] A good brief overview of this issue appears in Weinandy and Keating 2017, 44–47. See also Weinandy 2007, 91–96.

discussion among pro-Nicenes that had been going on for some time and seem more to express a growing consensus among that community than to lead the formulation of that consensus himself. As we see in the letter of Epictetus, eventually this Christological discussion, ongoing among theologians who assert in trinitarian contexts that the incarnate Word in his divine nature was *homoousios* with his Father, deploys the Nicene watchword in statements that consider whether Christ's humanity was *homoousios* with the divinity he received from the Father or with the humanity he took from his mother the Virgin Mary.[33] As we will see below, Apollinarius and his disciples were enthusiastic participants in the discussion this innovation generated, though we also have evidence of serious disagreements within the Apollinarian community about such claims.

The extension of this controverted Nicene term into Christological reflection is an important theological development that contributed to the formulation of Christological orthodoxy at the Council of Chalcedon in 451. Hence studying the uses of the key Nicene term *homoousios* in Apollinarius and his disciples is worthwhile for what it reveals about this development. This chapter will begin this study, first by surveying the use of the Nicene *homoousion* in trinitarian and Christological contexts in the works of Apollinarius and his disciples. Then, using what limited historical evidence we have, it will explore a hypothesis about when and under what circumstances the Nicene watchword became implicated in Apollinarius's Christological reflection. Exploring this will shed light not only on the development of Apollinarius's Christology but also help us better understand how the Christological controversies evolved out of the fourth-century trinitarian debates.

TRINITARIAN USES OF THE HOMOOUSION IN THE WORKS OF APOLLINARIUS AND HIS DISCIPLES

The *Homoousion* in Apollinarius's Trinitarian Works

Limiting ourselves to the works of Apollinarius contained in Lietzmann's edition (not including the numerous works under pseudonyms that have been attributed to Apollinarius over the past nearly seventy years), we see seven uses of the term *homoousios* in trinitarian contexts. The most obvious place for its appearance is Apollinarius's trinitarian treatise, the *KMP*, where it appears three times.[34] The text

---

[33]   Ath., *Epistula ad Epictetum* (*Ep. Epict.*) 2, 4, 9.
[34]   *KMP* 27.176.21; 33.180.13; 34.180.22.

also appears twice in Apollinarius's *De fide et incarnatione* (*On Faith and the Incarnation*),[35] and in two fragments from Apollinarius's *Apodeixis* (*Demonstration*)[36] that are preserved in Gregory of Nyssa's *Antirrheticus* (*Refutation of the Apollinarians*). Most of the trinitarian uses of *homoousios* in Apollinarius employ it as it originally appeared in the Nicene Creed: to describe the relationship between the first and second persons of the Trinity, the Father and the Son/Word. There is one instance in the extant works in which Apollinarius attributes the *homoousion* to the Holy Spirit.[37]

The use of the *homoousion* in *KMP* 34 specifically ties it to a condemnation of those who reject the term as "foreign to the Scriptures."[38] This comment has been used to set the *terminus ab quo* for the composition of the text to 357 with the emergence of the Homoian position on the doctrine of the Trinity and the outlawing of *ousia* language in trinitarian discourse, a development confirmed at the Council of Constantinople in January 360. I have argued that the *KMP* is an early statement of Apollinarius's support for the Nicene doctrine of the consubstantiality of the persons of the Trinity, perhaps articulated at the time of his accession to the episcopal see of Laodicea right in the period of Homoian ascendency, sometime in the autumn of 359 or early 360. I have also argued that it is likely to have been completed by 362. Such a date would coordinate well with the participation of monks representing Apollinarius at the Council of Alexandria in late spring 362, where the Nicene Creed was endorsed as the definitive statement of orthodox trinitarianism.[39] Another factor suggesting an earlier rather than later date for the *KMP* is the lack of specific attention to the Heteroousian theology that was emerging c. 360, though Jerome reports that Apollinarius wrote a treatise against one of its chief exponents, Eunomius of Cyzicus.[40]

Apollinarius only once explicitly links the consubstantiality of the Father and Son to the decisions of the Nicene council in his extant

[35] Apollinarius (Apoll.), *De fide et incarnatione* (*De fid. inc.*) 4.195.19; 6.197.18.
[36] Lietzmann 1970, Fr. 39.213.25; Fr. 40.213.29. Orton 2015, 93, translates the title as "The Demonstration of the Divine Enfleshment according to the Likeness of a Human Being."
[37] *KMP* 33.180.13.
[38] *KMP* 34.180.21–24: "And we think that those who have communion with persons who reject [the term] 'consubstantial' as foreign to the Scriptures and who say that any member of the Trinity is created and separate it from the divinity that is one by nature are outcasts and we have no communion with these sorts of men."
[39] Ath., *Tom.* 8–9.
[40] Jerome, *De uiris illustribus liber* 120.

works, in Fr. 39 from the *Apodeixis* according to the report in the *Antirrheticus* ("But he also recalled the teaching of Nicaea, at which the whole council of the Fathers proclaimed the *homoousion*").[41] However, his disciple Timothy of Berytus emphatically does this in his *Ecclesiastical History*, citing an authentic letter from Athanasius to the emperor Jovian (who ruled from summer 363 to February 364) in which the centrality of the *homoousion* to the teaching of the Nicene fathers is affirmed more than once.[42] Apollinarius does not mention Nicaea or the *homoousion* in his own extant letter to the emperor Jovian, who was reputed to be sympathetic to pro-Nicenes at the time of his accession.[43] Apollinarius's endorsement of the Nicene *homoousion* to describe the relationship of the Father and Son likely emerged in his public discourse in this critical period of pushback against the Homoian restrictions on trinitarian terminology, and this would explain its presence in the *KMP*.

The attribution of the Nicene *homoousion* to the Holy Spirit in the *KMP* also seems to fit in with theological discussion in this period. Integrating the Holy Spirit into a Nicene account of the Trinity was emerging as a concern in the pro-Nicene camp in the late 350s and early 360s, which Athanasius's letters to Serapion and the *Tomus ad Antiochenos* attest.[44] Apollinarius is more explicit on this point than Athanasius; while Apollinarius insists directly on the Holy Spirit's consubstantiality,[45] Athanasius instead states that the Holy Spirit is not foreign to or separated from the substance shared by Father and Son.[46] He does not attribute the *homoousion* directly to the Spirit. Elsewhere, I have suggested that Apollinarius may have had the priority in attributing divine consubstantiality to the Holy Spirit, since the anti-Marcellan theological influence so dominant in the Syro-Palestinian environment in which Apollinarius operated contained within it notions of the Spirit's created status that were starting to look suspect as the pro-Nicene theology of the Trinity advanced during the middle of the fourth century.[47]

---

[41] Apoll., Fr. 39.213.24–25. See Orton 2015, 135.
[42] Timothy of Berytus (Tim. Beryt.), *Historia ecclesiastica* in Lietzmann 1970, 279.23–283.10, especially 282.13 and 282.25 (the latter a direct quotation from the creed of Nicaea).
[43] Apoll., *Ad Jovianum* 250.1–253.14. The letter received extensive study in Drecoll 2015. On Jovian's interactions with Athanasius during his brief reign, see Barnes 1993, 159–61.
[44] Ath., *Tom.* 5.
[45] *KMP* 33.180.12–14.
[46] Ath., *Tom.* 5.
[47] Spoerl 2001.

The *Homoousion* in Trinitarian Statements of Apollinarius's Disciples

While Apollinarius may have been keen to attribute the *homoousion* to the Holy Spirit, we have no comparable occurrences of such usage in Apollinarius's disciples. All the uses of the *homoousion* employed in trinitarian statements in his disciples' works concern the relationship between the Father and the Son. We have one from bishop Vitalis,[48] four from works of Timothy of Berytus,[49] two from a disciple named Jobius,[50] two from one named Valentinus,[51] and one each from two works from Apollinarian circles (the *Ekthesis tēs pisteos* [*Exposition of the Faith*][52] and the *Quod unus sit Christus* [*That Christ is One*][53]), the provenance of which remains uncertain. Given that such works are likely to come from later in the fourth century (370s and 380s – Timothy was present at the Council of Constantinople in 381 and signed off on its decisions,[54] including those regarding the Holy Spirit) – it is perhaps surprising that the trinitarian statements within them do not integrate the Holy Spirit. However, this fact may be relevant: in both Apollinarius and the works of his disciples, there are far fewer references to the *homoousion* in trinitarian contexts than there are in Christological contexts. This likely shows that what the critics of Apollinarius and his school were interested in was not his trinitarian theology (likely *because* it conformed to later orthodoxy), but his problematic Christology. Hence the record on the trinitarian theology of the Apollinarian school is likely to have gaps that prevent fuller apprehension of its scope.

CHRISTOLOGICAL USES OF THE HOMOOUSION IN THE WORKS OF APOLLINARIUS AND HIS DISCIPLES

Christological Uses of the *Homoousion* in Apollinarius

This brings us to that aspect of Apollinarius's thought that was important for his own movement, but also for subsequent theology, namely, the idea that Christ is *homoousios*, consubstantial, with humankind according to his humanity, at least in some respects. In this section, I will examine (1) the appearance of such claims in Apollinarius's writings

[48] Vitalis, *De fide* (*About the Faith*) 273.12.
[49] Tim. Beryt., Fr. 181.279.8; *HE* 282.13, 25; *Epistulae ad Prosdocium* 285.18.
[50] Jobius 286.24; 287.1–2. See Leont., *Apoll.* 11, in Daley 2017, 534–35.
[51] Valentinus Apollinaristes (Val. Apoll.), *Capita apologiae* 1.287.32; 4.289.11–12. See also Leont., *Apoll.* 12 in Daley 2017, 536.6 and 538.10.
[52] *Ekthesis tēs pisteōs* 293.18.
[53] *Quod unus sit Christus* 7.299.12, 13.
[54] Mansi 1903, 568C; Lietzmann 1970, 153–54.

and those of his disciples and (2) the evidence that these claims generated discussion and division among those disciples.

Apollinarius uses the *homoousion* in Christological statements in various forms. For example, in *De unione* 8, he says that Christ is *homoousios* with God κατὰ τὸ πνεῦμα τὸ ἀόρατον (according to the invisible spirit), but also *homoousios* with human beings (πάλιν ἀνθρώποις ὁμοούσιος).[55] We have another reference to the idea that "God" (i.e., Christ) is *homoousios* with human beings in Fr. 126 (from *Against Diodore*), but with the specification κατὰ τὴν σάρκα (according to the flesh).[56] A statement appears in Fr. 41 (from the *Apodeixis*) that combines both the ideas that Christ is *homoousios* with God according to the spirit (κατὰ τὸ πνεῦμα) while *homoousios* with human beings κατὰ τὴν σάρκα.[57] In Fr. 163 (from the letter to Terentius), Apollinarius dispenses with the phrasing κατὰ τὴν σάρκα and simply says that Christ's flesh is not *homoousion* with God but *homoousion* with our flesh.[58] This matches a statement in the *Tomus synodikos* wherein Apollinarius and his followers decree that Christ's flesh is taken from his mother the Virgin Mary, and is *homoousion* with our flesh.[59] Significantly, in Fr. 161 (in a letter to Serapion of Thmuis commenting on Athanasius's letter to Epictetus of Corinth), Apollinarius twice asserts that the flesh the second person of the Trinity assumed in the Incarnation is *homoousios* with us "by nature" (φύσει).[60] This statement is of a piece with that in the *Tomus synodikos* wherein Apollinarius says that it is wrong to say that the flesh of Christ is of the uncreated nature (τῆς ἀκίστου φύσεως) and *homoousion* with God.[61]

The formulation of statements such as these, particularly those involving the paired assertions that Christ is *homoousios* with God according to the spirit but *homoousios* with men according to the flesh or body, point forward to the language of the Chalcedonian Definition of 451. However, it is clear that Apollinarius formulates the contrasting elements of Christ's being differently than the Definition. The latter talks of Christ's divinity and humanity; Apollinarius's focus remains more explicitly anthropological, concentrating on the components of Christ's person. What is divine about Christ is the indwelling spirit;

---

[55] Apoll., *De unione corporis et divinitatis in Christo* (*De unione*) 8.188.9–18.
[56] Apoll., Fr. 126.238.11. This claim is repeated at Fr. 146. 242.21 (also from *Against Diodore*).
[57] Apoll., Fr. 41.213.32–34.
[58] Apoll., Fr. 163.255.11–12. See Leont., *Apoll.* 9 in Daley 2017, 530–33.
[59] *Tomus synodikos* 262.28–29. See Leont., *Apoll.* 11 in Daley 2017, 532–33.
[60] Apoll., Fr. 161.254.21–22.
[61] *Tomus synodikos* 263.10–12. See Leont., *Apoll.* 11 in Daley 2017, 534.2.

what is human is the assumed flesh or body. The phrasing thus suggests the Apollinarian model of Christ as a divine mind in a human body. This is confirmed in his statement in Fr. 45 (from the *Apodeixis*), where he asserts that "[Christ] is not a man but like a man, because he is not *homoousios* with man according to the most authoritative part (κατὰ τὸ κυριώτατον)."[62]

It is clear from both the extant Apollinarian fragments and those of his disciples, as well as some external reports about Apollinarian circles, that the incorporation of the Nicene *homoousion* into Christological discourse struck many as problematic. The major concern that emerges from the fragments seems to be the fear that if one applies the *homoousion* to Christ's assumed humanity (restricted in Apollinarius's scheme to his human flesh/body), then one suggests that that physical human element is divine in and of itself, has a heavenly origin, or was changed into divinity at its assumption. In general, Apollinarius wants to quash any such notion and maintain the integrity of Christ's flesh as genuinely human and created, not divine. However, in some qualified sense he will allow Christ's flesh to participate in the consubstantiality of Christ's divinity with the divinity of God the Father.

Let us first consider those statements wherein Apollinarius maintains the authentically human quality of Christ's assumed flesh or body. Again, employing the language of nature, Apollinarius says at *De unione* 8 that "the nature of the body is not altered by its union with him who is *homoousios* with God."[63] In *De fide et incarnatione* 3, Apollinarius asserts that "neither we nor our synod nor any of those having human reason say or think that the body is *homoousion* [implied: with God] in and of itself (καθ' ἑαυτὸ)."[64] In Fr. 112 (from the *Syllogisms*), Apollinarius lays out the following argument: if the divine Word and the human flesh/body were *homoousios*, Christians would not be able to say of Christ (in the language of 1 John) that "we have seen and touched" him, because divinity is invisible and untouchable. But since Christians have had palpable experience of the physical, historical Christ, his spirit and his body must be of different οὐσίαι, one invisible and untouchable, one visible and touchable. "Consequently, the spirit of the Lord and the body are not *homoousion* [...] The one who says that the body is *homoousion* with God blasphemes the bodiless [God] as if he had a body."[65]

---

[62] Apoll., Fr. 45.214.28–29.
[63] Apoll., *De unione* 8.188.14–15; "[...] οὐκ ἀλλαττομένης τῆς τοῦ σώματος φύσεως ἐν τῇ πρὸς τὸν θεῷ ὁμοούσιον ἐνώσει [...]"
[64] Apoll., *De fid. inc.* 3.194.17–18.
[65] Apoll., Fr. 112.234.6–7. See Leont., *Apoll.* 10 in Daley 2017, 532–33.

The same conclusion is repeated at Fr. 162 (to Terentius).[66] Apollinarius takes an intriguing tack in Frs. 126 and 146 (from *Against Diodore*), employing not only the Nicene term *homoousion*, but the term *heteroousion*, in its trinitarian sense the polar opposite of the Nicene position, but used by Apollinarius in a Christological sense in a way compatible with Nicene orthodoxy. Fr. 126 runs: "Men are *homoousioi* with irrational animals according to the irrational body; but they are *heteroousioi* insofar as they are rational. So also God [i.e. Christ] is *homoousios* with human beings according to the flesh, but *heteroousios* insofar as he is Word and God."[67] Lastly, in Frs. 163 (from the letter to Terentius) and 164 (from the second letter to Dionysius), Apollinarius asserts that because the flesh is *homoousios* with our flesh, it is wrong to say that "it came down from heaven, and not that it was taken up by the one from heaven [. . .]"[68] These statements make it clear that Apollinarius did not agree with many of the claims his critics attributed to him and that his thought affirmed clear distinctions between the human and divine elements in Christ.

However, Apollinarius's works also contain statements that likely blurred these distinctions from the perspective of his readers. For example:

> Thus [Christ] is both *homoousios* with God according to the invisible spirit (even the flesh being included in the title because it has been united to him who is *homoousios* with God), and again *homoousios* with human beings (even the godhead being included with the body because it has been united to what is *homoousion* with us). The nature of the body is not altered by its union with him who is *homoousios* with God and by its fellowship with the title of "*homoousios*," just as the nature of the godhead has not been changed by its fellowship with the human body and by bearing the designation of the flesh that is *homoousios* with us.[69]

As Apollinarius makes clear, to say that the body is included in Christ's title as the one who is *homoousios* with God or that the godhead bears the designation of the flesh that is *homoousios* with us does not suggest a change in nature of either the godhead or the human body itself. Rather, a statement like this addresses the issue of attribution. While in

[66] Apoll., Fr. 162.254.31–255.9.
[67] Apoll., Fr. 126.238.9–12. We see the same sentiment at Fr. 146.242.19–22.
[68] Apoll., Fr. 163.255.11–14; see also Fr. 164.262.13–14. See the parallel to Fr. 164 in Leont., *Apoll.* 2.8 in Daley 2017, 550.2.
[69] Apoll., *De unione* 8.188.9–18.

strict analytical terms the body is *homoousios* with human beings, it is acceptable to say that it has some share in the assuming Word's consubstantiality with God the Father and so is *homoousios* with God too – because it is united to the Word who is *homoousios* with the Father. Likewise, Christ's godhead can be said to be *homoousios* with human beings because it belongs to the Word who assumes the body that is *homoousios* with human beings. The statement thus implies the communication of idioms that follows from the fact that the Word is one person. The union of human and divine in Christ is obviously the main theme of *De unione*, but Apollinarius does not resort in this text to the language of person to express this unity. This language does appear in *De fide et incarnatione*, where Apollinarius uses the term that he employs in the *KMP* for the different members of the Trinity, πρόσωπον:

> Let no one despise the masterful and saving flesh of our Savior on the pretext of the *homoousion*. For neither we nor our synod nor any of those having human rationality say or think that the body is *homoousion* [with God] in and of itself; yet neither do we say that the flesh of our Savior Jesus Christ was from heaven, but we confess that the God-Word has become incarnate from the holy Virgin Mary and we do not divide him from his own flesh, but [we say that] he is one person, one hypostasis, whole man, whole God.[70]

We see the reference to Christ's one person in Fr. 164 (from the second letter to Dionysius):

> And that no one can charge us with these things that are said against some, is clear from what we have always written, saying neither that the flesh of the Savior is from heaven, nor that the flesh is *homoousion* with God insofar as it is flesh and not God, but that it is God to the extent that it has been united in one person (πρόσωπον) to the godhead.[71]

Apollinarius is even clearer in conveying the idea of the communication of idioms in a statement in Fr. 153 (from a text called *Logoi*):

> Therefore the Lord Jesus Christ is sinless as God and with the flesh is *homoousios* with the only God, creator before the ages; but flesh as flesh of God is God, as belonging to [the one] who is *homoousios* with God [...] For God by the fellowship with the flesh is not man

---

[70]   Apoll., *De fid. inc.* 3.194.15–23.
[71]   Apoll., Fr. 164.262.12–16. See Leont., *Apoll.* 2.8 in Daley 2017, 548–51.

in and of himself nor is the flesh, by its fellowship with God, God in and of itself. God empowers the things that follow upon the flesh by virtue of his oneness with the flesh, while the flesh takes to itself things that are proper to God because of its union with God.[72]

The same idea appears in what remains of the correspondence Apollinarius conducted with Serapion of Thmuis. Though we do not have the letter of Serapion to which Apollinarius was responding, the latter seems to be commenting on a statement that Serapion made, remarking, "But to say that 'the flesh is not *homoousios* with us since it is the flesh of God' needs a little refinement. For it is better to say that [Christ] took to himself flesh that is *homoousion* with us by nature but he revealed it as divine by virtue of the union."[73]

In view of this evidence, the distinction seems to be clear in Apollinarius's mind between what one can say of the flesh/body *qua* flesh/body (not *homoousios* with the godhead incarnate in Christ) and what one can say of it as belonging to the one person of the assuming Word who is divine (as such, *homoousios* with the godhead because the Word to whom it belongs is *homoousios* with the godhead). But this is a subtle difference, relying upon a distinction between substance (οὐσία) and person (πρόσωπον) that is still unclear in the third quarter of the fourth century, with the added difficulty that some believed the term equally relevant to Trinity and Christology, ὑπόστασις, referred to substance, some to person. Indeed, it is not clear where Apollinarius falls out on this point.[74] In any case, while he is comfortable saying that one both can and cannot say that Christ's flesh is *homoousios* with his divinity, his disciples were not. What for Apollinarius was a both/and proposition becomes either/or for his disciples.

Christological Uses of the *Homoousion* among Apollinarius's Disciples

Among those who were willing to say that Christ's human body/flesh was *homoousios* with God was Timothy of Berytus, whose teacher, according to his opponent Valentinus, was Polemon.[75] Timothy makes the following statement in a work entitled the *Catechesis*:

---

[72] Apoll., Fr. 153.248.18–27. Compare with Leont., *Apoll.* 2.4 in Daley 2017, 546.12–20 and the accompanying translation on 547.

[73] Apoll., Fr. 161.254.20–23.

[74] See Ath., *Tom.* 5 and 6. Thdt., *Haereticarum fabularum compendium* 4.8 (PG 83: 425C) says that Apollinarius eventually endorsed the three ὑποστάσεις formula as equivalent to three πρόσωπα, but there is no unambiguous evidence for it in his works.

[75] Val. Apoll., *Capita apologiae* 3.288.21–25 (Leont., *Apoll.* 1.12 (Daley 2017, 535, renders the name Polemius.)

Called divine and confessed to be *homoousios* with God by virtue
of its union with God the Word, the flesh of the Lord remains
human by nature, and *homoousios* with us [...] It is fitting to
confess that [the flesh] is by virtue of the union the same as the
Word of God, and that it should be called by the divine title of the
Word and adored as the Word, and believed to be, as the Word,
homoousios with God.[76]

The other position among Apollinarius's disciples, who resisted
language of the flesh/body being *homoousios* with Christ's divinity,
was represented by figures such as Valentinus, Vitalis, Homonius, and
Jobius. For example, from Vitalis' *De fide*:

And further we also believe concerning the fleshly economy of the
Savior [...] that [he is] one and the same perfect God according to
[his] divinity and *homoousios* with the Father and the same perfect
man according to [his] birth from the virgin and *homoousios* with
human beings according to the flesh. And if someone says that
Christ has a body [that is] from heaven and is *homoousion* with
God according to the flesh, let him be anathema. And if someone
does not confess that the flesh of the savior is from the holy virgin
and *homoousios* with human beings, let him be anathema.[77]

We have a similar statement from Homonius: "I, Homonius, bishop,
confess that the Word of God took flesh from Mary that is *homoousion*
with us. But if someone says that the flesh that was united to the Word [is
homoousios] in the way as the Word is *homoousion* with God, let him be
anathema."[78] Jobius's statement seems to support a careful attribution
of consubstantiality of Christ's human and divine natures that anticipates significantly the Chalcedonian Definition: "I confess the Lord
Jesus Christ [...] *homoousion* with God according to the divinity that
is his from the Father's οὐσία, and *homoousion* with human beings
according to the flesh from human nature which was united to
him [...]"[79]

---

[76] Tim. Beryt., Fr. 181.279.6–8. See Leont., *Apoll.* 1.12 in Daley 2017, 536.1–3 and 4–6.
This translation is adapted from Daley 2017, 537.
[77] Vitalis, Fr. 172, 273.6–7, 11–17.
[78] Homonius in Timothy of Berytus, *Epistula ad Homonium* 278.3–6. See Leont., *Apoll.*
2.1 in Daley 2017, 544.6–9. His translation, 545: "And if anyone says that the flesh
united to the Lord, in any way at all, is of the same substance as God, we anathematize him."
[79] Jobius 286.19, 24–26. See Leont., *Apoll.* 1.11 in Daley 2017, 534.9–11 (Daley renders
the name Jovius).

Apollinarius's disciple Valentinus wrote an entire treatise against Timothy of Berytus and his teacher Polemon to attack the idea that Christ's body was *homoousios* with his divinity.[80] In one passage he asserts: "But the body which the Lord bore has become neither eternal nor incorporeal as a result of the union; because of this it is not *homoousion* with the ineffable and incorporeal οὐσία."[81] Valentinus also makes the distinction between the Incarnation's glorification of Christ's human corporeality and the substantial transformation that he accuses Timothy and Polemon of confessing: "The union glorified the nature for it does not make the body *homoousion* with God, as you, fantasizing, dare to say, having fallen away from the truth [...] saying it is *homoousion* with the impassible godhead because of the union."[82]

While Valentinus calls upon the example of Apollinarius for his claim that it is heretical to say that Christ's flesh/body participates in the divine consubstantiality of the Word/Son who assumes it, the fact of the matter is that the extant fragments of Apollinarius support both sides in the disputes of his disciples and in doing so, point the way to future syntheses.[83] However, Apollinarius represents an early stage in efforts to balance unity and duality in Christ, and his works reflect the lack of precision on this point typical of the initial stages of an important theological development. My point here is not to defend Apollinarius or one or another set of his disciples. What the summary above has shown is that Apollinarius participated in a debate in which the Nicene *homoousion* was integrated into Christological discussion in ways that would in the future lead to the formulation of Christological orthodoxy at Chalcedon.

WHAT PROMPTED APOLLINARIUS TO APPLY THE NICENE HOMOOUSION TO CHRISTOLOGY?

Having surveyed the use of the Nicene *homoousion* in both trinitarian and Christological spheres by Apollinarius and his disciples, I now ask: what triggered this critical "crossover" moment in Apollinarius's theology? Questions remain about how Apollinarius came to embrace the

---

[80] There is a whole collection of Apollinarian fragments collated by Valentinus to show that his opponents misunderstood the master's teaching, as well as Valentinus's own statement of faith in Leont., *Apoll.* 1.1–12 in Daley 2017, 526–43.

[81] Val. Apoll., *Capita apologiae* 4.289.8–10. See Leont., *Apoll.* 1.12 in Daley 2017, 538.7–9.

[82] Val. Apoll., *Capita apologiae* 5.289.22–28. See Leont., *Apoll.* 1.12 in Daley 2017, 538.19–24.

[83] Val. Apoll., *Capita apologiae* 9.291.14–15.

Nicene *homoousion* in trinitarian discourse in the first place, especially
in view of the fact that his theology was heavily influenced by the anti-
Marcellan tradition inaugurated by Eusebius of Caesarea, who was unen-
thusiastic about the conclusions of Nicaea.[84] But resolving that question
is made difficult by recent claims about the authorship and dating of the
Pseudo-Athanasian *Oratio Contra Arianos* IV and other issues that are
beyond the scope of this chapter.[85] The easier question to resolve now is
where Apollinarius might have found inspiration for incorporating the
Nicene *homoousion* into his Christological discourse. As we will see,
there are at least two possible sources for this inspiration, one of which
was very close to home in Syria in the late 350s.

The first candidate for the use of this term in Apollinarius is
Athanasius of Alexandria. Many readers will note that one finds
Christological uses of *homoousios* in his late letters to Adelphius
(370) and to Epictetus of Corinth (from 372). In the letter to Epictetus,
the term appears in a discussion that mostly centers on the question of
whether Christ's body is *homoousios* with his divinity. Athanasius
denies the claim, insisting that Christ's body comes from Mary.[86] In
these late letters, Athanasius does not use the term in a positive sense
to describe any aspect of Christ's humanity; he exclusively applies the
term *homoousios* in a positive sense to Christ's divinity vis-à-vis the
Father's, reiterating the central trinitarian claim of the Nicene Creed.
However, there is one place in the Athanasian corpus from earlier in the
bishop's career where *homoousios* is used positively in a Christological
sense.[87] Writing against "Arian" opponents, Athanasius offers an interpretation of Dionysius of Alexandria's biblical exegesis to support his
contention that Dionysius did not deny the incarnate Son's divinity,
but supported it. He claims that Dionysius applied some biblical passages to the humanity of Christ, and so in this way protected his divinity. The critical passage appears in his discussion of John 15:1 and the
extended metaphor there of the vinedresser, the vine, and the branches.
Athanasius states:

> The vinedresser is different in substance (ξένος ἐστι κατ᾿ οὐσίαν) from
> the vine, while the branches are of one substance and akin to it

---

[84] See the letter he wrote to his congregation about the creed in Socrates, *Historia
     ecclesiastica* 1.8 and Thdt., *HE* 1.12; translation in Stevenson 1957, 364–68.
[85] I refer here to Vinzent 2015, in which he proposes that the Pseudo-Athanasian *CA* IV
     was an early work of Apollinarius, *c.* 340, that pre-dated his meeting with Athanasius
     in 346.
[86] Ath., *Ep. Epict.* 4.
[87] Ath., *De sententia Dionysii* (*De sent. Dion.*) 10.3.

(ὁμοούσια καὶ συγγενῆ), and are in fact undivided from the vine, it and they have one and the same origin [...] If then the Son is of one substance with ourselves (ὁμοούσιός ἐστιν ἡμῖν), and has the same origin as we, let us grant that in this respect the Son is diverse in substance(ἀλλότριος κατ᾽ οὐσίαν) from the Father, like as the vine is from the vinedresser. But if the Son is different from what we are, and he is the Word of the Father while we are made of earth, and are descendants of Adam, then the above expression [i.e. John 15:1] ought not to be referred to the deity of the Word, but to his human coming.[88]

Perhaps significantly, Athanasius goes on to say that "we are akin to the Lord according to the body" (Ἡμεῖς γὰρ τοῦ Κυρίου κατὰ τὸ σῶμα συγγενεῖς ἐσμεν).[89]

Though this use of *homoousios* occurs in an exegetical context that is different from what one observes in Apollinarius, the basic idea that Apollinarius will go on to develop is there: the Son is *homoousios* with human beings according to the body. Given the relationship that had been developing between Apollinarius and Athanasius since the late 340s, it would seem likely that Athanasius is the source of this usage in Apollinarius. This may be all the more the case since Ute Heil has made a persuasive case for dating the *De sententia Dionysii* (and the *De decretis*, which she argues is earlier and the response to which prompted the composition of the *De sent. Dion.*) to the period between 357 and 359, after the autumn of 357 and the outlawing of *ousia* language in the second creed of Sirmium.[90] However, there is another place in the Greek-speaking world in the very same period where authors incorporate Christological language in trinitarian discourse in a way that might also have provided a catalyst for the use of the Nicene *homoousion* in Christological discussion in Apollinarius's thought: the Homoiousian documents of 358 and 359. The leaders of the movement were Basil of Ancyra and George of Laodicea.[91] Morales has recently questioned Epiphanius's attribution of the letter attributed to

[88]   Translation adapted from NPNF 4, 180. The Greek text may be found in Opitz 1935, 53, lines 12–20.
[89]   Ath., *De sent. Dion.* 10.5 (Opitz 1935, 54, lines 21–22).
[90]   Heil 1999, 26–30. It should be noted that Allen Brent has recently contested the notion that the outlawing of οὐσία-language occurred at a council in Sirmium in 357. He places the emergence of Homoian theology a few years later in 359: "Constantius II's Quest for an Inclusive Imperial Church and the Putative Synod of Sirmium" (paper presented at the Eighteenth International Conference on Patristic Studies, Oxford University, August 2019).
[91]   See the chapter in this volume by Mark DelCogliano, 262–63.

George,[92] yet the objection may not be critical to my hypothesis here because (1) the argument I will cite appears essentially unchanged in both the synodal letter of 358 from Basil's Ancyran synod and the letter attributed to George; and (2) this suggests a commonality of thought within the Homoiousian party that we may assume George shared with Basil. The relevant passages for our purposes are those in both documents in which the author(s) make the argument for their assertion that the proper term to define the ontological relationship between the first two members of the Trinity is *homoiousios*: the Father and Son are like in substance, but not the same in substance (hence, not *homoousios*). This is the case because they have different origins: the Father as source of the divine being transmitted to the Son in his begetting; the Son as the begotten offspring of that process.[93]

As Joseph Lienhard has noted, the argument is rooted in polemic tracing its origins back to Eusebius of Caesarea's seminal anti-Marcellan works of the late 330s.[94] What is significant about these documents for our purpose is that in making the argument for the appropriateness of the term *homoiousios* for the ontological relations between Father and Son, both texts use a Christological analogy. They say that just as it is correct to say that Father and Son are like but not identical in substance because they have different origins, so it is also correct to say that the incarnate Son is like human beings but not strictly identical to them because he, too, has a different origin from theirs: the conception by the power of the Holy Spirit instead of normal physical relations. The practical effect of this is that while the incarnate Word has the passions of the human flesh (for example, hunger and thirst), he has the ability denied to other humans to resist consistently the temptations to sin that can arise from those passions.[95] Hence, through the use of this analogy, the suggestion is made, though never made explicit, that just as the Son is *homoiousios* with the Father in his divinity, so he is *homoiousios* with the rest of humankind in his humanity.[96]

---

[92] The attribution has recently been contested and the letter's authorship reassigned to Basil of Ancyra in Morales 2018, which specifically takes issue with the attribution of the letter to George in DelCogliano 2011a.

[93] Epiph., *Pan.*, 73.5.7, 73.12.7, and 73.16.4.

[94] Lienhard 1999, especially 211, where he notes that "Eusebian theology ends with Basil of Ancyra and the Synod of 358," thus articulating the continuity of Homoiousian trinitarian thought with that of Eusebius's anti-Marcellan works.

[95] Epiph., *Pan.* 73.8.1–9.7 and 73.17.2–18.8.

[96] I am indebted to Weedman 2007, 157–79, for alerting me to the potential significance of these passages.

If one agrees with Heil's dating of the *De sent. Dion.*, these Christological passages in both Athanasius and the Homoiousians likely come out of the same historical context: the emergence in the late 350s of Homoian theology, which both Athanasius and the Homoiousians feared provided cover for the more radical trinitarian theories of Heteroousians such as Aetius and Eunomius. There had to be some kind of terminological decision defining the Son's relation to the Father. Obviously, Athanasius and Apollinarius on the one hand, and Homoiousians on the other, come to different decisions on this challenge. But, equally interesting, both parties felt the need in the moment, as they made their commitment to a certain trinitarian formula, to explain how that trinitarian formula would coordinate with their Christologies. Looking at this evidence, I propose that this period is the "crossover" moment for Apollinarius. Can we say who was the seminal influence: Athanasius or the Homoiousians? At this time, this is doubtful. Given that the exegesis in *De sent. Dion.* is consistent with his previous exegetical practices, and Apollinarius had been in contact and correspondence with Athanasius since at least the later 340s, it is perhaps more likely that Athanasian influence has priority. On the other hand, Apollinarius was directly on the scene in Laodicea and watching the unfolding events with attention; as clergy, he may have had access to Homoiousian documents. It is even conceivable that in correspondence with Athanasius, Apollinarius noted the Christological move in the Homoiousian documents and thus prompted Athanasius to do the same in *De sent. Dion.* Perhaps one should split the difference and say that both sides in the debate that emerged after Sirmium 357 likely contributed to the Christological use of *homoousios* in Apollinarius's thought.

If we cannot identify who influenced Apollinarius to apply Homoousion language to Christological discourse, identifying the likely moment when this development occurred may illuminate what we see of Apollinarius's development on this point in his extant works. The *KMP* confines itself to the critical matter in hand in the late 350s and early 360s: the assertion that the Son's divinity is *homoousios* with that of the Father, the central point in the Nicene Creed. Though Christology is important in the *KMP*, Apollinarius does not incorporate *homoousios* language in those parts of the text. Nevertheless, the example has been set by allies (Athanasius) and opponents (George of Laodicea). At some point, likely in the 360s, Apollinarius engaged with this claim along with others, which explains why the matter turns up in both Apollinarius's works from the 370s, the late Athanasian letters, as well as evidence from Serapion of Thmuis and Epiphanius. Significantly, in his letter to

Epictetus of Corinth, Athanasius notes that the debate about Christ being *homoousios* with human beings occurred among pro-Nicene churchmen,[97] and that certainly seems to be the case. The claim lent itself to all sorts of questions: if Christ's humanity is *homoousios*, is it divine and *homoousios* with the Father's οὐσία? Is it uncreated? Did it come down from heaven (a question also prompted by Apollinarius's references to the Pauline verse referring to Christ as "the man from heaven")?[98] Or is it of the same substance shared with other human beings? Later in the 370s, Epiphanius reports that the implications of attributing the Nicene *homoousion* to Christ's humanity led to odd debates among Apollinarius's disciples over whether Jesus had to excrete solid waste or not.[99] This seems like a trivial question and yet (1) it followed legitimately from Apollinarius's assertion that Christ's body/ flesh was *homoousios* with that of other human beings; and (2) the question of Jesus's digestion had already been implicated in Christological statements as early as the 320s, when Eustathius of Antioch used a physiological model deriving ultimately from Aristotle to argue for the presence of a human soul in Christ that would allow it – and not Christ's indwelling divinity – to be the subject of Christ's human weakness reported in the gospels.[100]

Many ironies follow from Apollinarius's assertion that Christ is consubstantial with human beings in his body. First, in doing so, Apollinarius likely sees himself as reasserting the anti-Docetism that Eustathius had made part of his anti-Arian trinitarian polemic nearly fifty years earlier with his assertion that Christ had a human soul. Second, it may have been the move to apply the term *homoousion* to the incarnate Word's humanity that forced him to be more explicit about what was *not* part of Christ's human consubstantiality – that is, the human rational soul. Again, this may have been a standard assumption in his own theological context going back decades, held by many without concern, and this is why the claim does not seem to have been a source of particular comment among Greek theologians *until* the 360s and 370s. Apollinarius may not have felt that he had to make any explicit statement of this view *until* he started asserting Christ's consubstantiality with men; then he *had* to offer that key qualification about the human soul. Third, this move then led to a final irony, which is that in denying

---

[97]   Ath., *Ep. Epict.* 3. Translation from NPNF 2.4, 571.
[98]   Apoll., Fr. 25.210.23–25: "Christ, having God as the spirit, that is to say, the mind, with the soul and body is rightly said to be 'man from heaven.'"
[99]   Spoerl 2017.
[100]   Spoerl 2016.

a human soul in Christ, Apollinarius, just like the "Arians" whom
Eustathius of Antioch denounced in the late 320s, ended up being
accused by Gregory of Nyssa in his *Antirrheticus* of Docetism, of denying the full reality of the divine Incarnation.[101]

CONCLUSION

These final points illustrate something that perhaps has not always been
appreciated about Christian theology in the fourth century. Trying to
make manageable such a vast array of materials composed over the
course of several decades, handbooks on patristic theology assert that
the controversy that Arius's preaching generated and the response
therein of the Council of Nicaea mark the initial stages in the "trinitarian" controversies, which are then said to be followed by the
"Christological" controversies, beginning with the emergence of
Apollinarius as the potential source of heresy for his "confusing" views
about Christ in the early 370s.[102] The fact is, Christology was implicated
in the trinitarian controversies from their inception, reflecting the reality that the nature of the debates involved considerations of the incarnate
experience of the Trinity's second person that affected perceptions of his
pre-incarnate status, which then affected assessments of his incarnate
experience. It was always a complicated feedback loop. This was the case
for Eustathius of Antioch, his enemy Eusebius of Caesarea (and likely
Theodotus of Laodicea), and Apollinarius. I suspect this dynamic is
traceable even further back to the third-century condemnation of Paul
of Samosata (the proceedings of which were attended by not one, but two
bishops of Laodicea),[103] whose modalist trinitarian theology was thought
to be twinned with an adoptionist Christology. But this survey shows
that the interplay between trinitarian theology and Christology was
operative shortly after the Council of Nicaea among figures who had
attended the council and continued to debate the issues raised (and not
really resolved) there. Partly because of the legacy of concerns he
inherited from his background in Syria, Apollinarius's extension of

[101]   This is clearly implied at *Antirrheticus*, as noted in Orton's translation (Orton 2015,
        145). For the Greek, see Mueller 1958, 164, lines 31–165, line 7. Orton 2015, 35–38,
        dates the text to the 380s. We also see this accusation surface in Gr. Naz., *Ep.*
        101.14–15, to Cledonius, in Gallay 1974, 76–79. He dates the letter to the summer
        of 382.
[102]   Bas., *Ep.* 263.4 (in Courtonne 1957–66, 3: 124–25) and *Ep.* 265.2, 128–31. See espe-
        cially the latter, 131, line 3.
[103]   DelCogliano 2008, 252–54, with regard to bishops Eusebius and Anatolius of
        Laodicea.

Nicene trinitarian terminology into the Christological sphere was seriously flawed. Nevertheless, though this study does not claim priority for Apollinarius's innovations in this domain, they represent an important advance that was influential both positively and negatively in the Church's efforts to better understand Christ's human and divine aspects and their proper interrelation.

SELECT REFERENCES

Bergjan, Silke-Petra, Benjamin Gleede, and Martin Heimgartner, eds. 2015. *Apollinarius und seine Folgen*. Studien und Texte zu Antike und Christentum 93. Tübingen: Mohr Siebeck.

Brennecke, Hanns Christof. 2015. "'Apollinaristicher Arianismus' oder 'arianischer Apollinarismus' – ein Dogmengeschichtliches Konstruct? 'Arianische' Christologie und Apollinarius von Laodicea." In Bergjan, Gleede, and Heimgartner, *Apollinarius und seine Folgen*, 73–92.

Daley, S. J., Brian E., ed. 2017. *Leontius of Byzantium: Complete Works*. Oxford Early Christian Texts. New York: Oxford University Press.

DelCogliano, Mark. 2008. "The Eusebian Alliance: The Case of Theodotus of Laodicea." *ZAC* 12(2): 250–66.

DelCogliano, Mark. 2011a. "George of Laodicea: A Historical Reassessment." *JEH* 62(4): 667–92.

Lietzmann, Hans, ed. (1904) 1970. *Apollinaris von Laodicea und seine Schule: Texte und Untersuchungen*. Tübingen: J. C. B. Mohr. Reprint, Hildesheim: Georg Olms.

Orton, Robin, trans. 2015. *St. Gregory of Nyssa: Anti-Apollinarian Writings*. FC 131. Washington, DC: Catholic University of America Press.

Spoerl, Kelley McCarthy. 1991. "A Study of the *Kata Meros Pistis* by Apollinarius of Laodicea." Ph.D. thesis, University of Toronto.

Spoerl, Kelley McCarthy. 1994. "Apollinarian Christology and the Anti-Marcellan Tradition." *JTS*, n.s., 45(2): 545–68.

Spoerl, Kelley McCarthy. 2001. "Apollinarius on the Holy Spirit." *StPatr* 37: 571–92.

Spoerl, Kelley McCarthy. 2015. "The Circumstances of Apollinarius's Election in Laodicea." In Bergjan, Gleede, and Heimgartner, *Apollinarius und seine Folgen*, 19–33.

Spoerl, Kelley McCarthy. 2016. "Eustathius of Antioch on Jesus's Digestion." *StPatr* 74: 147–58.

Spoerl, Kelley McCarthy. 2017. "Epiphanius on Jesus's Digestion." *StPatr* 96: 3–10.

Spoerl, Kelley McCarthy and Markus Vinzent, trans. 2017. *Eusebius of Caesarea: Against Marcellus and On Ecclesiastical Theology*. FC 135. Washington, DC: Catholic University of America Press.

Weedman, Mark. 2007. *The Trinitarian Theology of Hilary of Poitiers*. Supplements to Vigiliae Christianae 89. Leiden: Brill.

14 The Council of Ariminum (359) and the Rise of the Neo-Nicenes

D. H. WILLIAMS

By the time Constantius (II) called for a general council in 359, a doctrinal/confessional upheaval was already boiling over in the West. Passage and issuance of the Nicene Creed in 325 had not assuaged the problems it was intended to; rather, it functioned like a lightning rod that called for more acute clarification of multiple theological currents.[1] After Nicaea, a host of councils and creeds were promulgated with short-lived success. The debacle of Serdica (343) served as a useful indicator for the way doctrinal ideals were colliding, not at all congealing into a more unified stance between bishops and churches. To think of this dynamic as a division between East and West oversimplifies the various allegiances that existed between pockets of bishops with varying loyalties that were roughly divided into single substance terminology when it came to expressing the relation of the Father and the Son versus dyo-hypostatic.[2] Then there was the monarchial tendency, best known in the thought of Photinus of Sirmium. From hostile sources it seems that Photinus maintained that the Son did not exist until his incarnation at Bethlehem. By the late 340s, Photinus's teaching had come to be *the* demonstration of (adoptionist) monarchianism in the West.[3] While no one could articulate

---

[1] My use of "Neo-Nicene" is quite similar to "Pro-Nicene" except that the former is time related. As we will see, the term "neo-Nicene," while strictly a modern invention, has to do with the galvanization of pro-Nicenes once a movement against the Council of Ariminum was underway.

[2] Lienhard's division of the conflict as a division between trajectories is still valuable; mia-hypostatic and dyo-hypostatic is well known. See Lienhard 1987. The use of such parameters, however, cannot cope with the kind of ecclesiastical and doctrinal complexities that evolved by the later 350s as the very terminology of *ousia* (hypostatic) came under attack as a confessionally valid term.

[3] Eusebius of Vercelli (?), *De trinitate* 3.47 (CCSL 9, 42); Lucifer of Cagliari, *De non parcendo in Deum delinquentibus* 28 (CCSL 8, 250); Zeno of Verona, *Tractatus* 2.8 (CCSL 22, 177.37–38). In the earliest Latin handbook of heresy, "Fotinus" was highlighted as a heretic because "he denied that Christ is God with the Father before the ages." Filastrius (Filastr.), *Diversarum haereseon liber* 91.2 (CSEL 9, 257).

it at the time, the success of pro-Nicene theology was contingent upon its proving the dissimilarity between itself and monarchianism.

THE "BLASPHEMIA" AND ITS RESPONSES

We begin with Hilary of Poitiers,[4] who, as a western bishop in exile in Anatolia, was in a unique position to understand the complexity and variety of doctrinal perspectives among the eastern bishops.[5] In the *De synodis*, he sought to translate and comment on several "eastern" creeds to his episcopal confrères, as well as informing them about the enormity of a doctrinal explication that took shape in 357, as Hilary termed it, the "Blasphemia." He knows the councils of Ancyra (358) and Ariminum (359) are already planned and that western bishops will be attending. He wishes to warn them of "this most impious statement," which argues for one God and the Son begotten, not from the Father, but from nothing just as a creature (*ex nihilo ut creatura*).[6] As it concerned the begetting on the Son, Hilary snidely remarks that we are not supposed to know anything about it – "this Compulsory Ignorance Act" – except that the Son is of God. Hilary then quotes the "godless blasphemy" for his readers.[7] Curiously, nothing in the statement is said about the Son being begotten from nothing, nor that he is a creature, both of which Hilary claims to be the case. Although it could easily be divined from the sentence "[the] Son is subordinated to the Father, *together with all things* which the Father has subordinated to Him" (my emphasis)[8] that the Son partakes of the sane nature as "all things," Phoebadius of Agen also interprets the Manifesto as teaching that the Son is a creature.

This document is not a creed in the conventional sense nor is it framed as a creed by those who responded to it.[9] It is rightly regarded as a theological working or position paper meant for public presentation, a kind of theological manifesto that had the confidence of the emperor, who caused it to be widely distributed.[10] But this raises a question. Why have a position statement promulgated instead of a creed, which had

---

[4] For the pre-history of councils, bishops, and creeds during the 340–350s, see Kelly 1972 and Williams 2014.

[5] Writing in early 358, given that Hilary knows Basil and company have been received by Constantius in Constantinople (Hilary of Poitiers [Hilar.], *De synodis* [*De syn.*] 78).

[6] Hilar., *De syn.* 10 (PL 10:486B).

[7] Greek versions of the same are in Athanasius (Ath.), *De synodis Arimini et Seleuciae* (*De syn.*) 28; Socrates (Socr.), *Historia ecclesiastica* (*HE*) 2.30.

[8] Hilar., *De syn.* 11 (PL 10:489A).

[9] Though Hilary refers to the "Manifesto" as a *fides* (Hilar., *De syn.* 11; PL 10:487A).

[10] Ayres 2004, 139.

been the custom? The answer is linked to the expectation that the Manifesto was intended to have, namely, to prepare the ecclesiastical groundwork for acceptance of a later creed that reflects the Sirmium document. As the emperor Constantius sought to unify the empire, he also attempted to prompt unity of the various factions out of which could come a creed that the majority of bishops would accept.

The general response to the Sirmium document is unknown but appears to have been positive or neutral on the part of the majority of bishops. But it also raised immediate and virulent rejoinders from Hilary, Phoebadius, and perhaps Marius Victorinus, who saw treachery within it.[11] Nonetheless, it was officially issued under the emperor's aegis to eastern and western churches, probably with a cover letter, though it does not seem that subscriptions were required. It was said to be penned by Hosius and Potamius of Lisbon,[12] in the company of Valens of Mursa, Ursacius of Singidunum, and Germinius of Sirmium, who would have appealed to bishops with a doctrinal proclivity toward mia-hypostatic theology,[13] and Potamius for those who did not.[14] Was their aim to set aside the creed of Nicaea once and for all?[15] Undoubtedly this was part of the intent of the authors, and yet Nicaea's language was not the only one embargoed. Any terms containing *ousia* were to be shunned, including the short-lived *homoiousios*, a term which Hilary uses.[16]

There were responses to the "Blasphemia," although we ought not to think of these as well-defined groups. As the 340s and 350s showed, bishops changed allegiances in accordance with the latest developments.

[11] It is usually concluded that the first letter from Candidus to Victorinus and the latter's response (CSEL 83/1, 1–48) were motivated by the Sirmium manifesto, though there is virtually no internal evidence to substantiate such a date. Alternatively, this part of the correspondence may have been just as easily a product of the circumstances surrounding Liberius's exile (following the Council of Milan, 355), about which Victorinus would have taken a strong interest.

[12] Conti 1998, 17–18.

[13] A point Phoebadius of Agen (Phoeb.) observes in *Liber contra Arrianos* (*Ar.*) 28.1: "But even with all these [arguments of theirs] shattered and cast into the light of public knowledge, I am not unaware that the name of Hosius, that most elderly priest who always had such resolute faith, is now tempered to serve as a battering ram, one might say, against us in order to drive away the [seeming] rashness of our objections" (Wessel 2008, 62; PL 20:30B).

[14] Potamius of Lisbon, who sided with anti-ousian theology in the later 350s, is quoted as teaching, "in the flesh and spirit of Christ, coagulated through Mary's blood and reduced to a single body, was made the passible God" (*passibilem Deum factum*). Cited by Phoeb., *Ar.* 5.1. This is the only indisputable text that comes from Potamius.

[15] Barnes 2007, 279.

[16] Hilary also refers to this position as *similitudo essentiae configurata in genere* ("the similarity of substance conformed to the [Father's] nature") or *similis est Patri* ("He is like the Father") (Hilar., *De syn.* 25; PL 10:499).

Late twentieth- and twenty-first-century scholarship has demonstrated
that it is more useful to talk about theological trajectories. It is
a misnomer to imagine we are dealing with groups tightly knit around
a particular creed or doctrinal platform. This is demonstrated by the
loose coalitions of bishops that formed together in one context and
could be found in a new configuration in another context. At most we
can talk about theological trajectories as expressed above. Of course, it is
possible to go too far in a way that the subject becomes reframed according to post-modern exigencies such that doctrinal categories are too
unstable and pluriform to make any fundamental divisions in the religious landscape.

One response entailed a sharp reaction, as we witnessed with
Hilary's *De synodis*, which pushed back toward a mia-hypostatic/pro-
ousian direction, but without what Hilary called "the heresy which
arises from an erroneous interpretation of homoousian."[17] In the West
Phoebadius of Agen dashed off his *Liber contra Arrianos* (sic) regarding
the "Manifesto" as nothing less than a deceptive ploy in spreading
catholic doctrine: "I saw through this devilishly subtle deception –
a deception that had nearly taken over everyone's thoughts [...] I very
much desire to be able to reveal this heresy to the public conscience,
blind as it is with devilish deceit."[18] Certainly Phoebadius regarded the
"Manifesto" as a negation of Nicaea. There is no question that
Phoebadius is pro-Nicene – perhaps more than Hilary – when he calls
the Nicene creed the "fixed, perfect rule of universal faith with such
careful wording."[19]

Phoebadius's conviction about the Nicene creed did not appear out
of thin air. Whereas the Nicene creed had lain more or less dormant
during the 330s and 340s, it reappeared with a new surge of urgency as
bishops who supported a mia-hypostatic perspective were oppressed and
exiled in the councils of Arles (353), Milan (355), and others. These
synods reflected the emperor Constantius's efforts to establish ecclesiastical harmony by encouraging the inculcation of a formula that was the
least contentious. Constantius was not an "Arian" or a supporter of

---

[17]   That is, any form of Monarchianism associated with Photinus. Hilar., *De syn.* 84 (PL
       10:535C).
[18]   Phoeb., *Ar.* 1.1, 1.5 (Wessel 2008, 9–10; PL 20:13C–D). Sidaway 2013, identifies four
       interrelated tenets of Phoebadius's argument based on substance language: (1) God the
       Father and God the Son are of one substance; (2) the Son is eternally with the Father,
       without beginning and without end; (3) Father and the Son are distinct but indivisible,
       so the Son is equal in honor, greatness, dignity and majesty; and (4) the Son in his
       incarnate form has two natures, divine and human, which remain distinct.
[19]   Phoeb., *Ar.* 6.2. In 8.2 he more typically regards it as a remedy to heresy.

"Arianism." Nonetheless, the emperor now decided to take a firmer hand in the issues in contention – never resolved at Serdica. And we see that for him these issues were not so much theological, but ecclesiastical/political; in particular, the condemnation of Athanasius, Marcellus and Photinus.[29] After the Council of Arles, Liberius of Rome addressed the emperor in a letter requesting another council where reconsideration might be given to the decisions of Arles. Liberius had a very different vision from the emperor about what would best constitute unity among the churches and bring peace to the empire.[20] It was unnecessary to invent other formulas but necessary to return to that "exposition of the faith ratified between such great bishops at the Council of Nicaea."[21] When Eusebius of Vercelli presented the Nicene Creed for signatures at the synod of Milan,[32] an emotional outburst from Valens of Mursa easily scuttled the plot to introduce it, and the synod concluded with a majority of western bishops endorsing the decisions made at Arles. Constantius did not intercede in the way Liberius requested, but it probably would have made little difference. Few western bishops were prepared to sacrifice their sees by favoring a creed that they had little investment in anyways.[22]

In the year after the Manifesto, a group of eastern bishops led by Basil of Ancyra reacted to Aetius's more radical heteroousian (or anhomoousian) teaching – that the Son was an altogether different substance from the Father – and sought to propose yet another creed with yet another term that might mollify episcopal tensions. Just before Easter in the year 358, Basil of Ancyra and a group of like-minded bishops gathered at a council in Ancyra and approved a creedal document explaining that group's understanding of the Son's relation to the Father, to which they appended nineteen anathemas. It should be noted that these bishops never use *homoiousios*, but articulate several ways of expressing the mystery. Founded on the principle that the Son is the very image of God, he must be the Son according to essence. Like Hilary, Athanasius also expresses a positive opinion that the affirmations of Basil of Ancyra are consistent with the *homoousios*. Basil and company took their creed to Sirmium for imperial approval, and with it, a new formula for the

---

[20]   We must recall that Julius, Liberius's predecessor, had extended communion to Athanasius and Marcellus.

[21]   Hilar., *Collectanea antiariana Parisina* (*CAP*) A.7.6 (CSEL 65, 93).

[22]   Of the bishops that were deposed at Milan included Dionysius of Milan, Eusebius of Vercelli, Lucifer of Cagliari, along with two of his clergy. See Sulpicius Severus (Sulp. Sev.), *Chronicorum libri duo* (*Chron.*) 39.6–7; Rufinus, *Historia ecclesiastica* 1.20; Socr., *HE* 2.36; Sozomen (Soz.), *Historia ecclesiastica* (*HE*) 4.9.3.

empire. But it was not to be.[23] Very soon Basil and company would find it necessary to assimilate themselves into another confederation of bishops that produced another creed.

Meanwhile, the "Manifesto" was taking shape as Athanasius describes it, certifying whatever fears Hilary had that the "Blasphemia" would become the grounds for erecting a new doctrinal creed.[24] We do not know how many bishops favored the simpler theology of the Sirmium Manifesto, but it would have been far more than the few pro-Nicene. In only his first year as bishop of Antioch, Eudoxius held a council in the city of Antioch that openly endorsed it and the task of shrinking it into a concise definition of faith, dubbed by Athanasius as the "Dated Creed."

THE "DATED CREED"

One of the emphases in evaluations of the Nicene–"Arian" controversies over the last twenty years is how the Ariminum creed served as a confessional rallying point for the majority of western anti-Nicenes. In effect, it acted like a fulcrum on which sporadic and individualist defenses of the Nicene faith were raised to the level at which Nicaea came to function as a canonical statement of faith that superseded all others. As an alternative to the theology of consubstantiality and its interpreters, the Ariminum creed was accepted as an authoritative doctrinal standard by such leading bishops as Auxentius of Milan, Palladius of Ratiaria, and the renowned missionary to the Goths, Ulfila. Its fundamental place in Latin-speaking "Arianism" is perhaps best revealed when that same creed was named in a law issued by the pro-Homoian government of Valentinian II in 386 as a counter-standard of faith to the Nicene Creed.

Athanasius provides our earliest version of the "Dated Creed," wherein the logic of the "Manifesto" of 357 is repeated.[25] Concerning the Son it is stated that He is,

> [...] one only-begotten Son of God, who, before all ages, and before all origin, and before all conceivable time, and before all compre-hensible essence, was begotten impassibly from God: through

---

[23] There was no council held at Sirmium in 358. Soz., *HE* 4.15, presents a confused context with the various councils held in Sirmium as did Socrates.

[24] Ath., *De syn.* 29.

[25] The title was given by Athanasius because of the irregularity of ascribing a specific date to the issuances of the creed, "the eleventh of the Kalends of June" (= May 22). Ath., *De syn.* 8.3 (Martin and Morales 1985, 199).

whom the ages were disposed and all things were made; and Him begotten as the Only-begotten, Only from the Only Father, God from God, like to the Father who begot Him, according to the Scriptures; whose origin no one knows save the Father alone who begot Him [...]

But whereas the term *ousia* has been adopted by the Fathers in simplicity, and gives offense as being misconceived by the people, and is not contained in the Scriptures, it has seemed good to remove it, that it be never in any case used of God again, because the divine Scriptures nowhere use it of Father and Son. But we say that the Son is like (*homoios*) the Father in all things (*kata panta*), as also the Holy Scriptures say and teach.[26]

According to Athanasius, this formula of faith of 359 was also a kind of working paper, being drawn up in preparation for the ecumenical councils planned for Ariminum and Seleucia (in Cilicia). One notices that this statement draws on traditional language. Some features of the text hint at a kinship with the (second) Antiochene creed when it comes to "One only and True God" and "through whom the ages were fashioned."[27] But more significant is the reuse of the term *homoios*, which could have indeed functioned as a term mediating opposing groups. We will recall this was Athanasius's preferred word for talking about the Father and Son in his *Adversus Arianos*, for example, "If the Son is the offspring and Image and is like in all things to the Father" (1.21 cf. 1.40, 1.52, 2.17, 3.10–11, 3.20).[28] Hilary also uses it as designating essential likeness.[29] If the quest was to find a commonplace and familiar theological language, then it is arguable that the reintroduction of *homoios* makes good sense. There was nothing new, therefore, about employing *homoios* for doctrinal purposes.

Those architects of the "Dated Creed" are named, and the overlap with the "Manifesto" is not coincidental: Germinius, Auxentius of Milan, Valens, Ursacius, Demophilus, Gaius of Illyricum, and Mark of Arethusa, who acted as the final editor. No doubt Basil of Ancyra and his fellow delegates were disappointed not to see "like-in-substance," but the moment they agreed to the clause that the term *ousia* is too stark and causes more confusion than clarity, their doctrinal purpose was annulled. According to Epiphanius, Basil tried to compensate for this situation by

---

[26] NPNF 2.4, 454 (with modifications).
[27] Kelly 1972, 290.
[28] The expression that the Son was "like all things to the Father" also appeared in the so-called Long-lined Creed (*ekthesis makrostichos*), itself a document of rapprochement between East and West in 344.
[29] Hilar., *De syn.* 73.

adding a postscript that emphasized that the text "like the Father" must be qualified by "in all things" not merely in will but in essence (*hypostasis*), and in existence, and in substance (*ousia*). Little did Basil know that his creedal gloss would have no effect, since the qualifier of *similis* – "in all things" – would be expunged from the final version of the creed at Ariminum.

Was this event the beginning of the "Homoians" or at least the start of a Homoian theology? Maybe the second, but not the first. From the series of events we have just recounted, we are hard pressed to identify the crystallization of a "party" or "platform" known as the Homoians.[30] But we do see the resurgence of the term *homoios* (or *similis* in Latin), a term well known and sufficiently ambiguous to use for most of the theological trajectories of the time.[31] Neither was there a group of pro-Nicenes in any organized sense. It is more the case that those who called for the acknowledgement of the Nicene Creed were lone voices in the West. That Hilary exclaimed that he had even heard of the Nicene Creed recited before he went into exile (356) must have been a state of knowledge indicative of most Latin bishops.

THE COUNCIL OF ARIMINUM (RIMINI)

The decades of the 350s and 360s constitute a period of theological awakening and development in the West, as the controversies so long engaging the East become more prominent in the Latin-speaking world. Now the movement of events picked up speed in 359. The Council of Ariminum (Rimini) commenced in late spring, probably in the third or fourth week of May. Indecision over the eastern location made it impossible for enough bishops to converge at Seleucia until September.[32]

Not surprisingly Ariminum eventually came to endorse an edited version of the "Dated Creed" along with several qualifying statements that sparked such controversy in the West for the rest of the century. The best ancient source for the vicissitudes of this council is Hilary's *Liber contra Ursacium et Valentem* where it is Hilary's intention to show how an enormous maneuver of deceit was successfully perpetrated against the whole council by Valens and his associates.

---

[30] Contra Hanson 1988, 126, 347, 583 who sees the creation of the "Homoians" with the Sirmium "Manifesto."

[31] We would have to exclude, however, the Eunomians or Heteroousians for whom the Son is *dissimilis* from the Father.

[32] September 27, 359. Hilar., *In Constantium* 12.9–10; Socr., *HE* 2.39. The meeting of the easterners, around 150 bishops, will remarkably coincide with events at Ariminum.

The council's proceedings are divided into two parts. The first half bears witness that the warnings of Hilary, Phoebadius, and Liberius had had some impact on their western colleagues. The unveiling of the "Dated Creed" in the midst of the council by Valens and his fellows was rejected out of hand by the majority of bishops, though not because it was thought to contain heretical doctrine.[33] Rather, it was felt by the majority that no other creed or addition need be considered except "that which has been received from the beginning," namely, the Nicene Creed.

Such a decision split the council and made it impossible to fulfill Constantius's demand of the bishops: "to recognize the need for a discussion on faith and unity."[34] On the contrary, the members of the council proceeded to condemn and excommunicate Valens, Ursacius, Germinius, and Gaius. Ten delegates from the majority were sent to Constantius at Constantinople. The reporting delegation, whose decision was already made known to the emperor, was not given an audience and made to wait first in Hadrianople and then at Nikē in Thrace. In the meantime, pressure was laid on those delegates representing the majority of bishops at Ariminum to reach an agreement with the minority party; the result was a dramatic reversal on their part. By October 10, 359, the hard-line position of the majority had been overturned by its own delegates. Restutus (or Restitutus) of Carthage, the leader of the majority delegation, tells how the two groups met together (*in comminus positi*) at Nikē and explains that the excommunication of Valens, Ursacius, Germinius, and Gaius was a grave error that should be annulled. Furthermore, Restutus claimed they had also experienced mutual agreement over "the catholic faith in these matters according to their profession,"[35] which was none other than the formula recently drawn up at Sirmium. It declared that *ousia* should be abolished on the grounds that it was ambiguous and non-scriptural and confessed that "the Son was like the Father." Note that a small but significant alteration had taken place. The traditional phrase "in all things" (*kata panta*) had been removed, perhaps at the behest of Valens, who is said to have tried unsuccessfully to excise the phrase several months before at Sirmium.[36] A copy of the new formula that was approved at Nikē is preserved in Theodoret.[37]

[33] Socr., *HE* 2.37; Soz., *HE* 4.17.6–7.
[34] Hilar., *CAP* A.8.1 (CSEL 65, 94).
[35] Hilar., *CAP* A 5.3.2 (CSEL 65, 86.14).
[36] Epiphanius, *Panarion* 73.22.6.
[37] Theodoret (Thdt.), *Historia ecclesiastica* (*HE*) 2.21.3–7 (translation from NPNF 2.3, 184–85).

We believe in one only true God, Father Almighty, of Whom are all things. And in the only-begotten Son of God, Who before all ages and before every beginning was begotten of God, through Whom all things were made, both visible and invisible: alone begotten, only-begotten of the Father alone, God of God: like the Father that begot Him, according to the Scriptures, Whose generation no one knows except only the Father that begot Him [. . .]

But the word "the Substance," which was too simply inserted by the Fathers, and, not being understood by the people, was a cause of scandal through its not being found in the Scriptures, it has seemed good to us to remove, and that for the future no mention whatever be permitted of "Substance," on account of the sacred Scriptures nowhere making any mention of the "Substance" of the Father and the Son. Nor must one "essence" be named in relation to the person of Father, Son, and Holy Ghost. And we call the Son like the Father, as the Holy Scriptures call Him and teach.

But the exclusion of "in all things" was not the point of betrayal; the emphasis placed on the significance of its omission by modern historians is much overstressed. When both sets of the delegates returned to Ariminum, the majority was surprised, not so much that a new form of the "Dated Creed" was introduced, but that the Nicene faith had been omitted and replaced with another creed.

A second letter to Constantius, which was sent under the name of the whole council, tells how those who had endorsed the use of *ousia* and *homoousios* changed their minds, and agreed that such names were "unworthy to God, since they are never found in Scripture."[38] In the same letter, such denials give way to hyperbole: the use of these terms is potently described as a *sacrilegium* and are said to no longer have a place in sound doctrine. The council also indicated that its position was now unified with the eastern council (Seleucia), a claim which the pro-Homoian bishops may have used manipulatively.

The Council of Ariminum seems to have ended on a note of outward unity and harmony. Even certain resistant bishops finally subscribed to the Nikē formula, once Valens assented in dramatic fashion to a series of anti-"Arian" anathemas.[39] At this point, writes Jerome, "all the bishops and the whole church together received the words of Valens with

---

[38]   Hilar., *CAP* A.6.1.2 (CSEL 65, 87).

[39]   Phoebadius of Agen and Servatio of Tungri are mentioned as the leaders of those who had not yielded. Sulp. Sev., *Chron.* 2.44.1.

clapping of hands and stamping of feet."[40] The wording of the Ariminum creed, slightly modified, was ratified at Constantinople in the winter of 360 and thus designated as the confessional standard of the Roman empire.[41] Regrettably, no subscription list(s) of either council survives.

Among the anathemas affirmed in the assembly, Valens is said to have claimed that the Son of God was not a creature like other creatures. Despite the fact that the sincerity of his testimony was accepted *prima facie* by all, it is this statement in particular which Sulpicius Severus singles out as containing a secret guile:

> Then Valens [...] added the statement, in which there was hidden cunning (*occultus dolus*), that the Son of God was not a creature as was other creatures; and the deceit (*fraus*) of this profession bypassed the notice of those hearing. Even though he denied in these words that the Son was like other creatures, the Son was, nevertheless, pronounced to be a creature, only superior to other creatures.[42]

Jerome too claims that that underneath Valens' acclamation of orthodox-sounding anathemas, there was deceit. What the bishops failed to recognize at the time was the corollary to Valens' assertion at the council that if the Son was not a creature like other creatures he was nevertheless a creature and in this the Son is in fact *dissimilis* to the Father.[43] More importantly, herein lay the kernel of Homoian theology, that *homoios* was being harnessed to mark the unlikeness or at the very least a certain vagueness between the Father and Son, a usage which stood the traditional use of *homoios* on its head. It is unlikely that the western bishops at Ariminum realized they were subscribing against the Nicene faith. Nevertheless, Hilary sardonically refers to the difference between the two sessions: "They condemned the sound faith which they defended earlier, and received the treachery which they condemned earlier."[44]

---

[40] Jerome, *Dialogus contra Luciferianos* 18 (PL 23:171C–172A).
[41] The Homoian formula from Ariminum was endorsed by the synod and on February 15, 360, Constantius, along with the bishops present, consecrated the Great Church at Constantinople, named the "Sophia," which his father had begun a generation earlier.
[42] Sulp. Sev., *Chron.* 2.44.7 (CSEL 1, 97–98).
[43] Meslin 1967, has tried to present Valens and Ursacius, not as unscrupulous schemers, but as sincere theologians. His point, that Valens does unambiguously declare that he was no Arian, should be taken at face value. But it is hardly surprising that anyone in late fourth century should deny a connection to Arius or to the name "Arian." Another Homoian bishop, Palladius of Ratiaria, made the same denial at the Council of Aquileia in 381. Neither Valens nor Palladius saw themselves as points on a line that stretched back to Arius.
[44] Hilar., *CAP* A.5.2 (CSEL 65, 85).

Perhaps the most impugning testimony was that one of the signers of the "Dated Creed," Germinius of Sirmium, openly charged Valens with doctrinal vacillation and duplicity. It was Valens, Germinius testifies, who changed his position at Ariminum by declaring that the Son was like the Father but eschewing the important qualifier, "in all things."[45]

A decade later the great disparity between the two sessions of the council was still being rehearsed by Ambrose in his attack on Homoianism.[46] In a letter to Valentinian II, Ambrose bypassed the argument for the numerical superiority of Ariminum by explaining how sound decisions of the majority of bishops in support of the Nicene Creed were altered only by the illegitimate tactics (*circumscriptionibus*) of a few.[47] This Homoian theology that emerged from Ariminum became a standard around which its proponents rallied for the next two or more decades.

THE AFTERMATH OF ARIMINUM

The combination of foisting what were perceived as eastern creeds on western churches throughout the 350s, the exiling of western bishops, the *fraus* (deceit) committed at Ariminum, plus the prohibition of "sub-ustance" language for all subsequent theological language, contributed to an unparalleled counter-reaction in the West. A Neo-Nicenism that had slightly reared its head in the last decade now emerged in the 360s energized and ready to reclaim the field. This is certainly not meant to imply that the Nicene faith dominated the doctrinal minds of bishops throughout the Roman empire. But we will see the slow ascendancy of Nicaea, though in sharp conflict with the Homoian creed and theology that had now crystallized in theocratic style under the emperor Constantius. Indeed, the Homoian platform will vigorously contend with its opponents well into the fifth century, revealing that the hegemony of Neo-Nicenism is not a *fait accompli* by Constantinople 381. As late as 427/8, the authority of the Nicene and Ariminum creeds was still being contested.[48]

The immediate aftermath of Ariminum and Constantinople is quite telling. A gathering of bishops in Paris in 360 condemned Ariminum as a "deceit of the devil" and declared that those bishops who subscribed to the acts of the council did so out of ignorance.[49] This protest is echoed in

[45] Hilar., *CAP* B.6.3 (CSEL 65, 163).
[46] Ambrose, *De fide* 1.18.122.
[47] Ambr., *Epistulae* 75.15.
[48] Augustine, *Contra Maximinum Arianum* 2.14.3.
[49] Hilar., *CAP* A.1.1 (CSEL 65, 43).

the Roman bishop's (Liberius) general letter to the Italian bishops (AD 362/3) when he describes bishops at Ariminum as deceived and *ignorantes*.[50] Around this same time an unnamed gathering of Italian bishops professed (c. 363) that they had renounced the decrees of Ariminum; and in order for their episcopal colleagues to establish communion with them, the latter must not only subscribe to the Nicene faith but also disavow the Council of Ariminum without ambiguity.[51]

As the last letter shows, not only was Ariminum – not Constantinople – being rejected, but it was necessary to embrace Nicaea. The bishops at the Council of Paris further stipulated to their eastern colleagues that they had fully accepted the term *homoousios* as the proper way of speaking about,

> the true and genuine birth (*nativitatem*) of the only-begotten God from God the Father [. . .] God born from whole and perfect ingenerate God, and therefore confessed by us to be of one *ousia* or substance (*substantiae*) with the Father.[52]

We know that the decisions made at Paris were the tip of the stick. Later in 360, Gregory of Elvira penned a hostile attack entitled, *De fide orthodoxa*, on the proceedings at Ariminum and closed by wholeheartedly embracing the decisions of Nicaea.[53] Other similar pro-Nicene initiatives were taken.[54] The question that plagued the Neo-Nicenes, however, concerned the hundreds of bishops who had subscribed at Ariminum or Seleucia even if under false pretenses.

Constantius's death in November 361 meant the collapse of his ecclesiastical policy. Julian was now emperor of the entire empire, and following Constantius's death he wasted little time in undoing the religious policies of his predecessor. His ostensibly neutral attitude toward such matters had cloaked his zeal for pagan religion – at least for the first few months of his reign. Of the two general edicts published early in the new year, one declared a general amnesty for all bishops who were in hiding or in exile for religious offences.[55] Now the "confessors" of Arles and Milan, as well as bishops condemned at other councils under Constantius, were permitted to return to their towns and have their

[50] Hilar., *CAP* B.4.1 (CSEL 65, 157).
[51] Hilar., *CAP* B.4.2 (CSEL 65, 157).
[52] Hilar., *CAP* A.1.2 (CSEL 65, 44).
[53] CCSL 69.
[54] Hilar., *Liber contra Auxentium Mediolanensem* (*Aux.*); Filastr., *Diversarum hereseon liber*; Zeno of Verona, *Tractatus*; Gregory will produce a second version of his *De fide* in 361.
[55] *Historia acephala* 3.2 (Martin and Albert 1985, 150).

property restored. Still, the lineaments for continued discord were already well in place and the emperors Julian, Jovian, and Valentinian showed no interest in overriding the status quo. Except that Julian published an edict freeing all bishops who had been exiled on religious grounds, including western bishops, such as Eusebius of Vercelli and Lucifer of Cagliari, who were exiled in the East. Athanasius also returned to Alexandria where he called a small council of eastern and western bishops that met in mid-362 and issued a statement of faith that called for *homoousios* per the Nicene faith. But the real concern was to deal with those bishops who wished to dissociate themselves from the conciliar compromise that had been made in 359. Once the gravity of the situation was fully set forth to the bishops present, the synod agreed to extend a conditional pardon to the fallen bishops. In his letter to Rufinianus, written soon after the close of the synod, Athanasius describes this pivotal decision in concise terms: acquitting those "not deliberate in impiety, but drawn away by necessity and violence, that they should not only receive pardon, but should occupy the position of clergy."[56] Sulpicius Severus tells us that through frequent councils held in Gaul, nearly all the bishops publicly owned (and forsook) the error that had been committed at Ariminum.[57]

HOMOIAN CHRISTIANITY

It may be that Homoian communities were fewer in number than Nicene after the passing of Constantius, but they were no less cohesive and vibrant communities, spawning theological, exegetical, homiletic, and polemical literature of which sizeable fragments have come down to us today. In fact, it now appears, as Y.-M. Duval has observed, that this literature became more abundant from the moment when the Homoians were completely abandoned by imperial authority.[58] Western Homoianism was hardly a "lame duck" even after the death of Constantius and the temporary loss of imperial patronage. So widespread was pro-Homoian literature in the West, that Hilary of Poitiers, in his tract *Contra Auxentium* written under the reign of Valentinian I in 364, complains that the "Arian" opposition to the Nicene faith is considerably augmented: "all of the churches contain full records (*chartae*) of their most impious blasphemies, and even complete books."[59] Unless

---

[56] Ath., *Epistula ad Rufinianum* (PG 26:1180B–C).
[57] Sulp. Sev., *Chron.* 2.45.
[58] Duval 1969, 146.
[59] Hilar., *Aux.* 7 (PL 10:613B).

a bishop could be rightly accused of civil disturbance, Homoian bishops remained in their sees. Hilary of Poitiers discovered this when he tried to have Auxentius of Milan removed on heretical grounds. He failed to do so, and Auxentius remained bishop until his death in 374.[60]

An otherwise unknown Italian synod that met in Rome (c. 368) sent the results of its decisions to pro-Nicene bishops in Illyricum condemning publicly Auxentius and all supporters of Ariminum, but nothing came of it.[61] Similarly, Urbanus of Parma is said to have retained his episcopal see despite conciliar attempts to have him ejected as an "Arian."[62] In the early 360s, Florentius of Puteoli had been condemned by his peers for theological reasons that are almost certainly linked to the anti-Ariminum fervor that swept across Italy after 359. An isolated record of another unidentified Italian council complained to the emperor Gratian in 378 that Florentius was still active in the city, and "by his persuasive speech, corrupted a multitude of lost souls."[63] Earlier and more influential than Florentius was Epictetus of Centumcellae (Civitavecchia), bishop of an important city north of the Tiber. After Constantius's death in 361, we hear no more about Epictetus, although he likely remained in his see till death. The infamous and now aging Illyrian bishops, Valens of Mursa and Ursacius of Singidunum, had been repeatedly condemned by the assembly at Paris (360) and other synods in Gaul and Italy, and then at least on one other occasion by a Roman synod under Damasus in 371.[64] Nevertheless, Valens continued to preside over the see of Mursa as late as the reign of the emperor Valens (364–78), nor had the bishop's influence been abated by the series of condemnations. In 367, we find Valens, assisted by another Homoian bishop, Domninus of Marcianopolis (metropolitan of Moesia Secunda), successfully interceding on behalf of Eunomius with the eastern emperor. It is the last act of Valens known to us from the sources; presumably he died soon afterwards – still in control of his see. Ursacius also maintained a grip on his see until his death c. 366, and he was succeeded by another anti-Nicene, Secundianus, who joined the side of Palladius of Ratiaria at the Council of Aquileia.[65] But the clock was ticking for the continuance of most of these bishoprics.

---

[60] See Williams 1992.
[61] Soz., HE 6.23.7–15; Thdt., HE 2.22.
[62] Collectio Avellana, 13.6–7, Gratianus et Valentinianus Augg. Aquilino vicerio (CSEL 35, 55–56).
[63] CSEL 35, 56.7–8.
[64] Ath., Epistula ad Afros episcopos 3 (PG 56:1033B).
[65] See Williams 1995, 70–72.

COUNCIL OF AQUILEIA

By the time of the Council of Aquileia (381), Italy's bishops were almost solidly pro-Nicene, especially since the most influential sees – Milan, Aquileia, and Rome – were theologically united.[66] The identities of the bishops known to be at the council also reveal how the weight of episcopal authority had shifted to North Italy, largely due to the influence of Ambrose over the region. The Council of Aquileia was an event which Ambrose orchestrated to remove what he hoped were the last pockets of Homoian Christianity in Italy and Illyricum.

Only two Homoian bishops attended: Palladius of Ratiaria and Secundianus of Singidunum. Valerianus of Aquileia presided over the synodical proceedings as the host bishop, although the *gesta* record that Ambrose led the questioning of the accused, who were summarily condemned and excommunicated. But perhaps Ambrose's most influential activity was the consecration of new bishops in the cities of Como (Felix), Lodi (Bassianus), Ticinum (Profuturus?), and Aquileia (Chromatius). Besides these, there is from Ambrose's extensive correspondence positive reference to other north Italian bishops such as Gaudentius of Vercelli (c. 379) and Felix of Bologna, all of which provides us with a broader picture of the sphere of episcopal influence at the end of the fourth century.

Of course, the conflict between Neo-Nicenes and Homoians was also fought in the political area. Once Valentinian II had abandoned Milan for Ravenna, the political leverage that Homoians enjoyed in that city evaporated. This was especially the case once the pro-Nicene Theodosius defeated Maximus and stayed in Milan October 388 to the end of April 389.[67] Theodosius had already stipulated in Constantinople that only those who confess the Nicene faith would be considered Catholic (January 381). He enacted several anti-heretical (ant-Arian) edicts while in Milan and Rome.[68] The future of Homoian Christianity lay with the Gothic groups of peoples in the empire.

Toward the end of his life, Augustine was drawn into debate with an "Arian" bishop from Illyricum named Maximinus, who came to Africa with the Gothic commander Sigiswulf and a Roman army in 427.[69] This is quite likely the same Maximinus who later wrote against Ambrose's

---

[66]   Ironically, the church at Milan continued to experience discord between Nicenes and Homoians, exacerbated by the arrival of Valentinian II in the imperial residence. For the young emperor's pro-Ariminum policies, see Williams 1995, 259–71.

[67]   Seeck 1919, 235.

[68]   *Codex Theodosianus* 16.5.17–20.

[69]   The English translation is in Teske 1995.

treatment of Palladius and Secundianus at Aquileia. According to Maximinus, Sigiswulf had sent him to Hippo "with a view to peace" between Arians and Catholics. The advantage of this debate with Maximinus is that it contains one of the fullest extant presentations by an adherent of Homoian Christianity. As mentioned earlier, Maximinus appealed to the Council of Ariminum as his conciliar authority: "If you ask for my faith, I hold that faith which was not only stated but also ratified at Ariminum by the signatures of three hundred and thirty bishops."[70] The actual debate did not go well for Augustine, who claimed that his opponent monopolized all the time given to them. But the truth may also lie in the fact that the aged bishop was not prepared for a debater and exegete as knowledgeable as Maximinus. So Augustine wrote two books in response to his opponent's arguments.

NICAEA VERSUS ARIMINUM

By now it should be obvious that Latin "Arians" (Homoian Christianity) were not extinct at the end of the fourth century, but had lost most of their earlier vitality and certainly were in decline numerically.[71] And yet we continue to find pro-Homoian writings of self-defense, spirituality, and exegesis. In fact, a sizeable body of Latin "Arian" documents survived the imperial proscriptions of the later fourth and fifth centuries and have come down to the present. This literature can be divided roughly into two categories: (1) credal formulae and (2) homiletic, exegetical, and polemical treatises and fragments (some of them very large fragments). The bulk of Latin "Arian" literature which remains has been preserved in three collections: the Arian *scholia* from the Codex Parisinus ms. lat. 8907, an ensemble of short and complete texts from the ms. Verona LI,[72] and a series of fragmented palimpsests originally discovered in the library of Bobbio, now partly preserved in the Vatican library (ms. lat. 5750) and partly in the Ambrosian library (S. P. 9/1–2; 9/9).[73] Outside of these three groups of texts there are also extant a very lengthy and

---

[70]   Also in Teske 1995, entitled, "Debate with Maximinus" and "Answer to Maximinus."

[71]   Duval 1973, 183–92.

[72]   In Gryson 1982a. One finds in this collection an explanation of the names of the apostles (f. 2r–5v), a series of 24 homilies on the Gospels (f. 5v–39v), 15 sermons on the principal feast days of the year (f. 1r–1v; 40r–77v), a treatise against the Jews (77v–98v), a treatise against the Pagans, in two somewhat different recensions (98v–119r; 119v–132v), and a short polemical sermon directed against the doctrine that the *Pater et Filius aequales sunt* (133r–136r).

[73]   See Gryson and Gilissen 1980; Gryson 1982b; and Gryson 1983.

fragmented commentary on the Gospel of Matthew which was attributed to John Chrysostom throughout the Middle Ages but is now known
simply as the *Opus imperfectum in Matthaeum*,[74] an anonymous commentary on Job,[75] and an exposition or catechism of Homoian doctrine
known as the *Sermo Arrianorum* against which Augustine writes
a refutation.[76]

CONCLUSION

In the preceding historical reconstruction, we have seen that the West
had not always been sympathetic to Nicene Christianity nor was its
subjugation of Homoian "Arianism" accomplished only because of the
loss of its political support under the emperor Constantius. In the first
place, Nicene or Homoian "parties," that is, as conscious theological and
ecclesiastical identities, did not fully crystallize until after the councils
of Ariminum and Constantinople – events that marked the beginning of
the (Neo-)Nicene–Homoian conflict in the West. It is surely an exagger-
ation to call "Arianism" a "dying" religion after 360, or theologically
unable to sustain enduring devotion without political support any less
than the Nicene form of faith. Homoianism became increasingly isolated
in western communities in the 370s and 380s, but the ostensibly neutral
political policies toward religion under Valentinian I and Gratian's early
reign quelled any serious aggression by Neo-Nicenes or disgruntled
Homoians. And it was during this time that we charted a surge in
Homoian and pro-Nicene texts which provided insights into the ecclesi-
astical-doctrinal dynamics of the period. Hanson's general thesis that the
victory of pro-Nicene Christianity was established in 381 has long been
proven to be short-sighted, at least in the West.

It was not inevitable that the Nicene Creed or faith would become
the post-fourth-century church's way of confession. There were factors
that led to its hegemony in the West that were neither inexorable nor
necessary. This does not mean there were no fundamental agreements
about what constituted acceptable trinitarian expression, but simply
that there existed no uniform articulation which faith communities
were prepared to acknowledge as universally orthodox before 360. In
any case, by the time the Nicene faith became the primary doctrinal
expression among Latin churches, Neo-Nicenism in the later fourth and

---

[74]   CCSL 87B.
[75]   CSEL 96. See 1.73.40–41 and 1.11.6–14.
[76]   Against which Augustine composed the *Contra sermonem Arianorum* (in Teske
1995, 133–38).

early fifth centuries represented a considerable accretion to the doctrines articulated in 325, such as the consubstantiality of the Holy Spirit, as insisted by the threefold *homoousios* in the *Epistula Catholica* of the Alexandrian synod of 362, or how pro-Nicene Latin trinitarianism defined itself in sharp contradistinction to the Marcellan/Photinian tradition. Nicene theology and ecclesiology by this time meant something that had substantially evolved and expanded from what they meant in 325.

SELECT REFERENCES

Barnes, Timothy D. 2007. "A Note on the Term 'Homoiousios'." *ZAC* 10(2): 276–85.

Duval, Yves-Marie. 1969. "Sur l'arianisme des Ariens d'Occident." *Mélanges de science religieuse* 26: 145–53.

Duval, Yves-Marie. 1973. "Les relations doctrinale entre Milan et Aquilée durant la seconde moitié du IVe siècle: Chromace d'Aquilée et Ambroise de Milan." In *Aquileia e Milano*. Antichità Altoadriatiche 4, 171–234. Trieste: EUT Edizione Università di Trieste.

Gryson, Roger. 1982a. *Le recueil arien de Vérone (Ms. LI de la Bibliothèque Capitulaire et feuillets de la Collection Giustiniani Recanti): Étude codicologique et paléographique.* Instrumenta Patristica 13. Sint-Pietersabdij: Steenbrugge.

Gryson, Roger. 1982b. *Scripta Arriana Latina I: Collectio Veronensis, Scholia in concilium Aquilense, Fragmenta in Lucam rescripta, Fragmenta theologica rescripta.* CCSL 87. Turnhout: Brepols.

Gryson, Roger. 1983. *Les palimpsestes ariens latins de Bobbio: Contributions à la méthodologie de l'étude des palimpsestes.* Turnhout: Brepols.

Gryson, Roger, and Léon Gilissen. 1980. *Les scolies ariennes du Parisinus latinus 8907: Un échantillonage d'écritures latines du Ve siècle.* Turnhout: Brepols.

Lienhard, Joseph. 1987. "The 'Arian' Controversy: Some Categories Reconsidered." *Theological Studies* 48: 415–37.

Martin, Annick, and Micheline Albert. 1985. *Histoire "acéphale" et Index syriaque des Lettres festales d'Athanase d'Alexandrie.* SC 317. Paris: Les Éditions du Cerf.

Martin Annick, and Xavier Morales. 1985. *Athanase d'Alexandrie: Lettre sur les synodes.* SC 563. Paris: Les Éditions du Cerf.

Meslin, Michel. 1967. *Les Ariens d'Occident 335–430.* Patristica Sorbonensia 8. Paris: Éditions de Seuil.

Sidaway, Janet. 2013. "Hilary of Poitiers and Phoebadius of Agen: Who Influenced Whom?" *StPatr* 66: 286–90.

Wessel, Keith C. 2008. *Phoebadius of Agen: Liber Contra Arianos.* www .fourthcentury.com/wp-content/uploads/2010/09/Wessel-Phoebadius.pdf.

Williams, D. H. 1992. "The Anti-Arian Campaigns of Hilary of Poitiers and the *Liber Contra Auxentium*." *CH* 61(1): 7–22.

Williams, D. H. 1995. *Ambrose of Milan and the End of the Nicene–Arian Conflicts*. Oxford Early Christian Studies. Oxford: Oxford University Press.

Williams, D. H. 2014. "Italy and Its Environs." In *Early Christianity in Contexts*, ed. William Tabbernee, 407–11. Grand Rapids: Baker Academic.

Part V
The Long Reception

15 The Legacy of the Council of Nicaea in the Orthodox Tradition
The Principle of Unchangeability and the Hermeneutic of Continuity

PAUL L. GAVRILYUK

INTRODUCTION

The normative importance of the Council of Nicaea and its Creed in the Orthodox tradition cannot be overestimated. In the minds of the leaders and faithful of the Orthodox Church, whatever their doctrinal and political differences, the Nicene faith has been and remains an unshakable foundation. To clarify, the expression "Nicene faith" (πίστις) often refers to the doctrinal content that is broader than the "Nicene Creed" (σύμβολον).[1] The Nicene Creed is the original confession of faith and the associated condemnations of Arius and his followers set forth by the Council of Nicaea. By comparison, the "Nicene faith" refers to the teaching contained in the expositions of faith deemed compatible with but not limited to the Nicene Creed. For example, the Constantinopolitan Creed, whatever its historical origins and its exact relationship to the Nicene Creed, was received as an authentic expression of the Nicene faith.

Not all Christian communions in the West take the Nicene faith as a valid expression of the apostolic teaching. For the Christian East, the situation is quite different: while it is legitimate to consider new doctrinal questions in light of the Nicene faith, it is not legitimate to question the authority of the Nicene faith itself. In other words, the rejection of the Nicene faith is tantamount to the abandonment of Orthodox Christianity.

The Council of Nicaea was not the first gathering of bishops in the history of Christianity to issue canonical legislation. Before Nicaea,

---

[1] It should be noted that in some patristic sources the terms πίστις, σύμβολον, and ἔκθεσις ("exposition") had more fluid meaning and were used almost interchangeably in reference to the doctrinal content of Nicaea. For a nuanced discussion, see Smith 2018, 27, 195.

influential canons were issued, for example, by the councils of Ancyra
(314) and of Neocaesarea (315). While these councils were significant for
the development of canon law, the Council of Nicaea (325) established
itself as an event that provided a blueprint for future church councils,
especially those summoned by the Roman emperors. In the Orthodox
tradition, the reputation of the emperor Constantine and the Council of
Nicaea have followed parallel courses: Constantine, despite his controversial conversion and his personal defects, was eulogized, mythologized, and turned into a ruler "equal to the Apostles"; the Council of
Nicaea, despite the fact that the orthodoxy of its creed was strongly
contested by several fourth-century councils, was eventually made the
stuff of hagiography, hymnography, and iconography, and was recognized as the First "Ecumenical" Council.[2] Thus, Constantine was turned
into a Christian ruler whom all God-loving eastern Christian emperors –
Byzantine and Slavic alike – would be wise to emulate; the Council of
Nicaea inaugurated a succession of ecumenical and other significant
councils, all of which claimed their continuity with the faith professed
by the "318 Fathers" who gathered at Nicaea.[3]

The emperor Constantine had hoped that the Council of Nicaea
would provide a solution to the problem of church divisions and thereby
solidify the unity of his empire (divisive issues included the Arian controversy, conflicting calculations of the Easter date, and the Melitian
schism).[4] However, during the emperor's reign, Nicaea was a source of
turmoil rather than peace. While some local western councils defended
Nicaea, no fewer than eighteen eastern councils offered creedal alternatives to the Nicene Creed. As it is well known, the most vocal supporter
of the Nicene faith was Athanasius of Alexandria (d. 373), who tirelessly
promoted the Nicene Creed in the third quarter of the fourth century.[5]
However, during Athanasius's lifetime the Nicene faith had not been
decisively established as a common confession binding the Church
together.[6]

---

[2]   The first extant use of the adjective "ecumenical" (οἰκουμενική) with reference to the
      Council of Nicaea is in Eusebius of Caesarea (Eus.), *Vita Constantini* (*VC*) 3.6 (c. 338).
[3]   The traditional number of 318 episcopal participants was chosen for its symbolic
      significance as a number of male servants that were prepared to fight for Abraham in
      Gen. 14:14. This evocative biblical image turned the Nicene bishops into an army of
      the New Israel, the Church, ready to defend God by proclaiming the Son's consubstan-
      tiality with the Father. The first extant mention of the figure 318 in reference to Nicaea
      is in Hilary of Poitiers, *De Synodis* 86. See Aubineau 1966, and above, 92–96.
[4]   See Constantine's letter to churches in Eus., *VC* 3.17–20.
[5]   See Sara Parvis's chapter in this volume.
[6]   But see above, 264–79.

The defense of the Nicene faith was both a theological and a political task. After a succession of emperors who were not supportive of Nicaea, Emperor Theodosius undertook this task with great zeal in his decree *Cunctos populos* (380). This piece of legislation imposed the Nicene faith as a civic duty upon all law-abiding citizens of the Roman empire:

> It is our desire that all the various nations which are subject to our Clemency and Moderation, should continue to profess that religion which was delivered to the Romans by the divine Apostle Peter, as it has been preserved by faithful tradition, and which is now professed by the Pontiff Damasus and by Peter, Bishop of Alexandria, a man of apostolic holiness. According to the apostolic teaching and the doctrine of the Gospel, let us believe in the one deity of the Father, the Son and the Holy Spirit, in equal majesty and in a holy Trinity.[7]

The decree prudently avoided citing the still controversial Nicene Creed, while at the same time deferred to the authority of Pope Damasus and Archbishop Peter of Alexandria (Athanasius's successor), who were unflinching defenders of the Nicene faith in the face of strong opposition. The next imperial decree, issued on January 10, 381, was somewhat more explicit:

> The throngs of all heretics must be restrained from unlawful congregations. The name of the One and Supreme God shall be celebrated everywhere; the observance, destined to remain forever, of the Nicene faith, as transmitted long ago by Our ancestors and confirmed by the declaration and testimony of divine religion, shall be maintained. The contamination of the Photinian pestilence, the poison of the Arian sacrilege, the crime of the Eunomian perfidy, and the sectarian monstrosities, abominable because of the ill-omened names of their authors, shall be abolished even from the hearing of men.[8]

Notwithstanding such threatening rhetoric, the imposition of the Nicene faith as a requirement on all Roman citizens proved to be difficult to enforce, as the frequently repeated imperial proscriptions against heterodox Christian groups and non-Christian religions attest.[9] Nevertheless,

---

[7] *Codex Theodosianus* 16.1.2, trans. Bettenson 1943, 31.
[8] *Codex Theodosianus* 16.5.6, trans. Pharr 1952.
[9] While the state-sponsored persecution of the heterodox groups made their existence precarious, later historians register the fact that these groups have not disappeared altogether.

later imperial legislation, most especially the revision of the religious laws undertaken under the emperor Justinian, did not relax the requirement established by *Cunctos populos*, but repeatedly attempted to reinforce it. Byzantine and western medieval Christendom was erected upon the common metaphysical foundation enshrined in the Nicene faith.

All subsequent Ecumenical Councils of the Orthodox Church have emphasized their continuity with the Nicene faith. The Second Ecumenical Council in Constantinople (381) marked a turning point in establishing the normative status of the Nicene faith, which for the preceding part of the fourth century remained the subject of acrimonious controversy.[10] The first canon of the Council of Constantinople declares: "The Faith of the 318 Fathers assembled at Nicaea in Bithynia shall not be set aside, but shall remain firm."[11] This declaration was followed by condemnations of heresies that had appeared in the aftermath of Nicaea.

The main debates of the fifth century were no longer about the soundness of the Nicene faith, which was by then nearly universally accepted,[12] but rather about the *interpretation* of the Nicene faith in light of new challenges. These challenges clustered around the problem of how the properties of divinity and humanity could be clearly differentiated and ascribed to one subject, namely, the Son of God incarnate. The councils that addressed various aspects of this problem assembled in Ephesus (431), Chalcedon (451), and Constantinople (553 and 668). Like Nicaea, these councils were surrounded by a tempest of controversies, which led to enduring divisions. Those who rejected the Council of Ephesus became known as the Assyrian Church of the East; those who did not accept the Council of Chalcedon became known as the Oriental Orthodox Churches. While these divisions have not been fully healed to this day, these Churches share with the Eastern Orthodox Church a common Nicene legacy.

CYRIL OF ALEXANDRIA AND THE ASCENDANCY OF THE NICENE LEGACY

Among the fifth-century Christian authors, Cyril of Alexandria was both a witness to and a promoter of the ascendant authority of the Nicene faith. For Cyril, the Council of Nicaea was a divinely inspired moment

[10] No less than eighteen fourth-century synods offered alternatives to the Nicene Creed. See Pietras 2016, 197.

[11] "Canons of the Council of Constantinople," NPNF 2.14, 172.

[12] In the West, Arianism remained a live option well into the sixth century. In contrast, the Church in the eastern part of the Roman empire was more consistently pro-Nicene. See the discussion by Daniel Williams, above 312–22.

when the former holders of his archiepiscopal see, Alexander and then deacon Athanasius, demonstrated significant theological leadership. The Council of Nicaea could be trusted, because Athanasius was a man "worthy of trust and deserving of confidence," and he in turn could be trusted because he was close to bishop Alexander, whom Cyril also held in high esteem.[13] The Council of Nicaea boosted the authority of the Alexandrian bishopric at the time when its prestige was challenged by a newcomer, the archiepiscopal see of Constantinople. Cyril personally supervised the dissemination of the canons and the Creed of Nicaea from the archives of his church to other churches in the Roman empire.[14] It was Cyril also who "fostered the idea that no creed could claim equality with N.[icene]."[15]

Cyril made the Nicene Creed his point of departure in his argument against Nestorius of Constantinople. Cyril begins his second letter to Nestorius with an exposition of the Christological article of the creed. Specifically, Cyril argues that this article identifies one subject, namely, "one Lord Jesus Christ," who shares his divine nature with the Father and at the same time has typically human experiences of suffering, crucifixion, and death. Cyril builds a case for his Christology on the foundation of the second article of the creed and his interpretation of the kenotic hymn in Phil. 2:5–11. In his response, Nestorius does not challenge the foundational significance of the Christological article of the Nicene Creed.[16] Nestorius argues instead that Cyril's interpretation of this article does not do justice to the fact that the Son, who is equal to the Father, is also said to "become man" and, therefore, to suffer and die as a man, not as God. The particulars of their arguments need not concern us here. It is significant, however, that Cyril presents the Nicene faith as an undisputed foundation and Nestorius accepts his premise. Indeed, the controversy leading up to and culminating in the Council of Ephesus (431) has been aptly described as "a struggle over who could more convincingly present themselves as the advocates and defenders of the Nicene faith."[17]

---

[13] Cyril of Alexandria (Cyr.), *Epistulae* (*Ep.*) 1.9, trans. McEnerney 1987, 16. For Cyr., *Ep.* 39.7, loyalty to Nicaea was first of all loyalty to Athanasius.

[14] Cyr., *Ep.* 85.1.

[15] Kelly 1972, 322. As far as the Council of Constantinople and its creed were concerned, Cyril simply ignored the assembly that in its third canon elevated the archbishop of Constantinople above all other bishops in the eastern Roman empire, including his own see of Alexandria. Given the rising tension between the two archiepiscopal sees, Cyril was content to pass the Council of Constantinople over in silence.

[16] Nestorius, *Epistulae ad Cyrillum* 2.

[17] Smith 2018, 67.

The seventh canon of the Council of Ephesus summarizes this consensus position as follows: "[T]he holy Synod decreed that it is unlawful for any man to bring forward or write, or to compose a different Faith as a rival to that established by the holy Fathers assembled by the Holy Ghost in Nicaea."[18] After the council, a group of eastern bishops headed by John of Antioch and Acacius of Beroea demanded that Cyril abide by the principle of the sufficiency of the Nicene faith and on these grounds withdraw his critique of Nestorian teaching. Cyril replied, somewhat unconvincingly, that he did not put forth a new creed, but was obliged to correct the Christological tenet that, in his judgment, distorted the Nicene faith. Like the eastern bishops, Cyril held that the Nicene faith was unchangeable; unlike these bishops, however, Cyril could not accept that the profession of the Nicene Creed was *sufficient* since the new circumstance required a defense of the creed against its alleged misinterpretation.[19]

The Formula of Union, which Cyril signed with his opponents in 433, provided both a clarification of the Christological article and asserted the following about the Nicene faith:

> We will not allow the faith, or rather the Symbol of the faith that was defined by our holy Fathers who formerly came together in Nicaea, to be unsettled by anyone. We will not permit ourselves, or anyone else, to change one word of what is laid down there, or to go beyond even one syllable.[20]

In line with the seventh canon of the Council of Ephesus, this statement appears to go beyond the first canon of the Council of Constantinople that the Nicene faith must remain "firm." The Council of Constantinople put forth a hermeneutic of continuity; these fifth-century pronouncements assert the principle of unchangeability and even the principle of sufficiency of the Nicene faith, which is now more closely associated and sometimes simply identified with the Nicene Creed in its "pure" form and not any other confession of faith. While the principle of unchangeability was rhetorically powerful and psychologically compelling, when joined to the principle of sufficiency, it was also exceedingly difficult to put in practice, as the Council of Chalcedon and its aftermath would demonstrate. As Mark Smith observes:

[18] Council of Ephesus, canon 7, NPNF 2.14, 231.
[19] Cyr., *Ep.* 33.10, 37.1, 39.3, and John of Antioch, *Epistulae ad Cyrillum* 2. See also Smith 2018, 37–87.
[20] *The Formula of Union of 433. Ep.* 39.10 (*ACO* 1.1.4.20), in Hardy 1954, 356–58.

at the heart of the struggles over "Nicaea" lay the problem of how continuity with the Nicene past could be persuasively maintained, whilst the fresh challenges of new doctrinal contexts could be genuinely confronted. It was the dilemma, in other words, of how "Nicaea" could be both reaffirmed as sufficient and yet also acknowledged (even if not openly) as inadequate; of how the Creed could both remain inviolate and yet also be supplemented; of how the "great and holy synod" could both abide unchallenged and yet also admit (in some sense at least) to authoritative successors.[21]

At the Council of Chalcedon, the public reading of the "Exposition of faith of the 318 Fathers" was followed by acclamations: "This is the orthodox faith; this we all believe; into this we were baptized; into this we baptize," and so on.[22] After these acclamations, the "most glorious judges and great senate" ordered the reading of "what was set forth by the 150 holy fathers." This is a somewhat oblique reference to the creedal formula that would come to be accepted on the authority of the Council of Chalcedon as the one put forth by the Council of Constantinople. Since the *acta* of the Council of Constantinople are not extant, the matter of whether this episcopal assembly had indeed put forth any new creed in addition to the Nicene Creed remains uncertain. What is certain is that the Council of Constantinople saw its confessional stance as in keeping with the Nicene faith. The principle of the unchangeability of the Nicene faith did not preclude doctrinal development; on the contrary, this principle provided a robust metaphysical foundation for doctrinal development. If the Orthodox leadership had not come to the agreement over the Nicene faith, the debate over the foundations would have encumbered, or would have even rendered impossible, later doctrinal developments, especially in the area of Christology and doctrine of God. It was important for the Council of Constantinople to provide an authoritative moment of doctrinal "closure" for the Nicene faith, as it was equally important for the Council of Chalcedon to validate the Constantinopolitan Creed as a faithful expression of the Nicene faith.[23]

---

[21] Smith 2018, 3.

[22] Council of Chalcedon, Session II, NPNF 2.14, 249.

[23] The concept of doctrinal "closure" is developed by Cohen 2018. The validation of the Constantinopolitan Creed also had the unintended effect of challenging the Nicene Creed's uniqueness, although it did not relativize Nicaea's preeminence.

Post-Chalcedonian Orthodox tradition maintains that the Constantinopolitan Creed is an expanded version of the original Nicene Creed. Contemporary scholarship has challenged this tradition on textual and redaction-critical grounds, the particulars of which are considered in J. N. D. Kelly's classic study, *Early Christian Creeds*, and are beyond the scope of this chapter.[24] It is more relevant for our purposes that after the Council of Chalcedon, the Constantinopolitan Creed was gradually accepted and disseminated as an authentic and authoritative expression of the Nicene faith. The post-Chalcedonian prominence and wide distribution of the Constantinopolitan Creed attests to the fact that the principle of unchangeability of the Nicene faith, no matter how effective it was rhetorically and how often repeated, was in practice deployed rather as the principle of continuity. The church leaders gathered in Chalcedon were aware of the fact that the "faith of the 150 fathers" did not repeat the original Nicene Creed verbatim; nevertheless, they endorsed both formulations as valid. By implication, although without any explicit acknowledgement, they accepted the fact of doctrinal development and, in practice, had to set aside the principle of sufficiency of the Nicene Creed, which the Council of Ephesus put forth.

The main issue that the Council of Chalcedon had to determine was not the compatibility of the two creeds, but rather the agreement of the *Tome* of Pope Leo with the Nicene faith. The vast majority of the Council Fathers commented that in their judgment the *Tome* was indeed consistent with the Nicene faith. However, some expressed their reservations, which after the Council of Chalcedon would fester into a permanent division between the churches that accepted and those that rejected the Chalcedonian Definition and the *Tome* as its authoritative interpretation. This division shows that in the minds of some Christian leaders, the Council of Chalcedon was a departure from the Nicene faith, particularly its Christological aspect. Thus, the hermeneutic of continuity with the Nicene faith, professed by the subsequent councils, was itself a matter of controversy, which had enduring consequences. It is clear, then, that by building on the Nicene faith the Fathers of the Council of Chalcedon offered no mere repetition of Nicene orthodoxy, but rather attempted its Christological elucidation and re-expression. The fact that the non-Chalcedonian churches rejected the legitimacy of this development only confirms the point that the hermeneutic of continuity was no mere repetition. While its particular applications were strongly contested, the hermeneutic of continuity with the

[24]   Kelly 1972, 296–331.

Nicene faith was a principle that was shared by all parties that debated the outcome of the fifth-century Christological controversies.

THE NICENE LEGACY IN WORSHIP

Ironically, the original creed of the Council of Nicaea – in contrast to the Constantinopolitan Creed, or the Apostles' Creed – has never enjoyed a particularly broad ecclesiastical circulation. In fact, there is no evidence that the council's original creed was ever deployed in the context of worship. The Nicene Creed as well as the other fourth- and fifth-century conciliar creeds were not immediately proposed as replacements for local baptismal creeds. On the contrary, there is ample evidence to suggest that more than a century after the Council of Nicaea, various local creedal formulations continued to be used in the rite of baptism in different parts of the empire and beyond. Baptismal and conciliar creeds had somewhat different, although overlapping functions. Early baptismal confessions of faith varied widely, were drawn upon in baptismal catechesis, and were not formally debated at councils. In contrast, the Nicene Creed was the first conciliar attempt to establish a common standard of orthodoxy. As long as the local baptismal creeds could be interpreted as broadly agreeing with the Nicene faith, they continued to be used in catechesis and in baptism.

After the Council of Chalcedon endorsed both the Nicene Creed and the creed of the "150 Fathers gathered in the imperial city," the Constantinopolitan Creed, not the original formula of the Nicene Creed, began to replace local baptismal creeds. This development was gradual and by no means universal, with many churches continuing to adhere to their local ancient practices. The Constantinopolitan Creed had acquired this significance because it was widely believed to express the Nicene faith in light of the doctrinal challenges that arose in the aftermath of Nicaea. Just as the Council of Chalcedon was a defining moment for establishing the authority of the Constantinopolitan Creed, the Council of Constantinople was a defining moment for establishing the authority of the Nicene faith.

Prior to the sixth century, creedal formulae were not yet a regular part of the liturgy. Apparently, the first church leader to introduce the creed into public worship was patriarch Timothy of Constantinople. The patriarch, who was leaning in the miaphysite direction and was suspicious of Chalcedonian Christology, ordered that the Constantinopolitan Creed be recited during worship in Constantinople, wishing to increase the public significance of the creed and hoping, by implication, to decrease the doctrinal significance of the Chalcedonian Definition. However, Timothy's anti-Chalcedonian intentions were lost on his contemporaries, who embraced the practice of the recitation of the creed during the second part of the liturgy (the Liturgy of the Faithful, as it is known in the Christian East) without sharing his plan for consigning the Chalcedonian Definition to oblivion.[25] It is true, of course, that most eastern Christians today are more familiar with some version of the creed than with the Chalcedonian Definition, precisely because the former, but not the latter, is regularly recited in public worship. The introduction of the Constantinopolitan Creed into public worship at a relatively late date also explains why some non-Chalcedonian churches, such as, for example, the Armenian Apostolic Church, use a creed better suited for their traditions, rather than the Constantinopolitan Creed, in their worship.

The Nicene legacy in Orthodox worship is not limited to the recitation of the creed. In the church calendar, the Council of Nicaea is commemorated on three major occasions. The most prominent is the remembrance of the 318 Fathers of the First Ecumenical Council on the first Sunday after the Ascension. Second in order is the commemoration of the council itself on May 29. Finally, the Slavonic liturgical tradition also adds the Feast of the First Six Ecumenical Councils, which includes the Council of Nicaea.

The liturgical memory of the Council of Nicaea, as reflected in church hymnography, includes some curious hagiographic material. For example, the hymns of the Feast of St. Nicholas of Mira and Lycia (later turned into Santa Claus) have the saint confront Arius at the Council of Nicaea:

> Teaching incomprehensible knowledge about the Holy Trinity, thou wast with the holy fathers in Nicaea a champion of the confession of the Orthodox Faith. Thou didst confess the Son equal of the Father, co-everlasting and co-enthroned, and thou didst convict the foolish Arius. Wherefore the faithful have learnt to sing unto thee: Rejoice, sanctuary of prayer and devotion [...] Rejoice, thou who didst expel the demonic Arius from the council of the saints.

[25] Theodore the Reader, *Historia ecclesiastica* 2, frag. 32 (PG 86.1, 201): "Timothy ordered for the Creed of the 318 Fathers to be recited at every service in order to get even with Macedonius, as if he did not accept the creed. For previously the creed was recited only once a year, on the occasion of the catechetical instruction, which the bishop conducted on the Holy Friday" (translation mine).

The method of Arius's expulsion is specified in one hagiographic account, which has St. Nicholas growing so indignant with Arius as to strike the heretic on his face.[26] While this particular story was pure fiction, the reality of verbal abuse and occasional physical violence during the conciliar proceedings was not.

As a mythologized, or rather demonized character, Arius also provided ample opportunities for one of the most common rhetorical devices of Byzantine church hymnography, namely, antithesis. For example, the hymnography of the Sunday of the 318 Fathers of the First Ecumenical Council extols the theological achievement of Nicaea and pours pious vitriol on the waywardness of Arius, ascribing to him the following end:

> Arius fell into the precipice of sin, having shut his eyes so as not to see the light, and he was ripped asunder by a divine hook so that with his entrails he forcibly emptied out all his essence and his soul, and was named another Judas, both for his ideas and the manner of his death. But the Council in Nicaea loudly proclaimed you, Lord, to be Son of God, equal in rank with the Father and the Spirit.[27]

Whatever its literary qualities, the story filled a gap in popular imagination: the arch-heretic, who rejected the full divinity of the Logos, died the death of the betrayer of Jesus. Orthodox hymnography and hagiography of Nicaea reinforced in popular imagination the Athanasian interpretation of the council as primarily anti-Arian.[28]

In addition to these regular liturgical uses, the importance of adherence to the Nicene faith is in the rite of the consecration (ordination) of an Orthodox bishop.[29] This rite, the core of which was formed in the post-iconoclastic period, contains three confessions of the bishop-elect. In the first confession, the bishop-elect is asked by the senior bishop, who presides over his consecration: "What do you believe?" In response, the bishop-elect recites the Constantinopolitan Creed. In the second and third confessions, the bishop-elect summarizes the Christological doctrine of the Orthodox Church and promises to be faithful to the dogmas and canons of the seven Ecumenical Councils, as well as the provincial councils that have been approved by the Ecumenical Councils. The

[26] *Synaxarion*, trans. Holy Transfiguration Monastery 1997, 334.
[27] Quoted in Lash 2006, 155.
[28] For a significant corrective to this interpretation, see Ayres 2004, 105–30.
[29] "The Office of Confession and Answering of a Bishop (and the Laying-on of Hands)," trans. and notes St. Tikhon's Monastery 1998, 270–81.

bishop-elect then signs his three confessions in writing, promising to keep the peace and unity of the church. According to the rite, one of the main functions of the episcopal office is to preserve, teach, and transmit the Nicene faith in light of the canonical and dogmatic legacy of the councils. The canons of the councils, including the twenty canons of the Council of Nicaea, were collected and commented upon by the Byzantine and other Orthodox canonists. Among such collections, *The Rudder* (*Pedalion* in Greek) has proven to be the most widely used and influential over the past 200 years.[30]

THE COUNCIL OF NICAEA IN ORTHODOX ICONOGRAPHY

The artistic potential inherent in the figure of Arius as an antipode of the orthodox proponents of the Nicene faith was not lost on the iconographers. The first securely identifiable depiction of the Council of Nicaea in the Byzantine tradition belongs to the hand of Michael Damaskinos and is quite late.[31] Dated 1591, the icon, which shows strong western influences, depicts the council participants seated amphitheater style (in three rows of semicircles), surrounding the Gospel Book, which is enthroned in the center. Emperor Constantine is placed to the right of the throne with a papal figure (pope Sylvester?) seated in the same row to the left of the throne. Arius, defeated and condemned, is lying on the foreground in front of the seated bishops. To remove any doubt about his condemnation, the heresiarch holds an unrolled scroll with an inscription that says: "Arius enemy of God and the first of those who burn." The composition follows a relatively typical Byzantine and western scheme of presenting conciliar decisions. This general scheme, often with the emperor, rather than the Gospel Book, placed in the center, was also followed in the later centuries. In some versions of the icon, the open scroll features a part of the creed, specifically its second article with the assertion that the Son is consubstantial with the Father. Other later versions of the icon also feature St. Nicholas slapping Arius on his face (as we saw earlier, this episode came from hagiographic sources). Compared to the influence of hymnography, the iconographic tradition

---

[30] Cummings 1957. For a recent English-language commentary on the conciliar canons, including those of Nicaea, see L'Huillier 1996, 17–100.

[31] Walter 1991–92. The author notes earlier, thirteenth-century icons of the councils, which cannot be securely identified as those of the First Council of Nicaea. The earlier extant depiction of a church council is in the Menologion of Basil II (979?). The icon discussed here is the cover image for this volume.

of depicting the First Ecumenical Council was a relatively insignificant factor in shaping the popular reception of the Nicene legacy.

THE APPEAL TO THE NICENE FAITH IN THE FILIOQUE CONTROVERSY

While providing a common foundation for all Eastern Churches, the Nicene faith was also a part of the shared heritage of eastern and western forms of Christianity. Nevertheless, one controversy over the wording of the Constantinopolitan Creed has played a significant role in cementing the division between the Byzantine East and the Latin West. This difference, which had to do with the pneumatological article of the creed, became the subject of the Filioque Controversy of the eighth and later centuries.

The original form of the third article of the Nicene Creed of 325 was quite succinct: "And in the Holy Spirit." In light of the Pneumatomachian controversy, which challenged the divine status and hypostatic character of the Holy Spirit, the Creed of the Council of Constantinople (381) expanded the third article to read: "And in the Holy Spirit, the Lord, the Giver of Life, who proceeds from the Father," and so on. In the West, the clause "and from the Son" (*Filioque* in Latin) was added to some local versions of this creed. As one of the unfortunate accidents of history, it is the version of the Constantinopolitan Creed with the Filioque that became widely accepted in the West.

The creed with the Filioque was introduced into the Mass in the West under the following circumstances. Wishing to oppose the Arian heresy, the Visigothic king Reccared replaced the old Roman Creed, whose archaic formula rendered the precise relationship between the Father and the Son rather ambiguous, with the Latin text of the Constantinopolitan Creed, which included the Filioque clause. Ratified by the Council of Toledo (589), the king's original intention was to bring the Spanish Church in line with the "customs of the Greek Fathers" and to oppose Arianism, which was still strong in the Latin West. At the time that the Constantinopolitan Creed with the Filioque was introduced into the Mass, the difference between the Byzantine and western creedal formulae was lost in translation. Due to the isolation between the Greek-speaking East and the Latin-speaking West, the Filioque addition was at first ignored and became an international scandal only in the eighth century, with the Latins insisting on the legitimacy of the Filioque and the Greeks protesting against it.[32]

---

[32]   Louth 2007.

One of the strongest opponents of the Filioque in Byzantium was Patriarch Photius of Constantinople (c. 810 or 820–93). In *On the Mystagogy of the Holy Spirit*, Photius marshals a range of arguments against the theological implications of the double procession of the Spirit and the legitimacy of inserting the Filioque clause into the creed. Addressing the point of legitimacy, Photius cites the following decision of the Council of Chalcedon:

> After the exposition of the faith which the First and the Second Councils established and handed down, the Council [of Chalcedon] says: "Therefore, this wise and salutary Symbol (*symbolon*) of divine grace is sufficient for full knowledge and confirmation of piety." It says full, not partial, or requiring any addition or omission.[33]

In the conciliar decision, the term *symbolon* refers to three confessions: the Nicene Creed, the Constantinopolitan Creed, and the Chalcedonian Definition. Photius was aware of the fact that the Council of Constantinople did not leave the Nicene Creed unchanged and that by adopting the Constantinopolitan Creed alongside the Nicene Creed, the Council of Chalcedon implicitly accepted that the creedal formulae could be altered in light of new doctrinal challenges. However, for polemical reasons, Photius interpreted the decision of the Council of Chalcedon as an endorsement of the principle of unchangeability not just of the Nicene faith broadly conceived (which by then included both the Constantinopolitan Creed and the Chalcedonian Definition), but specifically of the Constantinopolitan Creed. Photius went on to argue that the Fifth and the Sixth Ecumenical Councils had reaffirmed the same principle.[34] In Photius's hands, the principle of unchangeability of the Nicene faith, stated by the Councils of Ephesus and Chalcedon, became a weapon against the inclusion of the Filioque clause into the Constantinopolitan Creed. Such an interpretation of Chalcedon's intention was appealing to Photius's Byzantine contemporaries, although it did strain the historical evidence.

The principle that a creed is unchangeable was on occasion invoked in the West too and, ironically, was used by some Latin Church Fathers in support of retaining the ancient Roman Creed or the Apostles' Creed in worship instead of the "newer" Constantinopolitan Creed. The weakness of such an argument, and this would also apply to Photius's argument

---

[33] Photius of Constantinople, *On the Mystagogy of the Holy Spirit*, 80, trans. Holy Transfiguration Monastery 1983, 104.

[34] Photius of Constantinople, *On the Mystagogy of the Holy Spirit*, 81, 82, trans. Holy Transfiguration Monastery 1983, 105–6.

for the unchangeability of the Constantinopolitan Creed, is that at earlier points in history the creedal formulae were regarded as more fluid and subject to alternation and expansion. As we mentioned earlier, by endorsing both the Nicene and the Constantinopolitan Creeds, the Fathers of the Council of Chalcedon by implication accepted the legitimacy of using two different confessional formulae in order to express one Nicene faith. While they insisted on the unchangeability of this faith, they also put forth a new Christological Definition, which some eastern church leaders interpreted as a departure from orthodoxy that made it necessary to separate from the Chalcedonian churches. In other words, the claim that Chalcedon offers a legitimate interpretation of the Nicene faith was not accepted universally; for the Oriental Orthodox Christians, the Nicene faith was indeed sufficient, especially when read in light of Cyril of Alexandria's Christology; the Chalcedonian Definition, and especially Leo's *Tome*, was superfluous at best and erroneous at worst.

The long-term outcome of the Filioque controversy was to turn the Nicene faith (and especially the Constantinopolitan Creed) from a shared doctrinal legacy into a field of theological battle between the Byzantine Church and the Latin Church.[35] The creed without the Filioque clause became a marker of the Eastern Orthodox identity, just as the creed with the Filioque clause became a marker of the Roman Catholic (and for some churches of the Reformation, also Protestant) identity. While the bulk of the Nicene legacy continued to be shared, the fixation on the difference over the Filioque under the sufficiently intransigent church leadership and in especially tumultuous political circumstances led in the eleventh century to a schism between the East and West. As a result, the Byzantines came to regard their western counterparts as compromising the Nicene faith; the two versions of the creed, with and without the Filioque, came to be deployed as weapons of identity politics in the subsequent confrontations between the Byzantine East and the Latin West, especially after the historical trauma of the Crusades. Behind the smokescreen of the Filioque, both traditions often failed to appreciate the significance of their shared Nicene legacy.

One historical example of this failure is the response of Patriarch Jeremiah II of Constantinople to the Lutheran theologians at Tübingen, who sent him the Augsburg Confession. The Lutheran theologians

---

[35] The Filioque controversy has not affected the Slavic Orthodox Churches to the same degree as it did the Byzantine Church. The main cause of disagreement between the East and West remains papal authority, rather than the Filioque.

mentioned in their letter that they accepted the seven Ecumenical Councils. Noting this matter with approval, the Patriarch pointed out the following:

> So then we affirm that your first article, which cites the dogmatic definitions, or sacred symbol, of the holy Synod of Nicaea [c. 325], concerning the one exceedingly holy essence and the three persons of the Godhead, is correct and has been piously proclaimed by you. However, this Synod of Nicaea and the others which agreed with it declared that the Holy Spirit proceeds from the Father. The confession of the sound faith of Christians, this most sacred symbol (which was first drawn up by the 318 God-bearing Holy Fathers at Nicaea, and completed by the 150 Fathers in Constantinople, and ratified by the other five Ecumenical Synods, without adding or omitting anything, inasmuch as they agreed with it, as the holy men who blazed forth during the years between those holy Synods, and distinctly confessed, and as we by the grace of God confess with them), most clearly reveals that the Holy Spirit proceeds from the Father.[36]

After citing the Constantinopolitan Creed without the Filioque in full, Patriarch Jeremiah added:

> This is the treasure of the true faith, which was sealed by the Holy Spirit, so that no one would omit anything nor introduce into it anything spurious. This divine, most sacred, and wholly perfect credo of our piety, the confession of all the Holy Fathers, the definition of Christianity, which we embrace and espouse, we boldly profess to preserve, unscathed and unadulterated to the end of time as the holy deposit [of faith] of the divinely inspired Holy Fathers.[37]

Several common features of the Orthodox approach to the Nicene faith are brought out with clarity and distinction in Patriarch Jeremiah's response: while the shared trinitarian faith is acknowledged, the creed of the Augsburg Confessions contains the offending Filioque and, therefore, departs from orthodoxy; the addition of the Filioque is unacceptable on the grounds of the principle of the unchangeability of the Nicene faith, which was "completed" by the Council of Constantinople (382)

---

[36] Patriarch Jeremiah II, "The First Answer of Patriarch Jeremiah [II] of Constantinople concerning the Augsburg Confession Sent to Tübingen [May 15] 1576," in Mastrantonis 1982, 32.

[37] Mastrantonis 1982, 32–33.

and "ratified" by the other five Ecumenical Councils. The Nicene faith, enshrined in the creed without the Filioque, is perfect as it stands and is "sealed" by the Holy Spirit in the sense that nothing could be added or subtracted from it. The principle of the unchangeability of the Nicene faith secures the continuity of the tradition. The patriarch's response is a classical expression of the way in which the Orthodox Church has viewed and continues to deploy the creed in the doctrinal discussions with the non-Orthodox. While some present-day Orthodox leaders may approach the dogmatic implications of the procession of the Holy Spirit with greater ecumenical sensitivity, the position of the Orthodox Church on the Filioque has remained fundamentally the same: the Nicene faith is unchangeable and the Filioque clause has no place in the creed.[38]

THE LEGACY OF NICAEA IN THE ORTHODOX CHURCH TODAY

The life of the Church is shaped as much by the controversies as by the matters that are taken for granted. The Nicene faith has been something that the Orthodox Church, beginning from the fifth century, has taken for granted as its unshakeable foundation. As we have seen, several Ecumenical Councils have both insisted on the principle of unchangeability of the Nicene faith and have attempted to follow the hermeneutic of continuity with Nicaea. For this reason, with the exception of the first-century Apostolic Council in Jerusalem (Acts 15:6–29), no council in the history of the Orthodox Church could rival the Council of Nicaea in its doctrinal significance and historical impact.

Several canons of the Council of Nicaea refer to the gathering as "the great and holy council," or "the holy and great council," or simply "the great council."[39] Building on this precedent, the 2016 Pan-Orthodox Council that met in Crete also called itself a "holy and great council." The Council of Crete was convoked by the Patriarchate of Constantinople and attended by delegations of ten out of fourteen self-governing Orthodox Churches. In the absence of the emperor, who in ancient times could enforce the participation of the delegates from different provinces of the

---

[38] For an important recent development, see The North American Orthodox-Catholic Theological Consultation, "The Filioque: A Church Dividing Issue: An Agreed Statement," at www.usccb.org/beliefs-and-teachings/ecumenical-and-interreligious/ecumenical/orthodox/filioque-church-dividing-issue-english.cfm [accessed June 30, 2018]. Also see Dunn's discussion below, 352–56.

[39] Council of Nicaea, canon 8, 14, 15, 17, 18; NPNF 2.14, 19, 31, 32, 36, 38.

Roman empire, four local churches (Patriarchate of Antioch, Russian Orthodox Church, Bulgarian Orthodox Church, and Georgian Orthodox Church) opted against attendance. This separatist impulse demonstrated that Orthodox conciliarity, while important in theory, is not always followed in practice. Following the pattern of the Council of Nicaea, the Council of Crete did not refer to itself as "ecumenical," for this would be both historically presumptuous and theologically erroneous. Instead, the Council of Crete chose the title "holy and great council," which was meant to signal its continuity with the Nicene faith.

Before the Council of Crete, influential traditionalist voices within the Orthodox Church raised objections against the legitimacy of any new Pan-Orthodox council by appealing to the principle of unchangeability. More moderate voices sided with the church leaders, who pointed out that the principle of unchangeability did not rule out the possibility of future conciliar gatherings. In fact, in some circumstances, this principle required the assembly of new councils in order to defend the Nicene faith in the face of new questions and controversies. There is no shortage of such questions and controversies in our time.

The Encyclical of the Council of Crete addresses the conciliar nature of the Orthodox Church in the following terms:

> The Orthodox Church, in her unity and catholicity, is *the Church of Councils*, from the Apostolic Council in Jerusalem (Acts 15.5–29) to the present day. The Church in herself is a Council, established by Christ and guided by the Holy Spirit, in accord with the apostolic words: "It seemed good to the Holy Spirit and to us" (Acts 15.28). Through the Ecumenical and Local councils, the Church has proclaimed and continues to proclaim the mystery of the Holy Trinity, revealed through the incarnation of the Son and Word of God.[40]

While the Encyclical does not mention the Council of Nicaea explicitly, the Nicene vision of God and Christ are foundational for the Orthodox understanding of the Trinity and Incarnation. If the Nicene faith had been compromised or distorted, the history of the Orthodox Church would have been very different. It is adherence to the Nicene faith that has been and remains the foundational marker of Orthodox Christian identity.

---

[40] "Encyclical of the Holy and Great Council of the Orthodox Church," par. 3, at www .holycouncil.org/-/encyclical-holy-council [accessed June 30, 2018].

The Council of Nicaea was an inspired experiment in communal truth-seeking and truth-articulating, which later councils sought to imitate, both "spiraling back"[41] to the Nicene faith and unpacking the content of this faith in light of new theological questions. In the realm of politics, the closest analogy to an assembly of this sort was the Roman Senate. However, political assemblies rarely, if at all, involved questions of metaphysics, which were typically addressed by the late antique philosophical schools. While such schools provided a framework for debate, they lacked sufficiently robust structures for public adjudication and dissemination of philosophical views. For example, late Platonist metaphysics has never been a matter of dogmatic definition or imperial legislation. Whatever means philosophers had of transmitting their teachings, they certainly could not rival the structures of the Church and the state, which ensured the teaching of the Nicene faith through her episcopate, the passing on of the creed in the rites of initiation, and the reaffirmation of the same faith in the liturgy and in imperial legislation. It is by these means – episcopate, baptism, liturgy, and councils (with the notable exception of imperial decrees) – that the Nicene faith continues to bear fruit in the life of the Orthodox Church.

SELECT REFERENCES

Bettenson, Henry, ed. 1943. *Documents of the Christian Church*. London: Oxford University Press.

Cohen, Will. 2018. "Doctrinal Drift, Dance or Development: How Truth Takes Time in the Life of Communion." *International Journal of Systematic Theology* 20(2): 209–25.

Coolman, Boyd Taylor. Unpublished. "Ongoing Re-Narration: A Catholic Practice of Historical Theology." Paper presented at the International Conference "Rethinking the Resources of the Christian Theological Tradition: Retrieval, Renewal, Reunion," University of St. Thomas, St. Paul, Minnesota, 11–15 July 2017.

Hardy, Edward R. 1954. ed. *Christology of the Later Fathers*. Philadelphia: Westminster Press.

Holy Transfiguration Monastery. 1983. *Photius of Constantinople: On the Mystagogy of the Holy Spirit*. Astoria, NY: Studion Publishers.

Holy Transfiguration Monastery. 1997. *Synaxarion*. Brookline, MA: Holy Transfiguration Monastery.

Lash, Ephrem. 2006. "Byzantine Hymns of Hate." In *Byzantine Orthodoxies*, ed. Andrew Louth and Augustine Casiday, 151–64. Aldershot: Ashgate.

Louth, Andrew. 2007. *Greek East and Latin West: The Church* AD *681–1071*. The Church in History 3. Crestwood, NY: St Vladimir's Seminary Press.

---

[41] See Coolman (unpublished).

Mastrantonis, George, ed. 1982. *Augsburg and Constantinople: The Correspondence between the Tübingen Theologians and Patriarch Jeremiah II of Constantinople on the Augsburg Confession.* Brookline, MA: Holy Cross Orthodox Press.

Smith, Mark S. 2018. *The Idea of Nicaea in the Early Church Councils,* AD *431–451.* Oxford Early Christian Studies. Oxford: Oxford University Press.

Walter, Christopher. 1991–92. "Icons of the First Council of Nicaea." *Δελτίον τῆς Χριστιανικῆς Ἀρχαιολογικῆς Ἑταιρίας* 16: 209–18.

16 Catholic Reception of the Council of Nicaea

GEOFFREY D. DUNN

To be tasked with investigating Catholic reception of Nicaea is not as easy as it first appears, especially as there is another chapter in this volume on Orthodox reception. Obviously there were distinctions between the "Catholic world" and the "Orthodox world" even before 1054, yet how much earlier should we start? We could simply look at the reception of Nicaea by the bishops of Rome or by the churches in the West. However, the initial part of that story, in the first fifty or sixty years after 325, belongs to the general Nicene story to be treated else-where in this volume.[1] In this contribution, therefore, attention is turned to how Nicaea was regarded during late antiquity and throughout Christian history from a Catholic perspective. In essence, this will mean looking at the bishops of Rome in the centuries immediately following the council and how the Catholic Church, once the splintering of Christianity became evident in later centuries, continued that recep-tion. Our interest will be in the profession of faith and the canons rather than the trinitarian controversy. The question of the date of Easter, which was of central concern to the bishops gathered at Nicaea, is also beyond our scope here.[2]

INITIAL ROMAN REACTION THE COUNCIL OF NICAEA

From Athanasius's *Apologia secunda*,[3] we learn that Julius, bishop of Rome (337–52), supported Athanasius during his second exile after his condemnation at the 335 synod in Tyre. Julius held a synod in Rome in

This project is funded by the Polish Minister of Science and Higher Education within the program under the name "Regional Initiative of Excellence" in 2019–2022, project number: 028/RID/2018/19, the amount of funding: 11 742 500 PLN.

[1] See the chapters in this volume by Sara Parvis, Mark DelCogliano, and Daniel Williams.
[2] On this, however, see the chapter by Daniel Mc Carthy.
[3] See Twomey 1982, 291–345; Barnes 1993, 192–95.

340/341, to which he referred in a letter of reply addressed to the Eusebian bishops from the Dedication Council in Antioch in 341, in which they had declined to participate in his synod in Rome.[4] Their letter itself was a reply to an earlier one from Julius, which had invited the eastern bishops to the synod in Rome, which, importantly for Julius's argument, was something they had requested.[5]

Julius reported that at Nicaea, described as the great council, it was decided that the decisions of one synod ought to be examined or confirmed (ἐξετάζεσθαι) by another.[6] This seems to be evidenced to some extent in canon 5 of Nicaea.[7] The synod met in Rome and dismissed the appeal, thus overturning the condemnation of Athanasius.[8] As Sozomen reports, Rome always upheld the decisions made at Nicaea.[9]

Following the death of Eusebius of Nicomedia, who had been translated to Constantinople from 338, Paul, the exiled bishop of Constantinople, tried to reclaim his see but was expelled by Constantius II and replaced by Macedonius. Paul, Athanasius, Julius, and Maximus of Trier petitioned Constans in Trier in 342 to get his imperial brother to agree to a synod to finalise matters of faith and the position of Athanasius and other bishops.

4   See Sozomen (Soz.), *Historia ecclesiastica* (*HE*) 3.8.4–8.
5   Athanasius (Ath.), *Apologia contra Arianos* (*Apol. sec.*) 21–35 = Julius I, *Epistulae* 2 (*Legi litteras*) (Thompson 2015, 38–80 = Sieben 2014, 1:88–128) = Jaffé 1885 (= JK), no. 186 = Jaffé 2016 (= J³), no. 431. At 36.1, Athanasius records this as a letter from the synod of Rome itself. See Soz., *HE* 3.10; and Twomey 1982, 398–425.
6   Julius I, *Ep.* 2.2 (Thompson 2015, 40–42 = Ath., *Apol. sec.* 22.2). Julius adds immediately that this παλαιὸν τυγχάνον was μνημονευθέν at Nicaea. The fact that the easterners asked Rome to reconsider the decision reached at Tyre in 338 meant that Julius could ignore the fact that a synod in Antioch in 339 had confirmed the excommunication of Athanasius (Julius I, *Ep.* 2.14 [Thompson 2015, 64 = Ath., *Apol. sec.* 29.3]) and repeated by the dedication synod in Antioch in 341, since Rome had agreed to be the review venue.
7   Council of Nicaea I (325), can. 5 (Alberigo 2006, 22). Twomey 1982, 403, is right to say that, "[c]anon V therefore itself demonstrates the way provincial synodal decisions were given final authority by means of their reception, and how this reception was not uncritical (merely a rubber stamp, as the Eusebians had demanded of Julius with regard to his reception of their decisions), and at the same time it establishes the principle of the necessary (universal) transparency of those judgements which involve the behaviour of individuals." However, the use of the word *reception*, even though qualified by *not uncritical*, can be somewhat misleading, especially when he writes at 402 that "the decisions of a synod became irreversible *once* they were implicitly or explicitly received by the universal Church." More clarity would be achieved for those unfamiliar with the precise nuances of *reception* if he had said that synodal decisions were *received* through a second confirmatory sentence in situations where the first decision had been appealed.
8   Julius I, *Ep.* 2.8–9 (Thompson 2015, 54–58 = Ath., *Apol. sec.* 26–27; and Ath., *Historia Arianorum ad monachos* (*Hist. Arian.*) 15.
9   Soz., *HE* 3.7.2.

When Constantius agreed, a synod met in Serdica (modern Sofia) late in 343. The presence of Athanasius and other exiled bishops split the synod into two.[10] Our interest is with the western gathering that remained in Serdica. The letter from Hosius of Cordova and Protogenes of Serdica does mention that the bishops who met there agreed with the creed produced at Nicaea.[11] The synod also produced twenty or twenty-one canons concerning episcopal elections, the translation of bishops, and ecclesiastical appeals,[12] which, although they did not mention Nicaea, built upon that earlier council. They will become important for our topic when our attention turns to Zosimus of Rome.

The question in these decades of the fourth century had become not whether or not one accepted the teaching of Nicaea but whether or not one held communion with Athanasius. Of course, the two are related topics, and it must be borne in mind that many argued that they accepted Nicaea even though they condemned Athanasius.[13] As Daniel Williams argues, we must not simply accept the idea of the fifth-century ecclesiastical historians that the West was always pro-Nicene.[14] Indeed, the rather pitiful story of Liberius (352–66), who succeeded Julius as Roman bishop, is apposite. While Liberius changed his opinion of Athanasius, admittedly under extreme duress, we know little about his attitude towards Nicaea itself.[15]

With this brief sketch of Rome's reaction to the 325 Council of Nicaea in the fourth century until the 381 Council of Constantinople, we may turn now to investigate Rome's attitude towards the first ecumenical council in the decades immediately following.

THE NICENE CREED IN THE CATHOLIC CHURCH

For the average Roman Catholic, the creed is encountered in the eucharistic liturgy and is the only part of Nicaea generally known, but probably without much grasp of its historical or theological context. Yet, the Nicene Creed used in the Catholic eucharistic liturgy is not the same as the creed of Nicaea. The creed produced at Nicaea grew out of the

---

[10]   See von Hefele 1871–96, 2:86–176; Barnes 1993, 67–81; Ayres 2004b, 122–26; Hess 2002, 95–113, for the history of the synod. See above, 228–29, 243–44, 260.
[11]   Julius I, *Ep.* 3 (*Meminimus*) (Thompson 2015, 94–96). On that creed see Hilary of Poitiers, *Libri tres aduersum Valentem et Ursacium* B.II.10–11.
[12]   On the textual issues with the canons see Hess 2002, 114–23.
[13]   See Ayres 2004, 177–86, 260–67.
[14]   Williams 1995. Also see his chapter in this volume.
[15]   See Ammianus Marcellinus, *Res gestae* 15.7; Ath., *Hist. Arian.* 35–40.

affirmations of faith handed over to catechumens and recited back (*tra-ditio symboli* and *redditio symboli*) and the baptismal interrogations used during the rituals of initiation.[16]

The idea that the council basically adopted the local creed of Caesarea Maritima with some minor adaptations is an interpretation no longer supported in careful scholarship.[17] The council of 381 in Constantinople produced its own creed, which was more than simply a modified version of the creed of Nicaea.[18] We do not know of this 381 creed until it, along with the 325 creed, was read into the *acta* of the second session of the 451 council at Chalcedon.[19] They were read again in the fifth session as part of the definition agreed to by the council.[20] Chalcedon accepted that the 381 creed was a slightly modified version of that of 325, although that is far from the entire truth, and hence that later creed is known as the Niceno-Constantinopolitan or simply Nicene (and here I distinguish between the 325 creed of Nicaea and the Nicene Creed).

It was this Nicene Creed that was then used in the West in the preparation of catechumens. The Gelasian Sacramentary and *Ordo Romanus XI* point to its use in Rome for the *traditio* and *redditio*,[21] although the older credal interrogations were used during the actual initiation ceremonies. As Kelly points out, in response to Gothic Arianism and the subjugation of the Roman church to the Byzantine, "[a]pparently the Roman church, which had been so proud of its age-long use of the same baptismal confession, laid it aside at some date in the sixth century and substituted C [Niceno-Constantinopolitan]."[22]

The first recorded use of this creed in the eucharistic liturgy seems to be in Antioch at the end of the fifth and early in the sixth centuries at daily eucharist in Constantinople under Timothy (although Theodore

---

[16] See Kelly 1972, 30–204; Ferguson 2009. Also see the discussion by Mark Edwards, above 143–44.

[17] Eusebius, *Epistula ad Caesarienses* = Urk. 22 = Socrates, *Historia ecclesiastica* (*HE*) 1.8.35–55 = Theodoret, *Historia ecclesiastica* (*HE*) 1.12.1–6. See Kelly 1972, 205–30; Davis 1983, 59; cf. von Hefele 1871–96, 1:288–92; Bezançon, Ferlay, and Onfray 1987, 11.

[18] Kelly 1972, 296–331; Davis 1983, 121–23.

[19] Schwartz 1933, 79; von Hefele 1871–96, 2:348–51, 3:315–19; Davis 1983, 182. See Price and Gaddis 2005, 2:11–13.

[20] *ACO* 2.1.2, 128; von Hefele 1871–96, 3:342–53; Davis 1983, 185. See Price and Gaddis 2005, 2:201–3, 2:191–94, for discussion about the textual variations in Chalcedon's presentation of the creeds.

[21] Mohlberg, Eizenhöfer, and Siffrin 1981, no. xxxv (para. 310–18) on 48–51; and Andrieu 1948, no. 65, with Andrieu's introduction on 377.

[22] Kelly 1972, 347.

refers to the creed of the 318, i.e. the creed of Nicaea). This was in opposition to his pro-Chalcedonian predecessor, Macedonius, in contrast with it having previously only been used once a year on Good Friday, as an anti-Chalcedonian move.[23] The first recorded appearance of the creed in western eucharistic liturgies comes from the second canon of the Third Synod of Toledo (589), when the Visigothic king Reccared renounced Arianism. The creed of the 150 bishops (of Constantinople in 381) was to be chanted before the Lord's Prayer throughout the churches of Gaul and Spain as a rejection of Arianism, in imitation of eastern practice.[24] The Stowe Missal of early ninth-century Ireland, under influence from Spain, incorporated the creed into the eucharistic liturgy, but placed it after the gospel.[25]

In the ninth century, Walafrid Strabo, abbot of Reichenau, reported on the introduction of the creed in the Carolingian Frankish world under Charlemagne. It was placed after the gospel and said to be in imitation of Greek practices, and that the Constantinopolitan version rather than that of Nicaea was used, perhaps because it was easier to set to music or better suited to countering the poisons of heresies. It was said to have come to the new western empire via Rome.[26] Smaragdus, abbot of Saint-Mihiel, who had been sent to Rome after the 809 synod at Aachen by Charlemagne to consult with Leo III (795–816) about the introduction of the Filioque into the creed, introduced the creed into the eucharistic liturgy following the gospel, after Leo had recently given permission for it to be used in the Carolingian world, possibly to counter the influence of the deposed adoptionist bishop, Felix of Urgel, who had been combatted by Alcuin of York and Paulinus of Aquileia.[27]

Rome appears to have resisted the use of the creed in the eucharistic liturgy for a few hundred years more. We have evidence in Berno, abbot of Reichenau, of the encounter between Emperor Henry II, the last of the Ottonians, and Pope Benedict VIII in 1014 for the emperor's coronation, and his surprise that the creed was not in the Roman liturgy. The pope's answer was that Rome was not subject to the influence of heresies and had no need for the use of the creed in the liturgy. However, since Benedict owed his position to Henry's support against his rival contender

[23] Theodorus Lector, *Historia ecclesiastica* 2, frag. 48 and frag. 32.
[24] Third Synod of Toledo (589), can. 2 (Martínez Díez and Rodríguez 1992, 110). See von Hefele 1871–96, 4:416–22; Thompson 1969, 94–101; Cecilio Díaz y Díaz 1991; Collins 2004, 63–69; Ferreiro 2014; Bishop 2016.
[25] Capelle 1934.
[26] Walafrid Strabo, *De ecclesiasticarum rerum exordiis et incrementis* 22 (PL 114:947).
[27] Smaragdus, *Notitia de colloquio Romano* (Werminghoff 1906, 240–44). Capelle 1929.

for the papal throne, Gregory VI, the pope agreed to follow the emperor's insistence that the creed be introduced into the Roman liturgy.[28] From there the creed continued to be used in the Roman liturgy throughout the Catholic Church, but restricted to Sundays and certain important feasts.[29]

The creed continues to be part of what was once called the ordinary of the mass (*Kyrie, Gloria, Credo, Sanctus/Benedictus,* and *Agnus Dei*). These were set to a variety of chants and in musical settings of the mass from the fourteenth century onwards, and these are the five parts included.

In terms of the creed in the liturgy today, the only other points of interest (as far as English speakers are concerned) is the change in the translations between the 1973 and 2011 versions prepared for the English-speaking world by the International Commission on English in the Liturgy (ICEL), the former for the 1970 first Latin typical edition of the missal and the latter for the 2002 third Latin typical edition. Following the fifth instruction of the Congregation for Divine Worship and the Discipline of the Sacraments on how to implement the use of vernacular languages in the liturgy (*Liturgiam authenticam* of 28 March 2001), the major difference is that the newer English translation is more literal. Thus, while the 1973 translation offered "We believe" for the Latin singular *credo*, in order to emphasis a more communal dimension to faith (and following the plural as found in the conciliar texts, πιστεύομεν), the current translation imposed "I believe" following the Latin liturgical text (*credo*).

FILIOQUE IN THE NICENE CREED

The most significant change to the creed of Nicaea – after its supposed modification and elaboration to create the creed of the council of 381 at Constantinople, the subsequent dislocation from its function as a statement of faith in an anti-Arian context, and its insertion into the liturgy as a proclamation of faith in general terms – was the addition of the Filioque clause.

While the 381 council had defined the Holy Spirit as divine by calling the Spirit Lord and giver of life, worshipped and glorified in equal measure with Father and Son, and proceeding from the Father (τὸ ἐκ τοῦ πατρὸς ἐκπορευόμενον in Greek, translated into Latin as *ex Patre procedentem*),

---

[28]   Berno of Richenau, *Libellus de quibusdam rebus ad missae officium pertinentibus* 2 (PL 142:1060–61).

[29]   See Jungmann 1951, 461–74; Cabié 1986, 131–32; Chapman 2005.

a fuller explanation of the relationships of all three persons within the Trinity was not provided.

Outside of episcopal synods, the issue of the Spirit's divinity and relationship with the other persons of the Trinity had received some discussion in theological works in both West and East. In the West, in the early third century, Tertullian had written that the Spirit is from the Father through the Son.[30] Augustine of Hippo in *De Trinitate* raised the question of what distinguishes the Son from the Spirit in terms of their relationship with the Father. Taking his starting point from John 15:26, Augustine stated that, while the Son was begotten of the Father, the Spirit proceeds (*procedit*) from the Father.[31] For Augustine, the procession of the Spirit as gift in the economy of salvation is from both Father and Son, as Jesus breathing out the Spirit in John 20:22 indicates.[32] Various bishops of Rome, like Leo I (440–61), Gregory I (590–604), and Agatho (679–81), taught the same.[33] Yet, it is also true that Augustine wrote of the Spirit originating from both Father and Son, but as from only one origin not two.[34] It is this kind of statement that would create problems in the East. Even that statement of Augustine was subject to later clarification when he stated that the Spirit proceeds principally or in origin (*principaliter*) from the Father, but also from the Son, which is true because the Spirit is the Spirit of them both, since this ability was given eternally to the Son by the Father.[35] The inclusion of the idea that the Spirit proceeds from the Son also is expressed in the Latin word *Filioque* ("and from the Son").

The East had a more subtle understanding. Gregory Nazianzus could speak of the Spirit coming forth from the Father (using the verb προϊέναι)

---

[30] Tertullian, *Adversus Praxean* 4.1 (CCSL 2, 1162): *quia Spiritum non aliunde puto quam a Patre per Filium*. One may note that Tertullian did not use the verb *procedere* but simply the adverb *aliunde*.

[31] Augustine (Aug.), *De Trinitate* (*De Trin.*) 1.3.5, 5.14.15, 9.12.17, 15.25.45.

[32] Aug., *De Trin.* 4.20.29, 15.26.45. See Hill 1985, 70–71, 108–21.

[33] Leo I, *Epistulae* 15.1; Gregory I, *Moralia* 1.22.30 and *Sermones* 26.2; and Agatho, *Epistulae* 3.

[34] Aug., *De Trin.* 5.14.15 (NBA 4, 258): *fatendum est Patrum et Filium principium esse Spiritus Sancti, non duo principia, sed sicut Pater et Filius unus Deus, et ad creaturam relatiue unus creator et unus dominus, sic relatiue ad Spiritum Sanctum unum principium*. This is where Kelly 1972, 359, puts his emphasis when he writes: "The logical development of his thought involved the belief that the Holy Spirit proceeded as truly from the Son as from the Father, and he did not scruple to expound it with frankness and precision on numerous occasions."

[35] Aug., *De Trin.* 15.17.29 (NBA 4, 674): *nec de quo genitum est Verbum et de quo procedit principaliter Spiritus Sanctus nisi Deus Pater. Ideo autem addidi, principaliter, quia et de Filio Spiritus Sanctus procedere reperitur. Sed hoc quoque illi Pater dedit, non iam exsistenti et nondum habenti; sed quidquid unienito Verbo dedit, gignendo dedit.*

not through being generated like the Son but through procession (using the verb ἐκπορεύεσθαι).[36] Thus, while the Spirit proceeds from the Father, the Spirit is from both the Father and the Son.[37] This idea of being from Father and Son is not used in any causal sense. Cyril of Alexandria also accepted that the Spirit came forth from or through the Son (using προϊέναι rather than ἐκπορεύεσθαι).[38] In the eastern tradition the Father is the only cause of the Spirit, so that the Spirit proceeds from the Father but through the Son.

Thus the single Latin verb could cover both of the meanings in Greek, and it was this terminological inexactitude that was going to cause later problems. As Walter, Cardinal Kasper points out, in words that deserve to be quoted at some length:

> The difference between the Greeks and the Latins began when the Vulgate translated *ekporeuetai* as *procedit*, for *processio* in Latin theology has a much more general meaning than *ekporeusis* in Greek theology. *Ekporeuesthai* means "emerge from, go forth from, stream forth from". In this sense the concept is applicable only to the Father, the first, unoriginated origin; the co-operation of the Son in the procession of the Holy Spirit, on the other hand, must be described by the verb *proïenai*. Latin does not make this fine distinction. According to Latin theology *processio* is a general concept that can be applied to all of the inter-trinitarian processes, that is, not only to the coming forth of the Spirit from the Father, but also to the generation of the Son and to the breathing of the Spirit through the Son. As a result, Latin theology is faced with a problem that does not have a parallel in Greek theology. For Latin theology too must hold fast to the distinction between the *processio* of the Son from the Father and the *processio* of the Spirit from the Father.[39]

Just what did Latin-speaking Christians mean when they said that the Spirit "proceeds from" the Father *and the Son* (*Filioque*)? Do they refer to the Son's involvement in the causation or origin of the Spirit or to the

[36] Gregory of Nazianzus, *Orationes* (*Orat.*) 39.12. See also *Orat.* 32.7–8.
[37] Gregory of Nyssa, *De Spiritu Sancto contra Macedonianos* 2 and 10 (PG 45:1310): ἐκ Πατρὸς ἐκπορευόμενον, ἐκ τοῦ Υἱοῦ λαμβανόμενον. The difference in English is captured here by distinguishing "proceeds from" and "from."
[38] Cyril of Alexandria (Cyr.), *Thesaurus de Trinitate* 34 (PG 75:585): τὸ Πνεῦμα [...] πρόεισι δὲ καὶ ἐκ Πατρὸς καὶ Υἱοῦ, πρόδηλον ὅτι τῆς θείας ἐστιν οὐσίας, οὐσιωδῶς ἐν αὐτῇ καὶ ἐξ αὐτῆς προϊόν (and PG 75:608, 612). See also Cyr., *De recte fide orat. alt.* 51; *Contra Nestorium* 4.1, 4.3; *De adoratione in spiritu et veritate* 1, to name only a few instances.
[39] Kasper 1983, 217.

role of the Son within the immanent Trinity (in such a way as to preserve causation by the Father alone) and in the sending of the Spirit into the economy of salvation?[40] Augustine and Leo can certainly be read in this second sense, although as we have seen Augustine certainly had passages that tended to suggest the former interpretation.

Once again, it was the Third Synod of Toledo in 589 under King Reccared and its overwhelming anti-Arianism and anti-Priscillianism that played a crucial part in the story of the reception of Nicaea (and its related creed) in the West. In the king's profession of faith it was asserted that the Spirit proceeded from the Father and the Son,[41] and in the third of the anathemas of the synod anyone who denied this proposition was condemned.[42] The point was to assert the consubstantiality of Father and Son more than to define anything about the Spirit. As yet, though, nothing in the Nicene Creed itself was altered.[43] In the middle of the seventh century, Martin I of Rome (649–53) professed the same thing, and this was criticized by his monothelite opponents in the East, most likely, as Maximus Confessor writes, because they read *procedit* as ἐκπορεύεσθαι rather than as προϊέναι.[44]

It was probably in Spain that the Filioque was inserted into the creed as used in the liturgy. Clarity is difficult because of later interpolations into earlier texts claiming the presence of the Filioque phrase. Alcuin of York brought this use to the Carolingian court. It was Charlemagne's view that the Filioque was part of the original formulation of the Nicene Creed and that the word had been dropped in the East. The king of the Franks and Lombards criticized Hadrian I of Rome (772–95) in 794 following a synod in Frankfurt for his endorsement of the creed of the Second Council of Nicaea in 787 that did not have the Filioque. The pope's reply was to inform Charlemagne that the non-inclusion of the Filioque was the ancient tradition and also observed in Rome.[45] Charlemagne held a synod in Aachen in 809, which ordered the inclusion of the Filioque in the creed as chanted at the eucharistic liturgy. We have

---

[40] See Congar 1983, 24–60.
[41] Synod of Toledo (589), *Regis professio fidei* (Martínez Díez and Rodríguez 1992, 55): *Spiritus aeque Sanctus confitendus a nobis et praedicandus est a Patre et Filio procedere.*
[42] Synod of Toledo (589), *Gothorum professio fidei* (Martínez Díez and Rodríguez 1992, 70).
[43] Manuscripts of this synod that include the Filioque in texts of the Nicene creed have been interpolated. See Burn 1908; Smith 2014.
[44] Maximus Confessor, *Opuscula theologica et polemica, Epistula ad Marinum.* On Maximus and Martin, see Neil and Allen 2003; Neil 2006.
[45] Hadrian I, *Epistula ad Carolum.*

already mentioned above the resistance of Leo III to the addition of the Filioque into the Nicene Creed, which was not used in the eucharistic liturgy in Rome at this point. Leo accepted the doctrine but added that not every doctrine needed to be added to the creed. One can think of the definition at Ephesus in 431 of Mary as *Theotokos*, which was not then added to the creed. Leo's solution was to suggest that the Carolingians ought to drop the creed from use in the eucharistic liturgy. He also had silver engravings of the creed in Greek and Latin without the Filioque hung at the entrance to the *confessio* inside St Peter's. By the time the creed was used liturgically in the eucharist in Rome in 1014, it included the Filioque.

Photius, bishop of Constantinople (858–68, 878–86), condemned the idea of the Filioque, even rejecting the idea of the Spirit proceeding from the Father through the Son.[46] The great schism of 1054 between East and West, with mutual excommunications between Rome and Constantinople that would not be lifted until the 1960s, had the use of the Filioque as one of the triggers. Cardinal Humbert was of the opinion that the Greeks had dropped the term from the creed, whereas the historical reality is that the Latins had introduced it.[47]

The Fourth Council of the Lateran (1215) and the Council of Lyons (1274), both considered ecumenical in the West, defended the use of the Filioque to express trinitarian belief, provided that it was recognized that there was only one origin of the Spirit in the Trinity (the Father) but that the Father and Son form a single principle in the procession of the Spirit. The Council of Florence (1439–45) defined Filioque as asserting that the Son is part of the causation of the Spirit but not as origin, such that *per Filium* ("through the Son") is acceptable so long as it is understood to be the same as *Filioque* ("and the Son"). There was much debate during the council about the authenticity of texts.[48]

Eastern churches in communion with Rome since the time of Benedict XIV (1740–58) use the Nicene Creed without the Filioque. The declaration of the Congregation for the Doctrine of the Faith "On the Unicity and Salvific Universality of Jesus Christ and the Church" (*Dominus Iesus*), issued while Cardinal Ratzinger (later Benedict XVI) was prefect on 6 August 2000, provided the Nicene Creed without the Filioque. This suggests that the phrase is becoming less of an obstacle in ecumenical dialogue with Orthodox Christians.

[46]   Photius, *Epistulae* 13.10–21. See Congar 1983, 58; and Louth 2007, 160–61, 185–66.
[47]   Louth 2007, 309–10, 315–16.
[48]   See Gill 1959, 145–65.

RECEPTION OF THE CANONS OF NICAEA IN THE WEST

The canons of Nicaea in 325 regulated the discipline and practice of church life on certain matters.[49] What is the status of those canons today? *Lumen gentium*, the Dogmatic Constitution on the Church, promulgated by the Second Vatican Council on 21 November 1964, stated that the teaching of an ecumenical council in matters of faith and morals is an example of an infallible teaching.[50] In the fourth century, Athanasius had written that the word of the Lord, spoken through Nicaea, was to remain for eternity.[51] In 381, the First Council of Constantinople reaffirmed the faith taught at Nicaea.[52] In 787, the Second Council of Nicaea asserted that the canons of the previous six ecumenical councils were to be held complete and without change.[53] What then is the relation of the canons of Nicaea in 325 with something like the 1983 Code of Canon Law? To what extent do the twenty canons of Nicaea remain in force for Catholics today?

Historically, the continual development of church structures, evidenced by a growing complexity and changing conditions for individuals and groups over the following decades and centuries, meant that a number of the canons of Nicaea became obsolete, unworkable, or in need of greater clarification. Also, the disregarding of some of the canons of Nicaea by individuals and churches in the West saw local synods and eventually Roman bishops repeating those canons as being still binding and needing to be obeyed, while other canons were barely mentioned again, which could indicate that they were not controversial and were adhered to or quietly forgotten. Church leaders faced the difficulties of being faithful to what Nicaea had enjoined and being responsive to fresh requirements. In this section I wish to consider the western reception of the canons of Nicaea in the first century after the council and then any vestiges of them today.

Damasus (366–84)

Collections of papal letters really begin with Damasus in the second half of the fourth century.[54] If we accept that the letter *Dominus inter cetera*

49   See chapter in this volume by Andreas Weckwerth on the canons of Nicaea.
50   Council of the Vatican II (1962–65), *Lumen gentium* 25 (Alberigo, Ganzer, and Melloni 2010, 317–19).
51   Ath., *Epistula ad Afros episcopos* 2.
52   Council of Constantinople I (381), can. 1 (Alberigo 2006, 64). See also the letters associated with the council: Thdt., *HE* 5.8.10, 5.9.10.
53   Council of Nicaea II (787), can. 1 (Alberigo 2006, 317–19).
54   On the collections of papal letters considered as decretals and combined with conciliar canons see Kéry 1999; Jasper and Fuhrmann 2001. The current edition of most of these

to the Gallic bishops was written by Damasus rather than Siricius or Innocent I,[55] we see some of the earliest reception of the canons of Nicaea in the West.

Canons 7 and 13 of that letter reflect canon 12 of Nicaea, although the former speak of eligibility for ordination,[56] while Nicaea spoke of the readmission to communion (without specifying clergy) of those Christians who had taken up their former civil/military offices.[57] Canon 16 on deposing translated bishops stems from canon 15 of Nicaea, while canon 17 on receiving deposed clerics relates to part of canon 5 of Nicaea. Canon 18 on bishops not interfering in other dioceses and on not hindering the metropolitan finds something of a parallel to canon 4 of Nicaea about the ordination of bishops in a province, as well as to canon 2 of Constantinople. Canon 19 on not ordaining in one church those laymen excommunicated in another relates to canon 16 of Nicaea, which was broader in that it applied to deposed clergy and excommunicated laymen.[58]

What we see here suggests that either the Gallic bishops were unaware of the regulations provided by Nicaea or had forgotten them, and the sense that Nicaea was binding on church life and practice, but that its provisions could be expanded to cover new and unforeseen circumstances.

Siricius (384–99)

Siricius's first preserved letter (*Directa*) was addressed to Himerius of Tarragona in response to a letter that had been sent to Damasus, who had died before a reply could be sent.[59] Canon 6, about the limited possibility for membership of the church for those who had returned to their former military/civil occupations, is closer to canon 12 of Nicaea than canons 7 and 13 of *Dominus inter cetera* are.[60] Yet, in *Directa* we find Siricius more interested in questions of clerical celibacy (canons 4–11) than what

papal letters, of which Sieben 2014 is a reprint with German translation, is still Coustant 1721, which is reprinted in various volumes of PL.

[55] Damasus, *Epistula ad Gallos episcopos* (*Ep. ad Gall.*) (*Dominus inter cetera*) (Sieben 2014, 1:238–62) = JK, 144 = J³, 586. See Duval 2005. Cf. Siricius, *Epistulae* (*Ep.*) 10; and von Hefele 1871–96, 2:428–30.

[56] Damasus, *Ep. ad Gall.* 2.7, forbade ordination for those who served in the military, and 2.13 (Sieben 2014, 1:254–56) permitted it only after penance for those who had held civil office.

[57] Council of Nicaea I (325), can. 12. See Duval 2005, 83–89, 102–9; and Dunn 2011, 159–62.

[58] Damasus, *Ep. ad Gall.* 2.16–19. See Duval 2005, 113–23; Sommar 2003.

[59] Siricius, *Ep.* 1 (*Directa*) (Sieben 2014, 2:302–26) = JK, 255 = J³, 605. See Hornung 2011; Zechiel-Eckes 2013; Hornung 2015; Ferreiro 2015.

[60] Siricius, *Ep.* 1.6.

is found in canon 3 of Nicaea.[61] Canon 12 on prohibiting the ordination of clerics without examination draws from canon 9 of Nicaea, but in such a way that the concern in 385 was more with a lack of examination about the ordinand's marital status. Canon 16 comes straight from Nicaea canon 3 about the prohibition of most women living with clerics, as the canon acknowledges specifically.[62] The whole question of the clerical *cursus honorum* (canons 13–14 and 17) was not a feature of Nicaea at all, except that canon 2 prohibits the appointment of neophytes to episcopal or presbyteral office, but we do see it in the West following the 343 synod at Serdica.[63]

Siricius wrote in 386 a letter (*Cum in unum*) after a synod in Rome to bishops who could not be present.[64] It is preserved in the acts of an African synod in Telepte or Zelle.[65] It refers to canon 4 of Nicaea explicitly, but expresses it in terms of a prohibition of only one bishop ordaining another instead of the minimum requirement of there being three.[66] Canon 3, like canon 7 of *Dominus inter ceteros*, relates to canon 12 of Nicaea; canon 6 derives from canon 16 of Nicaea (in terms of the ordination of transients); canon 7 about deposed clerics not being received in another church mirrors canon 5 of Nicaea; and canon 8 relates to canon 8 of Nicaea about the reception of Novatianists back into communion.

Siricius made explicit mention of Nicaea in his letter to Anysius of Thessaloniki (ancient Thessalonica in the province of Macedonia),[67] and to the Italian bishops.[68]

Innocent I (402–17)

When we turn to the letters of Innocent I we see an even more explicit and extensive interest in defending and expanding the disciplinary canons of Nicaea. Innocent was a thoughtful and careful administrator, and this is reflected in his correspondence.[69] He appealed to divine law contained in Scripture, the decision of synods, particularly Nicaea, and the precedents set by his predecessors as he answered queries from

---

[61] See Dunn 2014, 294–300.
[62] Siricius, *Ep.* 1.16.
[63] See Hunter 2011; Dunn 2013a, at 121–27. See Synod of Serdica (343), can. 13 (Latin). See Hess 2002, 157–61.
[64] Siricius, *Ep.* 5 (*Cum in unum*).
[65] CCSL 149, 59–63. See von Hefele 1871–96, 2:386–89.
[66] Siricius, *Ep.* 5.II.2. On this see Dunn 2011, 155–59.
[67] Siricius, *Ep.* 4 (*Etiam dudum*).
[68] Siricius, *Ep.* 6 (*Cogitantibus nobis metum*).
[69] See Green 1973.

colleagues about how to deal with situations, many of which presented a new dimension to an old problem or even new problems. So extensive are Innocent's references to Nicaea that it is worth a study in its own right.

Suffice it here to mention that like the two of his predecessors mentioned above, Innocent held the council of 325 to be authoritative, but that Rome was being appealed to from various parts of the empire with questions not anticipated a century earlier. Much the same issues (clerical marriage, eligibility for ordination, as well as the appeals process against synodal decisions) dominate the correspondence that was incorporated into later decretal collections (and which may therefore reflect more about later editorial selections than about any limited focus of topics addressed by the Roman bishop at the time). Innocent therefore referred to Nicaea as interpreted by Damasus and Siricius, as well as Nicaea as interpreted by Serdica, expanding on that as he thought necessary. Indeed, as Hess shows, the conflation of the canons of Nicaea with those of Serdica might have occurred already under Innocent.[70] Innocent's reliance upon the precedents created by Nicaea (as recently reinterpreted by other synods and his own predecessors) ensured that his management of Rome's responsibilities were seen as even-handed and in accord with acceptable tradition.

Zosimus (417–18)

Zosimus had a very different personality and practice from his predecessor. He was less cautious and more assertive of his own authority, not only within his own sphere of immediate responsibility but beyond, especially in Africa and Gaul.

In his letter to Hesychius of Solin, which was within Rome's traditional area of responsibility, Zosimus referred to the teaching of his predecessors and the teachings of the fathers at a synod with regard to clerical progression through the *cursus honorum*.[71] As we have seen, the synod that discussed this topic was not Nicaea but Serdica.

Zosimus was at his most innovative when it came to the ecclesiastical hierarchy of the churches in Gaul. It needs to be stressed that Zosimus did not develop the new arrangements on his own initiative but was responding to a request or suggestion from Patroclus of Arles to augment his authority over his fellow Gallic bishops in a number of provinces. Only days after his election Zosimus wrote to Patroclus

---

[70] Hess 2002, 125.
[71] Zosimus, *Ep.* 9 (*Cum et in praesenti*). See Dunn 2013a, 129–32; Dunn 2015b, 86–89.

endorsing the latter's idea that he should be metropolitan over not only Viennensis (replacing Simplicius as metropolitan), for which he had some right (as well as Proculus of Marseille, who from the time of the Synod of Turin had exercised a personal metropolitan status[72]), but Narbonensis Prima (replacing Hilary of Narbonne [ancient Narbo]), Narbonensis Secunda (replacing Remigius of Aix-en-Provence), and possibly Alpes Maritimae as well, for which Patroclus had no right.[73]

Although Zosimus nowhere mentions it, this grab for power by Patroclus was based in part upon canon 4 of Nicaea, where the metropolitan bishop was given right of veto over the election of bishops within his province. Tacitly accepting Nicaea, Patroclus sought to neutralize Nicaea's intention by redefining his province.

Most of the affected metropolitans opposed this demotion and reacted negatively. We see from Hilary's letter (responded to in *Mirati admodum*) that he continued to assert that Patroclus was a foreign bishop from a neighbouring province and not the metropolitan over Narbonensis Prima. Zosimus wrote to these bishops, upset not so much at their disapproval of the proposed changes but at their rejection of his authority to endorse and/or decree them.[74] While Zosimus threatened and belittled the recalcitrant bishops, appealed to the dubious historical precedent of Trophimus of Arles, and boasted of his own power, unsurprisingly he did not refer to Nicaea, since that council had nothing of relevance to the particulars of this situation, except in a letter to Patroclus against Proculus of Marseille (*Quid de Proculi*), in which he asserted that the latter had disregarded canonical procedures by becoming a bishop too soon after baptism (which we find regulated in canon 2 of Nicaea) and without progressing through the *cursus honorum* (which we find in Serdica and in previous Roman episcopal letters). This demonstrates that the antipathy with which Zosimus would be held came in part from his failure to ground his acceptance of Patroclus's innovations in Nicaea.

In writing to the Africans, Zosimus was concerned principally with the Pelagian controversy, in which he reversed the Roman position held by Innocent,[75] and lifted the condemnation of Caelestius and

---

[72] See von Hefele 1871–96, 2:426–28; and recently Kulikowski 1996; Mathisen 2013.

[73] Zosimus, *Ep.* 1 (*Placuit apostolicae*) (= *Liber auctoritatum ecclesiae Arelatensis, Ep.* 1). See Dunn 2013c and Dunn 2015c. Contrast Frye 1991, that Zosimus owed his election to Patroclus or Flavius Constantius, the power behind Honorius's throne.

[74] Zosimus, *Ep.* 4–7, 10–11, 19. I leave aside *Ep.* 18 (*Reuelatum nobis*), the authenticity of which is disputed. See Dunn 2015d; Dunn 2015e; Dunn 2016; Dunn 2019.

[75] See Innocent I, *Ep.* 29 (*In requirendis*) (= Aug., *Ep.* 181); 30 (*Inter caeteras*) (= Aug., *Ep.* 182); and 31 (*Fraternitatis uestrae*) (= Aug., *Ep.* 183 = *Collectio Avellana* (*Coll. Avell., Ep.* 41).

Pelagius.[76] There is no reference to Nicaea in these particular letters. Where Zosimus did refer to Nicaea with regard to the African churches, we find one of the more interesting aspects of the Roman reception of the council. It concerns Apiarius, an African presbyter from Le Kef, who in 418 appealed to Rome against a judgement given against him in Africa, contrary to the sentiment, if not the precise legislation, of African church law.[77] Evidence comes from a letter written by the African bishops in 419 to Zosimus's successor, Boniface I.[78] The basis for Zosimus's assertion that the Roman bishop had the right to hear overseas appeals and that lower clergy had the right to appeal against sentences issued by their own bishop was because it was held to be Nicene. In fact, they come from canons 7 and 17 of Serdica.[79] The Africans complained that they could not find these canons in their version of the acta from Nicaea. Hess has argued that Rome was not being deceitful or forgetful, but genuinely believed that material from Serdica to be Nicene because the canons from the two synods had been conflated as Nicene some time previously, as is evidenced by the ninth-century MS from Chieti (Biblioteca Apostolica Vaticana, Reg. lat. 1997) faithfully reflecting that earlier situation, although by the time of Dionysius Exiguus at the end of the sixth century this confusion had been resolved. The authority of Nicaea as a council of pre-eminence and authority (and the sense that Serdica was a synod to affirm Nicaea) is evident in this conflation.[80]

The Africans were suspicious of Zosimus's claims and seem to have eliminated the legitimacy of Serdica from their memory.[81] The acta of the synod of Carthage of 25 May 419 indicate that Alypius of Thagaste (in the province of Numidia) revealed that the canons upon which Zosimus relied could not be found in the version of Nicaea in Africa and that the Africans and Boniface, Zosimus's successor, both should secure fresh

76 Zosimus, Ep. 2 (Magnum pondus) (= Coll. Avell., Ep.); 3 (Posteaquam a nobis) (= Coll. Avell., Ep. 46); 122 (Quamuis patrum) (= Coll. Avell., Ep. 50). See Carefoote 1995; Dunn 2013b.
77 See Merdinger 1997, 111–35; Dunn 2012. The African bishops in May 418 forbade lower clergy going overseas on appeal against judicial sentences imposed on them in Africa (Registri ecclesiae Carthaginensis excerpta, can. 125). The question that has divided scholars is whether Apiarius went before or after the promulgation of this canon.
78 Synod of Carthage (26 May 419) (Quoniam domino) = Boniface I, Ep. 2.
79 Synod of Serdica (343), can. 7 (Latin) (Hess 2002, 214–16) = can. V (Greek) (Hess 2002, 228) = can. T7 (Theodosian) (Hess 2002, 244); and can. 17 (Latin) (Hess 2002, 222–24) = can. XIV (Greek) (Hess 2002, 236) = can. T18 (Theodosian) (Hess 2002, 250–52).
80 Hess 2002, 127–29.
81 Aug., Ad Cresconium grammaticum partis Donati 4.44.52; Ep. 44.3.6.

copies of the canons of Nicaea to see if these canons were to be found, although they would accept Zosimus's canons until they were proven not to be from Nicaea, which the Africans fully anticipated.[82] Indeed, the reply from Cyril of Alexandria (*Scripta uenerationis*) confirmed the Africans' belief.[83]

1983 Code of Canon Law

It may seem odd to jump straight from an early fifth-century Roman bishop to the 1983 Code of Canon Law, which regulates the functioning of the Catholic Church today. Space does not permit us to examine the intervening centuries and the bookended presentation suffices to establish the picture of the role of the canons of Nicaea in the life of the churches of the West.

Canon 1 of Nicaea about clerics who castrate themselves being removed from the clergy and the prohibition of those who castrate themselves being ordained is to be found in canon 1041 §5, although only with regard to grave and malicious mutilation (as well as attempted suicide) making someone ineligible for ordination. Dismissal from the clerical state for self-castration (or other forms of mutilation) is not mentioned specifically.[84]

The prohibition in canon 2 of Nicaea about the newly initiated being ordained soon afterwards (based on 1 Timothy 3:6) is found today in canon 378 §3 and §4, where a bishop must be at least thirty-five years old and ordained a priest for at least five years, and canon 1031 §1 where presbyters are required to be at least twenty-five years old, have been a deacon for at least six months, and have sufficient maturity. However, an interval after initiation is no longer specified. Canon 3 forbidding a cleric to live with a woman who is not a relative is now expressed in canon 277 § 2 as a directive to clerics to be prudent in associating with persons who could endanger their obligation to sexual continence or cause scandal.[85]

---

[82] Synod of Carthage (25 May 419). See Merdinger 1997, 116.

[83] Cyr., *Scripta uenerationis*.

[84] Council of Nicaea (325), can. 1. See L'Huillier 1996, 17–100, for commentary on the canons of Nicaea. Gilbert 1985, 713–36, at 730, wondered why this would not be considered under 1041 §1 about psychic defects. He seems to have overlooked the historical origins of this provision. Geisinger 2000, 1193–233, at 1218, instead, points out that mutilation can be culturally relative and asks whether a vasectomy would qualify as an irregularity for the reception of ordination.

[85] Canon 133 of the 1917 *Codex Iuris Canonici* was closer to Nicaea.

The election and ordination (καθίστασθαι) of bishops by the other bishops of his civil province and the confirmation (κῦρος τῶν γινομένων δίδοσθαι) by the metropolitan and the minimum number of ordaining bishops being set as three has now become a combination of canon 377, giving the choice of bishop to the pope after some consultation, and canon 1014, which requires three bishops for legality of the consecration of a bishop. The specific role of the metropolitan and the bishops of the same province is no longer specified.

Canon 5 about excommunicated people from one province not being received in another and about there being two provincial synods of bishops each year has now become canon 440 §1 about there being a provincial meeting as often as appropriate (with more attention being paid to national conferences of bishops in canons 447–59) and canon 269 about the excardination and incardination of clerics (with canon 1331 stating that an excommunicated person cannot discharge any office). Somewhat related to this is the question of the translation of clerics forbidden by canon 15 and the need to return such men to their own churches in canon 16 of Nicaea. The 1983 code permits such authorised movements in canons 265–72, and indeed, the fact that the pope has been a bishop elsewhere before becoming bishop of Rome, contrary to the provisions of Nicaea, shows the extent to which the Nicene prohibition later became a regulated possibility.

Canons 6 and 7 of Nicaea about the areas of responsibility of the bishops of Alexandria, Antioch, and Jerusalem do not feature in the 1983 Code of Canon Law, where instead we find canons 331 and 333 about the universal ordinary power of the pope. The enormous implications of this for ecumenism are beyond our scope here, in particular because the code does not attempt to regulate the life of non-Catholic churches. While one may speculate that any church that comes into communion with Rome in the future would be expected to accept this authority of the Roman bishop (especially given the Roman view that this authority was there since the time of Peter), the historical reality that Nicaea did not endorse the notion of Roman supremacy over the whole church gives Rome wiggle room for developing alternative patterns of authority if and when ecumenical communion with the Orthodox and other churches is better realized.

The permission of Novatianists to be received back into communion through reconciliation with clerics remaining in office in canon 8 of Nicaea is not in the 1983 code. However, canon 1364 §1 mentions that apostates, heretics, and schismatics incur automatic excommunication and, if clerics, can be subject to the penalties mentioned in canon 1336, which can include dismissal from office and dismissal from the clerical state.

The requirement in canon 9 that a candidate for the presbyterate must be examined prior to ordination survives in canon 1051 of the 1983 code. Canon 10 of Nicaea about removing one who is an undiscovered apostate (or whose known apostasy was ignored by the ordaining bishop) prior to ordination as a cleric relates to the previous canon about the due diligence to be undertaken prior to ordination to ascertain impediments to ordination, so it is different from canon 8 in that apostasy and schism (at least the Novatianist schism) were treated differently. Canon 1364 or canon 1044 §2 of the 1983 code would not be the appropriate canon here since it refers to a problem occurring after ordination.[86] Canon 1041 §2 about the ineligibility of an apostate, heretic, or schismatic to be ordained (associated with canon 290 §1 about a declaration of invalidity of ordination) would be more relevant to the situation described at Nicaea.

Canon 11 about the reconciliation process of apostates during the Licinian persecution has no direct parallel in the 1983 code. The closest thing would be the canons (1354–63) about the cessation of penalties. The restoration of lapsed catechumens eventually to the catechumenate of canon 14 of Nicaea has no equivalent in the 1983 code apart from those canons just mentioned.

We have considered above canon 12 of Nicaea about the reconciliation of those who returned to their former ways of life incompatible with being Christian and how, in the hands of the Roman bishops of the late fourth and early fifth centuries, this had been extended to questions about eligibility for ordination. This last point is seen in canon 285 §3 of the 1983 code about clerics being forbidden from assuming civil office (although it does not specify that one who has held civil office is ineligible from being ordained).

The importance of *viaticum* for the dying in canon 13 of Nicaea is repeated in canon 921 §1 of the 1983 code. Canon 17 condemning clerics being involved in usury is not to be found in the 1983 code.[87] Canon 18 about prohibiting deacons from distributing communion to a presbyter and regulating when they are to receive communion and where they are to sit during the liturgy is not specified in the 1983 code.

---

[86] See Cox 1992.

[87] On the church's changing attitude to usury over the centuries (although without mentioning usury by clerics), see Koyama 2010.

Canon 19 on the rebaptism and reordination of Paulianists (the followers of Paul of Samosata is not found specifically in the 1983 code. The recent code is concerned more broadly with the validity of sacraments (canon 841 in general, canon 845 §2 with regard to baptisms that could be invalid, and canon 1047 about dispensation from an irregularity such as having committed apostasy, heresy, or schism, as mentioned in canon 1041 §2). Canon 20 about standing rather than kneeling in the liturgy on Sunday when praying is not repeated in the 1983 code.

CONCLUSION

The Council of Nicaea has been of great importance in the history of the Catholic Church, and continues to be. Its creed, albeit modified by the Council of Constantinople in 381 and by the insertion of the Filioque after 589, inspired by Reccared, was introduced to the imperial liturgy in 809 by Charlemagne and to the liturgy in Rome by Benedict VIII in 1014, and continues to be used on Sundays and major feasts. The canons of Nicaea were held by Roman bishops in the centuries that followed 325 to be the most important church law, even though the canons from a synod like that of Serdica in 343 were incorporated into what Rome believed the canons of Nicaea to be, creating problems with Rome's dealings with the African churches. Over time, as new situations arose not envisaged by the regulations issued by Nicaea, the Roman bishops added, readjusted, and reinterpreted those canons to address them. What we have today are traces of the Nicene canons in the current law of the Catholic Church, albeit modified in most instances with the passage of time and changing circumstances.

SELECT REFERENCES

Bezançon, Jean-Noël, Philippe Ferlay, and Jean-Marie Onfray. 1987. *How to Understand the Creed*. Trans. J. Bowden. London: SCM Press.

Cabié, Robert. 1986. *The Church at Prayer: An Introduction to the Liturgy*. Vol. 2, *The Eucharist*. Trans. Matthew J. O'Connell. Collegeville, MN: The Liturgical Press.

Capelle, Bernard. 1934. "Alcuin et l'histoire du symbole de la messe." *Recherches de théologie ancienne et médiévale* 6: 249–60.

Chapman, Mark D. 2005. "Why Do We Still Recite the Nicene Creed at the Eucharist?" *Anglican Theological Review* 87(2): 207–23.

Congar, Yves. 1983. *I Believe in the Holy Spirit*. Vol. 3, *The River of Life Flows in the East and in the West*. Trans. David Smith. London: Geoffrey Chapman.

Davis, Leo D. 1983. *The First Seven Ecumenical Councils (325–787): Their History and Theology*. Wilmington, DE: Michael Glazier.

Dunn, Geoffrey D. 2011. "Canonical Legislation on the Ordination of Bishops." In *Episcopal Elections in Late Antiquity*, ed. Johan Leemans, Peter Van Nuffelen, Shawn W. J. Keough, and Carla Nicolaye, 145–66. Arbeiten zur Kirchengeschichte 119. Berlin: De Gruyter.

Dunn, Geoffrey D. 2013a. "The Clerical *Cursus Honorum* in the Late Antique Roman Church." *Scrinium* 9: 120–33.

Dunn, Geoffrey D. 2014. "Clerical Marriage in the Letters of Late-Antique Roman Bishops." In *Men and Women in the Early Christian Centuries*, ed. Wendy Mayer and Ian J. Elmer, 293–313. Early Christian Studies 18. Strathfield, NSW: St Pauls.

Dunn, Geoffrey D., ed. 2015a. *The Bishop of Rome in Late Antiquity*. Burlington, VT: Ashgate.

Ferreiro, Alberto. 2014. "*Sanctissimus idem princeps sic venerandum concilium adloquitur dicens*: King Reccared's Discourses at the Third Council of Toledo (589)." *Annuarium Historiae Conciliorum* 46(1–2): 27–52.

Hefele, Karl von. 1871–96. *A History of the Councils of the Church, from the Original Documents*. 5 vols. Trans. W. R. Clark. Edinburgh: T&T Clark.

Hess, Hamilton. 2002. *The Early Development of Canon Law and the Council of Serdica*. Oxford Early Christian Studies. Oxford: Oxford University Press.

Hill, Edmund. 1985. *The Mystery of the Trinity*. Introducing Catholic Theology 4. London: Geoffrey Chapman.

Jungmann, J. A. 1951. *The Mass of the Roman Rite: Its Origins and Development (Missarum Sollemnia)*. Vol. 1. Trans. F. A. Brunner. New York: Benziger Brothers.

Kasper, Walter. 1983. *The God of Jesus Christ*. Trans. M. J. O'Connell. London: SCM Press.

Smith, Shawn C. 2014. "The Insertion of the *Filioque* into the Nicene Creed and a Letter of Isidore of Seville." *JECS* 22(2): 261–86.

Appendices

APPENDIX I: THE SIGNATORIES

The Bishops at Nicaea, 325
Ian Mladjov, Bowling Green State University

According to tradition, the Council of Nicaea was attended by 318 fathers of the Church. There now survive several versions of the list of signatories of this first ecumenical council, in Greek, Latin, Syriac, Coptic, Armenian, and Arabic. In keeping with the vagaries of a long manuscript tradition and the use of different scripts, these lists disagree on various details, ranging from precise orthography, to the choice between alternate place names, to the very inclusion or omission of prelates. None of the surviving lists actually includes 318 bishops or anything close to that number without having resorted to the insertion of duplicate names and sees or other additions, some of them motivated by political or historical considerations (such as the inclusion of the bishops of Rome and Constantinople). Various explanations have been proffered for the genuine names failing to reach the canonical number of attendees, for example, that not all who subscribed to the council's decisions, or that the cited number reflected all those invited, whether they attended or not. Editors generally contented themselves with pointing out specific variants in the lists available to them, until Ernst Honigmann attempted to restore the original list of the fathers of Nicaea.[1] The list below is based primarily upon his, although the numbering differs, registering in continuous sequence all the 199 names that could be considered part of an authentic, original listing. This is not to say that additional prelates did not attend the council, and Honigmann concluded that between 200 and 250 as the number of attendees is well attested in the earliest sources. The names have been rendered in Anglicized or Latinized forms, and more recognizable historical place

---

[1] Honigmann 1939.

names have been added or substituted in some instances. Chorepiscopi ("rural bishops") who had no specific seat are labeled with *. Among other later interpolations or duplications, two bishops from Libya, Secundus of Ptolemaïs and Secundus of Tauchira, found in some of the lists, have been excluded by Honigmann as staunch Arians.

1. Hosius/Ossius of Cordoba
2. Vitus and
3. Vincentius, presbyters representing the Bishop of Rome

Eparchy of Egypt
4. Alexander of Alexandria
5. Paphnutius (omitted in some lists)
6. Harpocration of Alphocranon (Naucratis?)
7. Adamantius of Cynopolis
8. Arbition of Pharbaithus
9. Philip of Panephysis
10. Potamon of Heraclea
11. Dorotheus of Pelusium
12. Gaius of Thmuis
13. Antiochus of Memphis (omitted in some lists)
14. Tiberius of Tanis
15. Atthas of Schedia

Eparchy of the Thebaid (Upper Egypt)
16. Tyrannus of Antinoopolis
17. Plusianus (Volusianus?) of Lycopolis

Eparchy of Libya (two eparchies: Upper Libya and Waterless Libya)
18. Dachius of Berenice
19. Zopyrus of Barca
20. Serapion of Antipyrgus
21. Titus of Paraetonium

Eparchy of Palestine
22. Macarius of Jerusalem
23. Germanus of Neapolis (Nablus)
24. Marinus of Sebaste (Samaria)
25. Gaianus of Sebaste
26. Eusebius of Caesarea
27. Sabinus of Gadara
28. Longinus of Ascalon
29. Peter of Nicopolis

30. Macrinus of Jamnea
31. Maximus of Eleutheropolis
32. Paul of Maximianopolis
33. Januarius of Jericho
34. Aetius of Lydda
35. Silvanus of Azotus
36. Patrophilus of Scythopolis (Beishan)
37. Asclepias of Gaza
38. Peter of Aela (Elath)
39. Antiochus of Capitolias

Eparchy of Phoenicia
40. Zeno of Tyre
41. Philocalus of Paneas
42. Aeneas of Ptolemaïs (Acre)
43. Magnus of Damascus
44. Theodore of Sidon
45. Hellanicus of Tripolis (Tripoli)
46. Gregory of Berytus (Beirouth)
47. Marinus of Palmyra
48. Taddhoneus (Anatolius?) of Emesa (Homs)

Eparchy of Coele-Syria
49. Eustathius of Antioch
50. Zenobius of Seleucia
51. Theodotus of Laodicea
52. Alphius of Apamea
53. Philoxenus of Hierapolis (Manbij)
54. Selamanes (Solomon?) of Germanicea (Marash)
55. Piperius (Papirius?) of Samosata
56. Archelaus of Doliche
57. Euphratius (Euphrantius?) of Balanea
58. Phaladus (Palladius?) *
59. Zoïlus of Gabala
60. Bassus of Zeugma
61. Basianus of Raphanea
62. Gerontius of Larisa (Shaizar)
63. Manicius of Epiphanea (Hamath)
64. Eustathius of Arethusa
65. Paul of Neocaesarea
66. Syricius of Cyrrhus
67. Seleucus *

68. Peter of Gendarus
69. Pegasius of Harba-Kedem
70. Bassones of Gabbula

Eparchy of Arabia

71. Nicomachus of Bostra
72. Cyrion of Philadelphia (Amman)
73. Gennadius of Heshbon
74. Severus of Soada/Dionysias
75. Sopater of Errhe of Batanea

Eparchy of Mesopotamia

76. Aeithalas of Edessa (Ruha, Urfa)
77. Jacob of Nisibis
78. Antiochus of Resaïna
79. Mareas of Macedonopolis (Birtha)
80. John of Persis

Eparchy of Cilicia

81. Theodore of Tarsus
82. Amphion of Epiphania
83. Narcissus of Neronias
84. Moses of Castabala
85. Nicetas of Flavias
86. Eudaemon *
87. Paulinus of Adana
88. Macedonius of Mopsuestia
89. Tarcondimantus of Aegae
90. Hesychius of Alexandria (Alexandretta)

Eparchy of Cappadocia

91. Leontius of Caesarea (Kayseri)
92. Eupsychius of Tyana
93. Erythrius of Colonia
94. Timothy of Cybistra
95. Ambrosius of Comana
96. Stephen *
97. Rhodon *

Eparchy of Armenia (two eparchies: Armenia Minor and Armenia Major?)

98. Eulalius of Sebastea (Sivas)
99. Euethius of Satala

100. Eudromius *
101. Theophanes *
102. Aristaces *?

Eparchy of Diospontus
103. Eutychius of Amasia (omitted in some lists)
104. Elpidius (Helpidius) of Comana
105. Heraclius of Zela

Eparchy of Pontus Polemoniacus
106. Longinus of Neocaesarea
107. Domnus of Trebizond
108. Stratophilus of Pityous

Eparchy of Paphlagonia
109. Philadelphus of Pompeiopolis
110. Petronius of Ionopolis
111. Eupsychius of Amastris

Eparchy of Galatia
112. Pancharius of Ancyra (Ankara)
113. Dicasius of Tabia
114. Erechthius of Gdamaua
115. Philadelphus of Juliopolis

Eparchy of Asia
116. Theonas of Cyzicus
117. Menophantus of Ephesus
118. Orion of Ilium (Troy)
119. Eutychius of Smyrna
120. Mithres of Hypaepa
121. Paul of Anaea

Eparchy of Lydia
122. Artemidorus of Sardis
123. Seras of Thyatira
124. Hetoemasius of Philadelphia
125. Pollion of Baris
126. Agogius of Tripolis
127. Florentius of "Iron" Ancyra
128. Antiochus of Aurelianopolis
129. Mark of Standus

Eparchy of Phrygia
130. Nunechius of Laodicea
131. Flaccus of Sanaus
132. Procopius of Synnada
133. Pisticus of Aezani
134. Athenodorus of Dorylaeum
135. Eugenius of Eucarpia
136. Flaccus of Hierapolis

Eparchy of Pisidia
137. Eulalius of Iconium
138. Telemachus of Adrianopolis
139. Hesychius of Neapolis
140. Eutychius of Seleucia
141. Granius of Limenae
142. Tarsicius of Apamea
143. Patricius of Amblada (omitted in some lists)
144. Polycarpus of Metropolis
145. Academius of (Mustene/Pappa)
146. Heraclius of Baris
147. Theodore of Uasada

Eparchy of Lycia
148. Eudemus of Patara

Eparchy of Pamphylia
149. Callicles of Perge
150. Heuresius of Termessus
151. Zeuxius of Uarbe
152. Domnus of Aspendus
153. Cyntianus of Seleucia
154. Patricius of Maximianopolis
155. Aphrodisius of Magydus

Eparchy of the Islands
156. Euphrosynus of Rhodes
157. Meliphthongus of Cos

Eparchy of Caria
158. Eusebius of Antiochea
159. Ammonius of Aphrodisias
160. Eugenius of Apollonias

161. Letodorus of Cibyra
162. Eusebius of Miletus

Eparchy of Isauria
163. Stephen of Batata
164. Athenaeus of Coropissus
165. Aedesius of Claudiopolis
166. Agapius of Seleucia
167. Silvanus of Metropolis
168. Antonius of Antiochea
169. Nestor of Syedra
170. Hesychius *
171. Cyril of Humanada
172. Anatolius *
173. Gordianus *
174. Paul of Laranda
175. Quintus *
176. Tiberius of Ilistra
177. Aquilas *

Eparchy of Cyprus
178. Cyril of Paphus
179. Gelasius of Salamis

Eparchy of Bithynia
180. Eusebius of Nicomedia
181. Theognis of Nicaea
182. Maris of Chalcedon
183. Cyrion of Cius
184. Hesychius of Prusa
185. Gorgonius of Apollonias
186. George of Prusias
187. Euethius of Adrianopolis
188. Theophanes *
189. Rufus of Caesarea
190. Eulalius *

Eparchy of Europa
191. Phaedrus of Heraclea

Eparchy of Dacia
192. Protogenes of Serdica (Sofia)
193. Mark of Tomis (in Scythia Minor?)

Eparchy of Mysia

194. Pistus of Marcianopolis

Eparchy of Macedonia

195. Alexander of Thessalonica
196. Pudens (Budis?) of Stobi

Eparchy of Achaea

197. Pistus of Athens
198. Strategius of Hephaestias (Lemnos)

Eparchy of Thessaly

199. Cleonicus of Thebes (in Phthiotis)

APPENDIX I.I.: Select Bishoprics Represented at Nicaea, 325 (map by Ian Mladjov). Used with permission.

APPENDIX 2: LETTER OF THE SYNOD OF NICAEA
TO THE EGYPTIANS

The bishops assembled at Nicaea, who constitute the great and holy synod, greet the church of the Alexandrians, by the grace of God holy and great, and the beloved brethren in Egypt, Libya and Pentapolis. Since the grace of God and the most pious emperor Constantine have called us together from different provinces and cities to constitute the great and holy synod in Nicaea, it seemed absolutely necessary that the holy synod should send you a letter so that you may know what was proposed and discussed, and what was decided and enacted. First of all, the affair of the impiety and lawlessness of Arius and his followers was discussed in the presence of the most pious emperor Constantine. It was unanimously agreed that anathemas should be pronounced against his impious opinion and his blasphemous terms and expressions which he has blasphemously applied to the Son of God, saying "he is from things that are not", and "before he was begotten he was not", and "there once was when he was not", saying too that by his own power the Son of God is capable of evil and goodness, and calling him a creature and a work. Against all this the holy synod pronounced anathemas, and did not allow this impious and abandoned opinion and these blasphemous words even to be heard. Of that man and the fate which befell him, you have doubtless heard or will hear, lest we should seem to trample upon one who has already received a fitting reward because of his own sin. Such indeed was the power of his impiety that Theonas of Marmarica and Secundus of Ptolemais shared in the consequences, for they too suffered the same fate.

But since, when the grace of God had freed Egypt from this evil and blasphemous opinion, and from the persons who had dared to create a schism and a separation in a people which up to now had lived in peace, there remained the question of the presumption of Meletius and the men whom he had ordained, we shall explain to you, beloved brethren, the synod's decisions on this subject too. The synod was moved to incline towards mildness in its treatment of Meletius, for strictly speaking he deserved no mercy. It decreed that he might remain in his own city without any authority to nominate or ordain, and that he was not to show himself for this purpose in the country or in another city, and that he was to retain the bare name of his office.

It was further decreed that those whom he had ordained, when they had been validated by a more spiritual ordination, were to be admitted to communion on condition that they would retain their rank and exercise their ministry, but in every respect were to be second to all the clergy in each diocese and church who had been nominated under our most honoured brother and fellow minister Alexander; they were to have no authority to appoint candidates of their choice or to put forward names or to do anything at all without the consent of the bishop of the catholic church, namely the bishop of those who are under Alexander. But those who by the grace of God and by our prayers have not been detected in any schism, and are spotless in the catholic and apostolic church, are to have authority to appoint and to put forward the names of men of the clergy who are worthy, and in general to do everything according to the law and rule of the church.

In the event of the death of any in the church, those who have recently been accepted are thereupon to succeed to the office of the deceased, provided that they appear worthy and are chosen by the people; the bishop of Alexandria is to take part in the vote and confirm the election. This privilege, which has been granted to all others, does not apply to the person of Meletius because of his inveterate seditiousness and his mercurial and rash disposition, lest any authority or responsibility should be given to one who is capable of returning to his seditious practices.

These are the chief and most important decrees as far as concerns Egypt and the most holy church of the Alexandrians. Whatever other canons and decrees were enacted in the presence of our lord and most honoured fellow minister and brother Alexander, he will himself report them to you in greater detail when he comes, for he was himself a leader as well as a participant in the events. We also send you the good news of the settlement concerning the holy pasch, namely that in answer to your prayers this question also has been resolved. All the brethren in the East who have hitherto followed the Jewish practice will henceforth observe the custom of the Romans and of yourselves and of all of us who from ancient times have kept Easter together with you. Rejoicing then in these successes and in the common peace and harmony and in the cutting off of all heresy, welcome our fellow minister, your bishop Alexander, with all the greater honour and love. He has made us happy by his presence, and despite his advanced age has undertaken such great labour in order that you too may enjoy peace. Pray for us ill! that our decisions may remain secure through almighty God and our lord Jesus Christ in the holy Spirit, to whom is the glory for ever and ever. Amen.[2]

[2]   Translation from Tanner 1990, 16–19.

Bibliography

The most important collection of sources related to the "Arian" controversy and the Council of Nicaea is:

Opitz, Hans-Georg, ed. 1934. *Athanasius Werke*. Vol. 3, pt. 1. *Lieferung 1–2: Urkunden zur Geschichte des arianischen Streites*, 318–28. Berlin: De Gruyter.

And a more recent reevaluation, expansion, and reordering of these documents can be found in:

Brennecke, Hanns Christof, Uta Heil, Annette von Stockhausen, and Angelika Wintjes, eds. 2007. *Athanasius Werke: Dokumente zur Geschichte des arianischen Streites*. Vol. 3, pt. 1. *Lieferung 3: Bis zur Ekthesis Makrostichos*. Berlin: De Gruyter.

Brennecke, Hanns Christof, Annette von Stockhausen, Christian Müller, Uta Heil, and Angelika Wintjes, eds. 2014. *Athanasius Werke: Dokumente zur Geschichte des arianischen Streites*. Vol. 3, pt. 1. *Lieferung 4: Bis zur Synode von Alexandrien 362*. Berlin: De Gruyter.

PRIMARY SOURCES

The following bibliographic entries for sources cited in the contributions to this volume are arranged according to author or text, but preceded by "Canons," "Councils," and "Creeds" (see below). Citations of volumes from the Patrologia Graeca and Patrologia Latina are simply given as PG and PL respectively, with corresponding volume numbers.

Canons

Joannou, Périclès-Pierre, ed. 1962. *Discipline générale antique (IIe–IXe s.)*. Vol. 1 , *Les canons des conciles oecuméniques*. Fonti: Pontificia commissione per la redazione del codice di diritto canonico orientale ser. 1, 9.1. Grottaferrata (Roma): Tipografia Italo-Orientale "S. Nilo."

——— ed. 1963. *Discipline générale antique (IVe–IXe s.)*. Vol. 2 , *Les canons des Pères Grecs*. Fonti: Pontificia commissione per la redazione del codice di diritto canonico orientale ser. 1, 9.2. Grottaferrata (Roma): Tipografia Italo-Orientale "S. Nilo."

Martínez Díez, Gonzalo, and Félix Rodríguez, eds. 1984. *La coleccion canonica hispana. Tomo IV: Concilios galos. Concilios hispanos, primera parte.* Monumenta hispaniae sacra, Serie 3ª subsidia 4. Madrid: Consejo Superior de Investigaciones Cientificas.

——— eds. 1992. *La coleccion canonica hispana. Tomo V: Concilios hispanos. Segunda parte.* Monumenta hispaniae sacra, Serie 3ª subsidia 5 (Madrid: Consejo Superior de Investigaciones Científicas.

Councils

Alberigo, Giuseppe, ed. 2006. *Conciliorum Oecumenicorum Generaliumque Decreta.* Vol. 1, *The Oecumenical Councils, From Nicaea I to Nicaea II (325–787).* Turnhout: Brepols.

Alberigo, Giuseppe, and Hubert Jedin, eds. 1991. *Conciliorum Oecumenicorum Decreta.* Bologna: Edizione Dehoniane.

Alberigo, Giuseppe, Klaus Ganzer, and Alberto Melloni, eds. 2010. *Conciliorum Oecumenicorum Generaliumque Decreta.* Vol. 3, *The General Councils of the Roman Catholic Church, From Trent to Vatican II (1545–1965).* Turnhout: Brepols.

Gryson, Roger, ed. 1982. *Scripta Arriana Latina I: Collectio Veronensis, Scholia in concilium Aquilense, Fragmenta in Lucam rescripta, Fragmenta theologica rescripta.* CCSL 87. Turnhout: Brepols.

Lamberz, Erich, ed. 2016. *Acta Conciliorum Oecumenicorum, Series Secunda.* Vol. 3, *Concilium Universale Nicaenum Secundum.* Part 3, *Concilii Actiones VI–VII.* Berlin: De Gruyter.

Mansi, Johannes Dominicus, ed. 1903. *Sacrorum conciliorum nova et amplissima collectio.* Vol. 3. Paris: H. Welter.

Munier, Charles, ed. 1963. *Concilia Galliae a. 314–506.* CCSL 148. Turnhout: Brepols.

——— ed. 1974. *Concilia Galliae a. 345–525.* CCSL 149. Turnhout: Brepols.

Ohme, Heinz, ed. 2013. *Acta Conciliorum Oecumenicorum, Series Secunda.* Vol 2.4, *Concilium Constantinopolitanum a. 691/2 in Trullo habitum (Concilium Quinisextum).* Berlin: De Gruyter.

Price, Richard, and Michael Gaddis, eds. 2005. *The Acts of the Council of Chalcedon.* 3 vols. TTH 45. Liverpool: Liverpool University Press.

Schwartz, Eduard, ed. 1933. *Acta Conciliorum Oecumenicorum.* Tome 2, *Concilium Uniuersale Chalcedonense.* Vol. 1, *Acta Graeca,* Part 2, *Actio Secunda, Epistularum Collectio B. Actiones III–VII.* Berlin: De Gruyter.

Tanner, S. J., Norman P., ed. 1990. *Decrees of the Ecumenical Councils.* Vol. 1. London: Sheed & Ward.

Wohlmuth, Josef, ed. 1998. *Dekrete der ökumenischen Konzilien.* Vol 1. Paderborn: Ferdinand Schöningh.

Creeds

Kinzig, Wolfram, ed. 2017. *Faith in Formulae: A Collection of Early Christian Creeds and Creed-Related Texts*, 4 vols. Oxford: Oxford University Press.

Agatho (Pope)

PL 87.

Alexander of Aphrodisas

Hayduck, M., ed. 1891. *Alexander of Aphrodisias: Commentary on the Metaphysics*. Berlin: Reimer.

Ambrose of Milan

Faller, Otto, ed. 1962. *Ambrosius: De fide ad Gratianum Augustum*. CSEL 78. Vienna: Hoelder-Pichler-Tempsky.

Zelzer, Michaela, ed. 1982. *Sancti Ambrosii Opera, Pars 10, Epistulae et Acta, Tome 3*. CSEL 82. Vienna: Hoelder-Pichler-Tempsky.

Ammianus Marcellinus

Rolfe, John, trans. 1935–40. *Ammianus Marcellinus*, 3 vols., LCL 300, 315, 331. Cambridge, MA: Harvard University Press.

Apollinarius of Laodicea

Lietzmann, Hans, ed. (1904) 1970. *Apollinaris von Laodicea und seine Schule: Texte und Untersuchungen*. Tübingen: J. C. B. Mohr. Reprint, Hildesheim: Georg Olms.

Apostolic Constitutions

Metzger, P. Marcel, ed. 1987. *Les Constitutions apostoliques*. Vol. 3, *Livres VI–VIII*. SC 336. Paris: Les Éditions du Cerf.

Asterius

Vinzent, Markus, ed. 1993. *Asterius von Kappadokien, Die theologischen Fragmente: Einleitung, kristischer Text, Übersetzung und Kommentar*. Supplements to Vigiliae Christianae 20. Leiden: Brill.

Athanasius

Camplani, Alberto, ed. 2003. *Atanasio di Alessandria, Lettere festali; Anonimo, Indice delle Letter festali: Introduzione, traduzione, e note*. Letture cristiane del primo millennio 34. Milan: Paoline Editoriale Libri.

Heil, Uta, ed. 1999. *Athanasius von Alexandrien. De sententia Dionysii. Einleitung, Übersetzung und Kommentar.* Patristiche Texte und Studien 52. Berlin: De Gruyter.

Martin, Annick, and Micheline Albert, eds. 1985. *Histoire 'acéphale' et Index syriaque des Lettres festales d'Athanase d'Alexandrie.* SC 317. Paris: Les Éditions du Cerf.

Martin, Annick, and Xavier Morales, eds. 1985. *Athanase d'Alexandrie: Lettre sur les synodes.* SC 563. Paris: Les Éditions du Cerf.

Opitz, Hans-Georg, ed. 1935. *Athanasius Werke.* Vol. 2.1: *Die Apologien (Lieferungen 1–7).* Berlin and Leipzig: Walter de Gruyter.

Robertson, Archibald, trans. 1892. *Athanasius: Select Works and Letters.* NPNF 2.4. Edinburgh: T. & T. Clark.

Stockhausen, Annette von, ed. 2002. *Athanasius von Alexandrien: Epistula ad Afros. Einleitung, Kommentar, und Übersetzung.* Patristische Texte und Studien 56. Berlin: De Gruyter.

Augustine

Beschin, G., ed. 1973–87. *Trinità.* Nuova Biblioteca Agostiniana. Rome: Città Nuova Editrice.

Teske, Roland, S. J., trans. 1995. *Arianism and Other Heresies.* Works of Saint Augustine: A Translation for the 21st Century 18.1. Hyde Park, NY: New City Press.

Basil of Caesarea

Courtonne, Yves, ed. 1957–66. *Saint Basile, Lettres.* 3 vols. Paris: Société d'Édition "Les Belles Lettres."

DelCogliano, Mark, and Andrew Radde-Gallwitz, trans. 2011. *St. Basil of Caesarea: Against Eunomius.* FC 122. Washington, DC: Catholic University of America Press.

Pruche, Benoit, ed. and trans. 1947. *Basile de Césarée: Traité du Saint Esprit.* SC 17. Paris: Les Éditions du Cerf.

Bede

Jones, Charles, ed. 1943. *Bedae opera de temporibus.* Cambridge, MA: Medieval Academy of America.

Berno of Richenau

PL 142.

Boniface I

PL 20.

Claudian

Platnauer, Maurice, trans. 1922. *Claudian* 2. LCL 136. New York: Putnam's.

Claudius Ptolemy

Toomer, Gerald J., trans. 1998. *Ptolemy's Almagest – Translated and annotated*. Princeton: Princeton University Press.

Collectio Avellana

Günther, Otto, ed. 1895, 1898. *Epistulae Imperatorum Pontificum Aliorum, Inde Ab A. CCLXVII Usque ad A. DLIII Datae, Avellana Quae Dicitur Collectio*. CSEL 35.1–2. Vienna: Tempsky.

Cyprian of Carthage

Weber, R. and M. Bénevot, eds. 1972. *Cyprianus: Opera 1*. CCSL 3. Turnhout: Brepols.

Cyril of Alexandria

McEnerney, John I, trans. 1987. *Cyril of Alexandria: Letters 1–50*. Washington, DC: Catholic University in America.

Epiphanius of Cyprus

Amidon, S. J., Philip R., trans. 1990. *The Panarion of St. Epiphanius, Bishop of Salamis, Selected Passages*. New York: Oxford University Press.

Holl, Karl, ed. 1922. *Epiphanius III, Panarion haer. 65–80 De fide*. GCS 31. Leipzig: J. C. Hinrichs'sche Buchhandlung. Rev. ed. Jürgen Dummer. Berlin: Akademie Verlag.

Eusebius of Caesarea

Amerise, Marilena, trans. 2005. *Eusebio di Cesarea. Elogio di Costantino. Discorso per il trentennale Discorso regale*. Letture cristiane del primo millennio 38. Milan: Paoline Editoriale Libri.

Cameron, Averil, and Stuart G. Hall, trans. 1999. *Eusebius: Life of Constantine*. Oxford: Clarendon Press.

Drake, H. A., trans. 1976. *In Praise of Constantine: A Historical Study and New Translation of Eusebius' Tricennial Orations*. Berkeley: University of California Press.

Ferrar, William John, trans. (1920) 1981. *The Proof of the Gospel: Being the Demonstratio Evangelica of Eusebius of Caesarea*. London: Society for Promoting Christian Knowledge. Reprint, Grand Rapids: Baker Book House.

Heikel, Ivar A., ed. 1902. *Eusebius Werke I. Über Das Leben Constantins: Constantins Rede an die heilige Versammlung. Tricennatsrede an Constantin.* GCS 7. Leipzig: J. C. Hinrichs'sche Buchhandlung.

——— ed. 1913. *Eusebius Werke VI. Die Demonstratio Evangelica.* GCS 23. Berlin: Akademie Verlag.

Klostermann, Erich, ed. (1906, 1972) 1991. *Eusebius Werke IV. Gegen Marcell. Über die kirchliche Theologie. Die Fragmente Marcells.* GCS 14. Leipzig: J. C. Hinrichs'sche Buchhandlung. Rev. ed. Günther Christian Hansen. Berlin: Akademie Verlag.

Lawler, Hugh, and John E. Oulton, trans. 1928. *Eusebius Bishop of Caesarea: The Ecclesiastical History and the Martyrs of Palestine.* 2 vols. London: Society for Promoting Christian Knowledge.

Maraval, Pierre, trans. 2001. *Eusèbe de Césarée. La théologie politique de l'Empire chrétien. Louanges de Constantin (Triakontaéterikos). Introduction, traduction et notes.* Paris: Les Éditions du Cerf.

Mras, Karl, ed. 1954. *Eusebius Werke VIII. Die Praeparatio Evangelica.* GCS 43.1. Berlin: Akademie Verlag.

Schwartz, Eduard and Theodor Mommsen, ed. 1903–9. *Eusebius Werke II.1–3. Die Kirchengeschichte.* GCS 9.1–3. Leipzig: J. C. Hinrichs'sche Buchhandlung.

Spoerl, Kelley McCarthy and Markus Vinzent, trans. 2017. *Eusebius of Caesarea: Against Marcellus and On Ecclesiastical Theology.* FC 135. Washington, DC: Catholic University of America Press.

Stevenson, James, ed. 1957. *A New Eusebius: Documents Illustrating the History of the Church to* AD 337. London: S.P.C.K.

Williamson, G. A., trans. 1965. *Eusebius: The History of the Church from Christ to Constantine.* Baltimore: Penguin.

Winkelmann, Friedhelm, ed. (1991) 2008. *Eusebius Werke I.1. Über das Leben des Kaisers Konstantin.* 2nd ed. GCS. Berlin: De Gruyter.

Eusebius of Vercelli

Bulhart, V. et al., eds. 1957. *Opera Quae Supersunt.* CCSL 9. Turnhout: Brepols.

Eustathius of Antioch

Declerck, José H., ed. 2002. *Eustathii Antiocheni, patris Nicaeni, opera quae supersunt omnia.* CCSG 51. Turnhout: Brepols.

Filastrius of Brescia

Bulhart, V. et al., eds. 1957. *Opera Quae Supersunt.* CCSL 9. Turnhout: Brepols.

Gelasius of Caesarea

Wallraff, Martin, Jonathan Stutz, and Nicholas Marinides, eds. 2018. *Gelasius of Caesarea: Ecclesiastical History. The Extant Fragments, with an Appendix*

Containing the Fragments from Dogmatic Writings. GCS, N.F., 25. Berlin: De Gruyter.

Gelasius of Cyzicus

Loeschke, Gerhard, and Margaret Heinemann, eds. 1918. *Gelasius Kirchengeschichte.* GCS 28. Leipzig: J. C. Hinrichs'sche Buchhandlung.

Gregory I

PL 75–76.

Gregory of Elvira

Bulhart, V., J. Fraipoint, and M. Simonetti, eds. 1967. *Opera Quae Supersunt.* CCSL 69. Turnhout: Brepols.

Gregory of Nazianzus

Gallay, Paul, ed. 1974. *Grégoire de Nazianze: Lettres théologiques.* SC 208. Paris: Les Éditions du Cerf.

Gregory of Nyssa

Mueller, Frederick, ed. 1958. *Gregorii Nysseni Opera Dogmatica Minora.* Vol. 3.1. Leiden: Brill.

Orton, Robin, trans. 2015. *St. Gregory of Nyssa: Anti-Apollinarian Writings.* FC 131. Washington, DC: Catholic University of America Press.

Hadrian I (Pope)

Dümmler, Ernst, and Karl Hampe, eds. 1898–99. *Epistolae Karolini Aevi.* Monumenta Germaniae Historica. *Epistolae.* Vol. 5. Berlin: Weidmann.

Hilary of Poitiers

Feder, Alfred, ed. 1916. *S. Hilarii Pictavensis Opera Pars IV: Tractatus Mysteriorum, Collectanea Antiariana Parisina (Fragmenta Historica) cum Appendice (Liber I ad Constantium), Ad Constantium Imperatorem (Liber II ad Constantium), Hymni, Fragmenta Minora, Spuria.* CSEL 65. Vienna: F. Tempsky.

Wickham, Lionel, ed. and trans. 1997. *Hilary of Poitiers: Conflicts of Conscience and Law in the Fourth-Century Church, Against Valens and Ursacius: The Extant Fragments, Together with His Letter to the Emperor Constantius.* TTH 25. Liverpool: Liverpool University Press.

Hippolytus
Stewart-Sykes, Alistair, trans. 2001. *Hippolytus: On the Apostolic Tradition.* Popular Patristics Series 22. Crestwood, NY: St Vladimir's Seminary Press.

Historia Acephala
Martin, Annick, and Micheline Albert, eds. 1985. *Histoire 'acéphale' et Index syriaque des Lettres festales d'Athanase d'Alexandrie.* SC 317. Paris: Les Éditions du Cerf.

Innocent I
PL 20.

Jerome
Helm, Rudolf, ed. 1956. *Eusebius Werke VII. Die Chronik des Hieronymus. Hieronymi Chronicon.* 3rd ed. GCS, N.F., 47. Berlin: Akademie Verlag.

John Scholastikos
Beneševič, Vladimir, ed. 1937. *Ioannis Scholastici Synagoga L titulorum ceteraque eiusdem opera iuridica.* Abhandlungen der Bayerischen Akademie der Wissenschaften: Philosophisch-Historische Abteilung, Neue Folge 14. Munich: Verlag der Bayerischen Akademie der Wissenschaften.

Julius of Rome
Thompson, Glen L., ed. and trans. 2015. *The Correspondence of Pope Julius I.* Library of Early Christianity 3. Washington, DC: Catholic University of America Press.

Lactantius
Creed, John, ed. and trans. 1984. *Lactantius: De mortibus persecutorum.* Oxford: Clarendon Press.

Leo I
PL 54.

Leontius of Byzantium
Daley, S. J., Brian E., ed. and trans. 2017. *Leontius of Byzantium: Complete Works.* Oxford Early Christian Texts. New York: Oxford University Press.

Lucifer of Cagliari

Diercks, G., ed. 1978. *Opera Quae Supersunt*. CCSL 8. Turnhout: Brepols.

Marcellus of Ancyra

Vinzent, Markus, ed. 1997. *Markell von Ankyra: Die Fragmente und der Brief an Julius von Rom*. Supplements to Vigiliae Christianae 39. Leiden: Brill.

Marius Victorinus

Henry, P., and P. Hadot, eds. 1971. *Marius Victorinus: Ad Candidam Arrianum, Adversus Arium, De homoousio recipiendo, Hymni*. CSEL 83.1. Vienna: Österreichischen Akademie der Wissenschaften.

Nicephorus Callistus

PG 146.

Notitia Dignitatum

Seeck, Otto, ed. 1876. *Notitia dignitatum: accedunt notitia urbis Constantinopolitanae et latercula provinciarum*. Berlin: Weidmann.

Optatus of Milevis

Edwards, Mark, trans. 1997. *Optatus: Against the Donatists*. TTH 27. Liverpool: Liverpool University Press.

Panegyrici Latini

Nixon, C. E. V. and Barbara Saylor Rodgers, eds. and trans. 1994. *In Praise of Later Roman Emperors: The Panegyrici Latini*. Transformation of the Classical Heritage 21. Berkeley: University of California Press.

Philostorgius

Amidon, Philip., S. J. 2007. *Philostorgius*: Church History. Writings from the Greco-Roman World 23. Atlanta: Society of Biblical Literature.

Bidez, J., ed. 1913. *Philostorgius, Kirchengeschichte*. GCS 21. Leipzig: Hinrichs.

Phoebadius of Agen

Wessel, Keith C. 2008. *Phoebadius of Agen*: Liber Contra Arianos. www.fourthcentury.com/wp-content/uploads/2010/09/Wessel-Phoebadius.pdf.

Photius of Constantinople

PG 107.

Hoegenroether, J., ed. 1869. *Monumenta graeca ad Photium eiusque historiam pertinentia*. Regensburg: Manz.
Holy Transfiguration Monastery. 1983. *Photius of Constantinople: On the Mystagogy of the Holy Spirit*. Astoria, NY: Studion Publishers.

Priscillian of Avila
Conti, Marco, ed. 2010. *Priscillian of Avila: The Complete Works*. Oxford Early Christian Texts. Oxford: Oxford University Press.

Pseudo-Justin Martyr
Pouderon, M. Bernard, ed. 2009. *Exhortation aux Grecs, Discours aux grecs, Sur la monarchie*. SC 528. Paris: Les Éditions du Cerf.

Rufinus of Aquileia
Simonetti, M., ed. 1961. *Opera*. CCSL 20. Turnhout: Brepols.

Sebeos
Thomson, Robert, and James Howard-Johnston, trans. 1999. *The Armenian History Attributed to Sebeos*. TTH 31. Liverpool: Liverpool University Press.

Siricius
Zechiel-Eckes, Klaus. 2013. *Die erste Dekretale: Der Brief Papst Siricius' an Bischof Himerius von Tarragona vom Jahre 385 (JK 255)*. Monumenta Germaniae Historica, Studien und Texte 55. Hanover: Hahnsche Buchhandlung.

Smaragdus
Werminghoff, Albert, ed. 1906. *Concilia aevi Karolini*. Vol. 1, pt. 1. Monumenta Germaniae Historica, Legum Sectio 3.1.1. Hanover and Leipzig: Hahn.

Socrates
Hansen, Günther, ed. 1995. *Sokrates: Kirchengeschichte*. GCS, N.F., 1. Berlin: Akademie Verlag.
Zenos, Andrew C., trans. 1890. *Socrates, Sozomenus: Church Histories*. NPNF 2.2.

Sozomen
Hansen, Günther Christian, ed. 1995. *Sozomenus: Kirchengeschichte*. GCS, N.F., 4. Berlin: Akademie Verlag.

Sulpicius Severus

Halm, C., ed. 1866. *Opera*. CSEL 1. Vienna: Geroldi.

Tertullian

Gerlo, A. et al. 1954. *Opera* 2. CCSL 2. Turnhout: Brepols.

Theodore the Reader

PG 86.

Theodoret

Papadopoulos-Kerameus, Athanasios, ed. 1895. Θεοδωρήτου ἐπισκόπου πόλεως
Κύρρου πρὸς τὰς ἐπενεχθε σας αὐτῷ ἐπερώθησεις παρά τινος τῶν ἐξ Α γύπτου
ἐπισκόπων ἀποκρ σεις. Saint Petersburg: Kirschbaum.

Theophanes

de Boor, Carl Gotthard, ed. 1883. *Theophanis Chronographia Recens*. Leipzig:
Teubner.

Walafrid Strabo

PL 114.

Zeno of Verona

Löfstedt, B., ed. 1971. *Tractatus*. CCSL 22. Turnhout: Brepols.

Zosimus

Mendelssohn, L., ed. 1887. *Zosimi Comitis et Exadvocati Fisci Histora Nova*.
Leipzig: Teubner.

Other Texts

Beneševič, Vladimir. (1906) 1974. *Drevne-slavjanskaja kormcaja XIV titulov bez
tolkovanij (Syntagma XIV titulorum sine scholiis secundum versionem
Palaeo-Slovenicam, adjecto textu Graeco e vetustissimis codicibus
manuscriptis exarato*. St. Petersburg, 1906. Reprinted Leipzig:
Zentralantiquariat der Deutschen Demokratischen Republik.

Bettenson, Henry, ed. 1943. *Documents of the Christian Church*. London: Oxford
University Press.

Brown, Dan. 2003. *The Da Vinci Code*. Doubleday: New York.

Bucherius, Aegidius, ed. 1633. *In Victorium Aquitanum Canonem*. Antwerp:
Plantin.

Catholic Church. 1994. *Catechism of the Catholic Church*. 2nd ed. Vatican City: Libreria Editrice Vaticana.

Coustant, Pierre, ed. 1721. *Epistolae Romanorum pontificum et quae ad eos scriptae sunt a S. Clemente I usque ad Innocentum III*. Vol. 1, *Ab anno Christi 67 ad annum 440*. Paris: L.-D. Delatour.

Cummings, Denver, trans. 1957. *The Rudder*. Chicago: Orthodox Christian Educational Society.

Holy Transfiguration Monastery. 1997. *Synaxarion*. Brookline, MA: Holy Transfiguration Monastery.

Jaffé, Philipp, ed. (1851) 1885. *Regesta Pontificum Romanorum ab condita ecclesia ad annum post Christum natum MCXCVIII*. Berlin: Veit et Socius. Vol. 1, *A S. Petro usque ad annum MCXLIII*, 2nd ed. Rev. ed. Wilhelm Wattenbach et al. Leipzig: Veit.

————— ed. (1851, 1885) 2016. *Regesta Pontificum Romanorum ab condita ecclesia ad annum post Christum natum MCXCVIII, Tomus Primus: A S. Petro usque ad a. DCIV*, 3rd ed. Ed. Markus Schütz. Göttingen: Vandenhoeck & Ruprecht.

Maier, Jean-Louis, ed. and trans. 1987–89. *Le dossier du Donatisme*. 2 vols. Berlin: Akademie Verlag.

Mastrantonis, George, ed. 1982. *Augsburg and Constantinople: The Correspondence between the Tübingen Theologians and Patriarch Jeremiah II of Constantinople on the Augsburg Confession*. Brookline, MA: Holy Cross Orthodox Press.

Musurillo, Herbert, ed. 1972. *Acts of the Christian Martyrs*. Oxford: Clarendon Press.

Pharr, Clyde, ed. and trans. 1952. *The Theodosian Code and Novels and the Sirmondian Constitutions*. Princeton: Princeton University Press.

Presbyterian Church (U.S.A.). 2016. *The Constitution of the Presbyterian Church (U.S.A.). Part I: Book of Confessions*. Louisville, KY: The Office of the General Assembly.

Sieben, Hermann-Josef, ed. and trans. 2014. *Vetustissimae Epistulae Romanorum Pontificum. Die ältesten Papstbriefe*. 3 vols. Fontes Christiani 58.1–3. Freiburg: Herder.

St. Tikhon's Monastery. 1998. *The Great Book of Needs*. Vol. 1. South Canaan, PA: St. Tikhon's Seminary Press.

Steinhauser, Kenneth, ed. 2006. *Anonymi in Iob commentarius*. CCEL 96. Vienna: Österreichischen Akademie der Wissenschaften.

Turner, Cuthbert Hamilton, ed. 1904. *Ecclesiae Occidentalis Monumenta Iuris Antiquissima*, 2 vols. Oxford: Clarendon.

Van Banning, J., ed. 1988. *Opus imperfectum in Matthaeum*. CCSL 87B. Turnhout: Brepols.

Warntjes, Immo. 2010. *The Munich Computus: Text and Translation*. Stuttgart: Franz Steiner.

MODERN SCHOLARSHIP

The bibliography of modern studies on all aspects related to the Council of Nicaea is, of course, massive (and ever growing). The titles listed below gather together all works cited in the chapters in this volume, and together represent a thorough survey of relevant scholarly works, each of which when consulted will certainly lead to other works absent from this list.

Abbasoğlu, Haluk, and Inci Delemen. 2003. "Remains from Ancient Nicaea." In Akbaygil et al., İznik throughout History, 189–97.

Abramowski, Luise. (1975) 1992a. "Die Synode von Antiochien 324/25 und ihr Symbol." ZKG 86: 356–66. Repr. and trans. in Abramowski, Formula and Context, III.

—— (1976) 1992b. "Gregory Thaumaturgus' Confession of Faith in Gregory of Nyssa and the Problem of Its Genuineness." ZKG 87: 145–66. Repr. and trans. in Abramowski, Formula and Context, VII.

—— (1982) 1992c. "Dionysius of Alexandria (d. 268) and Dionysius of Rome (d. 264/5) in the Arian Controversies of the Fourth Century." ZKG 93: 240–72. Repr. and trans. in Abramowski, Formula and Context, XI.

—— 1992d. Formula and Context: Studies in Early Christian Thought. Aldershot: Ashgate.

Adams, Edward. 2015. The Earliest Christian Meeting Place: Almost Exclusively Houses? Edinburgh: T&T Clark.

Ağtürk, Tuna Şare. 2018. "A New Tetrarchic Relief from Nicomedia: Embracing Emperors." American Journal of Archaeology 122(3): 411–26.

Akbaygil, Isýl et al., eds. 2003. İznik throughout History. Istanbul: Türkiye İş Bankası Kültür Yayınları.

Alexopoulos, Stefanos. 2017. "Proskynesis." In RAC 28: 360–72.

Anatolios, Khaled. 1998. Athanasius: The Coherence of His Thought. London and New York: Routledge.

—— 2011. Retrieving Nicaea: The Development and Meaning of Trinitarian Doctrine. Grand Rapids: Baker Academic.

Andrieu, Michel. 1948. Les Ordines Romani du haut moyen âge. Vol. 2, Les textes (Ordines I–XIII). Spicilegium Sacrum Lovaniense 23. Leuven: Spicilegium Sacrum Lovaniense.

Angelov, Alexander. 2014. "Bishop over 'Those Outside': Imperial Diplomacy and the Boundaries of Constantine's Christianity." GRBS 54: 274–92.

Arce, Javier. 1997. "Emperadores, palacios y villae (A propósito de la villa romana de Cercadilla, Córdoba)." Antiquité Tardive 5: 293–302.

—— 2016. "Imperial Journeys in the 4th Century: Burdens and Utilitas Publica." Antiquité Tardive 24: 149–56.

Athanasiou, Fani et al. 2013. Γαλεριανό Συγκρότημα: Μία εικονική περιήγηση (The Galerian Complex: A Visual Tour), Thessaloniki: Ephorate of Antiquities of Thessaloniki City.

Aubineau, Michel. 1966. "Les 318 serviteurs d'Abraham (Gen., XIV, 14) et le nombre des pères au concile de Nicée (325)." RHE 61: 5–43.

Ayres, Lewis. 2004. Nicaea and Its Legacy: An Approach to Fourth-Century Trinitarian Theology. Oxford: Oxford University Press.

Barnes, Michel René. 2001. The Power of God: Δύναμις in Gregory of Nyssa's Trinitarian Theology. Washington, DC: Catholic University of America Press.

Barnes Michel René, and Daniel H. Williams, eds. 1993. *Arianism after Arius: Essays on the Development of the Fourth Century Trinitarian Conflicts.* Edinburgh: T&T Clark.

Barnes, Timothy D. 1978. "Emperors and Bishops, AD 324–44: Some Problems." *American Journal of Ancient History* 3: 53–75.

1981. *Constantine and Eusebius.* Cambridge, MA: Harvard University Press.

1982. *The New Empire of Diocletian and Constantine.* Cambridge, MA: Cambridge University Press.

1993. *Athanasius and Constantius: Theology and Politics in the Constantinian Empire.* Cambridge, MA: Harvard University Press.

2007. "A Note on the Term 'Homoiousios'." *ZAC* 10(2): 276–85.

2011. *Constantine: Dynasty, Religion and Power in the Later Roman Empire.* Chichester: Wiley Blackwell.

Beatrice, Pier Franco. 2002. "The Word 'Homoousios' from Hellenism to Christianity." *CH* 71(2): 243–72.

Beaver, R. Pierce. 1936. "The Organization of the Church of Africa on the Eve of the Vandal Invasion." *CH* 5(2): 168–81.

Beeley, Christopher A. 2008. *Gregory of Nazianzus on the Trinity and the Knowledge of God.* Oxford Studies in Historical Theology. Oxford: Oxford University Press.

Behr, John. 2001. *The Way to Nicaea,* Formation of Christian Theology 1. Crestwood, NY: St Vladimir's Seminary Press.

2004. *The Nicene Faith: Formation of Christian Theology* 2. Crestwood, NY: St Vladimir's Seminary Press.

Bellen, Heinz. 1997. "Christianissimus Imperator. Zur Christianisierung der römischen Kaiserideologie von Constantin bis Theodosius." in *Politik – Recht – Gesellschaft: Studien zur Alten Geschichte,* ed. Leonhard Schumacher, 151–66. Historia Einzelschriften 115. Stuttgart: Franz Steiner Verlag.

Bergjan, Silke-Petra. 2015. "Theodoret von Cyrus, Apollinarius und die Apollinaristen in Antiochien." In Bergjan, Gleede, and Heimgartner, *Apollinarius und seine Folgen,* 229–58.

Bergjan, Silke-Petra, Benjamin Gleede, and Martin Heimgartner, eds. 2015. *Apollinarius und seine Folgen.* Studien und Texte zu Antike und Christentum 93. Tübingen: Mohr Siebeck.

Bezançon, Jean-Noël, Philippe Ferlay, and Jean-Marie Onfray. 1987. *How to Understand the Creed.* Trans. J. Bowden. London: SCM Press.

Bindley, Thomas Herbert. 1899. *The Oecumenical Documents of the Faith.* London: Methuen.

Bingham, Joseph. 1840. *Origines ecclesiasticae or the Antiquities of the Christian Church* 6. London: Parker.

Bishop, Chris. 2016. "Assessing Visigothic Latinity in the Late Sixth Century: The Contribution of Reccared's Letter to Gregory I." *JAEMA* 12: 35–52.

Bjornlie, M. Shane, ed. 2017. *The Life and Legacy of Constantine: Traditions Through the Ages.* London: Routledge.

Bleckmann, Bruno. 2010. "Licinius." In *RAC* 23: 137–47.

2015. "Constantine, Rome, and the Christians." In *Contested Monarchy: Integrating the Roman Empire in the Fourth Century AD*, ed. Johannes Wienand, 309–29. Oxford: Oxford University Press.

Bogaert, Raymond. 1976. "Geld (Geldwirtschaft)." In *RAC* 9: 843–90.

Bowman, Alan K. 2005. "Diocletian and the First Tetrarchy, A.D. 284–305." In *The Cambridge Ancient History, Second Edition, Volume XII: The Crisis of Empire, A.D. 193–337*, ed. Alan K. Bowman, Averil Cameron, and Peter Garnsey, 67–89. Cambridge: Cambridge University Press.

Bracht, Katharina. 1999. *Vollkommenheit und Vollendung: Zur Anthropologie des Methodius von Olympus*. Studien und Texte zu Antike Christentum 2. Tübingen: Mohr Siebeck.

Brennecke, Hanns Christof. 1988. *Studien zur Geschichte der Homöer: Der Osten bis zum Ende der homöischen Reichskirche*, Beiträge zur historischen Theologie 73. Tübingen: J. C. B. Mohr [Paul Siebeck].

1997. "'An fidelis ad militiam converti possit?' (Tertullian, De idolatria 19,1). Frühchristliches Bekenntnis und Militärdienst im Widerspruch?" In *Die Weltlichkeit des Glaubens in der Alten Kirche, Festschrift Ulrich Wickert*, ed. Dietmar Wyrwa, 45–100. Berlin: De Gruyter.

2010. "Die letzten Jahre des Arius." In *Von Arius zum Athanasianum: Studien zur Edition des Athanasius Werke*, ed. Hanns Christof Brennecke and Annette von Stockhausen, 63–83. Texte und Untersuchungen zur Geschichte der altchristlichen Literatur, 164. Berlin: De Gruyter.

2015. "'Apollinaristicher Arianismus' oder 'arianischer Apollinarismus' – ein dogmengeschichtliches Konstruct? 'Arianische' Christologie und Apollinarius von Laodicea." In Bergjan, Gleede, and Heimgartner, *Apollinarius und seine Folgen*, 73–92.

Brennecke Hanns Christof, and Uta Heil. 2012. "Nach hundert Jahren: Zur Diskussion um die Synode von Antiochien 325: Eine Antwort auf Holger Strutwolf." *ZKG* 123 (1): 95–113.

Brakke, David. 1995. *Athanasius and the Politics of Asceticism*. Oxford: Oxford University Press.

2006. *Demons and the Making of the Monk: Spiritual Combat in Early Christianity*. Cambridge, MA: Harvard University Press.

Brown, Peter. 2015. *The Cult of the Saints: Its Rise and Function in Latin Christianity, Enlarged Edition*. Chicago: University of Chicago Press.

Bruns, Peter. 2000. "Bemerkungen zur Rezeption des Nicaenums in der ostsyrischen Kirche." *Annuarium Historiae Conciliorum* 32(1): 16–22.

Burgess, R. W. 1997. "The Dates and Editions of Eusebius *Chronici Canones* and *Historia Ecclesiastica*." *JTS*, n.s., 48(2): 471–504.

2008. "The Summer of Blood: The 'Great Massacre' of 337 and the Promotion of the Sons of Constantine." *DOP* 62: 5–51.

Burn, A. E. 1908. "Some Spanish MSS of the Constantinopolitan Creed." *JTS* 9: 301–3.

1925. *The Council of Nicaea: A Memorial for Its Sixteenth Centenary*. London: Macmillan.

Burns, Dylan M. 2014. *Apocalypse of the Alien God: Platonism and the Exile of Sethian Gnosticism*. Divinations: Rereading Late Ancient Religion. Philadelphia: University of Pennsylvania Press.

Burrus, Virginia. 2000. *"Begotten, Not Made"*: *Conceiving Manhood in Late Antiquity*. Stanford: Stanford University Press.

Cabié, Robert. 1986. *The Church at Prayer: An Introduction to the Liturgy*. Vol. 2, *The Eucharist*. Trans. Matthew J. O'Connell. Collegeville, MN: The Liturgical Press.

Calderone, Salvatore. 1988. "Il pensiero politico di Eusebio di Cesarea." In *I cristiani e l'impero nel IV secolo. Colloquio sul cristianesimo nel mondo antico, atti del convegno (Macerata 17–18 Dicembre 1987)*, ed. Giorgio Bonamente and Aldo Nestori, 45–54. Macerata: Università degli studi di Macerata.

Camplani, Alberto. 1989. *Le lettere festali di Atanasio di Alessandria: studio storico-critico*. Rome: C.I.M.

Capelle, Bernard. 1929. "L'origine antiadoptianiste de notre texte du symbole de la messe." *Recherches de théologie ancienne et médiévale* 1: 7–20.

——— 1934. "Alcuin et l'histoire du symbole de la messe." *Recherches de théologie ancienne et médiévale* 6: 249–60.

Carefoote, P. J. 1995. "Augustine, the Pelagians and the Papacy." STD diss., Katholieke Universiteit Leuven.

Carlà-Uhink, Filippo. 2017. "Thinking through the Ancient World: 'Late Antique Movies' as a Mirror of Shifting Attitudes towards Christian Religion." In *A Companion to Ancient Greece and Rome on Screen*, ed. Arthur J. Pomeroy, 307–28. Malden, MA: Wiley-Blackwell.

Carter, T. J. 2011. *The Apollinarian Christologies*. London: Hamley King Publishing.

Cartwright, Sophie. 2015. *The Theological Anthropology of Eustathius of Antioch*. Oxford Early Christian Studies. Oxford: Oxford University Press.

Cecilio Díaz y Díaz, Manuel. 1991. "Los discursos del rey Rearedo: el 'tomus'." In *Concilio III de Toledo: XIV Centenario, 589–1989*, ed. M. González Martín, 223–36. Toledo: Arzobispado de Toledo.

Cereti, Giovanni. 1991. "The Reconciliation of Remarried Divorces according to Canon 8 of the Council of Nicaea." In *Ius sequitur vitam: Law Follows Life, Studies in Canon Law Presented to P. J. M. Huizing*, ed. James H. Provost and Knut Walf, 193–207. Annua Nuntia Lovaniensia 32. Leuven: Peeters.

Chadwick, Henry. 1958. "Ossius of Cordova and the Presidency of the Council of Antioch 325." *JTS*, n.s., 9 (2): 292–304.

——— 1960. "Faith and Order at the Council of Nicaea: A Note on the Background of the Sixth Canon." *HTR* 53: 171–95.

——— 2003. "The Council of Nicaea." In Akbaygil et al., *Iznik throughout History*, 89–103.

Chapman, Mark D. 2005. "Why Do We Still Recite the Nicene Creed at the Eucharist?" *Anglican Theological Review* 87(2): 207–23.

Cobb, Stephanie. 2016. *Divine Deliverance: Pain and Painlessness in Early Christian Martyr Texts*. Berkeley: University of California Press.

Cohen, Will. 2018. "Doctrinal Drift, Dance or Development: How Truth Takes Time in the Life of Communion." *International Journal of Systematic Theology* 20(2): 209–25.

Collins, Roger. 2004. *Visigothic Spain 409–711*. A History of Spain. Oxford: Blackwell.

Congar, Yves. 1983. *I Believe in the Holy Spirit*. Vol. 3, *The River of Life Flows in the East and in the West*. Trans. David Smith. London: Geoffrey Chapman.

Coolman, Boyd Taylor. Unpublished. "Ongoing Re-Narration: A Catholic Practice of Historical Theology." Paper presented at the International Conference "Rethinking the Resources of the Christian Theological Tradition: Retrieval, Renewal, Reunion," University of St. Thomas, St. Paul, Minnesota, 11–15 July 2017.

Cowdrey, H. J. 1997. "Eleventh Century Reformers' Views of Constantine." *Byzantinische Forschungen* 24: 63–91.

Cox, C. A. 1992. "Processes Involving Regularities and Impediments to the Exercise of Orders." In *Clergy Procedural Handbook*, ed. Randolph R. Calvo and Nevin J. Klinger, 178–205. Washington, DC: Canon Law Society of America.

Cox Miller, Patricia. 2009. *The Corporeal Imagination: Signifying the Holy in Late Antiquity*. Divinations: Rereading Late Ancient Religion. Philadelphia: University of Pennsylvania Press.

Cross, F. L. 1939. "The Council of Antioch in 325 AD." *Church Quarterly Review* 128: 49–76.

Crouzel, Henri. 1978. "Les *digamoi* visés par le Concile de Nicée dans son canon 8." *Augustinianum* 18: 533–46.

Crow, James. 2001. "Fortifications and Urbanism in Late Antiquity: Thessaloniki and Other Eastern Cities." In *Recent Research in Late-Antique Urbanism*, ed. Luke Lavan, 91–107. Journal of Roman Archaeology Supplementary Series 42. Portsmouth, RI: Journal of Roman Archaeology.

2017. "Fortifications." In *The Archaeology of Byzantine Anatolia: From the End of Late Antiquity until the Coming of the Turks*, ed. Philipp Niewöhner, 90–108. New York: Oxford University Press.

Dagron, Gilbert. 1974. *Naissance d'une capitale: Constantinople et ses institutions de 330 à 451*. Paris: Presses universitaires de France.

2003. *Emperor and Priest: The Imperial Office in Byzantium*. Trans. Jean Birrell. Cambridge: Cambridge University Press.

Dainese, Davide. 2011. "Συνέρχομαι – συγϰρότησις – σύνοδος. Tre diversi usi della denominazione." *Cristianesimo nella storia* 32: 875–943.

Daley, S. J., Brian E. 1993. "Position and Patronage in the Early Church: The Original Meaning of 'Primacy of Honour'." *JTS*, n.s., 44 (2): 529–53.

Davis, Leo D. (1983) 1990. *The First Seven Ecumenical Councils (325–787): Their History and Theology*. Wilmington, DE: Michael Glazier. Reprinted Collegeville, MN: Liturgical Press.

Daunoy, Fernand. 1925. "La question pascal au concile de Nicée." *Échos d'Orient* 24: 424–44.

De Clercq, Victor C. 1954. *Ossius of Cordova: A Contribution to the History of the Constantinian Period*. Studies in Christian Antiquity 13. Washington, DC: Catholic University of America Press.

De Decker, Daniel. 1968. "La politique religieuse de Maxence." *Byzantion* 38(2): 472–562.

2005. "Eusèbe de Nicomédie: pour un réevaluation historique-critique des avatars du premier Concile de Nicée." *Augustinianum* 45(1): 95–170.

DelCogliano, Mark. 2006. "Eusebian Theologies of the Son as the Image of God before 341." *JECS* 14(4): 458–84.

2008. "The Eusebian Alliance: The Case of Theodotus of Laodicea." *ZAC* 12(2): 250–66.

2011a. "George of Laodicea: A Historical Reassessment." *JEH* 62(4): 667–92.

2011b. "The Promotion of the Constantinian Agenda in Eusebius of Caesarea's *On the Feast of Pascha*." In *Reconsidering Eusebius: Collected Papers on Literary, Historical, and Theological Issues*, ed. Sabrina Inowlocki and Claudo Zamagni, 39–68. Supplements to *Vigiliae Christianae* 107. Leiden: Brill.

2015. "Asterius in Athanasius' Catalogue of Arian Views." *JTS*, n.s., 66(2): 625–50.

2018. "How Did Arius Learn from Asterius? On the Relationship between the Thalia and the Syntagmation." *JEH* 69(3): 477–92.

De Sena, E. C. 2014. "Constantine in the Imperial Palace at Serdica." In *Constantine, Sirmium and Early Christianity (Proceedings)*, ed. Nenad Lemajić, 7–24. Sremska Mitrovica: Institute for the Protection of Cultural Monuments.

Dey, Hendrik. 2015. *The Afterlife of the Roman City: Architecture and Ceremony in Late Antiquity and the Early Middle Ages*. New York: Cambridge University Press.

Di Berardino, Angelo. 1992. "L'imperatore Costantino e la celebrazione della Pasqua." In *Costantino il Grande dall' antichità all' umanesimo, Macerata, 18–20 Dicembre, 1990*, ed. G. Bonamente and F. Fusco, 363–84. Macerata: Università degli studi di Macerata.

Digeser, Elizabeth DePalma. 2000. *The Making of a Christian Empire: Lactantius and Rome*. Ithaca: Cornell University Press.

2014. "Why Has the Edict of AD 311 Been Ignored?" In *Serdica Edict (AD 311): Concepts and Realizations of The Idea of Religious Toleration*, ed. Vesselina Vachkova and Dimitar Dimitrov, 15–28. Sofia: Tangra.

Di Marco, Michele. 2014. "La figura di Costantino in Occidente fra tardo antico e alto Medioevo (s. IV ex.–VIII in.)." *Gregorianum* 95(2): 365–91.

Dockter, Hanno. 2015. *Klerikerkritik im antiken Christentum*. Bonn: Bonn University Press.

Domagalski, Bernhard. 1980. "Römische Diakone im 4. Jahrhundert: Zum Verhältnis von Bischof, Diakon und Presbyter." In *Der Diakon: Wiederentdeckung und Erneuerung seines Dienstes*, ed. Josef G. Plöger and Hermann J. Weber, 44–56. Freiburg: Herder.

Donciu, Ramiro. 2012. *L'empereur Maxence*. Bari: Edipuglia.

Dossetti, Giuseppe. 1967. *Il simbolo di Nicea e di Constantinopoli: Edizione critica*. Rome: Herder.

Drake, H. A. 2000. *Constantine and the Bishops: The Politics of Intolerance*. Baltimore: Johns Hopkins University Press.

2006. "The Impact of the Constantine on Christianity." In *The Cambridge Companion to the Age of Constantine*, ed. Noel Lenski, 111–36. Cambridge: Cambridge University Press.

2013. "Il 313: Costantino e i cristiani." In *Costantino I, enciclopedia costantiniana sulla figura e l'immagine dell' imperatore del cosiddetto editto di Milano, 313–2013*, 1: 167–75. Roma: Istituto della Enciclopedia Italiana.

2016. "The Emperor as a 'Man of God': The Impact of Constantine the Great's Conversion on Roman Ideas of Kingship." *História* (São Paulo) 35: 1–17.

Drecoll, Volker Henning. 2013. "How Binitarian/Trinitarian was Eusebius?" In *Eusebius of Caesarea: Tradition and Innovations*, ed. Aaron P. Johnson and Jeremy Schott, 289–305. Washington, DC: Center for Hellenic Studies Press.

2015. "Apollinarius, *Ad Iovianum*: Analyse und Bedeutung für die Apollinariuschronologie." In Bergjan, Gleede, and Heimgartner, *Apollinarius und seine Folgen*, 35–57.

Duchesne, Louis. 1880. "La question de la Paque au Concile de Nicée." *Revue des questions historiques* 28: 5–42.

1908–10. *Histoire ancienne de l'Église*. 3 vols. 4th ed. Paris: A. Fontemoing.

Dunn, Geoffrey D. 2011. "Canonical Legislation on the Ordination of Bishops." In *Episcopal Elections in Late Antiquity*, ed. Johan Leemans, Peter Van Nuffelen, Shawn W. J. Keough, and Carla Nicolaye, 145–66. Arbeiten zur Kirchengeschichte 119. Berlin: De Gruyter.

2012. "The Appeal of Apiarius to the Transmarine Church of Rome." *JAEMA* 8: 9–29.

2013a. "The Clerical *Cursus Honorum* in the Late Antique Roman Church." *Scrinium* 9: 120–33.

2013b. "Did Zosimus Pardon Caelestius?" In *Lex et religio in eta tardoantica, XL Incontro di studiosi dell'antichità cristiana, Roma 10–12 maggio 2012*, Studia Ephemeridis Augustinianum 135, 647–55. Rome: Institutum Patristicum Augustinianum.

2013c. "Zosimus and the Gallic Churches." In *Religious Conflict in Early Christianity to the Rise of Islam*, ed. Wendy Mayer and Bronwen Neil, 169–85. Arbeiten zur Kirchengeschichte 121. Berlin: De Gruyter.

2014. "Clerical Marriage in the Letters of Late-Antique Roman Bishops." In *Men and Women in the Early Christian Centuries*, ed. Wendy Mayer and Ian J. Elmer, 293–313. Early Christian Studies 18. Strathfield, NSW: St Pauls.

ed. 2015a. *The Bishop of Rome in Late Antiquity*. Burlington, VT: Ashgate.

2015b. "The Emergence of Papal Decretals: The Evidence of Zosimus of Rome." In *Shifting Genres in Late Antiquity*, ed. Geoffrey Greatrex, Hugh Elton, with Lucas McMahon, 81–92. Burlington, VT: Ashgate.

2015c. "*Placuit apostolicae* (*Ep.* 1) of Zosimus of Rome and the Ecclesiastical Reorganization of Gaul." *JECS* 23(4) 559–81.

2015d. "*. . . quid habuerit antiqua consuetudo*: Zosimus of Rome and Hilary of Narbonne." *RHE* 110(1–2): 31–55.

2015e. "Zosimus' Synod of Rome in September 417 and His Letter to Western Bishops (*Cum aduersus*)." *Antiquité Tardive* 23: 395–405.

2016. "The Ecclesiastical Reorganisation of Space and Authority in Late Antique Gaul: Zosimus' Letter *Multa Contra* (JK 334 = J³ 740)." *JAEMA* 12: 1–33.

2019. "Epistolary Sleight of Hand: Diplomatic Manipulation in Zosimus' Letter to Patroclus of Arles (*Quid de Proculi*)." *VC* 73(3): 254–70.

Duval, Noel. 1978. "Comment reconnaître un palais impérial ou royal? Ravenne et Piazza Armerina." *Felix Ravenna* 108: 27–62.

Duval, Yves-Marie. 1969. "Sur l'arianisme des Ariens d'Occident." *Mélanges de science religieuse* 26: 145–53.

1973. "Les relations doctrinale entre Milan et Aquilée durant la seconde moitié du IVe siècle : Chromace d'Aquilée et Ambroise de Milan." In *Aquileia e Milano*. Antichità Altoadriatiche 4, 171–234. Trieste: EUT Edizione Università di Trieste.

2005. *La décrétale Ad Gallos Episcopos: son texte et son auteur.* Supplements to Vigiliae Christianae 73. Leiden: Brill.

Dvornik, Francis. 1951. "Emperors, Popes, and General Councils." *DOP* 6: 1–23.

Earle, Timothy. 1997. *How Chiefs Come to Power: The Political Economy in Prehistory.* Stanford: Stanford University Press.

Edwards, Mark. 1995. "The Arian Heresy and the Oration to the Saints." *VC* 49 (4): 379–87.

1998. "Did Origen Apply the Words *Homoousios* to the Son?" *JTS*, n.s., 49(2): 658–70.

2006. "The First Council of Nicaea." In *The Cambridge History of Christianity*. Vol. 1, ed. Margaret M. Mitchell and Frances M. Young, 552–68. Cambridge: Cambridge University Press.

2012. "Alexander of Alexandria and the *Homoousion*." *VC* 66(5): 482–502.

2013. "Why Did Constantine Label Arius a Porphyrian?" *L'Antiquité Classique* 82: 239–47.

2015. *Religions of the Constantinian Empire.* Oxford: Oxford University Press.

Ehrman, Bart. 2004. *Truth and Fiction in the Da Vinci Code: A Historian Reveals What We Really Know about Jesus, Mary Magdalene, and Constantine.* Oxford: Oxford University Press.

Elm, Susanna. 1994. *'Virgins of God': The Making of Asceticism in Late Antiquity.* Oxford: Oxford University Press.

Ferguson, Everett. 1997. "Subintroductae." In *Encyclopedia of Early Christianity* 2, 1092. New York: Garland Publishing.

2009. *Baptism in the Early Church: History, Theology, and Liturgy in the First Five Centuries.* Grand Rapids: Eerdmans.

Ferreiro, Alberto. 2014. "*Sanctissimus idem princeps sic venerandum concilium adloquitur dicens*: King Reccared's Discourses at the Third Council of Toledo (589)." *Annuarium Historiae Conciliorum* 46(1–2): 27–52.

2015. "Pope Siricius and Himerius of Tarragona (385): Papal Intervention in the Fourth Century." In Dunn, *The Bishop of Rome in Late Antiquity*, 73–85.

Fıratlı, Nezih. 1974. "An Early Byzantine Hypogaeum Discovered at Iznik." In *Mélanges Mansel*, 919–32. Ankara: Türk Tarih Kurumu Basımevi.

Fischer, Joseph Anton, and Adolf Lumpe. 1997. *Die Synoden von den Anfängen bis zum Vorabend des Nicaenums.* Konziliengeschichte Reihe A: Darstellungen. Paderborn: Schöningh.

Foss, Clive. 1977. "Late Antique and Byzantine Ankara." *DOP* 31: 29–87. Reprinted in Clive Foss. 1990. *History and Archaeology of Byzantine Asia Minor*, VI. Aldershot: Ashgate.

1996a. *Nicaea: A Byzantine Capital and Its Praises: With the Speeches of Theodore Laskaris, "In Praise of the Great City of Nicaea," and Theodore Metochites, "Nicene Oration."* Archbishop Iakovos Library of Ecclesiastical and Historical Sources 21. Brookline, MA: Hellenic College Press.

1996b. *Survey of Medieval Castles in Anatolia II. Nicomedia.* London: The British Institute of Archaeology at Ankara.

2003. "The Walls of Iznik 260–1330." In Akbaygil et al., *İznik throughout History*, 249–62.

Foss, Clive, and David Winfield. 1986. *Byzantine Fortifications: An Introduction.* Pretoria: University of South Africa.

Francis, James. 2009. "Verbal and Visual Representation: Art and Text, Culture and Power in Late Antiquity." In *A Companion to Late Antiquity*, ed. Philip Rousseau, 285–305. Oxford: Oxford University Press.

Frank, Georgia. 2000. *The Memory of the Eyes: Pilgrims to Living Saints in Christian Late Antiquity.* Transformation of the Classical Heritage 30. Berkeley: University of California Press.

Frankfurter, David. 1994. "The Cult of Martyrs in Egypt before Constantine: The Evidence of the Coptic *Apocalypse of Elijah*." *VC* 48(1): 25–47.

2009. "Martyrology and the Prurient Gaze." *JECS* 17(2): 215–45.

Frend, W. H. C. 1952. *The Donatist Church: A Movement of Protest in Roman North Africa.* Oxford: Clarendon Press.

1972. "The Monks and the Survival of the East Roman Empire in the Fifth Century." *Past & Present* 54: 3–24.

Frye, David. 1991. "Bishops as Pawns in Early Fifth-Century Gaul." *JEH* 42(3): 349–61.

Gaddis, Michael. 2005. *There Is No Crime for Those Who Have Christ: Religious Violence in the Christian Roman Empire.* Transformation of the Classical Heritage 39. Berkeley: University of California Press.

Galvão-Sobrinho, Carlos R. 2013. *Doctrine and Power: Theological Controversy and Christian Leadership in the Later Roman Empire.* Transformation of the Classical Heritage 51. Berkeley: University of California Press.

Gaudemet, Jean. 1958. *L'Église dans l'empire Romain (IVᵉ–Vᵉ siècles).* Histoire du Droit et des Institutions de l'Église en Occident 3. Paris: Sirey.

Geisinger, S. J., Robert J. 2000. "Title VI: Orders (cc.1008–1054)." In *New Commentary on the Code of Canon Law*, ed. John P. Beal, James A. Coriden, and Thomas J. Green, 1218. New York: Paulist.

Gelzer, Heinrich, Heinrich Hilgenfeld and Otto Cuntz, eds. 1898. *Patrum Nicaenorum nomina Latine Graece Coptice Syriace Arabice Armeniace sociata opera.* Leipzig: Teubner.

Gibbon, Edward (1776–88) 1909–14. *The History of the Decline and Fall of the Roman Empire.* Ed. J. Bury. 7 vols. London: Methuen.

Gilbert, E. J. 1985. "Title VI: Orders (cc. 1008–1054)." In *The Code of Canon Law: A Text and Commentary*, ed. James A. Coriden, Thomas J. Green, and Donald E. Heintschel, 730. New York: Paulist.

Gill, Joseph. 1959. *The Council of Florence.* Cambridge: Cambridge University Press.

Girardet, Klaus M. 1993. "Der Vorsitzende des Konzils von Nicaea (325) – Kaiser Konstantin d. Gr." In *Klassisches Altertum, Spätantike und frühes Christentum. Adolf Lippold zum 65. Geburtstag gewidmet*, ed. K. Dietz, D. Hennig, and H. Kaletsch, 331–60. Würzburg: Selbstverlag des Seminars für Alte Geschichte.

2001. "Die Teilnahme Kaiser Konstantins am Konzil von Nicaea (325) in byzantinischen Quellen." *Annuarium Historiae Conciliorum* 33: 241–84.

2010. *Der Kaiser und sein Gott: Das Christentum im Denken und in der Religonspoitik Konstantins des Grossen*. Berlin: De Gruyter.

Goltz, Andreas. 2008. "Der 'mediale' Konstantin: Zur Rezeption des ersten christlichen Kaisers in den modernen Medien." In *Konstantin der Große: Das Bild des Kaisers im Wandel der Zeiten*, ed. Andreas Goltz and Heinrich Schlange-Schöningen, 277–308. Cologne: Böhlau.

Graf, Georg. 1944. *Geschichte der christlichen arabischen Literatur, 1: Die Übersetzungen*. Studi e Testi 118. Città del Vaticano: Bibliotheca Apostolica Vaticana.

Grant, Robert M. 1972. "Eusebius and His Church History." In *Understanding the Sacred Text: Studies in Honor of Morton S. Enslin on the Hebrew Bible and Christian Origins*, ed. John Reumann, 235–47. Valley Forge, PA: Judson.

Green, Malcolm R. 1973. "Pope Innocent I: The Church of Rome in the Early Fifth Century." DPhil thesis, Oxford University.

Gregg, Robert C. 1985. *Arianism: Historical and Theological Reassessments. Papers from the Ninth International Conference on Patristic Studies*. Patristic Monograph Series 11. Philadelphia: Philadelphia Patristic Foundation.

Gregg, Robert C., and Dennis Groh. 1981. *Early Arianism: A View of Salvation*. Philadelphia: Fortress Press.

Grig, Lucy, and Kelly, Gavin, eds. 2012. *Two Romes: Rome and Constantinople in Late Antiquity*. Oxford Studies in Late Antiquity. Oxford: Oxford University Press.

Grünewald, Thomas. 1990. *Constantinus Maximus Augustus: Herrschaftspropaganda in der zeitgenössischen Überlieferung*. Historia Einzelschriften 64. Stuttgart: Franz Steiner.

Gryson, Roger. 1972. *Le ministère des femmes dans l'Eglise ancienne*. Recherches et Synthèses. Section d'histoire 4. Gembloux: Éditions J. Duculot.

  1982. *Le recueil arien de Vérone (Ms. LI de la Bibliothèque Capitulaire et feuillets de la Collection Giustiniani Recanti): Étude codicologique et paléographique*. Instrumenta Patristica 13. Sint-Pietersabdij: Steenbrugge.

  1983. *Les palimpsestes ariens latins de Bobbio: contributions à la méthodologie de l'étude des palimpsestes*. Turnhout: Brepols.

Gryson, Roger, and Léon Gilissen. 1980. *Les scolies ariennes du Parisinus latinus 8907, un échantillonage d'écritures latines du Ve siécle*. Turnhout: Brepols.

Gwynn, David M. 1999. "Constantine and the Other Eusebius." *Prudentia* 31(2): 94–124.

  2007. *The Eusebians: The Polemic of Athanasius of Alexandria and the Construction of the "Arian Controversy."* Oxford Theology and Religion Monographs. Oxford: Oxford University Press.

  2009. "The Council of Chalcedon and the Definition of Christian Tradition." In Price and Whitby, *Chalcedon in Context*, 7–26.

  2010. "Eusebius of Nicomedia: A 'Court Bishop' for Constantine?" *StPatr* 46: 289–94.

2012. *Athanasius of Alexandria: Bishop, Theologian, Ascetic, Father.* Christian Theology in Context. Oxford: Oxford University Press.

Hall, Stuart G. 1985. "The *Thalia* of Arius in Athanasius' Accounts." In Gregg, *Arianism: Historical and Theological Reassessments*, 37–58.

1998. "Some Constantinian Documents in the *Vita Constantini.*" In Lieu and Montserrat, *From Constantine to Julian*, 86–103.

Hanson, R. P. C. 1988. *The Search for the Christian Doctrine of God: The Arian Controversy, 318–381.* Edinburgh: T&T Clark.

Hardy, Edward R. 1954. ed. *Christology of the Later Fathers.* Philadelphia: Westminster Press.

Harris, William V. 2005. "Constantine's Dream." *Klio* 87: 488–94.

Hauben, Hans. 1998. "The Melitian 'Church of the Martyrs': Christian Dissenters in Ancient Egypt." In *Ancient History in a Modern University.* Vol. 2, *Early Christianity, Late Antiquity and Beyond*, ed. Thomas W. Hillard et al., 329–49. Grand Rapids, MI: Eerdmans.

2012. *Studies on the Melitian Schism in Egypt (AD 306–335)*, ed. Peter Van Nuffelen. Farnham: Ashgate.

Hefele, Karl von. 1871–96. *A History of the Councils of the Church, from the Original Documents.* 5 vols. Trans. W. R. Clark. Edinburgh: T&T Clark.

Hefele, Karl Joseph von and Henri Leclercq. 1907. *Histoire des conciles d'après les documents originaux.* 1.1. Paris: Letouzey et Ané.

Heil, Uta. 2002. "... bloß nicht wie die Manichäer!" Ein Vorschlag zu Hintergründen des arianischen Streits." *ZAC* 6(2): 299–319.

Hekster, Olivier. 2015. *Emperors and Ancestors: Roman Rulers and the Constraints of Tradition.* Oxford Studies in Ancient Culture and Representation. Oxford: Oxford University Press.

Henderson David E., and Frank Kirkpatrick. 2016. *Constantine and the Council of Nicaea: Defining Orthodoxy and Heresy in Christianity, 325 C.E.* Chapel Hill, NC: Reacting Consortium Press.

Henderson, John B. 1998. *The Construction of Orthodoxy and Heresy: Neo-Confucian, Islamic, Jewish, and Early Christian Patterns.* Albany: State University of Albany Press.

Hess, Hamilton. 2002. *The Early Development of Canon Law and the Council of Serdica.* Oxford Early Christian Studies. Oxford: Oxford University Press.

Heurtley, Charles Able. 1911. *De Fide et Symbolo.* Oxford: Parker.

Hildebrand, Stephen M. 2007. *The Trinitarian Theology of Basil of Caesarea: A Synthesis of Greek Thought and Biblical Truth.* Washington, DC: Catholic University of America Press.

Hill, Edmund. 1985. *The Mystery of the Trinity.* Introducing Catholic Theology 4. London: Geoffrey Chapman.

Hinschius, Paul. 1869. *System des katholischen Kirchenrechts mit besonderer Rücksicht auf Deutschland.* Vol. 1. Berlin: Guttentag.

Honigmann, Ernst. 1939. "La liste originale des pères de Nicée: à propos de l'Évêché de 'Sodoma' en Arabie." *Byzantion* 14(1): 17–76.

1942–43. "The Original List of the Members of the Council of Nicaea, the Robber Synod and the Council of Chalcedon." *Byzantion* 16(1): 20–80.

Hornung, Christian. 2011. *Directa ad decessorem: Ein kirchenhistorisch-philologischer Kommentar zur ersten Dekretale des Siricius von Rom.*

Jahrbuch für Antike und Christentum, Ergänzungsband Kleine Reihe 8. Münster: Aschendorff Verlag.

2015. "Siricius and the Rise of the Papacy." In Dunn, *The Bishop of Rome in Late Antiquity*, 57–72.

2016. *Apostasie im antiken Christentum: Studien zum Glaubensabfall in altkirchlicher Theologie, Disziplin und Pastoral (4.–7. Jahrhundert n. Chr.)*. Supplements to *Vigiliae Christianae* 138. Leiden: Brill.

Hort, Fenton J. A. 1876. *Two Dissertations*. Cambridge: Macmillan.

Hughes, Amy Brown. 2016. "The Legacy of the Feminine in the Christology of Origen of Alexandria, Methodius of Olympus, and Gregory of Nyssa." *VC* 70 (1): 51–76.

Humfress, Caroline. 2007. *Orthodoxy and the Courts in Late Antiquity*. Oxford: Oxford University Press.

2008. "Citizens and Heretics: Late Roman Lawyers on Christian Heresy." In *Heresy and Identity in Late Antiquity*, ed. Eduard Iricinschi and Holger M. Zellentin, 128–42. Texts and Studies in Ancient Judaism 119. Tübingen: Mohr Siebeck.

Humphrey, John H. 1986. *Roman Circuses: Arenas for Chariot Racing*. Berkeley: University of California Press.

Humphries, Mark. 2008. "From Usurper to Emperor: The Politics of Legitimation in the Age of Constantine." *JLA* 1(1): 82–100.

Hunter, David G. 2011. "Clerical Marriage and Episcopal Elections in the Latin West." In *Episcopal Elections in Late Antiquity*, ed. Johan Leemans, Peter Van Nuffelen, Shawn W. J. Keough, and Carla Nicolaye, 183–202. Arbeiten zur Kirchengeschichte 119. Berlin: De Gruyter.

Ideler, Ludwig. 1825–26. *Handbuch der mathematischen und technischen Chronologie*. 2 vols. Berlin: A. Rücker.

Irshai, Oded. 2011. "Fourth Century Christian Palestinian Politics." In *Reconsidering Eusebius: Collected Papers on Literary, Historical, and Theological Issues*, ed. Sabrina Inowlocki and Claudio Zamagni, 25–38. Supplements to Vigiliae Christianae 107. Leiden: Brill.

Jan, Johann Wilhelm. 1718. *Historia cycli Dionysii cum argumentis paschalibus et aliis eo spectantibus*. Wittenberg: Literis Gerdesiansis.

Jasper, Detlev, and Horst Fuhrmann. 2001. *Papal Letters in the Early Middle Ages*. History of Medieval Canon Law. Washington, DC: Catholic University of America Press.

Johannessen, Hazel. 2016. *The Demonic in the Political Thought of Eusebius of Caesarea*. Oxford Early Christian Studies. Oxford: Oxford University Press.

Johnson, Aaron P. 2004. "Ancestors as Icons: The Lives of Hebrew Saints in Eusebius' *Praeparatio Evangelica*." *GRBS* 44(3): 245–64.

2014. *Eusebius*. London: I. B. Tauris.

Johnson, Gary J. 1984. "Roman Bithynia and Christianity to the Mid-Fourth Century." PhD diss, University of Michigan.

Jungmann, J. A. 1951. *The Mass of the Roman Rite: Its Origins and Development (Missarum Sollemnia)*. Vol. 1. Trans. F. A. Brunner. New York: Benziger Brothers.

Kannengiesser, Charles. 1982. *Holy Scripture and Hellenistic Hermeneutics in Alexandrian Christianity: The Arian Crisis.* Colloquy 41. Berkeley: Center for Hermeneutical Studies in Hellenistic and Modern Culture.

Karababa, Idil Ucer. 2008. "Function and Architecture of the Principal Residences of the Tetrarchy: An Assessment of Their Capitalness." PhD diss, Bryn Mawr College.

Kasper, Walter. 1983. *The God of Jesus Christ.* Trans. M. J. O'Connell. London: SCM Press.

Kelly, J. N. D. 1972. *Early Christian Creeds.* 3rd ed. London: Longmans.

Kéry, Lotte. 1999. *Canonical Collections of the Early Middle Ages (ca. 400–1140): A Bibliographical Guide to the Manuscript and Literature.* History of Medieval Canon Law. Washington, DC: Catholic University of America Press.

Kinzig, Wolfram. 1999. "*. . . natum et passum* etc. Zur Geschichte der Tauffragen in der lateinischen Kirche bis zu Luther." In *Tauffragen und Bekenntnis: Studien zur sogenannten "Traditio Apostolica", zu den "Interrogationes de fide" zum "Römischen Glaubensbekenntnis,"* ed. Wolfram Kinzig, Christof Markschies, and Markus Vinzent, 75–183. Arbeiten zur Kirchengeschichte 74. Berlin: De Gruyter.

Kinzig, Wolfram, and Markus Vinzent. 1999. "Recent Research on the Origin of the Creed." *JTS*, n.s., 50(2): 535–59.

Kirin, Asen. 2000. "The Rotunda of St. George and Late Antique Serdica: From Imperial Palace to Episcopal Complex." PhD diss, Princeton University.

Kirsten, Ernst. 1954. "Chorbischof." In *RAC* 2: 1105–14.

Klaassen, Walter. 1981. "The Anabaptist Critique of Constantinian Christendom." *Mennonite Quarterly Review* 55: 218–30.

Klauser, Theodor. 1957. "Diakon," *RAC* 3: 888–909.

Knight, Jonathan. 2012. "The Origin and Significance of the Angelomorphic Christology in the *Ascension of Isaiah.*" *JTS*, n.s., 63(1): 66–105.

Kolb, Frank. 2001. *Herrscherideologie in der Spätantike.* Berlin: Akademie Verlag.

Kopecek, Thomas. 1979. *A History of Neo-Arianism.* 2 vols. Cambridge, MA: Philadelphia Patristic Foundation.

Kötting, Bernhard. 1957. "Digamus." In *RAC* 3: 1022–23.

Koyama, Mark. 2010. "Evading the 'Taint of Usury': The Usury Prohibition as a Barrier to Entry." *Explorations in Economic History* 47(4): 420–42.

Krautheimer, Richard. 1979. *Early Christian and Byzantine Architecture,* 3rd ed. New York: Penguin.

Krusch, Bruno. 1880. *Studien zur christlich-mittelalterlichen Chronologie: Der 84jährige Ostercyclus und seine Quellen.* Leipzig: Veit.

    1938. *Studien zur christlich-mittelalterlichen Chronologie: Die Entstehung unserer heutigen Zeitrechnung.* Abhandlungen der Preussischen Akademie der Wissenschaften 8. Berlin: Verlag der Akademie der Wissenschaften.

Kulikowski, Michael E. 1996. "Two Councils of Turin." *JTS*, n.s., 47(1): 159–68.

Lafontaine, Paul-Henri. 1963. *Les conditions positives de l'Accession aux Ordres dans la première législation ecclésiastique (300–492).* Ottawa: Éditions de l'Université d'Ottawa.

Lash, Ephrem. 2006. "Byzantine Hymns of Hate." In *Byzantine Orthodoxies*, ed. Andrew Louth and Augustine Casiday, 151–64. Aldershot: Ashgate.

Laubscher, Hans Peter. 1975. *Der Reliefschmuck des Galeriusbogens in Thessaloniki*. Archäologische Forschungen 1. Berlin: Mann.

Le Boulluec, Alain. 1985. *La notion d'hérésie dans la littérature grecque IIe–IIIe siècles*. Paris: Études Augustiniennes.

Leemans, Johan, Wendy Mayer, Pauline Allen, and Boudewijn Dehandschutter. 2003. *"Let Us Die That We May Live": Greek Homilies on Christian Martyrs from Asia Minor, Palestine and Syria (ca. AD 350–AD 450)*. London: Routledge.

Leithart, Peter. 2010. *Defending Constantine: The Twilight of an Empire and the Dawn of Christendom*. Downers Grove, IL: Intervarsity.

Lenski, Noel, ed. 2006. *The Cambridge Companion to the Age of Constantine*. Cambridge: Cambridge University Press.

Lenski, Noel. 2016. *Constantine and the Cities: Imperial Authority and Civic Politics*. Philadelphia: University of Pennsylvania Press.

2017. "The Significance of the Edict of Milan." In *Constantine: Religious Faith and Imperial Policy*, ed. A. Eduard Siecienski, 27–56. London: Routledge.

Leppin, Hartmut, and Hauke Ziemsen. 2007. *Maxentius: Der letzte Kaiser in Rom*. Mainz am Rhein: Von Zabern.

Leroy-Molinghen, Alice. 1968. "La mort d'Arius." *Byzantion* 38(1): 105–11.

L'Huillier, Peter. 1996. *The Church of the Ancient Councils: The Disciplinary Work of the First Four Ecumenical Councils*. Crestwood, NY: St Vladimir's Seminary Press.

Lienhard, S. J., Joseph T. 1983. "The Exegesis of 1 Cor 15: 24–28 from Marcellus of Ancyra to Theodoret of Cyrus." *VC* 37(4): 340–59.

1987. "The 'Arian' Controversy: Some Categories Reconsidered." *Theological Studies* 48: 415–37.

1989. "Acacius of Caesarea: Contra Marcellum. Historical and Theological Considerations." *Cristianesimo nella Storia* 10: 1–22.

1993. "Did Athanasius Reject Marcellus?" In *Arianism after Arius: Essays on the Development of the Fourth Century Trinitarian Conflicts*, ed. Michel R. Barnes and Daniel H. Williams, 65–80. Edinburgh: T&T Clark.

1999. Contra Marcellum: *Marcellus of Ancyra and Fourth-Century Theology*. Washington, DC: Catholic University of America Press.

Lieu, Samuel N. C., and Dominic Montserrat, eds. 1996. *From Constantine to Julian: Pagan and Byzantine Views*. London: Routledge.

eds. 1998. *Constantine: History, Historiography and Legend*. London: Routledge.

Lim, Richard. 1995. *Public Disputation, Power, and Social Order in Late Antiquity*. Transformation of the Classical Heritage 23. Berkeley: University of California Press.

Linck, Heinrich. 1908. *Zur Übersetzung und Erläuterung der Kanones IV, VI und VII des Konzils von Nicaea*. Gießen: Münchow'sche Hof- und Universitäts-Druckerei.

Logan, Alistair H. B. 1989. "Marcellus of Ancyra and anti-Arian Polemic." *StPatr* 19: 189–97.

Löhr, Winrich. 2006a. "Arius Reconsidered (Part 1)." *ZAC* 9(3): 524–60.

2006b. "Arius Reconsidered (Part 2)." *ZAC* 10(1): 121–57.

Loofs, Friedrich. 1905. *Nestoriana: Die Fragmenta des Nestorius.* Halle: Niemeyer.

Lorenz, Rudolf. 1979. *Arius judaizans? Untersuchungen zur dogmengeschichtlichen Einordnung des Arius.* Forschungen zur Kirchen- und Dogmengeschichte 31. Göttingen: Vandenhoeck & Ruprecht.

1983. "Die Christusseele im arianischen Steit: Nebst einigen Bemerkungen zur Quellenkritik des Arius und zur Glaubwürdigkeit des Athanasius." *ZKG* 94: 1–51.

Louth, Andrew. 2007. *Greek East and Latin West: The Church AD 681–1071.* The Church in History 3. Crestwood, NY: St Vladimir's Seminary Press.

Lübeck, Konrad. 1901. *Reichseinteilung und kirchliche Hierarchie des Ostens bis zum Ausgange des vierten Jahrhunderts: Ein Beitrag zur Rechts- und Verfassungsgeschichte der Kirche.* Kirchengeschichtliche Studien 5.4. Münster: Schöningh.

Luibhéid, Colm. 1982. *The Council of Nicaea.* Galway: Galway University Press.

Luijendijk, Annemarie. 2008. "Papyri from the Great Persecution: Roman and Christian Perspectives." *JECS* 16(3): 341–69.

Lyman, Rebecca. 1989. "Arians and Manichees on Christ." *JTS*, n.s., 40(2): 493–503.

1993. *Christology and Cosmology: Models of Divine Activity in Origen, Eusebius and Athanasius.* Oxford Theology and Religion Monographs. Oxford: Oxford University Press.

2008. "Arius and Arians." In *The Oxford Handbook of Early Christian Studies*, ed. Susan Ashbrook Harvey and David Hunter, 237–57. Oxford: Oxford University Press.

Maassen, Friedrich. 1853. *Der Primat des Bischofs von Rom und die alten Patriarchatskirchen.* Bonn: Henry & Cohen.

1870. *Geschichte der Quellen und der Literatur des canonischen Rechts im Abendlande bis zum Ausgang des Mittelalters.* Graz: Leuschner & Lubensky.

Mac Carthy, Bartholomew. 1901. *Annála Uladh: The Annals of Ulster.* Vol. 4. Dublin: Alex Thom.

MacCormack, Sabine. 1981. *Art and Ceremony in Late Antiquity.* Transformation of the Classical Heritage 1. Berkeley: University of California Press.

MacMullen, Ramsay. 1969. *Constantine.* New York: Dial Press.

1976. "Two Notes on Imperial Properties." *Athenaeum* 54: 19–36.

2006. *Voting About God in Early Church Councils.* New Haven: Yale University Press.

2014. "Religious Toleration around the Year 313." *JECS* 22(4): 499–517.

Magdalino, Paul, ed. 1994. *New Constantines: The Rhythm of Imperial Renewal in the East, 4th–13th Centuries. Papers from the Twenty-sixth Spring Symposium of Byzantine Studies, St Andrews, March.* Society for the Promotion of Byzantine Studies, Publications 2. Aldershot: Ashgate.

Mango, Cyril. 1994. "Notes d'épigraphie et d'archéologie: Constantinople, Nicée." *Travaux et Mémoires* 12: 343–57.

2005. "The Meeting Place of the First Ecumenical Council and the Church of the Holy Fathers at Nicaea." *Deltion* 26: 27–34.

Marcone, Arnaldo. 2002. *Pagano e cristiano: vita e mito di Costantino.* Roma: Editori Laterza.

Marschall, Werner. 1971. *Karthago und Rom: Die Stellung der nordafrikanischen Kirche zum apostolischen Stuhl.* Päpste und Papsttum 1. Stuttgart: Hiersemann.

Martimort, Aimé Georges. 1982. *Les diaconesses: essai historique.* Bibliotheca Ephemerides Liturgicae, Subsidia 24. Roma: Edizioni liturgiche.

Mathews, Thomas. 1993. *The Clash of Gods: A Reinterpretation of Early Christian Art.* Princeton: Princeton University Press.

Mathews, Thomas, and Norman E. Muller. 2016. *The Dawn of Christian Art in Panel Paintings and Icons.* Los Angeles: Getty Publications.

Mathisen, Ralph W. 2013. "The Council of Turin (398/399) and the Reorganization of Gaul ca. 395/406." *JLA* 6(2): 264–307.

Mattei, Paul. 2013. "Novatian." In *RAC* 25: 1145–59.

Mc Carthy, Daniel. 1993. "Easter Principles and a Fifth-Century Lunar Cycle Used in the British Isles." *Journal for the History of Astronomy* 24: 204–24.

1994. "The Origin of the 'Latercus' Paschal Cycle of the Insular Celtic Churches." *Cambrian Medieval Celtic Studies* 28: 25–49.

2011. "On the Arrival of the *Latercus* in Ireland." In *The Easter Controversy of Late Antiquity and the Early Middle Ages*, ed. Immo Warntjes and Dáibhí Ó Cróinín, 48–75. Turnhout: Brepols.

Mc Carthy, Daniel and Aidan Breen, eds. 2003. *The Ante-Nicene Christian Pasch "De ratione paschali": The Paschal Tract of Anatolius, Bishop of Laodicea.* Dublin: Four Courts.

McGuckin, John A. 2001. *Gregory of Nazianzus: An Intellectual Biography.* Crestwood, NY: St Vladimir's Seminary Press.

2003. "The Legacy of the Thirteenth Apostle: Origins of the East-Christian Conceptions of Church-State Relation." *St. Vladimir's Theological Quarterly* 47(3–4): 251–88.

McHugh, Michael P. 1997. "Chorepiscopus." In *Encyclopedia of Early Christianity* 2, 242. New York: Garland Publishing.

Meier, Mischa. 2003. "Göttlicher Kaiser und christlicher Herrscher? Die christlichen Kaiser der Spätantike und ihre Stellung zu Gott." *Das Altertum* 48: 129–60.

Merdinger, J. E. 1997. *Rome and the African Church in the Time of Augustine.* New Haven: Yale University Press.

Meslin, Michel. 1967. *Les Ariens d'Occident 335–430.* Patristica Sorbonensia 8. Paris: Éditions de Seuil.

Miles, Graeme. 2015. "Stones, Wood and Woven Papyrus: Porphyry's *On Statues.*" *Journal of Hellenic Studies* 135: 78–94.

Miles, Richard, ed. 2016. *The Donatist Schism: Controversy and Contexts.* TTH, Contexts 2. Liverpool: Liverpool University Press.

Millar, Fergus. 1971. "Paul of Samosata, Zenobia and Aurelian: The Church, Local Culture and Political Allegiance in Third Century Syria." *JRS* 61: 1–17.

1977. *The Emperor in the Roman World (31 BC–AD 337).* London: Duckworth.

Mohlberg, Leo C., Leo Eizenhöfer, and Petrus Siffrin, eds. 1981. *Liber Sacramentorum Romanae Aeclesiae Ordinis Anni Circuli (Cod. Vat. Reg. Lat. 316/Paris Bibl. Nat. 7193, 41/56) (Sacramentarium Gelasianum)*. Rerum Ecclesiasticarum Documenta, Series Maior, Fontes 4. Rome: Herder.

Möllers, Sabine. 1994. *Die Hagia Sophia in Iznik/Nikaia*. Alfter: Verlag und Datenbank für Geisteswissenschaften.

Morales, Xavier. 2006. *La théologie trinitaire d'Athanase d'Alexandrie*. Études Augustiniennes, Série Antiquité 180. Paris: Institut d'Études Augustiniennes.

2018. "Basil of Ancyra's Treatise on Faith: Confirming the Authorship." *VC* 72 (1): 71–92.

Morlet, Sébastien. 2009. *La* Démonstration évangélique *d'Eusèbe de Césarée. Étude sur l'apologétique chrétienne à l'époque de Constantin*. Collection des Études augustiniennes, Série Antiquité 187. Turnhout: Brepols.

2019. "Συμφωνία: Symphonic Exegesis from Origen to Eusebius of Caesarea." In *Origeniana Duodecima: Origen's Legacy in the Holy Land – A Tale of Three Cities: Jerusalem, Caesarea, and Bethlehem*, ed. Brouria Bitton Ashkelony, Oded Irshai, Aryeh Kofsky, Hillel Newman, and Lorenzo Perrone, 359–74. Bibliotheca Ephemeridum Theologicarum Lovaniensium 302. Leuven: Peeters.

Morlet, Sébastien, and Lorenzo Perrone, eds. 2012. *Eusèbe de Césarée. Histoire ecclésiastique. Commentaire*. Vol. 1, *Études d'introduction*. Paris: Les Belles Lettres.

Moss, Candida R. 2010. *The Other Christs: Imitating Jesus in Ancient Christian Ideologies of Martyrdom*. Oxford: Oxford University Press.

2012. *Ancient Christian Martyrdom: Diverse Practices, Theologies, and Traditions*. New Haven: Yale University Press.

Mosshammer, Alden. 2008. *The Easter Computus and the Origins of the Christian Era*. Oxford: Oxford University Press.

ed. 2017. *The Prologues on Easter of Theophilus of Alexandria and [Cyril]*. Oxford: Oxford University Press.

Motia, Michael. 2017. "The Mimetic Life: Imitation and Infinity in Gregory of Nyssa." PhD diss., Harvard University.

Muehlberger, Ellen. 2015. "The Legend of Arius' Death: Imagination, Space and Filth in Late Ancient Historiography." *Past and Present* 227(1): 3–29.

Muth, Robert. 2004. "Kastration." In *RAC* 20: 284–342.

Neil, Bronwen. 2006. *Seventh-Century Popes and Martyrs: The Political Hagiography of Anastasius Bibliothecarius*. Studia Antiqua Australiensia 2. Turnhout: Brepols.

Neil, Brownen, and Pauline Allen, eds. 2003. *The Life of Maximus the Confessor: Recension 3*. Early Christian Studies 6. Strathfield: St Pauls.

Niewöhner, Philipp. 2016 "Church Building in Anatolia during the Reign of Constantine and His Dynasty." In *Costantino e i Costantinidi: l'innovazione costantiniana, le sue radici e i suoi sviluppi, Pars I (Acta XVI congressus internationalis archaeologiae christianae (Romae 22–28.9.2013)*, ed. Olof Brandt, Vincenzo Fiocchi Nicolai, Gabriele Castiglia, 295–308. Studi di Antichità Cristiana 66. Città del Vaticano: Pontifico Istituto di Archeologia Cristiana.

Norderval, Øyving. 1988. "The Emperor Constantine and Arius: Unity in the Church and Unity in the Empire." *Studia Theologica* 42: 113–50.

Nothaft, C. Philipp E. 2012. *Dating the Passion: The Life of Jesus and the Emergence of Scientific Chronology (200–1600)*. Time, Astronomy, and Calendars: Texts and Studies 1. Leiden: Brill.

Novak, Ralph Martin. 2001. *Christianity and the Roman Empire: Background Texts*. Harrisburg, PA: Trinity Press.

Ohme, Heinz. 1998. *Kanon ekklesiastikos: Die Bedeutung des altkirchlichen Kanonsbegriff*. Arbeiten zur Kirchengeschichte 67. Berlin: De Gruyter.

———. 2004. "Kanon I (Begriff)." *RAC* 20: 19–25.

———. 2012. "Greek Canon Law to 691/2." In *The History of Byzantine and Eastern Canon Law to 1500*, ed. Wilfried Hartmann and Kenneth Pennington, 24–114. Washington: Catholic University of America Press.

Özgenel, Lale. 2007. "Public Use and Privacy in Late Antique Houses in Asia Minor: The Architecture of Spatial Control." In *Housing in Late Antiquity*, ed. Luke Lavan, Lale Özgenel, and Alexander Sarantis, 239–81. Late Antique Archaeology 3.2. Leiden: Brill.

Pack, Edgar. 1998. "Italia." In *RAC* 18: 1049–1202.

Parsons, Mikeal. 2006. *Body and Character in Luke and Acts: The Subversion of Physiognomy in Early Christianity*. Grand Rapids: Baker Academic.

Parvis, Paul. 2006. "Constantine's Letter to Arius and Alexander?" *StPatr* 39: 89–95.

Parvis, Sara. 2006. *Marcellus of Ancyra and the Lost Years of the Arian Controversy, 325–345*. Oxford Early Christian Studies. Oxford: Oxford University Press.

———. 2008. "'Τὰ τίνων ἄρα ῥήματα θεολογεῖ;': The Exegetical Relationship between Athanasius' *Orationes contra Arianos* I–III and Marcellus of Ancyra's *Contra Asterium*." In *The Reception and Interpretation of the Bible in Late Antiquity: Proceedings of the Montréal Colloquium in Honour of Charles Kannengiesser, 11–13 October 2006*, ed. Lorenzo DiTommaso and Lucian Turcescu, 121–48. The Bible in Ancient Christianity 6. Leiden: Brill.

———. 2010. "Joseph Lienhard, Marcellus of Ancyra, and Marcellus' Rule of Faith." In *Tradition and the Rule of Faith in the Early Church: Essays in Honor of Joseph T. Lienhard, S.J.*, ed. Ronnie J. Rombs and Alexander Y. Hwang, 89–108. Washington, DC: Catholic University of America Press.

Perrone, Lorenzo. 1996. "Eusebius of Caesarea as a Christian writer." In *Caesarea Maritima: A Retrospective after Two Millennia*, ed. Avner Raban and Kenneth Holum, 515–30. Leiden: Brill.

Person, Ralph E. 1978. *The Mode of Theological Decision Making at the Early Ecumenical Councils: An Inquiry into the Function of Scripture and Tradition at the Councils of Nicaea and Ephesus*. Theologische Dissertationen 14. Basel: F. Reinhardt.

Peschlow, Urs. 2003. "The Churches of Nicaea/Iznik." In Akbaygil et al., *İznik throughout History*, 201–18.

———. 2017. "Nicaea." In *The Archaeology of Byzantine Anatolia: From the End of Late Antiquity until the Coming of the Turks*, ed. Philipp Niewöhner, 203–16. New York: Oxford University Press.

Pietras, Henryk. 2016. *Council of Nicaea (325): Religious and Political Context, Documents, Commentaries.* Rome: Gregorian and Biblical Press.

Poschmann, Bernhard. 1951. *Buße und letzte Ölung.* Handbuch der Dogmengeschichte 4.3. Freiburg: Herder.

1954. "Bußstufen (Bußstationen)." In *RAC* 2: 814–16.

Poster, Carol. 2007. "A Conversation Halved: Epistolary Theory in Graeco-Roman Antiquities." In *Letter Writing Manuals and Instruction from Antiquity to the Present,* ed. Carol Poster and Linda C. Mitchell, 21–51. Columbia, SC: University of South Carolina Press.

Potter, David. 2013. *Constantine the Emperor.* Oxford: Oxford University Press.

Potz, Richard, Eva-Maria Synek, and Spyros Troianos. 2007. *Orthodoxes Kirchenrecht: Eine Einführung.* Freistadt: Plöchl.

Prestige, G. L. 1956. *St. Basil the Great and Apollinaris of Laodicea.* London: S.P. C.K.

Price, Richard, and Mary Whitby, eds. 2009. *Chalcedon in Context: Church Councils 400–700.* TTH, Contexts 1. Liverpool: Liverpool University Press.

Puche, Josep M., and Jordi López. 2017. "Centcelles: aproximación al monumento a través de su arquitectura. La métrica y la proporción." In *Modelos constructivos y urbanísticos de la arquitectura de Hispania: Definición, evolución y difusión del periodo romano a la Antigüedad tardía (MArqHis 2013–2015),* ed. Lourdes Roldán Gómez et al., 169–81. Documenta 29. Tarragona: Institut Català d'Arquelogia Clàssica.

Rabbel, Wolfgang et al. 2015. "Discovery of a Byzantine Church in Iznik/Nicaea, Turkey: An Educational Case History of Geophysical Prospecting with Combined Methods in Urban Areas." *Archaeological Prospection* 22: 1–20.

Radde-Gallwitz, Andrew. 2018. *Gregory of Nyssa's Doctrinal Works: A Literary Study.* Oxford Early Christian Studies. Oxford: Oxford University Press.

Rapp, Claudia. 1998. "Imperial Ideology in the Making: Eusebius of Caesarea on Constantine as 'Bishop.'" *JTS,* n.s., 49: 685–95.

2005. *Holy Bishops in Late Antiquity: The Nature of Christian Leadership in an Age of Transition.* Transformation of the Classical Heritage 37. Berkeley: University of California Press.

Ricken, Friedo. 1969. "Nikaia als Krisis des altchristlichen Platonismus." *Theologie und Philosophie* 44: 321–41.

Robert, Louis. 1977. "La titulature de Nicée et de Nicomédie: la gloire et la haine." *Harvard Studies in Classical Philology* 81: 1–39.

Robertson, Jon M. 2007. *Christ as Mediator: A Study of the Theologies of Eusebius of Caesarea, Marcellus of Ancyra, and Athanasius of Alexandria.* Oxford Theological Monographs. Oxford: Oxford University Press.

Robertson, Paul. 2018. "The Polemic of Individualized Appellation in Late Antiquity: Creating Marcionism, Valentinianism, and Heresy." *Studies in Late Antiquity* 2(2): 180–214.

Rose, Peter. 2005. "Spectators and Spectator Comfort in Entertainment Buildings: A Study in Functional Design." *Papers of the British School at Rome* 73: 99–130.

Roth, John D., ed. 2013. *Constantine Revisited: Leithart, Yoder, and the Constantinian Debate.* Eugene, OR: Pickwick Publications.

Rousseau, Philip. 1994. *Basil of Caesarea*. Transformation of the Classical Heritage 20. Berkeley: University of California Press.

Röwekamp, Georg. 2003. "Gelasius von Cyzicus." In *Lexikon der antiken christlichen Literatur*, 280. Freiburg: Herder.

Rowett, Catherine. 2012. "Christopher Stead (1913–2008): His Work in Patristics." *StPatr* 54: 1–14.

Rubenstein, Richard E. 1999. *When Jesus Became God: The Struggle to Define Christianity During the Last Days of Rome*. Orlando: Harcourt.

Russell, Norman. 2007. *Theophilus of Alexandria*. The Early Church Fathers. London: Routledge.

Şahin, Mehmet Çetin. 1981. *Die Inschriften von Stratonikeia*. Part 1, *Panamara*. Inschriften griechischer Städte aus Kleinasien 21. Bonn: Habelt.

Şahin, Sencer. 1979–87. *Katalog der antiken Inschriften des Museums von Iznik (Nikaia)*, 4 vols. Inschriften griechischer Städte aus Kleinasien 9–10.3. Bonn: Habelt.

——— 2003. "Iznik (Nicaea) in the Hellenistic and Roman Periods." In Akbaygil et al., *İznik throughout History*, 3–23.

Saliou, Catherine. 2000. "A propos de la ταυριανὴ πύλη: remarques sur la localisation présumée de la Grande Eglise d'Antioche de Syrie." *Syria* 77: 217–26.

Salzman, Michele Renee. 1990. *On Roman Time: The Codex-Calendar of 354 and the Rhythms of Urban Life in Late Antiquity*. Transformation of the Classical Heritage 17. Berkeley: University of California Press.

Scarpi, Paolo, ed. and tr. 2009–11. *La rivelazione segreta di Ermete Trismegisto*. 2 vols. Milan: A. Mondadori Editore.

Schmid, Joseph. 1905. *Die Osterfestfrage auf dem ersten allgemeinen Konzil von Nicäa*. Theologische Studien der Leo-Gesellschaft 13. Vienna: Verlag von Meyer.

Schneider, Alfons M. 1943. *Die römischen und byzantinischen Denkmäler von Iznik*. Istanbuler Forschungen 16. Berlin: Archäologisches Institut des Deutschen Reiches.

Schneider, Alfons F., and Walter Karnapp. 1938. *Die Stadtmauer von Iznik (Nicaea)*. Istanbuler Forschungen 9. Berlin: Archäologisches Institut des Deutschen Reiches.

Schwartz, Eduard. 1905. *Christliche und jüdische Ostertafeln*. Abhandlungen der königlichen Gesellschaft der Wissenschaften zu Göttingen, philologisch-historische Klasse, Neue Folge, vol. 8, no. 6. Berlin: Weidmann.

——— 1959. *Zur Geschichte des Athanasius*. Gesammelte Schriften 3. Berlin: De Gruyter. Articles originally published 1904–11 in *Nachrichten der königlichen Gesellschaft der Wissenschaften zu Göttingen*.

Schwartz, Eduard. 1911. *Bußstufen und Katechumenatsklassen*. Schriften der Wissenschaftlichen Gesellschaft in Strassbourg 7. Strassburg: Trübner.

Seeck, Otto. 1919. *Regesten der Kaiser und Päpste für die Jahre 311 bis 476 N. Chr.: Vorarbeit zu einer Prosopographie der christlichen Kaiserzeit*. Stuttgart: J. B. Metzlersche Verlagsbuchhandlung.

Seibt, Klaus. 1994. *Die Theologie des Markell von Ankyra*. Arbeiten zur Kirchengeschichte 59. Berlin: Walter de Gruyter.

Shahîd, Irfan. 1984. *Byzantium and the Arabs in the Fourth Century.* Washington, DC: Dumbarton Oaks.

Shaw, Brent D. 2011. *Sacred Violence: African Christians and Sectarian Hatred in the Age of Augustine.* Cambridge: Cambridge University Press.

Shaw, Gregory. 2014. *Theurgy and the Soul: The Neoplatonism of Iamblichus.* 2nd ed. Kettering, OH: Angelico Press.

Sidaway, Janet. 2013. "Hilary of Poitiers and Phoebadius of Agen: Who Influenced Whom?" *StPatr* 66: 286–90.

Sieben, Hermann Joseph. 1979. *Die Konzilsidee der Alten Kirche.* Paderborn: Schöningh.

Siecienski, A. Edward. 2010. *The Filioque: History of a Doctrinal Controversy.* Oxford Studies in Historical Theology. New York: Oxford University Press.

Simonetti, Manlio. 1975. *La crisi ariana nel IV secolo.* Studia Ephemeridis "Augustinianum" 11. Rome: Institutum Patristicum "Augustinianum."

Singh, Devin. 2013. "Disciplining Eusebius: Discursive Power and Representation of the Court Theologian." *StPatr* 62: 89–101.

  2015. "Eusebius as Political Theologian: The Legend Continues." *HTR* 108(1): 129–54.

Skarsaune, Oskar. 1987. "A Neglected Detail in the Creed of Nicaea (325)." *VC* 41 (1): 34–54.

Smith, Andrew. 1994. "*Hypostasis* and *hyparxis* in Porphyry." In *Hyparxis e hypostasis nel Neoplatonismo: atti del 1°Colloquio internazionale del Centro di ricerca sul neoplatonismo, Università degli studi di Catania, 1–3 ottobre 1992,* ed. Francisco Romano and D. P. Taormina, 33–41. Florence: Leo S. Olschki Editore.

Smith, Geoffrey. 2015. *Guilt by Association: Heresy Catalogues in Early Christianity.* Oxford: Oxford University Press.

Smith, Mark S. 2018. *The Idea of Nicaea in the Early Church Councils, AD 431–451.* Oxford Early Christian Studies. Oxford: Oxford University Press.

Smith, Shawn C. 2014. "The Insertion of the *Filioque* into the Nicene Creed and a Letter of Isidore of Seville." *JECS* 22(2): 261–86.

Solomon, Jon. 2001. *The Ancient World in the Cinema.* New Haven: Yale University Press.

Sommar, M. E. 2003. "Pragmatic Application of Proto-canon Law: Episcopal Translation." In *Confrontation in Late Antiquity: Imperial Presentation and Regional Adaptation,* ed. Linda Jones Hall, 89–101. Cambridge: Orchard Academic.

Speigl, Jakob. 1975. "Das entstehende Papsttum, die Kanones von Nizäa und die Bischofsernennungen in Gallien." In *Konzil und Papst. Historische Beiträge zur Frage der höchsten Gewalt in der Kirche. Festgabe für Hermann Tüchle,* ed. Georg Schwaiger, 43–61. Munich: Schöningh.

Spoerl, Kelley McCarthy. 1991. "A Study of the *Kata Meros Pistis* by Apollinarius of Laodicea." Ph.D. thesis, University of Toronto.

  1994. "Apollinarian Christology and the Anti-Marcellan Tradition." *JTS,* n.s., 45(2): 545–68.

  2001. "Apollinarius on the Holy Spirit." *StPatr* 37: 571–92.

  2008. "Two Early Nicenes: Eustathius of Antioch and Marcellus of Ancyra." In *In the Shadow of the Incarnation: Essays on Jesus Christ in the Early Church in Honor of Brian E. Daley, SJ*, ed. Peter W. Martens, 121–48. Notre Dame, IN: University of Notre Dame Press.

2015. "The Circumstances of Apollinarius's Election in Laodicea." In Bergjan, Gleede, and Heimgartner, *Apollinarius und seine Folgen*, 19–33.

2016. "Eustathius of Antioch on Jesus's Digestion." *StPatr* 74: 147–58.

2017. "Epiphanius on Jesus's Digestion." *StPatr* 96: 3–10.

Stead, G. Christopher. 1961. "The Significance of the *Homoousios*." *StPatr* 3: 397–412.

1977. *Divine Substance*. Oxford: Clarendon Press.

1978. "The *Thalia* of Arius and the Testimony of Athanasius." *JTS*, n.s., 29(1): 20–52.

1982. "The Scriptures and the Soul of Christ in Athanasius." *VC* 36(3): 233–50.

1983. "The Freedom of the Will and the Arian Controversy." In *Platonismus und Christentum: Festschrift für Heinrich Dörrie*, ed. Horst-Dieter Blume and Friedhelm Mann, 245–57. Münster: Aschendorffsche Verlagsbuchhandlung.

1988. "Athanasius' Earliest Written Work." *JTS*, n.s., 39(1): 76–91.

1994. "Arius in Modern Research." *JTS*, n.s., 45(1): 24–36.

1997. "Was Arius a Neo-Platonist?" *StPatr* 32: 39–52.

1998. "The Word 'From Nothing'." *JTS*, n.s., 49(2): 671–84.

Stefan, Alexandra. 2005a. "Le titre de *Filius Augustorum* de Maximin et Constantin et la théologie de la tétrarchie." In *Prosopographie et histoire religieuse. Actes du Colloque tenu en l'Université Paris XII – Val de Marne les 27 & 28 octobre 2000*, ed. Marie-Françoise Baslez and Françoise Prévot, 329–49. Paris: De Broccard.

2005b. "Un rang impérial nouveau à l'époque de la quatrième tétrarchie: *Filius Augustorum*. Deuxième partie: considérations historiques." *Antiquité Tardive* 13: 169–204.

Stefaniw, Blossom. 2016. "A Disciplined Mind in an Orderly World: Mimesis in Late Antique Ethical Regimes." In *Metapher-Narratio-Mimesis-Doxologie*, ed. Ulrich Volp, Friedhelm W. Horn, and Ruben Zimmerman, 235–56. Contexts and Norms of New Testament Ethics 7. Tübingen: Mohr Siebeck.

Stephens, Christopher W. B. 2015. *Canon Law and Episcopal Authority: The Canons of Antioch and Serdica*. Oxford: Oxford University Press.

Stephenson, Paul. 2009. *Constantine: Roman Emperor, Christian Victor*. New York: Overlook.

Stevenson, James. 1929. *Studies in Eusebius*. Cambridge: Cambridge University Press.

Streeter, Joseph. 2006. "Appendix: The Date of the Council of Elvira." In *Christian Persecution, Martyrdom and Orthodoxy*, ed. Michael Whitby and Joseph Streeter, 99–104. Oxford: Oxford University Press.

Strobel, August. 1984. *Texte zur Geschichte des frühchristlichen Osterkalenders*. Münster: Aschendorff.

Struck, Peter T. 2004. *Birth of a Symbol: Ancient Readers and the Limits of Their Texts*. Princeton: Princeton University Press.

Strutwolf, Holger. 1999. *Die Trinitätstheologie und Christologie des Euseb von Caesarea*. Forschungen zur Kirchen- und Dogmengeschichte 72. Gottingen: Vandenhoeck & Ruprecht.

Sünskes, Julia. 1983. "Eine Brückenbauinschrift unter Konstantin und Licinius aus der Umgebung von Kyzikos." *Epigraphica Anatolica* 2: 99–105.

Swain, Simon, ed. 2006. *Seeing the Face, Seeing the Soul: Polemon's Physiognomy from Classical Antiquity to Medieval Islam*. Oxford: Oxford University Press.

Tetz, Martin. 1993. "Zur strittigen Frage arianischer Glaubenserklärung auf dem Konzil von Nicaea (325)." In *Logos: Festschrift für Luise Abramowski zum 8. Juli 1993*, ed. H. C. Brennecke, E. L. Grasmück and C. Markschies, 200–38. Berlin: de Gruyter.

Thompson, E. A. 1969. *The Goths in Spain*. Oxford: Clarendon Press.

Torres Guerra, José B. 2017. "Image and Word in Eusebius of Caesarea (*VC* 3.4–24): Constantine in Nicaea." In *Rhetorical Strategies in Late Antique Literature: Images, Metatexts and Interpretation*, ed. Alberto J. Quiroga Puertas, 73–89. *Mnemosyne*, Supplements 406. Leiden: Brill.

Troianos, Spyros. 2012. "Byzantine Canon Law to 1100." In *The History of Byzantine and Eastern Canon Law to 1500*, ed. Wilfried Hartmann and Kenneth Pennington, 115–69. Washington, DC: The Catholic University of America Press.

Twomey, Vincent. 1982. *Apostolikos Thronos: The Primacy of Rome as Reflected in the Church History of Eusebius and the Historico-Apologetic Writings of Saint Athanasius the Great*. Münsterische Beiträge zur Theologie 49. Münster: Aschendorff.

Ulrich, Jörg. 1994. *Die Anfänge der abendländischen Rezeption des Nizänums*. Patristische Texten und Studien 39. Berlin: De Gruyter.

Urbainczyk, Theresa. 1997. *Socrates of Constantinople: Historian of Church and State*. Ann Arbor: University of Michigan Press.

Uytterhoeven, Inge. 2007a. "Housing in Late Antiquity: Thematic Perspectives." In *Housing in Late Antiquity*, ed. Luke Lavan, Lale Özgenel, and Alexander Sarantis, 25–66. Late Antique Archaeology 3.2. Leiden: Brill.

2007b. "Housing in Late Antiquity: Regional Perspectives." In *Housing in Late Antiquity*, ed. Luke Lavan, Lale Özgenel, and Alexander Sarantis, 67–93. Late Antique Archaeology 3.2. Leiden: Brill.

Vaggione, Richard. 1989. "Arius: Heresy and Tradition by Rowan Williams: A Review Article." *Toronto Journal of Theology* 5(1): 63–87.

Vaggione, Richard. 2000. *Eunomius of Cyzicus and the Nicene Revolution*. Oxford: Oxford University Press.

2007. *The Roman Revolution of Constantine*. Cambridge: Cambridge University Press.

2010. *Rome and Constantinople: Rewriting Roman History during Late Antiquity*. Waco, TX: Baylor University Press.

2011. *Remembering Constantine at the Milvian Bridge*. Cambridge: Cambridge University Press.

2014. "'Constantine's Beautiful City': The Symbolic Value of Constantinople." *Antiquité Tardive* 22: 83–94.

2018. "Eastern Aristocracies and Imperial Courts: Constantine's Half-Brother, Licinius's Prefect, and Egyptian Grain." *Dumbarton Oaks Papers* 72: 1–24.

van der Hagen, Johannes. 1733. *Observationes in Prosperi Aquitani Chronicon* [...] Amsterdam: Johannem Boom.

1736. *Dissertationes de Cyclis Paschalibus* [...]. Amsterdam: Johannem Boom.

Van Nuffelen, Peter. 2013. "Eusebius and Images of Truth in the *Life of Constantine.*" In *Eusebius of Caesarea: Tradition and Innovations,* ed. Aaron P. Johnson and Jeremy Schott 133–49. Washington, DC: Center for Hellenic Studies Press.

——— 2017. *Penser la tolérance durant l'Antiquité tardive.* Collection Les Conférence de l'École Pratique 294. Paris: Éditions du Cerf.

Verdoner, Marie. 2011. *Narrated Reality: The Historia Ecclesiastica of Eusebius of Caesarea.* Early Christianity in the Context of Antiquity 9. Frankfurt: Peter Lang.

Vilella, Josep. 2014. "Constantino y Osio: la última etapa del conflicto arriano preniceno." *Antiquité Tardive* 22: 27–33.

Vinzent, Markus. 2015. "Pseudo-Athanasius, Oratio contra Arianos IV: Apollinarius's Earliest Extant Work." In Bergjan, Gleede, and Heimgartner, *Apollinarius und seine Folgen,* 59–70.

Vogt, Josef. 1968. *Coetus sanctorum: der Kirchenbegriff des Novatian und die Geschichte seiner Sonderkirche.* Theophaneia 20. Bonn: Hanstein.

Vössing, Konrad. 2015. "Paulus von Samosata." In *RAC* 26: 1250–64.

Walch, Christian. 1770. "Decreti Nicaeni de Paschate Explicatio." *Novum Commentarium Societatis Regiae Scientiarum Goettingensis, commentationes historicae et philologicae* 1: 10–65. Göttingen.

Wallace-Hadrill, Andrew. 1982. "Civilis Princeps: Between Citizen and King." *JRS* 72: 32–48.

Wallraff, Martin. 1997. "Geschichte des Novatianismus seit dem vierten Jahrhundert im Osten." *ZAC* 1(2): 251–79.

Walsh, Maura and Dáibhí Ó Cróinín, eds. 1988. *Cummian's Letter 'De Controuersia Paschali' Together with a Related Irish Computistical Tract 'De Ratione Conputandi'.* Toronto: Pontifical Institute.

Walter, Christopher. 1991–92. "Icons of the First Council of Nicaea." Δελτίον της Χριστιανικής Αρχαιολογικής Εταιρίας 16: 209–18.

Ward Perkins, J. B. 1954. "Constantine and the Origins of the Christian Basilica." *Papers of the British School at Rome* 22: 69–90.

Warmington, B. H. 1985. "The Sources of Some Constantinian Documents in Eusebius' Ecclesiastical History and Life of Constantine." *StPatr* 18(1): 93–98.

Watts, Edward J. 2015. *The Final Pagan Generation.* Transformation of the Classical Heritage 53. Berkeley: University of California Press.

Weckwerth, Andreas. 2004. *Das erste Konzil von Toledo: Ein philologischer und historischer Kommentar zur Constitutio Concilii.* Jahrbuch für Antike und Christentum: Ergänzungsband Kleine Reihe 1. Münster: Aschendorff Verlag.

——— 2010. *Ablauf, Organisation und Selbstverständnis westlicher antiker Synoden im Spiegel ihrer Akten.* Jahrbuch für Antike und Christentum: Ergänzungsband Kleine Reihe 5. Münster: Aschendorff Verlag.

Weedman, Mark. 2007. *The Trinitarian Theology of Hilary of Poitiers.* Supplements to Vigiliae Christianae 89. Leiden: Brill.

Weinandy, Thomas G. 2007. *Athanasius: A Theological Introduction.* Burlington, VT: Ashgate.

Weinandy, Thomas G., and Daniel A. Keating. 2017. *Athanasius and His Legacy*. Minneapolis, MN: Fortress Press.

Weiss, Peter. 2003. "The Vision of Constantine." Trans. A. R. Birley. *Journal of Roman Archaeology* 16: 237–59.

Westra, Liuwe. 2002. *Apostles' Creed: Origin, History, and Some Early Commentaries*. Instrumenta Patristica et Mediaevalia 43. Turnhout: Brepols.

Whitby, Mary, ed. 1988. *The Propaganda of Power: The Role of Panegyric in Late Antiquity. Mnemosyne*. Supplements 183. Leiden: Brill.

White, L. Michael. 1996–97. *The Social Origins of Christian Architecture*. Vol. 1, *Building God's House in the Roman World. Architectural Adaptation among Pagans, Jews, and Christians*. Vol. 2, *Texts and Monuments of the Christian Domus Ecclesiae in its Environment*. Harvard Theological Studies 42. Valley Forge, PA: Trinity Press.

2017. "Early Christian Architecture: The First Five Centuries." In *The Early Christian World*, ed. Philip Francis Esler, 2nd ed., 673–716. London: Routledge.

Wienand, Johannes, ed. 2015. *Contested Monarchy: Integrating the Roman Empire in the Fourth Century AD*. Oxford: Oxford University Press.

Wiles, Maurice F. 1993. "A Textual Variant in the Creed of the Council of Nicaea." *StPatr* 26: 428–33.

1996. *Archetypal Heresy: Arianism through the Centuries*. Oxford: Oxford University Press.

Williams, D. H. 1992. "The Anti-Arian Campaigns of Hilary of Poitiers and the *Liber Contra Auxentium*." *CH* 61(1): 7–22.

1995. *Ambrose of Milan and the End of the Nicene–Arian Conflicts*. Oxford Early Christian Studies. Oxford: Oxford University Press.

2014. "Italy and Its Environs." In *Early Christianity in Contexts*, ed. William Tabbernee, 407–11. Grand Rapids: Baker Academic.

Williams, Michael Stuart. 2008. *Authorized Lives in Early Christian Biography: Between Eusebius and Augustine*. Cambridge: Cambridge University Press.

Williams, Rowan D. 1986. "Arius and the Melitian Schism." *JTS*, n.s., 37(1): 35–52.

(1987) 2001. *Arius: Heresy and Tradition*. London: Darton, Longman and Todd. Rev. ed. Grand Rapids: Eerdmans.

1997. "Angels Unawares: Heavenly Liturgy and Earthly Theology in Alexandria." *StPatr* 30: 350–63.

Willing, Meike. 2008. *Eusebius von Cäsarea als Häreseograph*. Patristische Texte und Studien 63. Berlin: Walter de Gruyter.

Wilson, Roger J. A. 2014. "Considerazioni conclusive." In *La villa restaurata e i nuovi studi sull'edilizia residenziale tardoantica*, ed. Patrizio Pensabene and Carla Sfameni, 691–702. Bari: Edipuglia.

Young, Frances. 2013. *God's Presence: A Contemporary Recapitulation of Early Christianity*. Cambridge: Cambridge University Press.

Young, Robin Darling. 2001. *In Procession before the World: Martyrdom as Public Liturgy in Early Christianity. The Pere Marquette Lecture in Theology, 2001*. Milwaukee, WI: Marquette University Press.

Zuidhoek, Jan. 2017. "The Initial Year of *De ratione paschali* and the Relevance of its Paschal Dates." In *Late Antique Calendrical Thought and Its Reception in the Early Middle Ages*, ed. Immo Warntjes and Dáibhí Ó Cróinín, 71–93. Turnhout: Brepols.

    2019. *Reconstructing Metonic 19-year Lunar Cycles (on the basis of NASA's Six Milllennium Catalog of Phases of the Moon)*. Zwolle: JZ.

REFERENCE WORKS

Blaise, Albert and Henri Chirat. 1954. *Dictionnaire latin-français des auteurs chrétiens*. Turnhout: Brepols.

Glare, P. 1968. *Oxford Latin Dictionary*. Oxford: Oxford University Press.

Lampe, Geoffrey. 1961. *A Patristic Greek Lexicon*. Oxford: Clarendon Press.

Liddell, Henry and Robert Scott. 1996. *A Greek-English Lexicon*, rev. Oxford: Oxford University Press.

Index

CPSIA information can be obtained
at www.ICGtesting.com
Printed in the USA
LVHW081127050622
720538LV00013B/797

9 781108 448116